OXFORD STUDIES IN MODERN EUROPEAN HISTORY

General Editors

MODEL NAZI

ARTHUR GREISER AND THE OCCUPATION OF WESTERN POLAND

CATHERINE EPSTEIN

OXFORD
UNIVERSITY PRESS

Great Clarendon Street, Oxford OX2 6DP

Oxford University Press is a department of the University of Oxford.
It furthers the University's objective of excellence in research, scholarship,
and education by publishing worldwide in

Oxford New York

Auckland Cape Town Dar es Salaam Hong Kong Karachi
Kuala Lumpur Madrid Melbourne Mexico City Nairobi
New Delhi Shanghai Taipei Toronto

With offices in

Argentina Austria Brazil Chile Czech Republic France Greece
Guatemala Hungary Italy Japan Poland Portugal Singapore
South Korea Switzerland Thailand Turkey Ukraine Vietnam

Oxford is a registered trade mark of Oxford University Press
in the UK and in certain other countries

Published in the United States
by Oxford University Press Inc., New York

First published 2010

Typeset by Laserwords Private Limited, Chennai, India
Printed in the U.S.A.

ISBN 978–0–19–954641–1

Book Club Edition

For Daniel and our children,
Nathan, Dora, and Stella

Contents

List of Illustrations

All reasonable effort has been made to contact the holders of copyright in materials reproduced in this book. Any omissions will be rectified in future printings if notice is given to the publisher.

List of Maps and Tables

Maps

Tables

List of Abbreviations

CdZ	Head of the Civil Administration (*Chef der Zivilverwaltung*)
DAF	German Labor Front (*Deutsche Arbeitsfront*)
DNVP	German National People's Party (*Deutschnationale Volkspartei*)
DSP	German-Social Party (*Deutsch-Soziale Partei*)
DUT	German Resettlement Trust Company (*Deutsche Umsiedlungs-Treuhand GmbH*)
DVL	German Ethnic Register (*Deutsche Volksliste*)
EWZ	Central Immigration Office (*Einwandererzentralstelle*)
Gestapo	Secret State Police (*Geheime Staatspolizei*)
HSSPF	Higher SS and Police Leader (*Höhere SS- und Polizeiführer*)
HTO	Central Trust Agency for the East (*Haupttreuhandstelle-Ost*)
IMT	International Military Tribunal
NSDAP	National Socialist German Workers Party (*Nationalsozialistische Deutsche Arbeiterpartei*)
POW	Prisoner of War
RKFDV	Reich Commissariat for the Strengthening of Germandom (*Reichskommissariat für die Festigung deutschen Volkstums*)
RM	Reichsmark
ROA	Reserve Officer Candidate (*Reserveoffizieranwärter*)
RSHA	Reich Security Main Office (*Reichssicherheitshauptamt*)
RuSHA	Race and Settlement Main Office (*Rasse- und Siedlungshauptamt*)
SA	Storm Troop (*Sturmabteilung*)
SD	Security Service (*Sicherheitsdienst*)
Sipo	Security Police (*Sicherheitspolizei*)
SPD	Social Democratic Party of Germany (*Sozialdemokratische Partei Deutschlands*)
SS	Protection Squad (*Schutzstaffel*)
UWZ	Central Resettlement Office (*Umwandererzentralstelle*)

VoMi	Ethnic German Liaison Office (*Volksdeutsche Mittelstelle*)
WVHA	SS Business Administration Main Office (*Wirtschaftsverwaltungshauptamt der SS*)
ZAfJ	Forced Labor Camps for Jews (*Zwangsarbeitslager für Juden*)

Note on Place Names and Terminology

Where place names have a commonly used English word (Warsaw), the English word is used throughout the text. Most place names are given in the form used by the prevailing political authorities at the time in question. I use Łódź, for example, when writing about the interwar period; Lodsch for the months November 1939 to April 1940; and Litzmannstadt for the period April 1940 through January 1945. The exception is Chełmno; since scholars typically refer to the extermination camp by that name, rather than the German Kulmhof, it is used here, too.

The German noun *Volk* (loosely translated as 'people') has ethnic, racial, and nationalistic connotations not easily rendered into English. The term and various compound forms—*Volksgemeinschaft* ('people's community'), *Volkskampf* ('ethnic struggle')—is used in italics throughout the text and generally not translated. Similarly, the adjective *völkisch* ('racial-nationalist') and the noun *Volkstum* ('ethnic-racial group') are used throughout the text, usually without translation.

Introduction

On a sunny Sunday morning in July 1946, a public hanging took place in the Polish city of Poznań. From dawn onwards, 15,000 Poles streamed toward the grounds of the Citadel, a fortress reduced to rubble in recent German–Russian fighting for the city. Shortly before 7 a.m., a car threaded its way through the throng. A tall man, blindfolded and dressed in a suit, emerged. Guided by two guards, he mounted the gallows that had been specially built for his execution. On the scaffold, hands tied behind his back, he mumbled prayers, but otherwise showed no sign of emotion. In his last moments, he offered no defiant slogans, no pleas for forgiveness, and no words of justification. Right on schedule, the executioner, clad in black save for white gloves, set about his grim task. Quickly and efficiently, he slung the noose around the condemned man's neck. He then sprang the wooden trap beneath the man's feet. The man dangled in the air, his head dropped on his neck, and he was soon dead. All the while, the crowd watched in intent silence.[1] At 7:20, the corpse was taken down and placed in a coffin. The hangman took off his white gloves and tossed them away in a grand gesture of disgust.[2]

Who commanded such revulsion? Why did 15,000 Poles come to see this man die? The man executed was Arthur Greiser, former Nazi Gauleiter (party territorial leader) of the so-called Warthegau, a part of western Poland annexed to Nazi Germany in 1939. Headquartered in Posen (the German name for Poznań), Greiser had carried out a ruthless Germanization of the area. As his Polish judges determined, he had used 'the new method of mass extermination of the Polish and Jewish population,' had engaged in the 'complete destruction of Polish culture and political thought,' and had brought about 'physical and spiritual genocide.'[3] In a cautious formulation, they even found Greiser guilty of 'new crimes against the interests of humanity'—one of the first times that a phrase so similar to the International Military Tribunal Charter's innovative 'crimes against humanity' charge was used in a court verdict.[4]

This biography tells the neglected story of an important Nazi leader and his brutal Germanization program in occupied Poland.[5] In transforming the Warthegau into a 'German' area, Greiser even initiated the first mass gassings of Jews in Nazi-occupied Europe. But he also pursued an extraordinary range of other measures to remake a Polish region into 'Germany.' He brought in some 500,000 ethnic German resettlers, and attempted to alter the built and natural environment of the Gau (Nazi territorial area). He deployed ruthless policies against Poles, including their deportation from the Gau and, when this was not possible, their segregation from Germans in all spheres of activity. His treatment of Jews was nothing short of atrocious: Greiser expropriated Jewish property, exploited Jews for their labor, and eventually had the vast majority of them murdered. Greiser's far-ranging Germanization program—including the importation of ethnic Germans and 'German' culture, the ethnic cleansing (forced removal of a people and its culture) of Poles, and the genocide (outright murder) of Jews—was the most ambitious in Nazi-occupied Europe.

Although Greiser's program was part of a much larger Nazi project to colonize eastern Europe, only the Warthegau saw so many and such cruel Germanization policies. The Nazi program, an outgrowth of Germany's longtime desire to dominate eastern Europe (the *Drang nach Osten*), was much more violent and exclusive than earlier attempted colonizations.[6] The Germans, the Nazis claimed, were a people 'without land.' To solve this alleged problem, Nazi bureaucrats pored over maps of eastern Europe, envisioning a massive transfer of Germans to historically non-German areas. To make space for these Germans, they intended to deport, resettle, or 'liquidate' over thirty million Slavs, Jews, and other peoples.[7] Save for the murder of Jews, most of these megalomaniac projects were never carried out—except in the Warthegau. Alone among eastern Nazi leaders, Greiser set in motion a wide-ranging Germanization project designed to transform a Polish province into a model of the Nazi future. His measures included everything from murder to the planting of oak trees, deportation to the changing of street names, and segregation to the designing of furniture styles.

To contemporaries, Greiser presented many different faces. Carl Burckhardt, the last League of Nations high commissioner in Danzig, where

Greiser served as senate president from 1934 to 1939, thought Greiser 'by nature soft.'[8] Ernst Ziehm, a conservative Danzig politician, recalled his 'soldierly nature.'[9] Duff Cooper, the conservative British politician, labeled him 'execrable.'[10] Józef Lipski, Polish ambassador to Berlin, viewed him as a 'well-balanced person.'[11] Anthony Eden remembered a 'truculent' Greiser.[12] Julius Hoppenrath, a Danzig Nazi, saw him as 'thoughtful, purposeful, and ruthless.'[13] The prosecutor at Greiser's trial, Mieczysław Siewierski, claimed that Greiser was 'no emotional type, he has no momentary emotions.'[14] Greiser's Polish housemaid, Danuta Groscholska, remembered that her boss 'was so vain, so full of himself, as if there was nothing above him—a god almost.'[15] And an opposition politician in Danzig, Hans Leonhardt, thought that 'Greiser was not so much a disruptive political fanatic as a type of a somewhat maladjusted mercenary who, under normal circumstances, could have made quite a useful citizen.'[16]

Given these contradictory contemporary descriptions, who was Greiser really? What motivated him to carry out his nefarious deeds? In the following pages, I trace how Greiser became the man who was hanged in 1946. I explore the personal, ideological, and career dynamics that accompanied his life trajectory. This is a complicated story, and one that illustrates choices, breaks, and discontinuities in Greiser's life history.

In trying to interpret Greiser, I looked to the major explanations of Nazi perpetrators that have emerged since World War II.[17] Was Greiser a psychopath or cold-blooded monster, as early postwar views of Nazi perpetrators suggested? Was he a soulless bureaucrat trying to make a career in a totalitarian dictatorship?[18] Did Greiser condone murder for seemingly rational purposes—to address food supply or other problems related to overpopulation?[19] Was he one of the smart, committed security officials who belonged to the 'war-youth' generation and saw themselves as pragmatic realists ruthlessly dedicated to Germany's national redemption?[20] Was he an 'eliminationist anti-Semite?'[21] Or was he an 'ordinary man' who, like most men, would participate in genocide if put in an actual killing situation?[22]

An exploration of his behavior and passions reveals that none of these explanations fits Greiser.[23] Rather, Greiser is an example of a particular kind of perpetrator: one shaped by a *völkisch* (racialized) nationalism rooted in the ethnic tensions of borderlands regions. Hitler and other Nazi perpetrators came from Austria; many others from Alsace, the Baltic countries, or eastern borderlands regions; and yet others witnessed the French occupation of the Rhineland.[24] A recent investigation of the geographical origin of Nazi perpetrators discovered that they 'were disproportionately drawn from lost territories or threatened borders;' it concluded that 'the origins of mass murder lay substantially in embittered ethnic imperial revisionism.'[25] This book builds on this finding by closely examining how a nationalism rooted in ethnic tensions played out in the life and career of a Nazi who came to rule over a borderlands region.

Born in 1897, Greiser came from the Prussian province of Posen—the birthplace of Generals Paul von Hindenburg and Erich Ludendorff and later, the rocket scientist Wernher von Braun. In Greiser's youth, the German minority made up the province's governing elite, but Poles constituted close to two-thirds of the population. Shortly after World War I broke out, Greiser volunteered for military service. Over the next four years, he served as a scout, aerial observer, and combat pilot. After years at the front, he saw the war end in a humiliating defeat for Germany. Moreover, in December 1918, a Polish uprising led to the de facto loss of Posen province to the new state of Poland. Greiser moved to Danzig, a port city on the Baltic Sea that, as dictated by the Versailles Treaty, had been decoupled from Germany. By the late 1920s, the National Socialist German Workers' Party (NSDAP) had secured a toehold in Danzig; Greiser joined the party in December 1929.

If not before, Greiser came to espouse a xenophobic German nationalism during his first years as a Nazi. Greiser's nationalism was neither sophisticated nor intellectual; he never moved in university or other circles that read and discussed chauvinist German screeds. Instead, he harbored a nationalism that was inchoate, visceral, and personal. It was also deeply anti-Polish. And it was very simple: above all, Greiser strove for Germany's national redemption. Germany, he hoped, would recover its former glory, along with its lost lands, especially those ceded to Poland. Greiser even believed that he would play a personal role in the restoration of German greatness. As he wrote to his mistress (and later wife) in 1934, 'I feel it ever more clearly . . . yet greater tasks will fall to me . . . My life doesn't belong to me, it belongs to Germany.'[26] Five years later, in the Warthegau, Greiser's 'greater task' became explicit. Hitler wished the Gau—now overwhelmingly Polish—'to become flourishing German land in ten years.'[27]

Greiser's experiences help illuminate why the Warthegau became a site of such dramatic ethnic-cleansing and genocidal policies. Some historians, though, doubt whether biography can teach us anything at all about genocide. As they argue, numerous studies support the conclusion that virtually anyone can and will become a murderer—provided that he finds himself in a situation in which he is called upon to kill. To such historians, the key to understanding why men murder lies in the concrete killing situation, not in individual men's biographies.[28] But such analysis cannot explain how and why genocidal situations arise in the first place. For this, leaders are necessary, leaders who incite others to murderous actions. And such leaders—like Greiser—are shaped by their experiences. They come to their hatreds and prejudices through real or perceived slights and injuries, all too often reactions to historical developments in which they found themselves on the 'losing' side. Biography, then, helps to explain the genesis of genocidal circumstances. Perhaps even more important, it ascribes responsibility for heinous crimes—to individuals, not just to impersonal situations.

While a brief summary of Greiser's life might suggest a straightforward radicalization from Posen youth to war veteran to anti-Polish Nazi zealot, this was not actually the case. In fact, right up to when Greiser joined the NSDAP, his life might have taken a very different direction. This biography underscores the notion that there was nothing inevitable about the rise of the Nazis or Germans' attraction to them. At the same time, while historians have long analyzed the factors that led individuals to join the NSDAP, they have only more recently focused on how Nazis underwent a 'cumulative radicalization' within the movement.[29] Greiser, for one, was probably radicalized more by his experiences within the party than those beforehand. In large part, this was due to a bitter power struggle in Danzig.

In 1930, Hitler sent Albert Forster, one of his young favorites, to be Danzig's Gauleiter. For the next nine years, Greiser served as deputy Gauleiter to Forster. For Greiser, this was galling: he had to play second fiddle to a man five years younger and much less tied to Danzig. Their rivalry was exacerbated after May 1933, when the Nazis won elections and thus ruled the city. While Forster controlled the Danzig NSDAP, Greiser became senate president and thus chief executive of the tiny Free City state in November 1934.

The Greiser–Forster rivalry is key to understanding the Nazi that Greiser became. This aspect of the Greiser story underlines the personal nature of politics in the Nazi regime. Greiser's career was fundamentally shaped by his fierce jockeying for power with Forster. Unfortunately for Greiser, the Danzig Gauleiter always had the upper hand: whenever necessary, Forster could turn to Hitler for help and support. Greiser, by contrast, was handicapped by the fact that he had joined the NSDAP relatively late for a high-ranking Nazi. Since he never enjoyed the sort of trust that Hitler placed in his old cronies, he sought to raise his profile in other ways. First, he found other patrons, most notably Heinrich Himmler, leader of the SS (*Schutzstaffel*, literally Protection Squad). Second, in hopes of distinguishing himself, Greiser sometimes advocated policies at odds with those of his rival Forster. In the late 1930s, he thus supported 'moderate' Nazi policies such as not insisting on the immediate removal of the Jews from Danzig. It was only after this moderation brought him political defeat—Greiser lost his Danzig positions in August 1939—that he played up his Nazi zeal by espousing 'radical' Nazi policies. All this complicates the man. How deep were Greiser's ideological passions? Was he just a rank opportunist? Or did he marry a pragmatic ambition with nationalist fervor?

In the Warthegau, Greiser joined the ranks of the Gauleiters, the leaders of the forty-one (later forty-two) Nazi Gaus.[30] Hitler viewed his Gauleiters as his most trusted lieutenants; unlike Greiser, many came from among his earliest and staunchest supporters. Given his late entry into the party, the fact that Greiser became a Gauleiter at all testifies to his political tenacity and to the fact that Hitler wanted a Gauleiter with borderlands experience in the Warthegau. While the Führer allowed all of his Gauleiters considerable free rein, those who served in the Old Reich (areas belonging to Germany before annexations began in 1938) held circumscribed powers.[31] In the annexed eastern Gaus, this was not the case. There, Hitler gave his Gauleiters extraordinary powers to Germanize their regions. In the Warthegau, Greiser was not only Gauleiter, but also Reichsstatthalter or governor, thus combining the top party and state positions in his person. By claiming that Hitler had granted him 'special powers' to Germanize the region, Greiser came to thwart virtually all meddling by Reich ministries in his Gau's affairs.[32]

Hitler reportedly once stated that 'every Gau should have its own face according to the personality of its leader and the particular problems of the population.'[33] Often, developments at the Gau level can be explained only with reference to the Gauleiter in charge. Among the annexed eastern Gaus, for example, Greiser set policies that differed significantly from those of his peers in Danzig–West Prussia, Upper Silesia, and East Prussia. While these differing policies partly reflected the unique conditions of individual Gaus, they also resulted from the Gauleiters' preferences. The Gauleiter in a particular region made a definite difference, often all the difference. As I argue throughout this book, Greiser—and no other individual or institution—was responsible for much of what happened in his Gau.

Shortly after coming to the Warthegau, Greiser declared that 'our distant goal . . . is to become a model Gau of the Great German Reich.'[34] He was not the only Gauleiter to entertain this ambition; many others claimed or aspired to 'model Gau' status.[35] Their Gaus, they hoped, would show the way to the Third Reich's future. But Greiser faced formidable challenges in meeting this goal. Although close to five million individuals lived in the Warthegau, almost 4.2 million of them were Poles, 400,000 were Jews, and just 325,000 were Germans.[36] To Greiser, however, the population's makeup was a source of opportunity: 'Here we are able to construct a truly National-Socialist Gau. Before us, we have a "virgin territory" in which the ideology of National Socialism must have a total breakthrough. What happens here is a drill for the Reich and a visiting card for the German East.'[37] Greiser neglected to spell out that the Warthegau could only become a 'virgin territory' if draconian methods were deployed to remove the Polish and Jewish populations. Precisely because it was so far from the Nazi ideal, Greiser's Gau did become a model—a model of Nazi brutality.

As the Nazi occupation unfolded, some of Greiser's policies and administrative practices were copied elsewhere. Greiser's mode of rule—by decree, free of Berlin ministerial interference—was emulated by other eastern Gauleiters. Many of his policies toward Poles were replicated in the other eastern Gaus. Perhaps most important, Greiser's Warthegau served as a model for the developing genocide of Jews. In early 1940, Gau authorities established the first major ghetto in Nazi-occupied Europe in Lodsch (soon renamed Litzmannstadt). The Litzmannstadt ghetto pioneered the systematic exploitation of Jews for their labor; eventually, it became the most industrialized of the Nazi Jewish ghettos. The Gau also saw the largest network of Jewish forced labor camps in occupied Europe. On Greiser's initiative, the first Nazi extermination camp—Chełmno—was built in the

Warthegau. In early December 1941, the first mass gassings of Jews took place there, some six weeks before the Wannsee Conference.[38] In all sorts of ways, then, Greiser's Gau proved to be a 'model.'

Why did Greiser end up leading with such a radical bent? No doubt, this reflected a hyper-nationalism incubated in his borderlands youth and his personal competition with Forster in Danzig. But there was more. Greiser's need to present himself as a zealous Nazi was also a response to deep-seated personal insecurities. From his youth onwards, Greiser craved attention and admiration. But for a Nazi, Greiser's pre-movement years, as well as the first part of his party career, contained shortcomings. To make up for these imperfections, I argue, Greiser as Gauleiter tried to act as a super Nazi by promoting the most extreme Nazi solutions to alleged problems. Indeed, while he explicitly aimed to make the Warthegau a 'model Gau,' he also tried to fashion himself into a 'model Nazi.'[39] To him, an exemplary Nazi leader was tough, radical, and brooked no compromise. In no small measure, then, this is a book about the self-conscious making of a mid-level Nazi actor. As the following pages show, Greiser expended much psychic and other energy to turn himself into what he believed his movement demanded.

As a start, Greiser manipulated his life story to shore up his Nazi credentials. He played up, altered, or even fabricated elements of his past life.[40] He touted a heroic war record, but his military career was subject to doubt. He supposedly fought in Free Corps units after the war, but his para-military activity was quite minimal. He joined several right-wing political groupings in Danzig, but his membership was all but nominal. While each such newly characterized detail might seem trivial, together they added up to a new autobiography.

But even more was at stake in these manipulations. The politics of biography were crucial in the Nazi regime. Biographical details served as excuses to both reward and discipline longtime Nazis.[41] Many Nazi 'old fighters' reaped the rewards of their revolutionary pasts with jobs and sinecures after 1933.[42] But for Greiser—and not a few other longtime Nazis—their past lives had the potential to derail their political careers. In the 1920s, for example, Greiser had been a Free Mason; Hitler absolutely detested Free Masonry. Greiser also joined the party very late for a high-ranking Nazi. And in 1934 he created a scandal by abandoning his wife and cavorting with his mistress, a professional pianist, shortly before the

Nazis needed to win an important election. That same year, the NSDAP undertook an investigation into his past life; nine years later, in 1943, another took place. Although cleared both times, Greiser remained vulnerable. At any time, he worried, some aspect of his past life might resurface, and he would be subject to another humiliating party investigation.

Greiser was not the only one to manipulate his life story. Shortly after World War II, West German revanchists circulated rumors about him to foment anti-Polish sentiment; they aimed to ratchet up calls for the return of lands taken by Poland in 1945. They claimed that prior to his hanging, Greiser was put in a steel cage and paraded around Poznań while angry Poles pelted him with rotten eggs and other noxious objects.[43] Although not true, it is the story that is best known about Greiser, and it has found its way into many of the brief biographical summaries published about him. Both during his life and after his death, Greiser's life story was the object of political manipulation.

In writing this biography, I have been able to use some remarkable—and previously untapped—sources. During World War I, Greiser wrote hundreds of letters home; in the 1930s, he wrote dozens of letters to his mistress and later wife; over the years, he wrote some letters to his children; and lastly, he wrote two letters to his wife from his Poznań prison cell in 1946. (Unfortunately, there are almost no personal papers pertaining to the years 1939-45, just when Greiser was at the height of his power. For these years, I have had to treat Greiser with a certain distance.) I was also able to interview four individuals who knew Greiser personally, including his daughter, his niece, his cousin, and his personal adjutant in 1945. The letters and interviews humanize Greiser; they bring out his sense of humor, his lively mind, and his sometimes rather pleasant qualities.

The more intimate sources also suggest that Greiser embodied the contradictory impulses that have now become a cliché about Nazi perpetrators—the oft-found combination of decency and cruelty, culture and barbarity, sentimentality and brutality.[44] To the world, Greiser was a cruel Nazi leader, but in his private life, he was a dutiful son, loving father, amorous husband, and good friend. To the world, he thundered his hatreds, but he was generally even-keeled and respectful in private interaction. To the world, he presented himself as a hard, soldierly Nazi, but he was always prone to anxiety, depression, and psychosomatic illnesses. To the world, Greiser projected himself as a man of culture, but he rarely read a book and he never finished secondary school. All this, however, is not really so peculiar. Like most Nazis (and, indeed, most of us), Greiser had a deep capacity to engage in contradictions, tolerate ambiguities, and compartmentalize his life.

Although he made a heady Nazi career, Greiser was surely not a man at peace with himself. He was not only torn by personal doubts and career ambitions, but also by conflicting political aims. Although a hard-bitten enemy of Poles, he could, when necessary, be a realist in his policy toward them; some of his policies thus complicate his reputation as a Nazi 'racial fanatic.'[45] Moreover, despite his eagerness to ethnically cleanse the Poles, he did not always want them deported; he needed Poles as workers. For the same reason, he sometimes tried to ameliorate Poles' situation. Greiser was also torn about his policy toward Jews. He wanted to maintain a Jewish workforce to carry out his Germanization projects and to otherwise generate funds for his Gau. Yet he also wished to have Jews killed so as to satisfy Himmler's murderous cravings. Greiser thus felt burdened by his crimes—but for all the wrong reasons.

Greiser's biography presents numerous absences, gaps, twists, and contradictions. But as we know from other biographies, individual lives do not always, or even usually, add up to a coherent whole. Greiser experienced deep ruptures in his life, largely brought on by circumstances beyond his control: World War I, Germany's loss of Posen province, Danzig's curious interwar situation, the rise of Nazism, World War II, and finally, Nazi defeat. The different pieces of his lived experience created a jagged life narrative, at least until he arrived in the Warthegau. There, the disparate parts of his biography coalesced into a dreadful Germanization project. But this, too, may impose too much unity on what in many ways remained an inconsistent biography. For Greiser, like most individuals, faced competing pressures that he responded to in different ways, at different times, and in different situations. At one time or another, he privileged ideology over pragmatism; ambition over ideology; and pragmatism over passion. As the historian Simone Lässig has written, 'heterogeneity is typical of *every* person.'[46] Greiser was no exception.

Like all biographies, this one is a product of its times. In recent years, historians of Germany have shifted their interest from the Nazi rise to power and the genesis of World War II to a preoccupation with the Holocaust and other Nazi crimes committed in occupied Europe. Decades ago, a biography of Greiser might well have included an extended discussion of Danzig affairs in the 1930s and how these contributed to the outbreak of World War II. While these matters are touched on, they are not the main focus of this book. We live in an era obsessed with the Holocaust and other cases of ethnic cleansing and genocide. I thus emphasize how Greiser became a Nazi leader eager to carry out vicious ethnic-cleansing and genocidal measures. I also devote considerable attention to the details of his Germanization project.

Greiser's life offers considerable insight into how some Germans became Nazi perpetrators. In Chapters 1 and 2, I describe Greiser as a young man and newly minted Nazi. These chapters illustrate how formative experiences flowed into Greiser's later political views; how longstanding resentments, insecurities, and personality traits fueled Greiser's Nazi persona; and how Greiser changed through his encounter with the Nazi movement. Chapter 3 recounts his tenure as Senate President in Danzig, including how his rivalry with Forster led him to adopt some 'moderate' Nazi policies. Chapter 4 offers an overview of his position in the Warthegau, and begins to explore how Greiser accumulated the powers that made it possible for him to carry out a radical Germanization program. Together, these chapters suggest how mid-ranking Nazi perpetrators were shaped by their experiences both inside and outside of the Nazi movement: their motives, their values and sensibilities, and their strategies for forging a career.

The heart of this book lies in Chapters 5–7. Here, I describe Greiser's policies toward Germans, Poles, and Jews. Rather than exploring the story of each of these groups in separate chapters (and thereby suggesting separate stories as most other historians have done), I present an integrated history of Greiser's Germanization program.[47] Examining the Holocaust in the context of a more general Germanization program may strike some readers as controversial or even loathsome. By definition, it would seem, this strategy must detract from the extreme suffering that Jews experienced. But as I hope readers will come to understand, the specific forms of persecution that Jews endured in the Warthegau had much to do with Greiser's more general Germanization policy. Policies toward incoming Germans led to the deportation of Poles, the removal of Poles prevented the deportation of Jews, and the impossibility of evacuating Jews led to their continued ghettoization and subsequent murder. Discrimination against Poles demanded an intricate system of ethnic classification that deeply affected Germans living in the Gau; it also underscored the very real difference between the discriminatory treatment of Poles and the murderous treatment of Jews in the Gau. Finally, transforming the Gau's natural, built, and cultural environment to make it 'German' depended on resources generated in large part through the expropriation of Polish and Jewish property, and the exploitation of Jewish and Polish labor.

An integrated approach exploring Greiser's policies toward Germans, Poles, and Jews holds many benefits. We can only appreciate the totality of his Germanization program by exploring these interconnections. Such an approach also reveals the ambition, minutiae, and inconsistencies of the Germanization project. Moreover, it makes clear that some Nazis, at least, saw non-Jewish 'foreign' population groups as just as threatening as Jews. It further reminds us that Nazi plans for the 'cleansing' of Nazi-occupied Europe went well beyond the Holocaust. Had the Nazis triumphed in World War II, the Third Reich would have seen a wholesale slaughter of many non-German peoples. For Nazis of Greiser's ilk—those imbued with a hyper-nationalism stemming from their experiences in borderlands areas—the Nazi project was about much more than 'just' the de-Judaization of continental Europe.

The final two chapters recount Greiser's downfall. In Chapter 8, I relate how Greiser lived and ruled as Gauleiter, particularly during the last war years; and how his power came to an abrupt end with the Red Army's arrival in his Gau in January 1945. In Chapter 9, I examine Greiser's Polish trial. In yet another reinvention of his past life, Greiser adopted an implausible defense strategy in which he claimed to have never been a 'true' Nazi. The trial made legal history: because Greiser was indicted after the Nuremberg proceedings began, but convicted before those verdicts were announced, he was the first person ever found guilty of 'crimes against the peace.' Finally, in a short Afterword, I locate this biography in the context of how historians' views of Nazi perpetrators and their regime have evolved.

In writing this book, I have often felt a deep discomfort. In small part, this is due to parallels between my own family history and that of Greiser and his family. Like Greiser's father, my great-grandfather was a German Protestant civil servant in a borderlands area—in this case not Posen, but Alsace. After World War I, my great grandparents and their children were expelled from what had become their homeland. Always nostalgic about their beloved Alsace, they were very bitter about Germany's loss of the province. Like Greiser, one of my grandmother's sisters became a very committed Nazi. While this great aunt didn't initiate the murder of Jews or the persecution of Poles, she nonetheless believed deeply in the Nazi cause. My grandmother, meanwhile, married a man of Jewish origins, and she and my grandfather left Nazi Germany, emigrating first to England and later the United States. Greiser's sister, too, married a man of Jewish origins, and that couple left Germany, first for Shanghai, and later for the United States. As all this suggests, the distance between the two families is not so great: members of both harbored the same resentments and shared the same fates. Could someone in my family have become Arthur Greiser?

Much more troubling is a whole other set of concerns. I have often been asked: 'How could you devote so much time to a person who created so much suffering?' Or 'Can you write a biography of someone without getting close to your subject?' Those working on perpetrators frequently face the objection that the very act of trying to explain perpetrators somehow justifies or even forgives their subjects' conduct. Understanding, in this view, becomes empathy. Alternatively, others fear that trying to explain human evil inevitably leads to contamination—that at the very least, I, as the biographer, will become callous or numb to my subject's deeds.[48] These are legitimate objections and fears. I have regularly needed to remind myself of all the awful crimes that Greiser committed—especially when writing about other parts of his life. Beyond such objections, I also wonder whether Greiser might best be forgotten by history. Why grant him the dignity of a biography? Nevertheless, despite misgivings, I believe that we should confront the lives of those who create enormous evil. The Nazi regime was not a unique example of barbarous crimes. Too often, genocide is perpetrated, only too recently in Yugoslavia, Rwanda, and Darfur. Understanding perpetrators should be viewed as a critical process: one that heightens our sensitivity to the circumstances (political, economic, social, and even psychological) in which people create great evil. Greater sensitivity toward those circumstances, I hope, will allow us to better see and contain the threat of genocide, before millions more have died.

Last but not least, I am left with a nagging doubt that may bedevil all biographers, but surely those working on perpetrators. The historian Volker Berghahn, for one, has suggested that 'the perpetrator ultimately may well remain impenetrable.'[49] Put otherwise, do I really 'know' Greiser? Do I have him right? After years of working on Greiser, I believe I do. Yet who can know for sure? Greiser is long since dead. Those who knew him as a family member—as a father or uncle—knew him as such, not as a merciless Nazi perpetrator. Those who knew him as a boss must have known or suspected some of his crimes, but they will not speak of them, lest they incriminate themselves. I know Greiser mostly through the extensive paper trail that he left behind. After working through reams of documents and listening to those who knew him, I have aimed to write a biography that is true to the man. I hope to have captured Greiser as he was—his strengths and weaknesses, his passions and interests, his motives and inclinations. Through much of my writing, I have tried to suspend judgment about him. But ultimately, Greiser and all other perpetrators must be explained and evaluated. Greiser's life trajectory, I believe, was bound up in a complex knot of xenophobic nationalism, career ambition, and personal insecurity. This, to be sure, is a miserable tangle. But within that knot, I believe, lies the explanation for how and why Arthur Greiser's life ended on the gallows that July morning in 1946.

I

'Child of the East:' Posen Province, World War I, Danzig

Nazis were made, not born. In the first thirty-two years of his life, Arthur Greiser lived the experiences that made Nazis out of many Germans. But he did not follow a straight path to Nazism. Indeed, Greiser was not preordained to be a Nazi. In every stage of his life, some of his actions belie those one might expect of a future fanatical Nazi. Later on, Greiser would also embellish or even fabricate some facts of his life so as to make them adhere to a heroic Nazi ideal. Untangling Greiser's early biography is thus no easy matter. Doing so, however, provides valuable insight into what led some Germans to become Nazis.

At the same time, evidence from Greiser's youth suggests personality traits that would play a role in his later actions as a Nazi. From an early age, Greiser displayed a liking for attention and admiration, a desire for the good life, and a near obsession with status. Such personal characteristics did not lead him to become a Nazi—that was due to his experiences in the decade after World War I. But they do help to explain the kind of Nazi that he became: vain and ambitious, eager to stand out, and jealous of his power and authority.

Arthur Karl Greiser was born in Schroda, in the Prussian province of Posen, on 22 January 1897.[1] His father, Gustav Greiser, was born in Gdingen (near Danzig) in 1861. The Greiser family had a glazier business. At an early age, however, Gustav hurt his hand and couldn't work in the family business.[2] Instead, he joined the Prussian civil service in 1885. As of 1893, he had a permanent position as a bailiff.[3] Arthur's mother, Ida Siegmund, was born in Kempen (Posen Province) in 1870. She was the daughter of a prosperous lumber merchant.[4] Gustav and Ida married in 1888.[5] In quick succession, the couple had three children—Wilhelm, Käthe, and Otto—in 1889, 1890, and 1891. Arthur, born six years later, was the baby of the family.

The Greisers belonged to a lower middle-class milieu. Although Gustav had entered the professional civil service, his social status remained similar to that of his craftsman background. The building in which Arthur was born, 1 Market Square, was a simple affair located on the town's market square. The Greisers' apartment consisted of just a kitchen and one other room.[6] Although never in dire financial straits, the Greisers lived frugally. In 1904, Gustav Greiser petitioned the Ministry of Justice to have the official length of his service changed; according to Gustav, it was possible to calculate his service in such a way that he would be entitled to a higher pay grade. 'Furthermore,' he wrote, 'I most humbly ask that you take into consideration that already three of my four children attend secondary school which is associated with significant costs.'[7] His petition, however, was rejected.[8] Although Gustav felt the pinch of educating his children, all four Greiser children continued their educations after the mandatory schooling age; Gustav and Ida encouraged the virtues of education and social advancement in their children. Arthur attended elementary school and the local classical high school in Hohensalza, a larger provincial town to which his father was transferred in 1900.

While little else is known about his youth, growing up in Posen province proved important for Greiser's Nazi career. In 1939, Hitler appointed Greiser Gauleiter in Posen not least because he was, as the Führer noted, 'a child of the East.'[9] Greiser, himself, it seems, came to think of himself as a 'child of the East' only after he joined the NSDAP; only then did he recast his lived experience into an anti-Polish, hyper-German nationalist narrative. Nonetheless, from his earliest days, Greiser knew something of Polish–German competition for hegemony in the area. He also became familiar with the repertoire of ethnic-cleansing measures available in the early twentieth century. In interwar Danzig, Greiser and the Nazis imitated Prussian economic measures to strengthen the German element in the Free City. And after 1939, Greiser looked to Prussian precedents to Germanize the Warthegau. In the end, though, he radicalized these measures beyond anything that Prussian authorities had ever envisioned.

In 1793, Poznania (the territory that made up the province of Posen) fell to Prussia in the second partition of Poland. Except for the brief period of 1807–15, the area remained under Prussian administration until the end of World War I. Throughout the nineteenth century, Poles made up 60–65 percent of the population. Prussian administrators vacillated between conciliatory and hard-line approaches to them.[10] By the last decades of the century, however, they had decided on more forceful Germanization measures that included language laws, official discrimination, building projects, and settlement programs. Germanization was to prevent the re-emergence of a Polish state that, in turn, could lead to German territorial losses.[11] In 1876, the Official Language Law made German the only official language in Prussia. Bilingual signs disappeared, and Polish place names were replaced with German names.[12] Schools were also affected: from the 1870s onwards, various laws sharply curtailed the use of Polish in elementary schools. In 1908 the Reichstag (parliament) passed an Association Law that decreed that all organizations—even those dedicated to Polish cultural endeavors—had to use German as their official language in counties in which at least 40 percent of the population was German.[13] Prussian Germanization measures also aimed to retard Polish economic advancement. Large public building projects, for example, employed only German laborers and used German materials produced in the area.[14] Prussian authorities made subsidies and loans available to needy German shopkeepers, doctors, and farmers. In addition, Prussian authorities hoped to attract Germans to the area by modernizing the province. They regulated the Warta River, built a port in Posen, and extended the rail network. In Posen, they erected numerous imposing public buildings to project German power and celebrate German culture. In 1899 the Hygiene Institute was opened, in 1902 the Kaiser-Wilhelm Library, in 1903 the Royal Academy and Bismark Monument, in 1904 the Kaiser-Friedrich Museum, in 1908 headquarters for the Prussian Settlement Commission, and in 1910 the City Theater and 600-room Posen Castle. The Castle, built as a royal residence for William II, later served as Greiser's headquarters.

Like the Nazis who would follow later, Prussian authorities hoped to alter the region's demographic makeup. Between 1885 and 1887, Bismarck oversaw the expulsion of some 30,000 Poles and Jews who were not Prussian citizens to Russia and Galicia.[15] In 1886, hoping to settle more Germans in the province, the government also founded the Royal Prussian Settlement Commission. According to the official act, it was 'for the strengthening of the German element in the provinces of West Prussia and Posen against attempted Polonization through the settlement of German peasants and workers.'[16] The Commission was charged with buying Polish land for resale to German settlers. Eventually, it spent 734 million Marks and, at the height of its activity, employed some 900 persons.[17] But its success was decidedly mixed. By 1918, the Commission had placed 21,886 settlers (with their families, 153,800 persons) in Posen and West Prussia.[18] Germans, however, were still just barely able to hold their own in Poznania; Poles continued to outnumber them by a ratio of two to one.[19]

Historians generally agree that Prussian Germanization measures backfired.[20] Rather than spawning a loyal Polish population, they strengthened the Polish nationalist movement. Polish nationalist leaders mobilized their constituents in opposition to Germanization policies. They also founded a variety of civil organizations to counter official discrimination. After 1886, for example, Poles created institutions to buy land for their countrymen so that Germans would not acquire it.[21] They maintained self-help institutions (known as Organic Work) to bolster Polish economic activity, including cooperative banks, lending libraries, a trade union system, a growing press, and a scholarship fund.[22] They also founded a variety of Polish political parties and a rich assortment of singing, sports, and other clubs to strengthen Polish nationalist loyalty.

By the time Greiser was born, Posen province was a hotbed of nationalist tensions. German and Polish nationalists vied against each other while also trying to mobilize their nationally indifferent neighbors. In 1894, militant German nationalists had founded the Eastern Marches Society in Posen. The society tirelessly lobbied Prussian authorities for ever harsher Germanization measures. In turn, in the late 1890s, Roman Dmowski founded the National Democratic movement to unite Poles across the partition regimes; it was headquartered in Posen. Prussian Germanization policy neither made Germans out of Poles, nor a German region out of a Polish area. Instead, it created a legacy of bitter German–Polish tensions.

It's not clear how much Arthur's father, Gustav Greiser, was caught up in these borderland tensions; the evidence is contradictory. Greiser family members believed that Gustav opposed the Germanization of Poles. As one family source put it, 'He [Gustav] was instructed to make good Germans of the Poles under his jurisdiction, including forcing them to speak German. He was a very humane individual, and it bothered his conscience that he was inflicting punishment of this kind, so he refused.'[23] There is some minor evidence to support this. In 1898, a civil-service decree obligated German bureaucrats to contribute to 'strengthening of

Germandom;' they were to speak only German at home, keep their children away from Polish influence, and profess German sentiments 'frankly and unambiguously.'[24] In violation of this decree, however, Gustav allowed Arthur to learn Polish; decades later, Arthur's Polish was still good enough to toast a Polish official visiting Danzig.[25] By contrast, a Polish author insisted that Gustav was militantly anti-Polish. Gustav, he claimed, worked as a official debt collector and used his position 'for his own ends, most often at the expense of Poles.' This same author continued, 'when his dirty machinations compromised his office ever more, his superiors officially transferred him to Inowrocław [Hohensalza].'[26] In all likelihood, Gustav neither sympathized with the Polish plight, nor used his official position to exploit Poles. But after he retired from the civil service in 1912, he became a director of cooperative associations for the Eastern Marches movement.[27] This commitment suggests that Gustav harbored strong German nationalist sentiments—of which Arthur certainly would have been aware.

Accounts of Arthur's sympathies, too, are inconclusive. Some Polish sources claim that as a youth, Arthur was violently anti-Polish. One, written around the time of Greiser's trial in 1946, claimed that 'little Arthur' embodied all sorts of negative features: 'Most of all he liked to fight. Eagerly he attacked Poles, he insulted them, he initiated rows, and he resorted to fist fights [with them] . . . Healthy, robust, and forceful, already then he tried to violently impose his will on others . . . To destroy and to give in to the lowest instincts—this unruly boy later transformed these specific traits into his passion.' As a secondary school student, this source continues, Greiser organized an anti-Polish club: 'On the grounds of the Inowrocław gymnasium he created a German organization with a distinct chauvinistic program. The struggle with the Polish element was the principal content of its activities. Young Greiser with his hatred of Poles initiated constant disturbances on the school grounds, creating an atmosphere of open nationalistic struggle.' The pedagogical board of the school—consisting of Germans—supposedly recommended that Greiser be expelled for his anti-Polish activity.[28] Another Polish source claims that Greiser *was* thrown out of high school for 'rowdy behavior, showing aggression toward his Polish fellow students and initiating fights with them.'[29] But in a curriculum vitae written for Nazi party authorities in the mid-1930s, Greiser never mentioned an expulsion.[30] Since the Nazis prided themselves on past persecution, it seems unlikely Greiser would have suppressed an incident which would have enhanced his militant image.

In fact, Greiser may not have shown much anti-Polish zeal as a youth at all. At his trial, a former Polish classmate testified about Greiser as a pupil. Before World War I, S. Kozielski recalled, Greiser was not hostile toward Poles: 'He acted like the majority of boys. In any case, before the war the times were totally different than during Hitler's rule.' As Kozielski suggested, Prussian school authorities did not do much to foster anti-Polish sentiment. The school atmosphere changed only after the outbreak of war when, Kozielski recalled, German pupils began to create German fraternities. According to Kozielski, Greiser was now reserved in relations with Polish schoolmates, but he was not one who hurled abuse on them.[31] Greiser's own reflections on his schooling also suggest that he had not been so caught up in Polish–German national tensions. In 1941, he returned to his former school on the occasion of its renaming as the 'Arthur-Greiser-School.' He now dwelt more on its earlier class distinctions than on racial matters. As he reportedly stated, 'at that time, only children of affluent parents could attend secondary school. At that time, pupils came for their school-leaving exam [*Abitur*] in a frock coat and top hat.'[32] Greiser himself, however, never completed that exam—and not because his family couldn't pay. Instead, at age seventeen, he was swept up in the patriotic fervor that accompanied the start of World War I. He soon volunteered for war, trading the boredom of school days for the dangers of military life.

On 28 June 1914, Archduke Franz Ferdinand, the heir to the Austro-Hungarian throne, was assassinated by a Bosnian Serb in Sarejevo. Longstanding tensions among the Great Powers in Europe soon burst into war. In the hope of benefiting from a military head start, Germany declared war on Russia on 1 August, and on France on 3 August. The next day, 4 August, Germany invaded neutral Belgium and Britain declared war on Germany. For the next four years, millions of men fought for their countries in a senseless war of destruction. Cowering in trenches, hungering in barracks, flying dangerous missions, or dying in no man's land—all were part of the lived experience of Europe's male youth. Like Greiser, many future Nazis, and not least Hitler, were veterans of this terrible conflagration. As many have argued, the Nazi movement was born of German defeat in World War I.

Greiser recorded his war experiences in a steady stream of letters that he sent home; many are now found at the Institute for National Remembrance in Warsaw. Most date from when he was stationed in

Flanders between 1915 and 1917. The letters suggest that Greiser was a confident youth, a dutiful son, a devoted brother, and a loyal comrade. Although no brilliant writer, Greiser had a flair for describing his daily happenings, whether a battle in the trenches or a day of amusement in Ostende. He had a fine sense of humor; the tone of his letters was often ironic or self-deprecating. While Greiser surely didn't relate everything to his parents, he was quite open with them. The letters thus record the vicissitudes of his wartime experiences: frustration as a new recruit, initial excitement at the front, ambivalence as the war took its toll, exhilaration when he joined the navy airmen, and a breakdown of sorts as the war drew to a close. The letters also suggest some of Greiser's less appealing traits: a desire for attention and admiration, a pronounced liking for the 'good life,' and a preoccupation with status and its symbols. The letters betray little inkling that he would become a cruel Nazi. Indeed, like the vast majority of future Nazis, Greiser seemed a well-adjusted and well-integrated young man.

Like so many others in summer 1914, Greiser eagerly volunteered for service at the front. He always claimed that he began naval service on 4 August. His choosing of this date was important. On that day, Germany not only invaded Belgium, but its emperor, Kaiser Wilhelm II, made a famous speech declaring that he no longer recognized political divisions in Germany, but 'only Germans.'[33] August 4 thus symbolized Germany's spirit of nationalistic unity. Both his letters and official military record, however, show that Greiser enlisted in the navy only a month later, on 7 September 1914.[34] Perhaps he volunteered in August, but was only officially enlisted in September. Greiser's earlier dating of the start of his service is the first of several elements of his past life that he later manipulated so as to make his biography appear more heroic.

Greiser was initially stationed in a naval artillery unit in Friedrichsort, a training area outside of Kiel. In spring and summer 1915, he was at the nearby Battery Laboe. On 25 September 1915, deemed ready for war, Greiser left for Belgium. The next morning, his excitement was palpable. En route to Flanders, he wrote, '602 men are on the train, the mood is marvelous. This past night I slept perfectly on three backpacks . . . As we ride by, the population cannot wave enough at us.'[35] Ten days later, he was part of a mine-clearing unit laying wire along the front.[36] He proudly noted: 'The work is dangerous, but we are almost finished . . . Here the air is damn thick, we haven't been out of our clothes in four days and we are near starving. At the moment we hear an English warship shooting at Zeebrugge.'[37]

Although in the navy, Greiser was always part of units that fought on land (or later in the skies). He was stationed along the coast of Belgium, near Ostende, roughly twenty miles northwest of Ypres, Langemarck, and Passchendaele, where some of the most famous battles in Flanders took place. As part of the Second Sailor Artillery Regiment, he fought in skirmishes to defend and extend the German front along the Yser River at its most northern point, at its mouth into the North Sea.[38] Indeed, Greiser once proudly wrote that 'When I'm out at the front now, I'm the first flank man of the officer scouts on the western front; our post is on the last dune toward the ocean before Nieuport-Bad.'[39] When not actually fighting, his duties alternated between scouting at the front and guard duty behind the lines.

From late 1915 until early 1917, Greiser was more or less in constant danger; his letters are filled with descriptions of the perils he survived. Around Christmas 1915, for example, he participated in a battle that raged during the holidays. On Christmas Eve, just when he and some comrades had put on their Christmas coffee, they received orders to attack the French. They were soon surrounded by '... an absolute racket; a roar as if hell had opened up; when we looked back we saw huge tongues of flame everywhere...' They did not wait long for the French response: 'Twice as much iron splinters around us as we sent over there... If I had all the money that flew over my head in this one hour, [it would be] a Christmas present for my whole life...'[40] The battle continued over the next days. On 2 January, the French attacked the Germans: 'I've really never experienced so much fire, smoke, and the stink of gunpowder, we couldn't see 15 meters ahead of us... then there was also a nice sandstorm, so that we couldn't do anything without glasses to protect us.'[41] A week later, Greiser wrote: 'At the moment I'm back at the front and happy to be alive, yesterday it was not nice in the gas mask and the idiotic mine fire.'[42] And later that month, Greiser wrote of his nineteenth birthday: 'On the 22nd I was in the battery; the day began with four grenades thrown behind us and ended with four bombs that they dropped in M[iddelkerke].' Two days later at the front: '... there was great confusion, heavy bombardment, mines, machine guns, and all death and devil. Three times on that day I had more luck than reason.' But the Germans were successful. They managed to destroy a tower in Nieuport that had allowed 'wonderful surveillance by the evil enemy.'[43]

Greiser endured the miserable conditions of front life. Often, he went without basic foodstuffs: 'Butter is a great rarity; in fact, there is none.'[44] On another occasion he begged: 'Provisions are flagging, if you have an extra egg, I would be very grateful.'[45] He sometimes complained bitterly about the heat and bugs: 'Is it so idiotically hot there as here? During the day I can hardly escape the flies and during the night mosquitos and gnats, without mosquito netting it can't be endured.'[46] His accommodations ran the gamut. When scouting, he lived in primitive shacks at various observation posts. But at other times, his lodgings were luxurious. 'I live like a king,' he wrote in December 1916. Indeed, just then his room was in a house on the grounds of the Belgian king's summer residence in Raversijde, a royal chalet built off the proceeds of King Leopold's brutally exploitative rubber-gathering practices in the Congo.[47] Greiser's room had a bay window, many mirrors, stone tiles, and six electric bulbs.[48]

In Belgium, Greiser first experienced harsh occupation methods. Although the German military committed war atrocities there, Greiser may well not have participated or even known about them. But he certainly knew about and engaged in requisitioning, which he recognized for what it was: robbery. On Christmas Day 1916, he noted that 'my flunky is roasting a duck for the holiday, stolen specifically for today.'[49] He seems to have had few qualms about taking things from the civilian population: 'Today I sent home... four nice Flemish pictures that I requisitioned here...'[50] At least one historian has suggested that occupied Belgium served as a 'forerunner of Nazi Europe.'[51] In the Warthegau, Greiser would condone an administration that was notorious for its robbery of Polish and Jewish property.

Greiser impressed his officers with his intelligence and diligence. In February 1916, he was thus chosen to take a course that would qualify him as a reserve officer candidate (*Reserveoffizieranwärter*, or ROA). Greiser preened: 'Yes, I have the peculiar luck of being the only one from my 6 comrades—all of whom already have the school-leaving exam and are older—to be ordered to the ROA course.'[52] Throughout his life, Greiser would emphasize his hard-won successes despite the fact that he had not completed high school. Yet as much as the distinction of being chosen for the ROA course flattered his vanity, Greiser complained non-stop about the workload: 'For the course I have a dreadful amount of work, some days in addition to regular service, five to six hours of lessons and when there's free time, we must really exert ourselves to digest all the stuff.'[53] The course included both practical and theoretical training. Greiser learned about artillery plans, shooting charts, naval gunnery, the military judicial system, and the organization of the navy.[54] He detested the theoretical aspects of the course: 'It's about time that it end, for nothing is more odious to me than intellectual work.'[55] Greiser's distaste for intellectual work accompanied him throughout his life. He probably volunteered for military duty so as to escape the school bench. In Danzig and Posen, he disliked the administrative aspects of rule; reading memoranda was never his idea of a good time. He thought of himself as a man of action, not a man of ideas—a sense that would become more pronounced during his Nazi career.

In his letters, Greiser showed a preoccupation with status and recognition; this, too, followed him through his Nazi career. 'I'm in the midst of colossal work,' he wrote in April 1916, 'A higher entity gave me a task and placed me as a guard at a new operation that is colossally important . . .' Greiser underscored the significance of his job: '. . . the success of the operation depends on my actions; I could come before a court martial if something goes wrong . . . This morning the commander of the sector said a nice word to me: "You are still young, the life and death of hundreds is in your hands, but my regiment and I trust you." Something like that is fun.'[56] In May 1916, when Greiser passed the ROA course, he wrote to his parents that the officer in charge 'said to me in confidence that I had written the best exams of all . . ., everything 5 and 4, that is, the best grades in the military. Very good and good.'[57] At the end of July, Greiser passed an additional course. 'I came off very well,' Greiser wrote home, 'they very much liked my calm during the live fire exercise and my improvement.'[58] He relished the approval of superiors.

On 24 November 1916, Greiser learned that he had been promoted to officer, to a petty reserve officer (*Vizefeuerwerker d. R.*).[59] He quickly dashed off a postcard to his parents, 'Just promoted. Today I went to the officers' mess for the first time.'[60] In August 1917, he was promoted once again to reserve ensign (*Leutnant d. R.*).[61] In peacetime, achieving officer status for someone of his youth and family background would have been all but unthinkable; the navy officer corps was made up of men from noble, military, or upper-middle-class families. During the war, such promotions were more common. Still, for Greiser, with his petit-bourgeois provincial background, becoming a reserve officer was a significant boost to his social status.

Greiser savored the recognition that came with being attached to a top-notch institution. For a year beginning in November 1915 he belonged to a battery that was considered a 'model' (*mustergültige*) battery, Battery Beseler of the 4./1. Battalion of the Second Naval Artillery Regiment. In April 1916, Greiser wrote that there was a 'great hullabaloo' when the division admiral and other dignitaries visited the battery: 'They showered us with colossal praise, since in the face of the enemy we were in every respect a model battery and in contrast to every other battery behaved very well.'[62] But, just after he became an officer, Greiser was moved to the Battery Cecilie. He was annoyed. 'I've been transferred to another battery that is not to my taste . . . even though it's a neighboring battery, the whole operation is so unmilitary, that doesn't make a good impression.'[63] Greiser worked to secure a transfer and, after a month, was successful.[64] He craved belonging to a 'model' institution.

Greiser's letters reveal warm relations with his parents. Although some family members recall Ida Greiser as a cold and unpleasant woman, she doted on her youngest son.[65] Greiser seems to have returned her favor. He was always very solicitous about his mother worrying about him at the front. 'I want to write immediately,' he noted in November 1915, 'so that Mama isn't frightened. When I don't have any time to write for a while, you shouldn't worry, I'm always doing well.'[66] Over and over again, Greiser reassured his mother that things were not so bad or so dangerous and that he, in any event, would make it through the war. As he once wrote, 'The time has to come when we'll once again all drink coffee together. No one will be missing, for it will take more than this to finish us lowly ones off (*Unkraut vergeht nicht*).'[67] Ida, in turn, spared no effort to ease her son's life at the front. Arthur invariably opened his letters with expressions of thanks for what he had received: ham, eggs, cheese, butter, lard, bread, chocolate, and nuts; roast duck, veal, and rabbit; and articles of clothing, including underwear, gloves, and knickers. At times, even he thought it was too much. 'Dear Mama,' he wrote in October 1915, 'please don't send me so much, when I need something, I'll write.'[68] But the packages continued. Gustav sent his son cigars and rum. He also obliged Arthur's frequent requests for money.

Arthur had close relations with his siblings, too. Wilhelm, or Willy as Arthur called him, lived in Kiel, and Arthur frequently saw him and his wife Helene while stationed in Friedrichsort and Battery Laboe. In January

1916, when Willy and Helene had their first child, Arthur wrote home, 'I fancy myself very important as an uncle.'[69] During the war, Käthe was a Red Cross nurse near Berlin. On several occasions, Arthur stopped off in Berlin to see her on his return trips to Flanders.[70] Arthur was closest to his brother Otto. Otto first visited Arthur in Flanders in November 1915: 'Yesterday Otto and I were together from early morning until the evening... The day was wonderful. He's still the old Otto. We ate in the navy officers' mess and spent the whole day out on the town and amused ourselves. With Otto, twenty to thirty Marks don't make any difference, I'd also like to be able to spend money like water. He bought me Luiser cigars and chocolate; now I'm well provisioned.'[71] Arthur admired the easy ways of his older brother. In summer 1916, Otto visited several times. On one such visit, the brothers spent the afternoon loafing on the beach. As Arthur wrote home, 'Well, you see there's no point in worrying about us, when you think that we could be in danger, we're happily traveling around the North Sea resorts and celebrating our fourth meeting in Flanders and Northern France.'[72]

All three of the Greiser brothers survived the war. That was no mean feat in a war that claimed so many lives. Perhaps it cemented their close relations. In the next decades, the brothers were in frequent touch. Willy, however, was always somewhat removed from the other two. He was seen as the 'serious' one. Unlike Arthur and Otto, he was never particularly attracted by Nazism. Otto, known as the 'fat' one, was much closer to Arthur in politics and temperament.[73]

Arthur was always eager for a good time. He often went to Ostende to go to parks, movies, concerts, cafes, or restaurants. He occasionally took day trips up and down the coast.[74] On one occasion, returning from a visit to Otto, his train stopped in Lille. *Lohengrin* was advertised, and Greiser decided to stay for the performance. He was enthralled by Wagner's music. 'It was superb; to hear such music is wonderful. In the mood that I found myself, the music made me totally crazy and I was completely indifferent about whether or not I returned late.' Due to the opera, he overstayed his leave, but no one noticed his tardiness.[75] Greiser also enjoyed playing and listening to music in his barracks. In summer 1916, he asked his mother to send his mandolin to the front, and Ida promptly sent the instrument.[76] He and his buddies sometimes played music together.[77] They also whiled away the time by listening to records.[78]

Even as a soldier, Greiser had a taste for the finer things in life. His desire for the best meant that he simply couldn't make it on his meager military wages. He had to buy his uniforms, pay for his amusements and good food, and subscribe to war bonds at a level that equaled roughly a third of his salary. 'I don't have any extra money,' he complained in 1916, 'I'm in a pickle because of the old war bonds that are deducted every month.'[79] A year later, he wrote, 'I think that in this war I'll never be able to get by with my money.'[80]

Whatever his activity, Greiser wanted the finest accouterment. Already as a young man, he had a passion for weapons and hunting. In March 1916, he wrote to his parents, 'I have a little weakness for nice weapons, I've ordered a pistol to be made for me...'[81] Greiser also smoked and drank, and when he did, he was partial to good cigars and better alcohol. In 1916, he noted that 'I just celebrated Papa's birthday by eating up the nice cake and filling myself up with the smoke of your nice cigars, really a pleasure after the constant smoking of the cigars donated for the troops.'[82] He was very pleased when a Bavarian unit opened a canteen that served 'very decent German beer.'[83] Throughout his life, Greiser had a fondness for drink. But he was large—1,82 meters (just shy of six feet)—and could hold his own during drinking sprees.[84]

Always concerned about his outward appearance, Greiser frequently wrote to his parents about clothing that he had bought, ordered, or wanted. In March 1918, for example, he planned his summer wardrobe: 'Next week I'll go to Bruges. I want to have a field gray linen suit made for me but then I also bought 2 meters of blue serge; it's very soft for eighteen Marks per meter, it should make a sailor's jacket and vest, so that I have something for the summer...'[85] For someone of Greiser's modest background, clothing—especially suits and uniforms—was quite an investment. But eager to show status, Greiser lost no opportunity to dress for an occasion. His preoccupation with external signs of success would continue throughout his Nazi career.

Greiser occasionally expressed profound ambivalence about his life at the front. Shortly after returning from a leave in Hohensalza, he wrote, 'I can't yet quite find myself here. I'm supposed to watch for planes, but again and again I find myself looking at the ocean, always so calm and steady.'[86] He also related an acute sense of the passage of time and place. In February 1917, just back from some leave, Greiser wrote: 'Four weeks ago today

I was drinking champagne at Albrecht's, *o quae mutatio rerum* [O what a change of things].'[87] When he had such moments, he found solace in his mandolin and in swimming. As he wrote shortly after he got his instrument, 'It's splendid that it's here, it comforts me during some hours.' The next sentence of his letter reads: 'As often as I can, I go swimming in the North Sea, that refreshes body and soul.'[88] Such passages reveal a more serious, reflective side of his personality. At the same time, they suggest that Greiser had a sense that the war for which he had volunteered was not the one he experienced. War, he learned, was a many-sided affair: camaraderie and excitement were accompanied by deprivation and melancholy.

Not infrequently, Greiser wrote home about the deaths of friends or fellow soldiers. His tone was a mixture of sadness and resignation. In June 1916, he wrote of the death of Gustav Grosskopf, a friend from Hohensalza: 'It's really too bad about him; he really could have become something. In the first moment I was very sad about it, but such feelings pass as necessity intervenes.'[89] Two months later, another Hohensalza friend died: 'That Kurt Marquardt is now dead is sad, but slowly this war will get everyone.'[90] As the war dragged on, Greiser developed friendships with men in his various units. They, too, were killed. In September 1917 Greiser wrote, 'Right away the evening that I came back here I lost a very good comrade.' The man's plane had not returned. 'Now I'm staying in his hut in Ostende and have arranged all of his papers, now I have to fulfill the sad duty of writing to his father and his relatives, letters that I don't like to write.'[91] Greiser was not cold-hearted or indifferent to the terrible loss of life all around him. But he developed psychological mechanisms to endure such losses. He simply refused to dwell on the deaths all too long. To him, 'necessity'—that is, life—had to go on.

In April 1917, Greiser was chosen to become a naval airman; the navy used airpower to prevent British ships from approaching Germany and to detect the laying of sea-mines. Greiser was enormously excited: 'I have had success with my good surveillance, indeed something has happened that I am very happy about and that I've wanted for a long time: I'm going to the naval airmen. This is an enormous distinction for a twenty-year-old vice [sergeant].' As always, Greiser proudly recorded the recognition that he received. He continued, 'I have been ordered by my regiment to the naval air station Flanders I (*Zeebrugge*) for training as an [aerial] observer. After the training I will fly as an observer for the two heavy batteries (28 cm and 38 cm) of my regiment... I joyfully agreed to this.' Always careful to reassure his mother, Greiser added: 'Mama should not worry about this, something like this is fun. In any event, it's the best Easter egg that I've been given...'[92]

The next months were a whirl of activity. In contrast to his earlier courses, Greiser thoroughly enjoyed training in navigation, nautical science, and radio telegraphy. As he wrote to his parents on 4 May: 'We have learned all sorts of nice things and it was lots of fun and now we are more or less done, but we still must practice radio telegraphy, I can already hear over sixty letters [per minute], but it has to be eighty and more; I can send out enough. Recently I flew for a torpedo boat, it was really interesting.'[93] Greiser may have enjoyed this course so much because of the distinction of being chosen as a naval airman. Perhaps he was also genuinely excited by airplanes and flying, then in their infancy. Then, too, during World War I aviators enjoyed enormous respect. Greiser surely enjoyed such close company with 'heroes of the sky.'[94]

Greiser was soon assigned to what became known as Christiansen's squadron. Friedrich Christiansen was famous as a naval flying ace.[95] Proximity to such a heralded war hero no doubt appealed to Greiser's sense of importance. Indeed, although Greiser never mentioned him in his wartime letters home, in June 1934, he noted that two 'old war friends,' Bruno Loerzer and Christiansen, 'greeted me especially warmly' when they made a stopover in Danzig.[96] In 1937, Christiansen became head of the National Socialist Flying Corps. On at least one occasion, he visited the Warthegau. Greiser's personal connection to the famed general was then touted in the Warthegau press.[97]

As an aerial observer, Greiser endured terrifying incidents. In July 1917, British sailors shot down his airplane. The pilot of his plane made an emergency landing, but the men were now stranded on the high seas. Greiser sent a cry for help via carrier pigeons that were carried aboard fighter planes. After eight harrowing hours, the men were saved in a dramatic rescue that involved some difficult maneuvers by fellow German airmen.[98] Greiser was not injured. In late July, his plane was attacked by four British fighters, but once again, he returned to safety.[99]

Greiser received a series of honors for his military exploits. In May 1917, he was awarded the Iron Cross Second Class medal: 'Yesterday morning they hung the Iron Cross Second Class on me; this was still from the regiment for the shooting during the last great hullabaloo.'[100] On 20

August, he received the Iron Cross First Class medal. William II, Germany's emperor, hung the medal around his neck.[101] In October 1917, Greiser received the Naval Observer Badge (*Marinebeobachterabzeichen*) and, at some point, the Naval Aviator Badge (*Marinefliegerabzeichen*).[102] Perhaps because of his successes, Greiser was introduced to various dignitaries visiting the naval base—just the kind of distinction that he enjoyed. In May 1917, he wrote that General Paul von Hindenburg, Supreme Commander of all the German armies, was coming to the naval station.[103] Three weeks later, he sent home a picture marked 'x is Hindenburg, xx is "*me*"!!!'[104] In July 1917, Greiser was introduced to Prince Heinrich, William II's brother. 'Today Prince Heinrich was here and I was introduced to him, he spoke with me and my pilot for about eight minutes, we then had coffee with him in the mess.' Greiser told the Prince about the time when he had been attacked by the four planes, but had made it back to Zeebrugge. According to Greiser, 'Prince Heinrich was very happy and very nice.'[105]

In Zeebrugge, Greiser had increased responsibilities. In May 1917, he wrote, 'Now, however, I don't know whether I'll be able to fly much in the next time, for I can no longer complain about much boredom. I've become the second adjutant and aide-de-camp to the commander of the naval airmen in Flanders; I'm a sort of "young man," I get to know all the ships and I stand in for the real adjutant when he flies or is away.' Greiser liked the job. As he continued, 'It's very interesting, for I get to know about everything behind the scenes and I learn the whole bureaucracy (*Schriftladen*) of the navy properly. I don't need to sit much in the office, I just need to take note of everything and to pass things along.'[106] After his promotion to reserve ensign in August 1917, Greiser noted: 'Now I have a little bit more to do. Unfortunately, I've become the leader of a squadron and have to do all the paperwork alone, but it's alright. The one advantage is that in the next days I will get a small motored vehicle or a small car, at least something.'[107]

In contrast to many other World War I combatants, Greiser did not view Allied soldiers as equals, as respected counterparts or worthy opponents. Instead, he saw the 'enemy' as a lesser being engaged in nefarious, below-the-belt tactics. On Christmas Day 1916, for example, he noted: 'Yesterday the uncles over there showed themselves altogether really shabbily, mines small and large and artillery light and heavy.'[108] Given his views of the 'enemy,' Greiser was quite surprised when he saw how the German military treated British prisoners of war (POWs). As he wrote in May 1917,

'Yesterday two English naval officers from the airforce [i.e., POWs] ate with us, they were essentially comrades in the mess . . . That irritated me no end, but among flyers that's the way it is, so that one gets something out of them.'[109] In Greiser's view, these POWs should have been treated more as prisoners than as equals. Even as a young man, then, Greiser held a ruthless attitude toward the 'enemy.'

During World War I, Greiser's ethnic, racial or other political views did not particularly stand out. While he never wrote home about Poles or Jews, he occasionally mentioned Russians and blacks. In 1915, when he arrived at a training camp, he noted how dirty the barracks were: 'When yesterday we took over the barracks where infantry units had been, they looked as though Russians had lived in them; the beds were full of rat droppings and the straw had all been taken away, totally filthy (*wüst*).'[110] At this time, Greiser viewed not Poles, but Russians, as the 'dirty' nation. Greiser also harbored racist sentiments about dark-skinned people. He knew that the French were using African colonial troops to help man their trenches. Once stationed on the western front, Greiser proudly wrote of German defense capabilities: 'Well, they [enemy soldiers] can try what they want, but where navy seamen are, no Englishman will come through, not to speak of the black rabble (*das schwarze Gesindel*) in the trenches.'[111] Such views, though, were par for the course among German soldiers during World War I.

Greiser was also not a particularly ardent German nationalist during the war. He was certainly proud of Germany and its military prowess. He was a patriot. But his love for Germany only went so far. He thus expressed ambivalence about placing the nation above all else. In early 1916, for example, Greiser wrote to his sister-in-law Helene about the name chosen for his nephew, Walther: 'That is a good name, I mean a good German name . . .' He continued (in response to her letter): 'That he shows so much love of the Fatherland in his outward appearance is very nice, hopefully he'll keep that in his inner self in later years . . .' But Greiser then added, 'only he shouldn't ever make too much use of it, he should always think of himself first, otherwise he'll be cheated by the others who first think about themselves and then about the Fatherland.'[112] Greiser perhaps feared that he might somehow be cheated if he placed Germany above all; he was bent on self-preservation.

Greiser held typical soldier resentments toward civilians at home. In 1916, he found a nice lace apron for a girl named Erna in Hohensalza, but he couldn't find anyone to take it to her. As he wrote home, 'Tell her that she must be patient. After all, there's a war going on here.'[113] On another occasion, he was pleased that his sister Käthe had received a Red Cross medal: 'It was her turn; in any event she has certainly earned it much more than the pack of aunts who parade their toilettes past the beds of the wounded.'[114] When he heard about the death of a friend from Hohensalza, he wrote 'It's a pity about him, but I'm only annoyed by one thing, that so many here have to give their lives and that so many shirkers and "those in occupations exempted from military service" (*Unabkömmliche*) are building their future on this.'[115] Greiser echoed an oft-held sentiment that those not fighting at the front were profiting at soldiers' expense. Such views culminated in the Stab-in-the-Back legend, that Germany lost the war not on the battlefield, but on the homefront—potent fodder for right-wing groups after the war.

In all of Greiser's preserved wartime correspondence, only one comment pertained directly to politics. It came in November 1917. A Mr. Stephan had sent Greiser some very nice cigars. Greiser commented: 'Hopefully he'll soon again have such good thoughts. We were all very happy that there are still such decent people in Germany. After all the events in the Reichstag, etc., we here at the front do not speak well of these jerks (*Armlöcher*) with big mouths. One should send a lieutenant with ten men there and immediately put the whole lot before the firing squad. It's a scandal...'[116] Greiser was perhaps referring to acrimonious Reichstag debates about naval mutinies that had occurred the previous August.[117] In any event, his proposed solution—to shoot the parliamentarians—was indicative of his later political methods.

During the war, Greiser put some thought into his postwar plans. At his 1946 trial, he claimed that his mother had wanted him to become a theologian. 'But,' Greiser told the court, 'with every fibre of my being I always wanted to be a soldier and to sail the seas.'[118] Indeed, as a new recruit, Greiser had hoped to become a naval engineer. In August 1915 he learned that this would entail two years of practical experience in the civilian sector. As he wrote to his father, this was very unappealing: 'After the war to go back to civilian life for two years, no, that I won't do. I very much want to remain a soldier...' Greiser looked around for other opportunities, and decided that his best prospect was to become an infantry officer.[119] But over the course of the war, his goals changed. In November 1917, Greiser still planned on a military career, but now with a colonial interlude. As he explained to his parents, he and another comrade had gotten to know a lieutenant captain who had spent six years in German East Africa (*Deutschost*): 'soon after the war he [the lieutenant captain] is going back to German East Africa and wants to set us up there; he thinks that right after the war young people eager to work will be much needed there.' Greiser continued: 'If he doesn't go immediately after the war, then I'll work for a time on a farm in Germany and then go out together with him.'[120] It's significant that at one time Greiser saw Germany's colonies as his future. When Germany lost the war and as a result, its colonies, he lost a career option.

In January 1918, Greiser's military career took another turn: he began pilot training. He was sent to Johannisthal, Germany's first airfield, opened outside of Berlin in 1909. Curiously, though, Greiser betrayed little excitement about learning to fly; perhaps he was all too cognizant of the dangers of battling in the skies. In late April, he learned that he was to go to another flying school in Langfuhr, a suburb of Danzig. He was downright disappointed. As he wrote to his parents, 'At the beginning of May I was supposed to go to W[ilhelms]haven, but the flight chief in Berlin has again changed everything around, now I do have to go to Langfuhr . . .; that's what I get since I can fly decently! In any event, I won't work so hard in Langfuhr as I have here, that's certain!'[121] On 17 May, Greiser began training at the Langfuhr Single-Seater Fighter Airplane School (*Kampf-Einsitzer-Schule Langfuhr*).[122] His instructor was Robert Reuter, who would bring Greiser to the Nazi party and, later still, turn against him.[123]

Greiser spent a bittersweet summer in Langfuhr. He had some sort of breakdown. Only the barest details of this can be gleaned from his letters. In June, Greiser noted that '. . . at the moment I'm again somewhat depressed.' He had just visited his mother in the Harz mountains where she was vacationing. 'The time in the Harz was apparently too short and I think that for a while I'll have to stay away from the flying business. It's very likely that I'll get leave soon.' He considered staying in Zoppot, a suburb of Danzig where some relatives lived. But as he wrote, 'To stay in Zoppot so long is pointless, for once I've been there for five to seven days, I won't be able to stand it and will go to Langfuhr and stick myself in a plane.' He had also received an invitation to go to Marienfelde in East Prussia. 'I haven't decided yet; probably I'll say yes, for there I'll have lots of quiet and very good food, and I'll be away from everything, furthermore

I can easily come from there to Hohensalza.'[124] Three days later, Greiser wrote home again: 'You don't have to worry, I'm doing very well.' He then explained, 'After four years of war one occasionally loses a little screw and one has to stop flying. For a while now I won't be able to see or hear anything about flying, otherwise the state will lose me. It's a good thing, though, that the people here understand this. I'll probably start my vacation this week and then continue my training here after three to six weeks . . . Now I'm not flying at all.'[125]

Greiser did not describe the manifestations of his depression. Yet clearly, his superiors had realized that he was not fit to continue training. In 1949, the former commanding general in the Warthegau, Walter Petzel, stated that he had seen evaluations written about Greiser during World War I. These, he claimed, concluded 'that he [i.e., Greiser] is not suitable to be a fighter pilot because at the decisive moment, when it's a real battle, his nerves fail him.'[126] But Petzel did not say why Greiser's superiors had reached this conclusion. Something was not quite right about Greiser's flying career.

The sweetness of that summer came from a different part of his life. The invitation to Marienfelde that Greiser was considering came from his future mother-in-law. Greiser first got to know Ruth Tripler in August 1917, when he was visiting relatives in Zoppot. The two met on a pier. That is, their shoes met. Walking along, each noticed that the other was wearing patent leather shoes, a rarity in wartime Germany. Having noticed each other's shoes, the two looked up at each other, and a flirtation began. Ruth, born in 1899, was just seventeen when she met Arthur. She was the daughter of a Lutheran minister who had died when she was a child. In his letters home, Arthur barely mentioned Ruth. But in December 1917 he sent her a picture of himself with a dedication to 'my dear girlfriend Ruth from her boyfriend on the front [of the picture].'[127] By June 1918, Ruth's mother had invited Arthur to come to her brother's estate. Greiser did go to Marienfelde. In late July, he wrote to his parents that 'my time here [i.e., in Marienfelde] has gone by very quickly, I've also recuperated somewhat.' In answer to his mother's inquiry about how long his vacation would last, Greiser wrote: 'Well, I would be happy if I had proper vacation, Berlin has not yet decided on the matter; and from Langfuhr I'm only on furlough, I had to leave there because I wasn't allowed to see a plane.'[128]

At the end of summer 1918, Greiser was deemed capable of flying, and he soon returned to Flanders. Very soon, however, on 3 September, his plane was shot down.[129] Greiser sustained serious injuries, including to his head. He was first brought to a military hospital in Bruges and later taken by hospital train to Hamburg. In Germany, he was treated at the military hospital in Frohnau/Mark; Käthe helped to nurse him back to health.[130] Greiser was still in hospital when, in November, revolution broke out in Germany. William II was forced to abdicate, and a new Social-Democratic government signed an armistice ending hostilities.

In his Warthegau days, Greiser made much of his time as a World War I combatant. He frequently appeared in navy uniform. He occasionally referred to himself as a 'World War aviator' (*Weltkriegsflieger*).[131] The Warthegau press celebrated his soldiering past.[132] But to some extent, Greiser presented a false version of his war record. He changed the dates on which he joined the navy and was shot down, the latter perhaps so as to lengthen his time in the skies. Far from the 'flying ace' remembered in Greiser family lore, Greiser flew missions from just 21 August to 3 September—in a piloting career that was as short as it was unspectacular.[133]

Much has been made of the 'Front Generation' and its contribution to the Nazi movement. After harrowing years at the front, soldiers returned home, only to face enormous difficulties in finding employment, forging relationships, or otherwise reintegrating into civilian life. Many war veterans thus came to long for what they saw as the stability of their youth and the comradeship of their soldiering days. Finding neither in the crisis-ridden Weimar regime, they turned to a radical alternative, Nazism.[134] As Hitler's first followers, members of the Front Generation made up a good part of the Führer's inner circle and the Nazi elite more generally.[135]

Greiser, however, should not be seen as an example of a bitter war veteran who turned to the Nazi movement. While his wartime letters can be read in such a way as to hint at a future predisposition to Nazism, this is largely because in knowing the man that Greiser became, the historian is tempted to tease out clues that intimate that future. His wartime depression and injuries notwithstanding, Greiser appears to have been a generally confident, insouciant youth. He came from a close-knit family, and he was clearly able to forge friendships and relationships.[136] The Greiser family also had a 'good' war. None of the brothers was killed, maimed, or otherwise saw his life chances ruined by wartime injuries. Greiser was one of the millions of war veterans who managed to adjust to the postwar order—that is, until the onset of the Depression, when he turned to Nazism with all the vengeance of the most bitter war veteran.

Greiser was released from hospital on 9 December 1918. Until the end of January, he was stationed in Johannestal and Langfuhr. Over the Christmas holidays, however, he was on leave in Hohensalza.[137] These were dramatic days in Posen province. On 27 December the Posen Uprising broke out; Poles demanded that the area belong to the newly created Polish state. Polish forces were successful, and the city (and soon most of the province) passed into Polish hands. When the Uprising began, Greiser immediately left for his naval unit.[138] That spring, he was attached to military units called Border Protection East (*Grenzschutz Ost*). He was then stationed in Johannestal until his official discharge from the German military on 31 July 1919.[139]

Greiser spent much of spring and summer 1919 in Danzig, cut off from his family. He now married Ruth. As he wrote home in late summer, 'Dear Käthe, you wanted very much to be at our wedding, yes, we waited so long and had hoped since March that one of you would come. We got married on 25 June, very quietly and small, and due to the prevailing conditions, that was really the best... From our side, the Zoppot relatives were there, from Ruth's, the grandparents, one uncle with wife and child, and her one best friend. That was all who couldn't be avoided.' Greiser added, 'I tried every day to telegraph you, but always unsuccessfully, I sent endless telegrams.' He didn't waste any more words on his wedding, but went on to describe his post-wedding travels. He and Ruth had gone to her home town in Thuringia, to the Harz mountains, to a friend in Goslar, and then to Ruth's uncle in East Prussia. Greiser further reported that he had a job lined up. 'I'm starting now at Benz as the second representative for the sales bureau in Danzig. After Mercedes, Benz is the largest car dealer and factory for motors in Germany and many are jealous that I got this position. I'm happy that I've found a job in a trade that I like. At the same time, I have good prospects with working in a factory in Thuringia about which I need to speak with Papa.' To his parents, he intimated domestic plans: 'Soon Dr. [Alfred] Kochmann [Käthe's future husband] will spend his four weeks of vacation with us as our first house-guest in our guest room on the third floor. We're looking forward to that. Of course, Käthe can also stay with us, but she'll have to sleep on a couch if Kochmann is still here...' He reported of Ruth: 'today, Ruth is canning cherries that we brought from the countryside.' Greiser concluded his letter, 'Here we'll become a Free City, but for the time being I'll stay here for sure, it will be good.'[140] While Greiser was optimistic about his future in summer 1919, he actually never started the job at Benz or at the Thuringian factory.

That same summer, the Allies imposed the Versailles Treaty on Germany. This Treaty had significant personal consequences for Greiser. With it, he lost his homeland: almost all of Posen province became part of the newly established Polish Republic. Even though Greiser was seemingly planning a civilian career, he nonetheless lost a potential military career. The German naval officer corps was reduced to a mere 1,500 men; as a low-ranking reserve officer, Greiser had no chance of being included.[141] He lost employment prospects: Germany was not allowed to maintain an air force, and so Greiser's piloting skills had little value. He also lost other potential opportunities: Germany had to relinquish its colonies, where Greiser, at least for a time, had hoped to go. And he lost residence in the German Reich: Danzig, where he now lived, was to be a 'Free City,' no longer part of Germany. Each of these losses had a tangible impact on Greiser; each limited his range of options.

Events in Posen province soon took their toll on the Greiser family. After the Posen Uprising, the Poles moved against Germans in the area.[142] They interned many German men, confiscated German weapons, removed German signs, opened German mail, and imposed a curfew on the German population. Greiser family members suffered these measures first hand. Gustav and Otto Greiser were captured by Polish insurgents and interned in a former POW camp at Szczypiorno near Kalisz. Arthur later described the camp as 'infamous.'[143] In winter and spring 1919, up to 8,000 Germans spent several months in this camp.[144] Writing home in late summer 1919, Gustav had been released, Arthur noted, but Otto had not: 'Considering the circumstances, I was very happy to hear that you are doing well. But I don't like that Otto is still not at home. Hopefully in the meantime he's arrived and both Papa and Otto are doing well.' In the same letter Arthur wrote, 'If you would just come, so that I'd know what all is going on, if you'll stay there or not, I'd like so much to do something for you and to prepare.'[145] Gustav and Ida Greiser soon moved to Danzig.[146] Although Otto initially returned to Inowrocław (as Hohensalza was now called), he soon realized that he had no future in the Polish Republic. He moved to Brandenburg in 1921.[147]

Map 1.1 Germany's Eastern Provinces and Western Poland in the Interwar Period.

The Greisers were part of a mass exodus of Germans from areas now ceded to the new Poland. At the time, this population movement was considered 'unprecedented.'[148] The Greisers left the Poznań (Posen) region for the same reasons that many other Germans did. They did not want to live in what had become a foreign country. Nor did they want to endure Polish discrimination. Indeed, Polish measures mirrored many of those that

Prussian authorities had earlier imposed on Poles.[149] Polish was the sole official language. German minority leaders were harassed. The number of German state schools was reduced. Land reform laws undermined German land ownership. Citizenship laws made the acquisition of Polish citizenship difficult. Germans were conscripted into the Polish Army (now fighting the Red Army, as well as Ukrainians and Lithuanians); many young Germans left to avoid the draft. In the end, Polish ethnic cleansing measures—unlike their earlier Prussian counterparts—had their desired effect: Germans left in droves. In 1910, 720,650 Germans had made up 34 percent of the population of Posen province.[150] By 1921, only 327,846 Germans, making up 16.7 percent of the population, remained in the area of Poznania ceded to Poland.[151] Ten years later, the German population was smaller still: 193,000.[152] When Greiser returned to Posen in 1939, the ethnic makeup of the region he had known as a youth was much changed; Germans made up a small, embattled minority.

Danzig, Greiser's new home, was at the epicenter of German–Polish conflict.[153] The city occupied a peculiar position in the international system. After the war, the Poles had wanted to incorporate the city into their new state so as to have an outlet to the Baltic Sea. But while Poland was given the Polish corridor (a strip of land separating East Prussia from Germany), Danzig did not become a Polish city—its population of roughly 410,000 was 96.5 percent German. Instead, Danzig became a Free City under the supervision of the League of Nations. The League appointed a high commissioner who, in turn, was to uphold Danzig's democratic constitution, mediate between Danzig and Poland, and protect Danzig from military incursions.[154]

Poland had many official rights in Danzig. The 1920 Danzig–Poland Agreement established that Danzig belonged to the Polish customs area, and that Poland had formal oversight of the city's foreign relations, owned and operated the main railway lines inside Danzig, had a small munitions depot on the Westerplatte peninsula in the Danzig harbor, and enjoyed unhindered access to the Danzig port. A joint Danzig–Polish harbor board, with a neutral president, regulated port matters. These Polish rights angered a German population that was seething about Danzig's separation from the Reich. The Danzigers were thus little inclined to cooperate with Poles. This, in turn, only heightened the city's economic woes. Poland, wary of the reliability of Danzig harbor workers, built another port nearby, in Gdynia. By the early 1930s, Gdynia handled more freight than Danzig—a clear threat to the Free City's economic viability.[155] In the 1920s, Danzigers fed on anti-Polish animosity, German chauvinistic nationalism, and a deep-seated resentment of the Treaty of Versailles.

Next to his childhood, Greiser's first decade in Danzig is the least well-documented time of his life. The paucity of sources, in turn, has made historians more dependent on Greiser's own accounts of this period. But Greiser obfuscated his biography. In the mid-1930s, for example, he wrote of the 1920s as follows: 'After the end of the war, founding of a fighter unit (*freie Jagdstaffel*), service in Border Protection East. Demobilization and discharge May 1921. Then trainee in an export company, founding of a trade representative company, due to pooling (*Vertrustung*) giving up of the firm in 1928. Then captain of a motorboat for passenger trips in the Danziger Bay.' As for his political activity, Greiser wrote: 'Since 1922 member of the German-Social Party [*Deutsch-Soziale Partei* (DSP)], mem[ber]-Nu[mber] 520.'[156] Elsewhere, Greiser noted that he had been a member of the *Stahlhelm* (Steel Helmet) from 1924 to 1926.[157] All this is only partially true. Greiser's biography was more complicated than this brief summary would suggest—especially for a later Nazi.

Greiser wrote that he participated in Free Corps activity from 1919 to 1921. The Free Corps were voluntary German military units founded in late 1918 at the initiative of the army and navy high command. Free-Corps volunteers were put into the service of right-wing causes: to save the new German Republic from left-wing insurrections, to protect Germany's eastern territories from Polish insurgents, and to halt the spread of Bolshevism in the Baltic countries. They celebrated violence, self-sacrifice, comradeship, and masculinity, the very qualities that would soon imbue the Nazi movement. Many historians have viewed participation in the Free Corps as an important step in the making of early Nazis.[158] But Greiser's role in the Free Corps remains questionable.[159] On several occasions, Greiser stated that he founded a fighter unit that was part of the Border Protection East, Free Corps units that were to prevent raids by Polish irregulars along the eastern border. In 1933, a member of his former unit wrote that 'at the first sign of Polish rebellion, under the leadership of the then lieutenant Arthur Greiser, now vice senate president of Danzig, we founded a flight escort formation (*Flugstaffel*) for the Border Protection East, equipped with fighter and surveillance planes . . . In late summer 1919 we were disbanded by the government.'[160] Curiously, though, there is no mention of Greiser founding such a unit in his official military record or in the large literature on the Free Corps.[161]

Greiser belonged to the Border Protection East under the German military from 1 February through 15 May 1919.[162] In 1939, a newspaper article noted that at the end of 1918, 'duty called him as a fighter in the Free Corps to protect his eastern homeland.'[163] The Border Protection East was active in the Poznań area in the first months of 1919. But if Greiser was there, his role was unimportant. In fact, he probably saw little—if any—active service in the various German–Polish border skirmishes that spring. He was mostly in Danzig, still recovering from his injuries, waiting to hear from his family, and anticipating his wedding. Since Greiser was discharged from the military in July, any additional Free Corps activity would have to have taken place independent of the German military.[164] Some sources suggest that Greiser belonged to a Baltic Free Corps unit.[165] Just when the Baltic campaign was at its height, though, in spring and summer 1919, Greiser married Ruth and was traveling around Germany. Greiser's own words that he served in the military until 1921 probably referred to his service in the Danzig Border Protection East that existed independently of the German military; this paramilitary unit was not disbanded until sometime in 1921.[166] Greiser thus appears to have elided his military service into his paramilitary service with the Danzig Border Protection East. A Polish source claims that Greiser served in a Free Corps unit from spring 1919 through 1920. In January 1920, as a pilot for such a unit, Greiser allegedly flew a plane over Danzig's Long Market and dropped leaflets sympathizing with demonstrators protesting the city's separation from Germany.[167] Later on, in the 1930s, Greiser frequently told this anecdote.[168] Still, Greiser was never mentioned in the extensive celebratory Free Corps literature published in the 1920s and 1930s. And, in 1940, when the official Nazi Warthegau newspaper, *Ostdeutscher Beobachter*, published a hagiographical portrait of Greiser that focused on his fighting prowess, it never mentioned his activity with the Border Protection East.[169] In all likelihood, Greiser's participation in the Border Protection East was utterly undistinguished; it certainly won no accolades. At war's end, it is safe to say, Greiser was no swashbuckling Free-Corps desperado.

Greiser joined a Free Mason lodge in 1921. In 1920, Otto, then still in Hohensalza, had become a Free Mason. Perhaps he urged Arthur to join. Much later, Arthur claimed that Otto joined the Free Masons because they stood 'at the center of German attempts to organize themselves' in Hohensalza.[170] Greiser reached the first degree (Apprentice) on 14 February 1921, the second degree (Fellow) on 9 January 1922, and the third degree (Master) on 19 February 1923.[171] While Free Masonry was supposedly apolitical, in Germany it tended toward conservatism. In the 1920s, most lodges espoused strong *völkisch* and anti-democratic views. Greiser's Danzig lodge was no exception. Its very name, '*Feste Burg im Osten* (Stronghold in the East),' betrayed its chauvinistic nationalism. In 1925, Greiser and some others founded a new Masonic lodge, and linked it with a mother lodge that had pronounced chauvinistic tendencies.[172]

Yet despite its right-wing tendencies, the Nazis distrusted Free Masonry. They (and many others) claimed that Free Masons were enemies of German nationalists and tools of the Jews. According to Hitler, 'the Jew' fights for religious tolerance so as to enhance his political position, and in this 'Free Masonry, totally enslaved to him, is a superb instrument.'[173] Heinrich Himmler, leader of the SS, was also convinced that Jews controlled the Free Masons.[174] These anti-masonic views meant that those Free Masons who wished to join the NSDAP had to abandon their lodges or else keep their Free Masonry secret from the party.[175] Among later high-ranking Nazis, very few had been lodge members; indeed, Greiser may well have been the highest-ranking Nazi with a Free-Mason past.[176] Greiser did his best to keep quiet that he had been a lodge member until 1929, just before he joined the Nazis.[177] In 1934, he even tried to minimize the time that he had been a Free Mason. As he wrote to a former fellow lodge member, 'thank God I already recognized this swindle ten years ago and left the [Free Masons] then.'[178] This would suggest that Greiser left the Free Masons in 1924—a fact that was simply not true.

What of Greiser's early political activity?[179] Greiser's right-wing inclinations are clear. He joined the radical DSP in 1922.[180] The Danzig party was allied with the Reich party of the same name, and was founded by Richard Kunze in November 1921. Kunze was militantly anti-Semitic; one of the party's main slogans was 'elimination of the Jewish hegemony in Germany.' The party was also dedicated to the 'exclusive rule of Germans in the German Empire' and for 'state independence' of Germans living abroad. In elections in Danzig in November 1923, the party won 10,000 votes and seven seats in the Volkstag (the Danzig city parliament).[181] By 1925, the party numbered 34,000 members, 5,000 of whom lived in Danzig.

Greiser boasted a relatively low party membership number, but he did not play a leadership role in the party's Danzig branch.

Other early political activity in Danzig confirms Greiser's nationalism. He helped found the Front Fliers' Group (*Danziger Frontfliegergruppe*) in 1922. He later wrote that this was 'a nationalist flying association [that] pursued flying and *völkisch* goals.'[182] Later on, an acquaintance recalled 'how we [i.e., Greiser and he] had wanted to go to Munich in November 1923.'[183] Perhaps they had fantasized about joining the Beer Hall Putsch, Hitler's 1923 attempt to come to power through a coup. Another acquaintance later wrote to Greiser 'how under your leadership in 1923 we with a handful of Stahlhelmers blocked an armed Sokół [Polish national youth group] march in Danzig . . . so that the planned Polish coup against Danzig was dashed.'[184] Early on, Greiser seems to have been involved in anti-Polish activity. In 1924, he also helped to establish the Stahlhelm in Danzig.[185] Founded by Franz Seldte in November 1918, it represented the political interests of World War I soldiers. It frequently flirted with right-wing putschists and gave covert support to anti-Republic activities. In light of Greiser's Free Masonry, it's noteworthy that the Stahlhelm didn't share the Nazi antipathy toward Free Masons; it viewed the lodges as 'nationally trustworthy.'[186]

Meanwhile, during this same decade, Greiser became a family man. Early on, Arthur and Ruth enjoyed an apparently happy marriage. They lived in Langfuhr, a lower middle-class community between the city of Danzig and the resort town of Zoppot. Family pictures suggest a dashing young couple. In all of the pictures, Ruth appears as a pretty, vibrant young woman. The Greisers had their first daughter, Ingrid, on 23 March 1920. Five years later, on 8 January 1925, they had a son, Erhardt. In 1929, the Greisers had another son, but the baby lived only a few hours. Ruth was soon pregnant again. On 11 October 1930, the Greisers had their third child, a daughter, Rotraut.[187] Rotraut has a series of pictures of Greiser holding each of his children as babies; in the pictures, he is very much the proud Papa. Notably, all of the Greiser children were baptized. Rotraut's christening took place at home before a makeshift altar that included both religious and nationalist motifs.[188]

It is difficult to evaluate Greiser's financial situation during the 1920s. Greiser is often said to have been down-and-out in the decade after World War I; long years of financial insecurity, so these arguments go, made him susceptible to Nazism.[189] Family members, however, tell a very different story: they claim that Greiser was a successful businessman in the 1920s. As Rotraut has related (from what her mother told her), a war comrade, a Mr. Bieber, convinced Greiser to do an apprenticeship in his import/export firm. Greiser did this for all of six months, after which he decided that he could do better on his own.[190] In American custody, Greiser gave a similar account: between 1919 and 1921, he noted, he continued to have medical treatment in Danzig, did occasional work in the harbor, and then did business apprenticeships with the Bieber and Zicke Company in Hamburg and a Dutch trading firm in Danzig. In 1923, he founded his own business agency, specializing in oils and fats.[191] According to Rotraut, Greiser's company flourished. Despite the Great Inflation, Greiser did well; he earned his money in English pounds and American dollars. In April 1924, the Greisers took a trip to Italy, leaving Ingrid with Arthur's parents. A card to Ingrid shows a smiling Ruth in front of a palm tree in Salo; on the back, Ruth noted that they had danced the previous evening away.[192] The Greisers also met up with a friend who later recalled how 'we merrily sat together in Venice in 1924.'[193] In another sign of financial success, Arthur had Willy open a branch of his business in Hamburg. When he and Ruth visited Hamburg, they supposedly stayed in the city's finest hotel, the Four Seasons on the Alster.[194]

It's possible that Ruth (as told to Rotraut) looked back on this time in a rosier light than was merited; she always viewed her years with Greiser as the best of her life.[195] But another family source concurs. Harry Siegmund, Greiser's cousin, recalls how Arthur and Ruth visited his family in Libau, Latvia, in 1926. According to Siegmund, 'After the war he [Greiser] became a salesman and lived as the owner of an agency in Danzig. Apparently, he wasn't doing badly. A visible sign of his then prosperity was the Fiat Cabriolet, in which they had come. He now took me and my brother Gunther on drives through the virtually traffic-free streets of Libau or—at the highest speeds—on the hard ground of the Baltic Sea beach so as to impress us.' As with his wartime superiors, Greiser was eager to impress his relatives. Siegmund continued, 'Arthur didn't only come to visit his Uncle Max, but also to participate in an international tennis tournament. In his [tennis] club in Zoppot he was among the best players. In Libau he won second prize . . .'[196] Indeed, in the 1920s, Greiser was an avid tennis player and active member in the Zoppoter Tennis Club. In 1934, the Club named Greiser an honorary member in recognition of 'your [e.g., Greiser's] many years of loyal membership, your willingness to serve on the board, your engagement on behalf of the sport of tennis and especially for our club...'[197] Greiser was very pleased with this honor, and only regretted that 'I am no longer able to actively play our nice sport as before...'[198] The trip to Libau, the sporty car, and the posh tennis club all suggest that Greiser enjoyed a certain prosperity—and that he still reached for the finer things in life.

Given the similar accounts of different Greiser family members—who are not themselves on speaking terms—it's likely that Greiser was fairly comfortable until 1928 or so. Other sources intimate the same. For a time, Greiser had as a client the Stettiner Ölwerke, a company dealing in oils and fats.[199] One Polish source, written in 1946, noted that people in Poznań still recalled the Greiser of the 1920s. At that time, Greiser 'was shrewd. He was able to sweeten his views and to convince. He earned well.' Furthermore, Greiser was a 'good merchant.'[200] In the 1926–7 registry for his Free Mason lodge, Greiser listed his occupation as salesman (*Kaufman*).[201]

In the mid-1920s, perhaps because he found his life quite satisfactory, Greiser's political engagement waned. He left the Stahlhelm for unknown reasons in 1926. In addition, his DSP ran out of steam in the face of the Nazi juggernaut. By 1927, the DSP had essentially become two: one that wished to amalgamate with the Nazis, the other not. Many DSP members joined the NSDAP in 1927 or 1928. Greiser, however, waited. This was probably not due to opposition to the DSP joining with the Nazis. Instead, Greiser was just not that interested in political affairs. Had there been no Great Depression, Greiser might well have permanently abandoned Danzig's radical right-wing fringe.

But Greiser did experience a serious financial setback in 1928–9.[202] He lost his company. Thereafter, he received a bit of help from business connections; in particular, Adolf Mazur, the Jewish owner of 'Oleo' (*Öl- und Fettfabrik AG*) that processed oils and fats, gave him work.[203] Yet in 1929, Greiser was unemployed.[204] After years of earning a decent living, this must have come as a terrible shock; moreover, the oncoming Depression made new employment all but impossible. This situation, in turn, may have reawakened his political interests—and led him to the Nazi party. It seems that Robert Reuter asked Greiser to come to a party meeting to check out the fledgling NSDAP in Danzig.[205] With time on his hands, Greiser accepted the invitation. Something about the meeting must have appealed to him: on 1 December 1929, he joined the NSDAP and, around the same time, the Storm Troop (SA).[206]

Greiser's party membership number was an unimpressive 166,635.[207] Although technically an 'old fighter' (*alter Kämpfer*), a pre-1933 NSDAP member, Greiser had not participated in the glory days of Nazi struggle. He was not a veteran of the Beer Hall Putsch. He had not joined in the party's aborted march on Berlin. He had not known the bloody Nazi bar and street-corner brawls of the 1920s. All this had significant repercussions for his Nazi political career: because he joined the party so late, Greiser never forged a close tie to Hitler, and so he never enjoyed the Führer's complete support or confidence. Among Nazi leaders, he always suffered from an inferiority complex.

Greiser's trajectory in the 1920s does not offer a self-evident explanation for why he became a Nazi. By the end of the decade, it is true, Greiser had lived the cumulative experiences that made Nazis out of many Germans: he had belonged to the 'Front Generation' that fought and lost World War I; he came from and now lived in borderlands regions lost by the German Empire; he was involved in right-wing political movements; and he suffered financial hardship in the late 1920s. But at the same time, other elements of his biography suggest that he might never have been drawn to Nazism. He was not one of those war veterans who joined the Free Corps because he was unable to reintegrate into civilian life. He moved in Danzig's right-wing circles but he was not particularly committed to either the DSP or the Stahlhelm. Greiser was perhaps more comfortable in the bourgeois associational life of his Free Mason lodge and tennis club than in the backroom smoke of Danzig's fringe right-wing milieu. He was also no down-and-out loser. For much of the 1920s, he was financially quite secure.[208] Even at the end of the decade, when he did run into serious financial difficulties, he did not rush to join the NSDAP.

But Greiser did join the party. He had long skirted Danzig's right-wing circles. At the same time, living in Danzig, a city clearly hurt by its extrusion from Germany, would only have bolstered his nationalist tendencies, all the more so once his business career soured. At his 1946 trial, he stated: 'I originally joined the Party because I, like so many at the time, was unemployed.' He then elaborated: 'When one has an empty stomach, one goes to the party and the organization that offers one work and bread. And hunger hurts and pains even more when one can't feed one's own children.' In the same statement, Greiser gave some political reasons for why he joined the party: 'From 1919 onwards, all the other parties had been at the helm and had shown that they could not solve the distress in Germany or in the Free City of Danzig. For me, no program points or even foreign policy conceptions were decisive, only the solving of the great social questions. From everything that I knew about him, I trusted Hitler with solving this problem.'[209] Perhaps these reasons moved him to join the NSDAP. But in all likelihood, Greiser, now speaking to a Polish court, downplayed what he found truly attractive about the Nazi agenda: a fervent German nationalism, opposition to the Versailles Treaty, and disdain for the parliamentary system of the Weimar Republic.

Greiser was typical of mid-ranking Nazis in that he came from a (lower) middle-class background, just the stratum that had the most to lose in the crises of the Weimar years. Like many other future Nazi perpetrators, Greiser had enjoyed years of steady income only to find himself unemployed with little hope of securing a new job. As we know from his letters, Greiser was preoccupied with matters of status and was dependent on the admiration of others. In 1929, he must have felt deeply threatened by the steep decline in his fortunes and precipitous drop in social status.[210]

Greiser may have found the NSDAP attractive for other reasons, too. After a decade on his own that had ended poorly, he joined a structured organization that provided purpose, comradeship, and surety. In Robert J. Lifton's words, the party's ideology offered 'a promise of unity, oneness, fusion'—perhaps much-needed psychic balm after his recent difficulties.[211] At the same time, Greiser likely joined the party to alleviate stress caused by his financial problems. Indeed, as psychologists have now discovered, Nazi perpetrators were often 'deficient in stress tolerance;' 'needed more than usual amounts of external structure, guidance, and reassurance in managing their everyday lives;' and 'appear to have had low self-esteem with a tendency to view themselves as victims of circumstances'—all of which seem true of Greiser. Nazism offered him surety, an external structure that delivered direction and encouragement.[212]

The NSDAP proved Greiser's personal salvation. During the war, he reportedly stated that he joined the party when he did since 'this was the only thing that could still save him.'[213] By 1929, Greiser was over thirty and few promising prospects lay before him. The Nazi party changed all that. Through the party, Greiser secured recognition: he was soon known as an effective Nazi activist. Through the party, Greiser secured the good life: although it took a few years, the party was his avenue to prosperity. And through the party, Greiser secured a mission: Germany. Reviving Germany, strengthening Germany, expanding Germany—this became his all-encompassing *raison d'être* .

2

'Little Maria:' Striving for Strength and Power in Danzig

When Arthur Greiser joined the NSDAP in late 1929, he was bankrupt and seemingly without a future. Nazism, however, offered him meaning and purpose—a messianic nationalism—that had eluded him in earlier decades.[1] Through the Nazi Party, Greiser came to believe, he could achieve greatness for both himself and his nation. Indeed, just five years later, he was already head of state in Danzig. In the intervening years, he became a Nazi, in every sense of the word. He adopted a Nazi persona—bossy, churlish, and aggressive. He adopted the Nazi political agenda, loudly attacking parliamentary democracy, Social Democracy, Poles and Poland, and the League of Nations. He adopted Nazi tenets and categories to interpret his goals and strivings. And he adopted dramatic changes in his personal life. In the early 1930s, Greiser refashioned his life—his attitudes, his politics, and his relationships—to fit his movement.

When Greiser joined the NSDAP in December 1929, the party was already four years old in Danzig. Hans Hohnfeldt had founded a party branch on 21 October 1925.[2] Hohnfeldt, however, proved unable to generate much support, and in local elections in 1927, the NSDAP won just 0.8 percent, or 1,483 votes.[3] In June 1928, Hohnfeldt resigned as Gauleiter, and Erich Koch, the newly appointed Gauleiter of East Prussia, was also entrusted with the leadership of the Danzig Gau.[4] In March 1930, Koch hired Bruno Fricke as a salaried business manager. Fricke, the SA-leader in Danzig, enjoyed great popularity among local Nazis. He was also a follower of Walter Stennes, the SA leader for eastern Germany. Stennes and Koch, however, had a tense relationship. In summer 1930, a Koch–Fricke conflict split the Danzig Gau leadership into two: those in the 'political' camp (who believed that the party should have the upper hand) and those in the 'SA' camp (who, like Stennes, advocated a more militant, street-brawling Nazism). Older party leaders such as Hohnfeldt rallied to Koch's side. So, too, did Greiser.

Early on, Greiser caught the attention of leading Danzig Nazis. He had business skills and had gained a reputation as a speaker; he stood out among the decidedly mediocre and colorless Danzig party members. Greiser must have found his sudden rise to prominence in the NSDAP gratifying. Now, however, he became a pawn in the Koch–Fricke conflict. Fricke insisted that SA men pledge their allegiance first and foremost to the SA. He could then exercise authority over them—to the detriment of the Gau political leadership. In July 1930, Hohnfeldt noted that Fricke used Greiser's membership in the SA to his advantage: 'According to my information, Fricke has forbidden our two Gau speakers up to now, Member Greiser and Member Dr. Thimm . . . to speak . . . This measure against the Gau speakers means a *systematic driving away of speakers vis-à-vis the Gau, so as to render it unable to work*, while the SA is able to have its members hold independent political lectures.'[5] That same month, Koch suspended Fricke from his position, and appointed Greiser as Gauleiter. Greiser, in turn, left the SA, and soon became an implacable enemy of its Danzig branch.[6]

Greiser was now in the thick of Danzig Nazi intrigue. Koch convinced the party leadership in Munich to suspend Fricke from the NSDAP. Fricke and his supporters, however, refused to back down. On 1 September, Munich party headquarters expelled Fricke, and disbanded the Danzig Gau. Koch was told to reorganize the branch. On 16 September, a new organization called the 'National Socialist German Workers Party (Hitler Movement)' was formed. According to the organization's minutes, 'Mr. Arthur Greiser opened the meeting at 8:15 p.m. as the deputy charged by Gauleiter Erich Koch in Königsberg for the founding [of the group].' The document also noted that Greiser was chairman, Hohnfeldt secretary, and Wilhelm von Wnuck treasurer.[7] Fricke, however, refused to give up. He, too, chose a new Gau leadership. For both factions, time was of the essence: elections to the Volkstag were scheduled for 16 November.

Hitler, concerned about this state of affairs, charged Hermann Göring, his special emissary for Polish–German relations, with settling matters in Danzig. In the next years, the flamboyant, mercurial Göring would oversee Nazi developments in the Free City. Although Göring and Greiser shared a passion for hunting and a past as World War I fighter pilots, they had bumpy relations. Already on 30 September, Göring heard from Fricke supporters about Greiser's alleged political shortcomings. One, Meller, claimed that Greiser was a 'Gauleiter without a Gau,' and had 'unjustifiably redirected [party] mail to his apartment.'[8] When Göring came to Danzig on 3 October 1930, he recognized the depth of Fricke's support and decided to broker a compromise. Göring confirmed Koch's choice of Greiser as Gauleiter, but only until a new man could be sent from the Reich. He also decided that Fricke supporters would serve as Greiser's deputy and as heads of the SA and SS. Greiser was very disappointed. As he wrote to Göring, 'yesterday left a crack in my pure, spiritual notion of the idea of Adolf Hitler . . . I cannot quite accept the fact that our principle of command and of the authority of leadership had to be sacrificed to the demand of a majority, embodied through the will of the SA.'[9] Greiser clearly didn't like Göring's democratic method. But he was probably also bitter because he had been passed over as permanent Gauleiter.

To Göring, Greiser lacked the necessary fanaticism to lead the Danzig Nazis. As Göring soon told Hitler, 'only through a fanatical leader personality could change be effected here [in Danzig].'[10] Thanks to Göring, Greiser spent the next nine years in the shadow of another man. During those same years, though, he developed the fanaticism that Göring thought missing.

On 24 October 1930, Albert Forster, clad in lederhosen and knee socks, pulled into Danzig's central train station. Greiser and other local Nazis met him on the platform.[11] The new Gauleiter was tall, lanky, and just twenty-eight years old.[12] Five years younger than Greiser, Forster was a far more important and, as Göring had correctly noted, fanatical Nazi. Forster came from Fürth, a small city in Franconia. In September 1923, he joined the NSDAP as a zealous political novice. He was soon known as a talented, provocative speaker who worked tirelessly to drum up support for the Nazis. By spring 1925, Forster led the Nazi party branch in Fürth. He joined the SS in 1926, and held the prestigiously low SS number of 158.

Anti-Semitism was at the core of Forster's Nazi commitment. Early on, he got to know Julius Streicher, the editor of the virulently anti-Semitic *Der Stürmer* (The Stormer); Forster would later style himself as 'Julius Streicher's beloved disciple.'[13] Streicher, in turn, made it possible for his young protegé to meet Hitler; when the Führer came to Nuremberg, Forster served as his personal escort. In 1930, Forster entered the Reichstag as part of the new 107-man Nazi delegation following the 30 September elections. But his Reichstag career was soon on the back burner. At the first meeting of the newly elected parliament, Göring supposedly told him, 'Forster, you have to set things right in Danzig. Get the files, and get going—on the first fast train to Danzig.' Forster was the youngest Gauleiter that Hitler would ever appoint.[14] When he arrived in Danzig, he was what Greiser was not: a proven, fanatical Nazi; a hard-core anti-Semite; and, most important, a man trusted by the Führer.

By all accounts, Forster turned around the fortunes of the Danzig NSDAP. With just three weeks to the Volkstag election, he imitated the electoral strategy that had proven successful in the Reich: a blitz of rallies, meetings, and demonstrations, culminating on election eve when Joseph Goebbels, the future Reich Minister for Public Enlightenment and Propaganda, spoke at Danzig's Sports Hall. The rash of activity paid off. The Nazis won 16.1 percent of the total vote in Danzig—not too much behind the 18.3 percent that they had won in the Reich. In the Volkstag, the Nazis went from one seat in 120 to twelve seats in 72 (as a cost-cutting measure, the number of seats in the Volkstag had been reduced). The NSDAP was now the second largest party—after the Social Democratic Party of Germany (*Sozialdemokratische Partei Deutschlands* or SPD)—in the Volkstag. Forster traveled to Munich to confer with Hitler and Göring about whether the Nazis should join a coalition government. Due to foreign policy considerations, Hitler decided no. Instead, the Danzig Nazis were to support a conservative–Catholic minority government. Ernst Ziehm, a conservative, became president of the senate, the Free City's government. In just three years, the NSDAP had jumped from a fringe movement to the arbiter of Danzig politics.

Under Forster's leadership, Greiser held a number of party positions. He was deputy Gauleiter from 1930 to 1939. Until May 1933, he was Gau business manager and leader of the NSDAP faction in the Volkstag. From 1930 to 1933, he was also delegate to the harbor board; this board, made up of equal numbers of Germans and Poles with a neutral president, regulated the affairs of the Danzig harbor.[15] After Forster founded an official weekly Gau newspaper, *Der Vorposten* (The Outpost) in February 1931, Greiser served as its editor-in-chief until 1 June 1933. On its masthead, the newspaper shrilly proclaimed: 'Back to the Reich—Against the Injustice of Treaties.'[16] By 1932–3, it had a weekly circulation of 8,000–12,000.[17]

Greiser soon enjoyed rapid promotions in the SS. He joined the SS on 29 September 1931 with membership number 10,795.[18] He was a junior storm leader (*Untersturmführer*), and commanded the SS Standard '36' flight squadron with three light planes.[19] In September 1932 he jumped an SS rank to become a head storm leader (*Hauptsturmführer*). On 2 June 1933, Werner Lorenz, who supervised SS activity in Danzig, asked Heinrich Himmler to promote Greiser again. Greiser, Lorenz wrote, had 'in an exemplary way started up and organized the flying storm troopers.' Moreover, 'Greiser has always done much for the SS, provided work for unemployed SS comrades and given monetary and economic support to the local SS.'[20] On 20 June Greiser was promoted to storm unit leader (*Sturmbannführer*).[21]

The years 1930–2 were the heyday of the Danzig NSDAP. Forster moved the party's offices from a shabby building in a lower-class neighborhood to a patrician town house on one of Danzig's finest streets, 11 Jopen Lane.[22] He revved up Nazi agitation in the city. Still an opposition party, the NSDAP did not need to curb its militant style or agenda to still international or other concerns. SA thugs fought street brawls with communists and attacked individual Poles and Jews with impunity. Economic and political developments aided Forster's initiatives. In December 1930, 25,000 Danzigers were unemployed; two years later, the number had grown to 39,000. Trade with Poland dropped significantly, and the port of Gdynia continued to take away a share of Danzig's harbor activity. The Danzigers felt ever more insecure, and Forster capitalized on their fears. The party swelled to over 5,000 members in late 1931; a year later, it had virtually doubled again, to 9,519 members.[23]

When Hitler made a brief appearance at the Danzig-Langfuhr airport on 9 April 1932, the strength of the Nazi movement in the Free City was on full display. Thousands of cheering Danzigers greeted the Führer.[24] One of the few extant pictures of Hitler and Greiser stems from this occasion. In the photograph, Greiser, flanked by two of his children, twelve-year old Ingrid and seven-year old Erhardt, stands tall and proud in his navy uniform. Hitler and Greiser shake hands while their eyes meet. But they are standing very far apart from each other; the handshake is a stretch for both. The photograph captured the formal, distant relationship that Greiser always had with his Führer.[25]

In the early 1930s, Greiser still lacked a steady income. Earnings from his party and other posts were meager. Hohnfeldt later recalled just how strapped Greiser was: 'I know party member Greiser from the time of struggle (*Kampfzeit*). Together we enjoyed some of the joys of struggle, but we also went through all of the suffering of this time. We knew each other's circumstances . . . We [i.e., Hohnfeldt and his wife] knew that party member Greiser suffered from serious economic worries and that with his family he had to struggle painfully hard for a living. Only after his entry into the government [in June 1933] did party member Greiser have an ordered economic existence for the first time again.'[26]

To earn money, Greiser tried a new venture. In 1930, he procured a small motor-boat with a loan received from his sister Käthe and her husband Alfred Kochmann, who had married in 1921. Kochmann, a Protestant doctor of Jewish origins, had a good practice as an ear-nose-and-throat specialist in Berlin.[27] Greiser thus borrowed money from an in-law of Jewish origins *after* he became a Nazi. He named the boat 'Ingrid' and claimed that it was the fastest in Zoppot.[28] Officially, at least, he used the boat to ferry tourists around the Danzig Bay, among them Jewish tourists who came to Zoppot to escape the anti-Semitism found in Polish resorts.[29] Greiser's political opponents questioned whether he put the boat to other purposes, too. In October 1930, the German general consul in Danzig, Edmund Baron von Thermann, alluded to Greiser's 'not totally irreproachable business methods.'[30] Perhaps the baron had heard unsubstantiated rumors that Greiser smuggled currency.[31] Others claimed that Greiser used the boat to transport urine for sale to various pharmacies.[32] Whatever his actual doings, the boat venture was not very successful; after about a year, Greiser gave it up.[33]

The failure of the motor-boat venture may have led Greiser to redouble his efforts to advance in the Nazi movement. A more aggressive Greiser now emerged: rude, quarrelsome, swaggering, even vicious. He adopted a commanding tone toward those he deemed his underlings. In June 1931, for example, he tried to coerce a fellow Nazi and high-ranking police official, Dr. Larsen, to expedite a naturalization application. Larsen complained to Forster that Greiser's conduct was 'extraordinarily alarming and unfortunate' and violated the Criminal Code.[34] Greiser assumed a similarly imperious air toward other leading Danzig Nazis. In August 1931, Hohnfeldt, who was the Gau expert on civil-service matters, wrote to Greiser that he had not been informed about inter-party discussions on the reduction of civil-servant salaries. Hohnfeldt demanded that he participate in all such negotiations.[35] Greiser immediately responded that no such talks had taken place, but were planned for the following Monday. He then added, though, 'I must refuse your request to participate in inter-party meetings with the Senate, for 1. experts are not to make requests of the Gau leadership, but at most to be asked for something and 2. after hearing the views of our party delegation, the Gauleiter or I reserve for ourselves [the right] to perhaps seek your view.'[36] Hohnfeldt was furious, and angrily complained to Forster.[37] But Greiser had shown Hohnfeldt that he and Forster—and not the old party hacks—were running the show. No doubt, he relished his newfound ability to boss around others.

Greiser was menacing toward 'enemies,' too. In June 1932, he wrote an article in *Der Vorposten* claiming that the harbor board—to which he was a delegate—served only Polish interests and should be disbanded. The newspaper continued in this vein throughout July. In early August, the professional association of Polish harbor-board employees passed a resolution criticizing the Nazi attacks. It also warned that Greiser would be held responsible for any future 'incidents.' A few days later, Greiser visited a harbor-board engineer who was active in the Polish association, and told him that he viewed the resolution as a threat. According to one historian, 'The Nazi [i.e., Greiser] then displayed a revolver, playfully tossed it about, and claimed that he was ready for any attack.' The Polish side—the press and Commissioner-General Kazimierz Papée—argued that Greiser had threatened the engineer. But the Danzig Senate supported Greiser. It claimed that the whole matter was a harmless joke.[38]

Greiser's aggressiveness was mirrored in the large number of criminal court proceedings initiated by or against him. Between 1930 and 1932, Greiser was involved in at least twelve separate legal proceedings in Danzig. On two occasions, he stood as the accuser. In 1930, he charged that the SPD newspaper, the *Danziger Volksstimme* (Danzig People's Voice) had libeled him in one of its articles. The next year, he claimed that he had been threatened by an unidentified letter writer. Nothing came of either case. In every other instance, Greiser was the accused.

Most of the cases against him involved libelous accusations in *Der Vorposten*; as editor-in-chief, Greiser was responsible for the paper's content. In March 1931, a Mr. Feibusch accused him of libel for the article 'The Profiteer Jew Feibusch.' A civil servant, Eugen Dunkern, felt libeled by the article 'Tax Bureaucrat as a Carcass Hunter of Agriculture.' Another civil servant, Dr. Drum, initiated libel proceedings for the article 'How They Lie!' The general consul of the Turkish Republic, Julius Jewelowski, began a case against Greiser for an article called 'Jewelowski in the Ranks of the Traitors.' The article titles suggest the nature of the libelous allegations; they also intimate the tone of the screed that Greiser edited. Most of the cases ended without conviction. But for the article 'How They Lie!', Greiser received a fine of 500 gulden in lieu of a one-month prison sentence. This penalty was lifted by an amnesty that the Nazis granted (after they had come to power) on 27 June 1933.

Two other proceedings involved disruptive or abusive conduct on Greiser's part. In March 1931, Greiser was accused of leading a disturbance at a meeting of the nationalist Young German Order (*Jungdeutscher Orden*) in Tiegenhof; the case was soon dropped. In September 1932, he also allegedly coerced and insulted policemen guarding the police station in Danzig-Langfuhr. This case ended with the June 1933 amnesty, too.[39]

Greiser also faced prosecution in Germany for making anti-state remarks against the Weimar Republic. On 8 June 1931, at a NSDAP rally in Elbing (in Germany), Greiser declared that 'The Front soldiers did not fight so that we could live today in a sick (*koddrigen*) Republic.' He also thundered 'During the war Mr. von Hindenburg was a good general field marshal; but for the post of president of the Reichstag [*sic*] he is too old. We are sick of allowing ourselves to be enslaved by old fools (*Trotteln*) for years on end.'[40] Soon after, on 21 July, Greiser gave another speech in Marienburg (also in Germany). There he stated: '100 kilometers from here, at the very same hour in which we are gathered in this garden, those ministers who have decided on Germany's downfall are negotiating with our ministers about the fate of this sixty-million people. They [e.g. our ministers] are representatives or ministers of the party of high treason. They can sell off this Republic for another three months, but then the collapse will come... Brüning will then seek protection with us... This Republic has been built on high treason.'[41] Greiser was referring to SPD members who, in an official capacity, were negotiating reparations payments. While Brüning and the Reich foreign minister, Julius Curtius, declined to have Greiser tried for insult, prosecutors in Elbing chose to pursue Greiser for his contemptuous statements about the Republic.[42] For a year and a half, the case dragged on as various courts parsed precisely what Greiser had said. In the end, he was fined 200 Marks.[43]

As a leading Danzig Nazi, Greiser now became known for his militant polemics against Poles, Social Democrats, the League of Nations and, to a lesser extent, Jews.[44] In the very first issue of *Der Vorposten* (6 February 1931), he took aim at all four. He claimed, for example, that the NSDAP had not joined the government since both the League of Nations and Poland 'hate us National Socialists like the plague. Had we gone into the government, then both sides would have tried to make us all possible difficulties in order to say—rightly so—that in Danzig a National-Socialist government is at the helm and achieves nothing.' Greiser also insisted that the previous Social-Democratic government had left a shortfall of 16.5 million gulden and thus made the city vulnerable to Polish intervention. According to Greiser, it had 'seen as its main task to bring its unemployed bigwigs and little bigwigs [*Bonzen und Bönzlein*] to the state's manger.' As a result, Greiser claimed, the city had lost its creditworthiness and could only secure loans from 'the Jewish banking houses Warburg in Hamburg and Mendelssohn in Berlin.' Due to the previous government's alleged profligacy, the city had also almost declared bankruptcy. 'We know very well,' Greiser insisted, 'that our neighbors [the Poles], with whom we are for the time being forced to live in a customs union, would not have lost the opportunity... to emphatically point out in Geneva [to the League of Nations] the danger to "its" railroad in Danzig, "its" postal service in Danzig, "its" harbor and waterways in Danzig and "its" oppressed fellow countrymen in Danzig and within 24 hours to get the permission of this peace assurance society [the League of Nations] to intervene in Danzig.' Greiser then added: 'Even if there had been no military occupation of Danzig, one would have had to reckon with the appointment of a Polish finance commissar, who would have squeezed the whole of the population like a lemon in order to recover in a year the millions that were frittered away.'[45] With such insinuations, Greiser tried to whip up anti-democratic, anti-Polish sentiment.

As leader of the NSDAP faction in the Volkstag, Greiser played no small role in turning the city parliament into a body that spilled venom from every side. He was out to irritate, to provoke, to anger—and with considerable success. In a March 1931 Volkstag session, for example, he ceaselessly heckled a Social-Democratic speaker, Johann Kruppke. Kruppke, in turn, made references to the Tiegenhof affair; the Social Democrat referred to the actions of a 'bunch of thieves and its leader.' Greiser interjected that the 'Social Democrats are too cowardly,' and a few minutes later, 'that the Social-Democratic bigwigs are too cowardly to make appearances in which they are personally exposed.' The Social-Democratic president of the Volkstag, Julius Gehl, had had enough. He began to reprimand Greiser but grew so angry that he kicked him out of the meeting. A parliamentary advisory committee, however, determined that Gehl had overreacted; Greiser had been acting within permissible, albeit raucous bounds. Gehl felt compromised and resigned as Volkstag president. A liberal newspaper noted sadly that Greiser's antics had led to the resignation of an individual bent on preserving parliamentary democracy in the city.[46] After Gehl stepped down, von Wnuck, a Nazi, was elected president of the Volkstag.

The Nazi assault on democracy in the Free City was now in full swing. Although the NSDAP officially backed Ziehm's government, it became increasingly unsupportive of the Senate's policies. In fall 1931, Forster and Greiser traveled to Tegernsee to confer with Hitler about a change of political course. The Führer, however, told them to hold their horses.[47] In summer 1932, Forster nonetheless decided that the Danzig party (like its Reich counterpart) was restless. To mobilize party supporters, Forster began a propaganda campaign against the Senate. The NSDAP introduced a motion to dissolve parliament, but it failed. The Nazis, however, kept up the pressure. In February 1933, newspaper accounts summarized Greiser's remarks in a Volkstag session. 'Unfortunately,' the gist of these remarks ran, 'the Poles flout the rights of Danzigers, and [the Senate] must energetically protest against such Polish rights violations.' Greiser further claimed that the Ziehm government was at the mercy of the Poles: 'The "Hanseatic spirit" has unfortunately been confused with liberalism, democracy, and a politics of rapprochement. That's why Danzig has been pushed into a totally fruitless defensiveness and the Poles have always determined the course of political developments.'[48] Democracy, Greiser suggested, had permitted Danzig to fall under Polish domination.

The Nazis soon manipulated a Polish provocation for their own ends. On 6 March the Poles landed a unit of 120 men to strengthen their garrison on the Westerplatte, a peninsula in the Danzig harbor; this act violated Polish–Danzig agreements. Danzigers feared that a Polish invasion was in the offing. The Nazis trumpeted these fears and claimed that only they could rescue the situation. Ziehm, hoping to gain a more supportive Volkstag, arranged for new elections on 28 May 1933. The Nazis conducted this election with their customary bilious zeal: provocative meetings and rallies, a series of featured speakers from the Reich, and even the broadcast of a radio message from Hitler. The results were impressive: the Nazis won an absolute majority, 50.03 percent of the vote. Hitler famously telegraphed: 'Forster! Magnificent!'[49]

The Nazi takeover of Danzig was an event of international significance. For the first time, the Nazis governed an area outside of the Reich. As Hermann Rauschning, the first Nazi senate president in Danzig, later wrote, the Free City was now 'the storm center of European politics.'[50] Many ongoing international conflicts touched Danzig: the fate of the Treaty of Versailles, Germany's relations with eastern Europe, and the rivalry between democracy and dictatorship. Although England and France were officially committed to protecting Danzig's constitution and the role of the League of Nations in the city, both were eager to mollify Hitler's Germany. At the same time, since the Danzig Nazis were quite rightly viewed as tools of the Third Reich, developments in the Free City were seen as a bell-wether of Nazi relations with western countries. This made Hitler cautious about pushing a Nazi agenda in the city. As the Führer insisted time and again, the Danzig Nazis were to subordinate their policies to Reich interests.

In the new Nazi government, Forster chose not to become senate president; this was deemed too much of a provocation to the western powers and the League. Instead, Rauschning, a gentleman farmer, became senate president. At heart, Rauschning was a conservative German patriot. He became a Nazi as a result of his frustration with the Ziehm Senate's inability to solve the problems of Danzig's farmers. After joining the NSDAP in 1931, Rauschning quickly became the Gau's agrarian expert; as such, he was instrumental in drumming up Nazi support in the countryside. But Rauschning was no typical Nazi. He was not a racial anti-Semite. He had little interest in the SA's street-brawling tactics. He advocated moderation in foreign-policy matters—particularly toward Poland. All this made Rauschning 'presentable' to the international community. At the same time, since he had no political base within the Danzig NSDAP, Rauschning—unlike Greiser—posed no threat to Forster.[51]

Rauschning and Forster soon disagreed on many points of policy. Shortly after the election, Hitler told the Danzig Nazis to seek better relations with Poland. This was quite a change from their virulently anti-Polish electoral platform. On 5 July, Rauschning and Greiser went for an official visit to Warsaw, the first such state visit by a Danzig senate president since 1921.[52] In August and September, representatives from Danzig and Poland negotiated agreements on the rights of the Free City's Polish minority and the use of the Danzig harbor.[53] But while Rauschning genuinely wanted better relations so as to create a favorable economic environment for Danzig, Forster viewed the new policy of rapprochement with Poland as a sham. The two Nazis also differed on budget priorities. Forster wanted to spend money on prestige projects such as a theater renovation, the construction of an indoor swimming pool, the modernization of garbage collection, and the building of fancy streets. Rauschning advocated an austerity program and the devaluation of the gulden.[54] The scene was set for a showdown.

What was Greiser up to? As deputy senate president and senator of the interior, he was at the forefront of the Nazi assault on the Danzig constitutional order. In August 1933 he complained to the Senate Department of Justice that some public prosecutors were following the letter of the law rather than Nazi political goals. Greiser demanded that the senator of justice 'dismiss or otherwise put away' at least two prosecutors 'so that it is no longer possible for them to work on political matters.'[55] In late October, Greiser gave a speech that created a political scandal. He reportedly stated that 'A police official who did not definitely accept the *National-Socialist State* would never hold a position under him. If the totalitarianism claimed by the National Socialist Party were not achieved, he, too, would be unable to achieve his object. Firm action would have to be taken to make the new regime a reality. There could no longer be any room in Danzig for parties or for members of the Socialist, Center [the Catholic party], or German National Groups. He could *promise that all parties would disappear.* He would keep a firm grip on the police and make it an instrument of the *National-Socialist State*.'[56] These sentiments suggested the Nazis' true agenda for Danzig: a dictatorship.

After learning of these remarks, the League high commissioner in Danzig, Helmer Rosting, requested a meeting with the senate president. Rauschning believed that it was his duty to defend the Nazis publicly, and he now supported his deputy. Greiser then upped the ante. He had the Danzig police president, Helmut Froböß, temporarily ban two newspapers that had editorialized against his remarks. As Greiser wrote to Forster, he had the *Danziger Volksstimme* banned for two months so as to 'let the paper run aground and to ruin it economically.'[57] In response to the ban, newspapermen petitioned Rosting for help. The high commissioner once again turned to Rauschning. But to no avail.[58] Indeed, the senate president now even sanctioned Greiser's decision to have the newspapermen taken into custody.[59] When the petition was discussed at a League of Nations meeting in Geneva in January 1934, League officials chose to trust Rauschning that banning the newspapers was necessary to uphold law and order in the Free City. As would become an unfortunate pattern, League authorities were loath to criticize Danzig Nazis, lest they antagonize Hitler's Germany.[60]

Just three weeks after his speech to the police, Greiser spoke about judicial independence to a Nazi group called Justice. Once again, he voiced unconstitutional sentiments: 'The issue of the present struggle is *whether the independence of the judges is or is not to remain*—that is to say, whether the objectivity of the judges is to remain the supreme legal consideration. Under the parliamentary system of party government it was reasonable to press for objectivity. *In the totalitarian National Socialist State, the subjective law of the National Socialist State must take the place of objective law*, since the National Socialist outlook is not based on objective treatment but on subjective assent. The National Socialist State must have National Socialist law.' The Danzig constitution, however, clearly called for independent judges. Accordingly, Rosting questioned Rauschning's office about Greiser's statement. The senate president's office issued a correction claiming that judicial independence would be retained. But it also noted that judges would confront 'a new conception of law' in the National Socialist state.[61]

Much as Greiser was bent on increasing Nazi power, he was also determined to consolidate his own. He was allergic to subordinates challenging his authority. In January 1934, he issued a memorandum to municipal officials under his control, declaring 'I am absolutely unwilling to tolerate directors of offices subordinate to me going over my head and turning to the president of the Senate, in either written or oral form, about a matter concerning or a complaint about another office.' He insisted that all matters first be brought to him, and that he would then decide what to forward to Rauschning. Greiser even threatened that 'I will suspend from service and pursue through disciplinary action any civil servant who in the future goes over my head and addresses the president of the Senate in written or spoken communication about work matters.'[62] In a pattern that reflected both his ambition and his insecurity, Greiser always sought new ways to expand his powers while vigilantly countering real or perceived challenges to his authority.

Greiser also worked to undermine what he saw as attempts to increase Polish influence in Danzig. In April 1934, for example, he wrote to Rauschning that he had recently become aware that Polish firms and professional associations in Danzig were either placing workers directly or threatening companies if they did not employ workers of 'Polish nationality.' Greiser claimed that the Polish companies and associations were thus violating 'legal official channels and bypassing the State Job Center.' He asked Rauschning whether 'while taking into account the foreign policy situation, one might use police intervention in this matter.'[63] Greiser even suggested that the offending parties be arrested. The upshot of the matter is unknown, but the request illustrates how Greiser intended to counter any growth of Polish influence in the city.

Until the 1930s, Greiser did not show any particular antipathy toward Jews. As a boy, his family had had contacts with Jews. In Schroda, Gustav Greiser was friendly with a Jewish merchant, Mr. Kaphan.[64] The Greisers maintained contact with Kaphan long after they left town; Arthur even made a passing reference to Kaphan in a 1917 letter.[65] In Danzig, Greiser had business dealings with Jews, and when he fell upon hard times, Jewish businessmen helped him out.[66] According to a Jewish source, well into the 1930s, he 'had a certain sympathy' for Jews such as Adolf Mazur, who had earlier aided him.[67] Nonetheless, once the Nazis came to power, Greiser, as a member of the Senate, generally countenanced measures that targeted Jews. New regulations, for example, made it impossible for doctors to move to the city (a measure against Jewish doctors from the Reich wishing to come to Danzig), and set up obstacles to Jews joining professional associations.[68]

Greiser's closest friendship with someone of Jewish origins was with Alfred Kochmann, his sister Käthe's husband. During World War I, the two men had gone to the theater together; in 1919, Kochmann was a houseguest in Danzig; and in 1930, Greiser had borrowed money from him to finance his boat. Once Greiser joined the NSDAP, he did not hide his new political activities from Käthe. As Käthe's daughter, Vera, has written, in 1932 Greiser 'invited my mother to come to a party meeting, knowing full well that my father, who was born a Jew, and converted to a Lutheran, would not fare well under the new regime.' Vera continued, 'I am not sure whether he invited her because he wanted her to hear all this first hand, or whether he did it to help convince his new "friends" of his sincerity in bringing more Germans into the party.' Perhaps Greiser brought Käthe to the meeting as a sort of warning. If so, it proved effective: after the Nazis came to power in Germany, Käthe immediately began to plan for her family's departure. Greiser now proved helpful. 'Accordingly, telling the "party" that it would further German interests, my Uncle Arthur arranged to have my father join a group medical practice of German doctors in Shanghai.' In December 1933, 'Uncle Arthur' even came to Berlin to see his sister off.[69] But it must have been a very strange farewell. After all, Greiser was an activist for the very movement causing Käthe to leave. Although Arthur aided her departure, he never communicated with Käthe again. By the mid-1930s, he was more than willing to sacrifice a close relationship for his Nazi ideals.

Did Greiser, too, sacrifice his marriage for his new career? In the early 1930s, his relationship with Ruth soured. Arthur began a series of affairs.[70] Perhaps to mitigate his own adultery, he also used flimsy evidence to accuse Ruth of having extramarital relations.[71] It seems that as Greiser became an ever more important Nazi, he came to see Ruth as weak, naive, and uninteresting. His vision of what he could attain had changed, and he now sought more glamour in his life. In late 1933 or early 1934 Ruth suggested that the couple go to a piano concert together. At a reception following the concert, Greiser met the pianist, Maria Koerfer. He was smitten, and his feelings were soon reciprocated. Arthur abandoned Ruth; Maria left her husband; and the Greiser children were forced to choose between their parents. Arthur's affair, though, sparked more than just a private drama. It became the stuff of political theater: Greiser's enemies hoped to use the chaos in his personal life to undermine his political career.

When Greiser first heard her play, Maria was married to Dr. Fredy Wessel, a Berlin veterinarian; she used her maiden name as her stage name. Born on 30 March 1908 in Cologne, Maria was the fourth child of an engraver, Johann Koerfer, and his wife Emilie. As a child, she attended Catholic primary school. At the age of ten, she began studying piano at the City Music School. She received private instruction in German, literature, English, and French. Beginning in 1925, she studied music at the College of Music (*Hochschule für Musik*) in Cologne. In 1931, she decided to specialize in the works of the composer Hans Pfitzner.[72] Pfitzner was a violent anti-Semite, a German chauvinist, and an enemy of the Weimar Republic.[73] He composed music in the style of late Romanticism, and he believed that his compositions espoused German national values. He even styled himself 'Hans Pfitzner the German.'[74] After World War I, Pfitzner had been forced to leave his posts as opera director and head of the conservatory in Strasbourg, and he moved to Munich. Once Maria decided to focus on his work, she went to Munich so that the composer could train her to interpret his piano works. For the next few years, Maria played Pfitzner's compositions all around Germany.

Maria was a fashionable, attractive blonde. Behind her soft, elegant demeanor, however, she was a strong, forceful woman. An in-law has characterized her as 'impressive (*beachtlich*).'[75] Several family members have described her as cold, particularly toward children; in this, Maria was rather like Greiser's mother, Ida.[76] Greiser was surely drawn to her youth, beauty, and artistic aura. Perhaps he was also attracted to her combination of moodiness and strong will. Obsessed with notions of German soul and strength, Greiser may have found Maria to be the embodiment of a 'German' woman. Maria also had a pert side. Shortly before they were married, the couple attended a party in Zoppot. There, a Mr. Boskamp asked Maria to dance with him. Maria agreed—but only under the condition that Boskamp made a donation of two hundred gulden (roughly $600 in 2008 dollars) to the Winter Relief Work (*Winterhilfswerk*). Greiser proudly passed on the check.[77]

Maria's attraction to Greiser is the greater mystery. She was, after all, an educated musician, falling for a man who had never completed high school. Perhaps Greiser seemed to her a shining knight, ready to liberate her from an unhappy marriage. He was certainly charismatic: tall and strapping, a war veteran and pilot, a self-made man, and increasingly important Nazi politician. Perhaps Maria, who was quiet, found Greiser's outgoing personality captivating—a case of opposites attract. She may also have been drawn to the lifestyle of leading Nazis; Greiser was her entry ticket into the social circles of the Nazi elite. And given her attraction to Pfitzner and his music, she must have found Greiser's deeply held nationalism appealing.

The romance between Greiser and Maria left a remarkable paper trail, dozens of letters that he wrote to her (very few of her letters to him are preserved).[78] These letters document how Greiser rationalized his love for Maria, the stormy circumstances that surrounded their affair, and the ups and downs of their relationship. They also show Greiser in a tender, vulnerable light—a side of his personality that complemented the provocative, aggressive public persona that he cultivated after joining the

Nazis. Far from being the mere traces of a love affair long past, Greiser's letters to Maria are key documents in understanding Greiser's personal and political trajectory; they reveal the man that Greiser had become by the mid-1930s, after almost five years in the Nazi movement.

The first extant letter from Arthur to Maria is dated 2 May 1934. By then, the two were intimate. 'I can't stop thinking about you,' Greiser wrote to Maria two days after their last dalliance, 'and, in all possible situations, conjuring up your picture before my spiritual eyes. Yesterday evening in a huge, overcrowded meeting, the fourth rally of the day, it was very clear and physically near to me and I immediately grew somewhat calmer.' Greiser already believed that Maria was his future. 'I feel it ever more clearly, you will be my fate and linked with this fate yet greater tasks will fall to me. I can only master these tasks if I can draw strength, and for this I need you, little Maria. Perhaps I demand too much from you, I don't know. My life doesn't belong to me, it belongs to Germany. But if it is to be lived, it must have a content through you and so you must live for Germany and me.'[79]

Later in the month, Greiser wrote a long letter in response to various concerns that Maria had raised. 'I know, little Maria,' Greiser wrote, 'that you will first bring me unhappiness, great unhappiness and much suffering. I'm completely aware of that . . .' But, he continued: 'You think that you cannot give me strength . . . Look here, from my own energy I must give strength in hundreds of meetings, in political courses, in huge parades not only to a broad mass of the people, but particularly to a selected stratum of leaders of the people and the state, for the present and for the future. Do you think that the energy source in me is inexhaustible? No, it sometimes also has to be recharged.' Greiser then claimed that this was Ruth's great shortcoming: rather than giving him strength, she sapped him of it. 'I am the source that my wife feeds on . . . I had little affairs, I admit that. Today I know that that was a search to find you.' In Greiser's view, however, Maria also needed him. 'I say perfectly clearly, you need me, in order through my work, my world view, my struggle, to stimulate and develop your creative strengths as an artist.'

Greiser also claimed that Nazi ideology demanded that he leave Ruth. 'According to our world view, what is ethically and morally higher? . . . Should I sacrifice myself simply so as to maintain the image of a respectable husband? No, according to the Nat[ional]-Soc[ialist] world view, never, for I must live not for myself alone or for a few others, but for Germany. I may also only die when it is for Germany.' Greiser insisted that no obstacles would stand in their way. 'That this path is long, that it is hard, that stones and dirt lie on it, that it leads over hills where it will be necessary to have a breather, I know all that. The movement and its struggle, about which I am very proud, have taught me to clear away obstacles and to wade through rivers of dirt and scorn and nastiness and, if necessary, even blood, but to never lose sight of the grand goal.'[80]

Greiser's bathetic analysis suggests that he now applied Nazi values to his personal life. Since Nazis abhorred weakness and celebrated strength, Ruth became the symbol of weakness, Maria that of strength. Indeed, because his task of reordering Germany was so great, the demands so high, and the sacrifices so enormous, he needed all the strength he could muster. Maria, he believed, would be his source of strength, a position that gave her—in his mind—an important role in the Nazi project. At the same time, Nazis saw themselves as involved in constant struggle. Greiser thus framed his relationship with Maria in terms of struggle; only by overcoming myriad obstacles would they be able to fashion their lives as they wished.

Even after Ruth learned of Arthur's affair, she wanted to preserve the marriage. Greiser nonetheless began divorce proceedings. He seems to have had some pangs about this. As he wrote to Maria, 'I did it for us. But I'm a little bit sad that I had to force through with such methods.'[81] All this personal upheaval caused Greiser stress. In summer 1934 he ended up under a doctor's care. He was told to lead a less hectic lifestyle.[82]

Greiser's letters to Maria also open a window onto political events in Danzig. On 1 May 1934, for example, Forster delivered a very anti-Polish speech, and Greiser and others had to deal with the fallout. As Greiser wrote the next day: 'High tension in domestic and foreign policy, my own administration comes with 1,000 wishes and questions to me, piles of files await, and the most urgent visitors are outside my door. In between, breakfast with the Polish Minister Papée and the German General Consul [Otto von] Radowitz and other men (only one schnapps as an appetizer, nothing more)—that's the momentary situation in which I'm writing this letter. I feel as though I'm a wild animal, penned in [and] yearning for a gate.'[83]

Nazi Party activities also claimed his attention. In June, Greiser attended a two-day party gathering. Greiser thrived on the recognition that the speech that he gave brought him: 'The best was my national ceremony for the police. The public was not invited. I had the state police [*Landespolizei*], the constabulary [*Schutzpolizei*] and gendarmerie assembled and spoke. It was surely the best speech of my life, everyone says that and was very moved. I spoke about the spirit of Prussian soldiering that in war overcame the horror of death and cold material and today finds its resurrection in the allegiant idea of our world view that overcomes materialism.'[84]

Later that summer, Greiser had a political thrill: he spent time with Hitler. On 2 August, President von Hindenburg died. On 7 August, the funeral and burial were held at the Tannenberg Monument, the East Prussian site that celebrated the general's great victory in World War I. On the day before the funeral, Greiser wrote to Maria, '. . . I was also in the personal company of the Führer. On Monday evening in Finkenstein I ate with him at the same table, only the Reichsführer [Himmler] sat between us. He also spoke with me about our outdoor opera and about much else, too . . . on Tuesday early with the Führer to Tannenberg. It was overwhelming, this picture of a military funeral parade. The ceremonial pomp and the guests, especially the many diplomats and military attachés with their gold-bedecked uniforms, were impressive. Then immediately back to Marienburg in an airplane. Before departure the Führer voiced his appreciation to me. You can imagine how much jealousy there is now . . .'[85]

Greiser's observation about jealousy was not idle. The Danzig Nazi movement was a hotbed of intrigue. In mid-August 1934, after a visit with Maria, Greiser returned home only to be confronted with a swirl of rumors. Within half an hour, he wrote, he had learned 'that because of problems at home I had poisoned myself with barbiturates; that due to grave differences I had had a duel with Forster and that he had therein shot my arm to pieces; that I as a representative of revolutionary nationalism had had a quarrel with Rauschning because of his treaties with the Poles and that this quarrel had become a physical bout in which I was injured because R[auschning] had called out to the guard that I . . . had stolen significant sums and that I had been bribed by Dr. [Robert] Ley, [head of the German Labor Front], with a sum of millions; that after my divorce I would marry a teacher; that there were grave internal differences that I could now only master; a hundred other things, too, but that incidentally I was indeed an interesting guy who would set everything right.'[86]

Most, if not all, of these rumors originated with Max Linsmayer, the SA-leader in Danzig. Greiser and Linsmayer detested each other.[87] Their mutual dislike was surely a local variant of the broader conflict between the SA and the SS for control of the Nazi coercive apparatus. But Greiser's dislike of Linsmayer also had more specific causes. In Danzig, the SA was unusually strong, not least because the local SS-leader, Dr. Alexander Reiner, was incompetent. Greiser had little use for the violent tactics of the storm troopers; they often presented a challenge to his police force. As he once told von Radowitz, 'it's happened on various occasions that the SA has failed just then when the state needed it.'[88] The conflict between Greiser and Linsmayer had reached a high point in late 1933. Greiser had criticized Linsmayer to Himmler, but was promptly formally reprimanded for this by Ernst Röhm, the head of the Reich SA, in Himmler's presence.[89] This surely humiliated and thus infuriated Greiser. Linsmayer, in turn, apparently feared that if Greiser were senate president, he would disband or otherwise weaken his SA. After the June 1934 purge of Reich SA-leaders, carried out by the SS, SA men in Danzig apparently considered killing Greiser. As Rauschning later recalled, an SA man who was 'aware of my dislike of Arthur Greiser,' visited him and mused 'that it would be a fit and proper thing to kill Greiser as an act of vengeance against the SS...'[90] Although Linsmayer didn't murder Greiser, his insinuations would soon threaten Greiser's political career.

Greiser's relationship with Maria was itself a potential weapon for his enemies. By the end of summer 1934, Forster and Greiser were ready to oust Rauschning and replace him with Greiser. Arthur's affair, however, complicated matters. As he wrote to Maria in late August, 'One wants to take down Rauschning, one needs me for that, I am to pull the chestnuts out of the fire of smouldering discontent.' But Greiser then explained the difficulties in this scenario: 'Now the calculation would be right [i.e., Greiser would be rewarded with the position of senate president], but a president who is getting divorced and who wants to marry a woman who does not love *me*, but rather my position, that is a mistake in the calculation that must be repaired.' Greiser's political enemies were suggesting that Maria was an opportunist. As Greiser further described the talk of Maria, 'And she has red lips, too, and is even an artist and in her arrogance takes walks arm and arm with me in Berlin.' He now claimed that he prized Maria above his political future: 'Tomorrow Forster will be back and I'll confront him immediately... One thing you must know for sure, my little Maria: I won't leave you, my life can only belong to the party and to Danzig if you preserve it. A separation from you would mean death for me, the severity of the struggle for our love gives me the certainty of victory in which our happiness lies.'[91]

The next day, Greiser vented his frustration with the fetid politics of the Free City. In a view typical of right-wing veterans of the Great War, he juxtaposed the pure world of soldiering with the sordid machinations of political life. 'Thank God that I was among soldiers yesterday. I drove out around 10:00 p.m. to the bivouac and spent the night in the open. This morning at 6:00 a.m. returned. Soldiers, weapons, bivouac fire, music, songs, also a juniper tree, it's another world and it's purer and nicer than politics and intrigues. It was nice and during the melancholy songs I thought only about you.'[92] In another letter written soon thereafter, Greiser alluded to the actions of others, perhaps former political supporters who had now deserted him since his political future seemed cloudy. 'When others now disappoint me, so be it. All the more you climb in my respect, since you predicted this all. One can learn to hate people, I'm in the process of that. For their personal advantage they betray others. Ugh!'[93]

Greiser's political enemies weren't the only ones to suggest his new relationship was problematic for a Nazi leader. Although Arthur was firm in his decision to leave his wife, Ruth still hoped to keep the marriage intact. On 12 October 1934, in sheer desperation, she wrote to Himmler: 'With all force, my husband wants to destroy our marriage and thus the parental home of our three children. A Mrs. Wessel . . . is pushing herself in the most unbelievable way into our marriage, [she]'s a typical Berlin figure who turns men's heads and brings about unforgivable disaster. Of course she has no children, and thus acts so unconscionably.' Ruth wrote that Greiser had forced her to lodge a suit against him. He had treated her so poorly that 'I'm no longer a person, I can't be anything for my children and more than once I have come to the decision to end my life. I need a husband more than almost any other woman, for I have no parental home and otherwise *no one* who can stand by me.' By the early 1920s, Ruth had not only lost her father, but also her brother and mother.[94] She further noted that 'my husband can forgive me the mistakes that I have made. I am treated with the greatest nastiness so that everything will happen quietly and three children will be deprived of their father. And that's in the spirit of the party? I can and will not believe that and ask you to speak with the Führer about whether a leader in my husband's position may *spiritually murder* the mother of his children and, if he does that, if he *has* to inform the party?' Ruth further claimed that 'all Danzig is outraged by this step and stands behind me. Every day I'm told how indignant all are that a wife who went through the hard times is abandoned in the good ones and is to be lonely and cannot have any share of the successes of the husband.' Ruth pushed what she thought were Himmler's buttons: the distress of an abandoned wife and fatherless children, the wiles of a fashionable lady, the need to keep Nazi leaders' private lives above reproach and, not least, public opinion. Marks on the letter suggest that receipt was never acknowledged. Himmler did nothing for Ruth.[95]

Three days later, on 15 October 1934, a Danzig court rendered its judgment in the divorce case. Greiser, in his case against Ruth, accused her of borrowing 100 gulden (roughly $300 in 2008 dollars) from his personal adjutant, Mr. Bühring, without his knowledge; ordering furniture for several hundred gulden without his consent; and telling others that Greiser was running after childless women so that he could get them pregnant.[96] In response to Greiser's suit, Ruth lodged a countersuit in which she claimed that Greiser had committed adultery with a prostitute in Munich. The prostitute's name was not known and the only witness to corroborate the encounter was Werner Lorenz, a close friend of Arthur's who had earlier overseen the Danzig SS. In all likelihood, Greiser put Lorenz up to making the statement. The judges deemed Greiser's suit without merit. But just as Greiser had wanted, they ruled in favor of Ruth. Greiser was declared the only guilty party and had to pay all legal costs associated with the case.[97] Soon thereafter, Himmler inquired about Greiser's marital situation. Greiser told him that 'For years I had had the intention of getting a divorce without knowing Mrs. Koerfer . . . I did not carry out my intention earlier because I was not in a financial situation to guarantee my wife economic security.' He then added: 'My divorce took place without coercion. I had numerous sufficient grounds to initiate a divorce, but . . . took upon myself sole blame so that my wife would have the opportunity to remarry.'[98] Greiser simply lied to Himmler.

Greiser hoped that with his divorce in place, all would be well with Maria. It was not to be. 'Today,' he wrote to her on 1 November, 'I received confirmation of the legality of my divorce and from you the phone message that you don't want to see me again. God knows, I imagined this day otherwise. For days I haven't drunk any alcohol, have not smoked, and barely eaten, my office is almost my apartment, I am thus totally cool in my judgment of everything that has happened. One gives every criminal the opportunity to defend himself. You don't give that to me, because my crime against you is that I cannot lie to you.' Given how Greiser would later treat accused criminals in the Warthegau (summary execution), it is striking that he once voiced the sentiment that those accused of wrongdoing should have an opportunity to defend themselves. Greiser then continued, 'First I wanted to be stubborn and to wait until you write. But I love you too much to make this first test of endurance of our love all too difficult. So I'm writing. But not an apology. He who apologizes, accuses himself. I'm ready to answer for what I did. But one must give me at least the opportunity to give an explanation for how it was that I did what I did.'

What had Greiser done? He had had sex with Ruth. Greiser claimed that he had been under enormous pressure because Ruth was threatening to appeal the case. 'Her hysteria grew from day to day. In this situation she would have made not only our marriage impossible, but also she would have totally undermined my existence and position. I had to cleverly but very quickly cut through the knot of all possible dangers.' Greiser noted that Maria had once done something similar with Fredy. As he continued, 'at all possible opportunities in life one uses the means of alcohol to attain one's goal. I used an even stronger means, the sexual frustration of a woman. Ice cold, I played with that *for hours*. And once I had the letter that I dictated I fulfilled my promise. But ice cold in my heart, without feeling, without an embrace, without a kiss, with disgust and closed eyes. A matter of a moment, the last of any respect that I had [for her] was then gone. Today I ask myself how it was possible that this woman could be the mother of my children.' Greiser, eager to get Ruth to write a letter, presumably stating that she would not appeal the case, blackmailed her with the promise of sex. Ruth still loved Greiser.

In his letter to Maria, Greiser continued: 'If I've committed a crime against you, good, then it should be expiated. But I do not come to ask for pardon because I don't feel myself guilty. What I did, I did for us and our future, it didn't move me, but rather further severed me from this woman.' Greiser also insisted that he would die if he lost Maria's love—and his work for his beloved Germany would also end. 'If you think that our love is not strong enough to survive this blow, then say it freely and openly to my face. Then I will hear it and be convinced by it. *Then life has lost its meaning for me, for I will be destroyed not just by this love, but also by the recognition that without you as power and force I cannot achieve anything more for my beloved Germany*. Germany will live even if we must die. Then I would rather die than sap this Germany.'[99] Perhaps Greiser was using his 'love for Germany' as a way to present himself as the person Maria wanted him to be. He was also, however, using his love for her to bolster him in the personality change he was undergoing in order to succeed as a Nazi.

The couple soon patched things up, but Greiser was now in the midst of an election campaign. Municipal elections were scheduled for Niederung and Grosses Werder on 18 November. 'You were yesterday at the movies,' Greiser wrote ten days before the elections, 'I don't have the time for that anymore. The election campaign is in full swing. Every day two meetings.'[100] For an unknown ailment, however, he was hospitalized. Since Rauschning was away, Greiser was in charge of Senate matters. 'From the Senate everyone comes here, so that I can govern from here. They also bring me piles of files.' Ingrid and Erhardt visited, too. Greiser was finally moving out of the family apartment, and Ingrid was packing his belongings so that he could go directly from the hospital to his new apartment.[101] Despite the hectic pace at his hospital bed, Greiser had some moments of quiet. As he wrote to Maria, 'I now dream much more often about you and afterwards yearn for you so much. Today, too. You are then so soft and lovely and sweet and I've never loved you so much.'[102]

The affair was not the only challenge to Greiser's position. As Arthur wrote to Maria from his hospital bed, 'After the [local] election the matter of Rauschning has to be taken care of, then I have to fight to the end with my special friends in the SA, and then we can both gradually accustom people that we belong together. Once again, I have to move cleverly so that we can reach our common goal and I can't offer any targets at the moment.'[103] Greiser's opponents were looking to undermine him by targeting his past and present activities. On 16 November, Arthur wrote, 'There's no quiet. The power struggle of the SA-leaders has reached a boiling point just as I predicted until the decision about the Rauschning matter. At all costs they want to prevent my presidency because they know exactly that then not only my current department—chiefly the police—will be denied to them as a playground but that just as in the Reich the gentlemen will have been totally outplayed. I told you once already about the fat report with lies and nastiness that they sent to [Rudolf] Hess in Munich. Now Hess has sent a special emissary to investigate. I'm happy about that, because I have a totally clean conscience vis-à-vis everything of which they accuse me.' While Greiser was writing this letter, Forster arrived at his sick bed. 'Forster,' Greiser continued, 'is beside himself in fury . . . All the more so because the local SA-leaders are conspiring with Rauschning. For personal political ends they place this already endangered state at risk. They are perhaps rogues and criminals. Unfortunately, one can't just shoot such rabble here. But my honest conscience will also be successful here. I have no fear about that.'[104]

Greiser was referring to a party investigation into his past life. Already in July 1934, his earlier Free Masonry had been examined by the party's Supreme Court. The outcome was favorable to him. As president of the court Walter Buch determined, despite his past membership, Greiser should still 'be used as a political leader in the party in Danzig.'[105] But now party investigators honed into other accusations, some of which originated with or were circulated by Robert Reuter, Greiser's former flight instructor who had brought him into the NSDAP. According to these insinuations, Greiser had supposedly passed himself off as having had a higher rank in the Navy reserves than was true because he wore an overcoat with the epaulette of a first lieutenant. He had allegedly belonged to a Free Mason lodge even after joining the NSDAP. He had supposedly permitted corruption in the Zoppot casino by extending the license for casino operations to two Jews, Wolff and Graetz. He also allegedly took a loan of 10,000 gulden from three Jews so as to support a lifestyle above his means—leasing hunting grounds, visiting the Zoppot casino, and belonging to the 'expensive' Red-White Tennis Club.[106] Although these accusations seem trivial, they had traction with the NSDAP; the party expected its leading members to live above reproach.

After examining the evidence about these and other (now undocumented) allegations, Hess's emissary, Baron Holzschuher, sided with Greiser. The baron decided that the rumors about Greiser's shortcomings came from the Rauschning and Linsmayer camps and were untrue. He nonetheless thought that from time to time Greiser's superiors had to 'rap him across the knuckles because of his somewhat thoughtless [*leichtsinnig*] disposition.' It's not clear what Greiser had been 'thoughtless' about—perhaps his affair, perhaps his finances, perhaps his dealings with Jews. Holzschuher also believed that one accusation merited further investigation in Berlin: that Maria 'has contacts with many foreigners, including French and Polish intelligence officers.'[107] In a letter to Greiser, the baron stated that 'in a number of instances you did not show necessary restraint.' Hess now issued

Greiser a formal censure. Holzschuher, however, emphasized that the 'censured actions were in no way based on dishonorable convictions.'[108] As Greiser gleefully wrote to Maria, 'honor has been saved, my honor and your honor. The enemy has been repelled in his attack, next week he will have to be crushed.'[109] Holzschuher's findings cleared Greiser's path to the senate presidency.

Rauschning's ouster had been brewing all fall. If Forster masterminded the operation, Greiser was the hit man. Greiser deployed all the unsavory political methods in his then arsenal: lies, rumors, threats, and faits accomplis. In early September, Forster and Greiser told Rauschning to reduce League influence, pursue a more anti-Polish foreign policy, and move more forcefully against domestic opposition. In response, Rauschning went on 'sick leave.' In fact, though, his health was just fine. He went to Berlin to plead his cause with Reich authorities. In a memorandum intended for Hitler, Rauschning outlined his views on the situation in Danzig. Since the Reich was unable to subsidize Danzig sufficiently, he argued, the city had to work closely with neighboring Poland. A League presence, in turn, was necessary to guarantee the Free City's independence from the Polish Republic. Forster's interference in senate matters, however, threatened Danzig's delicate international situation.[110] Rauschning noted that he wrote his memorandum in the German Foreign Ministry because 'in Danzig I was no longer safe from party spies.'[111] Foreign Minister Constantin von Neurath forwarded the memorandum to Hitler with the recommendation that the Führer demand that Forster cease meddling in Danzig's government. Hitler, however, refused to intervene. At the end of September, Forster sent Greiser to Rauschning in Berlin (conveniently, Greiser could also visit Maria). As Rauschning recorded, Greiser told him to ban three opposition newspapers for several months, arrest some Catholic priests, deport the editor of a Jewish newspaper, further destroy the opposition parties, and dismiss some senate employees who were his confidantes.[112]

Soon after delivering Forster's message, Greiser returned to Danzig to meet with the new League high commissioner, Sean Lester. Lester was a respected Irish diplomat who had taken up his post in January 1934.[113] In Danzig, he made it his mission to uphold the city's constitution and to maintain League rights in the city. In late September, he requested a meeting with Greiser to discuss the Rauschning situation. On 1 October, Greiser flat out lied to Lester, telling him that there was no conflict between the Gauleiter and the senate president. He even reiterated this statement in a letter to Lester the next day.[114] Greiser's cavalier treatment of Lester signaled the tenor of future Senate–League relations; in the next months and years, Greiser would do all he could to antagonize the well-meaning Lester.

Back in Berlin on 4 October, Greiser informed Rauschning that Forster demanded his resignation. The two men agreed that Rauschning would resign due to illness after another three weeks or so of sick leave.[115] Greiser and Forster now moved to strip Rauschning of his remaining influence. On 11 October Rauschning learned that Greiser had taken over the senate departments of foreign and economic affairs.[116] In a harsh letter to Greiser, Rauschning protested these developments.[117] But Greiser simply ignored the letter. Although Rauschning again requested that Forster be recalled from Danzig, Hitler continued to support the Gauleiter.[118]

Rauschning was out of options; his resignation was just a matter of time. His notion of honor, however, demanded that he submit himself to party discipline so long as he officially represented the Nazis. During fall 1934, he upheld the fiction that there were no political differences in the Danzig Nazi leadership. In addition, so as not to harm the party's electoral chances, he stayed in office until after the 18 November election. These elections proved the high-water mark of Nazi success in the Free City. The Nazis won 77 percent of the vote in Grosses Werder, and 81 percent in Niederung. But they had only won these margins through electoral intimidation. They had attacked Catholic priests, taunted and beat up poll workers for the Center party, and even fired shots into the bedroom window of a Center candidate. All the while, the police—Greiser's police—stood by and tolerated electoral abuses.[119] Election victory in hand, Greiser and the other Nazi senators threatened Rauschning that if he did not resign within forty-eight hours they would 'be compelled to take a further step of our own accord for the settlement of the whole matter.'[120] Rauschning refused to resign without following parliamentary procedure. He sought a vote of no confidence, and on 22 November, the Nazi parliamentary faction obliged.[121] Rauschning resigned the next day, announcing that he was leaving for 'special reasons;' he thereby signaled that his resignation was political.[122]

Rauschning's departure marked an important step in the Nazification of Danzig. He was the last head of the Free City to insist on following parliamentary rules. He was the last hope for Danzig to maintain itself as a

Free City, with some semblance of independence from the Reich, Poland, and the League of Nations. And he was the last honest man to head the city. Although he had an authoritarian bent and allowed himself to be a Nazi tool, he maintained a modicum of decency as senate president. Rauschning soon became a determined opponent of the Nazi regime; later, he emigrated to the United States, where he became a farmer in Oregon.

Greiser was the obvious choice to become Rauschning's successor. Although Linsmayer and von Wnuck tried to prevent his accession to the senate presidency, Greiser was Forster's choice; he was, after all, the best-known Nazi in Danzig after the Gauleiter himself. Perhaps Forster recognized that Rauschning's resignation would shake public confidence and did not want to further undermine the Nazi government's standing by choosing an unknown senate president.[123] He told von Radowitz in October, 'It will probably have to be Greiser, since I don't have anyone else.' Von Radowitz further noted that Forster would wait a few weeks so that 'clarity' vis-à-vis Greiser could be achieved—an allusion, no doubt, to the Holzschuher investigation.[124]

On 28 November the Volkstag elected Greiser as senate president. Of seventy-two representatives, forty-one were Nazis. Greiser received all of their votes—and not a single additional one. Only two other representatives deigned to vote, and both turned in invalid ballots. Foreign governments also expressed their reservations. Although many foreign representatives were usually present when a senate president was elected, only American, French, Danish, and Colombian representatives were there. As the German deputy consul noted, 'Contrary to custom, the [League] high commissioner and the Polish diplomatic representation sent no representative.'[125] The small number of foreign dignitaries was surely a snub to the Danzig Nazis.

In his inaugural address, delivered right after his election, Greiser offered a combination of lies and threats. He insisted that the change in senate president did not signal a new policy in Danzig. He claimed that his government had a resounding mandate: 'The government can . . . count on the will of the whole population as was demonstrated so strikingly in the elections in the countryside and as it embodies in a true way an ethical democracy . . .' He threatened Nazi opponents in the Free City. He claimed that he did not want to suppress criticism of the state leadership, 'but under criticism I do not understand the unlimited right of a tiny minority opposition to tear down all the work of the state leadership and to be only negatively critical . . .' He warned against 'saboteurs' spreading rumors, particularly concerning the economy. In this context, he added that all rumors to the effect that the gulden would be devalued were 'absurd,' and that the government would 'steadfastly hold on to the principle of maintaining the stability of the Danzig currency.' Finally, Greiser promised better relations with Poland: 'It's a pleasant duty for me to explicitly emphasize that nothing will change as concerns our attitude to our neighbor Poland, but on the contrary the stance of the National-Socialist Danzig government will be to endeavor to strive for and to develop an even further perfection and improvement of these mutual relations.' In a telling omission, Greiser made no mention of cooperation with the League of Nations.[126]

In early December, Greiser wrote to his old buddy, Werner Lorenz, now in Hamburg: 'in the last weeks, much, very much, has occurred in Danzig . . . I had to fight through the biggest battles and finally my friend Linsmayer has been exposed as a traitor. In a letter, it is impossible to describe to you the incredible strength of nerves that were necessary to survive the last weeks and months. Among other things, I was accused of earlier standing up for you [as the overseer of the Danzig SS] and this all was the subject of embarrassing proceedings in Munich.' Greiser was planning a vacation, 'so as with new strength to then use an iron broom as brutally as the constitution and laws of Danzig permit.' Greiser also commented that his relationship with Forster 'has finally entered the path that I have long wished . . . We work together in total trust and on this only possible basis we will be able to master the fate of Danzig.'[127] Shortly afterwards, Greiser and Forster arranged for Linsmayer's recall to the Reich.[128]

Greiser was now a head of state, albeit of the tiny Danzig statelet. He also took charge of the Foreign Relations Department while continuing to run the Interior Department.[129] For his thirty-eighth birthday, in January 1935, he was inundated with flowers and greetings. 'Too bad,' he wrote to Maria, 'that I can't send you all the flowers that are in my office . . . There are huge numbers of birthday congratulations and Warsaw and Geneva [to which he had made visits] have had a very good effect. My prestige has grown enormously. But not a single birthday congratulation from the SA.'[130] Two months later, Greiser described his trips through the region. 'It's always moving and thankful to see how much people support me. I am myself truly amazed at the enthusiasm everywhere. And the great pains that are taken when I come, everywhere festively decorated halls and music and flowers on the table or handed to me in bouquets. I wish that you could be there, too.'[131] Greiser relished his new job. Now an important politician, he enjoyed the deference he was accorded, as well as the trappings of power.

As senate president, Greiser continued to undermine democracy in the Free City. In February 1935, he rammed through a petition to dissolve the Volkstag, forcing new elections scheduled for 7 April. The Nazis were eager to secure a two-thirds Volkstag majority so that they could legally alter Danzig's constitution. They now tried to secure a landslide victory. Although parties were prohibited from gathering electoral funds, the Nazis received some 1,500,000 gulden from Reich party coffers. They prevented other parties from renting assembly halls or broadcasting on the state radio station. They confiscated opposition newspapers. They arrested four SPD Volkstag deputies—despite parliamentary immunity. They physically attacked SPD members. They taunted opposition candidates and supporters by writing slogans such as 'Here Lives a Traitor' on their homes. They organized special trains that brought Danzig residents living abroad to the city to vote. They blanketed the city with Nazi flags, swastikas, slogans, and pamphlets. Top Nazis came to speak at huge election rallies.[132] As Greiser wrote to Maria on 26 March, 'On Saturday the visits of [Reich] ministers begin and daily become more intensive until Hess, Göring, and Goebbels come in the last three days [before the election].'[133]

On 29 March, Gustav Greiser died in Berlin. Greiser had to interrupt his campaigning for several days. As he wrote to a relative, 'against my will, I will be in Berlin on Monday and Tuesday ... to organize the burial of my father.' Since his brother Otto had broken his foot and lay hospitalized in Brandenburg, Greiser felt he had to go to Berlin to help his mother.[134]

Back in Danzig for the final days leading up to the election, Greiser confidently told foreign diplomats that the NSDAP would win 90 percent of the vote.[135] In fact, the Nazis officially won just 59 percent of the vote—well short of the two-thirds majority that they needed to change the Danzig constitution. Forster was hugely disappointed; he allegedly broke down and wept on election night.[136] Beyond party circles, the results were also seen as a Nazi debacle. *The New York Times* published an editorial titled 'Nazi Defeat.'[137] After two years of NSDAP rule, many Danzigers were dissatisfied. The Nazis had failed to improve the Free City's precarious economic and international situation. Moreover, as Erich von dem Bach-Zalewski, the SS-leader in East Prussia and Danzig, believed, voters were alienated by the corruption and 'bosslike' conduct of

NSDAP officials. Danzigers, Bach-Zalewski thought, had been turned off by Greiser's divorce and Linsmayer's slander campaign.[138]

Although politics consumed much of his time and energy, Greiser remained preoccupied with his private life. In early 1935, he wanted custody over his two older children. But Ruth put up a battle. As she wrote to Greiser in February 1935, 'I... will not allow the sole right that I still have to be reduced. Following your constant pressure, I have relinquished home, house, and marriage. The children have been awarded to me.'[139] Greiser prevailed, however, in the sense that Ingrid and Erhardt chose to live with him; much later he assumed actual custody over them.[140] At the same time, Greiser seems to have felt threatened by his former wife. For several years, he had her actions and visitors observed—perhaps so as to have 'dirt' on Ruth should she ever try to compromise his political career.[141]

In spring 1935, Ingrid was confirmed. The minister who did the confirmation, Gerhard Gülzow, later recalled a striking episode about Greiser. Gülzow asked that all confirmands look with their parents for a Bible quotation fitting for the occasion. Ingrid came to Gülzow with 'In good luck proud, in bad luck tough as ebony.' When Gülzow asked her where she had found the quotation, Ingrid said that her father had made it up.[142] That Greiser thought that he could just make up a Bible quote is certainly telling of his hubris; it also foreshadowed his later campaign against organized religion.

Presumably to ease Maria's move to Danzig, Greiser sent both of his older children to live in the Reich in spring 1935. Ten-year-old Erhardt began the National-Socialist German Secondary School on Lake Starnberg (*Nationalsozialistische Deutsche Oberschule Starnberger See*), a Nazi boarding school in the Bavarian village of Feldafing. The school was the most elite of the Nazi elite schools, and was to educate the highest stratum of future Nazi leaders.[143] Greiser was surely taken with the notion of his son being educated along with the sons of top Nazi officials. Fifteen-year-old Ingrid, on whom Greiser doted, went to live with his mother, Ida, in Berlin. She first attended two year-long secretarial courses, and then did a half-year course of French foreign-language instruction. In November 1937, she took a secretarial job in the Air Force, but in March 1938 she transferred to a job in the Foreign Ministry.[144]

Of his youngest daughter, Rotraut, Greiser wrote to Maria in March 1935, 'For two days now I have always had a little girl in my bed in the mornings! Jealous? Rotraut is visiting and doesn't want to leave, she feels very comfortable in all the hurly-burly here [Greiser was just having the house renovated].'[145] Although Rotraut never lived with Greiser again, she regularly visited him in Danzig and Posen.[146]

Since he belonged to the SS, Greiser needed Himmler's permission to marry Maria. The couple now experienced a version of the invasive racial screenings that so many incoming ethnic Germans would later undergo in the Warthegau. According to the medical form that Greiser submitted to the Racial Office of the SS in 1935, he weighed 180 pounds at just under six feet tall. The doctor who examined him described his body type as 'muscular,' his posture 'tightly erect,' and his muscle tone 'strong.' The doctor had no reservations about Greiser's suitability for marriage.[147] The same was true of Maria. The doctor who examined her noted that she was twenty-six years old, stood five feet four inches, and weighed 123 pounds. Her body type was 'round, slender,' her posture 'erect,' and her muscle tone 'middling.' During the two years of her previous marriage, the doctor wrote, there had been 'a desired childlessness.'[148] Greiser and Maria were poster children of the perfect 'Aryan' couple. Himmler, of course, approved their marriage.[149] But, despite official encouragement to procreate, the couple never had any children.

In preparation for his marriage, Greiser rented a villa at 12 Lessing Street in Oliva, a residential quarter of Danzig. The house underwent substantial renovations. Banisters were removed, wood trim repaired, and doors and stairways altered. Although Greiser called the villa a 'little house' (*Häuschen*), it had a bedroom for Greiser and Maria, rooms for Ingrid and Erhardt and, at the very least, a music room and a dining room. It was outfitted with the most modern conveniences. Of the bathroom, Greiser wrote: 'a magnificent installation with three showers and a new large bathtub.' The house sported three telephone sockets and two telephones, along with an underground cable for the connection.[150] In the garden, three trees were cut down so as to make way for a garage, and the driveway was widened.[151] Greiser ordered a car from Stuttgart and had it delivered to Maria.[152]

Greiser's lifestyle was the talk of Danzig and beyond. During the election campaign in spring 1935, the SPD labeled Nazi leaders 'Brown Bosses' and luridly described their lifestyles; as one SPD handbill proclaimed, 'New autos and gold braid! The people have forgotten neither.'[153] Some years later, Rauschning ran into an acquaintance in Zurich who berated the Nazis. 'Just look at your successor, Greiser,' the man said to him, '—the make-believe gentleman . . . He's got to have one of the old historic houses in Danzig, and look how he's furnished it! Just fancy, a music room! Two grand pianos! His wife—the new darling, I mean—must have the right atmosphere round her.'[154] Besides his salary of 1,500 gulden per month (approximately $6,000 in 2008 dollars), Greiser received an expense allowance of 1,000 gulden per month, and an annual expense account of 30,000 gulden.[155] Greiser's taste for the good life would sow ill will not only in Danzig, but also in the Warthegau.

Not wanting to further fan the fires of Danzig politics, Greiser waited until after the 7 April election to wed Maria. Two days later, on Tuesday, 9 April, the couple was married in a civil ceremony. According to newspaper accounts, Greiser married the 'well-known pianist Maria Koerfer' at the registry office in Berlin-Wilmersdorf. Heinrich Himmler and Albert Forster served as witnesses.[156] Himmler's presence suggests that Greiser already had some standing with the SS-leader. And even though Forster had just suffered a crushing electoral defeat, he nonetheless attended his deputy's wedding. In spring 1935, the two top Danzig Nazis were still on reasonably good terms. The wedding party enjoyed a celebratory brunch at the Horcher Wine Restaurant.[157]

After marrying Greiser, Maria played only occasional concerts. On 8 December 1935 she was a soloist in a charity performance given by the Warsaw Philharmonic Orchestra and sponsored by the Polish Music Association in Danzig. Almost all of the Danzig senators, as well as Lester, Papée, and other diplomats listened as Maria played Liszt's E-flat major concerto.[158] A Polish newspaper commented on how Maria 'displayed a lively temperament, as well as a high degree of technical ability that aroused amazement . . .'[159] Maria played in several other well-received performances in 1936.[160] But, despite her concerting success, she retreated into private life. She took on little charitable or other honorary Nazi work. On 1 February 1937, however, when the party reopened its ranks to newcomers, she joined the NSDAP.[161]

In his recreational pursuits, Greiser remained a man's man. He continued to relish activities traditionally associated with masculinity—from driving fast cars to hunting in the wild. Greiser knew, though, that Maria (and Hitler, Himmler, and Martin Bormann) disliked the sport of hunting.[162] In January 1935, he thus noted, 'It's strange, although I love to go hunting, since I've had the sense that you don't like it so much [when I do it], I don't like [it] so much.'[163] But perhaps like no other activity, hunting spoke to his manly impulses. In June 1935, Sean Lester recorded a hunting expedition with Greiser, Maria, and several Danzig officials in the Sobbowitz Forest, near the border with Poland. Greiser was the only one of the party to take a shot. As Lester described: 'Greiser had two shots, with each of which he killed a buck. He is an excellent shot, and is also one of the Jaegers [hunters] who finish the job, which means not only the coup de grâce, given by sticking one of his sharp knives into the brain but the subsequent removal of the entrails.' Lester was disgusted by the operation; he hoped, though, that this didn't 'show itself too much to the enthusiastic Greiser.' Meanwhile, a close aide of Greiser, Viktor Böttcher, had a reaction similar to Lester's and 'had great difficulty in retaining his luncheon,' a fact not lost on Maria. As Lester wrote, 'Frau Greiser, who had also been a close spectator, with bright remarks to make, observing the convolutions of Dr. Böttcher's long form laughed very scathingly and said: "And he is a man!" '[164] For all that Maria may have found hunting distasteful, she seemingly delighted in her husband's masculinity—and Greiser, no doubt, savored this recognition.

Greiser's passion for hunting was later politicized and given a tendentious spin. Some Poles drew a connection between his zeal for hunting and the murder of Poles and Jews that eventually took place under his aegis. In the short 1969 film *Granica Zbrodni Arthura Greisera* (The End of Arthur Greiser's Crimes), Polish film makers spliced scenes of one of Greiser's hunting jaunts in Danzig with images of murdered Poles and Jews in the Warthegau.[165]

As his private life in the early 1930s suggests, Greiser was in many ways utterly typical. However one might judge his shabby treatment of Ruth, it was in keeping with that of husbands the world over who have fallen in love with other women. Greiser wanted Ruth out of his life, the sooner, the better. To accomplish his goal, he engaged in all possible tactics, including legal coercion and sexual exploitation. Greiser's conduct toward his children was also typical. He wanted to extricate himself from his marriage with his children at his side. He indulged Ingrid and Erhardt's pleas that they live with him. Greiser was also tender, affectionate, and vulnerable with Maria; he was no hard-bitten control freak.

Like many other Nazi perpetrators, Greiser led a highly compartmentalized life. Already in the 1930s, he applied different sets of values to his personal and his political lives. While he expressed tenderness to Maria, his public persona was rough and threatening. While he insisted that Maria give him the opportunity to justify himself when she felt wronged, he did not offer his political opponents a similar opportunity. And while he told Maria that he could only be honest with her, he engaged in all manner of deceptive and duplicitous political practices. Other aspects of Greiser's personal and psychological life were also typical of Nazi leaders or perpetrators. Many had close relationships with their children. Many also had extra-marital affairs.[166] And many were attracted to high culture.[167]

By the mid-1930s, Greiser had come to live his life according to Nazi tenets. Seeped in Nazi ideology, he now saw himself as a man destined to restore Germany to greatness. Indeed, his nationalist passions penetrated even the most intimate sphere of his life, his love life. Greiser rationalized his need for Maria by claiming that she would give him strength for his Nazi struggle for Germany, a struggle that was to end with German national redemption. While utterly self-serving, this justification was, to him, genuine. National Socialism had given him security, status, and importance. In just five short years, Greiser had gone from bankrupt businessman to head of state. In his black SS-uniform, he commanded authority and respect. Most of all, though, National Socialism had given him purpose. When Greiser wrote to Maria that he lived his life through and for Germany, he actually meant it. And this, in turn, helps to explain why the Germanization of the Warthegau was later so important to him.

After her divorce, Ruth used to say that the man she married in 1919 was very different from the one who abandoned her in 1934.[168] This remark was surely a reflection of her bitterness that Greiser had left her for another woman. But it also rings true. In the fifteen years following World War I, Greiser evolved from a German patriot to a radical German nationalist; from a pleasant fellow to a vengeful politician. Why this change? Greiser family members have suggested that perhaps head injuries were the cause. Greiser not only sustained a head injury when his airplane was shot down in 1918, but he also suffered a very nasty middle-ear infection in the early 1930s.[169] Head injuries are known to alter personality characteristics.[170] But Greiser's transformation more probably occurred through his participation in the Nazi movement in Danzig. Few places spoke more to the sense of German loss after World War I than Danzig, a German city separated from the Reich and surrounded by allegedly hostile Poles. And few political movements were as treacherous as the NSDAP in the Free City. In his first years in the Nazi party, Greiser went through a political schooling; he graduated as a hyper-nationalist, an inveterate schemer, and a tough political opponent. As senate president, Greiser would be all these and more. Not least, this was due to the bitter rivalry that he would develop with Forster—a rivalry that shaped his entire tenure as chief executive of the Free City.

3

'The Nicest Time of my Life:' Senate President

In November 1934, it seemed that Arthur Greiser, as a fanatical German nationalist and now senate president, would stop at nothing to Nazify Danzig. But curiously, as Danzig's chief executive, Greiser came to be seen as the face of Nazi moderation in the city. His actions in the mid-1930s complicate the man. To be sure, to his opponents, Greiser was nothing but a two-faced Nazi. He gave assurances to League of Nations officials in Geneva, but then violated them on his return to Danzig. He claimed to uphold the Danzig constitution, but then arrested opposition politicians and banned their newspapers. He seemed to reach agreement with Polish negotiators, but then fomented new provocations. He promised to help the Danzig Jews, but then threw up endless obstacles in their path. To others, however, many of whom knew him personally, Greiser was a decent, responsible force. Danzig city officials and not a few foreign diplomats found him a charming host, able negotiator, and reassuring confidante. This 'moderate' Greiser has even found literary rendition. In *The Tin Drum*, Günter Grass's masterpiece about the Nazi era in Danzig, Oskar Matzerath, the main character, recalled that 'Greiser never made much of an impression on me. He was too moderate ...'[1]

Greiser's new found 'moderation' stemmed from the pressures he faced in his role as senate president. As chief executive in Danzig, Greiser walked a fine line between Nazi and statesman; his loyalties as a National Socialist conflicted with his duties as senate president. His job as senate president was to uphold the status quo; moreover, his political power rested on Danzig's continued status as a Free City. At the same time, his rivalry with Forster forced him to establish his own political profile.

Both of these factors led him to vacillate on policy and, sometimes, to adopt 'moderate' Nazi measures. Greiser's political strategy was not out of character. His personality traits—his ambition, his desire for approval, his liking of attention—were all in play here. He was eager to be a successful Nazi and, for a time, he thought that a 'moderate' stance might help him attain his goal. Still, Greiser's political actions as senate president are difficult to square with the up-and-coming Nazi in the early 1930s, and even more so with the ferocious Gauleiter of later years.

In the mid-1930s, Danzig was both a cause and a microcosm of the political tensions of interwar Europe. Greiser and Albert Forster, Danzig's powerful Gauleiter, were eager to destroy the city's democratic opposition. The League of Nations stood in their way. Yet although the League pledged to uphold the city's democratic constitution, this commitment was only as strong as its member countries' concern about Danzig affairs. The two most important countries in this regard, England and Poland, were reluctant to insist on democracy in Danzig. Great Britain viewed the Free City as an irritant to British–German relations, while Poland did not want to jeopardize relations with Nazi Germany after the January 1934 German–Polish Non-Aggression Pact. Both countries, however, wished to preserve appearances. League officials thus frequently summoned Greiser to Geneva to account for Nazi actions in Danzig. At the same time, while German officials wished to uphold Danzig as a German city and Nazi outpost, they were wary of sowing tensions with Poland and the western powers. Nazi officials in the Reich thus tried to prevent a speedy Nazification or a rushed reintegration of Danzig into Germany. This, in turn, put them at frequent odds with Forster and, initially, Greiser.

Greiser first appeared at a League of Nations council meeting in January 1935. Several months earlier, two petitions concerning Nazi violations of the Danzig constitution had reached the council. Catholic officials claimed that members of their youth organizations had been unfairly forbidden to wear uniforms, while the Catholic Center Party objected to Nazi electoral abuses in the by-elections of November 1934. At the meeting, Anthony Eden, the League rapporteur for Danzig issues, gave a scathing report about the Senate's treatment of Catholic organizations. Greiser refused to accept the report. But in a pattern that would be repeated at upcoming League council meetings, he made a good impression by reiterating his government's commitment to the constitution and its eagerness to avoid conflict with Poland.[2] Eden, who did not wish to antagonize Nazi Germany, agreed to postpone discussion of the petitions, pending good-faith negotiations between the Senate and the petitioners. Back in Danzig, however, Greiser made sure that talks with Catholic officials got nowhere.

As new senate president, Greiser continued his assault on democracy in the Free City by targeting the League of Nations and its high commissioner in Danzig, Sean Lester. Lester was intent on fulfilling the League's role; he encouraged opposition politicians to insist on their democratic rights and, if necessary, to submit to him petitions about constitutional violations.[3] Already in December 1934, he intimated to Otto von Radowitz, the German general consul in Danzig, that Greiser was voicing unconstitutional sentiments.[4] For his part, Greiser complained that Lester was too involved in the minutiae of Danzig domestic politics.[5]

After Volkstag elections for April were called in February 1935, Greiser heightened his attacks on Lester. In campaign appearances, Greiser claimed, among other things, that the high commissioner was protecting 'the morbid and unshaven opposition parties' and thus 'interfering in the internal affairs of the Free City.'[6] On 26 March the two men met and, as Greiser wrote to his bride-to-be, Maria: 'With Lester I've had great trouble again, today we really squabbled for over an hour.'[7] Lester told Greiser that he had the right as well as the duty to listen to complaints voiced by opposition groups and, as he deemed appropriate, to act upon them.[8] *The New York Times* reported that Greiser 'lost his temper and told Mr. Lester, "You just wait until the same thing happens to you that happened to Knox in the Saar." '[9] Geoffrey George Knox, the last League of Nations president of the Governing Commission of the Saar, had left his post after the January 1935 plebiscite that brought the Saar back into the Reich; the Nazis hoped that something similar would happen in Danzig after the April elections. Lester was so irritated that he sent a report to the League general secretary in which he described Greiser as 'untrustworthy and incapable.' Somehow Greiser got wind of it. On 1 April, Reich Foreign Minister Constantin von Neurath recorded, 'Because of this [report] Mr. Greiser wants to bring about a public quarrel. I urgently advised him not to do this, since he would come out with the short end of the stick. In the end, Greiser agreed and said that for his part he would refrain from a further sharpening of differences.'[10] Reich officials had to temper Greiser's stance against Lester.

After the 7 April elections, the Nazis took a step that very nearly cost them their grip on the city. Danzig was dangerously low on cash. At the end of April, Hitler, Reich Bank President Hjalmar Schacht, Hermann Göring, and Forster decided to devalue the gulden; Greiser was not party to the talks. On 2 May 1935, Danzigers woke up to learn that their currency, and their savings, had been devalued by 42.37 percent. The gulden now equaled the Polish złoty in value.[11] Real prices for goods rose dramatically while wages and salaries failed to keep pace.[12] Financial panic ensued. The government ordered bank holidays and limited withdrawals. Nazi support in the city plummeted. Shortly thereafter, the Danzig Bureau of Statistics noted that the NSDAP could expect to win only 18 to 35 percent of the vote in new elections.[13]

In this situation, the Poles were eager to introduce the złoty as legal tender in Danzig so as to secure additional leverage over the city.[14] Greiser was dead set against this. 'Danzig will not sign its own death warrant,' he declared in the *Völkischer Beobachter*, 'Danzig's Germandom stands and falls with the gulden.'[15] On 20 May, Greiser and Forster met with Göring, von Neurath, Schacht, and several other high-level Nazis. The Danzig Nazis claimed that if the Reich did not come to their aid, financial woes would jeopardize Nazi rule in the city. But Reich officials were little moved.[16] Greiser later claimed that the Danzigers left the meeting in a 'depression.'[17] They felt betrayed: although the Nazis trumpeted German *Volksgemeinschaft*, they seemed ready to sacrifice Danzig.

But Hitler soon came to the Danzig Nazis' rescue. On 8 June the Führer held a meeting with top Reich officials, along with Forster and Greiser. Greiser later wrote, 'I noted . . . that as responsible head of government I was only willing to take the path to Warsaw [e.g., asking Poland for help] on the express orders of the Führer.' At this meeting, it was decided that Germany would not abandon Danzig, that Danzig would not seek help from Poland, and that the city would do all it could to minimize its expenditures. The Danzigers agreed that Dr. Helferich, a Prussian administrator, would have full powers to direct the city's economy. Greiser was very pleased with this outcome.[18] His great fear that the city would fall under Polish influence, and thus become *de facto* part of Poland, seemed assuaged.

On 12 June, Greiser announced a program of fiscal austerity. He planned to dismiss at least 500 officials and 100 teachers and to curtail other expenditures. He also extended an invitation of 'voluntary migration' to Germany to those who were dependent on Reich pensions or other monies. As Greiser declared, 'If these laws of the greatest need intervene in the fate of individual citizens, that is immaterial to me, for the fate of Danzig and its population is more important to me than the fate of individuals . . . Need not only bends theory; it breaks iron.'[19] These were tough words for tough times. Greiser further claimed that doing politics in the current situation meant 'a renunciation of popularity.'[20] Indeed, that summer, *The New York Times* reported that 'two years of Nazi government in Danzig has brought the Free City to the verge of ruin . . . Its trade has been crippled by foreign exchange restrictions, and business is preparing to move to the rival Polish port of Gydnia. There is a scarcity of certain manufactured goods and foodstuffs. The party in power has lost its grip on the population and the government has lost its authority.'[21] Nazi policies had cut deeply into NSDAP support in Danzig.

The Free City's precarious economy led to an escalation of Danzig–Polish tensions. To improve the city's financial situation, Greiser's Senate introduced foreign exchange controls. This, however, angered the Poles, who believed that such currency restrictions violated Danzig–Polish accords. On 21 July, the Poles responded: they issued an ordinance to the Danzig Customs Office (a part of the Polish Customs Service run by Danzigers) to stop collecting duties on all goods destined for Poland. These monies were to be collected only in Gdynia. This brought the Danzig harbor to a virtual standstill; since customs duties could not be paid, ships would not dock there. A furious Greiser told the Danzig Customs Office not to follow the Polish decree—a clear-cut violation of Poland's control over Danzig customs collection. A trade war ensued.

On 26 July, Greiser informed Richard Meyer, a high-ranking Foreign Ministry official, that the Polish representative in the City, Kazimierz Papée, wanted to hold talks. Greiser did not want to negotiate. Meyer, however, told him that it was necessary to secure Danzig's economy and for that, negotiations with Poland were essential. At this point, Meyer recorded, 'Mr. Greiser said that he could not simply obey this view; he would treat the matter in a dilatory manner in his conversation with Papée today . . .'[22] Greiser followed the letter of the Foreign Ministry's instructions, but not their spirit. Moreover, a few days later, at a meeting in the Foreign Ministry, he suggested that Danzig's cessation of collecting customs duties would pave the way for the Free City's economic reintegration in the Reich—a first step in the city's eventual reunification with Germany. But the chair of the meeting, State Secretary Bernhard von Bülow, insisted that all discussion of Danzig's political or economic reintegration into the Third Reich be avoided.[23] Göring now intervened. He called Greiser and told him to negotiate with the Poles. Soon thereafter, Göring summoned both Forster and Greiser to Berlin, and told them that Hitler had reached agreement with the Poles. On 9 August, a joint Polish–Danzig communique was issued; both the Polish customs decree and the Senate's countermeasures were lifted.[24] Despite this agreement, Greiser continued to oppose any concessions to Poland. As he reportedly told Lester on 17 August 1935, 'He [Greiser] has the task to maintain Germandom here. Even if the city were to become poor, it was preferable to him to maintain a German Danzig . . . than to allow Germandom to be destroyed and thereby enable an economically satisfactory situation for one or two years.'[25] In contrast to Reich officials, Greiser privileged keeping Danzig as a German redoubt even at the cost of the city's economic viability.

In May 1935, SPD and Center officials filed a motion with the Danzig Supreme Court questioning the legitimacy of the 7 April elections. Arguing that Nazi terror had compromised the election's outcome, the opposition hoped that the Supreme Court would annul the election and order a new one. The Nazis, by contrast, desperately wanted to avoid new elections. As they well knew, they would flounder at the polls. Their defeat, in turn, would be seen as a major blow for Nazism; not least, it would show the world that the Nazi juggernaut could be halted. But although the opposition tried to interest foreign authorities in its plight, it received little support from those who should have protected democracy in the Free City. Lester, too, brought the matter to the attention of English and Polish officials, but they were reluctant to jeopardize relations with the Third Reich over what they saw as domestic squabbling. Faced with indifference and with no force at his disposal, Lester could do little to support the opposition.

Meanwhile, Greiser kept up his attack on Lester, the League, and the political opposition. As he declared to the party faithful, 'Unlike my predecessors who glided into Geneva on velvet slippers, I prefer to appear solidly in my SS-boots.'[26] In late May 1935, the League Council met to discuss the two petitions from the Danzig Catholics, as well as one other from Jewish groups. It decided to send the petitions out to a commission of legal experts for adjudication. This was a limited victory for Greiser; once again, the League postponed discussion of the petitions' content.[27] At the same meeting, Greiser reassured participants that the Danzig Senate would abide by the Free City's constitution. He even carried out the motions of a personal rapprochement with Lester; the two men shook hands in a demonstration of friendship.[28]

Just a few weeks later, Greiser was back to his openly anti-constitutional actions. On 4 July, he publicly declared that 'no one will push us out of our political position of power in Danzig. No matter the parliamentary maneuvers and tricks that may be used to feign something for the population . . . National Socialism will not disappear in Danzig . . . So long as I am at the head of the government . . . I will take the rap so that Danzig will not become a second Austria.' Greiser also proclaimed: 'We National Socialists have not struggled in Danzig for years and did not come to power so as to be entangled in a jungle of constitutional paragraphs. In this respect, we have become clever as "parliamentarians" and have mastered the [constitution's] formal machinery (*Buchstabenmaschinerie*).'[29] Greiser's message was all too clear: regardless of the population's wishes, the Nazis would never give up power in Danzig—nor would they be strait-jacketed by the city's constitution.

In August 1935, Greiser caused a diplomatic brouhaha by publicly insulting Lester. When a German battleship, the *Admiral Scheer*, came to Danzig, Lester held a reception in honor of the ship's officers. Among others, he invited Hermann Rauschning, Greiser's predecessor and now vocal Nazi opponent. When Rauschning arrived, Greiser, along with a few senators and other National Socialists, stormed out of the party. The next day, the Nazi press claimed that the ship's captain and officers had also been insulted by Rauschning's presence. As the Polish press noted, though, the captain and officers stayed at the party.[30] Lester was furious with both Greiser's conduct and the Nazi attempt to manipulate military men in Danzig domestic politics. He met with Greiser who, he noted in his diary, was 'mild and apologetic.' Greiser claimed that party discipline demanded that he not have any communication with a former Nazi party member. Lester responded that Greiser could not compromise his Senate presidential duties by invoking party discipline.[31]

On 14 November 1935, the Danzig Court rendered its judgment on the 7 April elections. It found that the NSDAP had engaged in electoral abuses; its ruling documented numerous cases of voter intimidation. But it rejected arguments for a new election. Instead, it determined that the NSDAP should lose three percent of its city and ten percent of its rural vote; it was to give up one Volkstag seat to the SPD. Disappointed, the opposition filed a petition with the League seeking new elections. Greiser now declared: 'I know that one is trying to rope in the League of Nations against the Supreme Court's judgment and with that against the Danzig population . . . [Opposition] party leaders who do such a thing place themselves beyond the German *Volksgemeinschaft*.' He thus declared the opposition un-German. He also accused Lester of working with the opposition: 'I have been told by a very reliable source that the representative of the League of Nations in Danzig has made the wishes of the un-German opposition his own . . .'[32] Lester was dismayed by Greiser's speech, but he viewed Forster as the man behind the attack. He spent much of December 1935 traveling to Warsaw, Berlin, and Geneva trying to drum up support for a League investigation into the Danzig situation.[33] On 11 December, Lester met with von Neurath; he hoped to persuade the German Foreign Minister that Forster should be removed.[34]

In early January 1936, in anticipation of the League council meeting that would discuss Lester's report for the year 1935 and the opposition's petition for new elections, Greiser set out to charm the High Commissioner. He invited Lester to participate in an official state hunt. Shortly thereafter, Lester held a fancy dinner at which the brandy flowed freely. The Irishman even recorded that Greiser was 'really not a bad chap apart from his politics here.' At a subsequent dinner at the Danzig Town Hall, Greiser warmly welcomed Lester.[35] Both men soon left for Geneva, but Greiser went via Berlin to receive instructions from Hitler, Göring, and von Neurath. Hitler now told Greiser and Forster to force a confrontation about Lester's report; the Führer also hoped to pressure the British not to accept it. By contrast, Göring told Greiser to pursue a general course of good relations with the Poles, particularly with Polish Foreign Minister Jósef Beck, and to ignore pressures coming from Danzig 'party authorities' (read Forster) to raise tensions with the Poles. In Geneva, Göring wanted Greiser to be 'sharp and as unyielding as possible' about Lester's report, but at the same time to be 'correct, polite, and forthcoming' with the high commissioner.[36]

On the first day of the League council meeting, 22 January (Greiser's thirty-ninth birthday), Eden berated the Danzig government for its constitutional violations. Two days later, however, when discussion resumed, Eden declared that Greiser had promised to better the city's record on constitutional issues and that he was now satisfied with how matters stood in Danzig.[37] Why this abrupt turn-around? On 24 January, on Hôtel Beau-Séjour stationary, Greiser described to Maria what had happened. 'Now,' he wrote, 'everything is finally over. Eden spoke with Beck, the Frenchman, the Spaniard, the Portuguese, and [Soviet representative Maxim] Litvinov, and in the end, me. The report was accepted after a nighttime meeting with Eden that was very serious, [Viktor] Böttcher negotiated with [R. C. Skrine] Stevenson [a British advisor] for three hours, this morning I brought Berlin into the matter which made difficulties for me, negotiated with the Poles, and around mid-day, together with Eden and Beck, found a final clause.' Greiser summarized the results: 'Together with my proven luck, your good wishes helped, we gained far more than I ever expected, the struggle was really very hard and I must honestly say that we can be satisfied. Of course, we also had to give something up, but we pushed through our main points: no new elections, no investigating commission, and no powers for Lester.'[38] As Greiser suggested, Beck had brokered the compromise. The Polish foreign minister was less concerned about League authority in Danzig than about German–Polish relations. He believed in a 'direct talks' policy with Germany; involving third parties in German–Polish negotiations could only vitiate that policy. In this, Beck failed to recognize the importance to Poland of a League of Nations presence in Danzig; he might have used the League's authority to question the Danzig Senate and to confront Berlin about its nefarious actions.[39]

Following Beck's compromise, the council decided to postpone discussion pending a more detailed examination of the petition. No deadline was stipulated, however, and no such examination ever took place. In return, Greiser promised that the Senate would institute new regulations guaranteeing more freedom of the press and that two state employees who had lost their jobs for political reasons would be given compensation. On his return to Danzig, Greiser insisted that the concessions he had made were insignificant. And he was right. New press regulations did little to guarantee the opposition a public voice.[40] The League's unwillingness to insist on new elections squandered an opportunity to halt the further Nazification of the city. Instead, the opposition was handed a great defeat—by the very institution that was to guarantee the Free City's democratic constitution.

Relations between Danzig's two top Nazis—Forster and Greiser—had always been rocky. In the course of 1935, however, they soured beyond repair: both men wanted absolute power in Danzig. Before Greiser was senate president, Forster seems not to have felt so threatened by his deputy. But once Greiser became the city's chief executive, Forster faced a rival who had an independent power base. Forster was also jealous of Greiser's prerogatives as senate president; Greiser, for example, was accorded diplomatic and other recognition that Forster craved. Although the two men had earlier hewed to the same political line, this now began to change. In part, this was a reflection of Greiser's new job: as senate president, he was forced to play a more statesman-like role. But he also hoped to profile himself against Forster, not least by adopting positions that would secure the support of those who could aid him in his rivalry. All this points to a prominent feature of Greiser's career: political opportunism sometimes trumped political conviction. This feature made it possible for Greiser to be a 'moderate' Nazi in Danzig, yet a 'radical' Nazi in the Warthegau.

As both Gauleiter and a Hitler favorite, Forster had considerable advantages in this rivalry. Time and again, Hitler saved Forster—whether by active intervention or a passive letting of things blow over. Greiser never had the same sort of access to the Führer. As he stated at his 1946 trial, 'During my Danzig time, I could hardly ever speak alone with Hitler; in all these matters, he always referred me to Göring.'[41] Forster also had some institutional advantages. As Gauleiter, he was able to pursue personnel policies that consolidated his own rule while curbing Greiser's potential power. When Greiser became senate president, for example, Forster made Wilhelm von Wnuck head of the Senate Personnel Department; Wnuck was a man of his—and not Greiser's—choosing. Forster was also able to protect 'his' men in the Senate bureaucracy.[42] Finally, he exploited the situation that Greiser, as senate president, had to defend unpopular Nazi policies (such as cost-cutting measures or compromises in Geneva).[43]

But Greiser was not without advantages. Forster's zealous impatience—his eagerness to annex Danzig to the Reich, establish one-party rule, and 'free' the city of Jews—threatened Reich interests. Göring and Foreign Ministry officials thus supported Greiser as a useful counterweight to the Gauleiter. Greiser also enjoyed the support of SS circles in Danzig and Berlin. The SS, for example, resented Forster's attempts to separate the Danzig SS from its divisional headquarters in Königsberg.[44] Forster had notoriously poor relations with Heinrich Himmler; as the Gauleiter once famously quipped of the SS-leader's un-Aryan physique: 'If I looked like Himmler, I would not speak of race.'[45] Forster's enemy proved Greiser's friend; during his Danzig years, Greiser developed a closer relationship with the SS-leader.

Greiser also used his senate presidency to build a base of support. After von Wnuck's April 1935 resignation (on account of financial improprieties linked with devaluation), Greiser took over the Senate Personnel Department.[46] He also controlled the Senate Department of Foreign Affairs, headed by Viktor Böttcher, a longtime loyal lieutenant.[47] Finally, Greiser enjoyed popularity in Danzig. Even though he had not been born in the city, Danzigers viewed him as one of their own. Greiser took pains to underscore his roots in the city. Soon after the gulden devaluation, for instance, he noted his commonalities with 'those who like me on my father's side have been traditionally rooted in this home ground (*Heimatboden*) of Danzig for centuries.'[48] By contrast, Danzigers saw Forster as a foreign upstart; the Gauleiter's Franconian dialect never sat well with the city's population.[49]

In late October 1935, the Forster–Greiser rivalry burst out into public. A Swiss newspaper, the *Basler Nachrichten*, reported that Forster had called on Greiser to resign and planned to replace him with Wilhelm Huth, a Danzig Nazi leader loyal to the Gauleiter. According to the article, Forster felt himself responsible only to Hitler and was thus eager to introduce sharp measures against the opposition. On the other hand, Greiser, the newspaper alleged, felt some obligation to both the Danzig constitution and the League of Nations.[50] In November, Greiser denied rumors that he was about to resign. As he recorded, 'Minister Papée asked me whether the rumors were true that I would soon resign and go to the Reich, because the Polish government feared that there might be a change of course. I calmed him and emphasized that there was no truth to these rumors.'[51]

Events in the first half of 1936 also reflected Greiser's rivalry with Forster. In the January League Council meeting, at which Beck had worked a compromise, Greiser had been relatively conciliatory to the Poles and Lester. Moreover, once back in Danzig, Greiser had ceased his attacks on Lester. On 4 February, the Greisers even breakfasted with the Lesters at the high commissioner's home.[52] Lester, it seems, was now banking on Greiser to pursue a more moderate course against his rival. The high commissioner thus cooled his relations with the Danzig political opposition—already so weakened by League dithering on its petition. But Greiser's new-found moderation only widened his rift with Forster, since the Gauleiter was spoiling for a confrontation with the League. At a secret

NSDAP meeting in February, Forster attacked Lester and the League, forcing Greiser to defend his cooperative stance.[53]

Forster also worked to escalate political tensions within the city. On 12 June, Danzig SA members attacked participants at a local meeting of the German National People's Party (*Deutschnationale Volkspartei* or DNVP). A general melee ensued, in which a stormtrooper, Günther Deskowsky, died; Deskowsky did not die of injuries sustained in the commotion, but rather of causes linked to his advanced syphilis. Forster nonetheless gave him a 'hero's funeral.'[54] Lester met with the senate president about the matter; his biographer noted, 'as usual, Greiser told Lester in confidence afterwards that he was having difficulties with Forster.'[55] While Greiser tried to calm the political situation, Forster used Deskowsky's death to heighten the atmosphere of political terror in Danzig. Reich Foreign Ministry officials now became concerned. On 16 June, von Radowitz noted that 'the events of the last days have extremely endangered the political quiet and apparent improvement of the situation achieved through the deliberate conduct of the senate president.' Von Radowitz knew that Forster would see Hitler on 19 June. He thus wanted Greiser to meet with Göring beforehand.[56] Von Radowitz hoped that Göring, in turn, would exert influence on Hitler to curb Forster. On 18 June 1936, Greiser and von Radowitz visited Göring in Pomerania. The men supposedly discussed a palace revolution against Forster, but what exactly transpired at that or any further meeting with Hitler is not documented.[57] As subsequent events revealed, the Führer approved Forster's belligerent actions in Danzig.

Lester's initial term as high commissioner in Danzig was to end in early 1937. In May 1936, however, he agreed to a further one-year stay in the Free City. Greiser, independent of Forster and Reich officials, apparently caved in to League pressure to extend the high commissioner's term; perhaps he felt that Lester could provide a useful buffer to Forster's political ambitions.[58] Forster, however, found this extension unacceptable and, in alliance with Reich authorities, engineered a crisis to make Lester's continued presence in the city untenable.[59] On 25 June, a German warship, the *Leipzig*, sailed into the Danzig harbor. On such occasions, it was customary for the ship's commander to pay a courtesy call to the high commissioner. The commander, however, informed Greiser that he had received orders from 'on high' not to do so. Greiser sent a subordinate to inform Lester, who found the latter in formal garb awaiting his expected guests. The incident was intended as a great snub to both Lester and the League, and Lester, not surprisingly, was furious.[60] The situation also affected the Poles; arrangements for the warship's visit had been coordinated with them, and so the abrupt change in plans violated the Polish–Danzig Treaty of 1920, according to which Poland oversaw Danzig's foreign relations.[61] The '*Leipzig* incident,' as it was soon known, was a German assault on the Danzig status quo. Lester quickly brought both Nazi political violence and the *Leipzig* affair to the League's attention. Already on 4 July, the League was to deliberate these matters.

En route to Geneva, Greiser stopped off in Berlin to receive instructions. Hitler told him that he wanted 'a bombshell' of a speech.[62] Greiser now jettisoned his more conciliatory approach and exceeded his Führer's expectations. When he first entered the League Disarmament Building, he noisily declared 'It is high time a German bombing squadron came here.'[63] In his official speech, Greiser—'full of schnapps'—demanded nothing less than a change in Danzig's status.[64] *The New York Times* reported that his speech was 'delivered in German with rare insolence of manner. The whole performance surpassed in impudence anything ever known here before.' Greiser engaged in 'a bitter personal attack' on Lester and demanded that the Danzig statute be revised so that he would no longer have to appear in Geneva. 'With beetled brows and belligerent chin,' Greiser further declared 'I consider that my speech today is the first stage on the road of revision that we ask regarding relations between Danzig and the League of Nations . . . and if I have done it in public and before world opinion, I emphasize that it is not only in the name of the people of Danzig, but in the name of all the German people that I formulate this proposal. The German people expect from the League of Nations in the coming months resolutions that will permit me, as president of the Senate of the Free City of Danzig, to appear no more at Geneva.' But that was not all. Greiser ended his speech by giving the Nazi salute to Eden, Beck, and Joseph Avenol, secretary general of the League. The journalists found this a ridiculous provocation. 'A laugh or two' was heard in the press gallery. Moments later, 'Greiser then turned his back on the Council and as he left the room he thumbed his nose with a grimace of intense hatred, toward the press and the public. This plunged the hall into uproar and further incidents were narrowly avoided there and in the corridors.'[65]

Due to his nose-thumbing, Greiser attracted considerable attention. On the day after the speech, Joseph Goebbels approvingly noted: 'Greiser's speech was a bombshell. One must act. Then they knuckle under.'[66] But Forster, perhaps jealous of the attention Greiser received, cast aspersion on the senate president's conduct, if not his speech. Just then, he happened to be with Hitler in Weimar. As Forster later recalled, 'he had drawn the Führer's attention to how unbelievable the conduct of G[reiser] was in Geneva.'[67] Two days after Greiser's speech, Goebbels recorded: 'Greiser's speech in Geneva had a boorish effect. Demanded a new statute for Danzig. Massive attack against Lester. Sensation. Unfortunately afterwards he cocked a snook and stuck out his tongue. With that he threw away all of his success. Führer is very sad about this.'[68]

Greiser soon came to rue his gesture. As he wrote shortly thereafter to Himmler, '[Since I was] provoked to the extreme, from a National-Socialist perspective it can be understood, but from a diplomatic perspective it was a stupidity (*Dummheit*) that I recognize as such and for which I now have to swallow the accompanying displeasure.' Actually, though, Greiser was far more concerned about another matter: that Forster was taking the credit for his speech. In Weimar, Hitler had apparently talked at length about 'how good and how fantastic' the speech was. Forster had thus intimated to the Führer that he and Greiser had written the speech together. In letters to Göring, Himmler, and several others, Greiser now sought to set the record straight. He saw it as a matter of his honor: 'I can swallow anything if it's for the party or Danzig. But I cannot allow anyone to take away my honor and my spiritual property.' Göring, at least, was annoyed that Greiser wished to make a fuss about a seemingly trivial matter. As he wrote to the senate president, 'Don't let a nasty quarrel arise from this, rather you and Forster should together enjoy your common successes!'[69] In what was already and would continue to be a pattern, Greiser had to deny differences between himself and the Danzig Gauleiter so as to preserve an image of party unity. Forced to swallow his pride, though, he became ever more bitter and resentful of Forster.

Meanwhile, the international press was downright scathing of Greiser and his conduct. There was some discussion as to Greiser's precise gesture. While *The New York Times* claimed that Greiser had just thumbed his nose, other reports declared that he 'stuck out his tongue' or possibly 'waggled his fingers.'[70] The *Gazeta Polska* reported that as Greiser passed the press gallery, 'he raised his left hand to his nose, stuck out his tongue in the direction of the journalists and made an unequivocal gesture with fingers on the hand on his nose.'[71] Whatever the action that came to be known as 'cocking a snook' was, foreign newspapers were united in their disgust. In Britain, the *News Chronicle* described Greiser as an 'ill-mannered clown.'[72] *The Times* noted Greiser's 'touch of stupid schoolboy vulgarity.'[73] The *Morningpost* wrote that 'Herr Greiser delivered a carefully prepared soap-box tirade, punctuated with well rehearsed gesticulations of ecstasy and rounded off with a vulgar impromptu grimace as he swaggered out of the chamber.'[74] *The New York Times* viewed Greiser's gesture as one more expression of the primitive boorishness that characterized the Nazi movement.[75] In anticipation of the Nazi Olympics later that summer, the paper ran an editorial cartoon which showed a series of positive images emanating from Nazi Germany followed by one of Greiser, pictured as a buffoon, falling backwards with his thumb on his nose. This image was accompanied by the words of a pro-Nazi to an audience of one, 'Keep Calm Sir. This is only a short news reel.'[76] As the cartoon suggested, those eager to sell Nazism abroad were frustrated by Greiser's aggressive performance.

Despite the negative evaluation in the press, Greiser's speech achieved the desired ends. The July 1936 League meeting was a milestone in the Nazi suppression of the Danzig opposition.[77] In October, Lester took up the post of deputy secretary general to the League. While he remained high commissioner until his successor was named in January 1937, Lester was seldom in the Free City. Since the League refused to counter Greiser's challenge to its authority, the Nazis felt that they could act with impunity toward the opposition. Right after Greiser's return from Geneva, the Senate again suspended the *Danziger Volksstimme*, for three months (for publishing derogatory accounts of Greiser's conduct in Geneva).[78] On 16 July, the Danzig Senate passed a series of ordinances 'for the maintenance of public security and order.' These measures allowed for the dissolution of all associations, including political parties, in the event that an association 'propagates reports likely to endanger the state's interests.' Complaints addressed to the League of Nations were deemed 'treason.'[79] On 14 October 1936, the Nazi government banned the SPD. Even more ominously, Danzig policemen kidnapped Hans Wichmann, a popular SPD leader and Volkstag deputy in May 1937. Wichmann was soon murdered; several years later, Greiser admitted as much to Burkhardt.[80] The Wichmann case brought renewed international attention to political abuses in Danzig. But neither Great Britain, Poland nor any other state was willing to defend Danzig's political opposition.[81] In May 1937, the DNVP also dissolved itself. Five months later, the Nazis banned the Center party. And in November 1937, the Nazi government prohibited new political parties.[82] It took the Nazis four years to end all political opposition in the Free City. In the Reich, Hitler had accomplished this in just six months. The difference had been the League of Nations. Had the League been more forceful in upholding democracy in Danzig, a political opposition—and an unpleasant situation for the Nazis—could have endured in the mid-1930s. Instead, the League yielded, and the Nazis were able to suppress all political opposition.

In the mid-1930s, Greiser see-sawed between accommodation and confrontation with the Poles. This was largely a function of his official position; the senate president was often forced to temper his public anti-Polish stance. In January 1935, Greiser visited Poland twice, and both he and the Poles were at pains to show their best faces. During the first visit, Greiser met with Marshal Piłsudski for a half-hour audience in which they discussed problems surrounding Danzig and Gdynia. At meeting's end, Greiser wrote, 'the marshal, impulsively and in my view genuinely, emphasized that in future we should visit again not as enemies but as friends.'[83] A British diplomat recorded that Greiser had declared that 'his meeting with Marshal Piłsudski had been one of the greatest moments of his life, comparable only with his first meetings with Wilhelm II and Herr Hitler.' Furthermore, this report noted, Greiser had opined that 'it was a comforting thought that the frank speech of soldiers was more efficacious than the old type of diplomatic conference.'[84] Greiser later viewed it as a point of pride that he had been—so he claimed—the last foreign visitor received by the Marshal (in fact, though, Eden visited Piłsudski in early April).[85] Greiser also visited Ignacy Mościcki, the president of the Republic, at a hunting lodge in Spała. Telling Greiser that he was speaking to him as 'hunter to hunter,' Mościcki intimated his admiration of Hitler.[86] At the conclusion of the trip, *The New York Times* reported that 'Captain [*sic*] Greiser tried here to dissipate Polish fears and was even more conciliatory than his predecessor Dr. Rauschning...'[87] Later that January, Greiser took part in an official Polish state hunt in the Białowieża Forest.[88] There, Mościcki awarded him the Polish 'Great Golden Hunting Medallion.'[89]

But Greiser and the Poles did not always get along so well. In summer 1935, of course, they had a running battle over trade and customs matters. In early September, Polish officials expressed irritation with Greiser's seeming two-faced conduct. Von Radowitz forwarded to the Foreign Ministry a report written by an anonymous confidante with close ties to Polish officials. The author noted that Greiser, as senate president, had assured Polish officials that Danzig would abide by all international treaties. But at a Hitler-Youth sports festival, Greiser, as deputy Gauleiter, had declared that current treaties would soon be broken and that there would be a change in Danzig's international status (that is, Danzig would become part of the Reich). The source then noted: 'The question about who now speaks the truth, the deputy Gauleiter or the senate president, can be answered in the sense that Gauleiter Greiser had expressed his true convictions; in his capacity [as deputy Gauleiter], he is free from the restraints that burden him as senate president.' The author added, 'If this is the case, then from the Polish perspective the Danziger senate president is a political con-man (*Hochstapler*) . . . Negotiating with an adversary of such moral quality is for the Polish negotiating party unacceptable.'[90] But the Poles had little choice in choosing their German counterpart; after all, Greiser *was* senate president.

Greiser's see-sawing continued in early 1936. In February, he took part in another official Polish hunt in the Białowieża Forest.[91] He and Papée took the same train to the event.[92] At the time of the *Leipzig* incident, Greiser also sent soothing signals to the Poles. Coincidentally, the Polish Trade Minister, Antoni Roman, was just then on an official visit to Danzig. Greiser gave a reception in his honor and even gave a toast in Polish to Poland's president. This was widely seen as an indication that the Lester snub was not intended to threaten Polish interests.[93]

Despite his official stance, Greiser was vigilant about any Polish encroachments on what he saw as Danzig's rights. In October 1936, for example, he wrote to Forster that he believed that the Poles would use upcoming negotiations to extend their influence in the Danzig Customs Office (over which the Poles had ultimate control): 'earlier, in my view, unfortunately, the Poles were allowed too strong a measure of influence in the Danzig Customs Office.' This had afforded the Poles better opportunities to guard the city's borders. Greiser now warned, 'if we remain inactive . . . the time will soon come when the Poles will have the political prerequisites to strengthen their influence not only on the leadership, but also on the administration of the entire Customs Office. In my view, this absolutely cannot be allowed to happen . . .' Greiser then offered suggestions on how to counter any additional Polish influence.[94]

Greiser was also eager to undermine pro-Polish sympathies among Catholic church officials in Danzig. In the mid-1930s, the city's bishop, Count Eduard O'Rourke, offered staunch resistance to Nazi attempts to curtail religious instruction in the schools and to shut down Catholic youth organizations. In addition, O'Rourke tried to promote two Polish priests in Danzig, one of whom, Father Rogaczewski, was seen as at the center of the Polish spiritual community. When Greiser protested to the Vatican, O'Rourke indefinitely suspended the promotions. The bishop, however, made it known that he was considering resignation. Greiser now hoped to prevent a new bishop who might be sympathetic to Polish interests. In February 1938, the Vatican named F. Sawicki, a professor of theology in West Prussia, as the new bishop. Although an ethnic German, Sawicki was a Polish citizen with Polish sympathies. The Vatican sent his nomination certificate through the Apostolic Nuncio in Warsaw. The Senate protested both Sawicki's nomination and the alleged dependence of the Danzig diocese on Warsaw. Faced with such opposition, Sawicki declined the post.[95]

Greiser was now all the more concerned about O'Rourke's successor. In March 1938, he arranged a vacation in Italy so that he could meet with Cardinal Eugene Pacelli, state secretary in the Vatican (and future Pope Pius XII) about the matter. Pacelli, however, was in no hurry to see him. Greiser spent a few days in Rome in mid-March, but was unable to meet the cardinal. He and Maria then spent a week in Sicily. On his return trip, Pacelli received him on 30 March.[96] The meeting was friendly but inconclusive. In mid June, O'Rourke tendered his resignation. In his place, the Pope appointed Karl Maria Splett, the former administrator of the cathedral in Danzig-Oliva. Greiser was soon pleased with Splett; the bishop warded off Polish attempts at greater influence in the Danzig bishopric.[97]

Greiser's antipathy toward Poles was reflected in seemingly trivial matters, too. Late in his tenure as senate president, he wrote to the director general of the Danzig State Theater, Merz, that 'Danzig should and must become a bulwark of German culture in the East.' The issue at hand? Greiser had long been concerned about Polish-sounding names among German civil servants, and he had now discovered that the State Theater employed two bandleaders with Polish-sounding names. As Greiser wrote to Merz, 'in my view it is incompatible with the purpose of our whole cultural policy . . . when two bandleaders with Polish-sounding names are named to leading positions in the Danzig State Theater.'[98] Greiser demanded that the men change their names. Just two days later, Merz assured Greiser that the situation was being rectified.[99] To Greiser, any step—no matter how small—that could bolster the city's German identity was worthwhile.

Greiser also blew warm and cold toward the Free City's Jews. In 1933, there were roughly 10,000 Jews in Danzig; they made up some four percent of the city's population. Greiser's vacillating words and actions toward Jews reflected both his own ambivalence about anti-Semitism, and the tensions he felt between pursuing his Nazi ambitions and owning up to economic realities in Danzig. Greiser was reluctant to jeopardize Danzig's precarious economy by antagonizing Jewish businessmen. Furthermore, Danzig was dependent on Jewish tourist income; since many Polish Jews felt unwelcome in their own country's resorts, they came to enjoy the Zoppot hotels and beaches.[100]

The Nazi government first moved against the city's Jews through administrative methods, rather than laws (as in the Reich). In Danzig, for example, Jews were no longer elected to the boards of professional associations, some Jewish municipal employees were dismissed, and Jewish contractors were no longer given city jobs. Concerned by this administrative assault, two representatives from the Jewish community met with Greiser (then still vice senate president) on 21 August 1933. Greiser told his visitors that the rights of Jews would be respected; he also stated that neither a law precluding non-Aryans from being civil servants nor a boycott movement against Jewish business interests was in the offing.[101] But as one Jewish commentator later noted, 'For those who knew him, Greiser's declaration was too nice to be taken as truth.'[102]

Greiser was sometimes seemingly helpful to Jews. In 1933, for example, he intervened on behalf of at least one Jewish company, the Emil A. Baus Iron and Machine Company. For unknown reasons, Greiser insisted that the company continue to receive state contracts. In fact, though, the company received only very small jobs; either Greiser's intervention was half-hearted or Forster simply overruled him.[103] At the same time, Greiser also made very aggressive statements about Jews. On 1 June 1934, for example, he thundered anti-Semitic remarks at a rally. 'In the Weimar Republic,' Greiser declared, 'the stratum of the top ten thousand were scoundrels who had immigrated from Palestine. Through fraud and swindling they had money and more money. Thanks to their money bags they determined the cultural and spiritual direction of Germany. The German feeling was gagged.'[104]

In fall 1934, the Danzig Jews complained about official mistreatment to senate president Rauschning. On 16 October Greiser met with a Jewish delegation that included Adolf Mazur, with whom he had earlier had business dealings. During the meeting, he had a pistol lying on his desk. Greiser told the Jewish representatives that he was always ready to hear complaints, provided these had merit. The Jews raised a number of issues: they wanted a ban against the singing of anti-Semitic songs; they objected to Forster's call for a boycott against their businesses; and they wanted a law, promised by Rauschning, that would protect them from collective insults. In response, Greiser declared that Danzig was ruled by National Socialists, and that the Nazis would not change their attitude toward Jews. The Jewish delegation left disappointed and soon reported that the meeting has been 'without result.' Shortly thereafter, Greiser invited the delegation back. At this meeting, on 8 November, he apologized for the pistol. He then reported that Forster had agreed to a ban on the singing of anti-Semitic songs. But when the Jews demanded the law against collective insults, Greiser claimed not to know anything about it. He nonetheless reiterated that he would uphold the Danzig constitution; the government, he claimed, viewed Jews as having the same rights as the non-Jewish population. Greiser offered the Jews soothing words, but very little in the form of concrete promises.

In early 1935, the Jewish community sent in two new petitions, one complaining about official toleration of anti-Semitic measures, the other protesting boycotts against their businesses and the mounting of anti-Jewish posters. Greiser responded respectfully to the first. But to the second, brought on March 14, Greiser gave a brusque answer. He claimed that it had stated that the 'upholding of order in Danzig was no longer being accomplished.' This, Greiser insisted, 'includes . . . a serious disparagement of the government. The board of the synagogue community can no longer count on a response to petitions that lack an appropriate tone in communicating with the highest state authorities.' Greiser refused to answer any further petitions from the Jewish community.[105] Moreover, in a campaign rally on 24 March 1935, he called the League of Nations a 'Jewish organization.'[106] On 4 June, he also gave a speech, broadcast on radio, that blamed the Jews for the devaluation of the gulden. The Jews, he alleged, had methodically exchanged gulden for gold or hard currencies so as to destroy the Danzig currency.[107]

Yet that same summer, Greiser, in opposition to Forster's policies, objected to some anti-Jewish measures. In July, von Radowitz reported, a troop of men, some uniformed, harassed Jewish visitors at various Danzig swimming areas, and mounted posters stating 'The Jews are our misfortune.' Von Radowitz added 'that despite objections from the senate president and the Propaganda Department,' the Gau leadership did not intervene to stop the anti-Semitic provocations.[108] Forster tolerated and probably instigated the harassment of Jewish bathers. But Greiser objected; he was concerned about the impact of anti-Semitic provocations on Danzig's economy. Party and government officials now pursued somewhat different policies. As Paul Batzer, the senator for propaganda and a close confidante of Greiser, wrote to a group representing the hospitality industry in October 1935, 'after careful discussion, the government has decided that it must pursue a different line than the party can follow... As before, my view is that for economic reasons any pestering of a guest, even if he is a non-Aryan, must absolutely be avoided in Danzig restaurants.'[109] For the next two years, Greiser's views prevailed in Danzig; the Nazis introduced very little in the way of official anti-Semitic policies. The major exception was a senate decree of 16 July 1936 forbidding the kosher slaughtering of animals.

The upshot of the 4 July 1936 League meeting—the undermining of both the opposition and the League's presence in Danzig—meant that Greiser and Forster had fewer common enemies. This heightened their conflict. Ironically, by destroying democracy in the city, Greiser also jeopardized his own position. With Nazi rule unchecked, the office of senate president became less influential and Forster was able to strengthen his power. At the end of July, for example, Greiser was scheduled to do an interview with H. V. Kaltenborn, a CBS news commentator. On very short notice, the interview was canceled. Kaltenborn claimed that Forster was responsible.[110] Perhaps in response, one of Greiser's supporters, the senator for health, Dr. Helmut Kluck, circulated a memorandum critical of Forster to Reich party and state officials.[111] Kluck claimed that the Gauleiter intimidated the Free City's government. 'The president and senators, who number eight,' Kluck wrote, 'are completely powerless against the idiosyncracies of the

Gauleiter and his people . . . neither the president nor the senators dare to speak openly about their worries.'[112] This memorandum, however, cost Kluck, and not Forster, his position. Once Forster learned of it, he quickly replaced Kluck with one of his supporters.[113]

In 1936, there was another concerted attempt to undermine Greiser through rumors about his past doings. While it is likely that Forster was behind this, the evidence is inconclusive. In spring, a former SS-member, Karl Stangneth, criticized Greiser's role in supervising gambling activities at the famed Zoppot casino. Robert Reuter also repeated his earlier charges. Even though Baron Holzschuher had already dismissed these accusations in 1934, the insinuations were now again brought to Himmler's attention. In April, Greiser defended his actions in a letter to the SS-leader. He claimed that he had redirected the casino's profits from Jewish entrepreneurs to the city's coffers; that Reuter hated him because he had prevented Reuter from carrying out illicit money-making schemes at the casino; and that Reuter was on very friendly terms with his first wife Ruth, and that this had partly motivated the accusations.[114] Greiser now initiated party proceedings against Reuter for spreading 'libelous assertions.' The matter was settled in April 1937, when a Gau court supported Greiser and forced Reuter to state that he no longer believed his initial accusations. But acting on Forster's wishes, and with Greiser's consent, the court did not expel Reuter from the party.[115] In fall 1936, Greiser's past membership in Free Mason lodges also again became an issue when Himmler's officials were tipped off about the matter.[116]

That same fall, another set of rumors about Greiser was stewing: that in 1935 Greiser had known about the upcoming devaluation of the gulden and had acted to protect his assets. In October 1936, Hans Hohnfeldt admitted to the Supreme Party Court that he had told others about a rumor that Greiser's wife had bought a silver box just prior to devaluation.[117] Later, Hohnfeldt was also found to have said that Greiser had invested his assets in silver shortly before devaluation.[118] Again, Greiser went to court, and again, in June 1937, he was cleared. Hohnfeldt was forced to state that he regretted his words; he also received an official party warning and was banned from holding a party office for a year.[119] Greiser was clearly threatened by such accusations: he no doubt worried what else his political enemies might stir up about his past.

As the year wore on, the Danzig rumor mill churned rapidly, taking advantage especially of Greiser's absences. In late September and early

October 1936, when Greiser was on vacation, the foreign press once again reported that he was just about to resign. On 5 October, *The New York Times* wrote that 'Though he [Greiser] publicly defied the League of Nations at Geneva, he is now regarded as too moderate. Mr. Forster is expected to name one of his henchmen to the Senate post and proceed rapidly with plans for nazification of the Free City.'[120] The very next day, the newspaper wrote that 'Mr. Forster declared the party "comes first before the Senate," and that the Senate's function was to "execute the party's will." The party's leader, he added, ranks higher than the Senate's president. Thus Mr. Forster ... placed himself above the Free City's government.'[121] When Greiser returned, two days later, he and other leading Danzig Nazis publicly proclaimed that there was no difference between the party's demands and the Senate's intentions.[122] Whether by choice or capitulation, Greiser publicly accepted Forster's line that the party was in charge.

In private, however, Greiser stood up to Forster. In a private meeting on 9 October, Forster demanded that Greiser not make any personnel decisions without his express permission. Greiser refused. Forster then said that the two men should have a meeting with Hitler about this and other matters. But Forster prevented Greiser from going by claiming that he was leaving for Berchtesgaden even though he didn't have a firm commitment that the Führer would receive him. In fact, as Greiser bitterly noted in a memorandum, the meeting with Hitler was confirmed well before Forster left Danzig.[123] Greiser was left in the cold, unable to defend himself to his Führer.

Soon thereafter, Greiser left town again, this time for a four-week 'cure' in Bad Wildungen, Germany, where he received medical attention for his kidneys (another illness perhaps brought on by stress).[124] *The New York Times* reported that 'he [Greiser] will not return to his post and a new Senate President will try to block the Poles and through them the League of Nations.'[125] Some have argued that Greiser feigned illness in Bad Wildungen so as to stall Danzig–Polish negotiations about Polish rights in the city.[126]

But in late 1936 Greiser returned to Danzig to conduct the negotiations after all. As he later related to Himmler, 'I assume that you, my Reich leader, are still interested in foreign policy matters and so I allow myself ... to sketch out the course of Danzig–Polish negotiations in the last four weeks, which were to date the hardest of my life with the Polish government.' In December, Greiser wrote, the Poles had made a variety of demands on the Danzig Senate that would have led to increased Polish representation in the economic and political affairs of the city. Greiser believed that this would have meant 'a total restriction and paralysis of Danzig sovereignty.' He thus negotiated tooth and nail with Beck to have the Polish demands dropped: 'although the negotiations were sometimes razor close to breaking off, I believe that I was successful in pulling out the poison fangs and all Polish demands and wishes were either totally removed or clothed in vague expressions that say nothing.' Greiser also told Himmler that he intended to advance Nazi goals in the city 'step by step:' 'only by such a process could both the League of Nations and the Polish government . . . be distracted from the true goals of our domestic political wishes.'[127] Greiser was dead set against real accommodation with the Poles; moreover, he planned duplicitous methods to nazify the city.

Due to his rivalry with Forster, Greiser took on a new public persona: that of a 'moderate' force. This had nothing to do with a change of heart. Greiser advanced more temperate policies both to profile himself against his rival and to shore up his own political position. Forster hoped to take on formal executive power in the Free City. This, however, would require changing the Danzig constitution. To protect his own role, Greiser turned to the institution against which he had directed so much venom: the League of Nations. Greiser found an important ally in the Swiss historian Carl Burckhardt, Lester's replacement and the last League high commissioner in Danzig. As Greiser calculated, so long as the League had some voice in the Free City, the constitution would not be altered, and his position would be assured. In contrast to his earlier hounding of Lester, Greiser was very solicitous of Burckhardt. In 1959, Burckhardt published a famous account of his time in Danzig: *Meine Danziger Mission: 1937–1939*. Historians rightly question the accuracy of this memoir, particularly Burckhardt's narrative of how he allegedly helped Danzig's Jews.[128] But the book has much telling material on Greiser that, to the extent that it could be corroborated, is accurate.

Burckhardt arrived in the city on 1 March 1937. He was soon partial to Greiser, and later described him as 'agile, he had knowledge of economics, by nature he was soft, with kind traits, but when circumstances forced him to toughness, and this happened constantly, he exaggerated this toughness. In a well-ordered state under the rule of law, Greiser would have lived according to the rules of a professional ethos. He had an easy intelligence, he did not lack the ability to grasp and formulate objective connections.

When he spoke with foreigners, he could express intelligent criticism. Time and again this gave cause for viewing Greiser—in contrast to the Gauleiter—as an obliging and sensible person. It was always easy to discuss matters with him; with Forster, by contrast, there was no discussion.'[129] Burckhardt's description rings true.

From spring 1937 through fall 1939, Greiser's personal relationship with Forster was at the center of his concerns. He even kept notes on the slights and indignities he suffered at the Gauleiter's hands.[130] Initially, at least, Greiser wanted to patch things up so as to have a united Nazi front in Danzig. On 28 May 1937, just before he was to leave for a five-week stint of reserve military duty in Pillau, Greiser wrote to Forster: 'Mr. Gauleiter! Dear Party Member Forster! In recent times various incidents have hurt the feelings between us and have led to tensions that in turn have had a political effect damaging for Danzig. I would have liked to have discussed personally with you all these things and the consequences that they inevitably had for me. Just like earlier, I'd have liked to have come to you so as to resolve all these matters openly.' Greiser then stated that he had learned only from the press that Forster had undertaken a long trip and that such a conversation would not be possible now. 'But I confidently hope that after my return there will reign again an atmosphere and a foundation, in which I, as your oldest comrade-in-arms in Danzig will walk side-by-side with you—and not divided by middle men—on the so nicely begun path of unity between party and state.'[131]

But Forster was not interested in cooperating with Greiser. When Greiser returned to Danzig, he went straight to a welcome for an SA airforce unit visiting Danzig—in civilian clothing. Forster was in the midst of giving a rousing speech. Right after he finished speaking, he turned to Greiser and screamed 'What are you doing here?' Forster then berated the senate president for his 'listless manner' (perhaps due to his civilian clothing). The next day, Greiser spilled out his worries to Burckhardt. 'In great excitement,' the high commissioner later wrote, Greiser 'complained that everyone was conspiring against him. He had been invited by the Führer to attend the Bayreuth Week, but unfortunately this coincided with a visit by the German fleet in Danzig. He had summoned all his courage and personally called the Führer. He was now totally calmed, because he was able to talk about everything and Adolf Hitler had expressed heartening words of goodwill and trust. For him, this had compensated for much of the endured hardship.'[132]

Greiser felt himself pulled in too many directions at once. He wanted to satisfy his Führer, but did not have the wherewithal to do so. He wanted to be seen as a statesman, but his Nazi aims precluded diplomatic compromise. He wanted to be an independent force in the Free City, but he was bound by party loyalty to follow his Gauleiter. His see-sawing political actions speak to these competing demands. In June 1937, Greiser dropped in on the state secretary in the Reich Foreign Ministry, Ernst von Weizsäcker. Weizsäcker recorded that Greiser 'told me about his worries concerning a too drastic political tempo in Danzig . . .' Greiser also mentioned the Wichmann case and that Forster had initiated preparatory work so as to change Danzig's constitution. Greiser 'emphasized that the high commissioner also feared that with too drastic a tempo he would not be able to head off a Danzig debate in Geneva in September of this year.'[133] Greiser concerned about what the high commissioner thought? Greiser worried about too fast a Nazification of Danzig? What Greiser was this? The 'moderate' Greiser in action.

In early fall, things initially looked good for Greiser: it seemed that he might win out against Forster. As Burckhardt reported, Göring had supposedly arranged for Forster to join the staff of Richard-Walther Darré, the minister of agriculture.[134] But Forster saw Hitler, and the plan was scuttled.[135] Soon thereafter, on 25 October, Greiser signed a virtual death warrant on his own powers. Forster wanted a direct say in any legislation issued, and Greiser was unable to resist the Gauleiter's grab for additional control. 'With the ever more evident standardization of party and state in Danzig,' Greiser declared, 'it seems desirable both to the Gauleiter and to me that no directive and no law should be issued that has not first been thought over in its consequences for the interests of the party.' Greiser stipulated that no law or decree could come into effect unless he or his deputy and a representative of the Justice Department had co-signed it. The Justice Department, however, was ordered to discuss all draft laws and decrees with a representative from the party leadership, Marzian, who had been entrusted with this task by Forster; only with Marzian's approval would the Department co-sign a proposed law or decree.[136] This directive confirmed the Senate's complete subordination to the party; it no longer had an independent role. Greiser's capitulation to Forster was all but complete.

In December 1937, Greiser was depressed about his political future. In a report to a League official, Burckhardt noted: 'Should Greiser lose to his rival (Forster), he hopes for the job of a police president in the city of Hamburg as a best-case scenario, but in moments of depression, that are not so unusual for this once joyously combative man, he hopes for a consular position in Scandinavia.'[137] In early February 1938, Greiser was in for another rude shock. According to Burckhardt, he was ordered to Berlin. There, Forster told him that Hitler was unhappy with Franz von Papen as ambassador in Vienna. He, Forster, would now take over that position and Greiser would be both Gauleiter and senate president in Danzig. In an audience with Hitler, Greiser was told the same. According to Burckhardt, 'Greiser heaved a sigh of relief, made plans for the future, and decided A: to bring to an end the anti-Semitic measures in Danzig, B: to come to an understanding with the Catholics, C: to not permit any interventions in the constitution before elections to the Volkstag in 1939.' It's not clear whether Greiser just voiced these plans to Burckhardt or whether he really intended to carry them out. In any event, a disappointed Forster soon returned to Danzig; he wasn't to be ambassador in Vienna after all. Various attempts were made to find another post for Forster, but since he was little liked in the Foreign Ministry, this was a hard sell.[138] Greiser was left high and dry.[139]

In winter 1938, Burckhardt wrote, Greiser suffered from 'a sort of nervous breakdown.'[140] Greiser's political dilemmas were exacerbated by his fragile personality. He was not the hard and tough man of Nazi stereotype. Instead, he was vulnerable to anxiety and depression. Just as during earlier periods of tension in his life, he now succumbed to stress—so much so that he was unable to carry out his professional duties. In February 1938, Greiser left for Hintertux, an Austrian ski resort, to regain his mental calm. In a letter to Maria, he wrote: 'And because my recovery is going so slowly, I now realize just how done in I was. Even though I'm *only* living my recovery, I'm still very run-down. But in contrast to last week, I'm already a giant.' In Hintertux, Greiser got up late and spent his days alternating between short stints of skiing and lying in a deck chair. Otherwise, he ate healthily and drank little—not more than half a liter of Tyrolean wine per day. He claimed that he had stopped smoking.[141] Maria soon joined him. On 7 March, Greiser wrote to his daughter Ingrid that 'Life consists of sleep, sun and food and we are already as brown as Negroes.'[142] A few days later, the Greisers left for a three-week trip to Italy.

Back in Danzig, things were little better. According to Burckhardt, Greiser 'returned with deep worries. He felt that his position was getting weaker.'[143] Greiser was sent around Germany to agitate for the April 10 plebiscite on the union of Austria and Germany. On 4 April he was to speak in Uelzen, on 5 April in Bremerhaven (before a crowd of 30,000) and on 6 April in Celle.[144] He believed, though, that these party activities were not easily reconciled with his duties as senate president. Burckhardt also noted that Greiser felt that Hitler had 'stamped him as a sort of temporary figure.'[145] As Greiser keenly sensed, he had not yet consolidated his position within the Nazi movement.

In summer 1938, Greiser noted Forster's various steps against him. The Gauleiter, he recorded, had ordered that he be taken off the dinner-guest list at an official NSDAP event that featured the premiere of the film *Heimat*. At a meeting eight to ten days earlier with some party sub-district leaders, Forster had complained about the opulence of Greiser's new official residence; the garden, he claimed, had cost some 50,000 gulden, and Greiser had five domestics, all on the city payroll. Greiser further noted that Forster had told Polish officials that the Danzig government would be changed and that there would be a new senate president. Forster had also told a German official that an agreement that Greiser had worked out with Poland about the Danzig harbor amounted to treasonous activity.[146] Forster was even spying on him; he had ordered a Gau official to write a report about a speech that he, Greiser, was to give.[147] On 20 September, Greiser noted that on the previous day Forster had held a meeting of Danzig senators (i.e., the government) in his (party) office. Forster told the senators that they would now receive their work assignments from him; that they were to carry out their official duties in uniform; that every senator was to devote an evening a week to the party; and that, as of immediately, all senators were forbidden contact to Burckhardt who, in Forster's words, was a 'pig' and passed on everything to the British.[148]

As many—and not least Greiser—recognized, Forster had sharply limited the senate president's influence. But still, Forster could not remove Greiser. For Reich officials, Greiser was a useful antidote to the zealous Gauleiter. In June 1937, for example, Burckhardt told Greiser about a conversation that he had had with Göring. The Reich marshal had reportedly stated that Forster had lots of 'élan (*Schwung*)'—good for Nazi provocation purposes—but that the duplication of leadership in Danzig meant that Greiser could serve as a useful brake on the irascible Gauleiter.[149] Similarly, in December 1938, Burckhardt had a meeting with von Ribbentrop in which the foreign minister spoke approvingly about Forster, but nonetheless suggested that perhaps the Gauleiter could be removed from Danzig for a temporary period so that no tensions would arise in advance of the January 1939 League Council meeting.[150] With Greiser in charge, von Ribbentrop suggested, there would be no need to worry about the Danzig Nazis complicating German–Polish relations. The dual leadership in Danzig served Reich authorities well: when an aggressive stance was desired, Forster could deliver; when moderation was appropriate, Greiser could come to the fore.

In October 1937, after Forster accelerated his anti-Semitic course, Greiser adopted a 'moderate' stance regarding the treatment of Jews. Forster had Jews' stalls moved to special sections of Danzig markets; the Jews were then subjected to rough handling and verbal harassment. On 23 October, hooligans also vandalized roughly sixty Jewish stores and some private apartments. Burckhardt immediately demanded an explanation from Greiser.[151] Greiser telephoned Berlin to find out what line he should follow. As the high commissioner later wrote, the senate president told him that 'Göring was raging' and that the Foreign Ministry and the political police condemned the events. Greiser further stated that 'What clearly separates me from the Gauleiter is the Jewish Question. I won't give in.'[152]

According to Burckhardt, Greiser's attitude toward the Jews was primarily a reflection of his relations with Forster: 'Greiser's position in the whole matter was mainly determined by his rivalry with Forster. The opportunity to oppose his powerful competitor struck him as convenient. Again and again he had emphasized that the introduction of the Nuremberg Laws would have as a consequence the loss of economic influence and would thereby promote Polonization; since the Danzigers were not economically strong enough to take over Jewish businesses, Poland would feel it necessary to fill the vacuum through its own citizens.'[153] As Greiser well knew, Burckhardt, Göring, and Foreign Ministry officials all advocated a more measured stance against Jews in Danzig; these men could support him in his conflict with Forster. But at the same time, in an attitude that would pre- and post-date his rivalry with Forster, Greiser defined Poles, and not Jews, as his major enemy.

Still, Greiser was no friend to the Jews. At the end of October 1937, he met with a Jewish delegation and told it that both the party and the Senate had condemned the riots (which was nominally true). He also claimed that there was no intention of destroying the businesses of Jews who were long-time residents of the city. He did make clear, however, that the Senate intended to imitate Reich developments. In response, the Jewish representatives asked the Senate to simplify the red tape surrounding the granting of passports and other permits necessary for the Jews to emigrate. Greiser promised to help promote an 'orderly emigration' of Jews.[154] But, as one commentator icily noted, his promise of help turned out to be anything but. City tax officials stepped up their harassment of Jewish businessmen and, using various threats, pushed them to flee Danzig while leaving their assets behind.[155]

A year later, in one of the more curious steps of his political career, Greiser tried to delay the introduction of the Nuremberg laws in Danzig. Forster planned to decree the laws in November 1938. In October, however, Reich Foreign Minister Ribbentrop had proposed to the Polish government that the two countries 'clear up' all of their tensions; this would have included the return of Danzig to the Reich. That same month, Hitler made it clear that he was no longer particularly concerned about getting along with England; the Munich Conference in September 1938 had only heightened his contempt for the British.[156] Reich foreign policy considerations that had long dictated moderation in Danzig were no longer apposite. But Greiser failed to pick up on the change. In October he undertook two steps to halt the implementation of the Nuremberg Laws; both, however, were predicated on outdated Reich foreign policy considerations. He asked Burckhardt to inform the League's 'Commission of Three' (charged with monitoring Danzig affairs) that these laws were about to be introduced; he assumed that England and Poland would object and that the Reich would assuage these countries' objections. Burckhardt did as he was asked, and informed the 'Commission' on 4 October.[157]

Two weeks later, on 17 October, Greiser spoke with Weizsäcker in the Reich Foreign Ministry. As Weizsäcker reported, 'President Greiser then mentioned certain Jewish laws that were now being prepared in Danzig and asked about their foreign policy opportuneness. In an objective tone, he noted that Danzig could get by without such laws for six months or a year. The high commissioner was not a supporter of these laws. The reaction to these laws in England would not be particularly favorable, but one could probably ignore this point. By contrast, Poland with its Jewish–Polish citizens would undoubtedly be most affected.' Weizsäcker responded that it was unnecessary to worry about England, but that 'Polish sensitivity' should perhaps be examined. Greiser also hoped to get Ribbentrop to act against Forster: 'The senate president noted that in so far as we [the Foreign Ministry] also didn't want the laws to come into effect, it would be advisable if the foreign minister indicated such to Gauleiter Forster.'[158] Greiser, it seems, was trying to win the support of Burckhardt and ministerial officials in Berlin, perhaps so as to stage a coup against Forster. In fact, though, he seriously misjudged the situation; at this time, there was little reason for the Nazis to temporize in Danzig.

Greiser's efforts came to naught. On the evening of 23 October Forster had a long conversation with Hitler. If not before, the Führer now approved of Forster's planned actions against the Jews.[159] Several weeks later, Danzig saw events similar to those of 'Crystal Night.' Greiser's actions now suggested that he was promoting Forster's policies, while trying to appear otherwise to those who sought more moderate measures against the Free City's Jews. On 9 November, the police president of Danzig, Helmut Froböss, met with Greiser after some anti-Semitic incidents had occurred. As Froböss told another police official, 'I've just come from the senate president who condemns such attacks and will see to it that a repeat of this play with fire will be prevented.'[160] But beginning on 12 November, the Danzig Nazis burned synagogues, looted Jewish apartments, vandalized Jewish shops, and physically harassed many Jewish citizens. The police, controlled by Greiser, did nothing. Soon thereafter, on 21 November, the Nuremberg Laws came into effect.

Greiser tried to minimize the significance of both the incidents and the laws. In a letter to Marian Chodacki, the Polish representative in the city, Greiser insisted that the events of 12–15 November were not an organized pogrom, but rather 'individual occurrences that can never be completely avoided in any state. In any case, their repetition is out of the question. In this respect, state and party have issued the strictest guidelines.'[161] Greiser, of course, was mendacious: the party had instigated the anti-Semitic actions, and his police had allowed them to go on. It was only after the fact that Nazi party and state authorities claimed to be concerned about the events. As for the introduction of the Nuremberg Laws, Greiser claimed to Burckhardt that they would have little real effect on the Danzig Jews: 'It's hard to see how this decree could harm anyone. It's in keeping with the feeling of the great mass of the population and changes what had been customary law into formal law.'[162] Greiser was right that Jews had long been treated as second-class citizens in the Free

City. But the introduction of the Nuremberg Laws nonetheless marked a milestone in the Nazi persecution of the city's Jewish community.

On 17 December, the Danzig Jews met as a community and unanimously passed a resolution stating that they wished to leave the city as quickly as possible.[163] Greiser now pushed them to emigrate. In February 1939, for example, he complained to Burckhardt that the British were putting up obstacles to Jewish emigration.[164] But while he and other city officials urged Jews to leave, they also threw up obstacles to their emigration. The Jewish community was forced to sell its holdings to the city at a steep discount. Passport controls were tightened, making it harder for Jews to leave the city illegally. In March, Jews lost the right to administer their property and in July, all of their property was confiscated.[165] The decrees enacting these measures all bore Greiser's signature.[166] By 1 September 1939, barely 1,700 Jews were left in the city.[167] Greiser had done his part to destroy Danzig's Jewish community.

In the last year of the Free City's existence, the conflict between Greiser and Forster grew only nastier. Forster repeatedly stated that he intended to become head of state in Danzig. In March 1939, he planned to declare Danzig annexed to the Reich with himself as chief executive of the city at the end of the month. Greiser went to Berlin to make sure that this didn't happen. As he told Reich authorities, Forster's action would bring a Polish military response.[168] For the moment, Greiser was successful. In early April, Himmler came to Danzig and, on his return to Berlin, called for Forster's removal.[169] During these same months, Forster was very sick; he not only spent three weeks in hospital, but then went to Wiesbaden for a 'cure.' In May, Greiser told Burckhardt, 'Forster is really sick, he's in a sanatorium, it's too bad that he doesn't go away entirely.'[170]

Greiser, too, now spent a month away from the city; from 10 June through 9 July, he did reserve naval duty at Pillau. Forster tried to use his rival's absence to alter the status of Danzig; he planned to declare Danzig part of the Reich in mid-June. This time, Burckhardt managed—indirectly—to hold Forster off.[171] Forster nonetheless took the opportunity to make some personnel and administrative changes to undermine Greiser.[172] Sensing his boss's danger, Böttcher sent Harry Siegmund, Greiser's cousin and an employee of the Senate Department of Foreign Affairs, to inform the senate president about the ongoing intrigues. In Pillau, Siegmund later wrote, 'I found an enthusiastic Officer Greiser who took the matter lightly.' Greiser was holding a 'boozy party' on his boat and enjoying the company of 'his loyal officer comrades.'[173] Greiser nonetheless cut short his stay in Pillau; in a letter to an SS official, he vaguely alluded to the 'political situation in the territory of the Free City of Danzig' as the cause for his hasty return.[174]

On 16 July, after Greiser was already back, Forster insisted to Burckhardt that he 'now had the authority to make every decision and was the sole ruler in Danzig.'[175] But much to Forster's annoyance, Burckhardt would not respond directly to him. The high commissioner's view was that he was authorized to deal with state, but not party, authorities. A week later, Greiser had an unpleasant telephone exchange with Forster. As he noted, 'On the telephone, the Gauleiter was very angry with me and stated that he could not tolerate that the high commissioner comes to me when he receives directives from him, the Gauleiter. I told the Gauleiter that he would have to have it out with the high commissioner and not with me.'[176] This, of course, did nothing to mollify Forster.

In early August, Forster insisted that Greiser share all communication with the Foreign Ministry with him before sending anything off. Greiser told him that this was impossible, particularly since he often had to wait for up to a week before Forster would see him. The two men now agreed that when an important foreign policy decision was in the offing, Greiser would be able to contact Forster directly and immediately. But their relations continued to be very tense. On 18 August, Forster summoned Greiser and berated him for not having come to a rally earlier in the day. As Greiser described the meeting: 'The Gauleiter heatedly reproached me that I had not appeared at the parade and claimed that I hadn't come because I didn't want to be the second man next to him. He was going to tell the Führer about this. I answered just as heatedly and told him to do that. I further heatedly replied that I could not accept his reproaches. For ten years I had shown that next to him I was the second man in the Free City of Danzig and that I had done my job and done my duty.'[177] Up to the very last days of their time together in Danzig, the two men's power struggle remained at a standstill; neither was able to get rid of the other.

In the late 1930s, Greiser imparted some fatherly wisdom to his children Ingrid and Erhardt that reflected his concerns as much as theirs. On Ingrid's eighteenth birthday in March 1938, for example, Greiser wrote to his daughter: 'Freedom in life is nicest when one earns it through one's own work on oneself and for others, through the struggle for daily bread and [one's own] spiritual views.'[178] A year later, Ingrid had just taken a job on the personal staff of Reich Foreign Minister Ribbentrop, and Greiser congratulated her accordingly. But he added, perhaps somewhat ruefully: 'What a young person at your age dreams for her life will never totally come true and every life is full of disappointments. When, however, one is internally reconciled through work and the will to live, then one bears such disappointments better and I hope that you will suffer little from the unpleasant aspects of life.'[179] Greiser thus hinted at his own difficulties and how he stoically intended to overcome them.

In late spring 1939, Greiser received Erhardt's grades from the Nazi school that his son attended. He waited a few weeks before expressing his outrage at his son's poor performance: 'I was very angry about your grades . . . I was prepared for worse grades than I had expected, but that the school confirmed in black and white that you come into conflict with the external discipline and that you sometimes simply disregard the rules and beyond that are listless, sluggish and unwilling to engage in independent activities, and that the overall opinion confirms that in your conduct you do not fulfill the demands of the school, exceeds by far what I had expected and what I would consider acceptable.' He reminded his son that he and Maria had been very good to him at his confirmation earlier that spring. He also noted the sacrifices he had made on Erhardt's behalf: 'When under really great material sacrifice I'm prepared to send you for eight years to this school, then I do so solely for you, because with that you'll have for your whole later life the educational basis and springboard so that you can follow your life path securely and unchallenged.' Greiser made some comparisons to his own life: 'I myself have had it very hard since my youth and have had to make many sacrifices and have always had to work on myself in order to work myself up to the position in which I find myself today.' He further told his son, 'If you disappoint my good wishes for you and your life, then you are not worthy of being the son of a father who makes such sacrifices for you.' Although he himself had long enjoyed the sport, Greiser now expressed annoyance that Erhardt was playing so much tennis. 'No boy has ever become anything by getting money together and playing tennis. Boys only become men and fellows if they are hard-working, learn something competently and beyond that are bodily and sportily nimble and steeled, so that they become tough and quick.' If Erhardt was not able to adhere to these standards, Greiser threatened, then he should start an apprenticeship as a carpenter or metalworker. He finished this part of his letter by stating that 'I will give you once again a last chance, you know very well from the last years that I can be very kind (*lieb*), but also very tough (*hart*). It depends on you how we face each other in the next years.'[180] Greiser's words betray the resentments of a self-made man toward his children. In his view, he had struggled hard to attain his station in life. But to his great frustration, Erhardt was failing to make good on the opportunities for which he, Greiser, had supposedly sacrificed so much. Although Greiser threw down the gauntlet to his son, Erhardt refused to reply.[181]

By now, as he intimated to Erhardt, Greiser enjoyed the material laurels of his struggles. Sometime in 1937, he took over a manor house in the tiny village of Obersommerkau; this was his weekend house and hunting lodge. Burckhardt occasionally visited him there.[182] In May 1938, the Greisers also moved to another, larger house in Oliva, located in a very nice park.[183] Much work, however, was necessary to bring the villa up to snuff. As Greiser wrote to Ingrid: 'Workmen are simply always in the house. First the curtains are missing, then the right lamps, then the blinds, rugs, pictures, and furniture. Everything comes bit by bit. And in the garden a labor service (*Arbeitsdienst*) of forty men won't be done until the fall.'[184] A few weeks later, Ingrid was planning a short trip to Kiel and then a summer vacation in Danzig. Greiser wrote: 'I hope you won't lose any summer vacation because of that [Kiel trip]; you've never been in such a sanatorium as in our house.'[185] The implication was that Ingrid could not enjoy better accommodations than her father's new house; Greiser was delighted with his new living quarters.

Although later exaggerated at his trial (see Chapter 9), Greiser helped to heighten German–Polish tensions and thus create an excuse for the Nazis to unleash World War II. Until early 1939, Danzig–Polish relations were tense, but they retained a steely decorum. In May 1938, the Poles intimated to German authorities that they felt on 'more secure grounds' working with Greiser than with Forster, who they believed had a 'somewhat erratic nature.'[186] The Poles also made it clear to Greiser that so long as their rights in and about the city were not infringed upon, they would tolerate Nazi constitutional abuses. In a meeting on 17 December 1938, for example, Chodacki told Greiser that the Poles were really only concerned about threats to their army and to their access to the sea.[187] In mid-March, Greiser and Chodacki took up the matter of Volkstag elections that, according to the constitution, were to take place in spring 1939; the Nazis, of course, wished to put them off. Chodacki told Greiser that the Poles were indifferent as to whether or not the Nazis held the elections; it was fine with them, he suggested, if the Senate simply extended the Volkstag's legislative period by decree (which is what, in fact, happened).[188]

In spring 1939, this surface friendliness ended. Once the Nazis occupied Austria and what remained of the Czech state after the Munich Agreement, Hitler renewed his demands for the return of Danzig and the Polish corridor. As he told the Reichstag on 28 April, 'Danzig is a German city and wishes to belong to Germany.'[189] The Nazis now built up their military fortifications in and around the Free City.[190] Himmler—with Greiser's active engagement—formed an armed 'SS Home Defense Force (*SS-Heimwehr*)' of some 4,000 men.[191] In close consultation with Reich authorities, the Danzig Nazis heightened their attacks on Polish customs officials; these officials were trying to halt the smuggling of arms from East Prussia into the Free City. On 21 May, some Danzigers harassed Polish customs officials in Kalthof. In response, the chauffeur of the Polish commissariat-general killed a Danziger.[192]

On 3 June, Greiser lodged a vehement protest against the increasing numbers of Polish customs officials and their actions on Danzig territory. He also threatened to have Danzig customs officials swear allegiance to the Free City's constitution and government—a clear violation of the 1920 Danzig–Polish Agreement. The Polish government, in turn, insisted that if Danzig customs officials swore such an allegiance, it would introduce sharper customs measures. On 19 July, it also announced a trade war: customs officials were to prevent deliveries to Poland of certain Danzig agricultural products. Greiser responded by threatening to remove customs barriers between Danzig and East Prussia.

On 3 August, Chodacki officially complained that Danzig customs officials were smuggling arms and munitions. In response, Greiser ordered that as of 6 August, Danzig customs officials were to oppose the actions of their Polish counterparts on the Danzig–East Prussia border. On 5 August, however, Chodacki issued an ultimatum to the Senate: if Greiser didn't annul the orders, Polish customs inspectors would be armed and, should they be harassed in any way, his government would view this as a 'violent act' against the Polish state.[193] Greiser backed down, but the German government sharply protested the Polish ultimatum. This, in turn, raised a storm of protest in Warsaw. Just then, however, Hitler decided that he wanted quiet in Danzig; he did not want to draw attention to the city where he would soon begin war. On 11 August he summoned Burckhardt to Berchtesgaden. Soon thereafter, the high commissioner arranged for Greiser and Chodacki to begin negotiations that, in the event, got nowhere.

In late summer, Greiser alerted local officials about the state of the city's readiness for war. On 16 August, for example, he sent a directive to the president of the Postal and Telegraph Administration telling him to be ready to implement certain measures in the event of 'political tension' or 'defense.' These included an immediate halt to mail operations with Poland and 'enemy foreign countries;' the destruction of communications facilities that served 'enemy foreign countries;' surveillance of all letters, packages, telegrams, and long-distance telephone conversations; and the confiscation of all private transmitters.[194] On 22 August, Greiser wrote to State Police Headquarters that all of these and other measures could be immediately introduced.[195]

Since a German–Polish war was in the offing, Forster (and Reich officials) had no reason to allay British, League, or Polish concerns. Accordingly, on 24 August, with Hitler's consent, Forster carried out his goal of joining the position of Gauleiter and head of state in Danzig. This violated the Free City's constitution, since no official head of state (other than senate president) was foreseen. Although Greiser was only informed of the change on 22 August, to the outside world, Forster's assumption of state power occurred harmoniously: Greiser and Forster engaged in a pre-arranged exchange of letters published on 24 August. As Greiser wrote to Forster, 'The Senate has authorized me to request that you, Mr. Gauleiter, take on this office, so that in these difficult but wonderful days of decision the unity of the party and state will from now on be given outer expression . . .'[196] For Greiser, putting his signature on this letter must have been a bitter pill to swallow; he now sanctioned what he had spent years trying to prevent.

Although officially still senate president, Greiser was really a minister president under Forster's executive authority. He met with Burckhardt for the last time. Greiser reported of this meeting: 'We parted in a friendly way with the promise that we would sometime see each other again as private individuals in Switzerland or Germany.'[197] By contrast, the high commissioner described Greiser's desperation at this time: 'After the "takeover of power" by Forster,' Burckhardt wrote, 'Greiser ran around like a broken man.'[198] Among other humiliations, Forster insisted that Greiser give up his keys, and forbade his entry into the senate building.[199]

Both Poland and the League protested Forster's new violation of the Danzig constitution. They also refused to send officials to honor the German officers of the old battleship *Schleswig-Holstein* that sailed into the Danzig harbor on 25 August. That same day, Poland ordered a partial army mobilization. While France tried to prevent Poland from beginning military action, Great Britain and Poland signed a mutual assistance pact. Days later, Hitler began the war that he had long wanted. At 4:45 a.m. on 1 September, the *Schleswig-Holstein* opened fire on Poland's Westerplatte fortress in the Danzig harbor. A few hours later, Forster declared Danzig annexed to the Reich. The Free City was no more. And Greiser? As the senate president later told the story, he intended to serve as a naval officer in the German military.[200] But in fact, he was in search of a job—as well as more power and influence in the Nazi regime.

The Greiser–Forster rivalry was a key factor in Danzig politics during the 1930s.[201] It complicated and perhaps slowed the Nazification of the Free City. At different times, Greiser tried to hold back the imposition of anti-Semitic measures; advocated a less aggressive stance toward Poland; and cooperated with the League of Nations and its representatives. These political positions, however, were born of opportunism, not conviction; Greiser pursued them only so as to attain political advantage. At the same time, moderation is always a relative term, and Greiser was only 'moderate' in comparison to Forster. Moreover, his 'moderation' only went so far. In the end, he cooperated with Forster in Nazifying the Free City. Together, they suppressed the political opposition. Together, they undermined the role of the League of Nations in the city. Together, they militated against Polish influence in Danzig. And together, they dispossessed the Jews and forced all but the remnants of the community to leave the city.

If the Greiser–Forster rivalry did little to halt the eventual Nazification of Danzig, it did much to shape the Nazi who would lead the Warthegau. Due to his conflict with Forster, Greiser cultivated contacts among high-ranking Nazis, including Himmler and Göring, who could protect him against the Gauleiter's machinations. He worked hard to shore up his political base; among his underlings, he privileged loyalty above other qualities. Greiser was also eager to free himself from the fetters he faced in Danzig; as senate president, he had to follow Forster's orders, maneuver according to Reich interests, and circumvent demands made by the League of Nations. In the Warthegau, he would strive to rule independently of ministerial or other powers. Finally, Greiser learned an important political lesson. Never again would he position himself on the 'moderate' end of Nazi policy. As he saw in Danzig, the Nazi bent toward radicalization favored those who advocated more extreme positions.

Much later, at his trial, Greiser would say that the German invasion of Poland ended the 'the nicest time of my life.'[202] There was a certain truth in this. In Danzig, Greiser enjoyed spectacular career mobility. As senate president, he tasted political power for the first time. In November 1939, soon after he had left the city, Greiser declared: 'My National-Socialist crib stood in Danzig and I am thankful that fate allowed me to go through a unique ten-year schooling in the NSDAP and the state in Danzig...' His Danzig experiences, he insisted, had made it possible for him to tackle his new tasks: 'without the work in Danzig I could not approach this difficult work in the Warthegau. Here I became what I am today: through exposure to all areas of politics—domestic debate, foreign policy disputes, practical administration, and ideological objectives.'[203] As Greiser intimated, he would bring his Danzig schooling to his new position as Gauleiter of the Warthegau. Poles, Jews, and even Germans would soon feel the disastrous consequences of his rule.

4

The 'Model Gau:' The Warthegau

When Germany attacked Poland on 1 September 1939, Arthur Greiser had just suffered the biggest defeat of his political life. The war salvaged his Nazi career. It gave him a position, Gauleiter and Reichsstatthalter of the Warthegau, in which he could enjoy undisputed leadership. It gave him an opportunity to define himself as a Nazi can-do man. And it allowed him to carry out a mission near and dear to his heart, the Germanization of his childhood homeland that had fallen under Polish rule. His ambition soon knew few bounds. Early on, Greiser declared that his territory would become a 'model Gau'—an example for the rest of the Third Reich to emulate.[1] Eventually, he would describe it as 'the parade ground of practical National Socialism'—the area in which Nazi demographic and other experiments were to be carried out.[2] First, though, Greiser had to impose Nazi rule in the region; this proved as brutal as the ultimate goal was radical.

World War II began in Danzig. On 31 August, Greiser went aboard the battleship *Schleswig-Holstein* in the Danzig harbor. That evening he was told about the upcoming military action. Early the next morning, the battleship shelled the Polish Westerplatte fortress in the Danzig harbor. Around 7 a.m., Greiser inspected the ongoing fighting. According to his cousin, Harry Siegmund, who went with him, the tour was 'accompanied by the roaring salvos of the ship's heavy artillery and fierce rifle fire in the city.' In the next days, Greiser followed military developments in the Polish corridor. As Siegmund described, his cousin now 'sat inactive in his villa' while 'feverishly' listening to 'the news of victory on the radio.'[3]

Greiser was a man in search of a job. Three years later, he told an audience this story about the first days of the war: 'I had no idea that I was to go to this place [the Warthegau]. I had put on my uniform as a reserve officer in the Navy and was on my way to Kiel. I was supposed to take command over a boat in an active squadron. A telegram from Reich Marshal [Göring] reached me there, stating that I was to report and that the Führer had something else in mind for me. And so I—also unique in history—marched into Posen with the Army in a navy uniform.'[4] But the chain of events was otherwise. As so often before and after, Greiser reinvented his past.

In fact, Greiser actively sought a role in occupied Poland. As soon as war conditions permitted, he traveled to Berlin to speak with various contacts. According to Siegmund, who came along, 'Everywhere there were embarrassed shrugs, no one had any great interest in him and hardly anyone was ready to further help him . . .' In the Interior Ministry, 'He [Greiser] was received very kindly, but he was offered nothing more than the position of a district president in Köslin; this was unacceptable for him since he had been a head of state.'[5] At the Foreign Office, Ernst von Weizsäcker noted on 7 September, '. . . Mr. Greiser personally told me that he is looking for a new job and perhaps could be more useful in the area of occupied Posen than in the Navy where he is a reserve officer.'[6] That same day, according to Siegmund, Rudolf Hess, the deputy Führer, and Paul Körner, Göring's state secretary, alerted Hitler of Greiser's situation. The Führer now summoned Greiser and Albert Forster, and the two men were supposedly told that they would each become the Gauleiter and Reichsstatthalter of one of the two new Gaus to be created in western Poland. Siegmund later recalled that 'Greiser was overjoyed—he would now have a turn in the area where he had been born, the Prussian province of Posen, and he could finally count on the powerful position of a Gauleiter that he had lacked in Danzig.'[7]

The head of the Reich Chancellery, Hans Lammers, now informed the Interior Ministry that Hitler had approved Greiser's use in the administration of the occupied areas and thought him 'especially suitable' for the position of the head of the administration in Posen.[8] The Army High Command was also told that Greiser would become head of civil administration (*Chef der Zivilverwaltung* or CdZ) in Posen; CdZs were to aid the transition from military occupation to civilian rule in conquered areas.[9] The next day, Hitler officially nominated Greiser as CdZ.[10] Greiser now went to army headquarters in Zossen, where General von Brauchitsch handed him a signed certificate of appointment. According to Siegmund, Greiser was 'already in the euphoria of his future exercise of power.' Maria came to Berlin and the couple and Siegmund celebrated in a 'gourmet restaurant on the Kurfürstendamm with champagne, oysters, and caviar.'[11]

On 12 September, Greiser and Siegmund went to Frankfurt/Oder, where the CdZ staff for Posen was gathered. This staff had first formed in Potsdam at the end of August, and had moved to Frankfurt/Oder on 8 September.[12] Initially, Hans Bredow, the district president of Hildesheim, headed the staff. Siegmund claimed that once Bredow learned that Greiser would get the job, he 'departed in annoyance.'[13] On 11 September, August Jäger claimed the position.[14] But Jäger held this job for just one day; he would soon become Greiser's deputy. When Greiser appeared, both Jäger and Herbert Mehlhorn, deputy chief of the CdZ staff, viewed their new boss with suspicion. According to Siegmund, 'the leading men of the staff were uncertain, and they faced Greiser—in their eyes a pure party functionary—with visible reserve.'[15] Greiser greeted the staff as its new head at a 6 p.m. meeting. In the minutes of this meeting, Mehlhorn noted, 'Title of address for the chief: Mr. President.'[16] Late that evening or early the next morning, Greiser set out for Posen. He only arrived the next morning; although he later claimed that he marched into Posen with the Army (which came on 12 September), this was simply not true.[17]

Five years later, Eugen Petrull, a journalist for the *Ostdeutscher Beobachter*, the official Nazi newspaper for the Warthegau, published an account of Greiser's arrival in Posen. Around 10 a.m. on 13 September, Greiser, dressed in a black SS-uniform, came to the building that had served as the seat of the Polish governor of the region. 'Without a ceremonial welcome, only accompanied by his personal advisor [Siegmund], Arthur Greiser, the former senate president of Danzig, ... enters the arena of his first activity.' Petrull continued, 'The sight that he sees is dreary and unencouraging. The steps through the cloister-like broad halls are muffled, only occasionally does he see a low-level or middle-level Polish bureaucrat, there are empty shelves and tables in the offices, there are no pens or paper, and the Poles ... took all files and valuables.' Greiser immediately took charge of the situation. 'Instinctively Arthur Greiser's tall figure stiffens. As he goes from room to room giving the Polish bureaucrats their first directives, a plan and organization for the mastery of the gigantic task given to him form in his thoughts.' Petrull claimed that Greiser 'was thinking about how [the day before] he had telephoned his most loyal Danzig subordinates and ordered them to Frankfurt, from where they were all together to start the drive to Posen. But he did not await their arrival, he was too impatient to quickly find his new place of work. But now he needs them, without delay the work should begin. A few hours later they are there. Immediately he holds the first meetings and initiates the first measures.'[18] Although he gave a stylized account of a Nazi man of action, Petrull captured the situation: Greiser had to start from scratch, few men were available, and the offices at his disposal were in disarray. But no doubt he was more than eager to begin his new job.

While Greiser was busy securing his new position, German troops steadily advanced into what would become the Warthegau. By 7 September, the Eighth Army had moved into the vicinity of Łódź, the easternmost edge of Greiser's future Gau. On 13 September, Hitler made his only visit to what became the Warthegau; en route to the front, he halted briefly in Lodsch (as the Germans spelled Łódź), where jubilant Germans greeted him. The most significant military confrontation in the region took place near Kutno, close to the future border between the Warthegau and the General Government, the area of Nazi-occupied Poland just east of what became the Warthegau. By mid-September, twelve Polish divisions, representing more than one-third of the country's land forces, had gathered there. On 17 September, German troops encircled these forces and subjected them to heavy air attacks. Polish defenses collapsed, and some 40,000 prisoners were taken.[19] Greiser would later declare that 'the fate of this state [i.e., Poland] was decided in Kutno, which today belongs to the Warthegau. Kutno has thus become the symbol of the downfall of the Polish state.'[20] Ever eager to tote the Warthegau's importance, Greiser may have exaggerated the significance of military events in Kutno. But ten days after the Kutno defeat, Warsaw fell. And on 6 October, the last major Polish force was destroyed at Kock.

The speed with which the Wehrmacht moved into western Poland belied the ferocity of Polish resistance during the September campaign and the German repression it provoked. After the outbreak of war, Polish authorities used prepared lists of names to arrest the ethnic German elite. Some 10,000 ethnic Germans from the western Polish regions of eastern Pomerania and Poznania were arrested.[21] Most were then forced on treks eastwards into central Poland. Reliable estimates suggest that between 1,778 and 2,200 ethnic Germans died during or as a direct consequence of these forced marches.[22] Poles also murdered their ethnic German neighbors outright. The best known case of Polish rage directed at ethnic Germans took place in Bydgoszcz (Bromberg), a town that had belonged to the Prussian province of Posen, but would soon be joined to Danzig–West Prussia, Forster's enlarged Gau. On Sunday, 3 September, German diversionary insurgents entered the town and shot Polish soldiers and civilians. The Polish military commander then ordered a round-up of suspicious ethnic Germans.[23] In what became known as 'Bloody Sunday,' however, civilian Poles slaughtered 700–1,000 ethnic Germans on their own.[24] In response, the Germans 'pacified' the area. By 13 September military and police units had executed at least 1,000 Polish citizens.[25] When Greiser arrived in Posen, ethnic tensions and vicious anti-Polish measures were already in full swing.

On 14 September, General Alfred von Vollard-Bockelberg, the military commander of Posen, officially installed Greiser as head of the CdZ for the Posen area. Greiser demanded the Posen Castle for his headquarters. According to Siegmund, this request 'was greeted with an immediate refusal, and it was made clear to him that the general was number 1 and that he [i.e., Greiser] was his subordinate for the duration of the military campaign.'[26] General Vollard-Bockelberg established his own headquarters in the Posen Castle, but he gave Greiser two offices in the building.[27] Although the two men declared that they would cooperate, tensions were inherent in the very structure of military–CdZ relations.[28] On paper, at least, Greiser as CdZ was formally subordinate to the military. Yet in practice, he had considerable authority; he was, after all, a well-known Nazi leader, and Hitler had appointed him to his position. Moreover, many of those at work in his CdZ administration were high-ranking police officials, or else experienced civil servants from the Reich. Heinrich Himmler had even forced through an arrangement whereby the Order Police (*Ordnungspolizei*) was directly subordinate to the CdZ, and not to military authorities. The Wehrmacht's influence was thus somewhat limited.[29] But military authorities were nevertheless able to thwart some of Greiser's early aims. On 25 October, Greiser complained to Joseph Goebbels: 'the party cannot yet really act effectively so long as the military constantly prevents it [from doing things] . . .'[30]

Greiser immediately set about to consolidate German rule. He quickly appointed local officials to carry out administrative tasks. By 18 September, there were sub-district magistrates (*Landräte*) in twenty of twenty-one districts; a provisional lord mayor for Posen, Dr. Gerhard Scheffler; and a provisional police president for Posen, SS Brigade Leader Lambert v. Mahlsen-Ponikau.[31] Greiser set up a motorcycle courier service to facilitate administrative communication.[32] He also took steps to create a semblance of civilian life. He issued decrees regulating currency and banking matters.[33] To prevent price gauging, he set maximum prices for basic consumer goods.[34] He restored electricity, street car, and other basic services in the city of Posen. He organized food distribution.[35] He also initiated measures to bring in the harvest; to his relief, agricultural areas had suffered relatively light war damage, and so the harvest was 'in general good.'[36] Finally, he worked to restore industrial production. By 19 September, the largest industrial complex in the province, the H. Cegielski machine works, had already resumed limited production.[37]

Right from the start, Greiser displayed an uncompromising stance toward Poles. Shaped by his long experiences in the German–Polish borderlands—and the sense that Germany had been on the losing side of these tensions—Greiser now adopted vengeful policies toward Poles. All Polish political parties were banned. Many leading Polish politicians were arrested. All Polish newspapers and periodicals were shut down. Greiser also relegated Poles to a subservient role. At a rally in Posen on 21 September, for example, he declared that 'the Pole would never stand equal to the German in the new German areas, but rather he could only serve him...'[38] Greiser soon heard from Hitler that he had an even more radical task for the area. At a meeting on 28 September, the Führer reportedly told Greiser: 'On no account [Hitler stated] did he want even a small bit of Polish influence in Reich provinces. In thirty years someone driving through the country must not be able to notice that these areas were once disputed between Germans and Poles.'[39] Greiser's task was clear: using all means necessary, he was to turn an overwhelmingly Polish area into pure German territory.

Two weeks later, Greiser publicly echoed Hitler's ambitions for the region. He now declared that he had 'two goals, a short-term goal and a long-term goal.' The short-term goal was that 'the land must soon get back its old face of high culture and also the appearance of the people must soon be the same as it once was.' According to Greiser, 'all land that was once in German hands and robbed through Polish criminality must in the shortest time be returned in the same amount to German hands.' Greiser then discussed the long-term goal: 'Our long-term goal should be to become a model Gau of the Greater German Reich (*Großdeutscher Reich*), that in large measure guarantees the food supply for Greater Germany, that affords protection against Polish and Jewish invasion, and whose buildings correspond to the greatness of the Reich.' He continued, 'And the most important task before our eyes is the settlement of this land with people who will later know the term "Polish" as an historical memory.'[40] Greiser had made his (and Hitler's) long-term goal explicit: Germanization, a many-sided project that would include the reconstruction of the region, the immediate removal of all Polish and Jewish influence, and the transformation of the population through ethnic cleansing and genocide.

The imposition of Nazi rule was shockingly violent. By the time what became the Warthegau was annexed to Germany on 26 October 1939, some 10,000 individuals had been murdered in the area.[41] As Greiser told Goebbels the day before, 'There is not much left of the intelligentsia.'[42] Many of these murders were related to Operation Tannenberg, an SS-plan to eliminate the Polish elite by murdering the intelligentsia, clergy, and aristocracy. SS operational groups (*Einsatzgruppen*), directed from Berlin, initiated the killings. The SS, however, was aided by the Army and Greiser's civil administration.[43]

When Greiser met with Hitler on 28 September, the Führer's staff officer, Major Engel, recorded that Hitler was 'very satisfied with his discussion with Gauleiter Greiser. He [i.e., Greiser, according to Hitler] has the right policy in the Warthegau. As a child of the East he knows the Poles... Where he deems it necessary, he is liquidating the Polish intelligentsia. Since they earlier murdered us, now we should not be small-minded when it is necessary to remove centers of unrest.' While not too much stock should be placed in this summary of Hitler's words, the attribution of decision-making power to Greiser suggests that the new CdZ already had an important say in the area's policies. Engel's diary entry continues: 'He [i.e., Hitler] stated that he still has to speak with Greiser and Forster about the general course. The two do not hold identical views. Forster is no doubt softer, also vis-à-vis the Poles, and that's not good. It's no wonder, for he is also a Frank and he hasn't had much to do with the

Poles in Danzig...'[44] Already by this early moment, Greiser and Forster had reversed roles, at least as concerned Poles: Greiser, as a 'child of the East,' was now the 'radical,' Forster the 'moderate.'

As Hitler's words suggested, Greiser and his CdZ officials were already engaged in draconian actions against the Polish population. At the end of September, a member of the CdZ staff noted that in 'close cooperation' with the military it had been possible within a week 'to undertake a screening and cleansing of both the towns and the large majority of the rural sub-districts.' In a few cases, Poles who had not complied with the German demand to turn in their weapons had been executed. The report further stated that 'all elements that had committed violent acts against ethnic Germans insofar as they were still in the province were arrested and in the most serious cases were summarily shot.' The report's author regretted that 'the number of public executions... had unfortunately been only trifling.' He noted, however, that a newly instituted special court would sentence 'a large number of guerillas' to be 'shot publicly for intimidation purposes.'[45] Greiser, without informing General Vollard-Bockelberg, had established police court martials.[46] In mid-October, when unknown Poles tore down a swastika flag and hoisted a Polish flag on a government building in Ottorowo, vandalized the building's rooms, and took a weapon with ammunition, the Samter sub-district magistrate ordered a summary court to deliberate on the matter. This court sentenced ten men from Ottorowo to death. Within two days of the disturbance, five Polish men had been executed publicly on the Market Square; five more were executed on the following day.[47] Elsewhere, similarly harsh punishments were imposed.[48]

The short-lived Ethnic German Self-Defense Force (*Volksdeutsche Selbstschutz*) also massacred Poles in fall 1939. The Self-Defense Force was made up of ethnic Germans who provided additional police manpower in the first months of the German occupation. Although initiated by the SS, the Self-Defense Force retained some independence. It was particularly murderous in West Prussia, where it was led by the rabidly anti-Polish ethnic German SS-Senior Leader (*Oberführer*) Ludolf von Alvensleben.[49] The Posen region, however, also saw its share of Self-Defense–Force cruelty. From October 1939 onwards, Jürgen Stroop led the Self-Defense Force for the Posen area; later, Stroop would put down the Warsaw Ghetto Uprising. In jail after the war, he told a fellow prisoner that in the Posen region, some 45,000 ethnic Germans had been involved in the Self-Defense

Force. In winter 1939–40, however, the Self-Defense Force was disbanded in Posen and Danzig–West Prussia. Many military authorities and civilian administrators opposed its undisciplined actions; it also did not mesh well with other SS-structures. The Ethnic German Self-Defense Force is held responsible for some 10,000 murders in occupied Poland, most of which occurred in West Prussia.[50]

One of the more atrocious early crimes in the Posen region took place on the night of 22–3 October, just before the area was annexed to the Third Reich. A drunken thirty-year-old acting sub-district magistrate in Hohensalza, SA-leader Otto Christian von Hirschfeld, forced his way into a local prison with two drinking buddies. There, he and his friends, along with prison officials whom they coerced, murdered fifty-six Polish inmates. Before killing his victims, von Hirschfeld forced some of them to perform degrading acts, including having sex with one another. News of von Hirschfeld's crimes reached abroad; a radio station in Strasbourg broadcast a story about 'the Bloody Sunday in Hohensalza.'[51] Von Hirschfeld's actions constituted a serious breach of discipline and damaged the reputation of the nascent German civilian occupation. Greiser, however, seems to have had few moral qualms about the crime. He pleaded with the Interior Ministry to go lightly on von Hirschfeld, asking it 'to settle this matter in the spirit of bureaucratic discipline without ruining the life of a talented young daredevil...' Greiser added that von Hirschfeld had given him his word of honor that 'for ten years he would not drink any alcohol.'[52]

Some Germans in the civil administration were appalled by von Hirschfeld's actions and Greiser's weak response. According to a memorandum prepared in the Reich Chancellery, 'a sub-district magistrate of the Reichsgau Posen came to the Interior Ministry and declared that a number of sub-district magistrates of the Gau would ask for their discharge from the civilian administration if von Hirschfeld stayed in office. Other sub-district magistrates have also labeled this event as a "nasty scandal (*Schweinerei*)."'[53] Some contemporaries and later historians erroneously believed that von Hirschfeld's only punishment was transfer to another sub-district magistrate position or a summons for active military service.[54] In fact, however, in July 1940 a special German court in Posen sentenced von Hirschfeld to a prison sentence of fifteen years and the loss of his civil rights for ten years.[55]

Siegmund later wrote of Greiser's response to von Hirschfeld's crimes: 'We could only understand Greiser's hesitation [in disciplining von

Hirschfeld] in that he already found himself totally dependent on Himmler and [Reinhard] Heydrich and that he feared that he would appear in an unfavorable light in these officials' eyes . . . if he imposed a legal judgement against the wrongdoer von Hirschfeld.' Given Greiser's propensity to kowtow to those whom he believed could advance his ambitions, there may be some truth in Siegmund's words. At the same time, though, Siegmund claimed to have been surprised by Greiser's willingness to tolerate this and other atrocities committed by the SS and Wehrmacht: 'I soon noted that the senate president, up to now politically so conciliatory and bent on reconciliation, showed wholly new character traits that had remained completely hidden from me and those close to him. Without personal responsibility for these excesses by the police, but apparently approving of them, Greiser received the reports of merciless SS-leaders. In these first few weeks as CdZ he tried to win authority through very aggressive and self-confident conduct.'[56]

Was this really a new Greiser? In his last years in Danzig, Greiser had showed a more conciliatory face toward League officials and Polish negotiators. But he was always merciless toward political opponents. The main difference between Greiser in Danzig and Greiser in Posen was not the man, but the situation. In Danzig, Greiser had been constrained by the Free City's constitution, the League of Nations, and his rivalry with Forster. In Nazi-occupied Poland, these no longer obtained. The methods Greiser employed in the Posen area were a dramatic escalation, rather than a new departure, of what he had advocated against 'enemies' in Danzig.

Although Hitler allegedly told Greiser that he would become Gauleiter in early September, this does not seem to have been a final decision. Instead, the matter was wrapped up in ongoing discussions about how best to organize Nazi rule in occupied Poland. Hitler briefly entertained the notion of a much reduced Polish state that would include the area around Posen. Next, he considered a longer period of military rule. In late September, Hans Frank, the future head of the General Government, took up the position of CdZ for all of occupied Poland. Greiser was thus briefly subordinate to Frank. For a short time, Frank's headquarters were even in the Posen Castle, the very same building in which Greiser worked; perhaps the tensions that marked these two men's future relations began then. In early October, however, Forster met with Hitler and urged him to expand the Danzig Gau through the annexation of West Prussia. By now the Führer had come to believe that a speedy end to military rule would allow for harsher anti-Polish policies in the occupied areas.[57] On 8 October, Hitler thus decreed that two new Reichsgaus of West Prussia and Posen would be annexed to the Third Reich on 1 November. This decree also stated that two other Polish territories, the districts of Kattowitz and Zichenau, would be annexed to the existing provinces of Silesia and East Prussia respectively.[58] On 21 October, however, Hitler decided to carry out the annexation of western Poland a week earlier than originally planned; 26 October was now the official annexation date.

Martin Bormann, deputy head of the NSDAP party chancellery, was instrumental in the final appointment of Greiser as Gauleiter in the Posen area.[59] The party needed to find Greiser a suitable position after his Danzig ouster; not least, the former senate president had enough of an international reputation that simply dropping him from the political scene might have caused foreign tongues to wag. Unsurprisingly, Forster opposed Greiser's appointment.[60] On 4 October, a memo stemming from the NSDAP Party Chancellery listed the names of various individuals under consideration for Gauleiter positions in the newly acquired Polish territories. It noted that 'the use of Greiser is probably already settled.'[61] Formally, however, Greiser was named Gauleiter only on 21 October.[62] The day before, the minister of the interior, Wilhelm Frick, wrote that the Führer had also decided on Greiser as Reichsstatthalter in the Warthegau.[63] Does the late date of these appointments have any significance? Perhaps some institution or person once again raised doubts about Greiser's suitability for high-ranking Nazi posts. Or perhaps the decision was made much earlier, but only officially approved at the later date. In any event, on 2 November, Frick came to Posen to inaugurate Greiser as Reichsstatthalter.

Greiser's installation as Reichsstatthalter on 3 November involved considerable pomp and circumstance. It was intended to underscore the fact that the old German East was now once again securely in the German fold. Throughout the Reich, newspaper coverage was devoted to the elaborate ceremony.[64] The day began when future members of the Hitler Youth and the League of German Girls sang songs to greet Greiser and Frick in front of the Hotel Bazar. The two men then proceeded to the Posen Castle courtyard, where they inspected Army, Air Force, and Self-Defense–Force units. The official state ceremony of inauguration took place in the throne room of the castle. Draped with Nazi swastika flags and other symbols of the Third Reich, the room was an imposing setting. As Siegmund later wrote: 'The stage management was exemplary. The muted lighting, the adroit placing of the sea of flags, the appropriate classical-heroic background music played by a large orchestra, and the predominantly uniformed, often highly decorated audience, produced an overwhelming impression...'[65] After church bells in Posen rang, the orchestra played Hayden's Emperor-Quartet. Thereafter, the general of the artillery, Walter Petzel, welcomed guests. After a cantata was played, Frick gave the keynote speech. As he told Greiser, 'You give the Führer and me the best confidence that as Reichsstatthalter you will master great tasks with a sure hand according to the will of the Führer and the Reich government. These will demand patience—and in these times, in which the very existence of the Fatherland is at stake—your every commitment.' In brief remarks, Greiser thanked Frick, and assured him that 'All of us in the new and youngest part of Reich territory promise that we will always devote all of our strength to completely fulfilling the expectations that the Führer has for us.' After the Gau propaganda leader, Wilhelm Maul, honored Hitler, the ceremony ended with the playing of the 'songs of the nation'—the first verses of the German national anthem and the Horst-Wessel song, the NSDAP anthem. Frick and Greiser then continued on to the Lukas Cemetery to lay wreaths on the graves of martyred ethnic Germans. They listened while the former leader of the German minority in Posen, Dr. Kurt Lück, described 'the sufferings of ethnic Germans under Polish frightful rule (*Schreckensherrschaft*).'[66] The day concluded with an evening tea reception in the town hall. With imperial imagery, Nazi symbols, German music, martial tones, pompous rhetoric, and a cult of the dead, Greiser formally initiated his rule of the Warthegau.

The Gau that Greiser now ruled was known as the Reichsgau Posen until renamed the Reichsgau Wartheland on 29 January 1940 (after the river, the Warta, that flowed through the region).[67] More commonly, the area was referred to as the 'Warthegau.'[68] In 1939, it had some 4.9 million inhabitants. These included 4,189,000 Poles, or 85.1 percent of the population, and 325,000 Germans, or 6.6 percent of the population. There were approximately 400,000 Jews, and 23,000 persons belonging to other nationalities (mostly Russians, Czechs, and Ukrainians).[69] This population lived on some 43,943 square kilometers of territory, roughly the combined land mass of Massachusetts, Vermont, and New Hampshire. 47.8 percent of all Polish land annexed to the Third Reich was included in the Warthegau.

Map 4.1 Districts and Sub-Districts in the Warthegau, 15 February 1942.
Source: Wolf Gruner, *Jewish Forced Labor Under the Nazis: Economic Needs and Racial Aims, 1938–1944* (Cambridge: Cambridge University Press, 2006), 179.

The Gau was the second largest of the forty-one (forty-two as of 1941) Nazi Gaus in terms of both territory and population; only Saxony had a larger population, and East Prussia a larger land mass.[70]

In contrast to much of Germany, the Warthegau was very rural. Roughly 50 percent of the population worked in the agricultural sector, and 81 percent of all land was used for agricultural purposes.[71] Industry, in turn, was relatively underdeveloped. The Warthegau had only two cities of note. Posen, located 150 miles east of Berlin, served as the Gau capital. In 1939, the city had a population of 273,000, including roughly 6,000 ethnic Germans. Łódź, the second largest city in Poland, also became part of the Warthegau. It had 684,000 inhabitants, including some 54,000 ethnic Germans.[72] It marked the eastern-most part of the Gau. Long an important center of textile production, it was the Gau's only important industrial region.

The Warthegau was divided into three districts, Posen, Hohensalza and Kalisch, each named after the city or town that served as district capital. These three districts, in turn, were divided into thirty-eight rural and six city sub-districts (*Kreise*).[73] Kalisch, however, soon proved impractical as a district capital; it was too small and faced a severe housing shortage. On 1 April 1940, the Kalisch district seat was moved to Lodsch, and the district was renamed accordingly.[74] Ten days later, Lodsch was renamed in honor of General Karl Litzmann, a Nazi supporter who had conquered the city during World War I. According to Goebbels, the renaming of Lodsch to Litzmannstadt took place 'on Greiser's suggestion.'[75] Greiser may have gotten the idea from the wife of Lodsch district president Friedrich Uebelhoer. Ingrid, Greiser's daughter, who was present at the renaming of the city, later wrote that 'This name stemmed from Mrs. Uebelhoer and the Führer immediately approved it...'[76]

The territorial makeup of the Warthegau had no historical rationale. Of the three districts, only Posen district had belonged entirely to Prussia prior to World War I. Roughly half of Hohensalza district and a small area of Litzmannstadt district had also belonged to Prussia. Most of the rest of this region had been part of the Russian Empire, but a small area of Litzmannstadt district had been located in the Austro-Hungarian Empire. These historical divisions remained important. The interwar Polish government was never able to even out the different levels of infrastructure that characterized the three former empires. As a former Prussian province, Posen was relatively well developed and thus more 'German' than other parts of the Gau. To many Germans, though, it was not up to Reich standards; twenty years of 'Polish mismanagement' had allegedly undermined Prussian achievements.[77] Most Germans thought Litzmannstadt utterly primitive. Large areas of that district lacked running water, paved roads, decent housing, and other basic amenities.[78] Reich Germans, adopting the Nazis' hyper-racialized categories, attributed the differing appearances of Posen and Litzmannstadt to the degree of Germanness (or lack thereof) in each. Melding the disparate areas of the Warthegau into a coherent 'German' region would prove a challenge for Nazi occupation authorities.

The decision to join Lodsch to the Warthegau was hotly disputed. The city was initially slated for inclusion in the General Government, and Hans Frank very much wished to leave it there. Greiser, however, wanted Lodsch in his Gau so that his territory would have an industrial base. He had the support of Hitler and Hermann Göring, who wished to have Lodsch in the Warthegau so that its industry could be more easily integrated into the Reich economy.[79] The ethnic Germans in Lodsch also clamored for their city's inclusion in the Reich. They insisted to Himmler, Goebbels, and Frick, all of whom visited the city between 28 October and 3 November, that they wanted to live inside the borders of the Third Reich.[80] Demographic considerations also played a role in the decision to add Lodsch to the Warthegau. The ethnic Germans in the city would add substantial numbers of ethnic Germans to the Gau, and would make their eventual resettlement to the Reich unnecessary.[81]

On 4 November 1939, Hitler told Hans Frank that Lodsch would become part of the Warthegau. Three days later, Greiser went to the city, where, according to newspaper accounts, the German population enthusiastically received him.[82] On 9 November, in celebration of the 1923 Beer Hall Putsch, Greiser officially annexed Lodsch to the Warthegau.[83] In a telegram to Hitler, he declared: 'I report to you the accomplished annexation of the Lodsch area to the Warthegau. For the first time, over 30,000 free and unhindered Germans of this city are gathered here today for a powerful rally and thank you for their final liberation from servitude and repression.'[84] Despite his satisfaction with the annexation, the addition of Lodsch to the Warthegau proved a mixed blessing for Greiser. It certainly worsened his relations with Frank—and in due time, Frank would get his revenge. While the city brought the Warthegau sorely needed industry, its infrastructure demanded enormously expensive improvements.

Lodsch and its surroundings also increased by fourfold the number of Jews in the Gau.[85] The city alone had approximately 227,000 Jewish inhabitants.[86] Greiser's eagerness to have Lodsch despite its Jewish population may be variously interpreted. He may have felt that economic benefits outweighed the city's negative racial makeup. Less outrightly anti-Semitic than other Nazis, he may have been willing to tolerate the presence of Jews in his Gau. He may also have assumed that the Jews would be gone soon anyway; by November 1939, plans to deport them were underway. Nonetheless, the inclusion of so many Jews in his Gau meant that Greiser would soon preside over the second largest ghetto in Poland and eventually the first mass gassings of Jews. But for Lodsch, he might never have played a 'motor' role in the Final Solution.[87]

While Greiser was successful in the annexation of Lodsch, he had no luck with other attempts to expand the Gau's territory. Throughout 1939 and 1940, he pestered central authorities to extend the borders of the Warthegau to both the east and the west. In March 1940, he wrote a letter to Frick in which he stated that he had agreed not to reopen border questions during the war. He complained, however, that Forster had grabbed lands that rightfully belonged to the Warthegau. Greiser was particularly annoyed that Forster had taken the Bromberg area since it had a large ethnic German population. As he wrote: 'This has significantly disadvantaged the Reichsgau Wartheland. This disadvantage becomes ever more noticeable during the reconstruction of the Warthegau, especially now during wartime, since favorable *völkisch* starting points, either in terms of material or personnel, are not present.' Greiser stated for the record that immediately after the war he wanted areas that had earlier belonged to the Prussian province of Posen to be joined to the Warthegau. He also wanted a small exchange of lands between the Warthegau and Silesia.[88] On 2 April, Greiser met with Hitler and, following the meeting, told Frick that the Führer had said that border changes pertaining to the western part of the Warthegau might be made during the war. Frick, however, objected to any such changes. He worried that if border issues were reopened, Forster might make additional claims. Frick was also concerned that the Warthegau would become too large and that legal difficulties—related to the fact that a different legal system obtained in the newly annexed areas—might surface. Frick thus squashed Greiser's efforts to alter the Warthegau's boundaries.[89]

But Greiser still did not give up. In 1940, he was eager to annex two sub-districts that were currently in the General Government, Petrikau and Tomaschow. Bormann intervened on Greiser's behalf, arguing that these two areas' textile industry was closely linked to Litzmannstadt and that the current border divided an area best administered as one. In addition, some 50,000 ethnic Germans lived in these sub-districts; this alone was a good reason to make the areas part of the Warthegau. In September 1940, Greiser had an apparent victory when, after a lunch with Hitler, the Führer ordered Petrikau and Tomaschow to be joined to the Warthegau. But Greiser's victory was short lived. Since Frank refused to relinquish the districts, Hitler asked Greiser and Frank to meet and resolve the issue. At their November 1940 meeting, Greiser shelved the annexation of the two sub-districts; he and Frank agreed that the resolution of all outstanding border issues would be postponed until after the war's end.

But the issue of Petrikau and Tomaschow came up once again in 1941, when Frank's territory was considerably enlarged through the annexation of Galicia to the General Government. It was now thought that Frank might be less sensitive to a loss of territory on his western border. Yet again, though, he refused to cede any land.[90] In December 1941, Lammers wrote a memorandum to all Gauleiters stating that Hitler did not want any Gau border changes for the duration of the war.[91] Despite all of Greiser's efforts, after the annexation of Lodsch in November 1939, no further border changes were made to the Warthegau.

Although the Warthegau was officially annexed to Germany, an important border remained between what was now called the 'annexed eastern territories' (*eingegliederte Ostgebiete*) and the 'Old Reich' (*Altreich*). The customs border was moved east to the border between the Warthegau and the General Government, but Himmler insisted on a police border between the Warthegau and the Old Reich. All individuals traveling to and from the Warthegau were subject to passport controls.[92] This prevented Poles from migrating to the Old Reich. It also served to control German population movement. Gau authorities were eager to keep certain Germans out of the Warthegau, particularly those with Polish relations who wished to intercede on behalf of their persecuted relatives. They were also anxious to keep certain Germans in the Warthegau, especially ethnic German resettlers who might prefer the Old Reich. The police border thus trapped some Germans in the Gau.

In September and October 1939, Greiser pulled together a staff that would help him run the Warthegau. Despite the upheaval of the war years, it remained remarkably constant. Greiser chose his cousin, Harry Siegmund, to run his office; Siegmund's title was personal advisor (*Referent*) to Greiser; he held a civil-service ranking of senior civil servant (*Oberregierungsrat*). With some brief interruptions for military service, Siegmund held this position until 1944. According to both his memoirs, *Rückblick* (Looking Back) and a 1966 statement given to state prosecutors, Siegmund kept Greiser's appointment calendar, received petitioners, served as head of protocol, and took care of all administrative tasks related to what he termed a 'president's office.' As contemporary documents show, however, Siegmund, as part of Greiser's official personal staff (*Adjutantur*), also issued directives on his boss's behalf to state officials.[93]

Map 4.2 Nazi Territorial Units, Central and Eastern Europe, late 1941.

Greiser brought much of his personal staff from Danzig to Posen. Fritz Harder, who had served in the Wehrmacht from 1934 to 1939 and then briefly in the Danzig police force, was his adjutant. In Posen, Harder had responsibility for Greiser's personal security. He also organized the fleet of Reichsstatthalter cars, received visitors and set up appointments, and took care of Greiser's personal matters.[94] Colonel Willi Bethke, the retired chief of the Danzig Uniformed Police (*Schutzpolizei*) also came to Posen; he had been the German commander in the infamous assault on the main Polish post office in Danzig at the start of the war.[95] One of Greiser's closest friends, the two men shared a passion for hunting; in 1943, Greiser named Bethke his successor as Gau master huntsman (*Gaujägermeister*).[96] Greiser's personal secretary in Danzig, Elsa Claaßen, arrived in Posen in September 1939. In 1966, she stated that her main responsibility was Greiser's personal correspondence.[97] Claaßen was the secretary who typed Greiser's letters to top Nazi leaders such as Himmler and Bormann. She also had charge of a safe in which she filed particularly sensitive materials. According to Siegmund, only Greiser had a key to this safe, and 'no one . . . saw the letters filed here that Greiser received or sent with the stamp "strictly secret Reich matter, only to be opened personally." '[98] Greiser also brought his cook and driver from Danzig.[99]

Numerous other Danzigers came to Posen. According to Siegmund, 'in the end the invasion from Danzig included more than fifty people, which aroused astonishment, but contributed to Greiser's prestige in the administration then forming in Posen.' Siegmund argues that those who came to Posen were 'loyal supporters of Senate President Greiser, mainly qualified experts, who had highly regarded and supported their former boss because of his more realistic and politically moderate state leadership. Because of this, many had more or less fallen into disfavor with Gauleiter Forster and they saw little chance of working successfully in the changed Danzig circumstances.'[100] Siegmund's assumption that these civil servants gravitated to Greiser because of his alleged 'moderate' policies is questionable; in the Warthegau, at least, they had few scruples about implementing Greiser's brutal policies. Those who came included the former head of the senate's Foreign Department, Dr. Viktor Böttcher, now district president in Posen; Helmut Froböss, the former Danzig police president, now president of the provincial high court; Dr. Karl-Hans Fuchs, former spokesman for the Danzig Senate, now head of the Gau Press Office; Ernst Kendzia, former head of the Labor Department in the Danzig Senate, now president of the State Labor Office; Erwin Olsen, former chief of personnel in the Danzig Senate (he had changed his Polish-sounding name Olschewski to Olsen), now sub-district magistrate in Rawitsch; and Paul Batzer, former senator for propaganda in Danzig, now Gau economics advisor. With the exception of Batzer, Greiser awarded all of these individuals, as well as Siegmund and Bethke, the 'Cross of

Danzig' medal in August 1940. As the award ceremony suggested, there was a Danzig clique in the Gau.[101] But although the Danzigers enjoyed privileged access to the Gauleiter, their influence should not be overstated. With the exception of Greiser, the most powerful officials in the Gau all came from the Old Reich.

August Jäger, Greiser's deputy Reichsstatthalter (but not deputy Gauleiter), enjoyed considerable influence in Gau politics. A veteran Prussian civil servant born in 1887, Jäger had joined the NSDAP in 1934.[102] The son of a minister, Jäger had, according to one author, 'a pathological case of church hatred;' he was even nicknamed 'hunter of churches' (*Kirchen-Jäger*), a pun on his last name, the German word for hunter.[103] As state commissar for the Lutheran Church in the Prussian Ministry of Culture, Jäger had been a central figure in the 1933–4 Nazi anti-church offensive.[104] Among other efforts, he had tried to introduce an oath in which all pastors would have had to swear loyalty to Hitler. Opposition to this was so intense, however, that Jäger lost his job so that Hitler could save face with Protestant leaders.[105] Jäger's placement in the Warthegau may have anticipated anti-church policies in the Gau.

By all accounts, Greiser and Jäger had an amiable relationship. Greiser trusted his deputy and gave him considerable decision-making latitude. In 1946, he wrote of Jäger: 'for five long years we stood faithfully side by side and he was always for me one of the best comrades. In any case, he belonged to those on whom I could inwardly depend and there were very few of those.'[106] While Jäger was loyal to Greiser, he nonetheless worked to extend his own authority. He issued, for example, a directive that all correspondence to the Reichsstatthalter 'is without exception to be conducted through my hands.' He also exercised a tight hold over access to Greiser. As he insisted, 'reports and consultations with the Reichsstatthalter are to take place only with my consent, unless the Reichsstatthalter directly demanded a report or ordered otherwise. In this case I ask that I be informed by telephone or personally before completion of the report or, if that is not possible, immediately thereafter. In addition, the result of a consultation with the Reichsstatthalter is in every case to be reported to me.'[107] Jäger remained deputy Reichsstatthalter throughout the Warthegau years.

Jäger worked closely with Dr. Herbert Mehlhorn. Mehlhorn developed excellent relations with both Himmler and Greiser and thus held considerable influence in the Gau.[108] Born in 1903, he was trained as a lawyer.

Mehlhorn joined the NSDAP in 1931, and joined the SS in 1933, after which he gave up his law practice for a career in the Security Service (*Sicherheitsdienst* or SD). Mehlhorn exemplified the well-educated, technocratic, and fanatically Nazi sort of police official recruited by Werner Best on Himmler's behalf.[109] In 1939, however, he fell into disfavor with Heydrich and was relegated to the CdZ staff for Posen. In the Warthegau, Mehlhorn headed Department I (General, Domestic, and Financial Matters) in the Reichsstatthalter agency. Mehlhorn formulated many of the decrees issued by Greiser. In 1941, he was also named responsible for all 'Jewish questions;' as such, he helped organize the murder of Jews in the Gau.[110] In 1943, Mehlhorn became acting district president in Oppeln (Upper Silesia).[111] The license plate numbers assigned to Jäger and Mehlhorn suggest their positions in the Warthegau hierarchy: Greiser's car bore the number P 1, Jäger's P 2 and Mehlhorn's P 3; Siegmund's was P 4.[112]

While state officials played an important role in shaping Warthegau policies, security officials carried out the ethnic-cleansing and genocidal measures that characterized the Gau. From 1939 to 1943, Wilhelm Koppe served as Himmler's higher SS and police leader (*Höhere SS- und Polizeiführer* or HSSPF) in the Warthegau. Born in Hildesheim in 1896, Koppe served in World War I. During the interwar years, he owned a wholesale food business. He joined the NSDAP in 1930 and the SS in 1932. He briefly headed the SS in Danzig in 1935–6. He then led the Gestapo in Saxony from 1936 to 199.[113] Koppe was known for his 'uncommonly hectic,' 'spontaneously aggressive,' and 'excessively restless' style of work; according to one official, Koppe's motto was 'whirl, whirl (*Wirbeln, wirbeln*).'[114] As Himmler's deputy in the Gau, Koppe had responsibility for all SS and police agencies in the Gau. In practice, however, he was not always able to control his underlings in the SD, the Security Police (*Sicherheitspolizei* or Sipo), the Order Police, the Central Immigration Office (*Einwandererzentrale* or EWZ), and the Central Resettlement Office (*Umwandererzentrale* or UWZ). In the first half of 1940, Greiser and Koppe also had a power struggle that the Gauleiter won.[115]

Once Koppe accepted his subordinate role to Greiser, the two men apparently got along well. Indeed, in 1943, when Koppe left the Warthegau, the *Ostdeutscher Beobachter* recorded the remarks each man made at a farewell ceremony. The Gauleiter 'recalled that already ten years ago, namely in the former Free City of Danzig, he had worked together with Senior Group Leader [*Obergruppenführer*] Koppe as the then leader of the general

SS. When they separated then, both had clung to the feeling that beyond a working relationship a strong tie of comradeship had grown up between them. And this comradeship had proven itself in an outstanding manner in the four years in which SS-Senior Group Leader Koppe had worked in the Reichsgau Wartheland.' Koppe was no less effusive. As he reportedly stated, 'When the Reichsführer-SS sent him to Posen on 30 September 1939, he happily followed this call with a joyful heart because he knew that a man named Arthur Greiser stood at the head of the Gau. The hope for an ideal cooperation that he then had was in reality surpassed by far.'[116] Even in a 1960 criminal investigation, when it was clearly disadvantageous to admit good relations with Greiser, Koppe stated: 'I had close professional contact with Gauleiter and Reichsstatthalter Greiser. I knew Greiser from my Danzig time when Greiser was senate president . . . I was on good terms with Greiser.'[117] As Koppe's Polish biographer has written, '. . . one thing is certain: both men cooperated harmoniously in the work of carrying out crimes against the people of the "Warthegau." '[118] The good working relationship between Greiser and Koppe after summer 1940 is one reason why the Warthegau saw such radical Nazi experiments; unlike in other Gaus, no conflicts between the Gauleiter and the HSSPF hindered the carrying out of the Final Solution or other demographic plans.

Several other security officials were also influential in the Gau. Ernst Damzog, the inspector of the Sipo and SD in Posen, eventually organized the personnel that staffed the killing center at Chełmno.[119] Albert Rapp, the head of the SD-Main Office (*Leitabschnitt*) in Posen, organized mass deportations of Poles and Jews from the Warthegau to the General Government in the winter of 1939–40. Rapp's successor, Rolf-Heinz Höppner, also served as deputy and later chief of the Gau Office for *Volkstum* Affairs (*Gauamt für Volkstumsfragen*); he played a crucial role in radicalizing the Gau's demographic policies. Helmut Bischoff headed the State Police Office (*Staatspolizeistelle*) in Posen in 1940–1, and Hermann Krumey headed the UWZ in Litzmannstadt. Heinz Reinefarth served as HSSPF in 1944–5.

Among leading officials in the Warthegau, it is striking how many had connections to the German East or Germany's former colonial empire.[120] Greiser, of course, grew up in the Posen area. The officials he brought from Danzig had all spent long years exposed to militant anti-Polish propaganda. Siegmund grew up among the German minority in Latvia.[121] Böttcher had served as a German colonial official in Cameroon.[122] Even many of the officials who came directly from the Old Reich to the Warthegau had links to the East. Koppe had briefly lived in Danzig in the mid-1930s. Damzog was born in Strasbourg and spent much of his career as a police official in eastern borderlands areas. Three other leading security officials, Bischoff, Krumey, and Reinefarth, had grown up in borderlands areas—respectively in Silesia, in the Sudetenland, and in Gnesen, the northern part of the Prussian province of Posen.[123] At the outbreak of war, Bischoff was chief of the Gestapo office in the West Prussian town of Köslin. In 1939, he headed the Task Force (*Einsatzkommando*) I/IV that committed various atrocities during the September campaign, including the murder of dozens of Poles in reprisal for the Bromberg 'Bloody Sunday.' Much later, Bischoff explained that for his Task Force he particularly liked men who had experience as police officials along the German–Polish border. As he stated: 'their many years of service on the border [had] accustomed them to the methods and character traits of the Poles.'[124] A similar dynamic seems to have been at work in Posen: men from the 'East,' it was presumed, would have the 'proper' attitude toward the Polish population.

In fall 1939, Reich, NSDAP, and Warthegau officials grappled with the issue of legal authority in the Warthegau (and Danzig–West Prussia). A variety of issues and interests were at stake. Interior Minister Frick wished to use the new territories to model his vision of a streamlined administration of the Third Reich. Like other Reich ministers, he wanted to protect his jurisdictional competence against any encroachments by powerful Reichsstatthalters. Party chancellery officials, however, viewed the newly annexed territories as staging grounds for new forms of Nazi rule and practice.[125] For them, it was crucial that Reichsstatthalters in the annexed areas have adequate authority to carry out the Nazi revolution. Greiser, of course, wanted to enhance his own personal autonomy. The definition of legal authority in the Warthegau thus addresses central questions: How much authority did Greiser really have? How much could he personally influence developments in the Warthegau? In large measure, the answers to these questions turned on the powers accorded Reichsstatthalters in the new Reichsgaus. And these, it turned out, were remarkably muddled.

In 1933, the Nazis created the position of Reichsstatthalter in the non-Prussian areas of the German Reich to represent central authority in local states (the similar position of Oberpräsident [senior president] had long been in place in the Prussian provinces). Initially, the Reichsstatthalters, subordinate to the Interior Ministry, were intended to undercut local parliamentary institutions. Frequently, but not always, the Gauleiter served as Reichsstatthalter. The borders of Gaus and local German states, however, were not the same. This led to a welter of overlapping Gau and local state jurisdictions. Gauleiters, for example, sometimes held state authority in only parts of their Gaus or even in other Gaus. For Frick, this situation represented administrative chaos. He attempted to rationalize party and state authority with the introduction of so-called Reichsgaus. This began with the 'Greater Hamburg Law' of 1937, and continued with the creation of six Austrian Reichsgaus and the Reichsgau Sudetenland in 1939. A Reichsgau was a territorial unit in which the Gau and local state borders were identical. The office of Gauleiter–Reichsstatthalter was combined, and the Gauleiter was directly subordinate to Hitler.[126]

In the newly annexed areas, Hitler insisted, the territorial chiefs were to be directly responsible to him.[127] No bureaucratic or other hindrances were to stand in the way of their carrying out the measures necessary to Germanize the areas.[128] In fall 1939, Greiser and Forster were thus given enhanced powers as Reichsstatthalters. In his 8 October decree (which incorporated the occupied western territories of Poland into the Reich), Hitler deemed that 'all administrative branches were to be subordinate' to the Reichsstatthalter.[129] Unlike in other Reichsgaus, for example, communication between the district presidents (*Regierungspräsidenten*) and Reich ministries was to go through the office of the Reichsstatthalter. Even more important, the new Reichsstatthalters had a general right to issue directives to the Reich justice, finance, railway, and postal administrations, which operated independently of the Reichsstatthalters in the other Reichsgaus. The Ministries of Justice and Finance opposed this expansion of Reichsstatthalter powers, but their objections were overridden.[130] In a December 1939 memorandum, Frick reiterated and justified the unusual powers of the Reichsstatthalters in the newest Reichsgaus: 'in light of the current difficult conditions, this arrangement was arrived at so as to secure for the period of reconstruction under all circumstances the unified and tight leadership of the entire administration in both Reichsgaus.'[131]

But for all the talk of streamlined administration, the lines of authority in the Warthegau were ambiguous; this situation was typical of the administrative chaos that prevailed in Nazi Germany. In his speech at Greiser's inauguration as Reichsstatthalter, Frick declared that the 'Reichsstatthalter carries out the state administration at the Reichsgau level as the representative of the Führer and on behalf of the Reich government.' Greiser, however, was also to follow the 'technical directives' of the Interior Ministry. Frick further elaborated that 'the Reichsstatthalter is responsible for all administrative branches. This means that the entire administration in the Posen and West-Prussian Reichsgaus is subordinate to the Reichsstatthalter. At least for the time being, there are no special administrations there...' In this passage, Frick meant special administrations pertaining to justice, finance, railway, and postal operations. But shortly thereafter, he mentioned that there would indeed be special administrations in the Warthegau: those related to the 'political, economic, and *volkstum*-related circumstances.'[132] These, it soon transpired, included the Central Trust Agency for the East (*Haupttreuhandstelle Ost* or HTO), which oversaw the plunder of Polish and Jewish property, and many agencies linked to Himmler's police empire, including the Ethnic German Liaison Office (*Volksdeutsche Mittelstelle* or VoMi), the EWZ, and the UWZ. At least initially, these institutions sharply limited Greiser's authority over demographic developments in his Gau. The administrative chain of command in the new Gaus was thus confused, if not downright contradictory. Greiser was directly responsible to Hitler, yet he was to follow Interior Ministry directives. He was to have total administrative control of his Gau, yet numerous Reich institutions might (and, as it turned out, would) maintain independent operations in his Gau. It's no wonder that Greiser spent his entire time in power feuding with other agencies and institutions.

These conflicts began immediately—indeed, they were well underway even before Greiser was officially named Reichsstatthalter. As early as 3 October 1939, Mehlhorn noted that the CdZ staff had headed off attempts by central authorities to interfere with civilian rule: 'The initial strong attempts by central Reich authorities to issue direct orders were thwarted by the strict order to all administrative departments to observe official channels [of command].' According to Mehlhorn, rather than accepting orders from Reich ministries, the various departments of the CdZ administration were told to follow orders issued only by the military commander in Posen and/or the CdZ administration.[133] Once Greiser became Reichsstatthalter, policy in his Gau became a matter of dispute between him and central authorities, as well as between rival Reich institutions.[134] While the Party

Chancellery wished to give Greiser unfettered power so that he could carry out Germanization measures, the Ministry of Interior was eager to maintain control over areas that it deemed under its authority. Greiser, for obvious reasons, generally allied himself with the Party Chancellery against the Ministry of Interior.

In fall 1939, conflict erupted over the appointment of sub-district magistrates in the Warthegau.[135] Greiser did not have enough men in his Gau to appoint individuals of his choosing to all open positions. He was thus forced to rely on men sent by the Interior Ministry. But Greiser (and the Party Chancellery) wanted magistrates who would simultaneously serve as the NSDAP sub-district leader (*Kreisleiter*), just as he served in the state position of Reichsstatthalter and the party office of Gauleiter. This was to ensure that the NSDAP would have a decisive grassroots influence in the new Reichsgau; no local administrative official, bound by a sense of law or precedent, was to stand in the way of the Nazi reordering of the Warthegau. Interior Ministry officials, however, believed that the job of magistrate demanded administrative experience, which most NSDAP activists did not have.

The stakes were high. In December 1939, Greiser removed some of the magistrates who had initially been appointed by the Interior Ministry. The Party Chancellery, in turn, sent a number of men to the Warthegau to serve as sub-district party leaders and also, as of January 1940, as magistrates. Frick was furious; he viewed these actions as an infringement of his ministerial authority. After communications among Frick, Göring, Greiser, and the Party Chancellery, a compromise was reached. Twenty-three magistrates would come from the Ministry of the Interior; seven of these were deemed insufficiently politically active, and so would not serve simultaneously as NSDAP sub-district leaders. At the same time, fifteen magistrates would come from the Nazi movement, many of whom had no administrative training.[136]

Greiser also had a personnel conflict with the Ministry for Food and Agriculture. At issue was who would occupy the post of head of the Office of Agricultural Policy. Greiser had chosen Heinrich Pehle, a Nazi activist and department leader in the Pomeranian administration. But Reich farmers' leader and minister for food and agriculture, R. Walther Darré, found Pehle unacceptable. Darré's state secretary, Werner Willikens, met with Greiser and thought that he had secured the Gauleiter's agreement that Pehle would not hold the position. Willikens then wrote to Greiser that he was sending Dr. Karl Wilhelm Reinhardt to be director of the Office. Greiser responded churlishly. He insisted that he had never agreed with Willikens on the matter. He then added, 'On no account will I be forced on personnel matters. In view of the course you have adopted I reject Dr. Reinhardt in principle and for always. I have instructed Pehle to take up his service with me again.'[137] Darré now asked Frick to intervene 'through appropriate measures vis-à-vis the Reichsstatthalter to create the necessary conditions so that a proper administration can be set up in the Warthegau.'[138] In December, Darré and Greiser reached an agreement that Pehle would occupy the position.[139] Greiser had prevailed.

The affair illustrates how determined Greiser was to thwart Reich ministerial interference in his Gau. In his conflicts with Berlin ministries, Greiser displayed unusual zeal and arrogance. As Siegmund reported, some of Greiser's letters 'were so aggressive and in their tone with a superior Reich minister so unusual,' that the state secretary in the Interior Ministry, Hans Pfundtner, asked him to have a moderating effect on his cousin since '[Greiser's] conduct was hurting his reputation.' Although Siegmund supposedly mentioned the matter to him, Greiser did not change his behavior.[140] Over the next years, Greiser pushed to expand his autonomy and, as subsequent chapters illustrate, was able to impose his wishes on the Ministries of Interior, Ecclesiastical Affairs, Foreign Affairs, and Armaments and War Production.[141]

Greiser's Reichsstatthalter position was also enhanced by the initial legal vacuum in the annexed territories. Nazi authorities delayed the introduction of German law, but Polish law was no longer valid. As a result, although ethnic Germans were considered German citizens and thus subject to German law, 'non-Germans' were not subject to any legal order during the first months of occupation.[142] Even some Nazis found this situation problematic. Justice Ministry officials, for example, were anxious to end the legal uncertainty. Bormann, however, opposed the wholesale introduction of German law. He preferred a scenario whereby the Reichsstatthalters would decree elements of German law as they deemed fit.[143] In June 1940, the German penal code was introduced into the newly annexed territories. The implementing decree, however, specified that in the application of law, jurists were to take into account the objectives of the ongoing ethnic struggle. Likewise, the German civil code was formally implemented in September 1941 with the understanding that 'ethnic interests' would shape the application of the law.[144] In practice, such provisos permitted sheer legal arbitrariness. In the end, just as Bormann wished, Greiser ruled the Warthegau largely by decree. This was particularly true of measures related to Germanization; Greiser regularly issued piecemeal legislation to advance Nazi ethnic-cleansing projects.

Greiser also used his position as Gauleiter to strengthen his authority. Kurt Schmalz, the deputy Gauleiter, later stated that there were between 35,000 and 40,000 party members in the Warthegau.[145] By September 1940, the party was organized into forty-one district organizations, 501 local chapters, 2,425 party cells, and 10,380 party blocks. There were also roughly 100,000 members in the NSDAP's various ancillary organizations (not including the youth organizations), but these likely included individuals with multiple such memberships.[146]

Greiser had complete control over the NSDAP in the Gau. He was very careful to ensure that no rivals to his authority could emerge from the party ranks; his first deputy Gauleiter, for example, was a notorious drunk.[147] Thereafter, Schmalz, who had joined the NSDAP in 1925, took over the position.[148] Schmalz was widely seen as lacking in leadership skills. Batzer later recalled that Greiser told him that he took on Schmalz 'because Schmalz could never become Gauleiter and therefore posed no danger for him.'[149] Since Greiser refused to make Schmalz deputy Reichsstatthalter, Schmalz had no executive authority. Apparently, Schmalz found his position so powerless that he volunteered for military service and was away from Posen for much of 1943 and 1944; no other deputy, however, was brought in to replace him.[150]

Greiser encouraged a personality cult of himself. In the first issue of the *Ostdeutscher Beobachter* on 1 November 1939 (the paper was actually just the continuation of the renamed *Posener Tageblatt* [Posen Daily]), the front page featured a portrait of Greiser in which the new, rather corpulent Gauleiter stared rigidly forward in his medal-bedecked uniform. It was accompanied by a hagiographic portrayal of Greiser's character and past deeds, written by Karl Hans Fuchs.[151] The following spring, another biographical portrait of Greiser was published. Titled 'He who wishes to live, thus fights . . .,' it recalled various episodes in his life in which Greiser had struggled against the English: as a World War I fighter pilot off the shores of Dunkirk as well as in the diplomatic negotiations with Anthony Eden in Geneva. According to the article, 'All of these episodes have their significance not in the personal, but rather in the exemplary.'[152]

Greiser was a conspicuous and, at first, beneficent leader. As Siegmund wrote, he 'liked to travel around his new territory and, like a potentate of earlier times, to personally concern himself with everything and to make decisions off the cuff.' Initially, Greiser distributed cash and other assistance to his subjects; the money for such disbursements came from a fund of confiscated Polish property that held roughly one million Reichsmarks (RM)—about $6,000,000 in 2007 dollars.[153] His cousin remembered, 'it became Greiser's obsession to give a cow to the countless resettled small farmers that he met on his trips through the countryside. That was talked about in Berlin . . . and state secretary Pfundtner asked me if possible to prevent this dubious practice.'[154] Greiser soon abandoned such largesse, but he was still frequently underway in his Gau. He wanted to be loved and admired by his subjects—or at least his German subjects.

Like other Gauleiters, Greiser linked his person to his Gau so as to enhance his personal authority.[155] He repeatedly emphasized his roots in the area. In December 1939, for example, he laid wreaths at the gravestones of his relatives in Hohensalza.[156] Two years later, his former high school was renamed the Arthur-Greiser School. At the ceremonial renaming, Greiser claimed that 'in that I give my name to this school, I feel myself even more closely tied to the city of Hohensalza than before.'[157] In 1942, he declared: 'I am a child of this area and I acknowledge this with pride.'[158] By underscoring his roots in the region, Greiser hoped to generate genuine support for his rule among the local German population.

Finally, Greiser benefited from the increasing independence that Gauleiters enjoyed during the war years. Beginning in 1939, for example, many Gauleiters were made Reich defense commissars for their Gaus. Göring named Greiser Reich defense commissar for the Warthegau in March 1940.[159] This gave Greiser the sole right to issue orders related to the defense of his Gau—if necessary, in advance of or even in opposition to military authorities.[160] By successfully expanding his powers as Reichsstatthalter and Gauleiter, Greiser was able to exercise considerable control over developments in the Warthegau.

Yet to bolster his position, Greiser also had to seek out patrons among high-ranking Nazis. He was, of course, most eager for Hitler's support. By all accounts, he was completely under his Führer's spell. Siegmund claimed that after being in Hitler's presence, his cousin behaved as if 'drunk.'[161] But Greiser didn't have easy or frequent access to Hitler, and the Führer never came to the Warthegau. Greiser had a personal audience with Hitler on 28 September and 14 December 1939 (when he swore an oath of loyalty to Hitler), and on 2 April, 16 September, and 31 October 1940. He also met with Hitler twice in late spring and summer 1941, on or just before 24 May and on 18 July.[162] This was just when he was implementing important anti-Polish measures and likely planning the murder of Jews in his Gau. All but the last personal meeting between Greiser and Hitler took place before the German invasion of the Soviet Union; thereafter, it appears, the Führer had more important things to do than see Greiser. Greiser sometimes saw Hitler in larger groups, such as when the Führer appeared at Gauleiter meetings or other events.[163] At these gatherings, personal interaction with Hitler flattered Greiser's vanity—not least since it showed other guests that he enjoyed the Führer's attention. After one such occasion, Greiser even explained to Himmler why he had been unable to convey his birthday greetings personally: 'the Führer commanded me to be at his side during coffee and cake.'[164]

In the absence of Hitler's special favor, Greiser initially followed Hermann Göring's cue in the Warthegau. The Reich marshal, however, showed little interest in the agrarian Gau and, like Hitler, never came to Posen.[165] Greiser had to look elsewhere for a patron. Eventually, he settled on Heinrich Himmler. Already as senate president, Greiser had cultivated closer personal relations with Himmler. In April 1935, Himmler had been an official witness at Greiser's marriage to Maria. In early 1937, Greiser had also informed Himmler of his true intentions for Danzig.[166] During his first twenty months in the Warthegau, however, Greiser did not especially ingratiate himself with Himmler. He complained about the Reichsführer-SS to Goebbels; he opposed the expansion of Himmler's police authority in his Gau; and his agencies stood up to Himmler's in jurisdictional turf battles over resettlement matters.[167]

But, as the months of occupation stretched on, Greiser and Himmler increasingly had common cause. If Greiser was to fulfil his task of Germanizing the Gau, he needed the cooperation of Himmler's police apparatus. Himmler, in turn, wanted to make the Warthegau a playground of demographic experimentation. This was especially the case since none of the other eastern Gauleiters were promising partners: Forster had an intense dislike of Himmler; Erich Koch was more an ally of Martin Bormann (a Himmler rival); and Gauleiters Josef Wagner and then Fritz Bracht were not especially committed to Himmler's agenda.

Greiser humored Himmler. The SS-leader was an outsider who craved friends; Greiser knew just how to fawn over him. After his 1942 promotion to SS-senior group leader (*Obergruppenführer*), for example, Greiser wrote to Himmler: 'You can be sure that I will always and without reservation be at your disposal in all fields of my work.'[168] Greiser signed his letters to Himmler with 'Your always thankful Arthur Greiser' or even a handwritten 'Your always faithful Greiser.'[169] Greiser's obsequiousness was rewarded with Himmler's affection. The SS-leader eventually opened his letters to Greiser with the familiar 'My dear Greiser! (*Mein lieber Greiser!*)'[170] As a token of his friendship, Himmler gave Greiser a gelded fox named 'Sandmann' in August 1941.[171] Himmler also came to Posen surprisingly often. As Siegmund writes, 'The relationship of Greiser to Himmler . . . rested on mutual esteem . . . Greiser's willingness to subordinate himself to Himmler's interests could not be missed, and no Nazi dignitary was more often in the Warthegau than Himmler. On multiple occasions [Himmler] spent evenings in [Greiser's] house with a few close friends . . .' At such times, Maria, rather than the servants, took care of the honored guest's needs.[172] Himmler seems to have genuinely enjoyed Greiser's company. In May 1943, in response to an invitation to visit, he wrote to Greiser: 'I really hope that in the first half of this month I'll still be able to make use of your kind invitation. I very much look forward to then being able to be together with you.'[173]

Although he eagerly sought Himmler's favor, Greiser did not refrain from letting the SS-leader know when he was angry with him or disagreed with his policies. For example, Greiser was furious when Himmler left him out of communication channels. In July 1940, he complained bitterly that one of Himmler's decrees had been sent to him via Koppe: '. . . Once again I point to the fact that it is an impossible situation for me when I first receive decrees of the Reich commissar for the strengthening of Germandom [i.e., Himmler] via the higher SS and police leader . . . I cannot further approve of this situation.'[174] Perhaps this letter had its effect; Greiser doesn't seem to have complained about the issue again. He had less success, however, with another matter: the lifting of the police border between the Warthegau and the rest of the Reich in summer 1941. Desperate for manpower, Himmler decided to remove the police guarding that border. Greiser, fearing the consequences, angrily protested the decision: 'If it is carried out, I cannot take responsibility for the war-important tasks of the Warthegau . . . The carrying out of the *volkstums*-political tasks will also be made impossible . . .'[175] Himmler was unmoved by Greiser's dire warnings. The police stationed on the border were transferred, and Greiser had to use security police in the Gau to fill the breach.[176] But Greiser had not simply accepted the change; he had not shied away from voicing objections to the powerful SS-leader.

There has been considerable debate about how much control Greiser had over the police apparatus in the Warthegau.[177] In fact, the lines of police authority in the Gau were also very muddy. As Gauleiter or Reichsstatthalter, Greiser did not exercise formal authority over the various security agencies (such as VoMi, the EWZ, and UWZ) associated with the Reich Commissariat for the strengthening of Germandom (*Reichskommissariat für die Festigung deutschen Volkstums* or RKFDV). But in August 1940, Himmler named Greiser his deputy for the strengthening of Germandom in the Warthegau (a position initially held by Koppe).[178] Despite being Himmler's deputy, Greiser doesn't seem to have issued orders to agencies subordinate to the RKFDV until 1944, when hundreds of thousands of ethnic Germans crowded into the Warthegau from the Soviet Union. In the early years of occupation, Greiser had little influence over the police operations that dramatically altered his Gau's population.

But, in other police matters, Greiser had a much greater say. Although the power to issue police regulations in the annexed eastern areas was not actually formally vested in any authority, Greiser (like other eastern regional leaders), tacitly claimed it for himself—on the basis that he had comprehensive jurisdiction for the Warthegau.[179] Himmler also helped to enhance Greiser's police authority. He made Koppe 'personally and directly' subordinate to Greiser.[180] In October 1939, he raised Greiser's SS rank to that of group leader (*Gruppenführer*) so as to make it equivalent to Koppe's; the HSSPF could not pull rank on the Gauleiter.[181] In 1942, when Koppe went on vacation, Himmler named Greiser as Koppe's deputy for the duration of the HSSPF's absence.[182] Himmler also gave Greiser the right to issue directives to the Gau's Gestapo so long as these didn't contradict orders coming from the Reich Security Main Office (*Reichssicherheitshauptamt* or RSHA). Over the years, Greiser thus gave numerous orders to Koppe and the Gestapo; to the Security and Order Police in his Gau; and even to the police presidents in the cities of Posen and Litzmannstadt.[183]

Greiser was the rare Gauleiter who worked with the SS, rather than against it.[184] Besides his good relations with Himmler, Greiser generally got along with other security officials in and outside of his Gau, including all three of the HSSPFs who served in the Gau: Wilhelm Koppe (1939–43), Theodor Berkelmann (November–December 1943), and Heinz Reinefarth (1944–5).[185] The same was true of Greiser and the subordinates to the HSSPFs. When it came to carrying out mass crimes against Poles and Jews, cooperation was the general tenor of relations between Greiser's administration and police agencies in the Gau.

Because Greiser didn't have close relations with other men who really counted in Nazi Germany, he was very dependent on Himmler. This, in turn, had a significant impact on policy in his Gau. While Greiser had begun to carry out an agenda more radical than that of any other eastern Gauleiter as soon as he came to the Warthegau (perhaps to compensate for his 'moderation' in Danzig), he further radicalized his anti-Polish, anti-church, and anti-Semitic policies beginning in late spring 1941. By then Göring's power was on the wane, Himmler's on the rise. Greiser may have realized that Himmler's racial obsessions now dominated the Nazi agenda; he wanted to be on the winning side of the Nazi future. In the warped logic of the Nazi world in 1941, Greiser placed his bets on the right man.

In fall 1939, Greiser relished his new position as Gauleiter and Reichsstatthalter of the Warthegau. He welcomed visits from Nazi dignitaries. Frick, Goebbels, Himmler, German Labor Front leader Robert Ley, Hitler Youth leader Baldur von Schirach, and Finance Minister Lutz Graf Schwerin-Krosigk all came to Posen. These visits and the attendant media coverage underscored the importance that the Nazis attached to their new Gau and its leader. Goebbels came several times in fall 1939, and often visited the Warthegau in later years. His stepson, Harald Quandt, worked in Posen for his father, Günther Quandt (Magda Goebbels' first husband), the owner of the Gau's largest factory, the H. Cegielski Company, now renamed the German Weapons and Ammunition Factory (*Deutsche Waffen- und Munitionsfabrik*).[186] In early December 1939, Goebbels noted his approval of Greiser: 'Drive to Posen... In the castle a visit with Greiser... Talk with Greiser about the Reich propaganda agency. We agree on everything. Greiser is doing a good job. He has to overcome many difficulties.'[187]

At Hitler's insistence, Forster gave Greiser an official farewell in Danzig. This was to underscore Greiser's contribution to the Danzig Nazi movement despite Forster's unceremonious removal of his rival in August. The event took place on 28 November, the fifth anniversary of Greiser's assumption of the senate presidency. After an official farewell ceremony in the White Hall of the Danzig city hall, a rally celebrated Greiser in the Friedrich-Wilhelm Club House. According to the *Ostdeutscher Beobachter*, this rally had 'something of the atmosphere of the first National-Socialist meetings.' After Greiser entered the room, 'he received a welcome that only a few have experienced in this old National-Socialist site of struggle. Again and again stormy hails and clapping. The people jumped up on their stools and benches. Rally participants stretched out their hands to Gauleiter Reichsstatthalter Greiser. They waved to him and showed in every way the love and loyalty with which the Danziger National Socialists are attached to their former senate president.'[188] Although Greiser's years as senate president had been close to disastrous for his political career, this time was now whitewashed in nostalgic ecstasy.

For Greiser, the fall of 1939 was a time of exuberant hope. All his Nazi dreams had come true. Danzig was part of the Reich. His Posen homeland was once again under German rule. He had initiated the Germanization of the Warthegau. Indeed, as subsequent chapters show, by late fall 1939, he had begun all of the policies that would mark the Warthegau as a 'model' Gau: the influx of ethnic Germans, anti-Polish policies, measures against Jews, and the undermining of church authority. This all took place despite conflicting lines of authority, and the fact that no plans for the area had been worked out in advance of invasion. But after six years of Nazi rule in Germany, Hitler, Greiser, and other NSDAP officials knew how they would rule an area unfettered by German administrative traditions or international norms of conduct. What is often said of the Final Solution is true of many other aspects of Nazi rule as well: policies that took years to develop in the Old Reich (or Danzig) were telescoped into weeks or months in the annexed eastern areas. Nowhere was this more true than in the Warthegau: Greiser hit the ground running.

Greiser's autumn of political triumph, however, was followed by a winter of personal tragedy. On 20 December, Erhardt, Greiser's only son, was killed in a car crash.[189] Greiser had planned for his son to spend the Christmas holidays in the Warthegau; Erhardt was coming from his boarding school in Feldafing. Greiser sent a car and drivers to Frankfurt/Oder so that his son would not have to negotiate the poor railways in the new Gau. The car first dropped off a fellow student at that boy's family estate. The boy begged Erhardt to spend the night, but Erhardt was eager to see his father and wanted to leave as soon as possible. On the way to Posen, the car was hit by a fast-driving locomotive at a railway-track road crossing near Birnbaum that had no protective gates. Neither the car nor the train had lights on.[190] The two drivers, Lieutenant Hans Schulz-Wiedemann and administrative assistant Theodor Hey, were also killed. Both men had served on Greiser's personal staff in Danzig. Hey was Greiser's butler; Schulz-Wiedemann was said to be one of Greiser's 'closest colleagues.'[191]

Greiser did not hide his personal tragedy. On 22 December, he published a death notice in which he wrote that 'the belief in Germany and his Führer was the content of [Erhardt's] young life.'[192] A ceremony and burial took place on 23 December.[193] At the morning ceremony in the Reichsstatthalter office, only relatives of the dead and a few friends of the Gauleiter were present. Greiser refused to allow Ruth, his first wife and Erhardt's mother, to attend the ceremony.[194] Colonel Bethke gave the eulogy. According to a brief newspaper report, 'Colonel Bethke, as the closest friend and war comrade of the Gauleiter, spoke a few words during the simple ceremony that was framed by the tones of a string orchestra.' That afternoon, Erhardt and the others were buried at the Lukas Cemetery in Posen. At the burial, the Hitler Youth took part, as did the Uniformed Police. According to the *Ostdeutscher Beobachter*, 'At dusk, accompanied by the tones of the song of the good comrade and the crash of a salvo of a police honor guard, the coffins of the dead were lowered into the grave.'[195] In grieving for his son, Greiser placed Erhardt in a Nazi narrative: his son was a young soldier in the glorious Nazi cause, tragically struck down before his time.

Greiser was deeply moved by his son's death. In a personal letter in early January, he described the period surrounding Erhardt's death as 'the most difficult days of my life.'[196] The previous summer, as we know, he had had quite an altercation with Erhardt. After reprimanding his son for his less than stellar school performance, Greiser may not have seen Erhardt again. According to Siegmund, 'Greiser was affected so deeply by this turn of fate that one could not talk with him for days. Often in the next time I experienced him as still more reserved and pensive than before.' Siegmund also recalled a later episode that suggested Greiser's continued grief. Greiser and his party had returned by train to Posen very early one morning. Their sleeping car was placed on a railroad siding so that they could rest longer. At dawn, Greiser left the train and went to his son's grave, located in the immediate vicinity. A short time later, he was brought back, injured, by his escort commando. According to Siegmund, 'in order to reach his son's grave, [Greiser] had climbed over a fence, fallen, and had seriously hurt himself.'[197] Greiser was always haunted by Erhardt's death. When he fled the Warthegau in January 1945, he insisted on visiting Erhardt's grave in Posen and, en route to the Old Reich, he stopped at the site of his son's fatal accident.[198] In his final statement to the courtroom at his trial, Greiser asked that he be buried next to his son in Posen.[199]

On 21 December, Greiser gave a major speech at a rally in Posen. This speech, celebrating the winter solstice, was broadcast throughout the Reich. As the *Ostdeutscher Beobachter* wrote, 'Despite the tough personal blow of fate that hit him on the same day, Gauleiter Greiser appeared at the square before the Posen Castle in order to speak as the leading National Socialist of the Warthegau about the light that the Führer and the world view of National Socialism has brought to the German people.'[200] As Greiser told both the assembled crowd and the radio audience: 'We will draw from sun and light the strength to create from here the broadest living space for the German people in the East.'[201] In fact, for Greiser, not sun and light accompanied his cruel Germanization policies in the Warthegau, but rather a string of personal tragedies that began with Erhardt's death. In taking over his childhood homeland, Greiser sowed the seeds for his own personal destruction.

5

'A Blonde Province:' Resettlement, Deportation, Murder

When Arthur Greiser came to Posen in 1939, just 325,000 individuals, or 6.6 percent of the population in what would become the Warthegau, considered themselves German. As he later recalled, 'On 12 September 1939, right after the arrival of German troops, I drummed together the Germans who still remained in Posen. There were only 2,400 Germans. By contrast, when I left my homeland on 4 August 1914 as a child of the old province of Posen, Germans made up more than 50 of 100 persons in the province and city of Posen.'[1] Despite his biographical falsifications (Greiser couldn't possibly have held the rally on 12 September; he wasn't yet in Posen), his larger point was true: the German population had declined precipitously since 1914.[2] To reverse this process, Greiser spearheaded one of the most dramatic and sustained Nazi demographic experiments. Nowhere else saw such bold attempts at altering the population makeup; nowhere else saw so many people resettled, deported, murdered, or otherwise uprooted.[3] In his effort to 'Germanize' his Gau, Greiser even initiated the first mass gassings of Jews in Nazi-occupied Europe.

Germanization was an overarching project that included policies toward Germans, Poles, and Jews. While most historians have told separate stories about these population groups in the Warthegau (and elsewhere in occupied Europe), this has come at a conceptual loss.[4] Nazi policy toward each of these groups was profoundly different, but policy toward one group had a significant impact on one or both of the other population groups. The influx of ethnic German resettlers, for example, resulted in the deportation of Poles; the ethnic cleansing of Poles prevented the deportation of Jews; and the inability to remove Jews led to their ghettoization and, eventually, murder. This chapter is the first of three that explore Greiser's Germanization project *in toto*. This project constituted a veritable ethnic-cleansing primer. In making the land and people of the Warthegau German, Greiser adopted a dizzying array of measures: resettlement, deportation, and murder; segregation and anti-church policies; and the transformation of the Gau's natural, built, and cultural environment.

Nazi purists believed that the assimilation of allegedly lower races to Germandom was out of the question. As Hitler wrote in *Mein Kampf* (My Struggle), 'Germanization can only be applied to soil and never to people.'[5] According to this logic, to Germanize a region, Germans would have to replace non-Germans. On 7 October 1939, Hitler entrusted SS-leader Heinrich Himmler with the demographic reordering of the continent. To carry out his task, Himmler created the Reich Commissariat for the Strengthening of Germandom (RKFDV) and named himself commissioner.[6] To pave the way for German settlement, his officials now planned vast population movements. As the Nazis conquered ever more land, these plans, known as General Plan East (*Generalplan Ost*), Overall Plan East (*Gesamtplan Ost*), and General Settlement Plan (*Generalsiedlungsplan*), became ever more radical.[7] At their most phantasmagoric, they foresaw the deportation and/or extermination of some thirty-one million individuals (primarily Slavs) over a twenty-year period.[8] While most of this planning remained in the realm of Nazi fantasy, some remarkable population schemes actually took place in the Warthegau. In part, this was due to the Gau's situation: its outright annexation in 1939 (before the war soured for the Nazis), its close proximity to the Old Reich, and its past status as part of the German Empire. But it was also due to Greiser's personal engagement, and Himmler's willingness to give the Gau priority in its demographic reordering. As the SS-leader reportedly stated on a visit to Posen in December 1939, 'I want to create a blonde province here.'[9]

All of the Nazi plans suffered from a major logical flaw: where were the Germans who were to serve as colonists? The Nazis incessantly claimed that the Germans were a people without land (*Volk ohne Raum*). In fact, however, as the Wehrmacht conquered more and more parts of Europe,

Germany became a land without people (*Raum ohne Volk*)—or at least without German people.[10] Although there were small pockets of Germans abroad, there simply weren't enough Germans to people all the areas that the Nazis ultimately wished to Germanize.

In fall 1939, there was one ready source of ethnic Germans to populate areas newly conquered by the Nazis: ethnic-German leaders in the Baltic countries feared that their communities would experience the full brunt of Bolshevik terror if the Soviet Union took over their homelands (as seemed likely and soon occurred). They persuaded Himmler, who in turn convinced Hitler, that resettlement was necessary to protect these German minorities.[11] In a speech to the Reichstag on 6 October, Hitler announced that ethnic Germans living east of Reich borders would be moved to Germany.[12] Soon thereafter, Nazi Germany signed repatriation agreements with Estonia, Latvia, and the Soviet Union (for the return of Germans from eastern Poland, now occupied by the Red Army).[13] Ethnic-German leaders abroad trumpeted 'Back Home to the Reich' (*Heim ins Reich*) to their fellow countrymen. By 18 October, ships with ethnic Germans from Estonia and then Latvia were arriving daily in Stettin and other ports.

The resettlement of tens of thousands of Baltic Germans demanded considerable organization. Many agencies were involved in the resettlement process; most were formally or *de facto* part of Himmler's security empire. The RKFDV oversaw general resettlement policy. It determined which ethnic Germans abroad would be subject to repatriation and where they would be resettled in Nazi-occupied Europe. Numerous other agencies, often with overlapping jurisdiction, carried out the actual resettlement process. The Ethnic German Liaison Office (VoMi) coordinated activity among ethnic Germans abroad.[14] VoMi also ran the temporary camps that housed resettlers until they could be permanently settled. The Reich Security Main Office (RSHA) included the Gestapo, the Security Service (SD), and various subsidiary agencies. RSHA provided the police power necessary for the immigration process. A RSHA agency, the Central Immigration Center (EWZ), processed the resettlers once they arrived on Reich territory with regard to citizenship and other matters. Resettlers also underwent racial screenings carried out by another SS agency, the Race and Settlement Main Office (*Rasse- und Siedlungshauptamt*, or RuSHA).[15] These screenings categorized Germans into so-called O (*Osten*, or east) and A (*Altreich*, or Old Reich) cases. Those deemed racially suitable were given O status; resettlement in the East was an honor. All A cases were to be sent to the Old Reich, where they were confined in 'temporary' camps. The German Resettlement Trusteeship Company (*Deutsche Umsiedlungstreuhandgesellschaft* or DUT), represented resettlers' property interests in their old homelands and provided resettlers with equivalent property in the annexed territories.[16] Finally, the Central Trust Agency for the East (HTO), controlled by Hermann Göring, distributed commercial and agricultural property confiscated from Poles and Jews to the resettlers (as trustees, not owners).

Where was Greiser in all of this? RKFDV officials needed the cooperation of the Gauleiters; Greiser's role was thus critical. Albert Forster, the Danzig–West-Prussian Gauleiter, soon made it clear that he did not want resettlers: to him, the Baltic Germans (and later other ethnic Germans) were unnecessary mouths to feed and bodies to house.[17] Already on 25 October 1939, Martin Sandberger, head of the EWZ in Gotenhafen (Gdynia), noted: '... Gauleiter Forster is in principle in agreement that the great majority of the Baltic Germans not stay in West Prussia, but rather go on to Posen ...'[18] This was an understatement; Forster was downright opposed to taking in resettlers. On 26 October, Sandberger went to Posen. There, he reported, 'Greiser places great value on receiving ongoing transports of Baltic Germans immediately ... Gauleiter Greiser further declared that at his instigation, accommodations for the next weeks for roughly twenty thousand Baltic Germans ... had been prepared.'[19] Two days later, Sandberger wrote, 'My general impression is that the Gau Posen presents in much greater measure a guarantee for a successful and frictionless carrying out of the immigration action.' Greiser had just issued a directive ordering that immigration take priority over all other matters.[20]

In 1942, Greiser recalled his initial reaction to resettlement in his Gau: 'When, at the beginning of October 1939 the Reichsführer-SS ... called me and said that he had to send me 10,000 of the first Baltic resettlers, I had no idea how I was to accommodate them. Two days later I received a radio message that 25,000 would come, and the number later grew to about 60,000.' Greiser then related the difficulties he had faced: 'We had no buses or telephone or immediate operational possibilities. We had to establish improvised camps. Feeding [the resettlers] was a problem in and of itself.'[21] Greiser nonetheless continued to accept resettlers. In December 1939, Sandberger reported that while Forster had taken in approximately 6,000 to 7,000 Baltic Germans, he refused to accept any more. By contrast, 'Gauleiter Greiser has declared himself ready to take in all Baltic Germans who are capable of work . . .'[22] Greiser's readiness to take in ethnic Germans was rewarded. When Constantin von Neurath, the Reichsstatthalter in the Protectorate of Bohemia and Moravia, begged Hitler for more Germans, Hitler demurred—and told Neurath that western Poland would receive priority in the resettlement of ethnic Germans.[23]

To accommodate ethnic German resettlers, Nazi authorities planned the ethnic cleansing of Jews and Poles. Indeed, precisely because the Warthegau became the main site of ethnic German resettlement, it also became the main site of deportations of Jews and especially Poles. Already in the first weeks of occupation, Nazi authorities had confiscated the apartments of wealthier Jews and Poles so as to provide housing for Germans from the Old Reich who made up the core of the Gau's German administrative elite. Now, with German resettlers streaming in, Nazi authorities began a systematic program of ethnic cleansing.

In November 1939, Himmler charged Wilhelm Koppe, the higher SS and police leader in the Gau (HSSPF), with overall responsibility for deportations in the Warthegau. On 12 November, Koppe declared that in addition to 'all Jews,' 'all those Poles who either belong to the intelligentsia or due to their national-political views might pose a danger to the carrying out and strengthening of Germandom will be deported.' Koppe then continued, 'the goal of the deportation is (a) the cleansing and securing of the new German territories, (b) the creation of apartments and work opportunities for the incoming ethnic Germans.'[24]

RSHA officials ran the deportation actions.[25] The Security Police (Sipo) established a Special Staff for the Evacuation of Poles and Jews to the General Government (*Sonderstab für die Evakuierung und den Abtransport der Polen und Juden in das Generalgouvernement*) in Posen, led by Albert Rapp. From 1 to 17 December, Rapp and his staff carried out the so-called 'First Short-Term Plan.' 87,833 Poles (some of whom were Polish Jews) were deported to the General Government.[26] In the early pre-dawn hours, security officials knocked on apartment and house doors and gave their inhabitants just minutes to gather necessary documents, clothes, bedding, and food supplies. Everything else was to be left for the new occupants. The deportees were loaded on trucks and brought to a transit camp, Lager Glowno.[27] From there, they were transported in unheated cattle cars, without provisions (sometimes even without water), to the General Government.

Despite the high numbers of individuals evacuated in December 1939, Nazi officials found the operations characterized by 'absolute organizational deficiency.'[28] Too often, the wrong individuals were evacuated; Poles quickly learned to avoid the deportations; too few trains were at the operation's disposal; Polish railway personnel created difficulties; officials on the receiving end refused to accept deportees; and finally, many of those deported soon made their way back to the Warthegau. Perhaps in response to these shortcomings, Rapp's staff was reorganized and renamed the Central Emigration Office (UWZ) in April 1940; Rolf-Heinz Höppner became its head. The center of UWZ activities, however, soon shifted to Litzmannstadt, where Hermann Krumey headed the branch office. In the next fifteen months, Nazi authorities carried out three further deportation campaigns—all of which were accompanied by similar organizational difficulties.

Greiser had little influence over the early evacuations, too little for his liking. In early December 1939, recognizing a fait accompli, he named Koppe as 'the party member solely responsible' for all matters related to deportations.[29] In January 1940, however, he complained to Joseph Goebbels that he was having 'many difficulties with Himmler, who especially in evacuation matters rules very high-handedly.'[30] In August, however, Greiser finally received an official role in the deportation process. After he won a power struggle with Koppe, Himmler named Greiser his deputy for 'strengthening Germandom' in the Warthegau.[31] In future, Greiser would invoke this title whenever he had conflicts with Himmler over evacuation or other Germanization measures.

From the very beginning, Hans Frank, the Nazi governor of the General Government, objected to the deportations. At an April 1940 meeting in Cracow (at which Greiser was not present), Frank declared: 'The Führer [at a meeting in Berlin] has further determined a period of ten years for the total Germanization of the Warthegau, Danzig, West Prussia and the south-European and Upper-Silesian areas. In this period everything was to be done so as to work up the German *Volk* community, especially in the Warthegau, which is very endangered. It was originally thought that this would be possible by simply deporting the Poles from Posen to the General Government. Gradually it was realized that this is not possible, since the General Government does not want to put up with this dominant Reich opinion.' Frank was unwilling to allow his area to become the dumping ground of the Third Reich's undesirables. As he continued, though, 'But in the General Government one will have to get used to the notion that initially, with the addition of Germans in the Warthegau and in West Prussia, the Polish, Jewish, gypsy and other populations in the General Government will have to find a home for years. It would be pointless, indeed it would go against the policy of the Führer, if one wanted to force a policy of Germandom in the General Government as is necessary in the Warthegau.'[32]

Frank was torn. As his words suggest, he grudgingly felt that he had to do his part to make the areas annexed to the Third Reich 'German.' At a 31 July meeting with Greiser and Koppe, he reiterated that 'he saw himself obliged to give the Warthegau absolute priority in upholding Germandom . . .'[33] But Frank's objections resurfaced again on 2 November, when he sent word to Greiser that the General Government would not take in any more Poles.[34] The very next day, Greiser and Koppe rushed to Cracow. Frank now convinced Greiser that his 'essential tasks' in the General Government were being hampered by the evacuations.[35] The next day, however, Frank met with Hitler. The Führer told Frank of his 'urgent wish' that the General Government continue to take in Poles.[36] Deportations from the Warthegau went on until 15 March 1941, when they were halted in preparation for the German invasion of the Soviet Union.[37] By then, some 272,834 Poles had been deported from the Warthegau to the General Government.[38] Many of the same German officials who carried out these deportations would soon be involved in the murder of Jews.[39] As one historian has argued, the deportation of Poles was a 'prelude to the Final Solution.'[40]

Both Nazi observers and later historians have claimed that Greiser was a fierce anti-Semite.[41] By the time he came to the Warthegau, Greiser certainly espoused typical Nazi anti-Semitic notions. But he was not bent on the immediate destruction of Jews. Instead, his position on Jews was more nuanced. Greiser, it should be recalled, was not drawn to anti-Semitism until he joined the Nazi party.[42] Before that, he had viewed Jews quite favorably; as noted in earlier chapters, he had good relations with both his brother-in-law (who was of Jewish origins) and Jewish businessmen in Danzig. As senate president in Danzig, Greiser voiced anti-Semitic propaganda but also embraced a pragmatic approach to the 'Jewish Question.' Unlike Forster, who wished to rid the Free City of Jews immediately, Greiser was willing to tolerate Jews if this benefited Germany's international position. In the Warthegau, his stance was similarly pragmatic. If Jews could further Germanization measures, Greiser was willing to tolerate their presence. But if not, he was all too ready to see them 'liquidated.'

That said, Greiser made his fair share of nasty anti-Semitic remarks. On 11 November 1939, for example, at a rally in Lodsch celebrating the city's incorporation into the Reich, Greiser declared: 'Yesterday, during a tour through certain parts of the city, I had the opportunity to encounter figures who can scarcely be credited with the designation "person" (*Mensch*) and that are still present in much too great a number. In their faces live criminal instincts that stamp them as individuals of a fifth or sixth order. For us, and this I can assure you, the Jewish Question is no longer a problem, even when it confronts us in massed form, like here. It's only there for us to solve, and it will be solved.'[43] In just a few short sentences, Greiser managed to pack in anti-Semitic stereotypes: Jews were barely human, criminal by nature, and of a lower order than other peoples. He also proclaimed his intention of 'solving' the 'Jewish Question' in the Gau. He did not spell out how. Nor, in fact, did he know. When he made his statement, he assumed that the Warthegau Jews would be deported eastwards. But solving the 'Jewish problem' would prove much more difficult than Greiser expected.

In the first months of German rule, the Warthegau's Jews—some 385,000–435,000 individuals—experienced terrible persecution.[44] Greiser condoned this violence, but he didn't initiate it. In Turek, for example, local German authorities forced a group of Jews into a synagogue and then set the building afire.[45] Artillery General Walter Petzel, chief of the Military Commando XXI (Posen), reported another cruel incident there: 'A number of Jews were forced into the synagogue where they had to crawl through the benches while SS-people constantly whipped them. Then they were forced to let down their pants so as to be whipped on their naked bottoms. One Jew was so scared that he shat in his pants. He was then forced to smear his excrement in the faces of the other Jews.'[46] Local Germans also vandalized synagogues and other Jewish sites. As Greiser noted in a situational report, 'the interior of the [Wrongowitz] synagogue was destroyed and the wood was used by both the German and the Polish population for home firewood.'[47] On 10 November, the four largest synagogues in Lodsch were burned down.[48] Germans also arbitrarily seized and assigned Jews to work details. As one German civil servant later recalled, when he needed to load files and maps onto a truck during a snow storm, he simply ordered Jews who happened to be passing by to help him.[49]

In the Warthegau, legal regulations concerning Jews were often harsher than those in effect in the Reich or other parts of occupied Poland; Greiser was responsible for some of these. On 14 September 1939, for example, the very first day of his official duties, Greiser decreed that Jews could withdraw only 100 złoty weekly from their bank accounts; elsewhere, the limit was considerably higher.[50] On 11 December, Greiser ordered all Jews in the Warthegau to wear a 10-centimeter yellow Star of David on both their backs and chests. Although local Gau officials had already issued similar ordinances, Greiser's decree came well before Jews in the rest of the Reich had to wear the Star. Stipulations pertaining to first-degree mixed-race individuals (*Mischlinge* with one Jewish parent) were also stricter in the Warthegau. Rapp, for example, decreed that such individuals were to be treated as full Jews.[51] The fact that Greiser immediately radicalized measures against Jews on arrival in the Warthegau shows his commitment to Nazi ideology. It also suggests that he now viewed anti-Semitism as an important arena in which he could remake his Nazi reputation.

Greiser and other Nazi authorities initially planned to dump the Jews of the Warthegau in the General Government. In October 1939, Himmler ordered all Jews from the newly annexed territories to be deported by the end of February 1940.[52] As part of the December 1939 'First Short Term Plan,' all of the Jews in Posen, some 1,765 individuals as of November, were sent away on 13 December.[53] Jews from the rest of the Posen district, as well as those in Hohensalza district's western sub-districts, were also deported; this made the western Warthegau virtually 'free of Jews' (*judenfrei*). In the eastern part of the Gau, where the vast majority of Jews lived, some 16,000 Jews were deported from Kalisz, and another 5,000 to 6,000 Jews from Lodsch were pushed over the border into the General Government. Thereafter, however, relatively few Jews left the Gau. In the next wave of deportations, lasting from 10 February to 15 March 1940, 40,128 individuals were deported, but just 2,018 Jews.[54]

Why were so few Jews deported? Resettlement had top priority—and it demanded the ethnic cleansing of Poles, not Jews.[55] Baltic Germans fast arriving in the Gau 'needed' the city apartments of middle-class Poles, while incoming ethnic German peasants 'needed' Polish farms. By contrast, tenement buildings in Lodsch were ill suited to the new arrivals. Moreover, since many Jews had lost their homes, jobs, and businesses already in fall 1939, deporting Jews after that created few opportunities for ethnic Germans.[56]

Even before it was clear that most Jews would stay put in the Gau, planning for a ghetto in Lodsch began. On 10 December 1939, Friedrich Uebelhoer, district president of what soon became Litzmannstadt district, sent around a memorandum announcing plans for a ghetto.[57] Greiser, however, soon took credit for it. In January 1940, he reportedly told officials in the NSDAP Treasury Office that 'He [Greiser] had now concentrated the Jews in a ghetto in Lodsch that will be surrounded by a wall that the Jews will have to build themselves. The Jews will remain there until what they have amassed to exchange for food is returned and then they (roughly 250,000) will be shoved over the border. Then the empty ghetto will be burned to the ground.'[58] These remarks contained many falsehoods. Greiser didn't initiate the ghetto, Uebelhoer did. The Jews were not yet 'concentrated' in the ghetto. Their numbers were exaggerated. And Greiser assumed that Jews were hoarding valuables that could be 'squeezed' out of them. In fact, the ghetto was established only weeks after Greiser's statement, on 8 February. It was located in the impoverished Bałuty suburb, in which 60,000 Jews already lived. In early March, another 100,000 or so Lodsch Jews were forced to move there.

For a time, before it was sealed off, the ghetto was a tourist site.[59] Greiser's daughter, Ingrid, visited the ghetto on 11 April. In a letter to her fiancé, she wrote: 'It's really fantastic (*toll*). A whole city district totally sealed off by a barbed-wire fence... You mostly see just riff-raff loafing about. On their clothes, they have to have a yellow Star of David both behind and in front (Daddy's invention, he speaks only about the starry sky of Lodz).' Ingrid described conditions: 'Actually the quarter is much too small for all the people, there are 300,000 Jews, and in every room there are surely ten to twenty people, I saw so many heads at the windows. There are epidemics there, and terrible air since everything is spilled into the drainage pipes [the ghetto had no underground sewage system]. There is no water, the Jews have to buy it for ten pennies a bucket, and so they surely wash themselves less frequently than usual. Just seeing this can make one sick.' Ingrid concluded: 'You know, one really can't have any sympathy for these people. I think that they feel very differently from us and therefore don't feel this humiliation and everything. If I were in such a situation, I would burst with rage and hate the people who did this to me. They surely hate us too, but for other reasons.'[60] Steeped in anti-Semitic stereotypes, Ingrid assumed that the Jews hated the Germans not for degrading them, but for cutting them off from their economic activity. She viewed the ghetto as an outrage, but as a Jewish, not a German, outrage.

Using specious reasoning, Greiser and other Nazi authorities justified the ghetto's isolation from the surrounding population. On 1 April 1940, Greiser declared that the ghetto had already seen an outbreak of typhus; that it was allegedly a 'shelter for . . . criminal rabble;' and that since Lodsch was cut off from its agricultural hinterland (in the General Government), it was impossible to provide the city with necessary foodstuffs if one permitted Jews the 'opportunity of black marketeering and hoarding of foodstuffs.'[61] Accordingly, the ghetto was sealed shut on 30 April: 164,000 Jews were now locked in, almost entirely cut off from the rest of the city's population.[62] The Litzmannstadt ghetto (Lodsch had been renamed earlier that month) was the first major Nazi ghetto and, as such, served as a model for all other Nazi ghettos.[63] Eventually, it became the second largest ghetto (after Warsaw) in all of Nazi-occupied Europe.

While the Jews of the Gau were herded into the Litzmannstadt and smaller ghettos, ethnic German resettlers streamed into the Gau. Throughout eastern Europe, they were uprooted from their homes and communities. Many of the resettlers could not speak German and had little sense of where they were going or why they were leaving their native areas. While the Baltic Germans came by boat and train, most of the other resettlers came on treks—on horse-drawn wagons loaded with their possessions. In chilling cold or beastly heat (Nazi officials tried to avoid trekking in spring and fall, since these were the all-important sowing and harvesting seasons), resettlers endured journeys that often lasted for weeks. It was not unusual for babies, young children, and the aged to die en route. Moreover, after they arrived in the Gau, the resettlers met a harsh welcome in a cold 'homeland.' With few exceptions, most spent months or even years in VoMi-run 'temporary' camps awaiting placement in the Gau. The resettlers were given little to do, and even less of a sense of what would come next.[64] Many suffered from health problems made worse by camp life.[65] They also endured a harsh disciplinary regime. At one time, for example, camp authorities forbade inmates from playing soccer 'in the interest of saving footwear.'[66]

On the same trip on which she visited the ghetto, Ingrid Greiser accompanied her father on a tour of a VoMi camp near Litzmannstadt. The camp that they visited, the Forest Peace (*Waldfrieden*) camp, was housed in a former cloister.[67] Ingrid noted: 'At 10 a.m. we left for a camp for Volhynien Germans. This was a model camp and everything was prepared for our visit. The people are really fantastic, they have a faith in the Führer and in Daddy that is simply touching. They are very simple, but nonetheless not servile, but rather free. They have all been through great difficulties, in every family children died, altogether 12 percent of the Volhynien German children have died. It's sometimes still very difficult for them now, some have to wait for a very long time, they are separated from their family members, etc.' Ingrid then went on to describe her father's interaction with the resettlers: 'But Daddy told them that later, when they have been settled, they will have it much better than in Russia. One man gave the Führer forty-five gold rubles, and when Daddy gave him 2,000 Marks in recognition [of this gift], he was totally insulted. Daddy spoke terribly nicely with the people, he can do that well, especially with the children . . .'[68] Ingrid presented a picture of her father that many Germans would have recognized. Greiser was personable and undoubtedly charmed many of the resettlers in the camp. Perhaps his visit bettered morale among the resettlers—at least for the short term.

At various times, Greiser tried to improve conditions in resettler camps. In September 1940, he threatened to remove from the Warthegau any officials who bodily mistreated resettlers.[69] Much later, he wrote to Werner Lorenz, now head of VoMi, complaining that conditions in the camps were 'beginning to stink to high heaven.' As he reported, the housing of resettlers in a camp in Zduńska Wola was 'irresponsible and depressing.' Some Lithuanian Germans had been in the camps for almost three years; almost nightly one or another tried to break out of the camp. Camp staff members were stealing food from the camp kitchens. Too many camp inmates remained idle. VoMi officials were turning away Gau representatives who wished to visit the camps. As Greiser noted, 'the catastrophic conditions of the camps are gradually causing alarm not only in my agencies but also among the population in the areas concerned.'[70] In a detailed response, Lorenz addressed the complaints. Except for the matter of food stealing, he believed that every complaint was exaggerated or taken out of context.[71] Greiser, however, remained unconvinced. As he replied to his old chum, 'there is developing here a serious political danger inside my sovereign territory (*Hoheitsbereich*).' Even though the camps fell under VoMi jurisdiction, Greiser claimed responsibility for them because they were in his Gau. He now asked Lorenz to intervene with Himmler to get the resettler camps disbanded. Greiser needed the camp space to house Berliners who had been bombed out of their homes.[72] But he probably also wanted the resettler camps closed because they threatened the image of the Warthegau as a well-ordered, 'model' Gau.

Greiser's concern could not mask a fundamental reality: the ethnic Germans were not being resettled, but languishing in camps. Gau and Reich officials had no idea where to put them. In part, this was due to Himmler's desire to save future resettlement opportunities for soldiers at the front. As a much touted slogan went, 'The Wartheland is to become the Gau of farmers and soldiers.'[73] The SS leader initially insisted that only 25 percent of the land in the annexed eastern territories be used for wartime resettlement. In December 1940, he raised this figure to 40 percent, and to 50 percent in May 1942.[74] But there still weren't enough farms to go around. This was due to several additional factors. Nazi authorities demanded a certain standard of farm for German resettlers; many Polish farms, they argued, were simply too small or primitive for Germans. At the same time, to make room for resettlers, Poles had to be removed from their farms, which involved another set of problems detailed below. Even as late as July 1943, shortly before a huge wave of ethnic Germans poured into the Gau, 27,000 resettlers were still living in VoMi camps.[75]

Those resettlers who received permanent homes also faced difficulties. Many Baltic Germans were disappointed by the economic and cultural infrastructure of the Warthegau. Most experienced professional setbacks.[76] They also saw their old communities widely dispersed in the Gau. But their difficulties paled in comparison with those faced by the poorer peasant resettlers from eastern Poland. These peasants suffered from a dire shortage of household items: sheets, blankets, dishes, cooking pots, utensils, tables, chairs, beds, and winter coats were all in very short supply.[77] Peasant resettlers often lived far away from their extended family and fellow compatriots, a situation aggravated by the poor state of roads in the Gau. Many were outraged by the arbitrary nature with which farms had been distributed. It was not unusual for resettlers who had left good farms to find themselves on utterly ramshackle holdings.[78] Resettlers also found a hostile environment. Deported Poles sometimes returned and, in revenge, burned barns, stole farm animals, and pilfered household goods (often, in fact, their former possessions).[79]

Greiser and other Gau authorities tried to alleviate these difficulties. Koppe ordered his settlement and work staff leaders to carry out ongoing inspections into resettlers' situations.[80] In addition, NSDAP women's and charitable organizations detailed 'settlement advisors,' a new kind of professional, to the annexed eastern areas.[81] These 'advisors' worked to secure resettlers the services that they needed. They also made sure that resettlers got the furniture, farm tools, and household goods to which they were entitled. They set up daycare and kindergarten groups for resettler children. And ironically, they taught resettlers to be 'German:' they tirelessly instructed their charges on Reich German manners, hygiene, customs, and holiday rituals. But Greiser was still disappointed with resettler care. In February 1941, he decreed that the party would take charge. He appointed the head of the Warthegau NSDAP Welfare Office, Werner Ventzki (soon lord mayor of Litzmannstadt), with coordinating welfare efforts among resettlers.[82] That same day, Greiser told a resettler group: 'You are the masters in this land, but you yourselves must work hard. Only in this way can you serve your people. But if you should have concerns, if at any time the shoe pinches, you should always come to me, so that I can look after your rights. We always want to have good camaraderie, for we must act together.'[83] In December, Greiser wrote to Himmler about 'the correctness of my decree as your deputy to bring the party as much as possible into the work of caring [for the resettlers].'[84] Whether, in fact, the party improved the situation remains open to debate. Most party work involved propping up morale. For resettlers, this was likely superficial balm for deep-seated difficulties.

Although eager to satisfy the resettlers, Greiser pursued policies that angered his Gau's new citizens. He was bent on breaking up resettler communities in order to create a 'great German' identity. In 1940, a confidential RSHA source reported that 'as Gauleiter Greiser has said several times, the Balts are to forget that they are Balts, the Bavarians that they are Bavarians, and so on. As he says, here they should all blend together as "great German people" through the great German task of forging the Reich's food supply.'[85] Resettlers were not permitted to maintain their own organizations, publish newspapers or newsletters, or come together as a group.[86] Greiser also forced resettlers to stay in the Gau. In spring 1941, when Himmler lifted police controls at the border between the Warthegau and the Old Reich, Greiser had Gau security officials step into the breach;

Table 5.1 Ethnic German Resettlers in the Warthegau

Date of Arrival	Place of Origin	Number of Resettlers
Fall 1939	Estonia, Latvia	76,786
Winter 1939–spring 1940	Galicia, Volhynia, Narew	97,020
Fall 1940–spring 1941	Lublin	24,545
Fall 1940	Bessarabia	47,892
Fall 1940	Bukowina	33,568
Fall–winter 1940	Dobrudja	11,150
1941	Rumania	1,612
Fall–winter 1942	Bosnia	3,184
1944	Crimea	241,194

Sources: Dirk Jachomowski, *Die Umsiedlung der Bessarabien-, Bukovina- und Dobrudschadeutschen: Von der Volksgruppe in Rumänien zur 'Siedlungsbrücke' an der Reichsgrenze* (Munich: Oldenbourg, 1984), 1; and Czesław Łuczak, *Pod niemieckim jarzmem* (*Kraj Warty 1939–1945*) (Poznań: PSO, 1996), 69–71.

among other fears, he worried that resettlers would leave the Gau for the Old Reich.[87] In addition, most resettlers were not allowed to return to their former homelands after Germany occupied Soviet territory. In 1941, Greiser emphasized that the 700-year history of the Baltic Germans abroad was over: 'A return to the old homeland is out of the question.'[88] In the Warthegau, resettlers were a captive population.

Altogether, some 536,951 ethnic Germans came to the Warthegau. As Table 5.1 shows, between fall 1939 and spring 1941, 290,000 resettlers came to the Gau from the Baltic countries, eastern Poland, and Rumania. Much later, in 1944, 241,194 ethnic Germans from the Crimea poured into the Gau in advance of Soviet armies. Greiser took in 85 percent of all resettlers brought to the annexed eastern areas.[89]

The resettlement program made resettlers victims and perpetrators at once. Every resettler lost a native homeland. Every resettler lost a community. Every resettler lost a home and property. But each one of these victims was also an accomplice. Nazi authorities compensated resettlers' losses in their former homelands with funds amassed from confiscated Polish and Jewish property.[90] In addition, resettlers often made their living from expropriated Polish or Jewish businesses. They lived in homes stolen from Poles or Jews; ate from Polish or Jewish dishes; and slept in Polish or Jewish beds, with Polish or Jewish sheets and comforters.[91] There is irony in that 'German' resettlers were to make their environment 'German' with plundered Polish and Jewish goods. But resettlers seem to have had few moral qualms about taking over stolen property. To them, perhaps, this seemed a just state of affairs; after all, they had lost their former possessions. But even if resettlers did face moral quandaries, they had little choice but to engage in the (im)moral economy of the Gau. How else were they to survive in their new surroundings?

In the Warthegau, Reich Germans—those from the Old Reich—made up the elite of a three-tiered German population that otherwise included resettlers and native ethnic Germans. Altogether, an estimated 194,000 Reich Germans made their home in the Warthegau.[92] Of these, approximately 6,000 were civil servants, while another 11,700 or so were other administrative personnel.[93] Some businessmen, craftsmen, and former soldiers also came to the Gau.

On balance, Reich German officials were an unsavory lot.[94] Greiser favored longtime party activists—rather than experts—in the distribution of posts.[95] At the same time, mediocre yet ambitious bureaucrats came to the Warthegau to further their careers.[96] The low caliber of personnel led to widespread absenteeism, tardiness, alcoholism, and corruption among Gau officials. Numerous decrees were directed against their miserable conduct. In November 1939, for example, Koppe reminded civil and police agencies that 'all confiscated Polish or Jewish property is for the benefit of the German Reich' and not, by implication, for personal enrichment.[97] In December, Greiser railed against corruption in Lodsch. There, a German businessman had been named general director of a firm at an exorbitant salary. Claiming that 'we absolutely refuse to be identified with this Polish corruption system,' Greiser had the man arrested on the spot.[98] In March 1941, Greiser reportedly warned against the dangers of alcoholism among officials: 'The Gauleiter emphasized that drunkenness not only seriously harms the reputation of the German population, especially that of officials, but is also often behind the committing of criminal acts.'[99] Greiser and others, however, were hypocritical: they expected officials to run a criminal Nazi regime while, at the same time, maintaining a high standard of conduct in their private lives. This simply overtaxed many bureaucrats.

Although Greiser hoped to create a harmonious German community, the Gau's three main German constituencies were deeply divided. Reich Germans looked down on ethnic Germans; ethnic Germans resented the Reich Germans; Reich Germans were often dismayed by the 'un-German' qualities of resettlers; the resettlers were angered by patronizing Reich

Germans; ethnic Germans were jealous of resettlers; and the resettlers felt ill at ease among the ethnic Germans. In no small measure, the Germanization project itself had created these tensions. The process of determining who was 'German' (see next chapter) rankled some Germans. The influx of resettlers placed additional pressures on already tight resources. The racial classification of individual resettlers and the propagation of resettler stereotypes (those from Bessarabia were viewed most favorably, those from Volhynia least favorably) fostered additional divisions.[100] Throughout the occupation, these tensions never subsided. In January 1943, a Reichsstatthalter department reported that 'the individual German groups in the Gau still haven't totally merged. They often distinguish themselves from each other, while maintaining very strong ties among themselves, so that the creation of a tightly obedient (*festgefügten*) *Volksgemeinschaft* is fraught with difficulties.'[101] A quip making the rounds in the Warthegau also captured intra-German tensions: 'The Baltic [Germans] speak Russian, the ethnic Germans Polish, the Poles German, the Reich Germans are speechless.'[102]

By March 1941, when deportations from the Warthegau to the General Government ceased, Nazi authorities still entertained many plans that demanded the removal of Poles from their homes and farms. They hoped to resettle thousands of ethnic Germans still awaiting homesteads. The Wehrmacht intended to build large training grounds, a project that would entail moving some 80,000 individuals. There were longstanding schemes to enhance the economic situation of (native) ethnic Germans by giving them Polish farms or businesses. There were also hopes of bringing in skilled German craftsmen from the Old Reich so as to bolster the German element of the Gau.[103] And finally, another project, the so-called Farm Creation Action, was to amalgamate smaller farms into larger ones for German resettlers.

For lack of a better solution, Greiser now decreed the 'displacement' (*Verdrängung*) of Poles within the Warthegau; unlike other evacuation projects directed by Berlin, this project fell squarely under his aegis (although it was carried out by UWZ officials). On 10 May 1941, Harry Siegmund wrote to Koppe that '[Greiser] has now agreed that the action of evacuating roughly 100,000 to 120,000 Poles can now begin, *but with the clear precondition that not a single one of these Poles will leave the Warthegau, that is, only a crowding together and transfer within the Gau may take place.*'[104]

Greiser was intent on preserving his Polish workforce, even though this meant a continued Polish presence in his Gau. Indeed, where Poles were concerned, he became more inclined toward upholding a segregation regime than forcing their removal from his Gau. Later that summer, Greiser reportedly told local party leaders that he 'demanded from the sub-districts the even harsher concentration of displaced Poles, even if there was a danger of the outbreak of disease and/or death for Poles.'[105] But he gave local officials no guidance as to where to put the Poles. In the end, many Poles were forced to fend for themselves; generally, they tried to find accommodations with already cramped relatives and friends. In July 1941, Krumey reported that Koppe had ordered up to 5,000 Poles to be put in UWZ camps (previously temporary housing for Poles awaiting deportation).[106] For a short time, Gau officials also experimented with reservations for Poles. In 1942, they chose an area of poor land—120 square kilometers in Kalisch sub-district—and forced some 3,947 Poles to move to the tight quarters of Poles already living there. Smaller reservations were also begun. But conditions were so poor that many Poles fled the reservations, and Gau officials soon gave up the idea.[107] Through October 1944, some 194,428 Poles were 'displaced' in the Warthegau.[108]

In another population transfer, Greiser saw 12.2 percent of the Gau's Polish population (some 450,000 Poles) sent to the Old Reich for forced labor.[109] Although Greiser was unable to refuse the Reich's huge demand for workers, he eventually managed to come up with his own inflection on this program. Beginning in 1943, he insisted that only entire families could be sent away for forced labor. He didn't want workers to leave, while their dependants became a burden on Gau welfare services. In negotiations with Reich officials, however, he promised that at least half of the members of families sent would be capable of work. In 1943, some 3,966 families, making up 16,722 individuals, were sent to France to work as field hands.[110] While Greiser lost able-bodied workers, he nonetheless furthered his ethnic-cleansing project.

A final element of anti-Polish ethnic cleansing was the 're-Germanization' program. This was an effort to rescue German 'blood' from Polish people (in accordance with Nazi ideology, any parallel effort to rescue German 'blood' from Jews was unthinkable). Himmler claimed that re-Germanization would not only bring 'racially valuable families' to the German work force, but also rob the Polish population of families of Nordic background that he believed produced its leading strata. To determine who might be subject to re-Germanization, officials of the RuSHA carried out racial screenings in UWZ camps where evicted Poles awaited deportation. Poles deemed potentially 'Re-Germanizable' were sent to yet another camp where they underwent a more detailed screening. RuSHA officials were very picky. In October 1940, between one percent and five percent of all screened Poles had received RuSHA ratings that allowed them to undergo re-Germanization.[111] In late 1941 Greiser agreed to have the entire Polish population of Wollstein sub-district, as well as two other smaller areas of his Gau, screened.[112] Of the 44,782 individuals examined, RuSHA officials determined that just 7.1 percent were potentially re-Germanizable.[113] Ultimately, some 17,243 Poles left the Warthegau for the Reich to undergo Germanization.[114] They made up a small percentage of the altogether more than 700,000 Warthegau Poles (about 18 percent of the Polish population) who were uprooted from their communities and forced to go abroad during the years of occupation.

While Poles endured terrible hardship, Jews fared even worse under Greiser's rule. Although Greiser didn't found the Litzmannstadt ghetto, he played a crucial role in its development. The ghetto was under municipal administration, with the Reich Ministry of the Interior having ultimate authority over it. But jealous as ever over his authority, Greiser insisted on intervening in ghetto developments in his capacity as Reichsstatthalter. In May 1940, Litzmannstadt officials set up an office for ghetto affairs; it was headed by Hans Biebow, a Bremen-based businessman who had owned one of Germany's largest coffee import companies.[115] Eventually known as the 'Ghetto Administration,' Biebow's office employed some 414 individuals in December 1941.[116] Greiser often dealt with Biebow directly, thereby circumventing local officials, the ghetto administrator's nominal superiors. For Uebelhoer in particular, this was a source of great frustration. In November 1941, one of his officials noted that 'Posen makes the mastery of the Jewish Question in the district more difficult by unobjective interventions (*unsachliches Hineinregieren*).'[117]

Initially, all Nazi officials assumed that the ghetto would be a temporary affair. As Uebelhoer declared in his initial decree on the ghetto, 'The creation of the ghetto is of course only a transition measure.'[118] On 1 April 1940, Greiser also emphasized that the founding of the ghetto presumed the deportation of Lodsch Jews in the second half of 1940.[119] But events soon overtook assumptions. Not only were the Germans unable to deport large numbers of Jews (since deporting Poles took precedence), but developments internal to the ghetto also favored its continued existence. In this, the interests of Biebow and the controversial chairman of the Jewish Council, Chaim Rumkowski, coincided. It seems that Biebow wanted to preserve the ghetto so that he could maintain his 'indispensable' (*unabkömmlich*) status that prevented his conscription.[120] Rumkowski's stance was more complex. The Jewish leader served at the mercy of the Germans. But at the same time, he instituted a dictatorial regime that benefited a small circle of his favorites at the expense of the vast majority of ghetto inhabitants. He also had messianic ambitions; he wished to go down in history as the savior of his people. Rumkowski soon believed that if Jews could be made essential to German war production, their lives would be spared—'salvation through work' (*Rettung durch Arbeit*).[121]

Rumkowski and his fellow Jews lived and died at the whim of Germans. Within strict confines, however, Rumkowski organized the ghetto in a way that may have saved some Jews' lives.[122] He pushed to make the ghetto an important production site. He created a semblance of normality: the ghetto had functioning schools, hospitals, orphanages, soup kitchens, and even its own currency and postal system. But Rumkowski also employed a Jewish police force that used brutal methods against 'wayward' Jews who protested his rule. And he foisted terrible moral choices on ghetto inmates. In September 1942, for example, when the ghetto's children and old people were deported, he promised that those who helped round up others would be able to keep their children. For their part, ghetto inhabitants also tried to carry on 'normal' lives. Many continued their prewar political associations. They performed or otherwise participated in concerts, readings, theater productions, and street happenings. Some wrote poetry, short stories, or diaries. In the end, though, this was a brutal situation: the Germans imposed conditions that led otherwise healthy Jews to die from cold, sickness, and starvation. Roughly one in four persons who passed through the ghetto died there—altogether some 43,725 individuals.[123]

In early summer 1940, Greiser still expected the quick removal of Jews from his Gau. But on 31 July, he met with Frank in Cracow. According to Frank's notes of the visit, Greiser told him that Himmler had informed him that there were plans to deport the Jews to Madagascar. But Greiser knew that these plans could not be carried out immediately. He thus told Frank that 'both for reasons of food policy and especially for policing epidemics it would be an impossible situation to keep the Jews who had been crammed together in the ghetto there through the winter.' Greiser wanted 250,000 Jews deported to the General Government. But his request that Frank take in Jews made just as little impression as his request that the general governor take in more Poles. After considerable discussion, Greiser conceded that Frank was in no position to accept any more Jews, 'even on an interim basis.' The upshot of the meeting: Frank and Greiser agreed that they had to await a 'basic decision' from Reich authorities.[124] Greiser was stuck. No solution to his 'Jewish Problem' was in sight. The negative outcome of the Cracow meeting spurred a change in his policy toward Jews. As described in Chapter 7, Greiser now sought to profit from Jews in his Gau 'capable of work.' Another fate, however, was in store for those deemed 'unproductive.'

Historians of the Holocaust recognize an explicit link between the 'euthanasia' campaign—the murder of asylum patients—in 1939–41 and the later mass murder of Jews. In the Reich, the same 'T4' office (code named for its address in Berlin, Tiergartenstrasse 4) planned the technical means of murder for both projects.[125] In the Warthegau, the link was even stronger: the same execution squad that carried out the murder of asylum patients in late 1939–40 went on to staff Chełmno extermination camp in 1941 and beyond. Already in September 1939 a 'euthanasia' campaign was underway in the Old Reich and Danzig–West Prussia. In October, a similar campaign began in the Warthegau.[126] Himmler and Reich 'euthanasia' experts seem to have had some involvement in the Warthegau murders.[127] At the very least, some of the same doctors traveled through the Reich, Danzig–West Prussia, and the Warthegau selecting patients for murder.[128] In the Warthegau, however, it was a Gau institution that organized the murders—the Gau Self-Administration (*Gauselbstverwaltung*), an NSDAP entity that supported Greiser's Reichsstatthalter agency. After placing German staff in psychiatric and other asylums, it received medical reports about the patients and, in turn, authorized the killing of some.[129]

No direct evidence links Greiser to the 'euthanasia' campaign.[130] But he had oversight over the Gau Self-Administration.[131] He also played an indirect role in determining the squad's victims; in August 1940, he ordered sub-district magistrates to register all individuals with hereditary or other illnesses that endangered their health.[132] Greiser likely condoned these murders because he didn't want to be seen as a laggard—particularly behind Forster—in the matter. Germanization also demanded a fit, active population; the mentally ill or physically handicapped could only be a drag on his ambitious program.[133] Greiser may also have wished to put the asylums to other uses: to house resettlers or convalescent soldiers.[134]

Through the 'euthanasia' campaign, the Warthegau became the site of experiments with new forms of mass murder. In October 1939, an SS chemist, Dr. August Becker, came to Posen; Becker later worked for the 'T4' office. In Posen, he experimented with either Zyklon-B (later used in Auschwitz) or carbon monoxide (later used in Chełmno) to murder prisoners in the Fort VII prison camp.[135] These were the first Nazi experiments that used poisonous gas to murder large numbers of individuals. While the identity of the initial victims remains unknown, on 19 November some Polish and Jewish inmates from the Treskau asylum were murdered. In the next month, hundreds of patients from other asylums were likewise killed.

Shortly after Himmler came to Posen on 13 December, gassings in Fort VII stopped. Instead, in early January, the 'SS-Special Commando Lange,' led by Herbert Lange, began to bring a mobile gas van, disguised as a Kaiser's Coffee truck, to murder inmates of insane asylums, hospitals, orphanages, and old-age homes.[136] Lange's batallion also worked beyond the Gau's borders. Later, in October 1940, Koppe demanded from Jakob Sporrenberg, the HSSPF in East Prussia, payment for murders carried out by the battalion the previous spring. An agreement had decreed that 10 RM would be paid for every patient 'evacuated.' Since the battalion had killed 1,558 individuals, Koppe now sought 15,580 RM (minus 2,000 RM paid in advance).[137] By summer 1941, Lange's battalion had killed at least 5,726 victims in the Warthegau, and another 1,808 victims in East Prussia.[138]

In past decades, historians of the Holocaust have engaged in intense debate about the role of central and regional officials in initiating the Holocaust. Did Hitler or the RSHA order killings in fall 1941? Or did regional officials independently begin killings, thereby radicalizing anti-Jewish policy on their own? By now, historians have reached a consensus: neither the center nor the periphery initiated while the other simply reacted. Instead, regional authorities, faced with what they deemed impossible pressures, made proposals to and sought guidance from RSHA officials. RSHA officials, meanwhile, carried on their own conversations, informed by regional proposals. In turn, they encouraged and perhaps even coordinated various local murder initiatives that emerged in late summer and early fall 1941.[139] The input of local authorities helps to explain why the Final Solution took on different forms in different areas. In some regions, Jews were ghettoized; in others, not. In some regions, Jews were exploited for their labor; in others, even 'productive' Jews were soon murdered. In some regions, there were extermination camps; in others, roving bands of SS-execution squads. In the Warthegau, Greiser successfully insisted that Gau authorities take charge of the Final Solution. Greiser was thus able to put his own imprimatur on the Holocaust there. Indeed, he provides an excellent example of a mid-level Nazi official who shaped the Final Solution in his territory and, in the process, more generally radicalized murderous policy toward Jews in Germany and Nazi-occupied Europe.

On 4 June 1941, Himmler came to Posen to confer with Greiser. Two days later, the two men drove through the Litzmannstadt ghetto.[140] During Himmler's visit, the two men must have talked about the demographic situation in the Gau. Perhaps they also discussed the upcoming war—the Germans would launch Operation Barbarossa just two weeks later, on 22 June—and the opportunities that it might provide to resolve the Gau's demographic 'problems.'

By summer 1941 Greiser knew only too well the seemingly insoluble demographic pressures that local Gau officials believed that they faced.[141] Thousands of ethnic Germans were languishing in resettler camps in the Gau; there weren't enough homes or farms for them. Since Poles were needed to work, they couldn't just be deported or 'displaced.' At the same time, Hans Frank refused to take in any more Poles or Jews. The Madagascar Plan had been shelved. With the exception of the First Short-Term Plan, all of the other deportation plans had come up short against the difficult realities of moving masses of people eastwards. Local officials in the eastern parts of the Gau were clamoring for 'their' Jews to be deported to the ghetto. But Litzmannstadt officials balked. To them, the already overcrowded ghetto posed a health danger to the German population. It was also a financial drain. Due to shortages of machines and raw materials, even Jews 'capable of work' couldn't. Children, the aged, and the sick were unable to work. Profits from Jews' work still didn't cover the costs of maintaining the ghetto (especially since Reich, Gau, and city agencies all insisted on taking a share of the profits).[142]

That same summer, Rolf-Heinz Höppner, head of the Posen SD office, was also considering the Gau's population pressures. On 16 July—after the invasion of the Soviet Union—he wrote a now infamous memorandum about the 'solution to the Jewish Question.' In recent meetings in the Reichsstatthalter agency, he wrote, various solutions had been aired. One option was to create a camp for roughly 300,000 Jews, preferably near coal fields. All the Jews in the Gau would be brought there. According to the police chief in Litzmannstadt, Karl-Wilhelm Albert, this would have security advantages. Höppner then listed other alternatives that might be pursued—including outright murder. As he noted, 'there is a danger this winter that all the Jews can no longer be fed. It is to be seriously considered whether the most humane solution might not be to finish off those Jews not capable of work by some sort of quick-acting agent. In any case it would be more pleasant than to let them starve.' He further proposed that all Jewish women of child-bearing age be 'sterilized so that the Jewish Problem will really be totally solved in this generation.'[143] In a cover letter to Adolf Eichmann accompanying the memorandum, Höppner wrote that 'The things sound in part fantastic, but would in my view be quite capable of implementation.'[144] Höppner's memorandum is ubiquitously cited in literature on the Holocaust. Historians point to the line about a 'quick-acting agent' to show that by summer 1941 officials at different levels of the Nazi hierarchy were toying with murder as a solution to the 'Jewish question' even in areas west of the Soviet Union.

Where was Greiser in all of these discussions? According to Höppner, 'the Reichsstatthalter had not yet spoken his opinion on these matters.'[145] In all likelihood, Greiser had not yet made up his mind about how to deal with the 'Jewish Question;' he was perhaps waiting for a signal from Berlin.[146] At the same time, Höppner's line may be interpreted quite literally. Greiser was barely in Posen during these weeks; he was on an extended tour of his Gau, possibly discussing the 'Jewish Question' with local officials.[147] He thus couldn't take part in the meetings and, as a result, couldn't voice his views.

On 16 July, the very day on which Höppner wrote his memorandum, Greiser interrupted his tour of the Gau so as to have an audience with Hitler in Rastenburg on 18 July. A few days later, he documented the results of this conversation in a memorandum circulated to his subordinates: 'The Führer has repeatedly and now again in his last conversation with me in the Führer headquarters told me that he holds the view that to carry out my unique tasks in the Reichsgau Wartheland I have to have at my disposal much greater powers than [NSDAP leaders in] other Reich areas.'[148]

Greiser now claimed that Hitler had granted him significant 'powers' over his 'unique tasks'—read Germanization—in his Gau. Perhaps this meant, as one historian has argued, that Hitler also empowered Greiser to solve the 'Jewish Question' in the Warthegau.[149]

If Hitler granted Greiser the initiative in taking on the 'Jewish Question' in their 18 July meeting, it is unlikely that he approved any specific murder plans. In the next six weeks, Nazi measures against Jews in occupied Soviet areas evolved dramatically. In mid-July Himmler's operational groups (*Einsatzgruppen*) were shooting Jewish men of military age as 'partisans.' By mid-August, the operational groups, along with other security and Wehrmacht personnel, were systematically massacring Jewish women and children.[150] Greiser likely knew about this and may well have begun to contemplate similar measures in his Gau. On 28 August, Ernst Kendzia, the head of the Department of Work in Greiser's Reichsstatthalter agency, proposed the transfer of at least 5,000 'unproductive' Jews to the Gestapo, presumably so that they could be executed. Biebow, however, opposed the transfer.[151] On 12 September Greiser noted that he had told an Interior Ministry official that 'the Jewish Question need not always be solved through first asking the Interior Ministry, but rather through energetic and responsible action there and then.'[152] In his view, decisions about the 'Jewish Question' could be made on the spot, without having to consult Reich authorities. Still, Greiser did not initiate steps to carry out the systematic murder of 'unproductive' Jews in his Gau.

In mid-September, Hitler made a decision that finally set Greiser on a murderous course. Up to then, the Führer had insisted that no Jews from the Reich be deported until Germany had won the war in the Soviet Union. But abruptly, he now changed course. On 16–17 September, he met independently with the Hamburg Gauleiter Karl Kaufmann; the German ambassador to France, Otto Abetz; and Foreign Minister Joachim von Ribbentrop. All wished to deport Jews from western Europe. Perhaps the repeated requests convinced Hitler that it was time to begin the deportation of Jews from the Reich. Or perhaps military events—the Germans were just then enjoying a string of successes—emboldened the Führer.[153] Late on 17 September, Hitler met with Himmler. The very next day, the SS-leader sent Greiser a telegram: 'The Führer wishes that the Old Reich and Protectorate [Czech lands] be emptied and freed of Jews from west to east as quickly as possible.' As a first step, Himmler continued, the Jews were to be brought to the areas annexed to the Reich in 1939; 'next spring' they would be moved further east. He then told Greiser: 'I plan to bring roughly 60,000 Jews from the Old Reich and the Protectorate to the Litzmannstadt ghetto to spend the winter; as I hear, the ghetto has room for them. This measure will surely bring your Gau difficulties and burdens, but I ask you not only to understand it, but in the interests of the whole Reich to support it with all efforts.'[154]

Himmler's telegram forced Greiser to act. As he knew, Litzmannstadt officials were dead set against bringing further Jews into the ghetto. In mid-July they had bitterly opposed his orders that some 2,900 Jews from Leslau be sent to the ghetto.[155] (The Leslau Jews, it seems, were sent to the ghetto so that Poles could take over their housing and, in turn, relinquish their homes to some of the 50,000 resettlers from Besserabia and Bukovina still living in resettler camps.)[156] At the same time, Greiser surely wanted to stave off an influx of Jews in his Gau; he probably figured, correctly, that 'unproductive' Jews would be among the first deported to Litzmannstadt. In the next few days, meetings took place between various interested parties.[157] The upshot: Himmler and Greiser agreed that 'only' 20,000 Jews and 5,000 gypsies would come to the Gau.

But there was more. Greiser, in exchange for accepting the Jews and gypsies, appears to have received permission to have 100,000 'unproductive' Jews murdered.[158] Evidence for this is found in future correspondence between Greiser and Himmler. On 28 October 1941, Greiser reminded Himmler about 'the agreement reached between us.'[159] The following spring, on 1 May, he mentioned that 'the operation of special treatment with regard to 100,000 Jews, approved by you in agreement with the chief of the Reich Security Main Office SS-Senior Group Leader Heydrich, will be able to be completed in the next two to three months.'[160] Greiser's use of the word 'approved' suggests that Himmler hadn't ordered the operation. But if the SS-leader hadn't, who had? Presumably Greiser himself. It was Greiser who initiated the murder of Jews in his Gau.[161]

Local Gau officials certainly saw Greiser as the one giving the orders for murder. On 9 December, a German air-force listening post picked up a conversation between Uebelhoer and Robert Schefe, the head of the Litzmannstadt State Police Office. Uebelhoer reportedly told Schefe that 'on the orders of the Gauleiter those sick in the ghetto were to be brought away. In response to the State Police Office's question about whether Berlin knew about this, an evasive answer was given.' Uebelhoer's comment suggests that Greiser not only ordered the murder of some Jews in the Litzmannstadt ghetto, but that he did so without express approval from Berlin. On 16 January 1942, when deportations from the ghetto began, the listening post picked up another conversation. The acting head of the Litzmannstadt Gestapo, Herbert Weygandt, stated: 'after a further resettlement (*Aussiedlung*) of Jews incapable of work, the Gauleiter intends to bring in [to the ghetto] 10,000 Jewish workers from the Warthegau.'[162] Similarly, on 9 June 1942 the Litzmannstadt State Police office wrote a situational report in which it noted that 'On instructions from the Gauleiter, all Jews unable to work were to be evacuated...'[163] Finally, years after the events in question, Günter Fuchs, the expert for Jewish matters in the Litzmannstadt Gestapo, testified that 'in relation to matters concerning Jews we never received instructions from Berlin, but always only from the Reichsstatthalter in Posen.'[164]

How had Greiser come to order the murder of 'unproductive' Jews? Surely this was not the ethic that he had grown up with in Hohensalza. Rather, after years in the Nazi movement, notions that earlier seemed inconceivable must now have seemed plausible. Although Greiser voiced typical Nazi anti-Semitic propaganda, his desire to murder Jews was probably not the result of long-held ideological views about the Jewish 'enemy.' Rather, Greiser made his decision at a particular time, in a particular situation. The heated circumstances of war and occupation. The closed atmosphere of high-level consultations. The terrible housing shortage brought on by resettlement. The lack of any real solution to demographic 'problems.' The financial pressures of the ghetto. The desire to profile himself with Himmler and Hitler. Then, too, Himmler's operational groups were engaged in wanton killing operations in the Soviet Union. Subordinate officials such as Höppner were pressing for radical solutions in the Gau. Greiser surely wanted to be in step with radical Nazi proposals—at least in how he dealt with 'unproductive' Jews. Indeed, precisely because he wanted 'productive' Jewish workers to labor in his Gau (see Chapter 7), he wished to keep face with Himmler by zealously advocating the murder of Jews 'incapable of work.' Finally, his calculations may have reflected his insecurities about his place in the Nazi regime; he wanted to prove that he was a true Nazi. With all this in mind, murder must now have seemed to him the right solution to the 'Jewish Question.'

Initially, Litzmannstadt officials were not informed about the conditions under which Jews and gypsies were to come to the ghetto. As a result, they raised a ruckus—not least because this was just when the Leslau Jews were actually brought to the ghetto; local authorities had procrastinated on Greiser's July orders. On 24 September Werner Ventzki, the lord mayor of Litzmannstadt, sent Uebelhoer a letter protesting the arrival of even more Jews. On 9 October, Uebelhoer sent this letter on to Himmler along with his own letter of protest. Himmler soon complained to Greiser about Uebelhoer.[165] But Greiser intervened on behalf of his district president. On 28 October, he told Himmler that he was convinced that 'Uebelhoer wanted the best.'[166] By then, Uebelhoer was already tackling the arrival of western Jews. Between 16 October and 4 November 1941, 19,837 persons from the Old Reich, Prague, Vienna, and Luxemburg came to Litzmannstadt.[167] As Greiser wrote, Uebelhoer had done everything so as to implement Himmler's orders.[168] He was anxious to defend Uebelhoer (a situation that would soon change). He didn't want his local officials to be seen as a 'problem;' he wanted Himmler to know that he could be counted on.

Meanwhile, preparations for the systematic carrying out of the Final Solution in the Gau began. Already on 20 September, Greiser charged Herbert Mehlhorn, the Reichsstatthalter official, as his point man for all matters related to the 'accommodation and work' of Jews and gypsies in the Gau.[169] Mehlhorn was an interesting choice: he did not get along with either Heydrich or Koppe, but he had excellent relations with Greiser and Himmler.[170] The coordination of matters related to Jews living and working in the Gau thus took place in Greiser's Reichsstatthalter agency, and not in the offices of regional security authorities or Litzmannstadt city officials.

By the end of September, the Lange battalion was back at work, this time with Jews as its target. Battalion members soon murdered all the Jews in Konin sub-district, some 4,500 individuals; many of these Jews were killed in mass shootings in the forests of Kazimierz Biskupi.[171] These Jews may have been killed so as to alleviate a housing shortage caused by plans to build army exercise grounds (a project soon abandoned).[172] Konin was also the westernmost sub-district of the Gau not yet 'free of Jews.'[173] These murders show just how much anti-Jewish measures had radicalized. In mid-July, Greiser had insisted that Jews in Leslau be sent to the ghetto. Not so the Konin Jews; they were killed straight off.[174]

Greiser escalated other murderous policy toward Jews. On 9 October the Gestapo in Posen informed a branch office that the 'Reichsstatthalter has no longer limited special measures against Jews in the case of fleeing camp, but has ordered the carrying out of special measures against Jews accused of other criminal activity such as agitation, revolt, money smuggling, etc.'[175] 'Special measures' was a euphemism for murder. And since the crimes had elastic definitions and Jews had only to be 'accused,' Greiser had licensed the easy murder of Jews.

In fall 1941, Nazi authorities in the Warthegau sought more efficient means of mass murder than bringing mobile gas vans to victims. Unlike in the occupied Soviet Union, mass shootings were not an option much used (Kazimierz Biskupi was an exception). Such executions were likely deemed unseemly in a region that was part of the Reich and in which relatively large numbers of Germans lived. Instead, the decision was made to found an extermination camp where Jews wouldn't be shot, but rather gassed (in gas vans, not stationary chambers).[176] It is possible that Lange began searching for a suitable site for an extermination camp as early as July, but he did not settle on a site until October 1941.[177] He chose an unoccupied mansion in Chełmno (the Germans called it Kulmhof) along the Ner River, some thirty-five miles northwest of Litzmannstadt. It was soon readied for its murderous function.[178]

Just then, similar developments were taking place elsewhere in Nazi-occupied Europe. In late October, preparations were begun to make Belzec an extermination camp for the Lublin district of the General Government. Site selection for camps near Mogilev and Riga was also underway. By summer 1941, Nazi anti-Semitism, combined with wartime opportunity, led Nazi authorities in a number of regions to arrive at murder as the solution to the 'Jewish problem.'[179] RSHA authorities encouraged these local murder initiatives. In fall 1941, for example, Himmler and Heydrich had repeated consultations with Greiser and Koppe. At the same time, the gas vans used by the Lange battalion belonged to the RSHA's motor pool.[180] Chełmno was thus one of several Nazi murder actions getting underway in fall 1941; it did not occur in isolation.

Lange was the first camp commander at Chełmno, but he held this position only until March 1942.[181] His successor was Hans Bothmann. Thereafter, the battalion was officially called the 'Special Commando Kulmhof;' occasionally, it was referred to as the 'Bothmann battalion.' A Polish source later claimed that Greiser was repeatedly at Chełmno, thereby suggesting that he somehow busied himself with the camp's daily operations.[182] More reliable sources, however, do not corroborate such frequent visits. Instead, Koppe directed the general activities of the battalion, while Ernst Damzog, the inspector of the Sipo and the SD in Posen, supervised its day-to-day operations.[183] Greiser, however, was not out of the loop. In addition to their regular pay, battalion members received an extra subsidy of twelve to twenty RM per day, as well as extra food, tobacco, and alcohol rations. Funds for these expenditures were drawn at least partially from a special Reichsstatthalter account.[184]

Mass killings at Chełmno began on 8 December 1941. Jews there were killed in one of three mobile gas vans, and then buried in mass graves at a forest site some four kilometers from the mansion. The first victims were inhabitants of five small communities in the surrounding area—perhaps because their homes were not in the ghetto and could thus be more easily readied for 'displaced' Poles.[185] In mid-December some 4,400 Sinti and Roma, whose camp in the Litzmannstadt ghetto had seen an outbreak of typhus, were murdered.[186] On 16 January, the first Jews from the ghetto arrived and were murdered.

The western Jews sent to Litzmannstadt in fall 1941 were initially expressly excluded from these murders; it seems that Hitler had not yet definitely determined their fate.[187] On 16–17 April 1942, however, Himmler came to Posen and met with Greiser and Koppe in the Hotel Ostland.[188] In all likelihood, the men discussed the murder of western Jews. These and other meetings held with Himmler in late 1941 and early 1942 suggest that Greiser could not just do what he pleased with the Jews in his Gau. While he may well have initiated ever more radical measures, he nonetheless had to, wanted to, or was expected to consult with Himmler.[189]

Beginning on 29 April, western Jews were included in deportations to Chełmno. In September 1942, another wave of deportations targeted children and the elderly. Thereafter, Greiser had achieved his goal: Jews 'incapable of work' had been murdered, while the Litzmannstadt ghetto was peopled with only 'productive' Jews. Up through March 1943, when Chełmno was first closed, some 150,000 persons were murdered there. Those killed included about 145,301 Jews (both from the Litzmannstadt ghetto and from smaller communities around the Gau); the 4,400 Sinti and Roma; and children from the Czech town of Lidice whose parents were murdered in retribution for the assassination of Reinhard Heydrich.[190] Greiser did not hide what was happening in his Gau. In May 1942, he went to Vienna, where he described 'how Jews were packed into cars and murdered by means of exhaust fumes.' Vienna's Gauleiter, Baldur von Schirach, and the assembled audience were shocked.[191]

In the history of the Holocaust, Greiser occupies an important role: he initiated the first mass gassings of Jews. Save for Hans Frank, Greiser was the Nazi leader with the largest number of Jews in his territory. At the same time, steeped in Nazi racial attitudes, he and his officials believed that they faced terrible population pressures that could be alleviated only by the murder of Jews. Unlike other eastern leaders, Greiser occupied a position in the Nazi hierarchy that made it possible—indeed, desirable—for him to act speedily: he had direct control over the Litzmannstadt ghetto; he had good and frequent contact with Himmler; he had the support of security personnel in the Gau; and, perhaps most important, he wanted to prove himself as a can-do leader to his Nazi superiors.

In spring 1942, Greiser attempted to extend the methods of murdering Jews to Poles. On 1 May, he wrote to Himmler seeking permission to murder 35,000 Poles with incurable tuberculosis. As he noted, there were 230,000 cases of tuberculosis among Poles in his Gau; of these, 35,000 were suffering from open tuberculosis. Many Germans, and particularly German children, had become infected. In addition, a number of leading men, especially in the police, had contracted the disease and were now unavailable for military service. Greiser also wrote, 'Even if in the Old Reich one cannot take such drastic measures against this people's plague (*Volkspest*), I think that I can justify proposing to you that in the Warthegau cases of open T[u]B[erculosis] within the Polish population be eliminated.' He added that 'of course' this would be done only in cases in which a doctor had categorized a Pole as incurable. Pressing the urgency of the matter, Greiser asked Himmler for a quick response. Himmler took his time, though, and responded to Greiser only on 27 July. The SS-leader wrote that he 'had no reservations' about subjecting Poles with incurable tuberculosis to the 'special measures' Greiser had suggested. But he asked that Greiser discuss the matter with the security police so that 'the carrying out [of the operation] can take place as discreetly as possible.'[192]

Some time later, on 18 November, Dr. Kurt Blome, the deputy director of the NSDAP's Main Office for People's Health, wrote to Greiser that he believed that Hitler's approval for the action was necessary; it would be impossible to keep it secret, and foreign countries and church authorities would condemn the action. If, as Blome believed, the Führer rejected such a radical solution, Greiser could resettle all tubercular Poles in an enclosed area or isolate the sickest Poles in asylums.[193] Greiser was outraged. Three days later he turned to Himmler to decide the issue. As he wrote, 'I myself do not believe that the Führer needs to be asked again in this matter, especially since at our last discussion with regard to the Jews he told me that I could proceed with these according to my own judgement.'[194] As Greiser told Himmler, he believed that he could do what he wished as concerned the Jews in his Gau; he now translated this to Poles. In early December, however, Himmler sided with Blome.[195] With that, Greiser's plan to murder tens of thousands of Poles came to naught. Greiser had received a rare slap in the face from Himmler. But the incident suggests that for him, the 'Final Solution' was not the whole 'solution' to his Gau's demographic ills. Had the Third Reich triumphed in World War II, Greiser would likely have adopted murderous policies toward Poles, too.

Just how successful was the Germanization of the Gau's people? Greiser, for one, viewed his population policy as a success. In 1942, he proudly noted that 'we mastered resettlement . . .' By then, some 60,500 families, roughly 300,000 individuals, had been settled in his Gau since late 1939. Greiser framed his achievement by comparing it with Prussian results. Between 1888 and the onset of World War I, the Prussian Settlement Commission—with a large budget and a huge administrative building—settled just 24,000 peasant families in the two provinces of West Prussia and Posen. By contrast, in the Warthegau, a few untrained officials in two years of war had settled 'more than double' the number of families that Prussian authorities had managed 'in roughly 30 peace years!'[196]

Two years later, in March 1944, Greiser sent a telegram to Hitler reporting that the Gau now had one million Germans: 'full of pride and joy I may report to you, my Führer, as the first success of this real Germanization process, that today the number of one million has been reached.' Greiser recited the steps that had led to this number: 'We started in September 1939 with roughly 250,000 Germans. With painstaking attention to the German blood of this land, we then added through the process of the Ethnic German Register [see next chapter] another 150,000 persons. Then we anchored Reich Germans from all the Gaus of the Greater German Reich in the reconstruction of the party, state, and economy. We then took in more than half of all the German resettlers from the settlement zones of Europe . . .' Later in the telegram, Greiser noted that 'save for a tiny remnant

Jewry has completely disappeared, and Polishdom has been reduced from formerly 4.2 million to 3.5 million persons.'[197] Less than a week later, Greiser claimed that Hitler had told him that 'no report in recent times had given him greater joy than this one.'[198] Due to the influx of resettlers and Reich Germans, the ethnic cleansing of Poles, and the murder of Jews, Greiser raised the percentage of Germans in the Warthegau from 6.6 percent of the population in 1939 to 22.9 percent by April 1944.[199] But these numbers actually suggest the futile nature of these population projects. After all the resettlement, deportation, and murder—the uprooting of at least 1,500,000 individuals—not even a quarter of the Gau's population was German.

6

'The German is the Master:' Segregation in the Warthegau

While Arthur Greiser is arguably best known for his role in the Holocaust, his anti-Polish policies are what most distinguished him from other Nazi leaders. To Greiser, anti-Polish measures were just as crucial for his Germanization program as the persecution and murder of Jews. The Warthegau thus saw the most severe anti-Polish policies in Nazi-occupied Europe.[1] Some of these policies were replicated in the other annexed eastern territories; in this respect, too, the Warthegau proved a Nazi 'model.' At the same time, as a sub-theme of this chapter suggests, Greiser used radical racial policies to accumulate additional personal powers and to strengthen his radical Nazi credentials.

Anti-Polish policy, though, posed a dilemma for Greiser: he was torn between ideological and pragmatic goals. The Warthegau had an overwhelmingly Polish population, but Greiser wanted a 'German' Gau—only possible through the ethnic cleansing of the Polish population. Yet he also wanted an economically viable Gau—only possible through maintaining a Polish workforce. Greiser sometimes tempered his harsh anti-Polish segregation policies so as not to further alienate 'working' Poles. Given his competing goals, his policies toward Poles vacillated; sometimes, they were even downright contradictory.

Just as the demographic reordering of the Gau involved policies that touched Germans, Jews, and Poles in interrelated ways, Greiser's segregation policies toward Poles had a direct impact on the Germans in the Gau. To create an anti-Polish segregation system, Gau authorities had to know just who was 'German' and who was 'Polish.' Since the ethnic fault line between Poles and Germans was blurry at best, this was no easy matter. To address this 'problem,' Greiser created a registration process for Germans; all those deemed 'German' were placed on the Ethnic German Register (*Deutsche Volksliste*, or DVL). Greiser set a high bar for DVL registration. Together with strict anti-Polish measures, this meant that the stakes of ethnic classification were very high; DVL categorization was fraught with tension. At the same time, many of Greiser's other measures—including anti-church policies carried out in the name of Germanization—fractured or otherwise alienated the Gau's German population. So while segregation policies divided Germans from Poles, they also exposed contradictions in Greiser's policies and ruptured the German community in the Warthegau.

Greiser claimed that his biography gave him special insight into the 'Polish question.' Unlike other refashionings of his life story, this one had genuine resonance. After all, the Poles had taken over his childhood home; had put great pressure on Danzig during the interwar years; had offered fierce resistance to the Nazi invasion; and, at the start of his rule, made up roughly 85 percent of his Gau's population. Shortly after Greiser came to Posen, the *Ostdeutscher Beobachter*, the official local Nazi daily, described one of his speeches: 'Arthur Greiser recalled that he himself had the opportunity throughout his whole life to learn the peculiarities of the Polish mentality: in Hohensalza as a pupil, as a soldier in the Border Protection East and especially as a politician in Danzig.' As he further explained, as senate president, he had negotiated with Polish leaders in Geneva: 'There we got wise to their tricks. They overestimate themselves and believe themselves to be a great power . . . '[2] Two years later, Greiser again linked his biography to his understanding of the true nature of German–Polish relations. 'As a child of this Gau,' he reportedly stated, 'he saw the Polish question in its true light. The Polish people should never again be allowed to succeed in rising up in the East. Here the struggle between the German and the Polish *Volkstum* is about survival or extinction (*sein oder Nichtsein*).'[3]

In an article published in the *Völkischer Beobachter*, the national Nazi newspaper, Greiser claimed that there were certain characteristics of the Polish nation that everyone should know: that the Polish people were incapable of maintaining a state; that they were always engaged in egoistic struggle; that they overestimated their potential; that they showed devotion when treated harshly and fairly, and 'sadistic cruelty' when under poor leadership; that they could display at once both 'kindness' and 'shiftiness;'

and that the intelligentsia, middle class, and clerics always brought forth great 'haters of Germany.'[4] On another occasion he declared, 'The Pole has a different mentality . . . He only remains decent so long as he is treated by us harshly and fairly. The moment that he realizes that we are soft and weak he becomes rude and allows his shifty and deceitful ways to come to the fore.' Greiser further claimed: 'The Pole also has a whole different attitude toward the things of daily life and to the culture in Europe . . . For Poles it is the best satisfaction, the utter height of feeling, when he [*sic*] can drink and gorge himself like an animal.'[5] In a similar speech, Greiser concluded that it was 'sheer lunacy to believe that there could be a bridging of the two peoples.'[6]

The belief that a great divide separated Germans from Poles led Greiser—like Hitler—to claim that assimilation was impossible. He thus castigated the Prussian policy of his childhood: 'The Polish policy before 1914 was not only wrong because it wavered and was uncertain and did not use all possible means for its goal of Germanizing Poles, but also because of the goal itself. Our *Volkstum* policy is borne by *völkisch* and racial necessities. Between Germans and Poles there can be no coexistence. A Germanization of Poles, besides a numerically few exceptions, is not only not desired, but also wrong in a National-Socialist sense. The Polish person cannot and may not be Germanized.'[7] In place of assimilation, Greiser entertained other, more radical solutions. Initially, he hoped to expel many Poles from his Gau. But as described in the previous chapter, deportation became impossible (due to the war) and undesirable (due to the need for a work force). Instead, Greiser chose another path: a strict segregation system. This system underscored his vision of German–Polish relations, voiced in his phrase: 'The German is the master in this area, the Pole is the serf!'[8]

For all the specious reasoning that Poles were categorically different from Germans, Nazi authorities were hard-pressed to distinguish between the two. On 28 October 1939, Greiser thus decreed the DVL in the Warthegau.[9] Dr. Karl Albert Coulon, the advisor in *Volkstum* matters in Greiser's administration, headed the central DVL office, located in the Reichsstatthalter agency.[10] All ethnic Germans who had held Polish citizenship and who had lived in the territory of the Warthegau on 1 September 1939 would be registered on the DVL. Those on the list would automatically be considered German. With the exception of Jews, Czechs,

Ukrainians, and some smaller national minorities, all other inhabitants of the Gau were deemed Poles. In November, Greiser issued guidelines for the criteria to be used for DVL registration (which was voluntary). Initially, he did not focus on racial attributes. Instead, the most important measure of 'Germanness' was the degree to which an individual had acted as a German during the interwar period: 'the fundamental prerequisite for German national belonging is the profession of German *Volkstum* during the time of *völkisch* foreign rule.' Greiser expressly stated that 'due to the conditions in the Reichsgau, racial characteristics could not be used as a sure principle of judgment.'[11] (This was similar to Reich policies that categorized Jews not by racial criteria, but by whether an individual's grandparents had been members of Jewish religious organizations.)[12]

DVL classification sowed dissension within the German community. Information on an individual's past German activity was ascertained through formal criteria such as membership in German organizations (including Lutheran churches) or the enrollment of children in German schools before 1939. But DVL authorities also relied on the testimony of trusted ethnic Germans, who vouched for or denounced their compatriots. Old antipathies came to the fore as activist ethnic Germans who had been frustrated by the national apathy of their compatriots testified accordingly. Moreover, ethnic Germans who had little interest in the German nationalist cause faced a moral dilemma: whether to side with the Nazis or to suffer persecution as Poles. DVL decisions also sometimes left individuals who were members of the same extended family on opposite ends of an artificially created national divide.

Initially, Gau authorities established just two DVL groups. Group A included individuals active in ethnic German parties, clubs, or associations in interwar Poland. Greiser's guidelines meant that an individual with two Polish parents who had actively engaged in German organizational life would be registered in Group A.[13] Group B included all individuals of German descent who had not publicly identified themselves as Germans, but who had continued to maintain a degree of Germanness—such as speaking German at home or socializing with other Germans.[14] Gau authorities, however, soon realized that these two groups failed to capture many potential ethnic Germans. Many individuals of German origin had become 'Polonized' during the interwar period; they now, for example, spoke Polish rather than German (not least because there had been so few German schools in the interwar Polish Republic). Gau authorities also faced other classification quandaries. How should they categorize individuals with one German and one Polish parent? Individuals who had four German grandparents, but had married Poles and raised their children as Poles? Individuals who were nationally indifferent and reluctant to self-identify as either Poles or Germans?

At different times and with somewhat different criteria, Warthegau authorities introduced three further DVL categories. Group C included individuals of German origin who had become at least partially Polonized, but who were considered racially fit to become full members of the German *Volksgemeinschaft*. This group also included individuals of Polish descent if they were married to Germans and had raised their children as Germans. Group D included individuals of German descent who had become fully Polonized, but who had not actively worked against Germandom. Group E included individuals of German descent who had acted in a manner hostile toward Germandom; it existed only in Litzmannstadt district. Members of Groups A, B, and C received Reich citizenship; Groups D and E did not.[15] DVL authorities also decided that all members of a nuclear family had to be included in or rejected from the DVL; individual family members, however, sometimes belonged to different groups within the DVL.

While the DVL legally separated Germans from Poles, Gau authorities were bedeviled by the fact that no obvious physical features distinguished Germans from Poles. Language was not foolproof. Because parts of the Gau had belonged to Prussia up to 1918, many Poles could speak German—often better than their native ethnic German counterparts or resettlers. Gau authorities deemed it unwise to have all Poles wear a symbol (such as Jews wearing the Star of David) since this would only underscore their ubiquity in the Gau.[16] Instead, they placed the burden of positive identification on Germans. In 1940, a Posen police official reminded the force that to visit pubs designated for Germans, individuals had to wear a uniform, or show some sort of German badge (such as a DVL or NSDAP badge). As the official noted, though, some Germans, especially women, refused to do so.[17] Germans, it seems, resented the burden of identification.

Gau authorities were not alone in contemplating racial policy. In November 1939, Erhard Wetzel and Günther Hecht, staff members of the NSDAP's Racial Political Office (*Rassenpolitisches Amt der NSDAP*), put together a widely circulated report on 'The Question of the Treatment of the Population in the Former Polish Areas according to Racial-Political Considerations.'[18] This report anticipated many of the anti-Polish measures soon put into place in the Warthegau. In May 1940, Heinrich Himmler wrote his own memorandum on the matter. He planned on racially screening the entire population so as 'to fish out of this broth the racially valuable and to bring them to Germany so as to assimilate them there.' All others were to receive an elementary education that consisted of 'simple arithmetic up to 500, the writing of one's name, and the teaching that it is a divine command to obey the Germans and to be honest, hard-working and good.'[19] Himmler ordered that Greiser and the other eastern Gauleiters were to get copies of his memorandum.[20]

By then, tough anti-Polish measures were already underway in the Warthegau. On 29 September 1939, for example, Greiser issued administrative guidelines on Poles. 'As a matter of principle,' he declared, 'Poles lounging about are no longer to be seen.' They were to be used as forced labor for emergency public work projects. Poles found with weapons were to be publicly executed. All monies belonging to Polish organizations were to 'be secured and used in the interests of the German nation and reconstruction work' (see next chapter). Ominously, Greiser ordered the compilation of lists of leading Poles—priests, teachers, large landowners, merchants, and industrialists; many were soon arrested.[21] Greiser also began a ferocious campaign against the Catholic Church (the vast majority of Poles in the Gau were Catholic).

On 7 November, in an attempt to regulate personal interactions between Germans and Poles, Greiser decreed that marriages between Germans and Poles 'should fundamentally not occur.'[22] Later, on 25 September 1940, he issued general guidelines on German conduct toward Poles. Germans, he insisted, had to be educated in 'the necessity of absolutely preserving a personal distance from Polish nationals.' They were not to interact with Poles beyond the minimum necessary for work-related purposes. Friendly relations with Poles were unacceptable. Greiser threatened arrest for individuals who violated these principles; having sex with Poles would be automatic cause for Germans to be arrested.[23] Other Gau officials exhorted German farmers not to eat with their Polish farmhands or told German university employees not to address Poles with the term 'Mr.' (*Herr*).[24]

In November 1939, Wilhelm Koppe, the higher SS and police leader (HSSPF) in the Gau, decreed that Polish men, when they passed German officials, had the 'duty' to 'greet' (*Grusspflicht*) them by removing their hats. Poles were also to make way for Germans on crowded sidewalks.[25] A host of local officials reiterated these or similar orders. In July 1941, however, while touring the Gau, Greiser noticed how rarely Poles greeted him, his entourage, or his car. This led August Jäger, the deputy Reichsstatthalter, to remind sub-district magistrates that in rural areas, at least, Poles had to greet Germans.[26] But many officials opposed this measure since it was so difficult to enforce. In August 1941, Greiser declared that Hitler would have to decide the matter and that until then, local officials could do as they wished.[27] A long while later—in 1943—the Party Chancellery decided against a general duty of 'foreign people' to greet German officials.[28] Greiser now told a meeting of NSDAP political leaders that the issue 'was not a matter of overriding concern.'[29] In a rare triumph, Poles' refusal to greet German officials quashed this discriminatory measure.[30]

Segregation measures were soon apparent in every sphere of Gau activity. In December 1939, Café Schwan in Posen advertised 'Entry for Germans only.'[31] In June 1940, the *Ostdeutscher Beobachter* carried pictures of a newly opened outdoor city pool on the Warta River; as the caption read, the pool, along with its playground and other facilities, 'is there just for Germans and awaits its happy guests.'[32] Similar restrictions were placed on public beaches.[33] Playgrounds and park benches were designated 'for Germans only.'[34] Poles were not permitted to use recreational boats.[35] They faced restricted hours during which they could use public baths. Keeping clean was to be a German privilege; limiting bath hours for Poles would help to uphold the stereotype of the 'dirty Pole.'[36] All inns and restaurants were designated for use by either Germans or Poles; in some cases, this led to German establishments becoming unprofitable since they didn't have a large enough clientele.[37] Poles were not permitted entry into museums, libraries, theaters, and concert halls. All Polish children were to be given a Polish name chosen from a pre-approved list; in addition, all Polish boys had to bear the name Kazimierz, Polish girls Kazimiera.[38] Poles were also separated from Germans in death: in October 1941, Greiser decreed that Poles and Germans could not be buried in the same cemeteries. Similar burial measures were later adopted in Upper Silesia and Danzig–West Prussia.[39]

Poles lost virtually all property rights (see next chapter). Many discriminatory measures applied to shopping. In some locales, Poles were not permitted to enter German shops or markets during the early morning hours, when the best goods were available.[40] If Germans and Poles were both in a store, Germans were to receive preferential treatment.[41] Poles' weekly rations were lower than those for Germans.[42] In 1941, Poles were forbidden to buy fruit and wheat flour, as well as cakes, pies, or other wheat-based products.[43] In 1942, Poles were not permitted to buy 'high-quality' vegetables—such as cauliflower, asparagus, and onions. In certain seasons, other vegetables, including lettuce, carrots, cucumbers, tomatoes, and beans, were categorized as 'high-quality.'[44] Poles were not permitted to buy fish and crabs or alcohol, cigarettes, or cigars.[45] They could purchase only limited amounts of coal, clothing, leather, and soap.[46] All these restrictions left the best goods to Germans. They also undermined the health and vigor of the Polish population (save for the ban on buying alcohol and tobacco products).

Gau authorities were divided on Polish-language use. Initially, they introduced piece-meal measures that banned Polish-language use in certain situations. Local post offices, for example, refused to deliver mail addressed in Polish.[47] The Posen trams sported signs 'Only German is spoken here.'[48] In German-run shops and restaurants in the western parts of the Gau, all transactions were to take place in German (even if between Poles).[49] In 1940, Gau authorities discussed a total ban on speaking Polish in public. Viktor Böttcher, district president of Posen, proposed banning Polish in stores, public squares, and streets in his district (where much of the Polish population still knew some German from Prussian times). As Böttcher argued, 'if the Warthegau is to become completely German, then it is necessary that the Polish language disappear as quickly as possible.'[50] His views, however, met with fierce disagreement. Walter Moser, district vice president in Litzmannstadt, argued that a ban on Polish would be impossible in the Gau's eastern areas. Between 80 and 90 percent of the population spoke only Polish; moreover, many ethnic Germans spoke fluent Polish, but only broken German. Forcing Poles to speak German would also give them more opportunities for subterfuge. And most important, Moser declared, 'such a ban would make the principle of absolute distancing from Polishdom, constantly emphasized by Mr. Reichsstatthalter [Greiser], completely illusory.'[51] Indeed, if Poles had to speak German, an important distinguishing feature between the two groups would be lost.

Greiser issued guidelines on the use of Polish in public only in February 1943. He sided with those who viewed language as a mechanism of separation. Noting that Poles could not become assimilated Germans,

Greiser declared that 'it would be wrong to forbid Poles from speaking Polish.' But he added some provisos. In German agencies and offices, only German could be spoken; Poles who didn't know German would have to bring along a translator. In schools for Polish children, pupils were to learn enough German so that they could eventually understand their German employers. Greiser insisted, though, that they be taught a pidgin German; as he declared, '[German] was not to be spoken grammatically correctly.' Poles were to learn German, but so poorly that they could never be mistaken for Germans. Greiser also stated that after the war Germans officials who had many dealings with Poles would have to learn Polish. This was 'not so that they could speak with Poles in Polish, but rather to make clear and to prove to the Poles that the German is also the master in terms of language.'[52]

Reich and Gau officials discouraged education for Poles.[53] In fall 1939, all Polish schools were closed, and Polish children were not allowed to attend schools for German children.[54] In 1940, Böttcher issued guidelines for schooling in his district. Polish pupils were to learn 'the simplest basic knowledge and skills in speaking, reading, writing, and arithmetic.' He insisted that 'the teaching of fundamental beliefs (German language instruction in a deeper sense, history instruction) is not to take place. It must always be prevented that Poles gain so much education that they could pass for Germans. Priority value is attached to the teaching of order, cleanliness, discipline, and decency.'[55] Böttcher's guidelines were eventually incorporated into a general directive on schooling for Polish children issued by Greiser's Reichsstatthalter agency in 1942.[56] All Polish children aged nine to thirteen were to attend school, but if labor needs were such, children aged twelve and above could work instead of going to school. The use of Polish in the schools was forbidden, and no Polish subject matters were taught. All Polish teachers were fired, and German lay teachers (with no pedagogical training) were brought in as instructors.[57] Polish youths enrolled in apprenticeship programs were also not permitted to learn many skills of their trade.[58]

In the Warthegau, Poles aged fourteen and above were forced to work in a very discriminatory environment. Gau authorities insisted that Poles not work in positions in which they would supervise Germans.[59] Poles also received lower wages and paid higher wage deductions (up to 30 percent of their salaries).[60] For the most part, they were not given pensions, and they were deprived of accident and life insurance.[61] In keeping with efforts to lower Polish birth rates, Poles did not get child or other family subsidies.[62]

In October 1941, Greiser flatly rejected a directive of the Reich minister of labor that would have improved wages for Poles. Invoking special powers he had recently received from Hitler (see below), Greiser declared the directive 'invalid in the Gau.'[63] A year later, Greiser's agency ordered that Poles were to receive no vacation time until war's end, a practice put into effect in the other annexed areas in March 1943.[64] German employers also exercised arbitrary disciplinary powers over their Polish employees. They could, for example, send delinquent workers to the Zabikowo penal camp for so-called 'weekend instruction.' From Saturday evening until Monday morning, these Poles (often youths) endured beatings, hard labor, and other tortures in the notorious police camp.[65]

Greiser and other Gau authorities sharply curtailed Poles' freedom of communication and movement; this was to hinder resistance activity. In 1942, Greiser forbade Poles to send telegrams except in 'urgent circumstances,' in which case a police permit was necessary.[66] Poles were generally forbidden to use public telephones, but when they did (with special permission, of course) their calls had to be made in German.[67] Curfew regulations provided that Poles were not allowed outside between 8 p.m. and 5 a.m. in winter months and 10 p.m. and 4 a.m. in summer months.[68] Bicycle riding was regulated.[69] So, too, was the use of public transportation. In Posen, Poles were not permitted to use street cars during morning rush hour.[70] At other times of the day, they were to give up their seats to Germans if the street car was full.[71] Although it proved impossible to organize tram cars so that Poles and Germans would not travel together, disappointed Gau officials hoped to solve this problem right after the war.[72] For long distance travel, Poles in Posen district had to have a permit to ride on trains and buses.[73] Poles traveling to the Old Reich also needed a permit but, after 1942, such permits were not issued.[74]

In the annexed eastern territories, Reich and Gau authorities played fast and loose with the German legal system. They decided that Poles were not citizens; since the Polish state had ceased to exist, they argued, Poles were stateless and thus had no citizenship rights.[75] Poles became 'protected subjects,' a category that, as Diemut Majer has written, 'served merely to subject the mass of the "non-Germans" to unlimited discrimination behind the facade of a specious legal concept.'[76] In November 1940, Bormann noted that the Führer had told him that 'he only demanded a report from the Gauleiters after ten years that their area was German, that is, purely

German. He would not ask about the methods they had used to make the area German, and it was immaterial to him if at some time in the future it was established that the methods to win this territory were not pretty or open to legal objection.'[77] Since Hitler was not concerned with legal niceties, Greiser soon managed to arrogate for himself and/or his Gau authorities the right to arbitrarily adjudicate many legal matters concerning Poles.

A case in point was police courts-martial. In 1940, Himmler hoped to reintroduce police courts-martial for Poles that had existed in the very earliest period of occupation. These would be in addition to special courts for Poles, under the jurisdiction of the Ministry of Justice, now in place throughout the newly annexed territories. Hermann Göring, as well as Reich Chancellery and military officials, all opposed Himmler;[78] Greiser, too, was against them. Indeed, in January 1941, an official of the Higher Regional Court (*Oberlandesgericht*) wrote that Greiser had 'openly stated that in his opinion the Reichsführer-SS, or more accurately, the head of the security police [Heydrich], wanted to seize for himself a new area [of competences].' Moreover, 'He [Greiser], when questioned, told me expressly that there was no need for a return of the police courts-martial and that he, the Gauleiter, viewed such a return as neither desirable nor permissible.'[79] Greiser was wary of enhanced SS-competences in his Gau.

But Greiser soon changed his mind. In May 1941, he reported to Hitler that just as he was giving a recent speech, an ethnic German gendarme in a neighboring village had been murdered. Greiser had immediately ordered the public hanging of the perpetrators, as well as twelve hostages. He did not, however, have the legal authority to carry out such measures. So as to be ready for such situations in future, Greiser now requested permission to reintroduce police courts-martial. He proposed that a local party official would serve as chairman, and that two officers of the Order and Security Police would round out the court. The courts-martial would make use of only two punishments: death or concentration-camp incarceration. At a meeting with Hitler on or just before 24 May, the Führer granted Greiser both the right to reintroduce police courts-martial and the right to pardon Poles.[80]

Greiser's new rights did not sit well with the Justice Ministry; both the special courts that tried Poles and the right of pardon lay within its jurisdiction. Roland Freisler, state secretary in the Justice Ministry, now proposed that the right of pardon be given to the Reich minister of the interior in conjunction with the Reich minister of justice. The Reich Chancellery objected. Freisler then negotiated directly with Greiser. On 24 June, the two men agreed on formulations that allowed the Ministry of Justice to save face. The Ministry would give its 'approval' for the Reichsstatthalter to introduce police courts-martial. It would also 'transfer' the right of pardon to the Reichsstatthalter for the duration of the war.[81] This occurred on 19 July. The right of pardon now lay with the 'Reichsstatthalter (Chief Public Prosecutor's Office),' that is, an office in Greiser's agency. Greiser, though, believed that he had the personal right to make pardons.[82]

In the meantime, Greiser had another audience with Hitler on 18 July. The two men discussed courts-martial, and perhaps also the murder of 'unproductive' Jews.[83] Indeed, Greiser introduced many of his most radical Germanization policies in summer and fall 1941; this underscores the interrelated aspects of the Germanization program. It also suggests that this was when Greiser made a fateful choice—to ally himself more forcefully with Himmler and Borman than with the more moderate Göring. At the same time, this radicalization was surely linked to the 22 June invasion of the Soviet Union; spurred on by wartime conditions, Greiser and the Nazis more generally radicalized their programs.

On 22 July (he had not yet received the 19 July decree), Greiser told Freisler that 'the Führer in our last consultation at the Führer's headquarters unequivocally declared that he wishes to transfer to me personally all power and all responsibility for this area.' With the petulance he displayed when he felt particularly sure of himself, Greiser added: 'I therefore may ask you not to raise any objections to this decree, but in the future to leave the implementation to the practical handling that I will personally make sure is done very carefully.'[84] In no uncertain terms, Greiser declared that he had complete control of his Gau. He also circulated a memorandum to his Gau subordinates in which he stated that the Führer had given him 'greater powers' to carry out Germanization measures.[85] Greiser would frequently invoke the enhanced powers that Hitler had allegedly granted him. Now, for example, he ordered that all cases of sabotage be reported to him. 'I will then,' he declared, 'make the decision about how the case will be treated judicially.'[86]

But Greiser still wasn't satisfied with his enhanced powers. In a November 1941 letter to Hans Lammers, head of the Reich Chancellery, he complained that the Reich minister of justice had asked that in cases in which he, Greiser, had decided to change a death sentence for a Jew or a Pole into a term of imprisonment, the case should be submitted for the Führer's approval. (Greiser had unilaterally extended his authority to cover not just Poles, but also Jews.) He asked Lammers to drop that proviso.[87] Both the Reich Chancellery and the Reich Ministry of Justice acceded to his wishes.[88] In April 1942, after Gauleiter Fritz Bracht in Upper Silesia asked for similar powers, the Reich Ministry of Justice transferred the right of pardon for Jews and Poles to the Reichsstatthalters (or Oberpräsidents) in the other annexed eastern territories.[89] At a whim, the eastern chiefs could make life-and-death decisions about Poles and Jews. Greiser had arrogated to himself (and others in similar positions) a remarkable degree of totalitarian power.

Greiser also issued police guidelines for the treatment of Poles. In August 1941, he declared that police officials were to mete out harsher treatment to Poles than to Germans. 'I view it as necessary,' he declared, 'to point out that for the police treatment of Poles, even when dealing with only pure infringements of regulations (*Ordnungswidrigkeiten*), sharper and harsher measures are to be used than is normal in the treatment of police measures against Germans.' Greiser further added that police authorities were to be particularly strict in cases in which Poles had violated segregation measures. There was to be no limit as to the size of fines or the duration of custody that could be imposed on Poles. Poles could also be subject to forced labor. Finally, Greiser declared that Poles would be excluded from *all* forms of legal remedies against police orders.[90] Since the Reich Ministry of the Interior had overall responsibility for local police, Greiser did not actually have the authority to issue this decree. But in the face of his onslaught, the Ministry essentially abdicated responsibility for police matters in the Gau.[91]

All the while, Reich authorities were working to develop a general criminal law for Poles and Jews. This culminated in a Reich 'Decree on the Administration of Penal Justice against Poles and Jews,' issued on 4 December 1941. Among other things, it declared that Poles or Jews would be sentenced to death if they committed violent acts against Germans. In addition to extant special courts, the decree permitted courts-martial (with the approval of the ministers of Justice and Interior) when criminal activity 'seriously endangers German reconstruction work.'[92] Greiser, of course, had already superseded this provision for his Gau. Despite the latitude offered by this directive, Greiser still successfully expanded his Gau's judicial authority.

In August 1942, he demanded that the Peoples' Court (*Volksgerichtshof*) be excluded in cases in which Poles and Jews were being tried for high treason. Instead, jurisdiction for such cases was to lie with the Higher Regional Court in Posen. At the end of the year, his demand was granted.[93] Greiser also decreed that the Gestapo, and not judicial authorities, would prosecute Poles arrested on suspicion of resistance.[94] During the Warthegau years, then, Greiser reworked the legal situation of Poles in ways that devolved arbitrary legal authority on his person or his subordinates.

In the Warthegau, Poles received severe sentences for trivial offenses: five years of penal camp for writing anti-German comments in private letters; six years of penitentiary for listening to foreign broadcasts and circulating the information heard; and death sentences for smuggling flour and sugar (on Greiser's orders the convicted were hanged in the Leslau and Kutno market squares).[95] Memoirs and secondary accounts relate the agonizing conditions that Poles endured in Warthegau prisons: little food, constant beatings, forced labor, cold and dirty cells, limited toilet use, and the sound of frequent shootings. In 1943, Greiser gave a speech in which he summarized judicial actions against Poles in the previous year. 589 individuals had been sentenced to death; 566 had already been executed, while eight were pardoned (presumably by Greiser). As he added, 'In all of these proceedings value was placed on the greatest haste . . . In many cases, and not rarely even within twenty-four hours, it was possible to have the deed followed swiftly by the punishment.'[96] Only police courts-martial could have delivered such speedy verdicts. Through death sentences imposed by courts and occasional mass executions that served as reprisals for alleged resistance attacks (in Zgierz, for example, 100 Poles were publicly executed in March 1942), Greiser condoned the murder of thousands of Poles.[97]

During the occupation years, roughly fifty Polish resistance groups formed in the Warthegau.[98] Their aims ranged from armed struggle to informing Polish authorities abroad about conditions in the Gau.[99] These groups had limited success. In April 1940, for example, Poles blew up railroad tracks on the Ostrowo–Kempen line after which a freight train derailed, causing 'substantial property damage.'[100] In March 1942, as many as 108 balloons, all attached to canisters with flammable materials, were found in Hohensalza district.[101] In February 1943, some Poles managed to print up false ration cards.[102] But the Gestapo proved very effective at breaking up resistance groups. Year after year, waves of arrests decimated the resistance; altogether, roughly 6,000 Poles were arrested for such activities.[103] Greiser's Gau (unlike the General Government) was thus never really threatened by the Polish resistance.

While segregation measures in the Gau made life difficult for Poles, they did not produce the strict separation between Germans and Poles that Greiser so desired. In early 1941, a patrol of pubs in Posen showed that in the bars where Poles were permitted, the majority of guests were Reich Germans (often in uniform), and that many of these were in the company of Poles.[104] That same year, the sub-district magistrate in Kempen, Hans Neumann, was dismayed by how some Germans treated Poles during deportations: 'it was noted that as Poles were being evacuated, NSDAP members of formations giving assistance to the Gendarmerie said good-bye to them with a handshake and friendly words.'[105] In November 1941, Poles and Germans were holding joint drinking sprees in Posen district.[106] In early 1943, SD officials in Litzmannstadt district noted that cases of individuals violating segregation laws had more than doubled in 1942. As many as 1,212 individuals had been picked up by the police: 637 for sexual relations, fifteen for indecent conduct, and 557 for social interaction with Poles.[107]

Greiser was concerned about segregation violations. At the end of 1941, he issued a decree concerning those civil servants delegated to the East who had 'failed catastrophically with respect to *Volkstum*-political matters,' that is, who had engaged in 'improper interaction with foreign people.' These individuals were to receive a stamp in their personnel file stating that they were 'unsuited for deployment in the Reichsgau Wartheland.'[108] Greiser, though, was particularly vexed by Germans having sexual relations with Poles. In April 1941, he made an example of six NSDAP men who had had sex with Polish women. Two were sent to a concentration camp for an undetermined length of time; the other four were sent for a period of two weeks.[109] In June 1942, Greiser was confronted with a case in which a woman resettler, whose husband was a soldier, had forced a Polish farmhand to have repeated sexual encounters. As Greiser wrote to Freisler, he was able to punish the Pole, but he had no legal means to prosecute the German. He now asked the Justice Ministry to issue a regulation that would generally punish 'undignified racial (*volksunwürdiges*) conduct' of Germans toward Poles. Greiser even included a draft of such a regulation; it provided penitentiary or prison sentences for those found guilty.[110] In

May 1943, Greiser sought permission from the Party Chancellery and the ministers of interior and justice to issue the decree for the Reichsgau Wartheland.[111] (Since the decree was directed against Germans, Greiser did not feel that he could issue it on his own.) Some weeks later, a Justice Ministry official informed Greiser that such a regulation was in the works, and asked him to hold off on issuing a decree.[112] But no Reich decree ever appeared.

Although Greiser was unable to uphold a complete separation of Germans from Poles, the Warthegau was known as the area in which the harshest discriminatory policies against Poles obtained. In March 1942 a local Gau Office of *Volkstum* Affairs reported that 'since the Poles know about the good treatment [of Poles] in Danzig–West Prussia, they yearn to move there.'[113] In December, Goebbels noted that Greiser 'deals with this problem [the 'Polish Question'] with somewhat stricter and harsher methods than Forster. As congenially as Forster judges individual cases, Greiser's methods, in principle, strike me as correct. In any event he can point to significant successes for the correctness of his practice.'[114] As these comments underscore, Greiser was now the Nazi radical, Forster the Nazi moderate. Greiser's strict segregation had also had 'successes.' Many segregation measures were on the books, and Germans and Poles led largely separate and very unequal lives in the Warthegau. Poles, once proud citizens of a sovereign nation-state, were now downtrodden Helots under a savage occupation regime.

Even though segregation measures were fast institutionalized in the Warthegau, Gau authorities continued to have difficulties in classifying the population. In fall 1940, Himmler wrote to Greiser about complaints that he had heard concerning DVL practice in the Gau. Himmler claimed that individuals seeking DVL status were often treated callously or simply ignored. To rectify this situation, he asked Greiser for a 'comradely and smooth cooperation with your Ethnic Register offices.'[115] Greiser responded churlishly. Reminding Himmler that he was his deputy for strengthening Germandom in the Gau, he declared: 'It remains singly and alone my responsibility to entrust others with carrying out matters in my Gau. I do not intend to solve *Volkstum* proceedings with the offices of the police and the SS, but rather singly and alone with the offices of the party and the state. For that matter, it is not necessary to have the cooperation that you wish with individual offices, rather the cooperation

1 Ida Greiser, Arthur's mother (undated).

2 Gustav Greiser (seated), with his three sons, Wilhelm, Otto, and Arthur, 1917.

3 Ruth Tripler and Arthur Greiser, 1918.

4 Ruth and Arthur Greiser, with children Erhardt, Rotraut (baby), and Ingrid, 1931.

5 Maria and Arthur Greiser on their wedding day, 9 April 1935. Heinrich Himmler speaks to Greiser.

6 Arthur and Maria Greiser, 1936.

7 Arthur Greiser (left) with Ignacy Mościcki in Spała, 8 January 1935.

8 Arthur Greiser (left) and Albert Forster, 10 August 1939.

9 Arthur Greiser, 1 October 1939.

10 Walter Petzel, Wilhelm Frick, and Arthur Greiser inspect army and police units in the courtyard of Posen Castle, 3 November 1939.

11 Wilhelm Koppe (left), Arthur Greiser, and Adolf Hühnlein (leader of the National Socialist Motor Corps) in Posen, 21 October 1939.

12 Arthur Greiser (far left) with Adolf Hitler (far right) in Rastenburg on 18 July 1941. Martin Bormann stands to the left of Greiser. This is one of only two known pictures showing Greiser with Hitler.

13 Arthur Greiser shakes hands with the farmer designated the millionth German in the Warthegau, Litzmannstadt, 17 March 1944. Heinz Reinefarth stands between the two men.

14 Arthur Greiser, Poznań, 4 July 1946.

15 Arthur Greiser, Poznań, 21 July 1946.

will be initiated by me in the form that I in my responsibility as deputy of the Reich commissioner [for the strengthening of Germandom] deem desirable.'[116] Greiser's blunt response shows how jealously he guarded his authority on Germanization matters in his Gau—even against Himmler.

On 12 September 1940, Himmler decreed a uniform DVL throughout the annexed eastern territories. The Warthegau DVL was the explicit model, but Himmler's decree foresaw just four DVL groups. For Groups I, II, and III, the criteria for inclusion was similar to that of the Warthegau DVL's Groups A, B, and C. In Group IV, however, Himmler included those ethnic Germans who had become politically active on behalf of Polishdom. As he noted, 'With the registration of members of Group IV the principle must be that no German blood can be made available to a foreign people.'[117] Himmler attached greater importance to racial or biological criteria than did Greiser. Himmler's decree appeared in codified form on 4 March 1941.[118] Nine days later, Interior Minister Wilhelm Frick issued DVL guidelines.[119]

Greiser now had to adapt his DVL to the Reich version. As would become a pattern, though, he did so in a way that radicalized the whole procedure. On 6 April, Greiser issued a decree that in principle individuals who had been categorized in the Warthegau Groups A–C should now be classified as members of DVL Groups I–III. Groups D and E would be subsumed into the single category Group IV. But matters were not so simple, largely because DVL authorities in the Warthegau had paid little attention to German ancestry. As Greiser now recognized, the 'circle of persons who belong to Groups I–III is somewhat broader than had generally been the case in [Warthegau] practice.' He thus ordered that all registrations in DVL Groups B–E, as well as those denied registration, be reviewed. At the same time, the definition of German origin was not clear in Frick's guidelines. Greiser took the matter into his own hands and declared: 'For the Reichsgau Wartheland I have decided that only individuals who have at least 50 percent German ancestry can be recognized as of German origin.'[120] In August, Greiser further clarified his position. He now said that the 50 percent ancestry pertained only to individuals classified in Groups III and IV. This was because some individuals in his Groups A and B did not have 50 percent German ancestry, but had proven themselves in the interwar ethnic struggle. These individuals, he now said, were to be categorized in Group II (rather than in Group I as before).[121] This was an uneasy mix of Greiser's desire to privilege those who had sided with

Germans in the interwar period with Himmler's emphasis on racial purity. But the requirement of a high percentage of German ancestry for Groups III and IV was in keeping with Greiser's overall policy of adopting a strict interpretation of who was German.

Despite proclaiming a harsh policy, Greiser did not always hold to it. In August 1941, Rolf-Heinz Höppner, head of the Posen SD office, noted that the Gauleiter had given a speech in Kutno that 'had in part had a bewildering effect.' Greiser had reportedly stated that 'every drop of German blood' had to be preserved through the DVL. This had led some sub-districts to allow individuals with less than 50 percent German origins into the DVL. In Kolmar sub-district, roughly 5,000 mixed marriage cases now had to be reexamined.[122]

Greiser had some disagreements with Himmler about DVL policy. One point of contention involved racial screenings of persons categorized in Group III. In September 1941, Himmler ordered racial examinations for Group III (or potential Group III) individuals if they could not provide certain evidence of German ancestry. Those who failed racial screenings were to be removed from or not allowed to join the DVL.[123] Even before this decree was announced, Greiser and his subordinates lined up against this provision. As they argued, the DVL process in the Warthegau was more or less complete. Most individuals in Group III had already received their DVL identity cards. Racial screenings would lead to new decisions about DVL membership. This, in turn, would confuse the line drawn between Germans and Poles, and undermine the authority of those who had made earlier decisions. Coulon now proposed that racial screenings take place only once it was planned to send individuals to the Old Reich for re-Germanization.[124] Greiser agreed. As an official reported to Himmler: 'it is . . . the view of the Gauleiter that the racial-political question, especially the weeding out of the foreign-blooded, need not be solved in a short time. It must, however, be solved before the members of Category III and IV of the DVL are set to move to the Old Reich for the purpose of re-Germanization.'[125] The issue was resolved when Greiser achieved a 'special agreement' (*Sonderregelung*) with Himmler: racial screenings in the Warthegau would occur independently of the DVL process. Those individuals found to be racially unsuitable would be noted in a card index, and they would be taken off the DVL when they actually left the Warthegau.[126] Greiser got his way: racial screenings would occur, but they would not lead to an immediate removal of individuals from the DVL.[127]

As the episode suggests, Greiser was not forced to acquiesce to Himmler's dictates; rather, he was a tenacious Gauleiter who successfully stood up to the SS-leader.

In 1942, Greiser and his agency anticipated several DVL procedures that soon became Reich policies. In early January, Jäger sent out a memorandum that limited the time period to one month in which appeals of DVL decisions could be lodged. As Jäger noted, the initial Reich DVL guidelines did not prescribe any such time limit. This meant that questions about national belonging could continue ad infinitum—thus heightening tensions in the Gau.[128] Five months later, the Interior Ministry in Berlin issued a decree in which individuals were given just two weeks to appeal DVL decisions.[129] Even more strikingly, on New Year's Day 1942, Greiser issued a circular on the 'Treatment of Persons Taken into Categories III and IV of the German Ethnic Register.' Just six weeks later, on 9 and 16 February 1942, Himmler issued decrees on Groups III and IV of the DVL. Greiser's circular was very similar to Himmler's decrees. The opening paragraph even noted that it would be valid only until Reich regulations came into effect. Greiser presumably knew of Himmler's planned regulations and perhaps had some familiarity with their content.[130] The very existence of Greiser's circular raises intriguing questions that archival documents do not answer. Was the circular a trial balloon of sorts? By rushing these provisions into effect, was Greiser trying to influence Himmler's regulations? What role did Warthegau authorities play in the formulation of Himmler's decrees?

According to Himmler's decrees, members of DVL Groups III and IV were to be resettled in the Old Reich. In addition, they faced a host of legal restrictions. Their property was subject to confiscation. Group III members could not join the NSDAP or become civil servants. They could marry each other or individuals in a higher DVL category, but not those in Group IV or foreign peoples. They could enroll in technical or trade schools, but university study required permission from Himmler's main staff office. They were to undergo indoctrination so as to reenforce their German identity.[131] Members of Group IV had even more limited rights. If they were deemed very anti-German, their children could be taken away and placed with German families. They needed permission from the HSSPF of their Gau to move, to marry, or to enroll in technical or trade schools. To become 'German,' they were to undergo 're-education.' Only through individual naturalization could they receive revocable German citizenship.[132] In a separate decree, Himmler ordered that individuals of German origin who did not apply for DVL registration were to be taken into protective custody and sent to concentration camps.[133]

Despite such brutal policies, Greiser let Himmler know that he thought that the SS-leader was insufficiently hard-line on DVL matters. On 2 April 1943, for example, Greiser complained about decisions made by the Supreme Court for Questions of Ethnic Origin (*Oberste Prüfungshof für Volkszugehörigkeitsfragen*); Himmler generally chaired the court's deliberations. Greiser was vexed with a Court decision that permitted individuals with just 25 percent German ancestry admittance to the DVL if they had passed strict racial scrutiny: 'I personally believe that racial suitability where little German descent is present cannot lead to [a situation in which] entry into the Ethnic German Register comes into question.'[134] While Greiser was earlier willing to accept individuals with Polish ancestry as Germans if they had 'struggled' on behalf of Germandom, he was unwilling to accept individuals as Germans if the exception was due to racial criteria.

While Greiser challenged Himmler on some DVL matters, the SS-leader's subordinates in the Warthegau questioned some of the Gauleiter's policies. In particular, Höppner, who became head of the Gau Office of *Volkstum* Affairs on 1 February 1943, took Greiser to task for various alleged policy deviations.[135] In March, Greiser had decided—against Reich policy—that Czechs should be treated like Poles (as opposed to having a more privileged status). Höppner declared that 'the decision of the Gauleiter must be changed. The Czech question cannot be solved in the Warthegau, but only in the Reich.'[136] Nine days later, Höppner wrote that Greiser was now in sync with Reich policy.[137] In January 1944, Höppner tallied up a list of 'wrong things' that Greiser had said in a speech to some generals. These included statements to the effect that individuals classified in Group IV of the DVL were 'renegades, in whom we have no interest;' and that individuals in DVL Group III who were particularly good soldiers had always been transferred into Group II.[138]

As these reports suggest, Höppner watched Greiser's every move. This was a Reich-wide phenomenon: an SD liaison officer was attached to every Gauleiter staff.[139] Given, however, Greiser's good relations with Himmler, it is somewhat odd that Höppner and others (see below) were writing up reports about the Gauleiter. After the war, a Warthegau economics functionary wrote that 'the SD was very vigilant toward the Gauleiter. It always recorded his overstepping of authority and always also reported to the SD in Berlin those matters that the Gauleiter had not treated correctly.'[140] At his trial, Greiser claimed that he had been spied upon; in his words, 'in Germany slowly all the walls in offices and official residences had ears.'[141] Perhaps he had Höppner in mind. For unknown reasons, Höppner left the Gau and took up a position in the RSHA in Berlin in July 1944.[142]

Of the eastern Gauleiters, Greiser adopted the strictest DVL policy. Gauleiters Forster and Fritz Bracht in Upper Silesia enrolled as many individuals as possible into the DVL. In part, this was due to a shortage of 'Germans' to people all areas under Nazi occupation. Faced with necessity, Forster and Bracht adopted assimilation as their Germanization strategy. Forster admitted much of the West-Prussian population to Group III of the DVL, even though these individuals were widely viewed as Poles. In Upper Silesia, Bracht was eager to maintain industrial capacity; any mistreatment of workers, he feared, would lead to production disruptions. He thus had many industrial workers categorized in DVL Groups I and II.[143] By adding so many individuals to the DVL, Forster and Bracht were also able to increase the pool of potential soldiers for the Wehrmacht.

Greiser bitterly objected to DVL policies in Danzig–West Prussia, Upper Silesia, and even the General Government. On 16 March 1943, he wrote to Himmler that Hitler had given him the task of Germanizing the Warthegau, yet he (Greiser) refused 'to realize a cheap success.' As he reminded the SS-leader, he allowed only individuals with at least 50 percent German origins into DVL Categories III and IV. Greiser went on to note that 'my *Volkstumspolitik* [population policy] is . . . endangered by that in Reichsgau Danzig–West Prussia in that ongoing attempts there for the time being will strike superficial observers as more promising.' Greiser also told Himmler that he had heard that the General Government was planning similar measures. There, children with just 12.5 percent German blood were allegedly considered German.[144] On 3 April, Himmler wrote to Greiser: 'I believe that the policy that you have pursued in this matter is still the only one possible.' He thanked Greiser for alerting him to rumors concerning the General Government and noted that 'if even in part they are true I will turn with all possible means against the policy there.'[145] On 15 April, Greiser acknowledged Himmler's reply: 'I was particularly happy because of the renewed confirmation of the correctness of my *Volkstum*-policy.'[146]

In March 1943, at a conference of the Gau Office of *Volkstum* Affairs, Greiser further criticized Forster and Bracht's policies. Referring to how to fill the area with Germans rather than Poles, he declared: 'If the question is asked, if one couldn't come to the same result in a faster and easier way such as is being done in Danzig–West Prussia and Upper Silesia, then I say no!' Greiser quoted the Nazi propagandist Julius Streicher: 'If you dip a herring in wine, by no means will a better fish come out!' And he continued: 'Simply on the basis of his whole mentality, if you give a Pole who has no German blood in his veins a Group III or IV DVL identification card and put the children in the uniform of the Hitler Youth, he [and his children] will by no means be Germans; that is a racial matter alone. The inner value of a person is not conditioned by his territorial location.' Greiser also took aim at the policy of adding soldiers to the Wehrmacht through the DVL registration of Poles. Apparently, he feared that Poles might constitute a fifth column within the army's ranks.[147] Publicly, however, he declared: 'In the *Volkstum* struggle we must remain consistent. I believe that we will provide our *Volk* with a couple of thousand fewer soldiers, but apart from that we will serve the German *Volk* more through the radical exploitation of Polish workers. [For our *Volk*] we will also have achieved a stable foundation where the coming generations will feel comfortable in the next centuries. We all want to make sure that we build on granite here in the Gau Wartheland, while all around us is being built on sand.'[148] Building on granite rather than sand—the metaphor captures Greiser's view of his actions. Beleaguered yet undaunted, Greiser wished to forge ahead in making his Gau a fortress of Germans.

DVL numbers speak for themselves. As Table 6.1 indicates, aside from the much smaller Zichenau area, the Warthegau allowed the fewest number of individuals—both in proportional and absolute terms—into the DVL.[149] In contrast to the Warthegau, both Danzig–West Prussia and Upper Silesia had more individuals classified as 'Germans' than as 'Poles and others.' Greiser was much more restrictive than Forster and Bracht in admitting individuals to Group III. Ironically, his hard-line approach unwittingly benefited many Poles after the war. In 1945, Polish authorities paid virtually no attention to whether DVL membership had been voluntary or coerced; anyone listed in the DVL was considered German and treated accordingly.[150] Greiser's policies had the unintended effect that relatively few individuals in the Warthegau region were caught up in the postwar expulsions of the German population.

Table 6.1 Ethnic Registration in Annexed Territories of Occupied Poland, January 1944

	Warthegau	Danzig–West Prussia	Zichenau (East Prussia)	Upper Silesia
DVL I	218,000	113,000	9,000	97,000
DVL II	192,000	97,000	22,500	211,000
DVL III	64,000	726,000	13,500	976,000
DVL IV	19,000	2,000	1,500	54,000
TOTAL DVL	493,000	938,000	46,500	1,338,000
'POLES AND OTHERS'	3,450,000	689,000	920,000	1,040,000

Source: Elizabeth Harvey, *Women and the Nazi East: Agents and Witnesses of Germanization* (New Haven: Yale University Press, 2003), 79.

Greiser was the Gauleiter most eager to initiate and then radicalize the DVL. He was the first Gauleiter to introduce the DVL, and the only one to do so before it was introduced to all of the annexed eastern areas. As he wrote to Himmler in 1943, 'to fulfill the task given to me by the Führer—to Germanize the Reichsgau Wartheland—the first prerequisite was to decide which people who had lived here during the Polish time were to be treated as Germans and which as Poles. Not coincidentally, the ... German Ethnic Register ... was therefore developed in my Gau.'[151] Greiser also placed a high bar on who could be considered German. He proposed and/or initiated harsh measures against those deemed Polonized Germans. And he sharpened some technical aspects of the DVL so as to make it more difficult for individuals to dispute their classifications. Greiser even challenged Himmler on DVL matters; he was stricter than the SS-leader when it came to separating Germans from Poles. In contrast to other areas of policy, when it came to the DVL, Greiser privileged ideology over pragmatism.

Greiser's long-term goal, though, was not a strict segregation system, but the elimination of Poles from his Gau. Besides condoning the deportation and murder of Poles (see previous chapter), Greiser and other Nazis hoped to curb the Polish population's natural rate of growth. With Polish birth rates on the rise in the Warthegau, Reich and Gau officials discussed a variety of ways to lower them: raising the minimum age of marriage, allowing marriage only when couples were financially secure, taxing illegitimate births, sterilizing women who had several illegitimate children, refusing child subsidies or tax breaks for families with many children, permitting abortions for social (as opposed to health) reasons, and even taking away the children of women who had become pregnant during forced labor in the Reich.[152] Of all these measures, Greiser decided to focus on minimum marriage-age requirements. On 10 September 1941 he decreed a minimum marriage age for Polish men of twenty-eight, and for Polish women of twenty-five.[153]

Several years later, Greiser's policy was threatened by Reich officials who had become concerned about the different marriage-age policies in the annexed areas. In Zichenau, marriages between Poles were forbidden, Upper Silesia had minimum-age requirements (twenty-five for men, twenty-two for women), and Danzig–West Prussia had no special regulations. In April 1943, Frick called a meeting about setting a uniform minimum age of marriage for Poles; he planned to introduce the Upper-Silesian variant.[154] Greiser rushed off a dire response. He declared that he 'could not agree' with the planned measure. 'It is my duty to draw attention,' Greiser told the interior minister, '[to the fact] that a change in the marriage age in the proposed way would destroy the positive successes of our current *Volkstumskampf* and would seriously hamper the *Volkstumskampf* as such altogether.' Greiser further claimed that 'My representative will orally explain these successes as concerns especially the decrease in births among the Polish people.'[155] (In fact, Polish birth rates never substantially dropped in the Warthegau.) Greiser instructed his subordinates not to agree to any lowering of the marriage age unless they had received his express consent.[156] Herbert Mehlhorn represented the Warthegau at the meeting. Afterwards, he reported that he had convinced the others that only the Gau's higher minimum marriage ages would suffice for a uniform standard.[157] But on 4 May, the Interior Ministry issued a decree that set the minimum marriage age for Polish men at twenty-five, and Polish women at twenty-two. In a gesture to Greiser, however, a proviso allowed individual Reichsstatthalters to set higher minimum-age requirements. Greiser did just that. On 27 May he informed officials in his Gau that the original rule was still in effect.[158] Some months later, Greiser was actually successful in his quest for higher minimum marriage-age requirements throughout the annexed eastern areas. In January 1944, Himmler, now interior minister, raised the minimum marriage age for Poles to twenty-eight for men, and twenty-five for women. Once again, a Greiser policy had become the model for the rest of the annexed eastern areas.

Reichsstatthalter officials also advocated stringent maternity regulations for Poles: Polish women expecting a child could not refuse to work; most were to receive just four weeks off after birth; and peasant women would receive no maternity leave at all. As a memorandum on these matters noted, 'One has to realize that in ethnic struggle (*Volkstumskampf*) things are necessary that cannot be justified legally.'[159] In 1944, Jäger issued a decree on Greiser's behalf that Polish women could go back to work just two weeks after giving birth; at the outside limit, they had to return to work within six weeks.[160] Still, there was no significant drop in Polish birthrates. In part, this may have been due to other Nazi policies. Pregnant Polish women were not sent to Germany for forced labor. At the same time, since Gau entertainment and curfew policies prevented Poles from doing other activities, they had more sex.[161] Having children was also a form of resistance. Polish priests exhorted their parishioners to have children. As Greiser reportedly said in October 1941, 'It's ridiculous to grant Poles child subsidies after the Polish Holy Joes (*Pfaffen*) preach from the pulpits that the Polish people can only win their struggle against the Germans if they bring forth more and more children.'[162] Little could frustrate Greiser more. Losing the battle of births threatened the entire Germanization project.

In another attempt to deprive Poles of their people, Greiser condoned a Germanization program that took 'racially good' Polish children and raised them as Germans. In June 1941 (the same summer that so many other radical policies were enacted), Himmler wrote to Greiser that pursuant to their recent conversation, it would be 'right' if 'racially good' Polish children were taken from their families and put in children's homes. After a year or so, the children who had proven themselves would be placed in German families, while the others would be returned to their parents.[163] In November, the Interior Ministry stated that the program would begin with Polish children already in orphanages. According to instructions soon issued by the RKFDV, children who appeared to be 'racially valuable' were to undergo detailed racial, health, and psychological screenings. On behalf of the RKFDV, Greiser's Reichsstatthalter agency would then decide which children would undergo Germanization. Children aged between six and twelve years who passed muster would be put in German boarding schools; those aged between two and six would be placed in homes belonging to the Lebensborn e.V, and eventually in families of childless SS-men.[164] The roughly 300 Polish children who were subject to this form of Germanization lost their names and other identifying criteria; many were never able to return to their Polish families.[165]

Despite his severe policies toward Poles, Greiser realized that for the foreseeable future the great majority of his Gau's workforce would be Polish. To ensure the Gau's economic viability—not least so as to produce large quantities of food for the Reich—Greiser felt compelled to adopt more conciliatory measures toward working Poles. This stance was apparent early on. On 12 February 1940, at a meeting of all of the eastern Gauleiters and Himmler on 'eastern questions' at his Carinhall estate, Göring insisted that forced deportations of Poles could not get in the way of economic production. Greiser raised no objections.[166]

Greiser was also on record for advocating a relatively large Polish workforce for his Gau. In January 1941, an official in the Reich Agency for Spacial Planning (*Reichsstelle für Raumordnung*) disparagingly recorded Greiser's words at a meeting of resettlement officials. He noted that Greiser's stated goal was to Germanize the Gau within ten years. But, he emphasized, 'The Gauleiter sees Germanization as already complete when leadership, management, and supervision in all areas is in German hands and approximately 60 percent of the population is German. Apparently, the Gauleiter sees no danger in the fact that roughly 40 percent of the Gau will remain Polish.' The rapporteur continued, 'the Gauleiter places paramount importance on the food-political objective in the Gau and this means to him: the Gau Wartheland has to become even more than before one of the main bread baskets for the Greater German Reich.' Greiser reportedly believed that 50 percent of all agricultural lands should be held by large landed interests; only then could his Gau deliver large quantities of grain to the Reich. Such a distribution of land, however, would mean that relatively few German landowners would employ large numbers of Polish field hands. By contrast, Himmler's planning officials advocated small and middle-sized farms, worked by individual German farmers, that would create a human bulwark of Germandom.[167]

Just a few weeks later, on 4 February, Alexander Dolezalek, head of the Planning Department in the SS-Settlement Staff Office in Posen (*Planungsabteilung beim SS-Ansiedlungsstab Posen*), passed on 'dirt' about Greiser to his superiors (like Höppner). Dolezalek reported that Greiser had insisted on maintaining an agricultural structure that could produce large quantities of grain for the Old Reich. Hitler and Göring, Greiser claimed, had given him the task of producing 'grain, grain, and grain again, "a grain factory."' Greiser continued: 'therefore we need our large estates and therefore we need all workers! The workers, although they are Poles, must stay in the Warthegau. The current agricultural structure must not be changed. We have to have peace in the Warthegau. Peace for agricultural production.' Dolezalek also noted that Greiser had objected to the deportation of Polish forest workers. When Dolezalek proposed that at least their wives and children be deported, Greiser insisted that 'the capacity for work noticeably sinks when the workers are separated from their wives and children.'[168] With the ban on deportations to the General Government, such discussions were soon moot. But in early 1941, it is clear, Greiser privileged economic goals over demographic aims; his views were more in sync with Göring than Himmler. One historian has even suggested that Greiser was 'leaning toward a policy of economic rationality at the expense of his racist ideological goals.'[169]

Greiser, however, soon changed his views—in summer and fall 1941 he was eager to show Himmler his hardline attitudes. On 9 October he presided over a Posen meeting of Reich trustees for work in the eastern areas. He now insisted that ethnic struggle, and not economic production, was the Nazis' top priority. In a discussion that concluded that Poles must be treated harshly regardless of the effect it might have on their work, Greiser declared 'Either the Poles or we will live here in the East! There is no other possibility. Since we need this space, the German will have to triumph over the Polish *Volkstum*. Decisive is the question of *Volkstum*, not of work.' In the same meeting, Greiser declared of the Pole: 'He's nothing but a worker (*Arbeitskraft*) that we have to face without feeling.'[170] In the next months, Greiser forcefully expounded his views that Polish workers were to be ruthlessly exploited for their labor, and then simply discarded.[171]

Reports from around the Gau suggested that the miserable situation of Polish workers was jeopardizing the economy. In October 1941, for example, railroad officials complained that the displacement of Polish train employees was having a negative impact on their ability to keep trains running.[172] The following May, Litzmannstadt district officials stated that Polish wages, coupled with deductions, were insufficient for Poles to attain a subsistence level. 'The result,' they noted, 'is shown by the general waning not only of the will to work, but also, objectively seen, the capability to work.'[173]

Greiser gradually backed away from his hardline stance of October 1941. He seems to have realized that if his Gau was to be at the forefront of war production, Poles would have to be treated better. Over the course of 1942, he adopted a more conciliatory attitude toward working Poles (though not others). In late spring 1942, for example, he declared that 'the working Poles enjoy the protection of the German Reich.'[174] He also took some concrete steps to assuage Polish workers. No Polish workers—as opposed to 'asocial' or 'work-shy' Poles—were to be displaced.[175] In November, Greiser raised bread rations for Poles so that these equaled those of Germans.[176]

That same month (November 1942), unbeknownst to the public, Greiser helped prevent the introduction of an even more severe criminal regime for Poles. The Reich minister of justice, Otto Georg Thierack, had made an agreement with Himmler (with the consent of Hitler and Bormann) that all Poles liable to criminal prosecution would be turned over to the police (as opposed to judicial authorities) as of 1 January 1943. At a meeting on 13 November, Greiser, Bracht, and Forster objected. According to Wilhelm Stuckart, state secretary in the Interior Ministry, '. . . Greiser spoke forcefully against the planned regulation and explained his reasons: given the anti-Semitic views of the former Prussian Poles, the Criminal Law Decree for Poles that treated Poles and Jews in the same way was a severe psychological mistake.' Greiser also argued that if Poles were removed from the general judicial system, their enthusiasm and capacity for work 'would be diminished in the most alarming way,' especially since they would once again be treated 'together with the Jews.' Greiser stated that 'this was intolerable and endangered the political goal of gradually bringing those Poles willing to work to internally recognize the German leadership.' Greiser also said that the present judicial system was 'a sharply polished instrument in the hands of the political leadership and had worked quickly, successfully, and well.'[177] Greiser's argumentation is striking both for the anti-Semitism that he attributed to the Poles and for the importance that he attached to Poles' psychological situation. In the face of his and other Gauleiters' objections, Thierack dropped the proposed measure.[178]

Greiser also tried another tactic to win over Poles. In December 1942, he announced the founding of an Association of Achieving Poles (*Verband der Leistungspolen*) before a mixed German–Polish audience. It would, he claimed, 'advance the life and living together (*das Leben und Zusammenleben*) in the Gau in ordered ways.' Poles who 'had worked absolutely loyally under German supervision' would be invited to join. These 'Achieving Poles' would receive the same wages and rations as Germans and would eventually receive insignia that would allow them to be served before other Poles in stores and state agencies. Greiser further held out the promise that 'Achieving Poles' might eventually be allowed to visit German pubs and cultural institutions, and that their curfew hours would be extended.[179] His intention, it seems, was to give Poles an incentive to work hard.

But in March 1943, before a German audience, Greiser placed a very different spin on the association. He now claimed that it was to divide Poles. 'It's not clear to everyone,' he stated, 'that the founding of the Association of Achieving Poles is not an economic method, but rather a political method to disturb the unity of the Poles. By advertising economic methods we have found a very compact political means in order to disturb the Polish camp.'[180] Greiser apparently hoped that Poles' potential differences on the association would undermine Polish solidarity. Whatever his true intentions, the Association of Achieving Poles was a resounding failure. By October 1944, just 20,000 Poles had received identity cards as so-called L-Poles (*Leistungspolen*).[181] Gau officials found it difficult to convince Poles to join. Rightly so, many Poles were suspicious of Greiser's motives. Meanwhile, those who joined the association were shunned by their fellow countrymen.[182] Greiser's differing messages about the association were indicative of his torn attitudes toward Poles: he wanted to encourage Poles to work harder, but he didn't want to undermine his radical anti-Polish schemes. He never successfully resolved this dilemma—to the end, there were contradictions in his anti-Polish policy.

Greiser and the Warthegau were notorious for anti-church policies. These policies served a variety of functions—some closely linked to Germanization, others less so. Most important, they were to undermine Catholicism and its traditional role in fostering Polish nationalism. They were also to weaken organized religion as an alternative loyalty to Nazism. And they were to sap Reich control over the Gau—so that Greiser would have even more powers to carry out Germanization and other measures.

Greiser's anti-church stance is somewhat puzzling. He did not grow up in an overtly religious household; his anti-religious attitude was not a rebellion against an earlier all-enveloping worldview, as was the case with some other Nazis. Although his first wife Ruth was the daughter of a pastor, she also wasn't especially religious. As parents, Arthur and Ruth Greiser followed conventional religious rites. All three of their children were baptized. In the 1930s, after some half-hearted opposition, Greiser permitted Ingrid and Erhardt to be confirmed. Despite the Nazi regime's openly anti-church stance, Greiser himself didn't leave the church until long after he had become an important Nazi. As late as August 1937, he still described himself as 'Protestant' on official Nazi forms, rather than as 'believer in God' (*gottgläubig*), the official Nazi terminology for those who had left the church.[183] Only after becoming Gauleiter did he declare himself 'believer in God' and, even then, he still wrote '(ev) ggl.' (the German abbreviations for 'Protestant' and 'believer in God') on forms, suggesting that he still identified as a nominal Protestant. Nonetheless, from everything that we know about him, he had little personal interest in religion.

For Greiser, the persecution of the Catholic church was key to undermining Polish nationalism; it was necessary to destroy the institution that had done so much to uphold Polish national identity. In this context, however, his policies toward German Protestants are all the more startling. As even Greiser acknowledged, the Protestant church had played an important role in upholding the German community in interwar Poland. In a letter to Bormann dated 4 December 1939, Greiser noted that 'it cannot be doubted that some Protestant clergy proved themselves extraordinarily in the *Volkstum* struggle.' He nonetheless assured Bormann that he would follow his and Heydrich's instructions (he had received similar ones from both men) to eliminate church influence in the Gau.[184] Bormann saw organized religion as an alternative locus of loyalty for the German population, and was thus eager to eliminate it from German society.

Many of Greiser's anti-church measures originated in Bormann's offices.[185] On 12 December 1939, for example, Greiser received Bormann's assistant, Gerhard Klopfer. He told Klopfer that he was eager for the 'complete separation of church and state in his Gau area.' The churches would thus lose many of their rights and thus their influence. Klopfer recommended a 'Church Contribution Law' (*Kirchenbeitragsgesetz*) that would change the status of churches from public corporations to private associations. Deprived of state status, churches would no longer enjoy state financing, and would no longer have a connection to the Reich Ministry of Ecclesiastical Affairs. The two men also discussed the closing of confessional schools, training of teachers independently of denomination, and the transfer of church charities to the National Socialist People's Welfare (*Nationalsozialistische Volkswohlfahrt*).[186] In the next years, all these and many other anti-church measures were introduced in the Warthegau.

Bormann and Greiser soon sparred with the minister of ecclesiastical affairs, Hans Kerrl, about laws pertaining to religion in the annexed eastern areas. In February 1940, Greiser learned that clergy in Posen and Lodsch, in conjunction with the Ministry, planned to celebrate the amalgamation of their churches with the Old Prussian Union, the Reich association of Protestant churches. Greiser now brusquely told Kerrl that 'the powers that the Führer entrusted to me for the reconstruction of the Warthegau are such that in my Gau no matters of public life may be undertaken without my knowledge or against my will.' Greiser further told Kerrl that 'it has been left to me, in conjunction with the minister of the interior, to decide which legal system—the former Polish, the German or a specially devised one for the Warthegau—will be adopted for the reorganization of these matters.' In no uncertain terms, Greiser let Kerrl know that he did not intend to 'allow the reorganization of Church life in the Warthegau along lines valid in the Old Reich.' Turning to the immediate matter, he declared that 'whether the Protestant church in my Gau is joined with the German Protestant church . . . will never be decided behind my back, but singly and only with my agreement.'[187] In many ways, Greiser's letter is remarkable: for the tone he deployed with Kerrl, for his insistence that he controlled everything in his Gau, and for the suggestion that the Warthegau might well implement its own laws. Greiser relayed a copy of his letter to Kerrl to Himmler. Just five days later, the SS-Reichsführer declared, 'I not only fully agree with your views, but I'm downright happy about them.'[188]

True to his word, on 14 March 1940, Greiser decreed that the churches had no right to state financing in the Warthegau, and that all monies that they took in were subject to official approval and supervision. Greiser thus established the legal separation of the Warthegau Protestant churches from their mother church in the Reich. Many objected to this decree. Church officials in the Warthegau, Paul Blau and Alfred Kleindienst, heads of the Protestant churches in Posen and Lodsch respectively, were outraged. In the Reich, Dr. Friedrich Werner, president of the Protestant *Oberkirchenrat* (the highest advisory body for the Protestant churches) complained to Göring.[189] The Ministries of Justice and Ecclesiastical Affairs also objected.[190] Kerrl, of course, had not been consulted. As he now wrote to

Frick, Greiser had not gone through proper channels in issuing his decree. Moreover, Kerrl considered Greiser's act of separating the Warthegau churches from the Reich as 'intolerable.'[191] Despite his objections, Kerrl soon lost authority for church matters not only in the Warthegau, but in all of the annexed territories. Just one day after Greiser lunched with Hitler on 31 October 1940, Bormann noted that the Führer had stated that 'Kerrl has nothing more to do' in the areas beyond the Old Reich.[192] Yet again, Greiser had pioneered a development that stretched beyond his Gau's borders.

Greiser continued to push forward the anti-church agenda. In July 1940, he apprised Church officials of what became known as the 'Thirteen Points,' a set of anti-church measures originating in Bormann's office. In the Warthegau, Greiser indicated, churches would have the status of private associations. They could not uphold any ties to Reich churches or the Vatican. All youth and other church-affiliated organizations would be disbanded. No religious instruction would be given in the state schools. Poles and Germans would not be allowed to worship together, a proviso that flew in the face of the Catholic church's universalistic claims. Church property would be limited to actual churches, while all other buildings, houses, fields, and cemeteries would be confiscated. All monasteries and convents would be disbanded, their property confiscated. Individuals could not join a church at birth, but only after they had reached the age of majority. Finally, clergymen would have to come from the Warthegau and, in addition to their clerical duties, carry out another occupation.[193]

Putting the Thirteen Points into decree form proved no easy matter. Initially, Greiser planned to address church matters through a sweeping decree that would cover all associational life. But because of its far-reaching nature, the draft decree faced objections from many sides, including the Justice Ministry and the Reich Chancellery.[194] Instead, Greiser resorted to piece-meal anti-church decrees. In August 1940, he insisted that he be given the right to decide whether or not individual clergymen should be granted transit passes to enter the Gau.[195] In September, he issued a decree that all charitable institutions (many of which had been run by the churches) were now controlled by the office of the Gau Self-Administration.[196] A year later, on 19 August 1941, deputizing for Greiser, August Jäger promulgated a decree on religious instruction. Limited to German youths aged ten to eighteen, such instruction had to take place inside a church at sharply prescribed hours.[197] Finally, on 13 September, without consulting any of the interested ministries, Greiser issued the all-important 'Decree on Religious Associations and Religion Societies in the Reichsgau Wartheland.'[198] (This was yet another radical policy enacted in late summer 1941.) It was a milestone in the Nazis' anti-church campaign; it suggested how the Nazis would eventually 'de-church' German society.[199]

According to the decree, just four churches were officially recognized in the Warthegau, and all were designated private associations: The Posen Protestant church of German Nationality in Wartheland; the Litzmannstadt Protestant church of German Nationality in Wartheland; the Protestant–Lutheran church of German Nationality in Wartheland West; and the Roman Catholic church of German Nationality in Reichsgau Wartheland. In essence, Greiser founded new churches. At the same time, there was no provision for Polish believers at all: neither a Polish Catholic nor a Polish Protestant church was foreseen. This decree brought a total separation of church and state in the Warthegau—a new departure in German church–state relations. Unsurprisingly, church and other officials raised a new round of objections. Max Winkler, the head of the Central Trust Agency for the East (HTO), even questioned Greiser's authority to issue the decree: 'This decree of the Reichsstatthalter in the Warthegau is of the greatest significance. It creates a new church law in the Warthegau. I fail to see the legal basis on which this decree rests and how it is to be brought into accord with church law now valid in the Old Reich.'[200] Lammers was also concerned. He asked Bormann whether Greiser's policies really had Hitler's approval. Bormann responded that Greiser had discussed his plans with Hitler the previous winter. Lammers, still not satisfied, broached the matter with Hitler on 6 November 1941. The Führer had no objection to Greiser's decree.[201]

If Greiser's policies were tough toward Protestants, they were downright savage toward Catholics; this reflected his anti-Polish stance. Greiser sharply limited the hours in which mass, religious instruction, and confession could take place. In December 1940, a memorandum noted that 'on the directive of the Reichsstatthalter,' 80 percent of the monks in monasteries had been interned; soon thereafter, they were sent to concentration camps in the Old Reich. All Jesuits were deported to the General Government.[202] Gau authorities sent many nuns to concentration camps. They closed seminars for priests-in-training and all Catholic elementary and secondary schools.[203] They also decimated the ranks of the Catholic clergy. According to an October 1941 report, there had been 828 priests in the Posen Archdiocese (that covered only part of the Warthegau) in 1939. Of these, 451 were now in prisons or concentrations camps, 120 had been deported to the General Government, and seventy-four had been shot or had died in concentration camps. Only thirty-four were serving as priests for Poles, seventeen as priests for Germans. Gau authorities had also closed most Catholic churches. Of 441 churches in the Posen Archdiocese, only thirty were open for Poles, fifteen for Germans. The rest were either sealed shut or being used for other purposes. Of the thirty churches in the city of Posen, two were open for Polish and one for German Catholics. Thirteen were completely shut; six were being used for general storage purposes; four, including the cathedral, were being used to store furniture; and one each was being used as a music school, riding school, book-collection point, and theater-scenery workshop.[204]

Reich authorities received numerous complaints about the miserable situation of the churches in the Warthegau. In early 1941, Lammers asked Greiser to comment on one such report. Greiser justified his anti-church policies as necessary for the Germanization of his Gau. He insisted, for example, that limited hours for services were necessary because 'the Polish-Catholic churches are used for demonstrations and masses are misused for voicing political prayers against the German leadership.' The report had noted strictures on clergy entering or leaving the Gau. Greiser flatly declared that 'clergy who are in any way politically questionable do not receive a permit to go from here to the Old Reich.' He also addressed a complaint that various religious pictures and statues had been knocked down or otherwise removed. His response: 'the Führer did not send me here to use state power to protect yellowed pictures of saints, but rather to make this land a future land (*Zukunftsland*) for the German people. But these outdated monuments are in the way and their mere presence is a slap in the face to the German population.'[205] Greiser, a Reich Chancellery official wrote, had dispatched the complaints 'in a very spirited way:' 'the letter gives a vivid picture of Gauleiter Greiser's church policy of a separation of church and state in a Gau in which *Volkstum* policy must have first priority.'[206]

The Vatican envoy in Germany, Archbishop Cesare Orsenigo, repeatedly lodged complaints about the situation. This, in turn, raised the matter of the Vatican's jurisdiction in the newly annexed areas. Just as with the Ministry of Ecclesiastical Affairs, Greiser refused to recognize the Vatican's right to intervene in his Gau.[207] This led to a disagreement between Greiser and Ernst von Weizsäcker, state secretary in the Foreign Ministry. Weizsäcker argued that the Vatican's interest in Warthegau affairs involved an implicit diplomatic recognition of Germany's annexation of the eastern territories, which the Vatican had yet to give officially. He also believed that if special policies obtained in the Warthegau, this might suggest that the German government did not view the Gau as an integral part of the Third Reich.[208] But Greiser, the Party Chancellery, and the Reich Chancellery had a more antagonistic view: so long as the Vatican continued to accredit a Polish ambassador and refused to recognize Germany's annexation of Polish territories, it should not be allowed to interfere in the Gau.[209] Weizsäcker was ultimately overruled. In June 1942, the Führer determined that the Vatican's say in church matters in Germany was limited to the geographical areas covered by the 1933 Nazi–Vatican Concordat.[210] Just as Kerrl's influence had been limited to the Old Reich, so too was the Vatican's. Once again, Greiser had thwarted ministerial concerns. And once again, he had forged a policy that extended beyond his Gau.

Besides objecting to Greiser's anti-church policies per se, church authorities and others feared these measures as precedents. The Vatican, for example, assumed that developments in the Warthegau presaged those in the Old Reich. As the head of the Political Department in the Foreign Ministry, Ernst Woermann, noted in 1942, 'in the Vatican it is assumed that regulations being tried out in the Warthegau will also be valid later in the Old Reich.'[211] In all likelihood the Vatican was right: Greiser's anti-church measures might well have served as the model for a radical restructuring of church–state relations in a triumphant Third Reich. Of all of his policies, Greiser's anti-church measures aroused the greatest contemporary opposition from Germans and foreigners alike. Perhaps the fact that they affected Germans explains this outrage—an outrage never evident with regard to anti-Polish or anti-Jewish measures.

While Greiser was not fazed by ministerial or church opposition to his measures, he was concerned about the reaction of German citizens in the Gau. The SD reported widespread church-going among the German population.[212] Germans of all stripes had little understanding for the attack on organized religion. The Office of *Volkstum* Affairs noted that 'it's not easy for the resettlers and ethnic Germans to understand why the church, up to now the center of all *völkisch* work, is so flagrantly attacked.'[213] Ironically, anti-church policy threatened Germanization—the very project in whose name Greiser claimed it was necessary. As one Baltic minister wrote, 'The great majority of the resettled Balts remain loyal to the church that is now supported by voluntary contributions. But it's not surprising that many are very worried and harbor a strong wish to be allowed to leave the Wartheland as soon as possible.'[214] Faced with such reactions, Greiser decided to assuage some observant resettlers. In 1941, 155 German resettlers from Galicia sent him a petition asking for a German Catholic priest to minister to their needs. Greiser granted their request, and reportedly hoped that the resettlers 'would learn to love their new homeland and would live in it just as happily as in their former one.'[215] Even though he refused to buckle to demands made by Protestant church officials, the Ministry of Ecclesiastical Affairs, or the Vatican, Greiser acceded to some resettlers' religious demands.

In August 1940, Greiser removed some religious holidays—Good Friday, Ascension Day, and Repentance Day—from the list of official holidays. He thought such holidays unnecessary. In his words, 'the party also has its Good Friday—9 November 1923; it also has its martyrs—those who died for the Movement; it also possesses its altar—the Field Marshals' hall (*Feldherrnhalle*) in Munich.'[216] Many ethnic Germans complained bitterly about losing Good Friday as a holiday.[217] On Good Friday 1941, they filled Warthegau churches, even though the day was not an official holiday. The following year, the RSHA ordered that in German territories in which Good Friday was not an official holiday, services could be held only after 7 p.m. In the Warthegau, Good Friday worshipers gathered before locked churches early in the day, eagerly awaiting entry. As it turned out, shortly beforehand, the Gestapo, with Greiser's approval, had secretly decided not to uphold the ban on daytime church services. Worshipers were thus allowed into the churches.[218] Several church officials, however, were nonetheless disciplined because they held daytime services.[219] Greiser played a double game here. Since he didn't want to anger the general German population, he approved the Gestapo's decision not to uphold the ban on daytime services. Yet he also had church authorities disciplined with official Gestapo warnings for holding services. Perhaps the events of 1942 made Bormann and Greiser wary of future Good Friday battles. In March 1943, Bormann encouraged local officials to permit services all day on Good Friday, even in areas in which the day was not an official holiday.[220] Greiser agreed to this 'loosening' of restrictions.[221]

Opposition to Greiser's measures also surfaced in the hotly contested issue of whether Germans in the Warthegau were being forced to leave churches. Greiser—not Bormann—initiated these policies. The Decree on Religious Associations was worded so that Reich Germans who moved to the Warthegau did not belong to a church (since their churches in the Old Reich were not recognized in the Gau). To join a church in the Warthegau, Reich Germans would have to go to a police office and publicly declare their intentions. For many, this would serve as a strong deterrent.[222] In discussions of the draft of this law, Bormann rejected this clause on the grounds that it could lead to a plebiscite on regime policies.[223] While Bormann's fear was not borne out, the decree angered many Reich Germans. As the mayor of a Warthegau town, Franz Heinrich Bock (who wrote under the pseudonym Alexander Hohenstein), noted in his diary: 'this decree is an unprecedented, totally raw act of spiritual rape whose cynical unscrupulousness makes one tremble.'[224] Shortly thereafter, a movement was afoot to compel civil servants and party members to sign forms stating that the signatory did not and would never again belong to a church, even if he returned to the Old Reich. Refusing to sign could jeopardize one's job.[225] In April 1943, Bormann wrote to Greiser that he had received a complaint about party members being forced to sign these declarations. As he reminded Greiser, this practice had 'not been approved by me.' He now wanted Greiser to make clear to all Warthegau NSDAP offices that it was to end. In response, Greiser claimed that such compulsory declarations had not been demanded since mid-1942.[226] But this was not true. Apparently, with or without his knowledge, such statements were still occasionally forced upon individuals. In July 1944, Greiser finally circulated a memorandum in which he expressly forbade the practice.[227] The whole episode illustrates how little support radical Nazi anti-church measures had among the Gau's German population. It also shows that Greiser eventually softened his anti-church policies—presumably to boost morale as German military fortunes declined.

The anti-church policies in the Warthegau were unique in Nazi Germany. None of the other eastern Gaus had similar policies. While Greiser took his cue from Bormann, he also showed considerable initiative. He pushed for the separation of church and state. He permitted the extreme persecution of Catholic priests. He ensured that many other policies—from limiting religious instruction to using churches as storage facilities—went into effect. He, and not Bormann, decided to force Reich Germans to publicly declare their religious intentions. In carrying out his anti-church measures, Greiser ran roughshod over ministerial, Vatican, and Protestant church authorities. Only the opposition of his German population gave him pause.

Greiser was eager to use the Germanization of his Gau to profile himself as a radical Nazi, to forge the Warthegau into a model Nazi Gau, and to accumulate extraordinary powers as a Gauleiter. With his anti-Polish segregation policies, Greiser created the harshest anti-Polish regime in Nazi-occupied Europe. These policies proved a model; many were eventually adopted in the other annexed eastern areas. Likewise, he initiated the DVL and, eventually, put into place the most stringent DVL policies. His anti-church policies were also extreme; although not copied elsewhere, many thought that they presaged the future of church–state relations in the Third Reich. At times, Greiser was even more radical than Himmler or Bormann. Indeed, Greiser's challenging of Himmler on DVL policy and his willingness to go further than Bormann in anti-church policy suggest his increasing self-confidence as a hard-line Germanizer. Yet for all that Greiser was eager to profile himself as a radical Nazi, many of his policies foundered on realities that he simply could not overcome, such as his need for Polish workers or the support of Germans in his Gau. Although Greiser was deeply committed to Germanization, pragmatic necessities sometimes forced him to temper his highly ideological program. All these and other features of Greiser's rule were also evident in the final prong of his Germanization strategy: exploiting and expropriating Poles and Jews so as to make the Warthegau's land German.

7

'The Most Modern Streets:' Exploiting Poles and Jews to Make the Gau German

Arthur Greiser's chief aim in the Warthegau was to make its land and people 'German.' To win the ethnic struggle (*Volkskampf*) against Poles, he believed, Germans would have to settle there permanently. But they would do so only if they felt that they were in 'Germany,' not occupied Poland. Greiser thus attempted nothing less than a total transformation of the Gau's infrastructure, architecture, landscape, and public memory; no area of the built, natural, or cultural environment escaped his attention. Such reconstruction (*Aufbau*) measures, however, were costly, both in terms of money and labor. In large measure, Greiser financed his Germanization program through the expropriation and exploitation of Poles and Jews. Once again, his policies toward Germans, Poles, and Jews were deeply interconnected.

Just as with Poles, Greiser's attitude toward Jews was an inconsistent mixture of racial hatred and pragmatic concern. To him, Germanization demanded both the murder and exploitation of Jews. Even as he initiated the murder of 'unproductive' Jews, he was eager to use 'productive' Jews for Germanization purposes. Indeed, in October 1941, at a Posen meeting of Reich trustees for work in the eastern areas, Greiser reportedly made a most revealing remark: 'Of course, first priority must be given to winning the war. Therefore, for example, he [i.e., Greiser] was happy (*froh*) that he had 200,000 to 300,000 Jews in his Gau. They could do lots of the work that otherwise couldn't be done.'[1] Greiser's remarks were highly unusual: a high-ranking Nazi official proclaiming his happiness about the presence of

Jews! Although Greiser was steeped in Nazi anti-Semitism and was the first regional leader to initiate the systematic murder of 'unproductive' Jews, his main aim was the Germanization of his Gau—and for this, he was only too 'happy' to exploit the Jews in the Warthegau.

On arrival in the Gau, Greiser and other Nazi officials claimed to be dismayed by the utterly 'un-German' conditions. The cities and towns appeared dirty and shabby, the transportation infrastructure inadequate, agriculture and industry inefficient. Many buildings in the eastern parts of the Gau lacked running water or sewage systems. As Greiser once remarked, 'The area . . . does not yet have the face ... that it could and must have if German people are to feel at home there.'[2] Greiser, of course, blamed this situation on Poles. In their twenty years of rule, he insisted, the Poles had done nothing to improve the region. As he stated in 1942, '. . . the Polish state in those twenty years established nothing positive . . . In 1939 the streets looked exactly the same as twenty years earlier. I think that there were even the same potholes!'[3]

To Greiser and other Nazi authorities, 'German' meant modernity, order, cleanliness, and tastefulness. In October 1939, Greiser declared that 'German strength should flow to the east on the most modern streets of Adolf Hitler, the highways, . . . and with the best trucks and the fastest airplanes.'[4] A 'German' environment meant new factories, neat shops, and up-to-date home furnishings and appliances. It meant a sleek elegance in public buildings, and a cozy, homey provincialism in work canteens and rural living rooms. It meant a material culture that used indigenous plants and minerals: oak, elm, ash, and pine wood, for example, or stone mined from local quarries.[5] It meant a land rich with gardens, forests, and other greenery. 'German' also meant a sharp contrast from 'Polish:' paved German streets instead of dirt Polish roads, high-brow German culture instead of gauche Polish entertainment, modern German homes instead of ramshackle Polish slums, and rich German forests instead of barren Polish steppes.

During the German occupation, state-sanctioned robbery was the order of the day. On 5 October 1939, for example, Greiser issued a blanket authority to Gerhard Scheffler, city commissar and soon lord mayor of Posen, 'to confiscate buildings, plots of land and apartments in the area of the municipality of Posen . . . for the use of the civil administration or the

German economy.'[6] Nazi authorities soon imposed some order on their lawlessness. On 19 October, Hermann Göring decreed the establishment of the Central Trust Agency for the East (HTO).[7] The HTO oversaw the registration, administration, and eventual sale of all property confiscated from Poles and Jews (and virtually all Polish and Jewish property *was* confiscated). It worked closely with Heinrich Himmler's Reich Commissariat for the Strengthening of Germandom (RKFDV); altering property relations was key to the Germanization project.[8] In December 1939, Himmler also established a Land Office (*Bodenamt*) for the Warthegau; it registered all Polish and Jewish land in the Gau, and had the right to carry out confiscations of land.[9] The following September, Göring codified what was already established practice. The Polish Assets Decree (*Polenvermögensordnung*) made virtually all Polish property subject to confiscation. Polish property could be taken if 'needed for the public good, especially in the interest of defending the Reich or for the strengthening of Germandom.' Only small amounts of personal property and bank assets up to 1,000 Reichsmarks (RM) were excluded from potential seizure.[10] While many Poles continued to run their businesses (there weren't enough Germans to manage them all), their property was not their own.

Much Nazi wrangling accompanied the dispossession of Polish and Jewish property. To Greiser's irritation, HTO expropriations benefited the Reich, not his Gau. Gau authorities were thus left with confiscating the personal effects of Poles and Jews, usually during deportations: cash, jewelry, securities, and savings accounts. On 15 November, Greiser informed Fritz Ohl, director of the Posen Regional Bank and Central Clearing Bank (*Landesbank und Girozentrale*), that 'during the evacuation of apartments occupied by Poles certain sums of money are obtained that their owners are not allowed to take with them. These monies are to be paid into a special account... I have sole rights over this account.'[11] Years later, in 1944, the Reich Audit Office (*Rechnungshof des Deutschen Reichs*) investigated a tangle of accounts linked to Greiser. At that time, Greiser declared that the funds had 'since been totally used up,' and that he had reached an agreement about the matter with the president of the Audit Office. Audit officials were forced to acknowledge their inability to follow these particular money trails.[12]

While one historian has suggested that Greiser personally enriched himself with these funds, it seems instead that the monies were used to cover Gau expenses.[13] Initially, at least, Greiser financed his agency with confiscated funds. As a Reich Treasury official recorded in January 1940: 'Up to now Gauleiter Greiser has paid for the reconstruction of the Warthegau through monies that he has confiscated in his capacity as Reichsstatthalter. These were monies taken from evacuated Jews and Poles.' By that time, Greiser had taken in about 170,000 RM, or just over one million 2007 dollars.[14] In February 1940, Harry Siegmund, Greiser's cousin and personal advisor, issued an order that money and valuables confiscated during evacuations be deposited into the Reichsstatthalter's special bank account.[15] But the HTO also put a claim on these valuables, as did local authorities.[16] In April 1940, Greiser complained that 'the Central Trust Agency for the East is growing into a state within a state.'[17] That same month, his deputy August Jäger complained that the Reichsstatthalter agency had no influence over HTO dealings; all the confiscations, Jäger irritably noted, were benefiting the RKFDV and the HTO, but not the Warthegau.[18] Tensions between Greiser and the HTO persisted until February 1941. At that time, Göring stipulated that the Reichsstatthalters and Oberpräsidents were now in charge of HTO branch offices.[19] For Greiser, however, this was a Pyrrhic victory; by then, the HTO had confiscated and disposed of most Polish and Jewish property.

In addition to stealing homes, businesses, and real estate, Gau and other Nazi authorities confiscated Polish and Jewish consumer goods. These items were usually redistributed to Germans for household or business use. In early fall 1939, for example, Wehrmacht units in Hohensalza requisitioned furs, lingerie, feather beds, eau de Cologne, and 50 dozen condoms.[20] In early October, Greiser ordered the confiscation of all radios owned by Poles or Jews.[21] In March 1940 the Olympia Office Machinery Works advertised that it reconfigured Polish-language keyboards for German use; this made it possible for Germans to write on stolen typewriters.[22] In the next months and years, Poles and Jews saw their cars, motorcycles, cameras, binoculars, furs, silver coins, sewing machines, records and gramophones, and skis and ski equipment taken.[23] No Polish or Jewish property was safe from the grasping claws of occupation authorities.

While Greiser worked to secure funds, he also instituted measures aimed at making the land look 'German.' As a first step, he ordered the elimination of all easily removed signs of Polishness. On 18 September 1939, he instructed local officials to rename their locales according to the official pre-1918

German names. If no such German name existed, officials were to come up with appropriate German designations; these might sound similar to the Polish name, be a translation of the Polish name, or draw on the physical features of a given locale.[24] Five days later Greiser ordered the removal of all Polish-language signs and inscriptions on houses and businesses.[25] The Nazis also began to tear down Polish monuments. On the square next to the Posen Castle, for example, a religious statue that Greiser deemed a symbol of 'Polish hatred' was removed.[26] Although cosmetic, these changes strikingly altered the feel and appearance of the area. By the end of September, Greiser approvingly noted of Posen, 'the removal of Polish street names and signs on businesses shows that this city—German in its whole layout—has preserved its German character.'[27] A few months later, a member of the Polish underground wrote: 'Even I could hardly believe that it was the same city I had known before the war, so thoroughly had its face been remodeled.'[28]

In an effort to strip Poles of their cultural heritage, Nazi authorities took art and other valuable cultural objects from library, museum, and private collections. A December 1939 HTO decree declared that these confiscations were 'in the interest of the strengthening of Germandom and the defense of the Reich.'[29] In time, over 1.3 million Polish books were brought to a collection point at Posen University.[30] Even though these and other items were of Polish provenance, Gau authorities recognized their potential value. On Greiser's orders, museum staff eventually combed through all art works and other decorative objects confiscated from Polish estates. Those pieces deemed of museum quality were kept for exhibition purposes, while the rest were sold off to interested parties to benefit Gau coffers.[31] Greiser personally enjoyed some expropriated goods. A painting by a Flemish master, Roger van der Weyden's *Virgin on the Balcony*, stolen from one of the Skorzewski family estates, graced the walls of his office.[32] His country estate, Mariensee, was also allegedly furnished with confiscated items.[33]

Greiser and his officials also tried to erase Jewish sites from the Warthegau. In some cases, they transformed Jewish sites into German ones. The most remarkable example of this involved the New Posen Synagogue, originally opened in 1907. In fall 1939, city officials noted that Posen had no indoor swimming facility and approached Greiser with the proposal of turning the synagogue into a municipal pool. Greiser not only approved the project, but also made special funds available for it.[34] In September 1942, he officially opened the 25-meter pool and attended the first meet there.[35] Today, the former synagogue remains a swimming pool, a reflection of Nazi anti-Semitism, communist indifference, and present-day lack of funding.[36]

For Greiser, turning the synagogue into a pool surely held symbolic meaning. Germanization was to substitute the 'clean,' the 'beautiful,' and the 'healthy' for the 'dirty,' the 'ugly,' and the 'sick.' What better way to Germanize a synagogue then to turn it into a center of German health and vigor? In other cases, however, Warthegau officials transformed Jewish sites according to their association of Jews with squalor and crime. In Freihaus, the Jewish ritual baths were turned into a delousing station.[37] In Litzmannstadt, a former Jewish school housed not only workshops for the police, but also stalls for their horses.[38] At least one synagogue was turned into a prison. Other synagogues served more prosaic purposes such as storage depots or municipal multi-purpose rooms.[39] Many Jewish institutions were simply stripped of their valuables and destroyed. In Tuchingen, the Nazis leveled the Jewish cemetery and used the grave stones for paving roads and other infrastructural improvements.[40]

Greiser was eager to update the Gau's economy. The Warthegau, he insisted, was to become the 'largest breadbasket of the Greater German Reich.'[41] In February 1940, he argued that the Warthegau could produce 30–40 percent more agricultural produce if the Reich delivered sufficient quantities of fertilizer, machines, and seed.[42] Through October 1942, the Warthegau received some 100,000 machines and other tools from the Old Reich.[43] Greiser also worked to modernize factories. In the course of Aryanizing the Litzmannstadt textile industry, many small workshops were consolidated into larger, more efficient factories. The Gau's small machine and steel industries were also improved. A few new factories, including a large one that made hemp cord, were built.[44] In 1943, Greiser hoped to develop newly discovered coal fields near Konin.[45] As he well knew, the Warthegau could only be 'German' if its economy adhered to Reich standards.

To aid economic development, Greiser embarked on numerous modernization projects. Until the German invasion of the Soviet Union, he found Reich support for these measures. For fiscal year 1941, for example, the Interior Ministry requested an additional 30 million RM for the Warthegau and Danzig–West Prussia 'for the improvement of hygienic conditions through the building or expansion of hospitals, slaughter houses, sewage systems, and the water supply.' It was imperative, a memorandum argued, to create all 'the civilized institutions that are necessary so that the German people will feel comfortable in these areas and so as to incite a strong movement there from the Old Reich.'[46] Reich officials approved plans to widen the Warta River to allow more shipping and to build canals that would link major waterways.[47] Posen was also to have an expanded river harbor that would include large depot halls and cold-storage facilities.[48]

Most important, Gau and Reich officials planned to improve the road network. Reich officials intended to build highways from Berlin to Litzmannstadt and from Danzig to Breslau; both were to pass through Posen. In October 1940, Greiser announced that building on the highway stretch from Frankfurt/Oder to Posen was about to begin.[49] Three months later, Greiser stated that the Reich general inspector for streets foresaw a road network in the Warthegau of 200 kilometers of highways and 11,100 kilometers of streets; 300 kilometers had already been built.[50] In June 1942, he reported that in 1941 roughly 1,000 kilometers of streets had been readied 'that according to our standards could be described as driveable.'[51] Building roads and highways, however, was directly linked to the exploitation of Jewish labor.

In May 1940, Chaim Rumkowski, chairman of the Jewish Council in the Litzmannstadt ghetto, faced a dire problem: contrary to German belief, ghetto inhabitants were unable to pay for food and other supplies. He thus devised a strategy whereby Jews would produce goods for sale in exchange for foodstuffs. In the next months, he interested Litzmannstadt municipal authorities in his plans, especially since they, too, were concerned about how to pay for the upkeep of the ghetto's 160,000 inmates. Rumkowski and Hans Biebow, the German head of the Ghetto Administration, now sought machinery, raw materials, and contracts for ghetto workshops. Ghetto inmates soon produced Wehrmacht uniforms and parts, as well as underwear, hats, gloves, and stockings for private companies. They also made cabinets and other furniture, and maintained tannery, furrier and locksmith workshops.[52] Ghetto tailors made various articles of clothing for 'German dignitaries,' including Greiser.[53] Eventually, ghetto inmates produced ammunition and parts for military equipment.[54] All of this production had a relatively modest aim: preventing the city of Litzmannstadt (and the Reich) from having to subsidize the ghetto.[55]

In June 1940, Greiser received reports from inside the ghetto—perhaps from Rumkowski himself—suggesting that there was 'a large number of specialists' whose 'work potential had been wasted for months.' His interest was piqued. On 25 June, he asked Friedrich Uebelhoer, district president of Litzmannstadt, to determine how many workers were available in the ghetto and to what extent they could be mobilized in 'the interests of the war economy.'[56] Greiser's question presaged not only the extensive use of ghetto labor, but also the ominous categorization of Jews into those 'capable' and 'incapable' of work (which occurred in other Nazi-occupied areas, too). On 31 July, Greiser had a meeting with Hans Frank; as described in Chapter 5, Frank refused to allow additional Jews to be deported to the General Government. The negative outcome of the Cracow meeting spurred a dramatic change in policy. Making a virtue of necessity, Greiser sought economic benefit from the Jews in his Gau.

Although Jews had been used for forced labor since the start of the Nazi occupation, Greiser now initiated a more systematic exploitation of their work potential. On 6 August, the Department of Work in his Reichsstatthalter agency ordered private firms that employed Jews to pay regular wages and benefits for them. The greater part of these wages, however, was to be paid into the bank account 'Gauleiter, NSDAP Reconstruction Account' at the Deutsche Bank in Posen. Greiser thus intended that he—on behalf of the Gau—would be the major beneficiary of Jews working for private firms. Though it might seem that Greiser would reap a windfall, this was not the case. 90 percent of work done by Jews in the Gau was for Reich institutions, mostly the Wehrmacht; just ten percent was for private firms.[57]

The Reich Audit Office eventually tried to figure out what happened to funds paid into the 'NSDAP Reconstruction Account.' But Greiser had disbanded that account, and ordered all like payments to go to an association 'for the promotion of culturally important activity.' That association maintained a decentralized account system, permitting Greiser to create a web of slush-fund accounts. When an Interior Ministry official, Friedrich Karl Surén, wanted all income deducted from the wages of Jews to appear in the Gau's regular budget, Greiser complained that Surén was 'a typical exponent of the ministerial bureaucracy who through bureaucratic soullessness stands in the way of administrative effectiveness.'[58]

Greiser's new-found interest in using Jews as workers found many expressions. In early March 1941, he reportedly ordered that Jews capable of work were *not* to be deported to the General Government.[59] Once eager to rid his Gau of all Jews, Greiser now expressly forbade the deportation of those Jews 'capable of work.' This soon proved moot, since all deportations ended on 15 March. On 9 May 1941 Greiser visited the ghetto.[60] He liked how the Jews were working. As he reportedly stated: 'I would not have believed it if I had not seen it with my own eyes.'[61] In June, Greiser told a Nazi official that working Jews should receive the same rations as Polish workers.[62] In July, the mayor of Litzmannstadt, Dr. Karl Marder, wrote that 'the ghetto is no longer regarded as a labor or concentration camp of sorts, but rather as a significant element in the economic system, a kind of vast factory. To date, 40,000 of the 160,000 ghetto inmates are employed.'[63] In fact, the numbers of Jews employed in actual production was much smaller; in September 1941, just 17,936 Jews were producing goods for sale to outside entities. The rest, some 22,057 individuals, were employed by the Jewish Self-Administration to run the ghetto.[64]

Throughout the Gau, Jews now began to work on Germanization projects. In October 1940, when Reich authorities decided to build the highway from Frankfurt/Oder to Posen, Greiser told some journalists that this project would 'create work for a large number of unemployed Jews in the Warthegau.' It also, however, meant employing Polish Jews in the Old Reich, in areas technically 'free of Jews.' As far as Nazi racial purists were concerned, this was unacceptable. But with war in the offing, Reinhard Heydrich, the head of the Reich Security Main Office (RSHA), granted Fritz Todt, general inspector of the German Road and Highway System, a special dispensation. By early 1941, some 1,600 Jews from the Litzmannstadt ghetto had been sent to work on the highway building project in the Old Reich; another 119 Jews were sent to camps in Danzig and Straschin-Prangschin to work on highway building there.[65] Greiser soon sought to expand this program. In early February 1941 he worked out a proposal with the Reich Labor Ministry whereby some 73,000 Jews from the Warthegau would go to the Old Reich; had this plan been put into effect, the numbers of Jews in the Old Reich would have risen by roughly 40 percent.[66] Greiser's plans received Göring's indirect support: in mid-February the Reich marshal declared that for the duration of the war, racial considerations shouldn't preclude the use of available labor.[67] But both Hitler and the RSHA disagreed. As one RSHA official stated, 'It's simply unacceptable to move Jews out by exerting extraordinary force on one side, only to let them back in again on the other.' On 7 April,

Hitler struck the final nail in the project's coffin. He expressly forbade the scheme.[68] With that, Greiser's plan came to naught.

The highway camps for small numbers of Warthegau Jews in the Old Reich proved the start of an extensive network of Forced Labor Camps for Jews (*Zwangsarbeitslager für Juden* or ZAfJ) inside the Warthegau. Eventually, the ZAfJ became the largest such network in all of Nazi-occupied Europe.[69] These camps were under civilian authority, and so Greiser had authority over them. As with the highway camps, many were located in areas 'free of Jews.' Indeed, there were so many camps in and around Posen that many more Jews lived there now than in 1939—perhaps as many as 12,000.[70] Between 1941 and 1943, camp inmates did some agricultural and factory work. Mostly, though, they worked on projects to improve the Gau's infrastructure. Jewish workers were to make the face of the Warthegau 'German.' They did virtually all of the street and road improvement work.[71] They laid track and made other railroad improvements.[72] They worked on new sewage systems. In Posen, they worked on a central cemetery, the zoo, and several artificial lakes. They also worked on afforestation and other efforts to make Posen a greener, more 'German' city.[73] It is said that Jews built the road linking Greiser's country estate to a main street leading into Posen.[74]

In the second half of 1942, at the height of their existence, there were roughly 160 forced labor camps for Jews in the Warthegau; altogether, some 30,000 to 40,000 Jews passed through them.[75] Many more Jews, and for a much longer period, were used in labor camps in the Warthegau than elsewhere.[76] Camp conditions were atrocious.[77] In late 1941, the Ministry of Labor wanted to apply a Reich special labor law for Jews to the annexed territories; the law would have covered Jews working in public or private enterprises outside the ghetto. But at a November 1941 meeting, officials from the new areas vigorously objected—Jews in the annexed territories were already working under much worse conditions than the law envisioned.[78] One prisoner who worked in three labor camps in Posen later recalled: 'In general these three Posen camps were worse than Auschwitz. In Auschwitz, if you did your work correctly, you were left alone. In the Posen camps we were mistreated for no reason at all.'[79] Even contemporary German sources noted the poor conditions: food rations were very low; opportunities for washing limited; and medicines, bandages, and other necessities completely lacking.[80] After doing a stint of camp work, most Jews returned to the ghetto sick, exhausted, or otherwise physically spent.

Initially, Jews working in the camps received minuscule payment. Those laboring in the Old Reich were paid between thirty-five and seventy-five pennies per week, those inside the Gau less. That soon changed. According to guidelines issued by Greiser's Reichsstatthalter agency in June 1942, Jews working in ZAfJ camps were to receive no pay at all.[81] Instead, companies employing Jews were to pay their wages to the Litzmannstadt Ghetto Administration. This involved significant sums. Between mid-September and the end of November 1942, for example, the Ghetto Administration received almost 125,000 RM (roughly $740,000 in 2007 dollars) for Jewish labor in the Posen area.[82] After covering various costs, the Ghetto Administration channeled the remaining profits to the bank account 'Association of the Friends of the Warthegau,' personally controlled by Greiser.[83] Jews thus aided Germanization in two important ways. Given the general labor shortage, they provided a work force that carried out infrastructural improvements that otherwise would not have been accomplished. At the same time, their rank exploitation filled Gau coffers.

Although many Nazi officials favored the immediate murder of Jews and thus opposed his 'productivist' approach, Greiser had his supporters. In April 1942, for example, the local German air-force listening post recorded that 'on the directive of Reich Marshal Göring, who wants every worker to be used,' the Jews in the Litzmannstadt ghetto 'should be mainly employed with the production of goods for the Wehrmacht.'[84] Greiser himself expressed pride that he had put Jews to work. In June 1942, at the Institute for World Economics in Kiel, he proclaimed, 'We have tackled the problem of harnessing the work potential of Jews. I believe that we have solved the Jewish Question in a way that Jews and probably also Germans had never imagined. If one goes about matters in ways that are uncomplicated and non-bureaucratic, it's possible to make racially foreign workers useful for the German people.' Greiser then perhaps took a swipe against those who had wished to regulate Jewish labor: 'I do want to note, though—and this is not an accusation, just an observation—if we had used good Prussian bureaucrats to carry out this task, today the Jews probably would still not be working. But we used National Socialists who tackled the problem in a totally non-bureaucratic manner. So by using racially foreign workers we can do work now and prepare for huge planned projects for the postwar era that we could not have done with the existing workers in the Reich.'[85] Greiser may well have been suggesting that his method of dealing with Jews—exploiting them as workers—might serve as a model for the Reich. He was, perhaps, seeking legitimacy for a policy that Nazi racial purists found abhorrent.

Germanization meant far more than infrastructural improvements. Greiser hoped to project German power and might in the region. This was nowhere more evident than in the grand architectural plans made for the city of Posen: the Gau capital was to become the 'model city' for the 'model Gau.'[86] On a visit to Posen in January 1940, Joseph Goebbels commented: 'Checked reconstruction plans for Posen. Very generous and also reasonable. Greiser is making great efforts.'[87] In spring 1940, Gau officials unveiled an elaborate *Gauforum* plan. The governmental quarter in Posen was to include a renovated castle, a huge hall (with a standing room capacity of 40,000), an imposing building for the military, new police headquarters, a theater, an art museum, a new train station, and a building (with a tower) for the German Labor Front (*Deutsche Arbeitsfront* or DAF). The city was also to have a civilian airport, 40,000 additional apartments, an expanded zoo, a huge bridge across the Warta River, new indoor and outdoor swimming facilities, the 'most modern and largest' hospital in the German East, and a wooded cemetery on the outskirts of the city.[88] While their synagogue was turned into an indoor swimming facility, Jews labored on the zoo and cemetery projects, and possibly on others, too.

Of the most ambitious building projects, only one was realized: the renovation of the Posen Castle.[89] Originally completed in 1910 for Kaiser Wilhelm II, the castle had some 600 rooms, including a throne room, chapel, and private quarters for the emperor. When Greiser came to Posen, he was very taken with the castle, and he brought pictures and plans of it to his next meeting with Hitler. In September 1939, the Führer decided to turn the castle into one of his official residences. For Hitler, however, it was important that the castle represent Nazi aesthetics; it was thus to undergo a massive interior renovation. Since the building was also to house the office of the Gauleiter of the Warthegau, Greiser had a stake in the project's completion. This building project, however, absorbed enormous resources. Some Gau and Berlin Finance Ministry officials tried to stymie it. Irritated by what he saw as bureaucratic obstreperousness, Greiser wrote to Martin Bormann in June 1940: 'Despite the Führer's approval, the bureaucrats in my agency and those in the Reich Finance Ministry make the greatest imaginable difficulties in financially securing this building project which is estimated at roughly 6.7 million Reichsmarks . . . Please advise me on how I could best defeat the bureaucracy in this matter.'[90] Greiser's complaint seems to have had some effect. On this and several other occasions, Hitler personally intervened to ensure the project's continuation.

By December 1943, Greiser's suite of offices and personal living quarters, along with a casino, were completed. By then, the Castle renovation had cost some 20 million RM. At times, 400 to 500 Poles worked round the clock, using great quantities of stone, metal, and other precious resources. But Greiser, unrepentant, justified the costs. On 3 January 1944, for example, he declared that should the Führer come to Posen, 'no one will grouse that the castle was renovated, instead one will say, wow, we're good chaps, we can house the Führer in a worthy manner.'[91] In 1944, Albert Speer, Reich minister of armaments and war production, took away the castle's status as a 'war important building project.' Hitler, however, insisted that the work continue; he apparently considered using the castle as a temporary Reich Chancellery. But he never once came to Posen. The renovation of the Posen Castle exposed Nazi hubris and its illusions in the East. Although meant to be an imposing symbol of Germandom, it came to represent the unnecessary squandering of scarce wartime resources.

The Gau's largest city, Litzmannstadt, was also targeted for Germanization.[92] To the Nazis, it had a very 'un-German' population: in 1939, the city counted roughly 700,000 inhabitants, including 69,465 ethnic Germans, 361,358 Poles, and 227,067 Jews.[93] These demographics mirrored the supposedly unseemly face of the city. Factories dotted residential neighborhoods; much of the population lived in small, overcrowded apartments; and many neighborhoods lacked running water and sewage systems.[94] In 1939, Franz Schiffer, the lord mayor, declared that the 'most pressing task of the city administration' was to give Lodsch 'a German face.' The city was to receive a new city hall and new buildings for the NSDAP, the police, and the city military command.[95] Officials planned the construction of 35,000 apartments in the near future, and an additional 75,000 later.[96] In June 1941, Greiser explicitly linked the confiscation of Jewish and Polish property with the city's reconstruction: 'With the renovation and reconstruction of the city of Litzmannstadt the principle must be a generous treatment in the distribution of accumulated Jewish and Polish property. Bureaucratic and arithmetical objections may not in any way hinder the planned projects.'[97]

If new or renovated buildings were to project German might, cultural institutions were to radiate German erudition to the East. Greiser attached enormous importance to the founding of a German university. As soon as 26 October 1939, he turned to Hitler with a request to establish a university.[98] In December, Greiser informed Bernhard Rust, Reich minister of science, education, and popular culture, of the 'decision of the Führer to create in the shortest possible time a German university in Posen that in equipment and operations will represent German science in the East in exemplary fashion.'[99] In fact, Greiser had jumped the gun. On receiving the letter, Rust sought confirmation of Hitler's decision. As he now learned, the Führer had merely decided that a university in Posen 'should be prepared' (not yet opened).[100] Greiser and Rust, however, soon determined that Hitler's unwillingness to sanction a new university related only to the construction of new buildings. They thus decided to open university faculties in buildings that had first been used by the German Royal Academy (*Königliche Akademie*) and later by the interwar Polish university.[101] They designated 20 April 1941, Hitler's 52nd birthday, as the official opening date. Although they hoped the Führer would come, Rust was the keynote speaker at the university's grand opening festivities on 27 April.

The Posen University was one of four 'Reich universities' founded by the Nazis; the others were located in Prague, Strasbourg, and Dorpat. Besides fostering German knowledge, these universities were to inculcate National-Socialist ideology in new areas of the Reich.[102] In January 1941, Greiser declared that 'the crowning of our entire cultural work is the planning of the Reich University East in Posen. In its scale and its curriculum, [the university] presents a revolution in the area of education. For the first time, the demands that we National Socialists make for the education of the German person will be completely met here.'[103] The curriculum of the new university reflected its function as a 'Reich university.' The university had no theological faculty. In keeping with the Gau's rural character, university officials planned a strong faculty in agricultural science. Of the fifty to sixty professors who were to make up the university's faculty, at least twenty-one were to be in fields related to agricultural science. Faculty chairs were also planned in academic fields related to the German East: 'German Prehistory and German Folklore,' 'Border and Ethnic Germandom,' 'Race Politics,' and 'Political Study of Foreign Countries.' Most surprisingly, university officials foresaw a chair in 'The History and Language of Jews.'[104] In the event, neither the chair devoted to Jewish studies nor several of those focusing on Germanization were ever filled.[105] The university nonetheless grew apace. While 131 students attended the university in its first (summer) semester in 1941, 1,228 students were enrolled in summer 1944. The faculty (professors, instructors, and assistants) grew from forty-nine in 1941 to 118 in winter 1943–4.[106]

The university's focus on Germanization was evident in the selection and support of its students and faculty. Students were carefully screened for their past activities on behalf of the German ethnic struggle.[107] Both students and faculty had to sign a statement declaring that they were not related by birth or marriage to non-Germans living in the annexed eastern territories.[108] At the university's opening, Greiser announced a gift of 100,000 RM from Warthegau funds—roughly $600,000 in 2007 dollars)—that was intended to 'make it easier for German students during their studies to work on the problems of the East and to offer prizes for academic works that deal with the tasks of the German East.'[109] In fact, though, not many students made the German East the focus of their education; in 1943, more students were studying medicine than any other subject. The number of students studying agriculture never totaled more than one hundred.[110]

Just prior to the university founding, Greiser established the Reich Foundation for German Eastern Research (*Reichsstiftung für deutsche Ostforschung*), an institution closely linked to the university. Göring served as the foundation's official figurehead, Greiser as its president. Academic and administrative responsibility rested with the rector and provost of the Posen university. The foundation was funded through income from 24,000 hectares of land confiscated from the Polish National Foundation in Burgstadt, as well as from real estate that the Polish Prince Michael Radziwill was forced to bequeath Hitler. These holdings yielded a handsome income; in 1942, the foundation's forests provided a profit of some 400,000 RM (more than $2.3 million in 2007 dollars).[111] According to its statute, the foundation was 'to scientifically research, on the broadest basis, the area won in the East ... in its *völkisch*, cultural, political and economic conditions ...' Furthermore, 'through the evaluation of this research,' it was 'to establish the working bases for the reconstruction in the East and through planned schooling to convey these to all those working there ...'[112] In September 1941, a 'Research Group for the Reforestation of the East' was founded.[113] In January 1942, Greiser announced the opening of the foundation's Institute for Research into Eastern Law (*Institut für Ostrechtsforschung*). This Institute, already in operation, concerned itself with legal issues in the German East: the role of German law vis-à-vis Poles, the property situation of resettlers, and legal claims arising from the annexation and reconstruction of the eastern areas.[114] Eventually, the foundation included ten study groups and institutes, all covering practical matters regarding the settlement and exploitation of the German East.[115] The foundation also sponsored several prizes, including the Clausewitz Prize and the Prize of the Great King (in honor of Frederick the Great's settlement projects) for the best research into aspects of securing the German East.[116] Between the university and the foundation, few efforts were spared to promote a (pseudo-)academic understanding of the Germanization of the Gau.

Secondary and primary schooling was also crucial to the Germanization project. When Greiser arrived in Posen, there were only five German-language high schools in the entire Gau region. By May 1940, however, twenty-three high schools were available to German secondary-school students; by the following September, 5,330 students attended these schools. In the next years, the numbers of Germans enrolled in secondary education more than doubled.[117] The situation was even more dramatic in elementary education. In September 1939, there were just fifty-nine German elementary schools serving some 4,000 students. One year later, 100,000 pupils attended German elementary schools.[118] By April 1944, there were 2,032 German elementary schools in the Warthegau, serving some 144,000 pupils. Just 3,628 teachers taught all of these children; as a result, some 71 percent of all German elementary schools were single-class schools in which pupils of different ages were taught together.[119] The shortage of educators was constantly decried, but little could be done; it was simply impossible to recruit more teachers for the Gau.[120]

Greiser saw schooling as an important element of ethnic struggle. Many 'German' children—native ethnic German and resettler pupils—first learned the German language at school. They were also instructed in how to be 'German.' Teachers taught the children traditional German songs and dances, modeled German celebrations and ceremonies, and imparted 'German' values such as order, cleanliness, and personal hygiene.[121] Teachers were also expected to inculcate anti-Polish views in their pupils. In an October 1940 speech to teachers, Greiser reportedly declared, 'In addition to the love of the German race the educator must also sow abhorrence of the foreign race!'[122] Schooling in the Gau also served to differentiate German from Polish children; this was especially true when, as was often the case, they had played together since earliest childhood. As one Gau official noted in 1941, in every village where some German schoolchildren lived, it was necessary to set up a German school 'in which the German children were concentrated and thus separated from the Polish children.'[123] The organization of elementary schooling was intended to prepare Germans for their future roles as bosses of Polish laborers.[124] On at least one occasion, Greiser stated this explicitly to educators: 'But in this land, German teachers, you must educate our youth to dominate (*Herrentum*)!'[125] Schooling, then, aided the Germanization project by teaching children the language, customs, and attitudes of Nazi Germany.

Greiser saw the performing arts as another important 'weapon in ethnic struggle.' The main theater in Posen, soon designated the Reichsgau Theater, underwent a major renovation so as to bring it up to Reich standards. On 18 March 1941, Greiser and Goebbels celebrated its grand reopening. Greiser declared that the new theater 'was the hour of birth of a new cultural epoch for Posen and the Wartheland.' Goebbels reportedly stated that 'theaters and schools . . . are our medieval castles [*Ordensburgen*] and the firm strongholds of our will to colonization.'[126] In his diary, the propaganda minister noted: 'New theater . . . A tonic for the eyes. Magnificent colors and dimensions. Nice opening celebration. [Gau Propaganda Leader] Maul spoke well, Greiser very well. I explained the tasks of the East and received the greatest applause.'[127] In the next years, Germans in the Warthegau enjoyed many theater performances in this and other theaters. In the Reichsgau Theater, for example, 283 performances of plays, 147 of operas, and 166 of operettas were staged during the 1942–3 season. Litzmannstadt and several other towns had permanent theaters; traveling theater troupes served smaller municipalities. Gau authorities also established some sixty German cinemas in towns and larger villages. In addition, they arranged for a fleet of film trucks to drive around the countryside showing movies to the rural population; between 1939 and 1942, the Gau Film Office brought over 7,000 film showings to rural audiences.[128] The screened films included some of the Nazi regime's most notorious propaganda films, including the rabidly anti-Semitic *Jud Süss* and *Feinde* (Enemies), a film portraying Polish hatred of the German minority in interwar Poland.[129]

Greiser also placed music in the service of Germanization. In 1940, he began the 'Posen Music Week'—every September, a week of musical events showcased 'German' music. In November 1940, Maria Greiser played Hans Pfitzner's Piano Concerto in E-flat for a charity benefit; Pfitzner was the nationalistic composer under whom Maria had trained. The *Ostdeutscher Beobachter* gave a glowing account of Maria's only public performance in the Warthegau.[130] Perhaps on Maria's urging, Pfitzner was the principal during the 'Posen Music Week' of September 1942. Greiser convinced the composer to come, apparently giving him an even higher honorarium than he had demanded. According to historian Michael Kater, the event 'turned into an unabashed mixture of Pfitzner cult and Nazi propaganda.'[131] Greiser awarded the composer the 1942 Music Prize of the Reichsgau Wartheland; that year, the prize carried a whopping stipend of 20,000 RM (some $118,000 in 2007 dollars). In his speech awarding the Prize, Greiser reportedly stated that in Pfitzner, 'we see one of the great harbingers of German style and German cultural ethos.' In Posen, a street was renamed in the composer's honor. Greiser also created a 'Hans-Pfitzner Foundation,' endowed with 10,000 RM, to support music students.[132]

For Greiser, visual art was also an instrument of Germanization. On 21 January 1940, the Kaiser Friedrich-Museum reopened in his presence. The Museum took over the Polish Muzeum Wielkopolskie that had been housed in the original Kaiser Friedrich-Museum opened by Prussian authorities in 1904. Its permanent galleries featured painting, arts and crafts, folklore, pre-history, and natural history exhibits; many displays focused on the Gau region. 50,000 Germans visited the museum in its first year of operation; Poles were denied admission.[133] The museum mounted numerous temporary exhibitions designed to familiarize Germans with the Gau. In its first year, these included 'The German Wartheland,' 'The Beautiful City [Posen],' and 'German *Volks*-Awakening in the East of the new Wartheland Homeland.'[134] In winter 1940–1, museum curators planned 'The German Book in and from the East,' 'German Artists,' and 'German Buildings in the Wartheland.' The museum's Natural History section foresaw exhibitions on 'The Mineral Wealth of the Wartheland' and 'Our Winter Birds.'[135] In October 1941, the museum hosted an exhibition organized by the RKFVD, 'Planning and Reconstruction in the East.' It featured the ongoing planning for the future villages, farms, and rural homes and workshops that were to characterize the Gau.[136]

In October 1942, Greiser opened the exhibition 'Artists in the Wartheland.' In an effort to play up the natural beauty of the Gau, he had appealed to artists in the Reich to come and work in his Gau. Some, at least, followed his call. Seventy-six artists now displayed some 410 pictures. The *Ostdeutscher Beobachter* claimed that 'The displayed pictures are not only exceedingly valuable artistically, but they are also particularly alluring through their different views of our east German landscape.'[137] Rolf-Heinz Höppner, an important security official, reported that 'the exhibit accomplishes a great task, the awakening of a Heimat feeling (*Heimatgefühl*) for all of the German people (*Volksgenossen*) in the Reichsgau.'[138] Judging from the catalogue, spectators were treated to a sentimental, romantic image of the Gau that was intended to give them a warm, fuzzy feeling about their new homeland.[139]

Several Gau agencies focused on the 'scientific' documentation of German material culture in the region. In an effort to prove the German (as opposed to Slavic) origins of the area, the State Bureau for Pre-History (*Landesamt für Vorgeschichte*) gathered and sorted archeological evidence pertaining to the presence of ancient Germanic tribes. The Bureau also sponsored educational activities that, it claimed, had led to the discovery of a Viking cemetery in Lutomiersk.[140] According to Bureau Director Walter Kersten, the Viking graves were found when police destroyed a Jewish cemetery and discovered iron weapons and skeleton parts beneath the graves. These Viking graves, Kersten insisted, showed that the 'Polish state was not founded by the Poles themselves, but rather that its genesis lay with the Vikings, that is with Germans.'[141] The State Bureau for the Preservation of Historical Monuments (*Landesamt für Denkmalpflege*) also sponsored various excavations, including work on fifty Germanic graves and other cultural remains in Openholz, 150 Germanic graves in Konin, and the Viking graves in Lutomiersk.[142] It also preserved more recent German cultural artifacts. In Gnesen, the interior of the cathedral was 'liberated from Polish disfigurations,' and the cathedral in Tum, an outstanding example of eastern romantic architecture, was secured to prevent further collapse.[143]

Gau officials also worked to preserve sites associated with famous Germans. The most important of these was the birth place of Paul von Hindenburg, the celebrated World War I general and German president from 1925–34. Hindenburg was born in a house in the center of Posen in 1847. Already in 1939, a plaque was mounted on the building.[144]

Although Hitler wished the house to be made into a worthy memorial, the project never saw fruition. In part, this was because Reich and Gau building authorities deemed the project insufficiently important to merit construction funds during wartime.[145] Hindenburg's connection to Posen was nonetheless regularly recalled in the pages of the *Ostdeutscher Beobachter*. The street in which he had been born bore his name. In accordance with Greiser's wishes, the first newly established high school for boys in the Warthegau was named the 'Hindenburg Gymnasium.'[146]

Greiser and other officials also tried to create a new rhythm of holidays in the Gau. 26 October, the date on which the Warthegau was annexed to the Third Reich in 1939, became the 'Day of Freedom' (*Tag der Freiheit*). It was a legal holiday celebrated with great fanfare. In the days leading up to the holiday, numerous events took place. On the holiday itself, Greiser gave a major address in Posen. Gau authorities also decreed 9 November a legal holiday; this day commemorated Hitler's Beer Hall Putsch along with the sixteen early Nazis who had died in Hitler's abortive coup attempt.[147] According to Herbert Mehlhorn, a Reichsstatthalter official, this day had 'not yet been declared a legal holiday in the Old Reich;' his wording suggested that in this regard the Warthegau might also serve as a model for the rest of Nazi Germany.[148] While the Warthegau saw the addition of these two legal holidays, several religious holidays, including Good Friday, lost their status as legal holidays.[149] Gau authorities thus tried to forge an official calendar that downplayed religious observance while celebrating Nazi memory.

Gau authorities also played up 1 September, the date of the German invasion of Poland. The Hitler Youth organized an annual 'Freedom March' to Kutno that culminated with a large rally in the town on 1 September. Greiser was the keynote speaker from 1940 to 192.[150] The march and rally commemorated ethnic Germans who had been forced to march on the street from Kutno to Lowitsch and then on into central Poland in September 1939.[151] Kutno was also the site of a major defeat of the Polish Army by German forces in mid-September 1939. In his 1942 speech, Greiser announced plans for the postwar construction of a large memorial in Kutno that would both commemorate German suffering and celebrate German triumph.[152] Kutno was just the tip of the proverbial iceberg in the commemoration of German–Polish ethnic struggle. Gau officials aggressively publicized alleged atrocities committed by Poles against ethnic Germans. Greiser regularly visited the graves of murdered ethnic German and otherwise supported their memory.[153] Marią Greiser became titular head of a foundation established to help the orphans of murdered Germans.[154] Greiser also chaired an 'Association for Contemporary History,' charged with documenting the 'ethnic struggle and the reconstruction work in the Reichsgau Wartheland.'[155] The ethnic struggle with Poles was to shape public consciousness for a long time to come.

Germanization was not limited to the public sphere. Greiser and other Nazi officials viewed the private sphere—housing—as a site of ethnic struggle. The poor state of housing in the Gau made it difficult to attract Reich Germans to the Warthegau and, if they came, to keep them there. In 1941, Greiser noted that some Germans were leaving the region because of their poor housing situation. While he dismissed these individuals as 'not sufficiently idealistic to be deployed in our German East,' he did not question the importance of good housing for the successful Germanization of the region. As the *Ostdeutscher Beobachter* summarized his words: 'The Gauleiter outlined the necessity of giving the German person in the Wartheland a nicer and larger apartment than anywhere else in the Reich, if possible even a single-family home with its own garden. This fact, so he stated, would do more to bring German workers, employees, and bureaucrats to the Wartheland than bonuses or the so-called east subsidy.' On the same occasion, Greiser declared that 300,000 new apartments were necessary for the Warthegau. Their construction, however, would have to wait until after German victory. In the meantime, a much smaller program of building 5,000 apartments was underway.[156]

In their emphasis on good-quality German housing, Greiser and other Gau officials followed Robert Ley, head of the DAF and Reich commissioner of public housing from 1940 onwards. Ley believed that good housing would help German workers feel themselves true members of the German community.[157] In occupied Poland, however, good housing had a somewhat different function: it was to underscore German cultural superiority. Gau authorities thus insisted on modern, tasteful housing for the German population. Planners designed housing that was large by the standards of the time. Some apartments were to have three to five rooms (in addition to a kitchen and bathroom), and to measure seventy-five square meters or more.[158] German apartments were also to sport modern conveniences rarely present in Polish homes: running water, sewage systems, electricity and gas connections, up-to-date bathrooms, washing machines, refrigerators, and modern cooking appliances.[159]

Gau authorities devoted considerable attention to interior decoration. In the Old Reich, consumption policy, as the Strength Through Joy recreational program illustrated, aimed to paper over class conflicts and the rural-urban divide within the German racial community.[160] In the German East, however, consumption programs were part and parcel of the ethnic struggle between Germans and Poles: they were intended to create a cultural gulf between the two ethnic groups. As in all Gaus, the DAF Gau office in Posen included a Gau Home Bureau devoted to housing issues; within this bureau, a whole department, Beauty of Living (*Schönheit des Wohnens*), promoted tasteful interior decoration.[161] According to the head of the Gau Home Bureau in Posen, Willy Hornung, Beauty of Living's task was 'to substitute the omnipresent spell of Polish living culture through good German household objects, so that home interiors in the newly won living space in the East will as soon as possible receive a German character.' Hornung thus claimed: 'we must strive ... that in all housing in which Germans live, there are only household objects commensurate with the German character. It cannot be approved that poor furniture styles and otherwise kitschy household goods are further produced and sold on the market.'[162] To Hornung, the stakes of interior decoration were high. If Germans lived among attractive household goods, they would rise above their Polish rivals. If, however, their homes were decorated with Polish 'kitsch,' they would sink to the cultural level of their ethnic enemies.

In May 1941, Greiser, following up on a decree issued by Ley, established a working group 'Beauty of Living' that included representatives from many important party and state institutions.[163] That same month, he visited the offices of the Gau Home Bureau. Hornung gave him an overview of attempts 'to create a good *German living culture* in the Wartheland.'[164] In keeping with Greiser's pretensions to make the Warthegau a 'model Gau,' Hornung claimed that the design of household objects in the Warthegau could 'set an example for the Old Reich.'[165] His bureau worked to design all manner of tasteful yet inexpensive household goods, including cutlery, glassware, porcelain, pictures, lamps, clocks, rugs, and other textile products. In 1942, an exhibition of household objects designed or approved by the Beauty of Living Department and produced by Warthegau workshops opened in the Posen DAF headquarters; it was later on permanent display at the Kaiser-Friedrich Museum.[166] A report on this exhibition emphasized that 'the apartment is one of those places from which the German producer is to draw strength and power for his mission in the German East.'[167]

The Home Bureau also focused on furniture design. In 1940, an article explained that Beauty of Living 'wished to influence both the buyer and the producer to finally secure the production of furniture and appropriate household objects that would be both functional and match the taste of the modern German person.' This furniture, the article continued, was to be 'in a form worthy of our time that could survive centuries, without becoming "unmodern" like the sideboards and cupboards with nonsensical pillars and stilted legs or the monotonous steel-pipe furniture that one once wished to serve up to us as the "latest style" in functionality and beauty.'[168] In the Warthegau, furniture was to instill in its users a timeless German good taste and, in turn, a German sensibility.

Gau officials were particularly concerned with the rural German home. In this, they followed a nation-wide DAF program, 'the Beautiful Village' (*das schöne Dorf*), intended to improve rural housing conditions.[169] Farm architecture and furnishings were to reflect the particular conditions of the East. One local official suggested that the ideal farmhouse would be a '*stone, white-washed house with a bright red tile roof*.'[170] To Gau officials, the area needed simple, enduring, and cheerful farmhouses. Inside the farmhouse, Beauty of Living insisted that furniture 'relinquish any "peasant" romanticism.'[171] Kitchen cupboards were not to have too many open drawers; instead, they were to 'have easily locked cupboard doors' to protect their owners' possessions from pilfering Polish servants. The furniture was to be made from 'German' woods, but painted so as to vary its otherwise uniform appearance.[172] In the 1942 'Beauty of Living' exhibition, department officials displayed a model peasant home. It included a kitchen, living room, master bedroom, and two bedrooms for children. Officials attached particular importance to the fact that the kitchen was separate from the large living room: 'thus the German producer consciously sets himself apart from the one-room house of the Pole . . .'[173]

Beauty of Living ran parallel to the much better known Beauty of Labor (*Schönheit der Arbeit*) program that focused on the workplace. Just as Beauty of Living had a somewhat different function in the East, so too did Beauty of Labor. In occupied Poland, the Nazis did not link poor work conditions to their usual suspects of capitalism, Judeo-Bolshevism, or Americanization. Instead, miserable conditions were blamed on the Poles (or, in Litzmannstadt, Jews). German disdain of the allegedly Polish work environment is captured in a sixty-five-page account written by a German factory caretaker, Ernst Bährecke. Bährecke subtitled his work 'An

Attempt at Describing Polish "Cultural Conditions."' In October 1939, he took over the Glogowski and Son Machine Company and renamed it the Hohensalza Machine Factory. Within eight months, he claimed, he had cleaned up the factory. A series of before-and-after pictures showed the changes: the smithy, once dirty and full of broken machines, was now 'light, jolly, and clean;' the smithy roof, once filthy and leaky, had been cleaned and repaired; the office filing room, once a disorderly chaos, now sported neat filing cubicles; the storage hall, once full of unsorted junk, had been cleaned and emptied; the lavatories, once a row of holes in a board, were now real toilets; and a variety of new rooms, including a sick room, changing room, cafeteria, and kitchen, had been built.[174] In Bährecke's view, factory conditions also underscored the alleged cultural chasm between Germans and Poles.

Greiser and Nazi planners also believed that a 'German' landscape was an essential precondition to the successful settlement of Germans in the East. Greiser had long seen nature, particularly the ocean and the forest, as a source of regeneration; in letters, he occasionally noted how he found solace by communing with nature.[175] He shared this with many Nazis and indeed, many Germans.[176] To Germans, nature represented immortality, authenticity, seriousness, resurrection, and German 'willpower.'[177] Trees and forests occupied a particularly special place in the imagined German landscape: trees represented 'historical continuity and rootedness,' while forests symbolized 'national endurance over the centuries.'[178] A 'German' landscape thus involved an untouched natural environment, plants indigenous to German lands, and rich and abundant forests. But just as the built environment in the Warthegau struck Germans as 'un-German,' so too did the landscape. As a flat region with relatively few trees, bushes, or other natural landmarks, the Warthegau seemed cold, barren, and unwelcoming.

Nazi planners undertook a variety of measures to make the Warthegau landscape look 'German.'[179] Since the Warthegau had a smaller amount of forested land than any other Gau (just 16 percent of its surface area was forest), Gau authorities planned an ambitious reforestation program.[180] Some Nazis saw important ecological and economic benefits in forestation. Willibald Richert, the state planner of the Warthegau, believed that the lack of forests meant that the Gau had little dew, relatively little rain and snowfall, and few summer thunderstorms. Afforestation would bring more precipitation, and would also improve soil quality, help to contain soil erosion and runoff, and give birds a nesting habitat (important for pest control).[181] In the age of modern warfare, it would also provide the best possible natural defense cover. But forestation was also an ideological program. The Nazis believed that healthy forests in the East would remind Germans of their spiritual roots; help uphold the moral fiber of society (devastated landscapes were allegedly linked with higher crime levels); and attract and keep German settlers in the Gau.[182] In 1940, a Gau official (probably Richert) declared that once afforestation had occurred in the Warthegau, 'a considerable contribution to the Germanization of the landscape in the East will be achieved. A German land without sufficient forest is absolutely unthinkable. Such a land will never become home to German people. It will at most serve as home to a passionate moneymaker until he has earned enough and with his full pockets will go to where he can relax in a nicer environment.'[183]

Greiser supported afforestation efforts. He attended a conference put together by the 'Research Group for the Reforestation of the East.' There, he quoted the group's charter: 'At the hands of a Slavic population, the areas of the East have been deforested so extensively as to suffer severe climatic and economic damage. Moreover, the deforested landscape is in danger of losing the very aspect that is so familiar to the German. For that reason, the planting of new German settlers must be accompanied by the planning and execution of an orderly reforestation of the East.'[184] On another occasion, Greiser argued that the afforestation program in his Gau would be 'the biggest afforestation program ever achieved' and would do nothing less than 'create a new climate.' Within twenty years, he insisted, there would be at least 400,000 hectares of forest land. Greiser also announced plans to build the largest reservoir in the world. He claimed that this reservoir would 'be eleven times larger than the largest one in Germany and would be the largest of all in Europe, including Russian reservoirs.' It would hold one billion cubic meters of water and would be located at the source of the Warta River.[185] By creating a new climate through afforestation and a more plentiful water supply, Greiser believed, the Warthegau could become a truly rich farming area. That, in turn, would provide the livelihood for the millions of German farmers who were expected to people the Gau. It would also, of course, show how Germans—unlike Poles—had turned the Warthegau into a richly fertile region.

While little progress was made on the reservoir, Gau officials did manage to plant trees. In June 1943, Greiser visited a forest spanning some 50,000 hectares. Most of this forest had been present in 1939, but forestry officials had added another 1,500 hectares to one part, and 2,210 hectares to another part of the forest. By then, if Nazi numbers are reliable, German forestry officials in Leslau and Kowall had overseen the planting of over 38 million trees—29.5 million pine, 1.2 million spruce, 600,000 larch, 1.3 million birch, 1 million oak, 1.4 million alder and 3.9 million red oak, mountain ash, and other broad-leaved trees and shrubs.[186] Like so many other grand Nazi projects, reforestation involved a callous disregard of people—even Germans—who stood in its way. After the war, one German farmer recalled how authorities totally reforested his community, Neustein, in 1940–1. He had to leave his farm and move to another one nearby.[187]

Afforestation was also put to another use: masking German crimes. In spring 1942, Mehlhorn summoned a forestry official, Heinrich May, and told him to plant over the mass graves of Jews murdered at Chełmno. May soon planted gorse shrubbery and pine and birch trees over the Jewish corpses. But this proved insufficient. The stench from the graves was so severe that more drastic measures were necessary. Beginning in June 1942, the graves were opened and the decomposing bodies burned. Burning the corpses, however, demanded large amounts of scarce wood. May was thus forced to use up many of his wood reserves. A macabre, but telling example of how Greiser's various Germanization ambitions clashed.[188]

In the Warthegau, even the dead could not escape Germanization. German cemeteries were to allow the bereaved solace, serenity, and beauty. Accordingly, preliminary guidelines for German cemeteries in the Posen district demanded that all gravestones be made out of either stone or wood and that in any given cemetery, only *one* kind of wood or stone was to be used. The guidelines also included drawings of permitted gravestones; only simple, streamlined forms were allowed. The list of what was forbidden was long, and included all cement gravestones or decorations, graves made of terrazzo or black artificial stone, gravestones decorated with oil-based paint, photographs mounted on graves, or gravestone inscriptions that were 'not appropriate for the solemnity of the place.'[189] The ban on paint, photographs, and cement decorations was intended to remove Slavic 'kitsch' from German cemeteries. The choice of acceptable materials was also significant. Stone harkened back to the burial stones of prehistoric Germans, while wood reminded of forests. The emphasis on uniformity reiterated the importance of the nation over the individual, as well as the unity of the German people in an area long contested with Poles.[190]

Gau authorities also tried to integrate recreational activity into the Germanization project. They scoured the region for appropriate lakes, palaces, and swimming pools that might serve as attractive recreational destinations. Mehlhorn even suggested that at sites pertaining to the German–Polish ethnic struggle, memorials could be erected that would then become hiking destinations.[191] Posen city officials also did their bit to further hiking. The city's Traffic Bureau established an advice center for the 'encouragement and fostering of hiking.' The city administration also established a hiking group for its employees. According to an internal newsletter, this hiking group 'would not only serve our health and the preservation of our working strength, but through our presence in the countryside we strengthen our German *Volk*s-comrades . . . in the consciousness that the land will again become German.' As the newsletter suggested, hiking, too, could be a weapon of ethnic struggle. Ethnic Germans in the countryside surrounding Posen were now a small minority engulfed by Poles; if Germans hiked to the countryside, the ethnic Germans would not feel quite so alone.[192]

Finally, planners emphasized the importance of bicycle riding. In the Warthegau, cars were few and far between, and trams and buses serviced only limited routes. As a 1941 memorandum noted, the bicycle 'was *the* means of transportation for workers and employees.' Planners now rationalized its use. According to the same memorandum, 'The bicycle is just the best way to really get to know the new homeland (*Heimat*), to give to the German population a feeling and knowledge of their homeland, and with city inhabitants to achieve an attachment to the land. The Volkswagen will not be able to achieve this task . . . '[193] Through grand landscaping and climatic changes, as well as smaller measures that would allow Germans to more fully enjoy the natural environment, Greiser and his Warthegau planners hoped to both make the area 'German' and to foster a sense of belonging among the Gau's German population.

Following the German invasion of the Soviet Union in June 1941, Greiser could no longer depend on even limited Reich largesse for his Germanization measures. Indeed, beginning in January 1943, the Reich Finance Ministry even cut subsidies to the Gau by 500,000 RM per month; it justified these cuts by declaring that the Gau had received some 3 million RM (almost $18,000,000 in 2007 dollars) in profits from Jewish labor.[194] To secure funding for his Gau, Greiser now turned to an even more ruthless exploitation of Jews. He may even have received Hitler's tacit support for maintaining the ghetto and its exploitation of Jews. In November 1942, he wrote to Himmler about whether or not it was necessary to secure the Führer's permission to have Poles with incurable tuberculosis murdered (see Chapter 5). In Greiser's view, Hitler's permission was not necessary, 'especially since in our last conversation about the Jews, he told me that I could do as I liked.'[195] In analyzing Greiser's words, most historians have argued that Greiser was signaling that he had received permission from the Führer to have the Jews in his Gau murdered. But another interpretation is possible. Greiser's conversation probably occurred at one of two meetings of Reichsleiters and Gauleiters that took place on 1 October and 7–8 November 1942. By then, the vast majority of 'unproductive' Jews were dead. Greiser might well have discussed with Hitler the possibility of maintaining his 'productive' Jewish work force.[196]

In January 1942, Greiser issued a decree, 'De-Jewification of the Warthegau;' unfortunately, it has never been found. Contemporary references to it, however, note that it stated that the ghetto, a Reich institution, was run by the lord mayor of Litzmannstadt 'on behalf of and under the supervision' of the Reichstatthalter.[197] It seems that Greiser wanted to clarify and enhance his role vis-à-vis the ghetto. By winter 1942–3, ghetto income had soared. In 1941, the Ghetto Administration calculated that it had received 12,881,300 RM in wages for Jewish workers, and 3,312,400 RM from the sale of ghetto products.[198] In 1942, income was substantially higher: 27,682,200 RM.[199] But even so, these monies just barely covered ghetto costs, including living costs, updated machinery, and loan interest payments. Greiser pushed for higher profits. As Biebow wrote to Rumkowski in November 1942, it was necessary to generate higher profits from Jews' wages since 'those above me place great value on this.'[200] The following February, a sixty-hour working week was introduced for the Jews still alive in the ghetto. In the first half of 1943, the ghetto finally produced a surplus, three million RM—the only time that it actually turned a profit.[201] Even though recent historical research has shown that the ghetto was not very profitable, both later historians and, more important, Nazi authorities—and not least Greiser—long assumed that the ghetto was an important source of income for the Gau.[202]

Gau coffers also profited from the murder of Jews and from Jews working in forced labor camps outside of the Litzmannstadt ghetto. Unlike in the

General Government and Upper Silesia (where Auschwitz was located), the proceeds from the murder of Jews in the Warthegau did not go to the SS Business Administration Main Office (*Wirtschaftsverwaltungshauptamt* or WVHA), but rather to an account managed by the Ghetto Administration on behalf of Greiser's Reichsstatthalter agency. In February 1942, Reichsstatthalter officials came to Litzmannstadt to arrange for the setting up of a special account, 'Sonderkonto 12300,' at the *Stadtsparkasse Litzmannstadt*.[203] On 18 March 1942, Greiser decreed that all revenues from the 'evacuation' actions, including outstanding wages, were to be transferred 'without exception' to the Ghetto Administration that, in turn, deposited the funds into the 12300 account.[204] In addition, all personal effects, including cash and valuables (or the proceeds from their sale), that victims brought with them to Chełmno were deposited into this account. So, too, were the wages paid for Jews working in the various labor camps outside of the Litzmannstadt ghetto. Ghetto administration officials used these funds to pay all costs associated with the murder operations. Every month, however, they sent a statement of the account's activities to Reichsstatthalter officials. Periodically, large amounts of money were transferred from this account to the 'Association of the Friends of the Warthegau' account. In February 1943, for example, Greiser demanded four million RM for the 'Association' account; just then, he was trying to develop newly found coal beds in the Konin area.[205] By the end of 1944, at least eleven million RM (some $65,000,000 in 2007 dollars) had been deposited in the 'Association' account.[206] Since Greiser knew that his transactions would not pass muster with the Reich Audit Office, he prevented its officials from examining the ghetto administration's books.[207]

In some cases, valuables were also sent on to Greiser. In April 1944, a Litzmannstadt city inspector noted that 'especially valuable objects' had been transferred to the Reichsstatthalter. This was supposedly to prevent their acquisition by greedy officials and thus to 'preserve and promote the cultivation of thriftiness in the Warthegau.'[208] Greiser himself, however, didn't always abide by this precept. It is said that he personally received at least 1,000 RM of goods.[209] In January 1942, he had twenty-five kilograms of silver from the victims' remains sent to him. After the war, Biebow alleged that Greiser had a china dinner service made that was decorated with gold stolen from Chełmno victims.[210] Rudolf Kramp, a close associate of Biebow, later claimed that he had once brought two new leather suitcases to Hans Bothmann, the head of murder operations in Chełmno, who, in turn, was to fill and bring them to Greiser.[211] Both for his person, but especially for his Gau, Greiser profited from genocide.

For all the bold initiatives, the Germanization of the Gau's land was fraught with difficulties. Most important, there weren't enough workers (even Jews) or materials to complete even a fraction of the planned projects. Even before the invasion of the Soviet Union, these shortages were evident. When Greiser toured Posen building sites in September 1940, he saw only work on a man-made lake, a bridge over the Warta River, and some walking trails that led to a manor house (which he impulsively decided should become a pub).[212] The invasion of the Soviet Union further stretched the thin resources available for Germanization projects.

Some of Greiser's projects caused great resentment, even among the Gau's Germans. With a limited pie of available resources, prestige projects came at the expense of housing for ordinary Germans. Some local residents were furious about the squandering of available resources on the Posen Castle. In January 1943, in an anonymous memorandum titled 'Outrage in Posen!' they noted, 'Thousands of families and comrades are waiting for an apartment or living quarters and are herded together like sheep in a stall or herring in barrels . . . Building supplies, iron, metal, etc. are completely blocked for apartment building, but for the "castle renovation" . . . workers and building supplies of all kinds are available.' They concluded, 'The people in Posen and in the Warthegau who do not have apartments or who are looking for apartments protest against such a disgrace . . . and demand immediate remedy and the cessation of work on the castle renovation so that apartments can be built.'[213] Greiser's priorities, these frustrated citizens argued, were not their own.

Germanization also caused enormous administrative difficulties. The saga of Warthegau place names is particularly salient in this regard. Nazi authorities at all levels believed that giving German names to localities was important for re-enforcing a German consciousness in the area. In December 1939, Interior Minister Wilhelm Frick decreed that locales were to adopt their pre-1918 Prussian names. In the parts of the Gau that had not belonged to Prussia, new place names were to be invented according to strict guidelines.[214] In many cases, however, local officials or residents ignored the guidelines and renamed places on their own. In December 1940, Alexander Dolezalek, a planning official, complained about some of these names. Often, he claimed, the new names sounded Jewish ('Sterntal,' 'Egrenfeld'). Sometimes the names were not appropriate for the locale in question. A village named 'Wehrburg' (Defense Castle) was merely 'a hopeless row of mud huts,' while 'Adlershorst' (Eagle's Nest) was a 'miserable nest.' Another village, Malogeia, 'suggests Hawaii,' but was actually the first two letters of each name of the estate owner's four children (Marie, Lore, Georg, Ida). Dolezalek further noted that due to renamings, 'not even the locals can find their way around . . . ' Administrative, train, and postal service personnel were at wit's end.[215]

The Wehrmacht was also concerned: it only had interwar maps with Polish designations at its disposal. Without new maps, army officials argued, place names could not be changed. In April 1942, acceding to their wishes, the Interior Ministry halted the introduction of all new place names. At the same time, the Wehrmacht insisted that all places already renamed have signs with both the new German and the old Polish designation.[216] This, of course, defeated the purpose of the renamings: with the Polish names in full view, the built environment would not look German. This decision thus brought loud protests from local administrators.[217] Perhaps in response, the Interior Ministry gave Greiser and Albert Forster (but not the other eastern Gauleiters) special dispensations to continue place renamings—with the proviso, though, that place signs still bear the old Polish names. By June 1943, up to 1,100 names of places in the Warthegau had been changed, and new names for another 1,400 places were being considered. This led to renewed Wehrmacht objections. In August 1943, a meeting involving representatives of the Interior Ministry, the Wehrmacht, the Reich Postal Ministry, and the Reichsstatthalter in Posen took place in Berlin. There, the Wehrmacht representatives demanded that no place renamings go into effect until maps in various sizes had been readied. This remapping, they claimed, would take thirty to forty workers, and at least nine months.[218]

Undeterred, Gau officials continued to rename locales. In November 1943, Greiser wrote to his deputy Jäger that he had personally checked 'in so much as is possible at a desk' a list of new names for some 3,000 places. In some cases, he had not approved the changes, and Jäger was now to arrange for new place-name suggestions.[219] The following month, however, Greiser's agency grudgingly agreed that 'although *Volk*s-political reasons make the elimination of the current situation extremely urgent [i.e., the continued presence of Polish signs],' the name changes could be delayed until new maps had been readied.[220] Military demands now had the upper hand. In November 1944, just two months before the Warthegau fell to Soviet troops, Greiser, in his capacity as Reich Defense Commissioner for the Warthegau, insisted that all place name signs '*without exception*' bear both the new German and the old Polish place name. This was due to the 'especially urgent needs of the Wehrmacht . . . that almost exclusively has in its possession maps printed with the Polish names.'[221] The story of place renamings suggests the zeal with which Greiser and other Gau authorities pursued Germanization: even when the Wehrmacht objected and, moreover, necessary manpower could be utilized more effectively elsewhere, they insisted on continuing this Germanization project.

Yet another factor complicated Germanization measures: by 1943, Greiser faced an uphill battle to maintain Jewish workers. Himmler was always opposed to ghetto Jews working in manufacturing, and particularly in the production of war materials.[222] The Warsaw Ghetto Uprising in spring 1943 made Himmler all the more eager to shut down all ghettos and work camps or, at the very least, to transfer them to SS-control. On 2 August, he thus ordered all ZAfJ camps in the Warthegau to close. As one sub-district magistrate now told a district building office, 'In so far as possible, I recommend that you complete as quickly as possible work that has already been started.'[223] Himmler's measure meant the end of most Germanization projects in the Warthegau. Yet despite Himmler's orders, in August 1943, sixty-seven employers still paid 135,441.43 RM into the 12300 account controlled by Greiser. Even in December 1943—five months after Himmler's decree—six employers paid 21,621 RM into the account.[224] Due to financial and other benefits, Greiser may have delayed the cessation of some of the work projects. Between August and December, however, several thousand Jewish camp prisoners who had been working on construction, land improvement, or drainage projects were deported to Auschwitz.[225]

Greiser also faced the potential loss of income from the Litzmannstadt ghetto. On 11 June 1943, Himmler decreed that the ghetto was to become a concentration camp and thus come under SS-control (by definition, all concentration camps were SS-facilities). On 21 June, Odilo Globocnik, the higher SS and police leader (HSSPF) in Lublin, proposed that all of Litzmannstadt's skilled workers and machinery be transferred to concentration camps in his district. Between Himmler's decree and Globocnik's proposal, Greiser and the Warthegau would have been stripped of what they believed was the ghetto's financial potential. Nothing happened for several months. Over the summer, both the Wehrmacht's Weapons Inspectorate and Speer's Ministry of Armament and War Production registered objections to making the ghetto a concentration camp. Once again, nothing happened. On 3 December, Himmler again decreed that the ghetto would become a concentration camp and fall under the purview of the WVHA, headed by Oswald Pohl.

Greiser had not been informed and apparently had not consented to this decision.[226] Both the SS and Speer now sent representatives to the ghetto to determine its worth. In January 1944, Max Horn, the WVHA economics inspector, completed his investigation. He determined that from a financial viewpoint ghetto firms were 'uneconomical,' and that if the WVHA took over the ghetto, it would incur 'significant financial risk.' Horn was particularly bothered by the fact that Greiser's Reichsstatthalter agency assumed that the ghetto factories were profitable. Shortly thereafter, at a meeting on 9 February 1944 between representatives of the WVHA and the Reichsstatthalter, Greiser's subordinates demanded no less than eighteen to twenty million RM for the machines as well as a portion of the ghetto's future profits if the ghetto was to be transferred to SS-auspices. WVHA representatives objected.[227] The Reichstatthalter demands suggest that Greiser thought the ghetto lucrative.

Horn's report may have led Greiser to reconsider his position. On 12–13 February 1944, Himmler came to Posen to discuss the fate of the ghetto. While Greiser refused to cede control over the ghetto, he gave in to Himmler's wishes to begin its disbanding. Perhaps he was finally persuaded of the ghetto's unprofitability; perhaps he felt that Jews really should not be present in his Gau; or perhaps he wanted to curry additional favor with Himmler.[228] In any event, in a letter to Pohl, Greiser recorded the upshot of the meeting: the ghetto would remain a 'Gau-Ghetto of the Reichsgau Wartheland' under the auspices of his Gau administration. The ghetto population, however, would be reduced to the minimum necessary for continued war production. The Bothmann battalion, currently in Croatia, was to be recalled, so as to resume its killing operations in the Gau. Although he gave no date, Greiser wrote that 'after' the dissolution of the ghetto, its land would be returned to the city.[229] During spring 1944, Biebow's Ghetto Administration passed on incoming job orders to private firms while ghetto inhabitants finished up work on outstanding contracts.[230]

In early June, Speer briefly emerged as a the ghetto's defender. He spoke with Hitler about maintaining the ghetto so as to continue war production there. He also sent requests for information about the ghetto. When Greiser got wind of this, he immediately sent Himmler a telegram. After outlining Speer's activity, Greiser declared: 'Since I'm finished with the preparations for the clearing of the ghetto and have begun with the first evacuations, I'm duty bound to bring to your attention this attempt to thwart your orders.' Himmler immediately responded, 'Dear Greiser! Many thanks for your telegram of 9 June. I ask that you carry out the matter as before.'[231] Greiser had decided to side fully with Himmler. Speer's attempt to maintain ghetto production—a position that Greiser might earlier have embraced—was quashed.

Beginning on 23 June 1944, ghetto inmates were once again murdered at Chełmno. Between then and 14 July, some 7,196 Jews were killed. For unknown reasons, however, mass killings at Chełmno ended abruptly in mid-July. When deportations began again in early August, the remaining Jews—often survivors of over four years in the ghetto—put up resistance to their 'resettlement.' When Greiser visited the ghetto in mid-August, he saw the violent measures used to force ghetto inhabitants to collection points. These Jews were now deported to Auschwitz. Greiser had ordered most Chełmno personnel to take part in suppressing the Warsaw Uprising (see next chapter).[232] Auschwitz also offered more efficient murder facilities and could better serve as a transit camp for Jews slated for forced labor.[233] On 29 August, the last transport, carrying Rumkowski to his death, left the ghetto.[234] Roughly 1,300 to 1,500 Jews remained, some in hiding. Of these, about 600 were sent on to forced labor camps in the Old Reich, while just under 900 were engaged in clean-up operations when the Red Army arrived in January 1945.[235] Of the roughly 67,000 ghetto inmates deported to Auschwitz, more than 45,000 were gassed immediately. About 20,000 were 'selected' for work.[236] Many of these Jews escaped the gas chambers, although not necessarily death. It is believed that some 5,000 to 10,000 former inhabitants of the Litzmannstadt ghetto survived the Third Reich.[237]

Of all the Nazi ghettos, the Litzmannstadt ghetto lasted the longest: it was the first major ghetto established, and the last one to close. To the end and beyond, Greiser and other Gau authorities profited from the death of Jews. In fall 1944, the ghetto's remaining material goods were distributed to various interested parties: the city received the ghetto's land

and buildings; profits from the sale of remaining goods and machinery were paid into the bank account that Greiser controlled; and all of the Jews' left-over personal effects—from clothing to cutlery—was given to the Ethnic German Liaison Office (VoMi) for further distribution to ethnic German resettlers. Chełmno, the first Nazi extermination camp to go into operation, was also one of the last abandoned. In winter 1944–5, a Jewish work detail was cleaning up the camp. On the night of 17–18 January, with the Red Army fast approaching, the Germans set about killing the remaining forty-seven Jews. Some of these Jews, however, resisted their captors. Two SS-men were killed, while two Jews managed to flee the area. All the other Jews were murdered.[238] Ten days before Auschwitz, Chełmno was the second-to-last Nazi extermination site to be abandoned.[239]

Greiser's policy toward Jews is best understood as part of his ambitious Germanization program. Yet he faced a dilemma: Jews both aided and hindered his grand project. Their very presence, of course, undermined Germanization. How could a 'German' Gau contain large numbers of Jews? But Jews could positively advance Germanization. More than in any other area of Nazi-occupied Europe, the Jews in the Warthegau were thus exploited for their labor. As his Kiel speech suggests, Greiser made no secret of the fact that he believed that Jews aided the Germanization of his Gau. Not only did they do various improvement projects, but the Gau also profited from the Jews being paid scant (or, after June 1942, no) wages. Profits from the exploitation and later murder of Jews were put toward other Germanization projects. Ultimately, though, when Himmler insisted on the murder of his Gau's 'productive' Jews, Greiser acquiesced.

With or without Greiser, the Final Solution would have taken place in the Warthegau. In the end, almost all of the Jews there were murdered—just as everywhere else in Nazi-occupied Europe. But because Greiser insisted that the Jews of the Warthegau remain under his and not SS-control, he had a substantial impact on how Jews experienced Nazi rule. Without Greiser, there might not have been the same emphasis on exploiting Jewish labor; without Greiser, there might not have been mass gassings at Chełmno; and without Greiser, the Litzmannstadt ghetto might not have endured so long. Each of these developments shaped the torment of Jews in specific ways—and Greiser was responsible for all of them. Moreover, as a Gauleiter, Greiser's role in the Holocaust was unique. Although Adolf Eichmann couldn't remember his name, he later testified to Greiser's unusual role: 'In the Warthegau it was different [from other areas under Nazi occupation]. There, there was a special agreement between the Reichsführer-SS . . . and definitely the Gauleiter and a third man, the inspector of the security police and the SD in the Gau Wartheland [Damzog]. There, there was no Jewish expert [sent by the RSHA] since there was this special agreement . . . '[240] Greiser's role in the Final Solution mirrored the rest of his rule of the Gau. As a powerful Gauleiter who had arrogated 'special' powers to himself, he determined Gau policy: this was just as true for anti-Semitic policy as for many other Germanization policies.

With his Germanization program, Greiser showed a callous disregard for the human costs involved. Tellingly, even Germans suffered. The resettlement program tore 'Germans' from their homelands, planted families in a hostile environment, left many individuals interned in 'temporary' camps, and spawned nasty tensions among the Gau's various German constituencies. The DVL fractured communities, exacerbated longstanding tensions among ethnic Germans, and sowed artificial ethnic fault lines between neighbors and even extended family members. Of course, Poles and especially Jews paid the heaviest price for Greiser's Germanization project. Tens of thousands of Poles were murdered; hundreds of thousands were deported or sent to do forced labor; many others lost their homes and livelihoods. All were robbed of their property and subject to the Gau's terrible segregation system. Jews endured even worse: they were herded into ghettos, made to suffer a hunger regime, murdered if 'unproductive,' and otherwise forced to do slave labor. In the end, the vast majority of initially 'productive' Jews were also murdered.

Although Greiser's Germanization policies seemed to cohere—policies toward Germans, Poles, and Jews were deeply interconnected—they were also inherently contradictory. The influx of ethnic German resettlers brought in a population that many Germans viewed as decidedly 'un-German;' this sapped the unity of the German community. Deportation and segregation measures undermined Poles' willingness to work, thus jeopardizing the Gau's economy and efforts to modernize its infrastructure. Even more chillingly, Germanization demanded both Jews' slave labor and their murder. Combined with wartime constraints, these contradictions help to explain why Greiser's program failed. In the end, not even a quarter of his Gau's population was 'German.' At the same time, most of the planned building projects were barely begun, never mind completed; other Germanization projects—even place renamings—faltered, too.

In his Germanization measures, Greiser was more radical than any of the other eastern Gauleiters. His childhood roots in the area, his obsessive German nationalism, and his somewhat insecure position in the Nazi hierarchy made him the Gauleiter most attached to Germanization, and most willing to carry it out. He was the Gauleiter who most used the Germanization project to expand his arbitrary powers of rule. He was the one—and only one—who insisted on such wide-ranging Germanization measures. Although his efforts failed, their sheer ambition is significant. For Greiser, Germanization involved grand cultural programs, huge urban renewal projects, the redesigning of city apartments and rural homes, the alteration of the landscape and climate and, not least, the resettlement, deportation, and murder of hundreds of thousands of individuals. The scale (and minutiae) of the project was what was truly remarkable—a striking testament to Nazi ambition, if not to Nazi staying power.

8

'Feudal Duke:' Rule and Loss

In ruling the Warthegau, Greiser tried to fashion himself into the strong Gauleiter that Hitler envisioned for his eastern leaders. To the outside world, he was quite successful in this. In spring 1943, for example, Greiser and Fritz Bracht, the Gauleiter of Upper Silesia, met in Kattowitz. According to an SS-leader's report, the atmosphere was that of an 'old Germanic meeting of kings.' With his 'person and speech,' the report noted, Greiser 'had extraordinarily powerfully affected and impressed [his listeners]. One generally had the impression of a very strong leader personality.' Among other forceful remarks, Greiser had pointed to the future when 'the powerful domes of National-Socialist community houses would arch over church bell towers' that now dominate the eastern landscape. His statement that 'we will be the grandfathers of the generation of 1970' had 'given pause for serious reflection.' The rapporteur concluded that 'altogether Gauleiter Greiser made a thoroughly fighting impression' and that 'despite all the reservations against the new "feudal dukes (*Standesherzöge*)," it must be terrific fun to work with such a man.'[1] The report captured Greiser at the height of his power: on the face of matters, at least, he was an imperious, forceful ruler bent on an historic mission.

But despite the outward signs of strength, Greiser remained deeply concerned about his image and reputation. Ever anxious about his position in the regime, he attempted to project himself as a tough, in-charge Nazi. He tried to usurp the power of others—both those above and below him in the Nazi hierarchy. He jealously guarded his personal powers, and refused to subordinate himself to others, except to Hitler and perhaps Himmler. Ever eager to impress others, he used his material perks to charm visiting dignitaries, Gau functionaries, relatives, friends, and even acquaintances. As leader of the Warthegau, Greiser was out to prove that he was, indeed, a 'model' Nazi.

This chapter takes stock of Greiser as man and ruler in the heyday of his power. It then turns to his actions in the last fifteen months of rule, when the Warthegau faced extraordinary pressures brought on by total war and an advancing Red Army. Finally, it documents Greiser's decision-making in his last days of rule, including his precipitous flight from the Gau.

Greiser was eager to maintain a lifestyle that he believed befitted the Nazi leader of the largest annexed eastern territory. Like other Nazi leaders, he pursued a lavish lifestyle not just to enjoy riches, but also to show off his personal power status within the Nazi hierarchy. In the absence of electoral or other forms of legitimation, opulence became an important measure of success in the Nazi regime.[2] Greiser decorated his office with valuable furniture from the Posen Castle's collections. He occupied luxurious private quarters. Initially, he shared the official apartment of the Polish governor (*Woiwod*) of the Posen area with Harry Siegmund. This apartment was 'most splendidly appointed. Alone the extremely modern bath room was the size of a living room . . . '[3] And Greiser moved up from there. In fall 1939, he began to live in a house in an elegant section of Posen, 5 Tilsit Street.[4] The two-storey villa, initially confiscated from a Jewish or Polish industrialist, remained Greiser's town residence throughout his years in Posen.[5]

Greiser also sought an official country residence for the Reichsstatthalter in the Warthegau. In spring 1940 he settled on a lake-side property, formerly forest land owned by the Polish state, located some twelve miles outside of Posen.[6] Perhaps in imitation of Göring's Carinhall, Greiser renamed the lake, and soon the estate, after his wife Maria: Mariensee. Initially, he planned a relatively simple country home. Albert Speer, however, insisted on a more 'imposing' building that would reflect Greiser's status as governor of a large province.[7] Speer selected the Potsdam architects Otto von Estorff and Gerhard Winkler to do the project, and personally approved the building plans.[8] Surely not to his displeasure, Greiser's simple house turned into a stately mansion that was to project German superiority in the East. Mariensee cost over three million Reichsmarks (RM), the most costly Warthegau building project after the Posen Castle; in 2007 dollars, that would be roughly $13,743,000.[9] In justifying these costs, Hans Pfundtner, state secretary in the Interior Ministry, insisted that an official

Reichsstatthalter residence in the Warthegau 'must be equipped so that it meets the special representative and cultural demands of the eastern Gaus. With this in mind, a different standard as concerns the sum total costs will have to be used than was the case for obtaining official residences for the Reichsstatthalters in the Old Reich.'[10]

Besides the mansion, Mariensee included several out-buildings, as well as terraces, fountains, benches, a tennis court, a vegetable garden, and apple and cherry trees. Landscaping costs alone came to some 590,000 RM.[11] At first, a hedge was to surround the estate, but on Himmler's orders, a high wall was built instead.[12] When Greiser and Maria moved in on 22 May 1942, the elegant house featured living areas, guest quarters, and formal rooms for entertaining. The mansion was filled with fine furniture and lighting fixtures, some of which, at least, was plundered property.[13] Decorations included a bronze of Göring; a bronze relief of a huntress; and prints of Hitler, Frederick II, and Göring as hunter. Altogether, at least 164,133 RM was spent on interior design.[14] Hans Burckhardt, district president of Hohensalza, recalled the inside of Mariensee as 'very grand, if not royal.'[15]

The building of Mariensee was widely condemned. The German population criticized it as taking place at the wrong time, in the wrong place. An anonymous 1943 report, signed by 'an old fighter and a large number of German national comrades and members of the NSDAP,' wrote that 'the population rightly and with rage asks itself why Mr. Gauleiter is building a "manor house" outside of Posen at such enormous expense!? when other important things must be accomplished and completed?' Moreover, the report continued: 'There are not enough people available [to work] . . . but many must guard the "manor house" so that no one can swim in the lake or do ice sports. It must also be noted that with the "appropriation" of the property-manor house, a piece of land has been taken away from the Posen population that in former years served the general public for relaxation and weekends. What happened to the "slogan:" "*The public interest comes first?*"!?'[16] Greiser, the German population believed, was inexcusably squandering valuable resources on a luxurious home—in the midst of war and a serious housing shortage, in an area that was widely viewed as one of the nicest recreational areas in the Posen vicinity.

But for Greiser and Maria, life in Mariensee was good. Sitting on the terrace, they could contemplate a peaceful, quiet vista; hear the gentle lapping of the lake's waves; and view graceful birds flying overhead. Among other high-ranking guests, the couple hosted Heinrich Himmler, Joseph Goebbels, Finance Minister Lutz Graf Schwerin-Krosigk, and General Heinz Guderian there.[17]

Greiser and Maria also hosted family members at Mariensee. Antje Cordier, one of Greiser's nieces, recalls a summer afternoon visit in 1942. Twelve at the time, Antje came with her sister and a friend. Rotraut, Greiser's younger daughter who lived with her mother in Danzig, was also present; she had come for her annual summer vacation with her father. During the whole visit, Greiser was 'nice' and 'affable.' The party was served coffee and cherry pie with whipped cream on the terrace. Maria then disappeared into the house to the music room that held her white grand piano (a first-rate instrument stolen from a Polish apartment).[18] Those outside soon heard the tinkling of piano playing. Meanwhile, Greiser had changed for a hunting expedition, and now sported lederhosen and sturdy sandals. He wore no shirt; his burly chest and thick legs were covered in dark hair. Red-cheeked, Greiser seemed to Antje 'vital, healthy, ... and jovial.' While servants prepared the paddle boats, the children and Greiser's dog tumbled about in the grass. Everyone then piled into the boats. After a short ride, a flock of ducks was scared into the sky. Greiser fired several shots, and downed three ducks. The afternoon a hunting success, the boats returned to shore, and the visit soon ended.[19] Antje's memories ring true. Greiser, ever chummy, was pleasant and welcoming to his guests. He wanted his visitors to see and enjoy the lifestyle that his Nazi success had brought him.

Like many other Nazi satraps, Greiser engaged in nepotism. His eagerness to spread largesse among relatives suggests that he wanted to prove to them that he, the baby of the family, had made good. Given his past financial difficulties, Greiser must have found his new-found ability to provide for others very satisfying. Indeed, making positive things happen was part of his self-image: Greiser saw himself as benevolent and big-spirited.

Greiser used his contacts to help his older daughter, Ingrid. Beginning in March 1938, Ingrid worked in the Reich Foreign Ministry as secretary to Walther Hewel, the head of Joachim von Ribbentrop's personal staff; Hewel had close relations to Hitler.[20] Ingrid was now a twenty-something, a pretty blonde who wore fashionable clothes. She has been described as a 'lively one' (*eine flotte*).[21] In 1940, she was engaged to Kurt Birr, a naval officer whom Greiser had met while on reserve duty. Birr was twelve years older than Ingrid, but Greiser decided that he was the man for his daughter.[22] While Ingrid was preparing her trousseau, Greiser wrote to Friedrich Uebelhoer, district president in Lodsch (soon Litzmannstadt), about the possibility of his daughter buying some items there (by implication, from stocks of confiscated Jewish goods).[23] In April, Ingrid went. As she wrote to Birr: 'The best was the Lodsch-Department Store-Soc[iety]. Goods were piled up to the ceiling, room after room. I simply didn't know what to shop first . . . again and again, I saw something that I just had to have. And extraordinarily low prices . . . ' Ingrid went on several other shopping trips during her short stay in Litzmannstadt. In the end, she claimed, 'the cars almost collapsed under the burden of the packages; people stood around in astonishment.'[24] In July, Ingrid was married in the garden of Greiser's city villa in Posen. The married couple, however, spent only about two weeks together. Birr soon returned to his naval unit and, in November 1940, drowned in Amsterdam in the line of duty—another personal tragedy that Greiser endured as Gauleiter.[25]

Greiser's cousin, Harry Siegmund, served as his personal advisor and, in this capacity, ran his office and was party to many important decisions in the Gau. Greiser did Siegmund many good deeds. He managed to have Siegmund freed from active military service for much of the war.[26] He intervened to have Siegmund promoted within the SS.[27] Greiser also tried to have Siegmund's civil-service status backdated so that his cousin could enjoy salary and other perquisites. This effort proved unsuccessful, but not before it had become a divisive issue in Reich–Gau relations (more below).[28] As Siegmund writes, as a young, ambitious man, 'in the lee of a powerful boss,' he enjoyed heady years in the Warthegau.[29]

Otto Greiser profited from his younger brother's success. Otto and his wife Erna came to the Warthegau from Königsberg, where Otto had been a department head in a shipyard.[30] In the Warthegau, Otto ran a well-established business in Kutno—confiscated, of course, from its previous owners.[31] He also finally managed to join the NSDAP. For years, he had tried to secure entry into the party, but his past membership in a Free Mason lodge had stood in the way. In the early 1940s, Arthur intervened on his brother's behalf, insisting that his brother was 'worthy' of being a Nazi party member. On 14 December 1941, Hitler decided in Otto's favor.[32]

Arthur tried to convince his oldest brother Willy to come to the Warthegau. The managing director of the World Economics Institute in

Kiel, Willy declined. Never a Nazi, he probably wanted to keep his distance from his fanatical brother. But one of Willy's five children, Hildegrund, came to the Warthegau as a schoolteacher; she apparently had the time of her life in her uncle's Gau.[33]

Maria's brother, Hubert Koerfer, also benefited from his brother-in-law's position. Formerly a piano player in cafes and restaurants in Cologne, he now ran the largest textile shop in Hohensalza. Since he had no business experience, he used the former owner as an employee and right-hand man. Greiser protected Koerfer from military service until well into 1944.[34]

Greiser put relatives in charge of two of the four estates that he controlled and used as guesthouses.[35] The Schwarzenau Palace (*Czerniejewo*), a Skorzewki family possession, was the grandest. Greiser had Siegmund's brother-in-law, Siegfried Pluquet, run the estate; he had gotten to know Pluquet at Siegmund's wedding. Schwarzenau Palace included a fine library and large hunting grounds; it was updated during the Nazi years.[36] Greiser used the Palace to entertain various prominent Nazis. In January 1940, for example, Goebbels wrote of the Palace: 'An old, somewhat weathered and yellowed aristocrats' palace. The owners have fled. Here I had a truly good sleep.'[37] Himmler stayed there on 5 June 1941.[38] Greiser also invited Pfundtner for a weekend of hunting there; Pfundtner was Greiser's strongest supporter in the Interior Ministry. Pfundtner very much enjoyed his stay at the palace, even though, as he wrote to Greiser, he regretted that he had had no luck with bagging a deer.[39]

Greiser transferred ownership of another estate, Oberau (*Objezierze*), also confiscated from a Pole, to the Gau Self-Administration.[40] He then put his first wife's uncle, Adolf Waschau, in charge of the estate. Given how estranged Greiser was from Ruth, this was odd. But Greiser had developed his passion for hunting at Waschau's Workallen estate in East Prussia and so now, perhaps for old times' sake, turned to him to run Oberau.[41] Greiser invited all sorts of people to stay there, including young artists to enjoy a few weeks of undisturbed painting, and the widows of some of his fellow naval officers during World War I. He also invited Magda Goebbels and her children. Ever solicitous of the powerful, he sent Siegmund to enquire about Mrs. Goebbels' wishes.[42] Family members came to Oberau, too. In 1942, Greiser's niece Antje and her sister spent some weeks there. According to Antje, the main house was a 'huge old palace with marble floors;' it had, among other fine amenities, a built-in bathtub ('a huge thing') and a well-stocked library.[43]

Greiser had another property, a former guesthouse of the Polish president, Ciechocinek, transferred to his Reichsstatthalter agency. Renamed Hermannsbad, it served leading Gau officials who wished for rest and relaxation, not least through enjoying the nearby thermal baths. Greiser had a suite of rooms there prepared for his use.[44] Through his control of the various guest houses, he could distribute an attractive perquisite to those he wished to favor. He also furthered his reputation as a generous host and beneficent ruler.

Greiser used his position in the Warthegau to indulge his favorite hobby, hunting. Until 1943, he was 'Gau hunting master' (*Gaujägermeister*). At a meeting of sub-district hunting masters in April 1940, he discussed the 'essence of German hunting and the German hunter' and noted that 'here, too, despite great difficulties important reconstruction work must be accomplished.' He asked that Göring—the Reich hunting master—be informed that it is the 'will of the hunters to make the Warthegau a model Gau as regards hunting and hunters.'[45]

Greiser reserved several hunting preserves for his exclusive use.[46] Although Hitler and some other top Nazis disdained hunting, Greiser made no secret of his hunting passion. A schmalzy newspaper article, for example, declared: 'Despite a pronounced Prussian and therewith National-Socialist view of life, Arthur Greiser certainly doesn't have an aversion to the nice and friendly sides of life . . . He is most strongly drawn out when the deer bell in the foggy fall forest or the blackcock "rolls and romps" in the early summer mornings.'[47] Greiser ensured that no Gau policies interfered with his favorite pastime. In 1942, when Wilhelm Koppe, the higher SS and police leader (HSSPF) in the Warthegau, ordered Polish children to forage for wild mushrooms and blueberries, Greiser insisted that they be kept under close supervision so that they would not ruin potential hunting.[48] After the war, a Polish servant put a sinister twist on Greiser's love of hunting. In sworn testimony, he declared that Greiser, after a hunting expedition in which he had bagged stags and pheasants, told his guests that 'just as we shot and beat today, so we'll destroy the Polish filth.'[49] Whether or not Greiser really said this, the Polish imagination closely linked Greiser's hunting passion with his efforts to destroy the Polish people.

Greiser did not see himself as one of many Gauleiters. Rather, as Gauleiter of the Warthegau—with a special mission given him by the Führer—he was to enjoy rare privileges. Even though Hitler decreed that Gauleiters were no longer to use private railway cars as of December 1940,

Greiser eagerly sought his own private car. In June 1941, Martin Bormann won an exception for Greiser. According to Bormann, Greiser had to make frequent trips in his Gau to monitor reconstruction efforts. Outside of Posen, however, there were few, if any hotels suitable for the Gauleiter. Bormann now told Hans Lammers, head of the Reich Chancellery, that 'on demand, and with no ado, a private railway car should always be available' for Greiser. In September 1942, Greiser complained that he was having 'difficulties' getting access to a private railway car, and Lammers reminded the minister of transportation of Greiser's special situation. In 1944, the question arose of whether a private car, begun but never finished by the Poles, should be readied for Greiser. As Bormann wrote to Lammers, 'Greiser would be thankful if this happened: he pointed out that he now uses lots of fuel since he always has to drive back to Posen at night.' Together, Bormann and Lammers decided to ask Hitler about the matter. On 13 July 1944, the Führer agreed that a special railway car for Greiser 'should be finished so long as this is possible without special and extraordinary difficulties.'[50] The car was probably never finished. Greiser, however, had made his point: as a Nazi potentate in the German East, he was to enjoy special perquisites.

How grand was Greiser's lifestyle? A 1946 Polish account claimed that 'in the palace [i.e., Mariensee] there were often glittering receptions and parties. That's when Greiser felt himself in his element—after, incidentally, his "so demanding work." So this scoundrel spent the days of his useless existence.'[51] This description exaggerated Greiser's penchant for high living; it reflected the early postwar Polish attempt to portray him as a monster. Those who knew him, however, perhaps err in the opposite direction. They claim that Greiser lived very simply in his elegant surroundings. The meals at Mariensee were generally plain; a special meal might include wild boar (shot by Greiser) and beer, but not many courses of elegant dishes.[52] Greiser also never drank excessively.[53] As Siegmund has written, 'Even among his most trusted friends or hunting companions, Greiser was always in complete control of himself.'[54] Some of Greiser's larger parties, at least, were relatively simple affairs. Every October, he gave a party at Mariensee for leading officials of the Warthegau. As one guest later depicted the annual shindig, it was 'a beer evening of the simplest sort . . . As host he [Greiser] appeared very friendly and comradely. His wife also seemed perfectly natural and unaffected.'[55]

Greiser fostered an image of himself as a man of the people, enjoying simple pleasures. This was not a facade. Greiser relished beer, sausage, and back-slapping comraderie. But he also had a pronounced taste for luxury. As Goebbels wrote in July 1940, Greiser (and Forster) rule like 'the Pashas.'[56] While not personally corrupt (in the sense that he does not seem to have given political favors in return for material gifts), Greiser engaged in dubious financial practices that brought him considerable personal wealth. Besides his salary as Reichsstatthalter, Greiser served on the boards of various corporations. A Polish historian, Czesław Łuczak, estimated that Greiser's gross monthly income was a whopping 30,000 RM ($12,000 in 1941 or $325,000 in 2007 dollars).[57] After his arrest in 1945, Greiser stated that he had 400,000 RM in assets, including a 200,000 RM insurance payment following a hunting accident. In addition, he claimed that his salary as Reichsstatthalter was 3,000 RM per month ($1,200 in 1941 dollars, or $32,480 in 2007 dollars), along with a 2,000 RM per month expense account.[58] While Łuczak's estimate of his income is likely too high, Greiser's is likely too low.

As noted in the previous chapter, Greiser personally controlled bank accounts that held assets drawn from stolen Polish and Jewish property. The fact that he personally disposed of these assets suggests financial misdoing—although to what ends remains unclear. Greiser also profited from confiscated goods beyond those used to decorate his houses and office. Shortly after coming to the Warthegau, for example, he sent Siegmund to secure the famed wine cellars of the Hotel Bazar in Posen; the wine collection was worth some 1.5 million Polish złoty (or close to $300,000 in 1941 dollars).[59] According to the Polish man who oversaw the wine cellar, Greiser had bottles sent over two or three times a week and, in the weeks preceding Christmas, more often.[60]

Greiser also had the NSDAP give him the house in which he was born. A simple house, he surely never intended to live in it. But since he owned no other real estate, he may have been laying a financial nest egg. Perhaps, too, having the house reflected a desire to have a material connection to his childhood roots. The property, 6 Market Square in Schroda, was confiscated from its Polish owner and, in September 1943, bought by the NSDAP for 5,000 RM; shortly thereafter it was valued at 15,000 RM.[61] Greiser was ceremonially given the house by the NSDAP treasurer during one of Franz Xaver Schwarz's visit to the Gau. This 'present' irritated some Germans. As Burckhardt later wrote, 'It was noticed and Greiser was judged unfavorably for the . . . fact that the Treasurer Schwarz . . . gave the Gauleiter his birth house in Schroda. Astonished, some people wondered how the treasurer could give something as a present that didn't belong to him and how, in turn, the Gauleiter could accept it.'[62] Despite financial improprieties, Greiser's lifestyle is best described as luxurious, but not extravagant. This is especially true in comparison to other high-ranking Nazis; he was no Hermann Göring or Hans Frank.[63]

In descriptions of Greiser as Gauleiter, the same term is repeatedly used: he was a '*Persönlichkeit*,' usually translated as a 'strong character,' or a 'force to be reckoned with.' General Walter Petzel, the longtime commanding general in the Warthegau, later wrote: 'Greiser was doubtlessly a strong character. He had a marked talent as a speaker, and he understood how to captivate and fire up his audience with enthusiasm and to be convincing through a simple and natural way of speaking. In personal interaction he won one over with his quiet friendliness, objectivity, and modesty that stood in sharp contrast to the hooliganism and craving for recognition of other party big-wigs.' Petzel also found that Greiser 'never appeared as an autocrat, instead he was always objective, let everyone speak, and also allowed himself to be convinced.'[64] Similarly, Siegmund described his cousin as 'friendly and forthcoming to everyone, but always intent on an unbridgeable distance, he became an authority figure.'[65]

Other Germans found Greiser to be a strong presence, but without the more pleasant character attributes. Burckhardt, who had tense relations with Greiser, later wrote that 'one could never become "warm" with Greiser. Even when he projected a comradely manner, one saw that he jealously guarded his "authority" so that none of it would be lost; it also soon became apparent that he liked to pit individuals against each other or tried to beat them.' Greiser frequently gave promises 'that he already broke the next morning, he always had several irons in the fire and, at a given moment, pulled out the one that struck him just then as right.' Greiser also repeatedly emphasized that he was '*persona gratissima* with Hitler' and that he had Himmler's 'complete trust.'[66] Burckhardt's description, too, captures Greiser's personality. Regardless of where one stood in his estimation, Greiser was always a strong character. But in his forcefulness he could be pleasant, friendly, and affable—or haughty, nasty, and vengeful.

Greiser was bent on controlling all facets of life in his Gau. As Burckhardt noted, 'Greiser repeatedly emphasized that in his Gau nothing important could happen without his prior authorization and approval.'[67] Greiser's insistence on determining all developments in his Gau led to tensions with many others—from Reich ministerial authorities to Gau subordinates.

Greiser had a longstanding conflict with Interior Ministry officials about whether they could communicate directly with his three district presidents. According to stipulations worked out in fall 1939, the district presidents were solely responsible to the Reichsstatthalter. In 1941, Greiser was thus furious to learn that the Ministry had contacted them directly so as to declare one of his decrees invalid. As Greiser complained to Lammers, if he gave in to the Ministry, he would be 'reduced to a docile doll of the bureaucracy of the Interior Ministry.' Lammers was unwilling to decide the matter; instead, the parties involved agreed to a compromise whereby decrees would be sent to Greiser, who then would pass them on quickly to the district presidents.

Shortly thereafter, the Interior Ministry sent another decree directly to the district presidents. At about the same time, Greiser learned that Burckhardt had sent reports about the bad state of his district's roads to the Ministry and that, as a result, the head of the Ministry's Municipal Department had ordered extensive studies in conjunction with the General Inspector's Office. Since Greiser himself had just managed to arrange for the same studies, he was greatly annoyed by what he saw as the needless duplication of work. In his view, direct contact between district presidents and the Interior Ministry hindered rational administration of his Gau. Greiser won this issue—probably because the Reich Chancellery let the Interior Ministry know that it could not count on its support in this matter. On 24 November 1941, Interior Minister Wilhelm Frick signed a decree stating that any direct reporting from district presidents to the Ministry was to be limited to important, time-sensitive matters 'and therewith to exceptional cases.'[68]

Greiser had less success in another conflict. This had to do with the backdating of two men's civil-service promotions to 1940. The two men in question were none other than his cousin, Harry Siegmund, and the head of the Gau Press Office, Karl Hans Fuchs, the author of several hagiographical newspaper portraits about him. As senate president in Danzig, Greiser had illegally promoted them along with some 800 other civil servants on 23 August 1939. Frick reluctantly agreed to accept the two men's promotions as of 1 March 1942, but he refused to backdate them to 1 March 1940.

Frick even threatened Greiser that if he didn't drop his demand he would make Greiser personally responsible for the two men's back pay. Greiser responded that this would 'happily' give him the opportunity to raise the matter with the Führer. He refused to drop the issue.

In June 1943, Lammers wrote to Bormann that the matter had far more importance than the mere promotion of two civil servants. His words indicate how successfully Greiser had come to rule free of Berlin ministerial intervention: 'How difficult—if not to say virtually impossible—it has become for Reich central authorities to obtain validity for their decrees against certain authorities, even when these [decrees] express the will of the Führer, is well known. Against this background, the present matter is of a fundamental and serious nature, not an isolated case, but rather a symptom.' Lammers then continued: 'Were the Reich ministers of interior and of finance to give up their legitimate viewpoint, this would lead not only to an intolerable further loss of authority for these ministers, but of the Reich itself. If it's no longer possible to make valid Reich interests that encompass the whole against unreasonable special requests, then the just order that is especially indispensable under the difficult conditions of the war will no longer be seen as secured.' In Lammers' view, Greiser's efforts on behalf of his favorites threatened the integrity of the Reich. Bormann sent Klopfer to Posen, who, in turn, managed to convince Greiser to withdraw his request, no doubt arguing that with both Bormann and Lammers against him, he could not raise the matter with the Führer.[69]

Greiser tried to prevent Reich intervention by forbidding officials to inspect his Gau. In July 1942, he sent a letter to all party and state agencies claiming that 'all possible ministerial bureaucrats and consultants' were making visits to the Gau and that 'instead of Berlin supporting us in our complicated, arduous, and war-important reconstruction work, [our work] is hampered by constant visits and traveling around.' The Gau, he stated, would continue to welcome 'responsible men from the party and state,' but not those who were coming 'for social get togethers, dinners, and coffee breaks' for which 'in the third year of the war we really have no time.' Greiser further insisted that all official visits to the Gau were dependent on his personal permission. Although Lammers recognized the difficulties inherent in so many official visits, he was more concerned with Greiser's usurpation of authority. As he wrote to Bormann in August, 'I don't consider it permissible that a Reichsstatthalter makes an official visit in his Gau ordered by a Reichsminister dependent on his permission; I presume that you are of the same opinion as concerns an official visit ordered by a Reichsleiter [leading party official].' In September, Bormann sent someone (perhaps Klopfer) to discuss the matter with Greiser. Greiser now conceded that he could not insist on making official trips ordered by a central party agency dependent on his permission. But later that month, the Interior Ministry issued a decree restricting official trips to an absolute minimum. On 2 October, after meeting with Lammers a day earlier, Greiser sent another letter to all party and state agencies claiming that since the Interior Ministry's decree had made his first letter superfluous, it 'was to be seen as revoked.' He still requested, though, that he be informed of all official visits to his Gau.[70] While he could save face by pointing to the Interior Ministry's decree, he had lost the more important issue of whether he could issue commands to central state and party offices. Clearly, he could not. Doing so only irritated Lammers and Bormann who, in turn, were eager to show the wilful Gauleiter the limits of his power.

Greiser remained allergic to Reich interference in his Gau. In 1943, for example, a Ministry of Education official, Emil Pax, and his boss wished to do an inspection trip in Hohensalza. Pax had earlier documented the poor state of schools for Polish children. The two men announced their trip to the Reichsstatthalter's office, and were repeatedly asked not to come. Pax and his colleague nonetheless arrived in the Warthegau on a Sunday. The two men were then told that if they carried out their inspections, Greiser would order a 'coal-vacation' for all of the district's schools; with the schools closed, no inspections could take place. After frantic telephone calls from Hohensalza to Posen, Greiser agreed to the inspections, but only if the officials refrained from issuing orders on the spot.[71] Although this and some of the other episodes suggest that Greiser ultimately submitted to Berlin ministries, this was more the exception than the rule. Lammers' comment about how impossible it was for Reich central authorities to impose their will on 'certain authorities' (namely, Greiser) better captures the real state of affairs. As shown in earlier chapters, Greiser had conflicts not only with the Interior and Education ministries, but also with the Ministries of Finance, Justice, Ecclesiastical Affairs, Foreign Affairs, and Armaments. In virtually all of these battles, Greiser gained the upper hand. Only when he seemed to thwart Reich or party authority altogether—when Lammers or Bormann felt their own competences infringed—was he forced to retreat.

As Reichsstatthalter of the Warthegau, Greiser was virtually impervious to Reich authorities; in his Gau, he could do much as he pleased.[72]

Greiser's Gau was in some respects a microcosm of the Nazi regime as a whole: because lines of authority were up for grabs, everyone vied for a share of power. Just as Greiser tried to wrest authority from Reich superiors, he also tried to do so from Gau subordinates. Indeed, he was eager to centralize all Gau authority in his Reichsstatthalter and Gauleiter offices. The district presidents, however, put up a spirited defense against this attempted usurpation. Greiser thus had poor relations with two of his three district presidents, Hans Burckhardt in Hohensalza and Friedrich Uebelhoer in Litzmannstadt. (Viktor Böttcher, the district president of Posen, was a longtime Greiser ally from their Danzig days.) In their feuds with Greiser, the district presidents used methods similar to Greiser's. They tried, for example, to appeal directly to the Interior Ministry. This, of course, infuriated Greiser no end. In 1941, he dashed off an angry diatribe to Burckhardt, '...From now on I definitely can't tolerate your highhanded action. I have often repeatedly and unambiguously declared...that the district presidents are not to deal with a single Reich Ministry, not even the Reich minister of the interior, by bypassing my agency.' Greiser enumerated the various instances in which Burckhardt's officials had done just this. He then declared, 'Leaving aside the fact that this whole correspondence was totally unnecessary and that a telephone call to my responsible agency would have brought a better success, I am giving you a censure for the repeated highhanded conduct against my will.' Greiser threatened that if one of Burckhardt's officials did this again, he would have the man suspended and placed at the disposal of the Interior Ministry.[73]

Greiser was actually eager to disband the district-president administrations altogether. A Reichsstatthalter memorandum, for example, argued that the district presidents made up a superfluous layer of administration. In response, in May 1942, the district presidents signed off on a document in which they harshly criticized the Reichsstatthalter's administration. It opened with 'Every day the district presidents in Posen, Hohensalza and Litzmannstadt view with ever greater concern how the administration of the Reichsgau Wartheland is led.' It described the 'ever stronger splitting and fragmentation of administrative tasks to various offices,' making it difficult for decisions to be carried out in a rational way. It then referred to Interior

Ministry guidelines that stated 'The Reichsstatthalter with his agency should hold his head free for the big political, economic, and *völkisch* problems. He can only do this if he and his agency do not lose themselves in ongoing administration work, details, and particular occurrences.' According to the district presidents, just the opposite was happening in the Warthegau: 'The Reichsstatthalter administers more than he leads. He intervenes too much in individual decisions. The unavoidable consequence is a slow carrying out of business.' The seventeen-page document listed numerous examples of micro-management by the Reichsstatthalter agency. The district presidents were also angered that the Reichsstatthalter office had sometimes turned directly to the sub-district magistrates, bypassing their level of administration.[74] Despite their united front, they had little success in reining in Greiser. Meanwhile, in 1943, Greiser formally proposed the dissolution of Hohensalza and Litzmannstadt districts, but Hitler rejected this administrative change.[75]

Greiser eventually managed to have both Uebelhoer and Burckhardt removed. Although relations between Greiser and Uebelhoer had initially been good, they soured during 1941. Uebelhoer was eager to run his district—and particularly matters pertaining to the 'Jewish Question' in Litzmannstadt—independently of Posen.[76] In August 1941 (or sometime soon thereafter), Uebelhoer wrote up a document titled 'Consultation with Gauleiter.' As he wrote, 'You [e.g. Greiser] can shoot or let roebuck, deer, pigs and other animals, and Jews and Poles be shot. But you cannot and may not now shoot down old National Socialists . . . ' Uebelhoer seems to have been referring to a confidant, Prager, whom Greiser had somehow forced to leave the Gau. Uebelhoer further complained that in a meeting with Greiser he had apparently raised as his first question, 'Do I have a free hand?' and had received a positive reply. But as he noted, 'as of mid-1940 "uniform leadership" from Posen and Berlin. With that, inhibition of every initiative by ignoring the special circumstances in the Litzmannstadt area.' Uebelhoer claimed that between March and August 1941 he had been in Posen every week, a two-day long trip. But he had been able to accomplish little. He ended his notes with 'Back slaps: No serious work in Posen. The Gauleiter gives his ear to a Camarilla. One after the other can go to hell.'[77]

By October 1942, relations between Greiser and Uebelhoer had further deteriorated. Greiser now found a pretext to remove Uebelhoer. As he wrote to Frick, the district president had spent too much money on the purchase and renovation of a villa for his official residence; the money had gone to Uebelhoer's crony who officially administered the property. Greiser further claimed that the villa, valued at some one million Reichmarks, was much too grand for a district president. Due to what he claimed to be corruption, Greiser asked the Interior Ministry to dismiss Uebelhoer and, in the meantime, he suspended him.[78] In a letter to Hitler, Uebelhoer outlined his side of the story: Greiser, he claimed, 'insisted on his false view that we [in Litzmannstadt] were not working for the greater good, but rather for a division of the Gau.' He then described the false corruption case that Greiser had developed against him. In his words, the 'consequences' of Greiser's 'arbitrary actions are outrageous. A crippling horror has spread over the German people here . . . '[79] In fact, as concerned the villa, Uebelhoer seems to have been within the bounds of accepted Nazi practice. In 1943, after determining the accusations groundless, the Interior Ministry made Uebelhoer district president in Merseburg; a 1944 SS-investigation also uncovered no wrongdoing.[80] In Litzmannstadt, Dr. Hermann Riediger became district president; he stayed in the background and had no open conflict with Greiser.[81]

Greiser used different but similarly distasteful methods to remove Burckhardt. In 1944, Burckhardt's daughter was married in a Catholic church ceremony. Prior to the wedding, Burckhardt asked Greiser's office whether his attendance would be viewed as problematic (given the Gau's militant anti-church policies). Told no, he attended the wedding. But afterwards there was so much criticism within party circles (perhaps spurred on by the Gauleiter) that Burckhardt felt obliged to resign—surely not to Greiser's displeasure.[82] Burckhardt was succeeded by Karl-Wilhelm Albert, up to then police president in Litzmannstadt.[83] Greiser thus managed to remove several key subordinates whom he believed were too eager to run their districts independently.

Greiser treated the lower levels of his administration—his sub-district magistrates and mayors—in a similarly highhanded manner. He limited, for example, the powers of sub-district magistrates to issue police regulations; throughout the Reich, sub-district magistrates generally had this right. As of 31 July 1940, however, sub-district magistrates (and district presidents) in the Warthegau were required to receive authorization from the Reichsstatthalter for any police regulations that they wished to issue.[84] In another measure that stripped municipal officials of their powers, Greiser centralized the operation of his Gau's electricity works. He convened the Gau's mayors and, at the meeting, told them to show discipline. He then presented them with statements, already prepared for their signatures, that they would turn over their local electricity works to the Wartheland Electrical Works (*Elektrizitätswerke Wartheland AG*). All but the mayor of Posen did as ordered. Although Frick refused to recognize the new ownership structure, he nonetheless allowed the Wartheland Electrical Works to operate communal electricity for the duration of the war.[85] Local officials thus lost control of an important municipal resource.

Although Greiser's actions as a strong Gauleiter irritated ministerial authorities, they also attracted some positive attention in Berlin. For a time, at least, it seemed that Greiser might be given additional responsibilities, or even an altogether more powerful position. Lammers, Bormann, and Himmler were plotting to oust Hans Frank in the General Government; in their plans, Greiser would replace Frank.[86] On 7 May 1943, Goebbels noted in his diary that 'in the General Government things have gone so far that General Governor Frank cannot hold on to his position. The Führer will probably put Greiser in his position. Especially the most recent events in Warsaw have broken Dr. Frank's neck.'[87] Goebbels was referring to the worsening security situation in the General Government. Just then, the Warsaw Ghetto Uprising was taking place; the Germans were surprised by the ferocity of Jewish armed resistance. Moreover, after the German defeat at Stalingrad, Polish resistance became much more active.[88] On 9 May, Goebbels further noted: 'The Führer thinks very highly of Greiser. His Gau is led in an exemplary way. The Führer would like to transfer to him the things in the General Government and temporarily also leave him in his Gau; Greiser, of course, would be very reluctant to relinquish [his Gau].'[89] Despite Hitler's positive evaluation, neither Greiser nor anyone else ever replaced Frank.

Just a month later, in June, Goebbels noted that Hitler was dissatisfied with Frick and was considering making Greiser minister of the interior. Goebbels then commented: 'I think that Greiser has the ability to hold the position of an interior minister, but that he personally lives in a bit too grand a style and in wartime Berlin that would probably cause an unpleasant stir.' Goebbels added, though, that the Führer didn't wish to make any personnel changes just then.[90] Siegmund later wrote that when he asked Greiser about the matter 'he [Greiser] explained that he wanted under all circumstances to stay in the Wartheland; here, in his homeland, he wanted to fulfil the life's work that the Führer had entrusted to him.'[91] Greiser's coy reluctance to take on the ministry job might just have been a mask to cover any disappointment if not chosen. But he may also not have wanted the job. After all, he had done all he could to strip the Ministry of its powers. To him, the Nazi future involved ever stronger Gauleiters like himself—little Führers in their bailiwicks. Why take on a position that would advocate precisely the opposite? As matters developed, Himmler added the post of interior minister to his burgeoning portfolio.

Despite projecting strength, Greiser remained deeply insecure about his place in the Nazi regime. As noted in earlier pages, he did not have a close relationship with Hitler; he could never be sure of the Führer's support. He also did not have a long Nazi resume; he was something of an upstart in a regime that privileged longtime loyalty. And though he had successfully arrogated ever more powers to himself, he had also alienated potential supporters in Berlin. To counter these shortcomings, Greiser had adopted radical policies in the Warthegau and done all that he could to bolster his authority and power. But he was still worried—and not least about how his past life was viewed by party authorities.

In an attempt to mask his imperfect Nazi past, Greiser fostered a legend about himself: that he had been the target of an assassin, of none other than David Frankfurter, who murdered Wilhelm Gustloff, the Swiss NSDAP leader, in 1936. In 1940, Greiser reportedly stated in a speech that 'The [English] Secret Service had the bullet that the Jew David Frankfurter used to shoot Wilhelm Gustloff that was actually intended for the then Senate President Greiser, who only by coincidence escaped this assassination attempt.'[92] Greiser's garbled description suggests that the English Secret Service was behind the Gustloff murder, and that it had aimed to kill him. Perhaps because the accusation was so unlikely, Greiser did not repeat this often, or at least not publicly. No documentary evidence substantiates the claim.[93] But his eagerness to wear the Gustloff halo speaks to Greiser's anxiety about his biographical bona-fides.

Greiser was particularly sensitive about his past because it remained an issue throughout his Warthegau years. In June 1942, an official in the Reich Security Main Office (RSHA), Bruno Streckenbach, questioned whether it was already known that Greiser had been a Free Mason and, if so, whether Greiser had entered this information in the appropriate forms.[94] This inquiry does not seem to have had any negative consequences for Greiser. In April 1943, however, Robert Reuter, his old enemy in Danzig, coincidentally met Drendel, the chief public prosecutor (*Generalstaatsanwalt*) in Posen, at a speaking engagement. Reuter immediately inundated Drendel with negative information about Greiser. Drendel reported Reuter's accusations to Rolf-Heinz Höppner, the high-ranking security official in the Gau. Höppner, in turn, wrote to SS-Brigade Leader Otto Ohlendorf about the matter; Ohlendorf seems to have informed Himmler. Both Drendel and Höppner had tense relations with Greiser, and this may, in fact, have been an attempt to undermine the Gauleiter. Höppner, however, claimed that he passed on the information not to harm Greiser, but to have Reuter investigated.[95] Himmler, at least, viewed the situation this way: he wanted Reuter taken into protective custody so that he would no longer spread false information.[96]

Some of the accusations had already been raised and dismissed in the 1934 party investigation against Greiser. But Reuter raised some new ones. He questioned Greiser's Aryan origins. He suggested that during World War I Greiser had unnecessarily extended his flight-school course so as to avoid going back to the front (Reuter was perhaps referring to Greiser's breakdown in summer 1918). He insisted that Greiser did not have the right to wear an Iron Cross First Class medal because he did not have an official certificate for it. He also claimed that before Greiser joined the party, he had stated that 'he was eager to join the NSDAP, but that he had to be safe, he couldn't risk anything'—suggesting that Greiser was unwilling to sacrifice for the movement. Reuter related that once Hitler had made Greiser the 're-organizer' of the party in Gau Danzig in 1930, Greiser had not appeared in the Gau offices because he was afraid of the SA-opposition. Reuter also claimed that Greiser had given Danzig citizenship to a Jew. Finally, Reuter insinuated that Greiser had engaged in financial improprieties. Greiser, he claimed, had engaged in currency speculation in the early 1930s.[97] He had also supposedly made illicit profits with the help of individuals now employed in the Warthegau. Böttcher, Reuter claimed, had given Greiser the concession to run his motor-boat tourist operation, really a front for smuggling operations. Helmut Froböss, now the president of the provincial high court in Posen, had provided Greiser with forged passports to aid this operation. And Paul Batzer, a close associate, had allegedly been involved in Greiser's corrupt practices in the Zoppot Casino.[98]

How true were Reuter's allegations? Some were patently false. Reuter had no evidence that Greiser was not of 'Aryan' origins. Similarly, Reuter was simply wrong in stating that Greiser had not been awarded the

Iron Cross First Class medal during World War I. But some of Reuter's allegations, such as those concerning Greiser's actions in summer 1918, may have had an element of twisted truth. And some have never been cleared up. We just don't know whether Greiser was engaged in smuggling and corruption in Danzig in the early 1930s. In November 1943, however, a party court found Reuter guilty of 'totally vilifying conduct towards Gauleiter Greiser;' he had thus 'most seriously violated the duties of a party comrade.' As punishment, Reuter lost his membership in the NSDAP.[99]

But the matter was not yet over. In early 1944, Greiser spoke with Schultz, chairman of the First Chamber of the Supreme Party Court. The two men decided that Greiser should write a final statement about Reuter's allegations 'so that the matter could be cleared up.' Greiser didn't write the document until late May. Although he deemed the matter important, he noted that 'in the fifth year of war I also have other things to do besides deal with such matters.'[100] In his statement, Greiser declared that the gist of Reuter's accusations was that he, Greiser, had tried to avoid service at the front. He offered a passionate defense of his World War I military record. He insisted that 'I had one of the shortest periods of pilot training of that time, especially since I not only learned to fly, but concurrently was trained to be a fighter pilot. And all that in a little over half a year . . . Today one would need several years for that.' He explained that he had lost the original certificate of his Iron Cross First Class decoration when the British invaded Bruges; he had a notarized copy in his possession, and he was now sending along a copy of the copy to Schultz. He added that 'for an old World War I front soldier it is terribly sad when one has to defend oneself against such accusations . . . ' He also insisted that he had not profited from currency exchanges, but did not address the more detailed corruption charges.[101] A day after he sent the first letter to Schultz, Greiser wrote a second one in which he gave the names of individuals who could attest to his military prowess during World War I: Friedrich Christiansen, now military commander in Holland; a Pilot Ritter, now stationed with the Army High Command; and Carl Clemens Bücker, the owner of the Bücker Airplane Factory (*Bücker-Flugzeugwerke*) in Rangsdorf.[102] While all these details may seem trivial, Greiser felt threatened by attempts to cast aspersion on his past life—otherwise, he would not have bothered to defend his earlier actions.

October 1943 marked the zenith of Greiser's power and prestige. That month, Himmler came not once, but twice to Posen. At the beginning of the month, he gave several important speeches at meetings of high-ranking Nazis that took place in Posen. Greiser, who was in charge of the organizational details, basked in the glow of hosting so many prominent dignitaries. In Posen on 4 October, Himmler gave his infamous speech to SS-leaders in which he briefly mentioned the extermination of the Jews: 'Most of you know what it means to see a hundred corpses lying together, five hundred, or a thousand. To have stuck it out and at the same time—apart from exceptions caused by human weakness—to have remained decent fellows, that is what has made us hard. This is a page of glory in our history which has never been written and shall never be written.'[103] Two days later, the SS-leader spoke to the assembled Reichsleiters and Gauleiters.[104] On 24 October, Himmler was again in Posen to give the keynote address at the Fourth Annual 'Day of Liberation' celebration. Film footage of the day shows Greiser and Himmler striding along the parade ground, inspecting NS-formations against a backdrop of Nazi banners and flags.[105]

But despite the high-level attention he enjoyed that fall, Greiser's world soon began to unravel. On 24 November, he suffered a freak accident: during a hunt, bits of a bullet shot off by his brother-in-law, Hubert Koerfer, ricocheted off the ground and hit him in the left eye. One bit remained lodged behind his eyeball. Greiser was taken to the University Clinic in Breslau.[106] Hitler sent a telegram wishing him a speedy recovery. Himmler, too, expressed concern. On 12 December, he asked Ernst-Heinrich Schmauser, the HSSPF in Breslau, to look into Greiser's condition. If Greiser was still in Breslau, Himmler wanted Schmauser to visit him and to 'bring him my kind regards and wishes for a quick recovery.'[107] By 30 December, Greiser was back in his Gau.[108] Despite several operations, he never regained sight in his left eye. In spring 1944, he had a final operation in which he received an artificial eye.[109]

On 3 January 1944, Greiser broadcast a speech to Nazi party members from his office. He spoke quite openly about his accident. He first made use of Hitler's reaction to the event. Since the Führer's aversion to hunting was well known, Greiser presumed that some of his enemies had hoped that the accident might spell his political demise. But Greiser declared that such 'malicious joy' (*Schadenfreude*) was misplaced: 'Already in the first days of my injury I had such a warm telegram from the Führer at my sick bed that it alone speeded my recovery by at least four weeks.' Greiser also told his audience: 'You can rest assured—and my colleagues who are now sitting with me are witnesses to this—that even the seriousness of this injury will not get me down.' As so often, Greiser posed defiant. Yet in the very next sentence, he waxed philosophical: 'One has to pay for everything in life and so this injury must be the price for something that has happened or will happen. I don't know exactly.' Greiser's words suggest that perhaps he had something on his conscience. But he then continued his bluster: 'But in no way do I feel myself hindered in my work by the fact that at the moment I can't use my left eye. Now more than ever I will master the tasks that the Führer has set for me.'[110] His accident certainly didn't hamper his rule of the Gau. He was soon engaged in detailed negotiations about the fate of the Litzmannstadt ghetto. Moreover, it didn't stop his zeal for hunting: he was known to have hunted again and, according to his adjutant, hit his target.[111]

When Greiser picked up Goebbels in a private rail car on 26 January 1944, the propaganda minister recorded, 'We immediately began discussing the situation in the Warthegau; it's to be seen as extraordinarily consolidated.'[112] Indeed, Greiser was firmly in control of his Gau: he faced little opposition in his bureaucracy; Germans in the Gau were muted in their criticism of him; and, in the face of enormous repression, the Poles were unable to mount an effective resistance movement. But Goebbels' words belied important facts. The Warthegau did not exist in isolation. Nazi Germany was in peril. British and American bombers had devastated cities throughout the Old Reich. The Red Army had retaken many areas of the Soviet Union. Hans Frank was barely able to control Poles in the General Government, unrest that threatened to spill into the Warthegau. For all that Greiser's rule seemed strong, his Gau rested on a shaky basis.

Germany's precarious military situation had a deep impact on the Warthegau. Greiser's biggest challenge was taking care of Germans fleeing to his Gau for safety. While Posen was bombed once in May 1941, and would be twice again in April and May 1944, these attacks involved relatively little damage.[113] The Gau was thus an attractive destination for those escaping Allied bombings. In an organized action, fifty-seven trains brought tens of thousands of women and children to the Warthegau.[114] Most of the 're-quartered' (*Umquartierte*) were directed to strangers' homes. The Hitler Youth placed school-aged children—brought on sixteen additional trains—in camps all around the Gau.[115] Other individuals, seeking safety with relatives or friends, came on their own. Greiser soon claimed that 100,000 women and children 'endangered by the skies' had sought refuge in the Gau.[116] But the real number was probably closer to 60,000.[117] Another group also came to the Gau: at the end of 1943, thirty-nine military hospitals housed some 15,620 injured soldiers.[118]

At the beginning of 1944, a new wave of refugees poured in: several hundred thousand ethnic Germans from Russia. Referred to as 'Black-Sea Germans' or 'Russia Germans,' they were fleeing the Red Army's advance into areas occupied by the Nazis. In early January 1944, Greiser told Ulrich Greifelt, chief of staff in the Reich Commissariat for the Strengthening of Germandom, that he was willing to take in 100,000 ethnic German agricultural workers.[119] On 11 January, he issued a decree stating that he had agreed to take in 50,000 ethnic Germans and, 'under certain circumstances,' even more. In his view, 'the taking in of these persons . . . represents for us a onetime opportunity to enrich the Gau with a significant number of valuable German people.' Greiser noted that he knew that this operation would bring 'difficulties and in part even very great difficulties.' But, he added, 'a discussion about these difficulties is . . . pointless and in the current situation time-consuming. Instead of palaver about whether or not this order is correct, I expect speedy initiative. In the life of the National Socialist Party, difficulties have existed only to be overcome, and as quickly as possible.'[120]

For Greiser, the new ethnic Germans were a welcome addition. He wasn't sure, though, that he'd be able to keep those now streaming into his Gau. He thus begged for even more ethnic Germans to come to the Warthegau. As he soon wrote to Himmler, he wanted all 140,000 ethnic Germans slated for resettlement from Transnistria. In his view, this would be 'just compensation for the efforts and work done happily in earlier years as well as with the ongoing resettlement action, so to say as reward.'[121] In the spring, he extracted a promise from Himmler that all those from Transnistria would remain permanently in the Gau.[122]

Through 15 November 1944, some 241,000 ethnic Germans from Ukraine trekked into the Gau.[123] As Greiser stated, 'The Führer gave me the task of making the Reichsgau Wartheland a German Gau. Only through the bringing in of German people is it possible to achieve this goal.' Integrating the refugees, he insisted, was a 'question of leadership (*Menschenführung*).' This was a 'task of the NSDAP that was greater than any that had been put to another Gau.'[124] It was indeed a huge task—one that consumed Gau authorities until the very end of the occupation.

To come to the Gau, Black-Sea Germans had journeyed from three to five months; some, especially young children, had died en route.[125] Many arrived with tuberculosis or other serious diseases.[126] Once in the Gau, they were housed in schools, fire stations, sports halls—anywhere that space could be found.[127] They needed everything from clothing to cutlery to furniture to toys.[128] Like their predecessors, they languished in 'temporary' camps. In May 1944, Greiser forbade visits to these camps, presumably so as to prevent news of the situation from leaking out.[129] The resettlers faced other disappointments, too. If they received private housing at all, it was generally very primitive.[130] They were also employed as field hands, rather than given their own farms to work. And they were prisoners in the Gau. Worried that they wouldn't return, Greiser refused to let them go to the Old Reich for work or other purposes.[131]

The Warthegau was now bursting at the seams. In January 1944, the party declared that no more 're-quartered' individuals were to come to the Warthegau.[132] But those seeking safety still crowded in. All sub-districts was thus required to take a certain quota of individuals, even when they had no spare rooms, no spare supplies of clothing or furniture, and no spare goodwill to welcome any more refugees.[133] In contrast to the Nazi vision of a rural Gau neatly populated by soldiers and sturdy peasants, the Warthegau had become a Gau of resettlement camps, military hospitals, and overcrowded farms and cities. Moreover, since virtually all able-bodied men were at the front, the Gau's German population was largely made up of women, children, the wounded, and the elderly.

In the face of the desperate German military situation, Greiser tried to win over a population that he had done so much to alienate: Poles. Already following the February 1943 Stalingrad defeat, he had seemed to portend a relaxation of anti-Polish policy. He called for factories with better equipment and facilities; as he noted, 'to a considerable extent, these improvements would also benefit the Polish factory workers.'[134] That February, he issued a language decree that condoned the use of Polish. In March, he declared that Poles, provided that they had received identity cards from local civilian or police authorities, could use public telephones to convey business-related messages.[135] Later in the year, he loosened restrictions on Poles sending food packages to Polish prisoners and POWs.[136] He also issued a secret memorandum about Germans subjecting Poles to corporal punishment. Although Polish rumors were circulating that he had issued a ban on beatings, Greiser insisted that he had not and would not issue such a ban. Nonetheless, 'a German who wildly beats Poles,' Greiser threatened, 'will be criminally prosecuted.'[137] After the discovery of mass graves of Polish officers in Katyn in April 1943, Greiser undertook a number of measures that suggested official sympathy. He ordered a delegation that included some Poles to visit the site. According to the *Ostdeutscher Beobachter*, the delegation flew to Smolensk 'to gain a first-hand impression of the dreadful Jewish–Bolshevik mass murder of former Polish officers.'[138] In very scripted events, Polish delegation members then reported their impressions to Polish workers in factories.[139] Greiser also ordered the police to display posters calling upon Poles to bring forth documents, especially pictures, that would help to identify the murdered officers.[140]

But Greiser still vacillated on his Polish policy. In January 1944, Goebbels reported that 'Greiser is carrying out a more generous policy. He has brought the Polish people in his Gau to absolute quiet, and the Poles feel good. They have work and food. They have ended up in a subservient role, but that suits them well.'[141] Greiser, however, insisted that 'my policy toward Poles has not changed. As always, the Pole will be treated harshly but fairly.'[142] Harshly treated they were. By winter 1944, some Poles were working a seventy-two-hour week.[143] But were they treated fairly? In spring 1944, Poles were given the right to lodge formal complaints against their employer. Greiser's agency, however, secretly ordered that such complaints always were to be dismissed.[144]

When the Black-Sea Germans poured into the Gau, Greiser at first refused to antagonize Poles by making them give up homes or jobs for the resettlers. As he decreed, 'I place value on not displacing Polish agricultural workers.'[145] But once he learned that the ethnic Germans from Transnistria would settle in the Gau permanently, he changed his policy toward Poles. As he wrote to his sub-district magistrates in March 1944, 'Now that we can count on the Black-Sea Germans staying in the Reichsgau Wartheland, Polish workers can be withdrawn. For this purpose, I now approve that small Polish businesses and other Polish worker families be evacuated and made available for other kinds of work.'[146] But this was still a tricky situation. In general, Greiser couldn't do without Poles in his Gau. By 'evacuating' some Poles, how much would he risk alienating the rest of the Polish population? As so often, his various aims clashed.

In summer 1944, Greiser made a dramatic attempt to win over Poles. Tens of thousands of Poles were working on fortifications intended to halt the Soviet onslaught. They enjoyed better work conditions than their compatriots: they took their meals with Germans, had similar accommodations, and received the same wages. On 14 August, Greiser gave a much publicized speech in Litzmannstadt in which he praised these Poles' work. In his words: 'In the last seven days, I have inspected all of the work on fortifications. I can speak only highly about especially the Litzmannstadt Poles. They have conducted themselves obediently and conscientiously despite all the difficult and unusual aspects of this work.' Poles working on the fortifications, he now announced, would receive the same 'good food' as the Germans. After the work ended, these 'loyal Poles' would also receive the same rations as Germans.[147]

Greiser wanted the Polish population to enjoy some official acknowledgment. While most Poles viewed the speech as simply another clumsy attempt to get them to work harder, some 'thought it good that Greiser, who is otherwise known as a hater of Poles (*Polenhasser*), finally managed to make such a concession.'[148] Among German segregation enthusiasts, the speech caused consternation. Greiser thus issued a statement that 'the basic principles of my Polish policy have not changed in any way. This is especially true of my key phrase: harsh but fair.' As he explained, Germans were still expected to act in a superior manner toward Poles; whenever possible, the strict separation of the two nationalities was to be preserved; and generally, Germans were placed only in supervisory positions.[149] Despite the hoops that Greiser went through to justify his speech, saying anything positive about Poles was a new departure for him. Although his speech was a reaction to Germany's crumbling military situation, it compromised his hard-line anti-Polish policy.

Throughout 1944, the Nazi regime's worsening military situation strained Gau resources. In early January, Greiser claimed that no Gau had made a higher percentage of its men available to the Wehrmacht.[150] Personnel shortages were now felt in every area of Gau administration. Greiser lost some important staff members: in January, Herbert Mehlhorn moved to Oppeln; in June, Harry Siegmund went to the Wehrmacht; and in July, Rolf-Heinz Höppner was relocated to Berlin.[151] On 6 June, the day that Allied troops landed in Normandy, Greiser decreed that vacation time would no longer be approved.[152] In July, Goebbels, now special plenipotentiary for total war, demanded that all Gaus provide additional manpower for military needs. Greiser, in his capacity as Reich defense commissar for the Gau, decreed that all men and women in the Gau between the ages of 15 and 65 were 'temporarily required to do emergency work' (*notdienstverpflichtet*), effective on 1 August.[153] At the end of August, Greiser ordered a further reduction of the Gau's administrative staff. Individuals could only work in jobs that involved maintaining domestic order, securing the food supply, or producing materials necessary for the war effort. Everyone else was to join the Wehrmacht or work in the armaments industry.[154] That same month, the Gau Self-Administration listed institutions now closing. Many of these had been considered essential for Germanizing the Gau: the Kaiser-Friedrich Museum; the State Bureau for Pre-History; and the State Bureau for the Preservation of Historical Monuments.[155] In September, the Reichsgau Theater stopped its performances.[156] Greiser wrote to Himmler that he was also shutting down many administrative offices so as to free up Germans to supervise Polish workers laboring on Gau fortifications.[157]

Greiser now took steps to prevent Germans from fleeing in advance of a Soviet invasion. To him, an early evacuation would not only make the Gau seem weak and ill prepared, but might also suggest to Poles that Germans were no longer sure about eventual victory.[158] In July 1944, he sent around a circular in which he insisted that 'there is no reason in any part of Gau territory to take even partial evacuation measures or . . . to consider departures.' Any leading men, he threatened, who were preparing to send their family members or their possessions to the Old Reich would lose their jobs. In addition, any apartment 'whose owner lost nerve and left the Gau' would be confiscated and given to new occupants. Greiser also promised that 'should contrary to expectations any evacuation measures for parts of the Gau territory became necessary, timely directives will be issued.'[159] One official later recalled that train stations and post offices were carefully guarded to prevent anyone from leaving the Gau.[160] Some Germans were actually punished for violating the decree. A top customs official in Kutno sent a few boxes with personal items to the Old Reich; he soon found himself in a concentration camp.[161]

Greiser used the 20 July 1944 assassination attempt against Hitler to boost morale for the flagging Nazi cause. On the very next day, he gave a big speech at the university. With the Great Hall filled to capacity, his words were transmitted to crowds milling outside. Greiser reiterated his faith in Hitler: 'Especially in these hard times, especially now I can say that only Adolf Hitler with his statesmanlike and strategic talents has saved us.

Especially now in war every family has experienced what it means to be prey to the hatred and disfavor of our enemies . . . Now, just when everyone feels that our fate is in the balance, when it will be decided whether or not we will persevere in what we believe, our unshakeable confidence rests on knowing that only we have an Adolf Hitler.'[162] On 3 August, another Gauleiter meeting was held in Posen. Himmler, the keynote speaker, rallied the Gauleiters to new heights of defensive energy.[163]

But Himmler was in Posen for another reason, too. On 1 August, the Warsaw Uprising had begun—the Polish Home Army hoped to liberate the city before Soviet troops could arrive. In Posen two days later, Himmler gave the HSSPF in the Gau, Heinz Reinefarth, orders to go to Warsaw.[164] Reinefarth became chief of operations to Erich von dem Bach-Zelewski, the German commander of the battle for Warsaw. Reinefarth also led a force of some 8,000 men, including a militarized police battalion from Posen.[165] Some of these men had staffed the Chełmno death camp.[166] According to Polish estimates, in their first few days in Warsaw, these and other troops under Reinefarth's command massacred some 30,000 to 40,000 civilians in the Wola and Ochota sections of Warsaw.[167]

Greiser closely followed events in Warsaw. Since he had sent Gau police, he expected a quid pro quo: plunder from Poland's largest and wealthiest city. Around 20 August, he made a day trip to the city's outskirts. He first met with Reinefarth and then with Bach-Zelewski.[168] Immediately afterwards, the 'Warsaw Action' began. In Gau parlance, this was the transport of plundered goods to the Warthegau. Greiser fought bitterly with officials in the General Government over the booty. In a 1947 interrogation, Ludwig Fischer, the Nazi governor of Warsaw, described Greiser's greed: 'in roughly mid-August Gauleiter Greiser directed a huge column of trains and other transportation means filled with goods, furniture, textiles, and medical supplies from Warsaw to Posen.' Fischer also declared, 'during the whole time that fighting was ongoing Greiser evacuated not only gasoline, but everything that he could.'[169]

Back in his Gau, Greiser closely tracked the inflow of goods. On 21 August, a draft circular noted that the booty 'will initially remain at the continuous and personal disposition of the Gauleiter.'[170] Greiser refused to have any customs paid on the incoming goods.[171] He insisted that he get updates about the shipments every three days or so. He also micro-managed the distribution of goods.[172] Although the Warsaw Action provided the

Gau with a much-needed windfall (especially now that it could no longer profit from Jewish labor or death), Gau officials actually struggled with the massive intake. The sorting and registration of goods taxed stretched personnel.[173] Storage space was hard to find. Gau officials bickered with their Reich counterparts over who should control the goods.[174] Huge quantities were involved: all told, some 478 train cars filled with goods came to the Gau.[175] This included 1,502.5 tons of material, including 15 tons of medicine, 25 tons of soap, 352 tons of paper, 342 tons of steel goods, 62 tons of steel machine parts, 208 tons of agricultural machinery, 24.5 tons of leather goods, 265 tons of textiles, and smaller amounts of other items.[176]

From the German perspective, Greiser—together with the Reich railroad system—had accomplished a remarkable feat: rather than destroying the material or allowing it to fall into Soviet hands, he had saved enormous quantities of goods for German military and other use.[177] Greiser's actions, however, infuriated Hans Frank. Frank thus forced him on the defensive. In mid-September, Frank noted that Koppe, now HSSPF in the General Government, had told him that Greiser had emphasized that he 'had had no intention of interfering in the matters of the General Government.' During the Uprising, Greiser claimed, he had only 'sent some security commandos to the Warsaw district that had since been recalled.'[178] This, of course, totally downplayed his rapacious actions. Frank and Greiser bickered over this and other matters until the very end of the Nazi regime.[179] Even as defeat was fast approaching, Greiser antagonized fellow Nazis by taking steps that benefited primarily his Gau.

But other, even more urgent matters now occupied Greiser. With Soviet troops already outside of Warsaw, a mere 75 miles from Litzmannstadt, the military situation was ominous. On 25 September, Hitler announced the founding of the Volkssturm, a national guard made up of men between the ages of sixteen and sixty not otherwise in the military.[180] In the Warthegau, Greiser was named Volkssturm head; he, in turn, named Reinefarth as his chief of staff.[181] Reinefarth, however, was soon ordered to the western front and temporarily left the Gau. Fritz Harder, Greiser's trusted adjutant, did what he could to organize the militia, but he had many other tasks. The Gau's Volkssturm eventually counted roughly 100,000 men, but this was hardly a sign of strength. It lacked supplies, everything from weapons to bullets to footwear. Since the Gau was such a large geographical entity, Volkssturm units were also spread thin. Moreover,

Greiser and others assumed that the Volkssturm would not be needed until March 1945; limited preparations were carried out in accordance with an early spring deadline.[182]

Greiser had built his image as a can-do Nazi. He wanted to cement it by making the Warthegau a 'model' Gau in its defense against the Red Army. In mid-October, he spent two weeks traveling around the eastern sub-districts of his Gau. Everywhere he went, he voiced trust in the future, the Führer, and the German people. In Berntal, on the border to the General Government, he declared to the assembled crowd, 'I will depend on you just as you can depend on me!'[183] The *Ostdeutscher Beobachter* paraphrased Greiser's words in Warthbrücken: 'No *Volk*, as the Gauleiter said, has so developed a feeling for the homeland (*Heimatgefühl*) and so heartfelt a love for the fatherland as the German. And therefore no *Volk* is so resolute in fighting to the end for its homeland and Fatherland.' Greiser's words continued: 'No one asks today when the "V 2" or "V 3" will come. What's certain is that the whole *Volk* arms our soldiers so that they can deal with all enemies. But more important than all material weapons is the belief in our inner strength and the trust in our Führer as the executor of our Lord's will.'[184] In an effort to rally support among the German population, Greiser even made positive reference to religion.

Greiser continued to insist that victory was in the offing. On 26 October, the Gau marked its fifth anniversary. Normally, Greiser declared, this day would have been used to 'account for what has been achieved in the past time. But today we don't have any time for that.' Unlike in past years, the 'Day of Liberation' was not a paid holiday. Instead, Greiser called for an even more determined work ethic that would ensure triumph: 'We Warthelanders, rooted in the soil, have the will to remain fanatical in our faith, strong in our determination, enduring in our resistance and loyal in the struggle—an indisputable victory will then only be a question of time.'[185] The 'Day of Liberation' was belatedly celebrated on Sunday, 5 November. This year, it also honored the so-called 'Warsaw fighters,' those men in the 'Fighting Group Reinefarth' who had massacred Warsaw inhabitants and secured huge amounts of loot for the Gau. Himmler, General Heinz Guderian, and the head of the Order Police, Kurt Daluege, all came to Posen. On a beautiful fall day, units of the Volkssturm, Hitler Youth, and the Reich Work Service (*Reichsarbeitsdienst*) joined the 'Warsaw fighters' for a ceremonial march in front of the Posen castle's high walls.[186]

In fall 1944, work continued on the building of fortifications (the so-called *Ostwallbau*) along a 100-kilometer line. The project had become much larger than initially intended: according to Greiser, with the use of the 'most modern pioneering technical findings,' it had taken on the 'dimensions of a large-scale fortifications work.'[187] Greiser boasted that some 206,000 Germans and Poles had worked to build 9,306 machine gun nests and 470 anti-tank gun emplacements.[188] At the same time, though, he and Wehrmacht personnel expected that these fortifications would not be all that crucial in halting Soviet troops. They thought that the Red Army would aim for strategic military posts to the southwest and northwest of the Warthegau, and not for the Gau itself. Greiser was also told that some fourteen Wehrmacht divisions would be ready to defend his Gau.[189]

In late 1944, busy with inspections, Greiser was barely at home. As he wrote to his daughter Rotraut on 26 December, 'with the momentary situation on the eastern front, up to the last minute I had to take care of everything concerning the building of the eastern wall and the Volkssturm, for my Gau is not far from the front.—All this time I was underway in my eastern sub-districts.' Greiser further told her that 'yesterday and today I've been at home, now I'm taking care of the most important mail, and this evening I'll be on the road again in my mobile hotel. So to say in passing I can only thank you for your lines and wish you all best in the new year. Warmest always, your Daddy.'[190] Rotraut never heard from her father again. Greiser, meanwhile, continued his hectic inspections and exhortations.

On 12 January 1945, Werner Naumann, state secretary in the Ministry of Propaganda, visited Posen. At a meeting with local Nazi leaders, Greiser declared that the year 1945 would be the 'year of the fanatics.' 'The German Volkssturm,' he insisted, 'will contribute as best it can to defend and secure this area . . . '[191] Later, in the Great Hall of the university, Naumann claimed that 'Never before has the German Wehrmacht and the German *Volk* been so prepared for an attack by its enemies as with the offensive of the Russians beginning now (near Baranow). This offensive will end in a triumph for the German armies like none that has ever been seen before.'[192] That evening Greiser held a dinner for his high-ranking guest at Mariensee.[193] Two days later, Naumann told Goebbels about his visit. According to Goebbels, 'Greiser is absolutely in control in his Gau. The Warthegau is determined that in the event of an advance of the Bolshevik offensive it will not evacuate but rather defend every village. Greiser is a definite leader personality who's capable of doing things.'[194] Just one short week later, Goebbels would have a very different view of Greiser.

In the Warthegau, events now occurred with great rapidity. As Greiser's adjutant, Paul Ruge, stated much later about his boss, 'one slap in the face (*Ohrfeige*) followed another.'[195] At the 12 January rally, no one seemed to have realized the importance of the Red Army's offensive. During the next few days, however, the situation dawned on Greiser. His mood swung from desperation to depression, frustration to resignation. According to Harder, Greiser 'gradually fell apart spiritually.' Harder continued: 'This condition was surely also the cause of his conduct in the last days and hours in the Wartheland, so indecisive, so contradictory, so without initiative and an unwillingness to do anything on his own "without a Führer-order." '[196] Others had a somewhat different impression of the Gauleiter. Hugo Heiser, director of waterways in Posen, later wrote that 'every day Greiser drove in the direction of the front in order to inform himself personally [about the situation]. Evenings he held meetings and reported very openly about his impressions. From day to day, these reports became grimmer. In the end, Greiser did not hide from us all that the situation was completely hopeless. He actually used a much crasser term.'[197]

On Sunday, 14 January, Greiser was present at the ceremonial opening of an electric train between Pleschen and Jarotschin. In Jarotschin, he was warmly welcomed, and he held a two-hour speech that was often interrupted by cheers from the capacity crowd—or so the *Ostdeutscher Beobachter* reported.[198] Greiser rushed home to Posen, though, since the Russians had advanced deep into the territory of the General Government. On 15 January, he attended troop exercises called 'Defense of the Fortress Posen.' Ruge later wrote that on 16 January there 'were worries in Posen about the quick advance of Russian tanks. Everyone waits for a counterattack by the German divisions.' That day, Goebbels recorded that both Greiser and Forster implored him to send Berlin Volkssturm units to their Gaus.[199] By 17 January the situation was dire: the Russians were practically at the Gau's borders. Greiser tried to get a military report from General Petzel, but Petzel had no information. Greiser then decided to inspect the situation himself: he drove via Kutno to Litzmannstadt and then on to Kalisch.

On paper, at least, Greiser had an evacuation plan. The Gau had been divided into three zones: A (the eastern areas, including Litzmannstadt),

B (central areas, including Hohensalza), and C (western areas, including Posen). Were an evacuation to be necessary, the Gau was to be emptied of Germans from east to west. Prior to a general evacuation, the codeword 'Florian Geyer' would be given to signal the evacuation of women with small children and other needy individuals. The orders for a general evacuation were code-named 'Frundsberg.'[200] All the while, however, the *Ostdeutscher Beobachter* was reporting sanguine news about how the Russians were being held off. The civilian population had little idea of the dangers it faced.[201]

Greiser refused to give evacuation orders. He didn't want to face up to reality, and he certainly didn't want his Gau to be the first evacuated. He even failed to tell his brother the truth. During his 17 January trip, Greiser saw Otto in Kutno. That evening, Otto told a local official that Arthur had assured him that the front was in good shape and that there was no need to even consider an evacuation. Arthur's visit may well have spelled a death sentence for his brother. Otto, reassured, saw little reason to rush out of town. But shortly thereafter, when the Russians arrived, they heard that Greiser was there and serving in a Volkssturm unit. Mistaking Otto for Arthur, they shot him dead along with several others.[202]

When Greiser reached Litzmannstadt, he met with the lord mayor of the city, Hans Trautwein. Their meeting was twice disrupted by air raids. Greiser gave orders to stop industrial production and to prepare for evacuation orders that were given that evening.[203] He then drove on to Kalisch. En route, he noted that German troops were desperately needed, but virtually none were present. That evening, Greiser later wrote, he saw the 'running away of ten thousands of German soldiers, who had no leadership (I met only two officers) . . . During the night and then on the next day in the eastern districts of my Gau the same picture! Now I had the necessary overview of the situation!'[204] Greiser arrived in Kalisch close to midnight. From the mayor's office he made numerous phone calls—to the Party Chancellery, to military officials, to Himmler, and to several others. In the course of these calls, he seems to have sought and received permission to give the 'Florian Geyer' signal for Zone A.[205] Much too late, the evacuation of women with small children began.

After a short night of sleep, Greiser drove back to Posen. There, in a desperate act (but with Himmler's permission), he took over the military command of Posen military district. 'Generalkommando Greiser,' headquartered in the Posen Castle, was established on a day when Petzel was in Oppeln to discuss the military situation.[206] That afternoon, Greiser declared to his assembled staff that Posen would be defended.[207] According to a Hitler-Youth functionary, Karl-Heinz Klinter, 'the Gauleiter described the situation as very serious and threatening since no troops were available to halt the successful breakthrough [of the Red Army] along a 400-kilometer stretch.'[208] Indeed, despite the enormous work that had gone into building fortifications, no one was there to man them when they were needed.[209]

Petzel soon got wind of Greiser's command. As he later wrote, since he and Greiser had generally gotten along, he was greatly surprised by Greiser's action, which he saw as an 'attempt to stab me in the back.'[210] Within twenty-four hours, Petzel managed to reverse the situation, and Greiser was relieved of his command.[211] The next day, Klinter noted a change in Greiser: 'at least as concerned military measures, he was deliberately uninterested and viewed matters more as a spectator than as an actor.'[212] Moreover, Klinter later recalled, 'already on this day the general tone of Greiser's words was no longer "hold out to the end." The events of the last days seem to have awakened in him considerable doubts.'[213]

On Saturday morning, 20 January, Russian tanks reached the Warta River near Posen. Greiser came to Petzel's headquarters to discuss evacuation orders for Posen. It was decided, however, to seek the Führer's approval; just the day before, Hitler had issued a decree insisting that any important military decision receive his permission.[214] That same morning, Greiser had also received a telegram from Bormann stating that the Führer had ordered him to leave Posen. Greiser now called Hitler's headquarters. He was not permitted to speak with Hitler—only with Bormann. Witness accounts of this conversation make no mention of a discussion about evacuation orders. Instead, they focus on what Bormann said to Greiser about what he was to do, namely leave the city immediately for Frankfurt/Oder. Bormann assured Greiser that it was just a matter of time before the Warthegau would be reconquered.[215] As discussed in the next chapter, Bormann may well have 'tricked' Greiser into leaving the Warthegau.

Around noon, on his own, Greiser issued evacuation orders for Posen; all Germans were to leave the city by midnight.[216] Never one to dispute his Führer's orders, Greiser also made ready for his personal departure. He paid a final visit to his son Erhardt's grave.[217] At 6 p.m., he held a last meeting with his staff. Klinter, who was there with just twelve to fifteen others (the rest were already on their way out of town), later recalled: 'Before us stood a broken man, who began the meeting with the words, "Gentlemen, in one, at the latest two days, the Russians will be in Posen." He then spoke in moving words about how he had to leave the Wartheland with his life's work unfinished. He also added *that according to a Führer order he was personally being recalled to Berlin to do a special task for the Reichsführer-SS and was to leave this evening*.'[218] Greiser seems to have made this last part up; he wanted to counter doubts that he was leaving Posen to save his skin. Perhaps he sensed that fleeing the city would soon come back to haunt him.

Around 9:30 p.m., Greiser, accompanied by Ruge, left Posen. By then, the whole Gau was in chaos. The evacuation orders came too late to have any systematic response. Instead, Germans were frantically trying to leave the Gau. Despite earlier plans for an organized flight, there were very few trek leaders, no Order Police to regulate traffic, and little or no medical or other available assistance.[219] In freezing cold, people waited all night in Posen and other stations to get on trains.[220] Streets leading westward were completely clogged with cars and carts stuffed full of people and their possessions. All this apparently moved Greiser. As Ruge later wrote, 'Greiser barely spoke. I saw how difficult it was for him to carry out this order, especially since he saw the misery and desperate straits in the streets, yet couldn't help. Shortly before the border to the Old Reich, Greiser left the car and lingered a bit at the memorial stone for his son who had been killed there.' Greiser and Ruge went on to Pinne, where they spent the night at Air Wing (*Luftflotte*) headquarters as guests of Colonel-General Robert Ritter von Greim.[221]

In the Warthegau, some Volkssturm units fought valiantly for a few days, but then collapsed with heavy losses. A few officials remained behind in Posen or were sent in to organize basic necessities, but they had all left by 3 February.[222] Thereafter, General Ernst Mattern commanded 'Fortress Posen' with some 12,000 to 14,000 men of varying military capabilities.[223] Mattern was soon replaced by Major General Gonell. Surrounded and besieged, Gonell held out until 23 February. He shot himself just as the defense of the 'Fortress' became untenable. Mattern then signed the act of capitulation.[224] As Hitler allegedly commented: 'In contrast to Breslau,

Posen is no longer a German city.'[225] The comparison was very unfavorable to Greiser. Karl Hanke, the Gauleiter of Lower Silesia, led a fanatical defense of Breslau; months after Posen, and only on 6 May, Breslau fell to Soviet troops.

After the Nazi defeat, nothing angered former German residents of the Warthegau more than Greiser's actions during the last days of German occupation. Germans fled the Gau under truly awful conditions. There were no soup kitchens or other facilities for those trekking westward. Little children died of cold and hunger.[226] Many fleeing Germans were overtaken by Soviet troops. As they later wrote in hair-raising detail, they were raped, murdered, or otherwise terrorized by marauding soldiers.[227] An estimated 50,000 Germans died during their flight from the Gau.[228] Given these events, many Germans believed that Greiser had failed miserably just when his leadership should have been strongest. Some saw his flight from the Gau as an act of naked self-preservation.[229] Others thought that Greiser should have helped the fleeing population reach safety, and then sought a hero's death defending the city.[230] General Petzel, the commanding general in Posen, took another tack: he believed that Greiser's tendency to fail in challenging moments was a character flaw. He had seen reports about Greiser during World War I that suggested that he fell apart just when he needed to be strongest. 'And so too it was in his activity as Gauleiter of the Warthegau.'[231]

How justified were these criticisms? Certainly, Greiser should have started the evacuation sooner. Had the evacuation begun just a few days earlier, a more orderly flight might have occurred, and many Germans might have been spared an encounter with Soviet troops. Greiser could also have taken a more active role in directing the treks. This surely would have improved his Nazi reputation, and might have kept some Germans from suffering great misery. In January 1945, however, Greiser was trapped between ambition and reality. By trying to uphold his reputation as a strong, decisive Gauleiter, to avoid seeming 'defeatist,' he created a situation that led to enormous human misery. By delaying evacuation orders, Greiser forced Germans to flee under terrifying conditions. By insisting on following Hitler's orders to leave Posen, Greiser also came off as a coward, especially given the experiences of Germans leaving just a few hours later. Greiser's actions were a disastrous mix of authoritarian rule and passive subordination. Of all the blots that stained his Nazi biography, his flight from Posen proved the blackest. Then, too, his Gau, far from being a last-ditch redoubt, was the first to succumb to the Red Army. So much for a 'model defense' of the 'model Gau' by a 'model Nazi.' Greiser had fallen very fast and hard—and yet worse was still to come.

9

'Two Souls in My Breast:' Trial and Execution

When Arthur Greiser fled the Warthegau, his active life as a Nazi official was over. He would spend the rest of his life—eighteen months in all—defending his past actions to Nazi leaders and, later, to a Polish court. Until the end of the Nazi regime, Greiser desperately sought to make up for his alleged desertion of Posen. But everywhere he went, he was met with disbelief, odium, or worse. Once arrested, Greiser faced an entirely different set of problems: answering for his actions in the Warthegau. As in earlier life transitions, he now tried to reinvent his persona and past. Yet he did this so unconvincingly that he drew only further disdain. The paunch and bravura of his heady Gauleiter days were gone; Greiser became a pale caricature of his former self. His torment finally ended when he was hanged in July 1946.

On 21 January 1945, Greiser drove to Frankfurt/Oder. The next day, Monday, 22 January, was his forty-eighth birthday. Some later claimed that he enjoyed a wildly excessive birthday celebration on the night of 21–2 January.[1] But his adjutant, Paul Ruge, who kept a record of Greiser's activities between January and May 1945, has insisted otherwise. According to Ruge, there were 'no orgies,' and Greiser and Maria spent that night sleeping on a bare floor since no beds were available.[2] Greiser was also rumored to have brought thirty wagons full of furniture and other belongings with him when he left the Gau.[3] Ruge recalls one truck with an attached trailer that carried Greiser's belongings (including a good amount of red wine) from Mariensee to Frankfurt/Oder.[4] On the afternoon of his birthday, Greiser and a small staff drove on to Landsberg in

Mark-Brandenburg. There, they set up headquarters in Hotel Vater.[5] While his staff met incoming treks and directed them onwards, Greiser occupied himself with his own fate.

Greiser realized that he had to fight for his Nazi reputation. On 23 January, Goebbels noted a telephone conversation with him: '[Greiser] complains a great deal that in Berlin circles he is being accused of a premature evacuation of Posen and of desertion. One can't accuse him of this, since on Saturday he received an order from the Führer to leave Posen. I, though, would have tried to actively oppose such a Führer order.'[6] That same day, Greiser drove to Deutsch-Krone, where Himmler was quartered. The SS-leader wished him a belated happy birthday and gave him a large world atlas with a personal dedication that ended with 'Now we'll certainly win!' Himmler convinced Greiser that he would be back in Posen in six to eight weeks. Two days later, Robert Ley, head of the German Labor Front, came to Landsberg. He and Greiser had a long, private conversation, after which Greiser 'was very annoyed.'[7] As Goebbels later heard from Ley, 'Greiser wanted to explain to him [Ley] the correctness of his premature evacuation of Posen; but Ley refused to acknowledge these arguments.'[8] On 26 January, Greiser again visited Himmler. He begged to be allowed to fly into 'Fortress Posen,' or to be sent to the Navy. On 29 and 30 January, Greiser had additional, apparently inconclusive discussions with Himmler.[9] The SS-leader was reluctant to allow Greiser to engage in futile pursuits.

Greiser now became the defeatist Gauleiter who had abandoned his post. This must have been utterly debilitating. Among top Nazis, Goebbels was most scathing of Greiser. Just when the propaganda minister was urging the German population to stay the fight, Greiser had done the opposite. On 22 January, Goebbels commented that 'our Gauleiters in the East conduct themselves well; they show a courageous and manly posture, with the exception of Greiser, who inexplicably withdrew from Posen even though the city was not even threatened . . . I had not expected that from Greiser; indeed, the opposite, I was always convinced that he was a strong man, but as this example shows, that was apparently not the case.'[10] Two days later, Goebbels noted, 'Greiser must be totally ashamed of himself . . . But he doesn't belong to the old guard of Gauleiters. These stand when it burns at their posts and they do not allow developments to deter them at all.'[11] As Goebbels saw it, Greiser's past suggested, and his actions now proved, that he did not have true Nazi stuff. Goebbels even wanted Greiser executed. As he wrote on 26 January, 'The Führer is also very angry about Greiser's conduct. If I were in his position, I would put Greiser before a National Socialist People's Court and give him the punishment that he deserves.'[12] Hitler, however, refused to begin proceedings against Greiser.[13]

On 1 February, Greiser drove to Berlin and checked into the Hotel Adlon. He then went to the Reich Chancellery, but Bormann refused him an audience with Hitler. According to Ruge, 'Bormann claimed to be astonished to see Greiser in Berlin and not in Posen defending his Gau capital city as Hitler had ordered. When Greiser showed Bormann the telegram that he had signed and that stated that Greiser was to go immediately to Frankfurt/Oder, Bormann claimed that Greiser had misinterpreted it. He made it clear that Greiser would have to take responsibility for his actions. Greiser was beside himself...' Greiser, however, had a contact in the Reich Chancellery who showed him the original telegram in Borman's handwriting that conveyed Hitler's order. With that, 'every possible mistake was ruled out and it was absolutely proven that the telegram had been sent on Bormann's order.'[14]

The Bormann telegram and its significance has long preoccupied those interested in Greiser. Although Greiser and Bormann had often cooperated on Warthegau policy, tensions developed between the two men in the later years of the Nazi regime. In 1943 Bormann officially assumed the position of Hitler's secretary and, in this capacity, controlled all access to the Führer. Greiser was frustrated that Bormann kept him from Hitler.[15] In addition, in the waning days of the Third Reich, Himmler and Bormann became great rivals. Some have argued that Bormann 'tricked' Greiser into leaving the Gau so as to undermine Himmler; by showing that one of Himmler's favorites was a coward, Bormann hoped to weaken the SS-leader's position.[16] Others developed an even more elaborate explanation of Bormann's telegram to Greiser. They claimed that Himmler was pushing Hitler to make personnel changes, including naming Greiser interior minister. Bormann, however, not caring for this proposal, recalled Greiser to Berlin prematurely so that he would look bad to Hitler and Himmler's plans would be scuttled.[17]

In all likelihood, Bormann did want to harm Greiser, though his actions in response to the situation were mixed. Bormann actually defended Greiser in January and February 1945. As Goebbels recorded on 29 January (two days before Bormann told Greiser how surprised he was to see him in Berlin!), 'Bormann protects Greiser because Greiser supposedly received from the Führer instructions to leave Posen prematurely.'[18] On

12 February, Bormann also issued an official circular titled 'Rumors in Connection with the Evacuation Measures in Gau Wartheland.' In it, he stated that Greiser had acted honorably: 'Gauleiter Greiser, who reported that he would allow himself to be surrounded with the military garrison in Posen, left the city on the express order of the Führer.'[19] Bormann thus set the official record straight. It's unlikely, though, that this circular improved Greiser's negative reputation. More important, in February 1945 Bormann could have allowed Greiser a meeting with Hitler or found some other way to burnish his reputation. But he didn't.

In spring 1945, Greiser was still Gauleiter and Reichsstatthalter of the Warthegau. August Jäger, his deputy Reichsstatthalter, established an office of Gau affairs in Potsdam to deal with ongoing administrative matters.[20] Greiser, however, had little to do with the office. Instead, on 3 February, Bormann told Greiser that Hitler had decided that he was to go to an SS-military hospital near Karlsbad to cure a gall-bladder condition that had bothered him for years. The Warthegau would be back in German hands in six to eight weeks, Bormann claimed, and Greiser was to go back to his Gau 'healthy and rested.' For Greiser, Karlsbad was surely a miserable prospect: he was stripped of any possibility of proving himself a fanatical, heroic Nazi. But he readily followed Hitler's orders. He spent more than six weeks in Karlsbad, from 6 February to 26 March; Maria joined him there. Greiser now wrote a report about the Gau's Volkssturm and possibly others that have not been found.[21] He saw a great deal of Curt von Gottberg, the notorious higher SS and police leader (HSSPF) in Central Russia and Belarus.[22] On 17 March, Greiser also had a long meeting with General Andrey Vlasov; later in the spring, he unsuccessfully tried to see Vlasov again.

After his 'cure' was completed, Greiser went to Mitteldarching in Bavaria and three days later to Berlin. In the capital, he stayed at the Reich Physicians' Chamber headquarters in Berlin-Grunewald.[23] Ingrid, Greiser's daughter, was now a secretary for Professor Hellmut Haubold, an SS-officer and influential cancer statistician who headed the Chamber's Foreign Department.[24] Ingrid had left the Foreign Ministry in October 1944 to work for Haubold; the two were apparently romantically linked.[25] During his two-week stay in Berlin, Greiser tried again to see Hitler, but without success. On 8 April, he had a last, long talk with Himmler, but the content of the discussion remains unknown.

In Berlin, Greiser repeatedly saw Gottlob Berger, head of the SS-Leadership Main Office, and the man in charge of all POWs in German custody.[26] Curiously, after Greiser was arrested, an interrogation report noted: 'Subject stated that in April 1945 he was in Berlin and held a conference with Allied medical P[O]W's for the purpose of improving the health standards in German P[O]W camps. Stated that he arranged the escape [of] General Wannaman [*sic*] and Col. Fritzley [*sic*], aircorps, to Switzerland and gave them a plan for a German truce and that he also arranged for a plane to be at their disposal. The plan was that Germany would join the British and the Americans and make a combined drive on Russia.'[27] Given everything that we know about Greiser, this sounds far-fetched. But Greiser, it turns out, did not invent this story from thin air. In January 1945, before Greiser came to Berlin, Berger was involved with an operation that brought two Americans, Brigadier General Arthur Vanaman and Colonel Delmar Spivey, POWs in Stalag Luft III, to Berlin. Vanaman and Spivey, in turn, managed to get Berger to allow trucks with food for POWs to enter Germany from Switzerland. In addition, sometime in April, Berger held a conference in Berlin-Schwanenwerder about improving POW conditions. At the 1948 Wilhelmstrasse Trial in which Berger stood accused, Haubold described this conference.[28] Greiser obviously knew about the conference and the Vanaman and Spivey matter. But did Berger or Himmler actually involve him in these efforts? We don't know. Most likely, Greiser was simply told of them and, in custody, claimed participation in them as part of his unfolding defense strategy.

On 17 April, Greiser returned to Mitterdarching. He was accompanied by Ruge, as well as two Warthegau subordinates, Wilhelm Maul and Albert Derichsweiler. Ingrid and Haubold visited him there.[29] From Mitterdarching, Greiser was constantly on the move, trying to find a place for himself in the disintegrating Reich. He saw Berger, who was now also in southern Germany, on at least three different occasions. On 27 April, he visited high-ranking SS-leaders temporarily staying in an SS-Junker School in Bad Tölz. He then decided to go east to offer his services to Josef 'Sepp' Dietrich, the commander of the Sixth SS-Panzer Army. As Ruge recorded Greiser telling him: 'Later he didn't want to be accused of cowardliness. He regretted very much that he hadn't stayed in Posen and shared the fate of the city . . .' The next day, Dietrich told a 'disappointed' Greiser that he didn't expect any more fighting, and rejected his offer of service. On 30 April and 1 May, Greiser was in St. Johann in the Austrian

Tyrol, where the SS-Leadership Main Office was temporarily located. There he learned of Hitler's death. Ruge didn't record Greiser's reaction, but it must have been some mix of shock, grief, and desperation. On 2 May, Greiser met up with Heinz Reinefarth, the last HSSPF in the Warthegau. Reinefarth stayed with him until the German capitulation. Greiser spent his last days of freedom in Krimml, near Salzburg. On 10 May, Ruge bade farewell to his boss. At this time, he later wrote, 'Greiser expected the Americans any moment and had no fear of this meeting. Greiser was willing to answer to any court, for the decisions that he had made had been done for the good of Germany. If he was to be handed over to Poles or Russians, however, then he wanted to commit suicide beforehand, for there a big show trial would take place and one could expect only one judgement: death.'[30] Greiser accurately anticipated his fate.

On 16 May, Greiser was arrested by patrols belonging to the 242nd Infantry Regiment of the 42nd (Rainbow) Infantry Division. The Americans had been tipped off by a civilian close to the Austrian underground. Led by Major James Cunningham and Major B. J. Smith, the patrols found Greiser, together with Maria, 'hiding out in a lodge up in the mountains' in Krimml. At the time of his arrest, Greiser had 10,088 Reichsmarks (roughly $2,500 in 1941 dollars or $35,000 in 2007 dollars) and two briefcases of documents.[31] The papers mostly concerned Greiser's past, and included extensive documentation that he had pulled together in response to Robert Reuter's 1943 allegations about his past actions. He told the arresting agents that he had saved the papers so as to write a book. He also announced that he didn't want to be delivered over to the Russians: 'Subject stated that he is not afraid of a War Crime trial before an Allied Court but prefers to be shot before handed over to the Russians.' Greiser knew that he had things to answer for. He now began to construct a new biography for himself, one that he would flesh out during his trial: 'Further states that he is not responsible for atrocities or executions committed by the SS and Gestapo. There was no concentration camp in his Gau.'[32] While this last detail was technically true, Greiser was, of course, playing down his responsibility for what had occurred in the Warthegau. He also claimed that he had helped American POWs Vanaman and Spivey earlier that spring.

Two days after his arrest, Greiser arrived at an American internment camp in Bad Wörishofen, a Bavarian spa town.[33] On 1 June, he was questioned at the Seventh Army Interrogation Center. He now concocted sheer nonsense about his past. About his Danzig days, for example, 'Greiser describes Rauschning as a friend with whom he had stood in agreement on many political issues.' His attitude toward the party: 'Greiser maintains, even today, that the original platform of the Party was good. In practice, however, these original principles were greatly distorted and for several years already he claims to have been near desperation. Out of a feeling of "German loyalty," however, he stuck to his post. He claims often to have discussed these matters with his wife (the only person with whom he could speak freely) and that both had come to the conclusion that they must remain at their post until the war had been lost.' On the murder of Jews: 'Greiser claims to have been in complete disagreement with the Nazis' persecution of the Jews. He interpreted the original Party program as intending to break the hold of the Jews on German economy and cultural life. He never interpreted it as meaning the physical extinction of the Jews.' Greiser invoked his sister Käthe to give poignancy to his words: 'He states that his own sister had married a Jew who emigrated to New York and that his sister's fate had made a deep personal impression on him and caused him to do a lot of thinking.' Greiser also lied about the ghettos: 'Of the Ghettos in Poland he claims to have known and to have had the impression that the Jews there lived fairly comfortable [*sic*]; but he maintains that he had no knowledge of the existence of the so-called extermination camps and that he had only learnt of what went on in the concentration camps on his capture.'[34]

In an effort to bolster his version of his biography, Greiser wrote to Carl Burckhardt, the former League of Nations high commissioner in Danzig and now president of the International Red Cross: 'Today I have spent exactly ten weeks in American internment and am currently in Camp Augsburg. I know nothing about my further fate, just as little my wife and I have any possibility of sending each other news.' He asked Burckhardt to intervene on his behalf: 'You will surely happily confirm that not only in my work and in my official capacity in the Danzig Free City, but also personally in my most inner conviction, that I often and loudly enough raised a warning voice against the threatening developments that were pressing for war.' Greiser tried to style himself as a man of peace. He also expressed his hope that Burckhardt or one of his representatives might come to see him.[35] Greiser never got an answer; Burckhardt surely didn't want to compromise himself by helping a Nazi war criminal.

In Allied captivity, Greiser was a broken man. He had traded pride for public scorn, privilege for prison, plenty for privation. He was subject to stringent Allied guidelines that prisoners receive 'minimum clothing, accommodation and medical care' and a daily food intake of 1,550 calories.[36] In October, he was moved to Camp 75 Ludwigsburg.[37] Never resilient in times of stress, Greiser suffered terrible symptoms related to a recurrence of a middle-ear infection. A doctor recommended an immediate operation.[38] On 12 November, Greiser was taken to the Seventh Army Internee Hospital 2 in Karlsruhe.[39] He was treated there for four months.[40] He apparently also suffered from depression. At the end of March, Maria wrote to Greiser that she had received a letter from him dated 1 March, but that it had conveyed 'hopelessness.' She now tried to raise her husband's spirits: 'Arthur, if you really love me, then you have to pull yourself together and believe and want. You are not alone and lonely, I am there for you and I suffer much worrying about you.—Faith can move mountains and God will not totally abandon us!'[41]

On 23 October 1945, the Polish government asked that Greiser be delivered to Poland for trial as a war criminal. It was acting according to the Moscow Declaration, signed by Allied foreign ministers two years earlier, that stated that war criminals who had committed crimes in occupied countries would be sent back to those countries and stand trial and be sentenced on the basis of those countries' laws. On 20 December 1945, the Allied Control Council issued Law No. 10, regulations to cover such proceedings; those returned were to be tried and sentenced within six months of delivery.[42] After receiving the request for Greiser, American military officials channeled it through various agencies. On 21 February 1946, Charles Fahy, director of the legal division of the U.S. Group Control Council, authorized that Greiser be sent to Poland.[43]

On 13 March, Greiser was called out of an English lesson at the hospital and transferred to a German police jail in Frankfurt/Main. As he later wrote to Maria, he was outraged by the treatment he received at the hands of Germans: 'What foreigners have never done, Germans managed to accomplish. Germans! In my condition—I could barely stand—, detectives brought me to and from questioning in chains. For the first time in my life. This jail will always stay in my memory as a bee house, but instead of honey I had to starve terribly.'[44] Greiser could barely contain his anger against Germans who, to him, must have seemed turncoats; just a year earlier, they would have treated him with deference, but now they treated him with contempt. After two weeks in Frankfurt, Greiser was put on a plane to Warsaw.

Greiser arrived in Poland at 3:45 p.m. on Maria's thirty-eighth birthday, 30 March 1946.[45] Film footage shows Greiser in his prison cell in the Mokotów Prison in Warsaw. Although he had visibly aged and lost weight, he still gave the impression of a tall, strong, muscular man. Clad in a large sweater, he came out of his cell to receive a bowl of slop and then sat at the back of his cell at a little table eating his food. While he looked disgusted that he was being filmed, he also seemed resigned to his treatment.[46] The fact that his head was bandaged, presumably due to his recent middle-ear infection, may have been the source for later allegations that he had been mistreated in American captivity by interrogators of Polish origins.[47] Greiser himself wrote that he had been 'taunted and beaten' in one of his first interrogations in US custody.[48]

It is difficult to determine what Greiser's experience in Warsaw was really like. While Greiser later wrote that he enjoyed decent conditions there, *The New York Times* reported that he was part of a ' "circus" with two caged Nazis' in Warsaw.[49] As the Associated Press notice read, 'Polish militiamen are staging their own sideshow here, with Ludwig Fischer and Arthur Greiser . . . as the star attractions and food as the admission price. The men who governed Warsaw and Posen were placed in a cage, so all Warsaw could see them before their war-crimes trials a few weeks hence. A permit to look at the caged Nazis costs a loaf of bread and five eggs. The food is given to court workers as extra rations promised them.'[50] This account seems exaggerated. Perhaps a few individuals bribed prison officials to see Greiser and Fischer. But had there been a full-fledged 'circus,' Greiser surely would not have stated his satisfaction with Polish prison conditions.

This Associated Press report may have been the source for the most famous legend surrounding Greiser: that prior to his hanging he was paraded around the streets of Poznań (as Posen was now called) in a cage while the local population pelted him with rotten food and other objects.[51] Another version of this story, found in an unpublished memoir written by a German interned in a Poznań camp after the war, claimed that Greiser was displayed in the lions' and tigers' cage of the Poznań zoo for the admission price of 50 złoty.[52] These rumors about Greiser's supposed ill treatment were likely meant to fuel resentment against Poles for taking

German homelands; Germans emphasized the supposed barbarity of Poles so as to de-legitimize Polish rule of formerly German territory.

On 13 June, Greiser was brought to Poznań and held at the jail on Młyńskie Street.[53] Two days later, he wrote a letter that was intended as much for the censors as for its addressee, Maria. Greiser stated that he had enough to eat and, since he wasn't given any tobacco, he had stopped smoking. He claimed that Poland, more than the Reich, offered 'order and discipline and correctness,' and that should he be given a choice about the matter, he would prefer to live there than in the current Germany: 'But as strange as it may sound, I have the feeling that I've come home again and while I'm in prison I just haven't found the right apartment yet.' Greiser further wrote that he had twice read the Bible in Warsaw and now 'greatly regretted that Hitler had not held to and been advised by Solomon's maxims. Then years ago Poland would have been a sovereign state again and I would not be sitting in the dock! In any event, I have put my matter in the hands of our Lord God and humbly await his decision.'[54] On arrival in Poznań, Greiser had been given a copy of the indictment against him.[55] In his letter to Maria, Greiser proclaimed his total innocence of all the crimes with which he was charged.

In the same letter, Greiser wrote that he had seen a newspaper article showing that Mariensee had become a vacation home for the children of Poznań workers.[56] 'I'm sure,' he wrote to Maria, 'that exactly like me, you'll find favor in this truly socialist solution. I myself would be satisfied if for the rest of my life I could live in a hut, in a makeshift home, or even just in a room, if only you were with me! It's very hard to bear everything alone and not have anyone with whom I can speak, especially since the indictment gives me the feeling that it's a matter of life and death.'[57] With his letter to Maria, Greiser was trying to convey to Polish authorities that he was a friend of Poland; that he had found religion; that he was not responsible for the crimes committed; and that he wished only for a quiet future.

While Greiser sat in prison, Polish authorities prepared his trial. On 31 August 1944, the Polish Committee of National Liberation, the temporary government established by Stalin, had issued a decree that foresaw harsh punishment for participation in the murder or torture of civilians and POWs; the capture or carrying off of persons sought by the SS or the Gestapo; and the instigation of, or assistance in, such crimes. Following up on this decree, the government established a Supreme National Tribunal on Greiser's forty-ninth birthday, 22 January 1946. Major war criminals were to be brought before it. The Tribunal's decisions were final, with the proviso that the Polish president had the right of pardon.

Greiser's trial was the first of seven major trials held before the Tribunal. All were intended not only to determine the accused's guilt or innocence, but also to educate the Polish public about the Nazi occupation.[58] Each featured a particular aspect of Nazi crimes; in Greiser's trial, prosecutors showcased crimes committed against the Polish people.[59] At the same time, Polish communist authorities were eager to put on competent trials against Nazi war criminals, so as to show how their treatment of war criminals differed from Nazi judicial practice. Judges and prosecutors were also chosen for their legal prowess.[60] In addition, Polish authorities provided decent defense lawyers to the defendants.

Two prominent Poznań attorneys, Stanisław Hejmowski and Jan Kręglewski, were assigned to Greiser. Both asked to be released from the case. As Hejmowski noted in his petition, every Poznań family had suffered terrible losses during the occupation. He himself had been deported to the General Government, and the Germans had killed two of his brothers. The lawyers' pleas, however, were rejected.[61] Despite their loathing for their client, both attorneys made good-faith efforts on Greiser's behalf; they made persuasive defense arguments.

Although Greiser was tried according to the 1932 Polish Civil Criminal Code and the 31 August 1944 decree, the language and principles of the International Military Tribunal (IMT) deeply influenced the proceedings against him. Poland recognized the Four-Power Agreement of 8 August 1945 that established the IMT Charter. A Polish delegation was granted access to the Nuremberg proceedings and had a suite of offices in the IMT building. It had the right to inspect documents and other evidence dealing with Polish matters; it could also interview suspects who had been taken into custody. It could not, however, take part in the actual proceedings.[62] One of the two prosecutors in Greiser's trial, Jerzy Sawicki, was a member of the Polish delegation to the IMT.[63] Sawicki accompanied Hartley Shawcross, the lead British prosecutor at Nuremberg, when he visited Warsaw in mid-June; Shawcross apparently had a particular interest in Greiser's actions in Danzig.[64] Although plans were made for Robert Jackson, the chief prosecutor at the Nuremberg trial, to come to Posen to attend Greiser's trial, the visit did not take place.[65]

Polish jurists structured the indictment against Greiser according to the IMT's Charter. The three charges that they brought against Greiser included and combined the four main Nuremberg charges—the Common Plan or Conspiracy, crimes against peace, war crimes, and crimes against humanity. Greiser as 'one of the leaders of the . . . (NSDAP) took part in the activities of a criminal organization, which that party was, its purpose being through violence, waging of aggressive wars and the commission of crimes, to establish in Europe and in particular in the states bordering on Germany, among them that of Poland, the national-socialist regime . . .' Greiser had allegedly conspired to commit 'crimes against peace:' 'on behalf of the . . . . (NSDAP), he [Greiser] was in charge of its branch' in Danzig and 'conspired with the chief government organs of the German Reich . . .' to cause 'warlike activities' aimed at depriving the Polish state of its independence. Finally, the indictment combined the third and fourth charges at Nuremberg, even though it did not use those exact phrases. As it phrased it, by 'exceeding the rights accorded to the occupying authority by international law,' Greiser had violated the Hague Convention that defined the laws of war.

Moreover, by 'contravening the principles of the law of nations and the postulates of humanity and the conscience of nations, both on his own initiative and in carrying out the unlawful instructions of the civil and military authorities of the German Reich, he acted to the detriment of the Polish State and of its citizens, by inciting to, and assisting in the commission of, and by committing personally the following offenses: (1) Individual and mass murders of civilians and of prisoners of war; (2) Acts of ill-treatment, persecution and bodily harm against such persons, and other acts causing their ill-health; (3) Systematic destruction of Polish culture, robbery of Polish cultural treasures and germanization of the Polish country and population, and illegal seizure of public property; (4) Systematic and illegal deprivation of the Polish population of its private property.'

The indictment also charged that Greiser had repeatedly made statements about the 'cultural and social inferiority' of the Polish nation. He had participated 'in the persecution and wholesale extermination of Polish citizens of Jewish race or origin . . .' He had ill-treated Poles by ruining their health; locking them up in 'jails, prisons, and various camps;' deporting them to the General Government; and subjecting Polish children to Germanization. Greiser was also charged with introducing the German Ethnic Register (DVL); depriving Poles of civil rights; raising the marriage age for Poles; depriving Poles of the means to practice their religion; killing or deporting Polish clergy; exploiting Polish labor; and closing down all Polish cultural institutions.[66] Placing these charges in the context of Polish law, the indictment enumerated how each of these charges violated the 1932 Polish Civil Criminal Code and the 31 August 1944 decree.[67] Finally, in its longest section, the indictment turned to a host of specific accusations that were intended to bolster the main charges.[68]

The indictment included some factual errors. It did not recognize that Greiser and Forster had been arch rivals in Danzig; instead, it claimed, relations between the two men 'were so close that nothing was done that had not previously been agreed between them.' The indictment further stated that Greiser was 'in charge' of the NSDAP in Danzig; of course, Forster had been Gauleiter in the Free City. It also stated that Greiser aided Forster in his being named head of state in Danzig—surely a galling charge, since Greiser had tried to keep Forster from assuming such a position.[69] The section of the indictment dealing with Greiser's actions in Danzig was the least accurate part of the indictment. But on other matters, too, the indictment contained misinformation. It claimed, for example, that 300,000 Jews were murdered in Chełmno; 160,000 is the more accurate number.[70] It also asserted that the Sonderkommando Kulmhof, the execution squad at Chełmno, 'was directly subordinate to the accused Greiser.'[71] Greiser never had day-to-day control of the squad.

The indictment focused on issues that most concerned the prosecution. The Poles were deeply angered by the Nazi invasion and occupation of Poland. Accordingly, the indictment prominently featured Greiser's alleged actions in Danzig that had led to war. In addition, it focused on the suffering of Poles during the Nazi occupation. This may have been a reaction to Nuremberg; the Poles complained that the Nuremberg indictment paid scant attention to their countrymen's suffering (for which the British blamed the Soviets).[72] While the Greiser indictment did not ignore Holocaust crimes, it subsumed the Final Solution under crimes against the Polish people. It thus gave little sense that Greiser's anti-Semitic policies differed from those pursued against non-Jewish Poles.

To Maria, Greiser wrote: 'If I had done just a fraction of what I am now accused of, you would have to immediately divorce me and you couldn't continue to bear my name! You know best, my little doe, how much I suffered under the development of a police state with the Gestapo hierarchy, and how much slander and how many reports about me were brought to

Berlin. The truly guilty have evaded responsibility, especially Hitler and Himmler! You know best that we refused to do the same, because I did not allow myself to become guilty and had a good conscience. For these decent convictions I now sit in prison and have to take on myself the greatest psychological burden that consists of my not knowing if I will see you again.'[73] Greiser persisted in this unpersuasive defense throughout his trial.

On Saturday, 22 June 1946, the trial against Greiser began in the Great Hall of the university, the same auditorium in which Greiser had spoken at countless NSDAP rallies.[74] Greiser's former site of triumph was now his site of shame. The Great Hall had been remade into a court room and wired for the simultaneous translation of the Polish proceedings into English, Russian, French, and German. There was enormous local interest in the trial; a system was devised whereby tickets were issued to avoid scalping.[75] The American consul, Howard A. Bowman, later reported that 'great numbers of local citizens were present at all sessions of the Court.' Foreign interest was more muted; American, English, French, and Russian newspaper correspondents came only to the opening session.[76] Film footage shows a capacity crowd following the proceedings with rapt attention. A gaunt Greiser, wearing spectacles and visibly balding, seemed unhappy. He wore a loose, ill-fitting gray jacket, and dark trousers. Although he refused to look directly into the camera, a closeup focused on his quivering nostrils. Greiser appeared to be a man with the air knocked out of him; his once full, powerful frame had given way to a much slighter, trembling figure.[77]

Kazimierz Bzowski, the president of the Supreme People's Tribunal, presided over the proceedings. There were two other judges and four jurors.[78] The court was aware of its historic role. In an interview before the trial, the head Polish prosecutor for the Supreme People's Tribunal, Stefan Kurowski, stated that 'the proceedings were of great international importance. The sentence against Greiser would be pronounced before the end of the Nuremberg trials. It would set a precedent in the domain of various legal norms, including in the area of criminal preparations for aggression, and the recognition of aggressive war as criminal...'[79] As Kurowski emphasized, this trial was the first trial of a major war criminal carried out according to the principles of the IMT Charter. Although Greiser's trial started well after the Nuremberg proceedings began, it ended months before they did.

The Polish court entered a legal no man's land, facing a host of legal complexities that bedeviled Nuremberg and future war crimes tribunals, too. Bzowski reportedly stated that 'a peculiar characteristic of this trial was the fact that the accused had not taken part directly in many of the acts for which he is charged but has been responsible indirectly through his method of government.'[80] How should one judge a man who instigated crimes but did not personally bloody his hands? How should one judge a man when his actions at the time of the crimes reflected his regime's norms? And how should one judge a man who insisted that he was just carrying out orders and was therefore not responsible for his actions?

After opening statements, a parade of witnesses testified.[81] Not just Greiser, but German rule altogether, was on trial. The prosecution called a series of expert witnesses who testified about various aspects of German rule in the annexed territories. These included Dr. M. Pospieszalski, a lecturer at the university in Poznań, who later authored important studies and document collections about the Warthegau. In addition, Polish and Jewish victims in Danzig and the Warthegau testified against Greiser. These witnesses were unable to convincingly link Greiser to specific crimes, but they forcefully portrayed the terrible experiences that they had endured under regimes that he had run. Hans Biebow, the head of the Litzmannstadt Ghetto Administration, also testified for the prosecution. Now in Polish custody awaiting trial, Biebow claimed that he had tried to improve conditions for Jews in the ghetto, but that Greiser's Reichsstatthalter agency had blocked him from doing so. He insisted that Reichsstatthalter bureaucrats followed Greiser's prescriptions 'that the harshest measures be deployed against Jews, and thus always looked unfavorably on his [Biebow's] requests.'[82] While Biebow's testimony was self-serving, it was not incorrect. The prosecution bolstered the witness testimony by introducing as evidence documents abandoned by Greiser's administration. It also had the court listen to recordings of Greiser's speeches.

In trial, some witnesses presented dubious testimony. J. Duczmal, for example, secretary of the Polish Socialist Party in Krotoszyn county, claimed that Greiser visited Fort VII and, on a tour of the jail, asked a prisoner what crime he had committed. The prisoner replied that he was there because he was a Pole. Greiser allegedly retorted 'You Polish swine, thus you rot! (*Ty polskaświnio, i tak zgnijesz!*)'[83] Greiser in such close contact with Polish prisoners? Not likely. Another witness, Alojzy

Pilarczyk, the former president of the Polish Economic Association in Danzig, claimed that Greiser introduced Hitlerism to the Free City.[84] But as we know, Hans Hohnfeldt brought Nazism to Danzig. Despite these and other historical inaccuracies, the court nonetheless heard a reasonable overview of Greiser's crimes.

While Greiser had prepared a list of some 126 witnesses who could testify in his favor, only a few were brought to the stand.[85] Many on Greiser's list were either in Allied custody (such as Hermann Göring); had gone underground (such as Harry Siegmund); or would not, in any case, testify on his behalf (such as Clement Atlee or Carl Burckhardt). The major defense witness thus became August Jäger, now also in Polish custody and eager to avoid self-incrimination. Jäger's testimony was generally viewed as unconvincing. As the court later wrote, he gave 'wobbly, careful' answers.[86]

In his defense, Greiser insisted that his actions had been done on orders from Hitler and Himmler. He stated that he had been carefully supervised by authorities in Berlin, and that all of his speeches were subject to censorship. He claimed that the directives issued over his signature were written by officials in Berlin. Although many departments of state administration were located in his Reichsstatthalter agency, he insisted that they had received their orders and directives from the various ministries in Berlin, and not from him. Morever, Greiser asserted, these departments were authorized to issue decrees over his name. Since he had not authorized the orders, he could not now be held accountable for them. Greiser also insisted that he had no control over any police formations. Instead, all police in the Gau took orders directly from Berlin, and especially from Himmler. Greiser thus supposedly had nothing to do with the extermination of Jews, the deportation of Poles, or any other criminal activity committed by police in his Gau. As concerned his actions as senate president in Danzig, Greiser claimed that none contravened the Free City's constitution. Moreover, Hitler or other Nazi party authorities had ordered the measures that he had introduced. Greiser further claimed that he had tried to settle disagreements with Poland peacefully, and that he had opposed the use of force.[87] In effect, Greiser suggested, he had had no impact on policy either in the Warthegau or in Danzig.

The chasm between the evidence presented and Greiser's defense lent a surreal quality to the proceedings. When asked about a well-known decree of 22 September 1940 that he had signed—about how Germans should treat Poles—Greiser claimed that he was unable to explain from memory the circumstances in which the decree had arisen: 'I would have to have the opportunity to question those bureaucrats who formulated the decree and presented the project or text of it to me for my signature.'[88] Greiser further claimed that special courts for Poles were introduced against his wishes, and that he never used them.[89] He stated that he didn't know anything about Chełmno.[90] At times, his responses were so preposterous that the audience couldn't contain itself. At one point, Greiser claimed that 'officially' he didn't know anything about Radogoszcz, a work camp near Łódź. When the prosecutor asked him if he 'unofficially' knew about it, Greiser replied: 'I already said that I was accidentally notified of it (...) Had I known about the conditions in that camp—given here—even in the smallest measure, I would have been the first to speak against it.' The court transcript noted 'laughter in the room.'[91] When Greiser declared that he knew nothing about the mass execution in Zgierz in March 1942, the audience reacted with 'vivid agitation and restrained indignation.' Not wishing to look at the disbelieving crowd, Greiser turned his back on the court audience.[92]

In a speech given on 25 June, the fifth day of the trial, Greiser insisted that he had long been in disagreement with the party and its aims. He allegedly submitted his resignation as Gauleiter several times, but it was never accepted. He insisted that 'national and racial hatred were for me foreign concepts—testimony for this is my life up to now.' He also claimed that in 'my chest there were two souls: an official soul and my own soul.'[93] In defiance of what his own soul dictated to him, he was forced to do what his official soul ordered. His constant internal resistance was unable to find expression externally. As Greiser put it, 'in human life there are, however, strivings more powerful than ourselves.' Greiser also argued that he couldn't possibly have known about everything taking place in his Gau's administration. The Warthegau had a civil service more or less the size of Denmark's or Switzerland's. Would anyone, he questioned, expect the rulers of those two countries to know everything about what was going on in their administrations? He further claimed that in his Gau 'little Hitlers and Himmlers' were engaged in a constant struggle with him, all of which took place behind the scenes. As he described it, 'in the course of months and years I was just as surrounded and under surveillance as today, with the only difference that then I sat in a golden cage, and today in prison.'[94]

Greiser seemed to believe his own statements and that his testimony would sway the court.[95] Given the wealth of incriminating evidence against him, this was implausible. Perhaps Greiser lied because he thought that this would be the most effective defense strategy. But his dissembling may also offer insight into his psychological state. As Ian Kershaw has suggested, Greiser was somehow psychically unable to assume any responsibility for his past actions. In Kershaw's view, 'this self-delusion perhaps reflected both the total collapse of his own value system, as well as the destruction of his idealized picture of the Führer.'[96] Indeed, with the demise of the Third Reich, Greiser may well have been unable to make sense of his past actions; they no longer fit into a coherent world view. His dissembling may also have reflected long-standing insecurities. Always concerned about how others viewed him, he may have been dismayed that his past actions were now seen in such a negative light. In response to his new situation, Greiser rewrote his past life. In turn, by constantly reiterating this new past, Greiser perhaps came to believe it. Then too, he may have convinced himself that his long-held worries about his Nazi bona-fides were, in fact, justified: somehow, he had never been a 'true' Nazi anyway, and so he couldn't have committed the crimes of a 'true' Nazi.

Trial testimony ended on Tuesday, 2 July. After a two-day recess, the prosecution made its final statements on 5 July.[97] Prosecutor Mieczysław Siewierski tried out various metaphors to describe Greiser's character and influence. Greiser was like 'the leader of a modern army. He himself doesn't fire a gun, he doesn't participate in the attack, but he directs the whole of the total extermination action.' Siewierski added, 'The accused Greiser takes on . . . the figure of an electrician, who sits at a switchboard of a gigantic electrical works and who lets electricity circulate through the entire grid or of an electrician, who sits at his transmitter and sends out the waves to the entire transmitting area of his apparatus.' In relation to the Polish population, Siewierski likened Greiser to a hunter. 'One must view Greiser in connection with a hunter who pursues a noble animal. With his shots he tries to target the nerve and circulatory centers of the animal so as to rob it of all resistance power.' The implication was that Greiser had picked off the Polish elite and thus made it difficult for the Polish population to engage in resistance. According to Siewierski, Greiser did everything 'in cold blood, without agitation, just as during questioning in this trial. For Greiser is no emotional type, he has no momentary emotions.'

Siewierski also placed Greiser in a narrative of centuries' long animosity between Germans and Poles. To him, Greiser's actions were 'just one link in the chain of disputes that had taken place between Germans and Poles in this area for a thousand years.' Sierwierski correctly noted that while Greiser's policies were realized within the National-Socialist program, they 'had their own face' and were different from those pursued by Forster, the Party Chancellery, the Reich Chancellery, and even Himmler. Siewierski then sought to explain Greiser's psychological motivations. In his view, Greiser's anti-Polish policies were rooted in an 'inferiority complex' vis-à-vis Poles. This complex, Siewierski argued, stemmed from Greiser's early experiences in Posen province. Siewierski claimed that 'Greiser . . . understood very well that in this area he functioned only as the bearer of paper rights vis-à-vis the native population because he was not . . . rooted in this land. This stirred his inferiority complex.'[98] In the last part of his statement, Siewierski correctly emphasized Greiser's responsibility for virtually everything that had happened in the Warthegau. As he noted, the prosecution had shown that in 'all fundamental policies we can see the spirit, idea, leading hand, and leadership initiative of Greiser.' Siewierski gave numerous examples of how Greiser had determined policy in the Gau and, in the process, showcased Greiser's lies to the court. He also showed how Greiser had violated virtually every article in the Polish criminal code. For Siewierski, only one punishment was possible: death.[99]

Prosecutor Jerzy Sawicki dealt with basic legal issues presented by the case. As he stated, 'the administration of justice is not prepared for the sort of phenomena as N[ational]-S[ocialist] crimes in the last war.' Sawicki challenged the court to establish 'a juridical formula and appropriate punishment for crimes that to date are unknown.' The prosecutor asserted that individuals commit collective crimes; without individuals, there are no collective crimes. He also argued that it was necessary to establish a principle whereby crimes committed in a collective be punished more harshly than those done individually; an individual in a collective is much more dangerous than an individual acting alone. The prosecutor added, however, that this was no easy matter and would create a 'significant precedent' in international law. In this context, Sawicki addressed Greiser's defense that he had just been acting under orders. Since Greiser followed orders because he had chosen to join a collective, he bore responsibility—and a heightened one at that—for the collective's crimes. Finally, Sawicki raised the question of whether state-sanctioned crimes could be prosecuted. He answered affirmatively, arguing that states are part of a human community whose moral principles have found expression in international conventions.[100]

In two cogent statements, the defense tried to undermine the prosecution's case. Hejmowski focused on legal principles. Since the IMT had not yet pronounced its judgment, he refused to recognize the IMT Charter as an extant system of law. Hejmowski thus argued that no existing legal system viewed a war of aggression as a criminal activity. Moreover, international law bound states, not individuals. As concerned Greiser's activity in Danzig, Hejmowski raised jurisdictional issues: 'Can a member and later head of government of a foreign state be put on trial before a national court of another state due to his official activity carried out on his own state's territory . . .?' Hejmowski also pointed to a lack of legal precedent: never before, he stated, had a head of state been judged for his official activity by a court of another state. (In making these arguments, however, he ignored the IMT Charter that explicitly stated that heads of state could be held personally responsible for violations of international law.)[101]

As for alleged crimes in the Warthegau, Hejmowski noted that the prosecution had not presented any credible evidence that Greiser had personally committed a crime. Moreover, on the matter of taking orders, he claimed, Greiser had acted as a soldier. According to the attorney, pre-war Polish law did not hold soldiers criminally responsible for actions committed under orders, if these occurred under physical duress that could not be resisted. Why, he asked, should Greiser's deeds be viewed differently? Then, too, Greiser was being tried as a 'traitor to the Polish nation.' How could Greiser, never a Pole or a Polish citizen, be accused as such? Greiser was also charged with committing actions that Hejmowski deemed purely political—such as removing Polish signs and monuments. 'Do we,' the attorney questioned, 'have the right to judge Greiser because of his ideology?' Finally, he made the case that Greiser should not be executed, lest a German martyr be created. As he phrased it, 'Do not sow future "Artur [*sic*]-Greiser-Streets" in German cities!' He also argued that the purity of Polish jurisprudence was at stake; it should not be sacrificed for a momentary feeling of revenge. If the Poles executed Greiser, they would essentially be acting as Germans: 'But if we should proceed like Germans,' Hejmowski concluded, 'then we would have no moral right to sit in judgement over them.'[102]

Kręglewski, the other defense attorney, focused mostly on the problematic nature of the procedures and evidence used against the accused. Greiser, Kręglewski argued, had not been allowed to effectively defend himself. Most of his proposed witnesses had not been brought to the stand. Kręglewski also argued that Greiser had been denied access to the documentary evidence and had thus had to defend himself from memory. The attorney then walked the court through various witness statements, pointing out the inconsistencies and contradictions found in the testimony. Less convincingly, Kręglewski claimed that the documentary evidence against Greiser was weak. Greiser's signature, he argued, could not be linked with any death sentence, nor with the founding of any work, concentration, or extermination camp. The defense attorney also worked hard to shift the blame for anti-Polish policies to other Nazi authorities (Göring, the Gestapo, Berlin ministries, and so on).

Kręglewski, too, turned to more basic legal issues. He castigated the prosecution's use of the 1932 Polish criminal code. That code expressly prohibited prosecution in cases in which no law obtained at the time of the criminal deed. As Kręglewski argued, the Tribunal had to decide either to apply or not to apply that law. It couldn't, though, pick and choose aspects of the law while ignoring others. The case against Greiser, Kręglewski insisted, was a legal quagmire.[103]

Greiser was given the last word. Defiant, he showed no remorse and refused all responsibility for past criminal activity. He insisted that he had always advocated rapprochement with Poland and that he had been unable to develop his own initiatives. He pointed to his reconstruction achievements: over 1,000 kilometers of new roads, modernized railroad stations, new apartment buildings, and the renovated theater. In one of his more outlandish statements, he suggested that the fact that he had not been allowed to resign may actually have helped Poles; Himmler would have replaced him with a more fearsome anti-Polish leader. Were his life spared, Greiser told the court, he hoped to work for the 'understanding and rapprochement of our two peoples.' He would do so by writing books. He wanted to finish one on Danzig; another comparing what Hitler proposed in *Mein Kampf* to what he actually did in the Third Reich; a third on the 'The Social Question;' a fourth, titled 'Two Peoples on the Border,' on the failures of Prussian-German policies toward Poles; and finally, his memoirs. But Greiser assumed that he would be executed. As he told the court, he did not fear death: 'In any event, death for me has lost its terror and can at most save me from a life that in the long run is not a life anymore.' Should he be given the death sentence, however, he had two wishes: to be buried next to his son Erhardt (whose grave lay in Poznań); and to be executed as a soldier, with his eyes uncovered. Should he be allowed to live, he wished to 'be able to work for an uncompromising understanding of our two peoples.'[104] This closing statement was just as unconvincing as the rest of his trial performance. Given Greiser's past actions, everyone, save perhaps the defendant himself, found it unpersuasive.

The Tribunal delivered its verdict on 9 July. Greiser was found guilty of all charges, except that he did not personally commit any murders, carry out acts of cruelty, or inflict bodily harm. The court sentenced him to death, stripped him of his public and civic rights, and forfeited his property.[105] The Tribunal declared that it had been convinced by the expert testimony and voluminous documentary evidence. As concerned the first two charges (belonging to a criminal organization and conspiring to wage an aggressive war), it found the indictment 'fully justified.'[106] Although it admitted that the criminality of 'waging aggressive war' was controversial, it nevertheless lent its support to this extension of international law. It concluded that Greiser was 'one of the first, most active, and most trusted colleagues of Adolf Hitler in the realization of German power in east central Europe by means of warlike and biological aggression, including the cultural extermination (genocide) of neighboring peoples, especially the Polish people so hated by Germans.'[107] As Telford Taylor, the Nuremberg prosecutor, later wrote, due to his conviction on the charge of 'waging aggressive war,' Greiser had the 'dubious honor of being the first person ever convicted on such a charge.'[108]

For the third main charge ('contravening the principles of the law of nations and the postulates of humanity and the conscience of nations'), the court stated that it needed to address four legal issues. The first involved the 'actual character' of the Polish–German war in 1939. In the view of the court, the attack on Poland was 'criminal,' and the occupation nothing but 'an illegal annexation of a foreign territory.' This was important, because according to the IMT Charter, 'crimes against humanity' could only be justiciable if they were directly related to 'crimes against the peace.'[109] Insisting that the attack on Poland was criminal allowed the Tribunal to follow IMT logic.

Greiser's policies in the 'illegally' annexed areas related to the second issue: superior orders. On two grounds, the court rejected the plea that Greiser had been acting under orders. First, it simply didn't believe him. As the verdict stated: 'He was . . . an independent, ambitious, and ingenious initiator and organizer of the fascist, Hitlerite, cruel means that served the mass extermination of the local population . . .' But even if Greiser had been acting under orders, the court argued, 'such a defense would in no way lessen his responsibility for the crimes committed in the above circumstances. According to the modern theory and practice of comparative penal law, the subordinate may not carry out every "order of a superior." In military law, including German military law, obedience is the foundation of soldiering. But even this rigorous military law of discipline does not conceive of obedience in the sense of a blind obedience . . . to every order, but only to orders that are in accordance with the law, and not those that call upon him to commit crimes. Any such criminal order from a superior will always constitute a particular crime, *delictum sui generis*, for the execution of which the doer will be equally responsible with the issuer of the order.'[110] The court thus rejected Greiser's main line of defense.

The third legal issue involved the 'actual content of the incitement that induced others to commit crimes found in the Polish Criminal Code.' Here the court ascribed responsibility to 'the role of the intellectual perpetrator' who induces others to commit crimes. According to the court, recent legal doctrine suggested that this was neither a new 'collective responsibility for the guilt of others,' nor the 'abandonment of the principle of individual responsibility.' Instead, it recognized that 'a whole series of modern crimes occurred in larger or smaller criminal groupings' and that these 'involved different kinds of direct participation (inciters, physical perpetrators, helpers' helpers).'[111] By holding Greiser responsible for incitement to crimes, the court expanded Polish legal doctrine as the prosecution had sought.

Finally, the court ruminated about the 'actual meaning of the new crimes against the interests of humanity . . . in the form of murdering peoples (according to the latest Anglo-Saxon terminology: genocide).' It rehearsed all of the measures that Greiser had introduced to decimate the Polish population. It then stated that it had asked expert legal witnesses whether 'leaders and organizers' of such crimes should be viewed as executors of these crimes. The experts had given a positive response, and the court fully recognized 'their validity.'[112] Although phrased slightly differently—'new crimes against the interests of humanity'—the court thus declared Greiser guilty of what at Nuremberg were called 'crimes against humanity.' But in doing so, it did not venture its own judicial opinion, but instead declared expert opinion 'valid.'

Did Greiser get a fair trial? His trial stood in stark contrast to another Polish trial taking place at exactly the same time. On 4 July 1946, more than forty Jews were lynched in Kielce. A quick trial of twelve alleged perpetrators was held from 9 to 11 July; nine were sentenced to death. The sentences were carried out the very next day. The government's swift action in this matter—it claimed that the political opposition had incited the pogrom—angered a Polish population that believed that Jews were trying to impose communism on Poland. A central committee report on Łódź compared the general population's views on the government's treatment of Greiser versus that of the Kielce perpetrators: 'Slogans of revenge and terror from the moment of execution [of the convicted killers of Kielce] were heard in the shops. [They] compare the alacrity of the Kielce trial with that of Greiser who is still alive, though he is guilty of so many millions of victims...'[113] Much to the Polish population's annoyance, the government (alleged to be Jewish) moved much more quickly against those committing anti-Semitic crimes than those, such as Greiser, who had perpetrated enormous crimes against the Polish nation.

Given the kind of justice that the Polish courts dispensed in Kielce, Greiser was well served by the Tribunal. By western standards, though, he hardly had a fair proceeding. Greiser was unable to call many witnesses, and he was not given access to many of the prosecution's documents. In addition, the Tribunal found itself on some slippery legal ground. While the indictment and verdict were structured around principles found in the IMT Charter, the court tried to link Greiser's crimes with violations of the 1932 Polish Criminal Code or the 31 August 1944 decree. At times, this proved impossible. Polish war crimes legislation, for example, didn't have a provision concerning membership in criminal organizations.[114] Yet despite judicial flaws, the court arrived at a fair estimation of Greiser's crimes. In its finding, for example, that Greiser had not personally committed murder or other corporal crimes, it showed that it was discerning in its examination of the evidence. Ironically, the most notable feature of Greiser's verdict—that he was the first man ever convicted of 'crimes against the peace'—was based on the least credible evidence. In Danzig, Greiser was hardly engaged in an organized 'conspiracy' to wage aggressive war. Nonetheless, he did much to escalate German–Polish tensions in the years before World War II. The court was on much stronger grounds in condemning Greiser's activity in the Warthegau. As it rightly noted, Greiser—and none other—had initiated many of the crimes there. Decades of research on the history of the Warthegau has added much detail, but little new substance, to the record of Greiser's crimes. Despite the flaws of the proceedings, Greiser's trial served both justice and history reasonably well.

While the verdict broke new legal ground, it generated little international interest then or later. In part, this was due to the cautious nature of the Polish court's opinion: when treading on the new legal grounds established by the IMT Charter, the court offered precious little in the way of judicial opinion. Then, too, attention was focused on Nuremberg. Few international observers had any interest in a war-crimes verdict issued by a court behind the Iron Curtain. Excerpts of court materials from the case were not published in English until 1949, and have yet to be published in German. While the conviction was ignored by both international contemporaries and later scholars, the record should note: Greiser, not the Nuremberg defendants, was the first major war criminal convicted according to principles set out in the IMT Charter.

According to the Polish daily *Głos Wielkopolski*, 'When he heard that he had been sentenced to death, Greiser choked as if he had gotten the hiccups.' The only other visible sign of his distress was that 'the muscles of his face quivered.' The newspaper further commented: 'He did not regret the lives of thousands of human beings murdered in every camp, shot on marketplaces or squares, but it was clearly apparent that he very much regretted [the loss of] his own despicable life.' Once back in his cell, Greiser allegedly 'fell apart completely, burst into tears, and prayed for a long time.'[115] But he soon pulled himself together and did everything possible to save his life. He sought clemency from the president of Poland, Bolesław Bierut. He begged Sir Anthony Eden, the Pope, and others to intervene on his behalf. His defense attorneys also filed a petition for amnesty.[116] But Greiser had little time. In the end, just twelve days separated the verdict from his execution: twelve days of feverish activity and anguished waiting.

Already on the day of his verdict, 9 July, Greiser penned a short letter to Bierut. In it, he declared that he was innocent of the crimes for which he had now received a death sentence. As senate president in Danzig, he claimed, he had 'pursued efforts for a rapprochement with Poland as a pure and honest matter of the heart and did not know Hitler's ulterior motives and was also not party to his plans. This inner attitude was in accordance with my father's way of life and my whole upbringing in relationship to the Polish people.' Greiser next claimed that Hitler had personally ordered him to carry out harsh measures against the Poles in the Warthegau; that he had not participated in any way in Himmler's police organization; and that he had frequently used his right of clemency to pardon Poles sentenced to death. He further stated that he wished to devote his life to writing that would 'further the cause of truth and world peace.' He ended his unconvincing petition lamely: 'For all these reasons, I ask that you, Mr. President, make use of your right of pardon for me. I have the honor to be in deep devotion, Arthur Greiser.'[117] Just two days later, Bierut made his decision public: no pardon.[118]

Greiser next asked and received permission to appeal to Pope Pius XII, and British politicians Duff Cooper and Anthony Eden.[119] His telegrams to Cooper and Eden fell on deaf ears. Not so his plea to the Pope. Greiser had personally met Pius (as Eugenio Pacelli, then cardinal secretary of state) on a visit to Rome in 1938.[120] Given his militant persecution of the Catholic church, it's peculiar that Greiser should have turned to Pius now. Even more surprisingly, Pius urged the Polish government to grant Greiser clemency. (Later, he would do the same for Hans Frank, Albert Forster, and other convicted Nazi war criminals.)[121] As Pius wrote: 'Mr. Arthur Greiser, sentenced to death, beseeched in a message to the Holy Father to grant him his highest protection so that his life should be spared. The abovementioned has been one of the most severe foes of the Church in Warthegau, where he was Governor. Despite this His Holiness, following the divine example of our Lord, who, on the cross, prayed for his executioners, grants the sentenced man's request and addresses to the proper authorities his paternal request to spare his life.' The Polish government angrily rejected the Pope's plea: 'No Pole will have compassion for the bloody hangman of the Polish nation, Arthur Greiser. No Pole in his conscience will find the slightest shade of justification for the criminal who cold bloodedly depressed and destroyed hundreds of thousands of human lives. The greater is our astonishment at such unexpected intervention by the Vatican but the principle of justice will prevail. Arthur Greiser will be executed.'[122]

Pius' intervention for Greiser created a political scandal. Two hours before Greiser's execution, the Warsaw paper *Głos Ludu* published an article 'Pope defends Greiser.' The article declared, 'Flirtation continues between the Vatican and conquered Germany . . . It is evident that the Holy Father defends Germany.'[123] Initially, the Vatican denied all knowledge of any papal intervention, but on 22 July (after Greiser had been executed), it confirmed the news reports.[124] It now claimed that it would not have made the message public if Russia had not chosen to capitalize on it for anti-Catholic propaganda. As *L'Osservatore Romana* noted, Radio Moscow had broadcast a story titled 'Vatican defends Nazi criminals.' The Vatican insisted that the gesture had no political significance.[125] But the intervention was a slap in the face to the Polish communist government, and was greeted with widespread disbelief by Poland's strongly Catholic population.[126] Pius had nothing to gain by taking up Greiser's cause; he certainly had no special relation with or concern for Greiser. While Pius' plea for clemency was linked to his religious convictions, it mirrored his generally forgiving attitude toward Nazi crimes.

The Polish government had waited for the papal reply before going ahead with Greiser's execution. Once the Poles heard from Rome, they made final preparations for the execution. Decades later, in 1985, the man in charge of carrying out Greiser's sentence, Roman Śmielecki, gave a sworn statement about the days leading up to the execution. In 1946, he was deputy public prosecutor of the special criminal division of the county court in Poznań. On Thursday, July 18, Śmielecki declared, he received a phone call from the Justice Ministry telling him to arrange for the execution. First, he had to choose the place and date of the hanging. Śmielecki decided on the Poznań Citadel, not least since it would permit a large audience to view the event. He arranged for the building of special gallows. He also chose a casket for Greiser, the same as those used for Poles murdered by the Nazis. At a press conference on Saturday, 20 July, Śmielecki announced that the execution would take place at 7 a.m. the next morning. He had posters printed up in the same style that the Nazis had used to announce death sentences for Poles. Special tickets were prepared that permitted holders to stand in the first rows, nearest the hanging. Śmielecki also went to the Protestant cemetery where Erhardt was buried and ordered it to be tidied up. As he later noted, he wanted to make sure that foreign journalists would not have any reason to claim that 'as revenge for the crimes of Arthur Greiser the Poles had desecrated the grave of his son.'

Around 6 p.m. on Saturday, Śmielecki, along with a stenographer and translator, visited Greiser in his cell: 'The cell was large, clean, and bright. The convicted man wore only a shirt and shorts. When he saw us, he put on a jacket. He was surprised to see us—he assumed that we were there to tell him something important . . . In Polish, I asked if Arthur Greiser was in the cell and I received an answer in Polish—"yes." I knew German, but I thought that in such a situation a Polish public prosecutor should use only his native language. Greiser also knew Polish, for he had been born in Schroda and had gone to high school in Hohensalza. The news that he would be executed the next morning made a big impression on him.' Śmielecki continued, 'In this moment, one could see that he was reeling and he asked me how he would be executed. When I told him that he would be hanged, he immediately expressed the wish that he be shot, and declared that he was still a soldier. I then asked him if he had any wishes. One saw that he was still very numbed, he couldn't answer any question. I therefore suggested that he might wish to write a letter to his wife Maria Koerfer-Greiser... He immediately agreed.'[127] According to a newspaper account, Greiser first asked if he could see Maria, but was told that this was not possible 'for technical reasons.'[128] Śmielecki asked Greiser if he wanted a clergyman. Greiser responded in German 'I'm Protestant,' at which point the public prosecutor said that he would send in a Protestant minister. He also agreed to Greiser's requests to see Hejmowski, his defense attorney, and his fellow prison inmate, Jäger; Śmielecki stipulated, however, that a witness had to be present at the meeting with Jäger, and that the two men could not discuss political matters. As he left the cell, Śmielecki noted, 'Greiser reeled again and fell on his knees next to his bed.'[129] A newspaper story reported that Greiser met with Hejmowski for about 15 minutes; the condemned man gave his attorney some letters to his family. The meeting with Jäger lasted only about ten minutes, 'for Jäger didn't say much since there were witnesses at the meeting and he didn't want to say anything that could incriminate himself.' At 8 p.m., a Protestant minister came. Greiser spent the rest of the night writing to Maria and praying.[130]

In typed form, Greiser's letter to Maria is four-and-a-half single-spaced pages; many lines, however, note deletions by the censor. Right up to the end, Greiser refused to accept that he had committed atrocious crimes. As he told Maria, given the court's verdict that he had not personally murdered or otherwise caused bodily harm to others, 'I was actually sure that I would be pardoned.' He claimed, though, to be relieved that he 'would not have to testify against Germans in further trials. For I would have refused to reduce myself to this level...' Greiser also told Maria that 'I just took communion and will die tomorrow believing deeply in God and Jesus Christ.' In this vein, Greiser also wanted Maria to write two pastors in Karlsruhe to thank them for 'having brought me back to Christ.' Greiser told Maria that he had just met with Hejmowski. He was very satisfied with his defense lawyer: 'a touching, decent man . . . [who] truly did everything in his power to alter my fate.' He had instructed Hejmowski to relay financial and other information to Maria.

Greiser asked Maria to contact various family members about his death. He had a few words for each. 'I always loved my children and tried to be more of a friend than a father to them. Hopefully fate and the Good Lord will raise them as decent and hard-working people. Ingrid is already independent, but unfortunately I now can't help Rotraut study medicine which she so much hoped to do and I, too. Greet both very warmly from me—[CENSORS' CUT]—their father was no criminal, even if so many foreign newspapers should write that this was the case!' In a surprise gesture, Greiser wanted Maria to contact his first wife, Ruth: 'And in these last hours I have yet another wish: Please find conciliatory words for the mother of my children, for despite all that happened, I cannot simply cut this time out of my life.' Greiser mentioned his mother, who he hoped would not be plagued by illness in her old age, and his brother, Willy, 'the oldest of us three brothers and now the last one.' In another surprising twist, Greiser mentioned his sister Käthe, who had long ago fled Nazi Germany because her husband, Alfred, was of Jewish origins: 'And when you get Käthe's address in New York from Oma [his mother] or Willy, write her a few lines. Even though I never wrote to her, I thought about her often and she always remained in my heart my sister and Alfred my brother-in-law, too.' Finally, Greiser wanted Maria to convey his thoughts to her brother, Hubbi, the man whose shot had hit Greiser in the eye: 'You know my friendship to Hubbi. Even the loss of my eye couldn't shake it.' The mention of both Ruth and Käthe suggests that Greiser had not forgotten either woman. In his last hours, he sought to connect himself to earlier, more innocent days.

Greiser insisted on his undying love for Maria. His words, however, suggest that their marriage had been somewhat troubled: 'And now the most difficult thing for me is to take farewell of you, my little goat . . . I can only assure you that you are the great love of my life and will remain such to my last breath. The struggle for our love was not an easy one. Against all resistance we won it. Marriage to me was not always easy, for we are both strong-willed people. But I always loved you . . . For me the nicest hours and days were when I felt and noticed that you also loved me and when you could show me that.' Greiser further wrote that he had withstood his long months of prison only because he 'always had the goal of seeing you before my eyes.' Greiser hoped that Maria would return to her piano playing, a reflection of the 'immortal nature of German music:' 'And you, my little goat, are a tool of this eternal immortality. Remain thus, I'm no longer jealous, and I know that I will continue to hold my place in your heart . . .' Toward the end of his letter, Greiser wrote, 'but with my last thoughts I am with you, my little goat, my most beloved wife Maria and I greet you with the warmest hug the last time—[CENSORS' CUT]—and devotion—[CENSORS' CUT]—Your husband Arthur (*Arthurmann*).'

But the letter still wasn't done. In the last hours of his life, Greiser added six postscripts. In the first he wrote, 'What sort of a time is this! And for an old soldier there's not even a bullet, just a miserable rope! I don't understand the world anymore!' In the next: 'It will soon be 4 a.m. I heard from a newspaper notice this morning that the Pope had asked for my pardon. And still I'll be hanged . . .' In the third, Greiser said that he was attempting suicide: 'But I don't want to hang. Now I'm trying to slash my wrists with the top of my tobacco jar. God and you, too, forgive me for this sin, but I can't do otherwise.' In the next, 'It's not working. The guards sit in front of the door and watch carefully. The skin is thick and the metal is too blunt . . . Outside the morning grays, the last for me.' By his fifth postscript, he had given up on suicide: 'It's 5 a.m. I have to summon my last nerves. Still two hours and then it's over.' And in the last postscript: 'That was an anxiety attack with the veins. It's passed. It was the first since the trial began. Now it's almost 6 a.m. Even when I'm dying no one should see me weak! I greet you . . . —[CENSORS' CUT]—Mariawife, now for the last time, 'til we see each other up there. Always your Arthur.'[131] While Greiser was willing to reveal his weaknesses to Maria, he still wanted the outside world to see him as strong and manly.

On Sunday morning at 4 a.m., while Greiser was contemplating suicide, Śmielecki drove to the Citadel to inspect preparations for the execution. Soon, crowds of spectators were pouring in—so many that they blocked one of two access roads to the gallows.[132] Children were not allowed to attend the execution; for 'pedagogical and psychological reasons,' Polish authorities banned them from the site.[133] Śmielecki later described the hanging: 'Shortly before 7 a.m. Greiser was driven to the execution site. His eyes were covered. He was brought to the gallows. In order to follow formalities, I then asked the prison director if the man brought forth was really Arthur Greiser. After he confirmed this, I turned to the executioner with the words: "Citizen Executioner, I put Arthur Greiser into your hands.

Fulfill your duty." The executioner and his assistant then went about their activity. Punctually at 7 a.m. Greiser was hanged on the gallows.' Śmielecki further noted that BBC news reports had emphasized the punctuality of the execution.[134] Film footage offers a bleak sight: amidst a huge crowd that peopled the otherwise empty ruins of the Poznań Citadel, Greiser's body dangled in the air.[135] 'After 20 minutes,' Śmielecki continued, 'Greiser's body was taken down from the gallows.'[136]

Although Greiser had hoped to be buried next to Erhardt, his wish was not fulfilled. Instead, his body was cremated in the Anatomical Institute of the Medical Academy in Poznań—the same ovens used to cremate thousands of Polish and Jewish victims during the Nazi occupation.[137] The fate of his ashes, however, remains in doubt. Śmielecki claimed that the exact place where the urn with Greiser's ashes was buried was 'surrounded by secrecy.'[138] Others suggest that Greiser's ashes were simply scattered in an unknown area.[139] Polish authorities surely wished to prevent the creation of any potential pilgrimage sites associated with Greiser. But they needn't have worried. The vast majority of Germans had little interest in or sympathy for Greiser; they now linked him with defeat and flight from the East.

After her husband's arrest, Maria Greiser went to Bavaria, where she lived with her mother in Tegernsee and later, Munich.[140] She continued to play piano for herself and, very occasionally, for small audiences.[141] She lived in straitened circumstances, and spent years trying to get a widow's pension or other restitution based on Greiser's civil-service career. But her attempts were stymied by the fact that the 1951 West German law concerning '131ers' (civil-service employees who had lost their jobs in 1945 and thereafter) deemed Reichsstatthalters comparable to Reich ministers. Since Reich ministers were ineligible for amnesty, Reichsstatthalters were, too.[142] As Maria wrote to Ruge in 1956: 'For many years now I have known only sorrow and worries. One of these days it *has* to get better for me!'[143] In 1960, Maria and her mother moved to Bonn, to be near her sister. Maria occasionally encountered difficulties because of her connection to Greiser. In May 1960, for example, an invitation to play a concert in a nearby town was withdrawn after a swastika was found smeared onto a church door.[144] Neighbors also harassed her. As Maria once wrote to Ruge, 'And I was also hugely agitated by a wretched woman here in the [apartment] house who apparently knows about my "past."'[145] Maria never remarried and, for the next six decades, was supported largely by her family.

Maria always remained defensive about her husband. Indeed, at times she sounded rather like Greiser at his trial: 'I know that my husband always tried to moderate and head off the harsh measures toward Poles ordered from Berlin . . .' A few individuals, especially Ruge and Julius Hoppenrath, the former senator of finance in Danzig, tried to help her in her quest to secure some sort of pension. Maria was very bitter that other old acquaintances—notably Reinefarth—were unwilling to confirm Greiser's alleged good deeds in order to help her in her efforts: 'People are so nasty that they use all means to drag a dead man, who can no longer defend himself, through the mud. But in Posen my husband acted just as Dr. H[oppenrath] described him in his Danzig days, namely he tried to be conciliatory, moderate, and to weaken and avoid brutal orders!' But as Maria noted with resignation, 'Since my husband has been branded a "criminal," I'm still pursuing a quite hopeless struggle with the agencies [responsible for financial restitution] and, in addition, they are all scared about newspaper articles . . .'[146] To Maria, the bureaucrats that she faced lacked the civil courage to make an unpopular decision in her favor.

Like many old Nazis, Maria had trouble adjusting to postwar mores and the increasingly negative light in which Nazis and their era were viewed. She was, for example, hugely annoyed by Carl Burckhardt's *Meine Danziger Mission*: 'I'm horrified by how this man denies his close friendship with my husband. Although he actually always has to admit that my husband conducted himself in Danzig correctly and courageously, he obscures these facts through malicious remarks, as if my husband was a career opportunist at any price and that he carried out his actions directed against Forster (since he was the elephant in the china shop!) only out of jealousy [of Forster] . . .'[147] It's unclear whether Maria ever had a change of heart. In 2005, Harry Siegmund wrote to the author that Maria, now ninety-eight years old, 'doesn't speak about her marriage to Arthur Greiser and the time in Danzig and the Wartheland, but instead thinks about the time when she was a student of [Hans] Pfitzner and a celebrated piano virtuoso.'[148]

In one way or another, the other members of Greiser's immediate family also suffered from what the Nazis had wrought. Of Greiser's three children, two died before their father was hanged: besides Erhardt, Ingrid died in Munich in February 1946. The circumstances of her death have never been definitively determined. One family member says that she died from malnourishment, another from a botched abortion (of possibly her and Haubold's child).[149] Either way, Ingrid's death was likely the result of the terrible material conditions that obtained in immediate postwar Germany. Because word of her death never reached Greiser, he was spared what would have been a crushing blow.

Greiser's youngest child, Rotraut, fled with her mother from Danzig in February 1945. After a short interlude in Berlin with Ingrid, they went on to Saxony-Anhalt, where Ruth had family. Ruth never remarried. She and Rotraut spent the next eleven years in East Germany; Rotraut finished high school there in 1949. In 1956, Rotraut, unhappy in East Germany, left for Hamburg, and Ruth soon followed. Ruth died in Hamburg in 1984. Rotraut, who last worked as an office manager in a law firm, is now a pensioner. She and her husband divide their time between Hamburg and a summer home in Eckernforde. Since Rotraut has no children, she is the last living direct descendant of Arthur Greiser.[150]

Greiser had two brothers and one sister. As noted in earlier pages, the Russians killed his brother Otto during the invasion of the Warthegau in January 1945. Greiser's oldest brother, Willy, always somewhat frail, died in January 1951.[151] In the last years of her life, Greiser's mother, Ida, thus endured the deaths of all three of her sons, as well as of three grandchildren (Otto's son Horst died as a soldier during World War II).[152] Ida herself died in 1951.[153]

Greiser's sister Käthe had a rather different fate. She and her husband, Alfred Kochmann, fled Nazi Germany for Shanghai in late 1933. They came to New York City in 1936. After a difficult beginning, Kochmann became a successful doctor, and the couple and their daughter, Vera, lived comfortably. According to Vera, though, her mother 'never got over the fact that he [her brother Arthur] was one of "them" [i.e., Nazis].' Käthe was apparently distraught when she learned that her brother had been hanged: 'When the news came that he had been hanged by the American [*sic*] forces, very publicly, she cried bitterly.' Indeed, it must have been difficult for Käthe to square her image of her beloved brother—whom, after all, she had nursed during World War I—with that of the heinous perpetrator portrayed in *The New York Times*. Alfred Kochmann drowned during a vacation in Acapulco in 1959; Käthe died in 1966.[154]

Besides Greiser, several other Nazis active in the Warthegau ended up in Polish custody and were sentenced to death or long prison terms.

Biebow was hanged in Łódź in April 1947.[155] Jäger was tried in Poznań and sentenced to death on 21 December 1948. Albert Forster, Greiser's archenemy in Danzig, was tried and sentenced to death by the Polish Supreme National Tribunal in April 1948; his execution, however, was long delayed, and only took place secretly in February 1952.[156] Rolf-Heinz Höppner, head of the Posen SD office and the Gau Office of *Volkstum* Affairs, was sentenced to life imprisonment in Poznań in March 1949, but was pardoned and transferred to West Germany in April 1956.[157]

Some Nazi criminals in the Gau were killed or committed suicide at war's end. Herbert Lange, the first head of the execution squad at Chełmno, died fighting near Berlin in 1945. His successor, Hans Bothmann, hanged himself while in British custody in 1946. Ernst Damzog, the inspector of the Sipo and SD in Posen, was killed in fighting in 1945.

Many Nazis mentioned in earlier pages escaped justice or served relatively short prison terms in West Germany. Friedrich Uebelhoer, district president of Litzmannstadt, was interned by the Americans, released, and then disappeared under an assumed name. After 1945, Wilhelm Koppe, the HSSPF in the Gau until 1943, lived under a false name and was director of a chocolate factory in Bonn. After his true identity was found out in 1960, he was placed in police custody and arraigned in 1964. Deemed unfit to stand trial, he died in his bed, at home, in July 1975.[158] Similarly, Reinefarth was elected mayor of Westerland on the island of Sylt in 1951. In the mid-1950s, his murderous role in the Warsaw Uprising received considerable press attention. Despite a criminal investigation, Reinefarth evaded justice. In 1962, he was elected to the Schleswig-Holstein state parliament. He died at home in May 1979.[159]

Werner Lorenz, head of the Ethnic German Liaison Office (VoMi) and a longtime friend of Greiser, was a defendant in the Nuremberg trial of the SS-Race and Settlement Main Office. He was sentenced to twenty years of prison in 1948. In 1951, his sentence was reduced to 15 years, and he was released early in 1955. His daughter married Axel Springer, the conservative publishing magnate, thus giving him easy access to the West German elite.[160] Harry Siegmund, Greiser's cousin and personal adjutant, lived under an assumed name until 1950. He then had a long civil-service career in the West German Interior Ministry and the Ministry for Expellees, Refugees, and War Victims. In 2006, he was living in Heikendorf, on the Kiel fjords.[161] These men's trajectories confirm the obvious: in the end, many who had engaged in Nazi criminal or other heinous activity served reduced sentences, or simply got off scot-free.

What, ultimately, do we learn from the biography of a Nazi perpetrator such as Greiser? Put otherwise, how and why did someone like Greiser come to advocate murder as a way of improving the world? To countenance deportation and resettlement so as to better organize society? To classify and discriminate so as to achieve a more perfect polity?

During the interwar years, Greiser developed into a radical German nationalist. Although he was not steeped in nationalism in his youth, he became a hyper-German nationalist through the cumulative experiences of fighting in World War I, losing Posen province, living in Danzig, and making a career in the Free City's Nazi Party.[162] In the early 1930s, under the spell of his new party, Greiser came to believe that 'Germany' was his highest value, and that he would play a role in restoring German greatness. Given that his experiences had been determined much more by Poles than by Jews, Greiser viewed Poles as the main threat to his nationalist vision. Once he got to the Warthegau, his experiences, mediated through Nazi ideology, culminated in a vision of the German East that aimed to remake the Warthegau into a purely German area—'free' of Jews and especially Poles.

Greiser's zeal in pursuing this vision also stemmed from his character traits. Even as a soldier in World War I, he was eager to stand out, to attract attention, and to satisfy his superiors. As a Nazi, these same character traits were exaggerated by his sense that he had to live down various past shortcomings—the constant doubts about his war record, that he had belonged to a Masonic lodge, that he had joined the NSDAP relatively late. After 1939, Greiser also wanted to make up for his onetime 'moderation' in Danzig. In carrying out a ruthless Germanization program, he wanted to demonstrate that he was truly a 'model' Nazi—the right man with the right Nazi policy. In a sense, Greiser was not entirely his own man; he was hostage to his aspirations and his Nazi reputation. All this suggests that among Nazis, the weak and the vulnerable may well have been more dangerous than the strong and confident. Weak perpetrators had something to prove—a strong motive, it would seem, for countenancing or committing crimes.

Although obvious, it bears repeating that Nazi perpetrators such as Greiser were complex individuals. They were men, not monsters; humans, not automatons. Greiser's character was inconsistent, sometimes remarkably so. This was true of the gap between his personal life and his crimes as a

Nazi; despite his nasty divorce from Ruth, Greiser was rather decent to other family members. It was also true of his different personas as Danzig politician and Warthegau Gauleiter. While he pursued a more moderate stance toward Jews in Danzig in 1938 when he wanted to profile himself against Forster, he aimed to forge a 'model Gau' in the Warthegau when he wished to appear as a hard-core, fanatical Gauleiter. While this might suggest that Greiser was just a rank political opportunist, other elements of his story suggest that matters were not so simple. Although Greiser eagerly sought Himmler's favor, he frequently challenged the powerful SS leader. Then, too, he see-sawed on whether to privilege ideological aims or pragmatic realities. While he introduced a cruel segregation system against Poles, he eventually tried to improve the lot of Poles working in the Warthegau (even though he denied this to German audiences). And while he initiated the murder of 'unproductive' Jews, he also advocated exploiting Jews for their labor, thereby privileging financial benefit over ideological purity.

Despite the contradictions that he embodied, Greiser displayed a formidable ability to arrogate new rights to himself, a jealous insistence on keeping the powers he had won, and an arrogant attitude toward superiors and subordinates alike. There is no doubt that Greiser decisively shaped policy in his Gau; with a different Gauleiter, the region would certainly have seen different policies. Greiser's political strength rested both on the powers that he accumulated and the purposes to which he put them. Hitler wanted Reichsstatthalters in the eastern Gaus to have unfettered powers so that they could transform their regions into German Gaus. Greiser gladly took on these powers, and then used them just as Hitler wished. Had he, though, tried to use his power to halt or undermine Nazi programs, he would have been unsuccessful; he would have lost Hitler's, Himmler's and Bormann's support and with that, much of the police and other authority necessary for his continued exercise of power. Greiser's power, then, was not absolute. But given how he used it, Greiser was largely free to do as he pleased; his major constraint was the wartime situation, not limitations imposed by higher-ranking Nazis.

Greiser's many-sided, interconnected Germanization project set him and the Warthegau apart from other Gauleiters and regions. No other Gauleiter introduced such a wide-ranging Germanization program; no other region was the object of so many Germanization experiments.

Greiser's Germanization program was made up of a set of interlocking pieces. The influx of German resettlers 'necessitated' the deportation of

Poles and Jews, but the refusal of the General Government to take in deportees after March 1941 eventually spurred on the mass gassings of Jews in Chełmno. A system of segregation for Poles 'necessitated' the classification of the population into Germans and Poles—hence the founding of the DVL. To keep Germans in the Gau, Greiser initiated an ambitious program of 'positive' Germanization—a modern infrastructure for the region, buildings to display German might, institutions that propagated German culture, and a German lifestyle for the Gau—that 'necessitated' the forced labor of Jews, as well as the expropriation of Polish and Jewish property. Despite the unity of the program, Greiser's Germanization project ultimately foundered on internal contradictions and wartime realities.

Greiser's role in the Holocaust was also unique. Greiser insisted on maintaining control over the Jews of his Gau; he refused to cede authority on this matter to either SS or local officials. Like other regional security officials—but alone among Gauleiters—Greiser decisively shaped the persecution and murder of Jews in his Gau. Not only did he initiate the first mass gassings of Jews in Nazi-occupied Europe, but he also pursued an aggressive policy of exploiting Jews for their labor. The fact that Jews endured a worse fate than Poles in his Gau may not have been his priority; given a choice, Greiser might well have tried to 'eradicate' Poles first. But since he exercised power in the Nazi regime—that privileged anti-Semitism above all other negative values—he acted accordingly and, I suspect, with little regret.

It is with great unease that I end these pages. After years of working on Greiser, I know better who he was and what he did. But I cannot say that I understand him; that I've 'figured him out;' that his actions really make sense to me. There are, I believe, no pat answers to explain why individuals resort to such sordid actions; no easy analysis of such all-engulfing evil. Perhaps this is for the best. The very act of questioning what makes men (or the occasional woman) engage in such dreadful crimes helps to keep concern about such matters alive. Then, too, the events of our contemporary world—war, terrorism, genocide—will not let us forget. There seems little doubt that the impulses that motivated Greiser will persist. Greiser, then, serves as a warning for how some perpetrators are formed. He serves as an archetype for how some perpetrators act. And he serves as a model to which some perpetrators might aspire—at the risk, I hope, of universal condemnation.

Afterword

Why, until now, has no western historian written a biography of Arthur Greiser? While this absence may seem surprising, the answer to the question lies in how the history of the Nazi regime has been written.

In the immediate aftermath of the war, Nazi perpetrators were depicted as misfits, sadists, psychopaths, or worse. Psychologists sought to identify a specific Nazi personality; not least, this was so as to separate Nazis from the rest of humankind.[1] In this atmosphere, there was little chance that Nazi perpetrators would receive critical biographies. Early portrayals of Greiser were limited to two sensationalist articles by Polish journalists and a diabolical portrait rendered by his trial prosecutor.[2]

In the 1950s and 1960s, totalitarian accounts of the Nazi regime were highly influential. In such analyses, perpetrators embodied 'the banality of evil'—they were thoughtless automatons who had no will of their own. Mid-ranking Nazis such as Greiser were believed to have simply carried out orders. In this era, to the extent that Greiser was mentioned at all, he was depicted as the mere tool of Martin Bormann or Heinrich Himmler.[3] Passive cogs in the Nazi machine, however, hardly lend themselves to interesting analysis. Why write a biography about someone who just followed orders?

From the late 1960s onwards, the study of Nazi Germany underwent a sea change. Instead of a smooth-running, totalitarian dictatorship, the Third Reich was described as a chaotic system in which individuals and institutions vied for power and opportunity. Historians now argued that these and other structural features explained the regime's dynamics. In this vein, by the late 1970s, a new paradigm had emerged, captured in Ian Kershaw's phrase, 'working towards the Führer.' This interpretation suggested that in the absence of knowing exactly what Hitler wished,

Nazi bureaucrats did their best to do what they thought their Führer wanted. In the process, they radicalized Nazi policy, especially concerning the Holocaust, from below.[4] Given the new importance attached to mid-ranking Nazis, it now made sense to undertake biographical studies of them. Kershaw, in fact, published pioneering work on Greiser in the early 1990s.[5] Since his works appeared, virtually every general account of the Holocaust has mentioned Greiser—if only in a sentence or two.

Two other features of western scholarship on Nazi Germany still needed change to make a critical biography of Greiser possible. For decades, western scholars devoted relatively little attention to the Nazi occupation of eastern Europe. Language barriers and the difficulties of doing archival work behind the Iron Curtain kept all but the most stalwart western historians from venturing down this research path. Moreover, whereas Polish historians have published a steady stream of monographs and document collections on the Nazi occupation of the Warthegau ever since 1945, when western scholars focused on Nazi-occupied Poland, they tended to look at the General Government.[6] Since Hans Frank, the governor general, was tried at Nuremberg, considerable material on his regime was readily available in the west. The history of the General Government became synonymous with the history of Poland under Nazi occupation—and the Warthegau was virtually forgotten.

Similarly, before 1989, scholars, wearing Cold War blinders, ignored the role that ethnic tensions might have played in spawning Nazi perpetrators. This was true even though there were long rumblings about the high numbers of early Nazis, high-ranking Nazis, or Nazi perpetrators from borderlands areas.[7] But the events following 1989—the break-up of the Soviet Union and the ethnic wars in former Yugoslavia—reminded scholars of the potency of nationalistic passions. Historians and others now began to focus attention on the role of ethnic tensions in shaping the Nazi movement.

Following the collapse of communism, western scholars were able to undertake local studies of the Nazi occupation in Poland and points further east. In the process, they documented considerable regional variation in Nazi policies.[8] Some historians focused particularly on the Warthegau, exploring the deportation of Poles; the role of women in Germanization schemes; and, most important, the Final Solution.[9] Historians studying Nazi planning or racial/demographic policies in the East also looked at the Warthegau example.[10] All this brought greater attention to Greiser; he now received a paragraph or more in some historical monographs. Yet in the absence of a critical biography, factual errors about his life (in part, ones he himself had put into play) were repeated in the limited literature about him. Indeed, such inaccuracies—even the date of Greiser's hanging—are now found in very reputable historical works.[11]

To date, the only full biography of Greiser to appear is a slender volume by the Polish historian Czesław Łuczak titled *Arthur Greiser*, published only in Polish in 1997. Łuczak focused his entire research career on the Warthegau; he wrote literally dozens of works on Greiser's Gau.[12] Unfortunately, despite the wealth of his knowledge, this biography is disappointing. It includes factual errors, little overarching interpretation and, most egregious, no source citations. As a description of Greiser's life and deeds, it is of only limited value.

By the twenty-first century, it was high time for a critical biography of Greiser. The collapse of communism allowed western scholars ready access to important archival collections. At the same time, Greiser's policies proved a compelling subject for a generation of historians preoccupied with race, ethnicity, and the Holocaust. Given the upsurge in ethnic cleansing and genocide, Greiser's nationalistic pathos and its result, a vicious Germanization program, appeared apposite to contemporary affairs. Then, too, our era has been more attuned to the importance of human rights and individual responsibility. Although many historians still focus on structural processes that shaped the Third Reich, this biography has underscored the role of human agency in Nazi Germany. Men like Greiser—with their experiences, passions, and ambitions—mattered in the Nazi regime. Some six decades after his execution, a full-scale biography of Greiser finally seems timely and relevant.

Notes

ABBREVIATIONS FOR ARCHIVES CITED IN NOTES

APG	*Archiwum Państwowe w Gdańsku*
APP	*Archiwum Państwowe w Poznaniu*
BA	*Bundesarchiv*
BAB	*Bundesarchiv-Berlin*
BDC	Berlin Document Center (now housed in BAB)
GSA	*Geheimes Staatsarchiv Preussischer Kulturbesitz, Berlin*
IfZ	*Institut für Zeitgeschichte, Munich*
IPN	*Instytut Pamięci Narodowej, Warsaw*
IZ	*Instytut Zachodni, Poznań*
PA-AA	*Politisches Archiv des Auswärtigen Amts, Berlin*
NA	National Archives, College Park, Maryland
RGVA	*Rossiiskii gosudarstvennyi voennyi arkhiv, Moscow*
Stabi	*Staatsbibliothek zu Berlin Preußischer Kulturbesitz*
UNOG	United Nations Office at Geneva Library, Geneva
ZIH	*Żydowski Instytut Historyczny, Warsaw*

INTRODUCTION

1. '15,000 Poles Watch Greiser Execution,' *New York Times* (22 July 1946), 1.
2. Protokoll der Zeugenaussage, Roman Śmielecki, 26 August 1985, BA-Ludwigsburg, ZStL, AR 318/97, 17.
3. United Nations War Crimes Commission, ed., *Law Reports of Trials of War Criminals*, Vol. XIII (London: The United Nations War Crimes Commission, 1949), 113–14.
4. 'Urteil,' BA-Ludwigsburg, ZStL, Polen 365 h 2, 37 (of document).
5. While the story of what happened in the Warthegau has long been documented by Polish historians, it has been all but ignored by western historians.
6. Mark Mazower, *Hitler's Empire: Nazi Rule in Occupied Europe* (London: Allen Lane, 2008), 7.
7. See Mechtild Rössler and Sabine Schleiermacher, eds., *Der 'Generalplan Ost': Hauptlinien der nationalsozialistischen Planungs- und Vernichtungspolitik* (Berlin: Akademie, 1993).

8. Carl J. Burckhardt, *Meine Danziger Mission 1937–1939* (Munich: Callwey, 1980), 77.
9. Ernst Ziehm, *Aus meiner politischen Arbeit in Danzig 1914–1939* (Marburg: Herder Institut, 1950), 196.
10. Duff Cooper, *Old Men Forget* (London: Rupert Hart-Davis, 1954), 223.
11. Józef Lipski, *Diplomat in Berlin 1933–1939*, ed. Wacław Jędrzejewicz (New York: Columbia University Press, 1968), 385.
12. Anthony Eden, *The Eden Memoirs: Facing the Dictators* (London: Cassell, 1962), 388.
13. Julius Hoppenrath, 'Der Aufbau der deutschen Verwaltung und Wirtschaft in den Reichsgauen Danzig-Westpreußen und Wartheland unter dem Gesichtspunkt der Gegenüberstellung der Tätigkeit der beiden Reichsstatthalter und Gauleiter Forster und Greiser,' 3 March 1956, BA-Bayreuth, Ost-Dok. 8/145, 3–4.
14. 'Die Rede des Staatsanwalts M. Siewierski,' BA-Ludwigsburg, ZStL, Polen 365 h 2, 75.
15. *The Nazis: A Warning from History*, dir. Laurence Rees (Britain: British Broadcasting Corporation, 1997).
16. Hans L. Leonhardt, *Nazi Conquest of Danzig* (Chicago: University of Chicago Press, 1942), 222.
17. For overviews of the literature on perpetrators, see Jürgen Matthäus, 'Historiography and the Perpetrators of the Holocaust,' in Dan Stone, ed., *The Historiography of the Holocaust* (Houndmills: Palgrave Macmillan, 2004), 197–215; Gerhard Paul, 'Von Psychopathen, Technokraten des Terrors und "ganz gewöhnlichen" Deutschen: Die Täter der Shoah im Spiegel der Forschung,' in Gerhard Paul, ed., *Die Täter der Shoah: Fanatische Nationalsozialisten oder ganz normale Deutsche?* (Göttingen: Wallstein, 2002), 13–90; and Mark Roseman, 'Beyond Conviction? Perpetrators, Ideas, and Action in the Holocaust in Historiographical Perspective,' in Frank Biess, Mark Roseman, and Hanna Schissler, eds., *Conflict, Catastrophe and Continuity: Essays on Modern German History* (New York: Berghahn, 2007), 83–103.
18. Hannah Arendt, *Eichmann in Jerusalem: A Report on the Banality of Evil* (New York: Viking Penguin, 1963).
19. Götz Aly and Susanne Heim, *Vordenker der Vernichtung: Auschwitz und die deutschen Pläne für eine neue europäische Ordnung* (Frankfurt: Fischer, 1991).
20. See Ulrich Herbert, *Best: Biographische Studien über Radikalismus, Weltanschauung und Vernunft 1903–1989* (Bonn: Dietz, 1996); and Michael Wildt, *Generation des Unbedingten: Das Führungskorps des Reichssicherheitshauptamtes* (Hamburg: Hamburger Edition, 2003).
21. Daniel Jonah Goldhagen, *Hitler's Willing Executioners: Ordinary Germans and the Holocaust* (New York: Knopf, 1996).
22. Christopher Browning, *Ordinary Men: Reserve Police Battalion 101 and the Final Solution in Poland* (New York: HarperCollins, 1992). See also James Waller, *Becoming Evil: How Ordinary People Commit Genocide and Mass Killing* (Oxford:

Oxford University Press, 2002); and Harald Welzer, *Täter: Wie aus ganz normalen Menschen Massenmörder werden* (Frankfurt/M: Fischer, 2005).

23. As historians now recognize, no single explanation is able to cover all perpetrators. Donald Bloxham and Tony Kushner, *The Holocaust: Critical Historical Approaches* (Manchester: Manchester University Press, 2005), 157; Matthäus, 'Historiography,' 208; and Paul, 'Von Psychopathen,' 62.
24. Nazi perpetrators from Austria include Adolf Eichmann, Karl Hermann Frank, Odilo Globocnik, Ernst Kaltenbrunner, Arthur Seyss-Inquart, and Fritz Stangl. On these and others, see Peter R. Black, *Ernst Kaltenbrunner: Ideological Soldier of the Third Reich* (Princeton: Princeton University Press, 1984), 283. Alfred Rosenberg was a Baltic German, Theodor Eicke came from Alsace, and Erich von dem Bach-Zalewski was born in Pomerania. Werner Best experienced the French occupation of the Rhineland. See Herbert, *Best*, 31–4.
25. Michael Mann, *The Dark Side of Democracy: Explaining Ethnic Cleansing* (Cambridge: Cambridge University Press, 2005), 239, 227.
26. Arthur Greiser to Maria, 2 May 1934, IZ, I-941.
27. Helmuth Groscurth, *Tagebücher eines Abwehroffiziers 1938–1940*, ed. Helmut Krausnick and Harold C. Deutsch (Stuttgart: Deutsche Verlags-Anstalt, 1970), 381.
28. Bloxham and Kushner, *The Holocaust*, 157.
29. George C. Browder, 'Perpetrator Character and Motivation: An Emerging Consensus?' *Holocaust and Genocide Studies* 17 (2003): 495.
30. Although long neglected by historians, the Gauleiters are now being studied more intensively. See Peter Hüttenberger, *Die Gauleiter: Studie zum Wandel des Machtgefüges in der NSDAP* (Stuttgart: Deutsche Verlags-Anstalt, 1969); Jeremy Noakes, '"Viceroys of the Reich?" Gauleiters 1925–45,' in Anthony McElligott and Tim Kirk, eds., *Working Towards the Führer: Essays in Honour of Sir Ian Kershaw* (Manchester: Manchester University Press, 2003), 118–52; Ronald Rogowski, 'The *Gauleiter* and the Social Origins of Fascism,' *Comparative Studies in Society and History* 19 (1977): 399–430; and Walter Ziegler, 'Gaue und Gauleiter im Dritten Reich,' in Horst Möller, Andreas Wirsching, and Walter Ziegler, eds., *Nationalsozialismus in der Region: Beiträge zur regionalen und lokalen Forschung und zum internationalen Vergleich* (Munich: Oldenbourg, 1996), 139–59. For overviews of biographical studies on particular Gauleiters, see Magnus Brechtken, 'Kommentar und Forschungsforderungen,' in Jürgen John, Horst Möller, and Thomas Schaarschmidt, eds., *Die NS-Gaue: Regionale Mittelinstanzen im zentralistischen 'Führerstaat'* (Munich: Oldenbourg, 2007), 412; and Ziegler, 'Gaue,' 140–1. For a biographical dictionary of Gauleiters, see Karl Höffkes, *Hitlers Politische Generale: Die Gauleiter des Dritten Reichs: Ein biographisches Nachschlagewerk* (Tübingen: Grabert, 1986).
31. Noakes, '"Viceroys,"' 131.
32. Karol Marian Pospiezalski, ed., *Hitlerowskie 'prawo' okupacyjne w Polsce: wybór dokumentów: część I: ziemie 'wcielone' (Documenta occupationis V)* (Poznań: Instytut Zachodni, 1959), 274–80.

33. Ziegler, 'Gaue,' 139.
34. Czesław Madajczyk, *Die Okkupationspolitik Nazideutschlands in Polen 1939–1945* (Berlin: Akademie, 1987), 26.
35. On Gauleiters who wished to make their Gaus 'models,' see Ryszard Kaczmarek, 'Zwischen Altreich und Besatzungsgebiet: Der Gau Oberschlesien,' in John *etal.*, eds., *Die NS-Gaue*, 352; Martin Moll, 'Der Reichsgau Steiermark 1938–1945,' in John *etal.*, eds., *Die NS-Gaue*, 367–8; and Werner Röhr, '"Reichsgau Wartheland" 1939–1945: Vom "Exerzierplatz des praktischen Nationalsozialismus" zum "Mustergau"?' *Bulletin für Faschismus und Weltkriegsforschung* no. 18 (2002): 29–31. For a critique of the term 'model Gau,' see Frank Bajohr, 'Gauleiter in Hamburg: Zur Person und Tätigkeit Karl Kaufmanns,' *Vierteljahrshefte für Zeitgeschichte* 43, no. 2 (1993): 269.
36. The German and Polish population figures stem from Czesław Łuczak, *Pod niemieckim jarzmem (Kraj Warty 1939–1945)* (Poznań: PSO, 1996), 83. The Jewish population figure stems from Götz Aly, *'Endlösung:' Völkerverschiebung und der Mord an den europäischen Juden* (Frankfurt/M: Fischer, 1995), 68.
37. Michael Alberti, *Die Verfolgung und Vernichtung der Juden im Reichsgau Wartheland 1939–1945* (Wiesbaden: Harrassowitz, 2006), 85.
38. Alberti, *Die Verfolgung*, 5.
39. For a discussion of individuals fashioning their lives to accord with a highly ideological regime of mass mobilization, see Jochen Hellbeck, *Revolution on My Mind: Writing a Diary under Stalin* (Cambridge, Mass.: Harvard University Press, 2006).
40. Greiser was not the only Nazi to dress up his biography. See Bajohr, 'Gauleiter,' 273.
41. On the politics of biography, see Catherine Epstein, 'The Politics of Biography: The Case of East German Old Communists,' *Daedalus* 128, 2 (1999): 1–30.
42. See Frank Bajohr, *Parvenüs und Profiteure: Korruption in der NS-Zeit* (Frankfurt/M: Fischer, 2004), 17–34.
43. Carl Tighe, *Gdańsk: National Identity in the Polish-German Borderlands* (London: Pluto Press, 1990), 201.
44. Black, *Ernst Kaltenbrunner*, 32–3; and Joachim C. Fest, *The Face of the Third Reich: Portraits of the Nazi Leadership* (New York: Pantheon Books, 1970), 302.
45. *The Nazis*.
46. Simone Lässig, 'Introduction: Biography in Modern History—Modern History in Biography,' in Volker R. Berghahn and Simone Lässig, eds., *Biography Between Structure and Agency: Central European Lives in International Historiography* (New York: Berghahn, 2008), 8. Emphasis in original.
47. Aly first analyzed the interconnections among these policies. See Aly, *'Endlösung.'*
48. See discussion in Waller, *Becoming Evil*, 15–18.
49. Volker R. Berghahn, 'Structuralism and Biography: Some Concluding Thoughts on the Uncertainties of a Historiographical Genre,' in Berghahn and Lässig, eds., *Biography Between Structure and Agency*, 245.

1. 'CHILD OF THE EAST:' POSEN PROVINCE, WORLD WAR I, DANZIG

1. Czesław Łuczak, *Arthur Greiser* (Poznań: PSO, 1997), 3–4, 102; BAB, Former BDC Collection, Files on Arthur Greiser and Otto Greiser; and Vera Stroud to author, 3 May 2005.
2. Rotraut Fülleborn, interview with author, 30 May 2007.
3. Gustav Greiser to Justizminister, 4 March 1901, GSA, PK, I. HA Rep 84a Justizministerium, 26336, 194–5.
4. Harry Siegmund, *Rückblick: Erinnerungen eines Staatsdieners in bewegter Zeit* (Raisdorf: Ostsee Verlag, 1999), 7–8.
5. BAB, Former BDC Collection, RS Files on Arthur Greiser.
6. Łuczak, *Arthur Greiser*, 3.
7. Greiser to Justizminister.
8. Signature illegible to Gustav Greiser, 16 April 1904, GSA, PK, I. HA Rep 84a Justizministerium, 26336, 198–9.
9. Gerhard Engel, *Heeresadjutant bei Hitler 1938–1943: Aufzeichnungen des Majors Engel*, ed. Hildegard von Kotze (Stuttgart: Deutsche Verlags-Anstalt, 1974), 63.
10. William W. Hagen, *Germans, Poles, and Jews: The Nationality Conflict in the Prussian East, 1772–1914* (Chicago: University of Chicago Press, 1980), 324.
11. Brigitte Balzer, *Die preußische Polenpolitik 1894–1908 und die Haltung der deutschen konservativen und liberalen Parteien (unter besonderer Berücksichtigung der Provinz Posen)* (Frankfurt/M: Peter Lang, 1990), 290.
12. Richard Blanke, *Prussian Poland in the German Empire (1871–1900)* (Boulder: East European Monographs, 1981), 23–4.
13. Blanke, *Prussian Poland*, 231.
14. Robert L. Koehl, 'Colonialism inside Germany: 1886–1918,' *Journal of Modern History* 25, no. 3 (1953): 257.
15. Helmut Neubach, *Die Ausweisungen von Polen und Juden aus Preussen 1885/86: Ein Beitrag zu Bismarcks Polenpolitik und zur Geschichte des deutsch-polnischen Verhältnisses* (Wiesbaden: Otto Harrassowitz, 1967).
16. Balzer, *Die preußische Polenpolitik*, 58.
17. Blanke, *Prussian Poland*, 192; and Balzer, *Die preußische Polenpolitik*, 59.
18. Geoff Eley, 'German Politics and Polish Nationality: The Dialectic of Nation-Forming in the East of Prussia,' *East European Quarterly* 18, no. 3 (1984): 347.
19. Hagen, *Germans*, 324.
20. Blanke, *Prussian Poland*, 232–3; and Hagen, *Germans*, 320–1.
21. Koehl, 'Colonialism,' 267–8.
22. Hagen, *Germans*, 239–41.
23. Vera Stroud to author.

24. Blanke, *Prussian Poland*, 199.
25. Richard Breyer, *Das Deutsche Reich und Polen 1932–1937: Außenpolitik und Volksgruppenfragen* (Würzburg: Holzner-Verlag, 1955), 203; see also Arthur Greiser, Lebenslauf, BAB, Former BDC Collection, SSO Files on Arthur Greiser, Frame 46.
26. Albin Wietrzykowski, *Powrót Arthura Greisera* (Poznań: Nakładem Księgarni Wydawniczej Spółdzielni 'Pomoc,' 1946), 6.
27. Fragebogen zur Erlangung der Heiratsgenehmigung, 1935, BAB, Former BDC Collection, RS Files on Arthur Greiser, Frames 1690–2; and Łuczak, *Arthur Greiser*, 3.
28. Wietrzykowski, *Powrót*, 6–7.
29. Łuczak, *Arthur Greiser*, 4.
30. Fragebogen, Frames 1690–2.
31. Janusz Gumkowski and Tadeusz Kułakowski, *Zbrodniarze hitlerowscy przed Najwyższym Trybunałem Narodowym* (Warsaw: Wydawnictwo Prawnicze, 1961), 5.
32. '"Arthur-Greiser Schule" in Hohensalza,' *Ostdeutscher Beobachter* (3 December 1941).
33. Volker R. Berghahn, *Modern Germany: Society, Economy and Politics in the Twentieth Century*, 2nd edn (Cambridge: Cambridge University Press, 1987), 42.
34. Deutsche Dienststelle für die Benachrichtigung der nächsten Angehörigen von Gefallenen der ehemaligen deutschen Wehrmacht to author, 27 April 2006.
35. Arthur Greiser to Gustav and Ida Greiser, 26 September 1915, IPN, 63/1, 56.
36. Fragebogen, Frames 1690–2.
37. Arthur Greiser to Gustav and Ida Greiser, 5 October 1915, IPN, 63/1, 46.
38. Deutsche Dienststelle to author.
39. Arthur Greiser to Gustav and Ida Greiser, 12 December 1916, IPN, 63/2, 103–4.
40. Arthur Greiser, 'Weihnachten vor Nieuport,' undated [1915], IPN, 63/5, 1–6.
41. Arthur Greiser to Gustav and Ida Greiser, 4 January [1916], IPN, 63/1, 1–5. Greiser misdated this letter as 4 January 1915.
42. Arthur Greiser to Gustav and Ida Greiser, 10 January 1916, IPN, 63/2, 3–4.
43. Arthur Greiser to Gustav and Ida Greiser, 25 January 1916, IPN, 63/2, 1–2.
44. Arthur Greiser to Gustav and Ida Greiser, 13 February 1916, IPN, 63/2, 5–6.
45. Arthur Greiser to Gustav and Ida Greiser, 27 July 1917, IPN, 63/3, 43.
46. Arthur Greiser to Gustav and Ida Greiser, 13 August 1916, IPN, 63/2, 59–60.
47. Adam Hochschild, *King Leopold's Ghost: A Story of Greed, Terror, and Heroism in Colonial Africa* (Boston: Houghton Mifflin, 1998), 168.
48. Arthur Greiser to Gustav and Ida Greiser, 29 December 1916, IPN, 63/2, 103–4.

49. Arthur Greiser to Gustav and Ida Greiser and Geschwister, 25 December 1916, IPN, 63/2, 90–1.
50. Arthur Greiser to Gustav and Ida Greiser, 20 September 1916, IPN, 63/2, 75.
51. Larry Zuckerman, *The Rape of Belgium: The Untold Story of World War I* (New York: New York University Press, 2004), 2.
52. Arthur Greiser to Gustav and Ida Greiser and Geschwister, 3 March 1916, IPN, 63/2, 12–13.
53. Arthur Greiser to Gustav and Ida Greiser, 12 March 1916, IPN, 63/2, 18–19.
54. Arthur Greiser to Gustav and Ida Greiser, 17 April 1916, IPN, 63/2, 28–9.
55. Arthur Greiser to Gustav and Ida Greiser, 3 April 1916, IPN, 63/2, 21–2.
56. Arthur Greiser to Gustav and Ida Greiser, 5 April 1916, IPN, 63/2, 24–5.
57. Arthur Greiser to Gustav and Ida Greiser, 8 May 1916, IPN, 63/2, 34.
58. Arthur Greiser to Gustav and Ida Greiser, 27 July 1916, IPN, 63/2, 52.
59. Deutsche Dienststelle to author.
60. Arthur Greiser to Gustav and Ida Greiser, 24 November 1916, IPN, 63/2, 85.
61. Deutsche Dienststelle to author.
62. Arthur Greiser to Gustav and Ida Greiser, 17 April 1916, IPN, 63/2, 28–9.
63. Arthur Greiser to Gustav and Ida Greiser, 28 November 1916, IPN, 63/2, 94.
64. Arthur Greiser to Gustav and Ida Greiser, 29 December 1916, IPN, 63/2, 103–4. See also Deutsche Dienststelle to author.
65. Rotraut Fülleborn, interview with author, 26 May 2005.
66. Arthur Greiser to Gustav and Ida Greiser, 30 November 1915, IPN, 63/1, 26–9.
67. Arthur Greiser to Ida Greiser, 18 October 1915, IPN, 63/1, 38–41.
68. Arthur Greiser to Ida Greiser, 19 October 1915, IPN, 63/1, 32.
69. Greiser to Gustav and Ida Greiser, 25 January 1916.
70. Arthur Greiser to Gustav and Ida Greiser, 3 February 1917, IPN, 63/3, 4.
71. Arthur Greiser to Gustav and Ida Greiser, 26 November 1915, IPN, 63/1, 43–5.
72. Arthur Greiser to Gustav and Ida Greiser, 16 August 1916, IPN, 63/2, 61–2.
73. Fülleborn.
74. Arthur Greiser to Ida Greiser, 26 February 1916, IPN, 63/2, 9–10.
75. Arthur Greiser to Gustav and Ida Greiser, 19 December 1916, IPN, 63/2, 88.
76. Arthur Greiser to Gustav and Ida Greiser, 23 August 1916, IPN, 63/2, 65–6.
77. Arthur Greiser to Gustav and Ida Greiser, 20 September 1916, IPN, 63/2, 75.
78. Greiser to Gustav and Ida Greiser, 23 August 1916.
79. Arthur Greiser to Gustav and Ida Greiser, [1916], IPN, 63/2, 105.
80. Arthur Greiser to Gustav and Ida Greiser, 27 March 1917, IPN, 63/3, 27–9.
81. Arthur Greiser to Gustav and Ida Greiser, 11 March 1916, IPN, 63/2, 16–17.
82. Arthur Greiser to Gustav and Ida Greiser, 4 September 1916, IPN, 63/2, 69.
83. Arthur Greiser to Gustav and Ida Greiser, 2 November 1915, IPN, 63/1, 23–4.
84. BAB, Former BDC Collection, SSO Files on Arthur Greiser, Frame 29.

85. Arthur Greiser to Gustav and Ida Greiser, 31 March 1917, IPN, 63/3, 16–17.
86. Arthur Greiser to Gustav and Ida Greiser, 2 June 1916, IPN, 63/2, 41–2.
87. Arthur Greiser to Gustav and Ida Greiser, 20 February 1917, IPN, 63/3, 11–12.
88. Arthur Greiser to Gustav and Ida Greiser, 10 August 1915, IPN, 63/2, 58.
89. Arthur Greiser to Gustav and Ida Greiser, 11 June 1916, IPN, 63/2, 44–5.
90. Arthur Greiser to Gustav and Ida Greiser, 23 August 1916, IPN, 63/2, 65–6.
91. Arthur Greiser to Gustav and Ida Greiser, 12 September 1917, IPN, 63/3, 45.
92. Arthur Greiser to Gustav and Ida Greiser, 8 April 1917, IPN, 63/3, 18–19.
93. Arthur Greiser to Gustav and Ida Greiser, 4 May 1917, IPN, 63/3, 27–9.
94. For a discussion of the reverence paid pilots during World War I, see George L. Mosse, *Fallen Soldiers: Reshaping the Memory of the World Wars* (New York: Oxford University Press, 1990), 119–25.
95. 'Friedrich Christiansen,' at *http://en.wikipedia.org/wiki/Friedrich_Christiansen*, accessed 16 July 2009.
96. Arthur Greiser to Maria, 21 June 1934, IZ, I-941.
97. 'Korpsführer Christiansen beim Posener NSFK,' *Ostdeutscher Beobachter* (10 April 1940), 8.
98. Arthur Greiser to Gustav and Ida Greiser, 17 July 1917, IPN, 63/3, 42; Arthur Greiser to Gustav Blank, 22 September 1936, APG, 260/458, 381–4; and '"Wer leben will, der kämpfe also . . . ,"' *Ostdeutscher Beobachter* (17 March 1940), 3.
99. Greiser to Gustav and Ida Greiser, 27 July 1917.
100. Greiser to Gustav and Ida Greiser, 4 May 1917.
101. Arthur Greiser, Lebenslauf, 24 November 1933, APG, 260/328, 31–2; Duplikat Besitzzeugnis, 4 December 1926, NA, RG 319, Box 69.
102. Deutsche Dienststelle to author.
103. Arthur Greiser to Gustav and Ida Greiser, 27 May 1917, IPN, 63/3, 36–7.
104. Arthur Greiser to Gustav and Ida Greiser, 17 June 1917, IPN, 63/3, 39.
105. Arthur Greiser to Gustav and Ida Greiser, 27 July 1917, IPN, 63/3, 43.
106. Arthur Greiser to Gustav and Ida Greiser, 4 May 1917, IPN, 63/3, 27–9.
107. Arthur Greiser to Gustav and Ida Greiser, 28 September 1917, IPN, 63/3, 46.
108. Greiser to Gustav and Ida Greiser and Geschwister, 25 December 1916.
109. Greiser to Gustav and Ida Greiser, 27 May 1917.
110. Arthur Greiser to Gustav and Ida Greiser, 17 August 1915, IPN, 63/1, 17–18.
111. Greiser to Ida Greiser, 18 October 1915.
112. Arthur Greiser to Helene Greiser, [1916], IPN, 63/2, 10.
113. Greiser to Gustav and Ida Greiser, 3 April 1916.
114. Greiser to Gustav and Ida Greiser, 19 December 1916.
115. Greiser to Gustav and Ida Greiser, 11 June 1916.
116. Arthur Greiser to Gustav and Ida Greiser, 5 November 1917, IPN, 63/3, 52.

117. Holger H. Herwig, *The German Naval Officer Corps: A Social and Political History 1890–1918* (London: Oxford University Press, 1973), 218–24.
118. Arthur Greiser, Schlußwort des Angeklagten Artur [*sic*] Greiser im Prozess vor dem Höchsten Volksgericht, July 1946, BA-Bayreuth, Ost-Dok.13/452, 65.
119. Arthur Greiser to Gustav Greiser, 28 August 1915, IPN, 63/1, 19–22.
120. Arthur Greiser to Gustav and Ida Greiser, 25 November 1917, IPN, 63/3, 54.
121. Arthur Greiser to Gustav and Ida Greiser, 23 April 1918, IPN, 63/4, 13–14.
122. Deutsche Dienststelle to author.
123. Rolf-Heinz Höppner to Arthur Greiser, 22 November 1943, NA, RG 319, Box 69; and Fülleborn, interviews, 26 May 2005 and 30 May 2007.
124. Arthur Greiser to Gustav and Ida Greiser, 21 June 1918, IPN, 63/4, 19–20.
125. Arthur Greiser to Gustav and Ida Greiser, 24 June 1918, IPN, 63/4, 17–18.
126. Walter Petzel, 'Gauleiter Greiser,' 15 June 1949, BA-Bayreuth, Ost.Dok.8/ 401, 4.
127. Fülleborn, 26 May 2005.
128. Arthur Greiser to Gustav and Ida Greiser, 23 July 1918, IPN, 63/4, 21.
129. Deutsche Dienststelle to author.
130. Greiser, 'Lebenslauf;' and Deutsche Dienststelle to author.
131. Łuczak, *Arthur Greiser*, 6–7.
132. See Karl Hans Fuchs, 'Gauleiter Greiser,' *Ostdeutscher Beobachter* (1 November 1939).
133. Stroud to author; Deutsche Dienststelle to author.
134. Richard Bessel, 'The "Front Generation" and the Politics of Weimar Germany,' in Mark Roseman, ed., *Generations in Conflict: Youth Revolt and Generation Formation in Germany 1770–1968* (New York: Cambridge University Press, 1995), 122–7.
135. Today, however, historians emphasize the crucial role of the 'war-youth' or 'postwar' generation in forging Nazi institutions and projects, and especially those related to the Final Solution. See Ulrich Herbert, *Best: Biographische Studien über Radikalismus, Weltanschauung und Vernunft 1903–1989* (Bonn: Dietz, 1996); and Michael Wildt, *Generation des Unbedingten: Das Führungskorps des Reichssicherheitshauptamtes* (Hamburg: Hamburger Edition, 2003).
136. In this, Greiser was rather like Adolf Eichmann. See David Cesarani, *Becoming Eichmann: Rethinking the Life, Crimes, and Trial of a 'Desk Murderer'* (Cambridge, Mass.: Da Capo, 2006), 24.
137. 'Rede des Gauleiters Parteigenossen Arthur Greiser vom 20. Dezember 1942 zur Frage der Leistungspolen,' BAB, Former BDC Collection, PK Files for Arthur Greiser, Frames 2854–60.
138. Łuczak, *Arthur Greiser*, 6.
139. Deutsche Dienststelle to author.
140. Arthur Greiser to Gustav and Ida Greiser and Geschwister, [late summer 1919], IPN, 63/5, 7–8.
141. Herwig, *The German Naval Officer Corps*, 265.

142. On the treatment of Germans by Poles after World War I, see Richard Blanke, *Orphans of Versailles: The Germans in Western Poland 1918–1939* (Lexington: University Press of Kentucky, 1993); Anthony Komjathy and Rebecca Stockwell, *German Minorities and the Third Reich: Ethnic Germans of East Central Europe between the Wars* (New York: Homes and Meier, 1980), 65–101; Albert S. Kotowski, *Polens Politik gegenüber seiner deutschen Minderheit 1919–1939* (Wiesbaden: Harrassowitz, 1998); Hermann Rauschning, *Die Entdeutschung Westpreußens und Posens: Zehn Jahre polnischer Politik* (Berlin: Verlag von Reimar Hobbing, 1930); and Gotthold Rhode, 'Das Deutschtum in Posen und Pommerellen in der Zeit der Weimarer Republik,' in *Die deutschen Ostgebiete zur Zeit der Weimarer Republik* (Cologne: Böhlau, 1966), 88–132.
143. Volkmann to Reichsschatzmeister der NSDAP-Mitgliedschaftsamt, 3 April 1941, BAB, Former BDC Collection, PK files on Otto Greiser, Frame 100.
144. Blanke, *Orphans*, 17.
145. Greiser to Gustav and Ida Greiser and Geschwister, [late summer 1919], 7.
146. Fülleborn, 26 May 2005.
147. Volkmann to Reichsschatzmeister der NSDAP.
148. Blanke, *Orphans*, 32.
149. Blanke, *Orphans*, 65.
150. Hagen, *Germans*, 324.
151. Blanke, *Orphans*, 32.
152. Rhode, 'Das Deutschtum,' 99.
153. The following account is based on Komjathy and Stockwell, *German Minorities*, 65–6; and Herbert S. Levine, *Hitler's Free City: A History of the Nazi Party in Danzig*, 1925–39 (Chicago: University of Chicago Press, 1970), 9–17.
154. Levine, *Hitler's Free City*, 12.
155. Levine, *Hitler's Free City*, 17.
156. Fragebogen, Frames 1690–2.
157. BAB, Former BDC Collection, SSO Files on Arthur Greiser, Frame 30.
158. Bruce Campbell, *The SA Generals and the Rise of Nazism* (Lexington: University Press of Kentucky, 1998), 14–19; Michael Mann, *The Dark Side of Democracy: Explaining Ethnic Cleansing* (Cambridge: Cambridge University Press, 2005), 195–6; and Robert G. L. Waite, *Vanguard of Nazism: The Free Corps Movement in Postwar Germany 1918–1923* (Cambridge, Mass.: Harvard University Press, 1952), 264–81.
159. Kershaw assumes that Greiser was radicalized by his Free-Corps experiences. See Ian Kershaw, *Hitler: 1936–1945 Nemesis* (New York: Norton, 2000), 250.
160. Walter Rostin, Auszug aus einem Bericht an das Reichsbank-Direktorium, 8 August 1933, APG, 260/454, 473–4. See also Arthur Greiser to Walter Rostin, 2 August 1934, APG, 260/454, 481.
161. Deutsche Dienststelle to author. Lists of the most important units of the Free Corps do not include one headed by Greiser. See, for example, Appendix I

of Harold J. Gordon, *The Reichswehr and the German Republic 1919–1926* (Princeton: Princeton University Press, 1957), 431–5; and Appendix A of Nigel H. Jones, *Hitler's Heralds: The Story of the Freikorps 1918–1923* (London: John Murray, 1987), 249–65.

162. Deutsche Dienststelle to author.
163. Fuchs, 'Gauleiter Greiser,' 1.
164. Deutsche Dienststelle to author.
165. Jones, *Hitler's Heralds*, 267.
166. Armin Ziegler to author, 18 October 2008.
167. Łuczak, *Arthur Greiser*, 6.
168. Rüdiger Ruhnau, *Die Freie Stadt Danzig 1919–1939* (Berg am See: Kurt Vowinckel Verlag, 1979), 158.
169. See ' "Wer leben will, der kämpfe also . . ." ' 3.
170. Volkmann to the Reichsschatzmeister der NSDAP.
171. Aktenvermerk, Der Reichsführer-SS, Der Chef des Sicherheitshauptamtes, 5 October 1936, BAB, Former BDC Collection, SSO Files on Arthur Greiser, Frame 118.
172. The new lodge was called 'To the Seventh Light' and was linked with 'To the Three Globes.' Heinz Ziemer to Arthur Greiser, 15 July 1934, APG, 260/453, 777; Heinrich Himmler to Martin Bormann, 26 May 1943, NA, RG 319, Box 69; and Ralf Melzer, *Konflikt und Anpassung: Freimauerei in der Weimarer Republik und im 'Dritten Reich'* (Vienna: Braumüller, 1999), 101, 111.
173. Melzer, *Konflikt*, 47.
174. Melzer, *Konflikt*, 50.
175. Melzer, *Konflikt*, 77–8.
176. See Melzer, *Konflikt*, 147, 204.
177. Aktenvermerk, 5 October 1936.
178. Arthur Greiser to Heinz Ziemer, 23 April 1934, APG, 260/453, 771–2.
179. Łuczak portrays Greiser as an anti-Polish youth who quickly found Nazism after World War I. See Łuczak, *Arthur Greiser*, 9–10.
180. Unless otherwise noted, information on the Deutschsoziale Partei is from Dieter Fricke, ed., *Die bürgerlichen Parteien in Deutschland: Handbuch der Geschichte der bürgerlichen Parteien und anderer bürgerlicher Interessenorganisation vom Vormärz bis zum Jahre 1945* (Berlin: das europäische buch, 1968), Vol. I, 757–8.
181. Levine, *Hitler's Free City*, 19.
182. Arthur Greiser to Luftamt Königsberg, Abteilung IIa, 23 August 1934, APG, 260/454, 513.
183. Willy Hellwig to Arthur Greiser, 7 September 1933, APG, 260/452, 709–10.
184. Erich Zöller to Arthur Greiser, 19 January 1935, APG, 260/456, 487–91.
185. Łuczak, *Arthur Greiser*, 10; and Jones, *Hitler's Heralds*, 267.
186. Helmut Neuberger, *Winkelmaß und Hakenkreuz: Die Freimaurer und das Dritte Reich* (Munich: Herbig, 2001), 66.

187. Fülleborn, 26 May 2005; and 'Fragebogen,' BAB, Former BDC Collection, SSO Files on Arthur Greiser, Frame 40.
188. Fülleborn, 26 May 2005.
189. See Kershaw, *Hitler*, 250; Łuczak, *Arthur Greiser*, 106–7; and Arthur Greiser to Georg Deuser, 5 April 1934, APG, 260/452, 77.
190. Fülleborn, 26 May 2005.
191. Arthur Greiser, curriculum vitae, [1945], NA, RG 319, Box 69. On his oils and fats business, see Arthur Greiser [statement], 11 dzień rozprawy, 2 July 1946, IPN, 196/38, 862; and Maria Greiser to Paul Ruge, 25 October 1959, private collection of Paul Ruge.
192. Fülleborn, 26 May 2005.
193. Heinz Ziemer to Arthur Greiser, 17 February 1935, APG, 260/457, 155.
194. Fülleborn, 26 May 2005.
195. Fülleborn, 26 May 2005.
196. Siegmund, *Rückblick*, 35.
197. Zoppoter Tennis-Klub E.V. to Arthur Greiser, 6 March 1934, APG, 260/452, 535.
198. Arthur Greiser to Zoppoter Tennis-Klub E.V., 19 March 1934, APG, 260/452, 537.
199. Frank Fischer, *Danzig: Die zerbrochene Stadt* (Berlin: Propyläen, 2006), 333.
200. Wietrzykowski, *Powrót*, 8.
201. Aktenvermerk, 5 October 1936.
202. At his trial, Greiser claimed that the Dutch company Unilever destroyed his business. Since Unilever was founded only in 1930, Greiser probably meant one of its forerunners, the Dutch margarine producer Margarine Unie. See Greiser [statement], 11 dzień rozprawy, 862; and 'Unilever,' en.wikipedia.org/wiki/Unilever, accessed 25 July 2009.
203. Samuel Echt, *Die Geschichte der Juden in Danzig* (Leer: Verlag Gerhard Rautenberg, 1972), 173; and Erwin Lichtenstein, *Die Juden der Freien Stadt Danzig unter der Herrschaft des Nationalsozialismus* (Tubingen: Mohr, 1973), 33.
204. It is often said that Greiser now earned money by ferrying tourists around the Danzig bay. See Kershaw, *Hitler*, 250; Łuczak, *Arthur Greiser*, 107. In fact, he did this only *after* he had joined the NSDAP. See documents in NA, RG 319, Box 69.
205. Fülleborn, 26 May 2005 and 30 May 2007.
206. Personalbogen, [1936], BAB, Former BDC Collection, PK Files on Arthur Greiser, Frame 2882.
207. Fragebogen, Frames 1690–2.
208. In fact, financial security correlates better with future Nazi leaders than financial misery. See Ronald Rogowski, 'The *Gauleiter* and the Social Origins of Fascism,' *Comparative Studies in Society and History* 19 (1977): 401–2.

209. Greiser, Schlußwort, 22–3, 58–9.
210. Karin Orth, *Die Konzentrationslager-SS: Sozialstrukturelle Analysen und biographische Studien* (Munich: Deutscher Taschenbuch Verlag, 2004), 88.
211. Robert Jay Lifton, *The Nazi Doctors: Medical Killing and the Psychology of Genocide* (New York: Basic Books, 1986), 499.
212. Eric A. Zillmer, Molly Harrower, Barry A. Ritzler, and Robert P. Archer, eds., *The Quest for the Nazi Personality: A Psychological Investigation of Nazi War Criminals* (Hillsdale: Lawrence Erlbaum Associates, 1995), 108–16.
213. Kershaw, *Hitler*, 912, fn. 109.

2. 'LITTLE MARIA:' STRIVING FOR STRENGTH AND POWER IN DANZIG

1. Lifton has described how some Nazis, after joining the movement, took on new selves that involved a 'sense of mystical fusion with the German *Volk*, with "destiny," and with immortalizing powers.' Robert Jay Lifton, *The Nazi Doctors: Medical Killing and the Psychology of Genocide* (New York: Basic Books, 1986), 426.
2. Unless otherwise noted, the following account of the early days of the NSDAP in Danzig is drawn from Herbert S. Levine, *Hitler's Free City: A History of the Nazi Party in Danzig, 1925–39* (Chicago: University of Chicago Press, 1970), 18–30.
3. Marek Andrzejewski, *Opposition und Widerstand in Danzig 1933 bis 1939* (Bonn: Dietz, 1994), 21.
4. Zbigniew Ciećkowski, 'Powstanie i rozwój ruchu narodowosocjalistycznego w Wolnym Mieście Gdańsku do 1933 r.,' *Zapiski Historyczne* 30, no. 2 (1965): 50.
5. Hans Hohnfeldt to Parteigenosse Buch, 30 July 1930, APP, Hans Hohnfeldt/16, 108. Emphasis in original.
6. BAB, Former BDC Collection, SSO files for Arthur Greiser, Frame 30.
7. Sitzungsprotokoll, 16 September 1930, APP, Hans Hohnfeldt/16, 29.
8. Meller to Hermann Göring, 30 September 1930, BAB, Former BDC Collection, OPG files for Hans Hohnfeldt, Frame 2176.
9. Arthur Greiser to Hermann Göring, 4 October 1930, BAB, Former BDC Collection, OPG files for Hans Hohnfeldt, Frame 2262.
10. Dieter Schenk, *Hitlers Mann in Danzig: Gauleiter Forster und die NS-Verbrechen in Danzig-Westpreußen* (Bonn: Dietz, 2000), 32.
11. Hans Georg Siegler, *Danzig: Chronik eines Jahrtausends* (Düsseldorf: Droste, 1990), 330.
12. The following account of Forster's biography is based on Levine, *Hitler's Free City*, 31–3; and Schenk, *Hitlers Mann*, 15–30.
13. Christoph M. Kimmich, *The Free City: Danzig and German Foreign Policy 1919–1934* (New Haven: Yale University Press, 1968), 141.

14. Schenk, *Hitlers Mann*, 32–3.
15. Arthur Greiser [statement], 11 dzień rozprawy, 2 July 1946, IPN, 196/38, 862; and Levine, *Hitler's Free City*, 11–12.
16. Schenk, *Hitlers Mann*, 37.
17. Andrzejewski, *Opposition*, 28.
18. BAB, Former BDC Collection, SSO Files on Arthur Greiser, Frame 29.
19. Hans Hohnfeldt and Werner Lorenz to Reichsführung der SS der NSDAP, 20 July 1931, BAB, Former BDC Collection, SSO Files on Arthur Greiser, Frame 134.
20. Werner Lorenz to Heinrich Himmler, 2 June 1933, BAB, Former BDC Collection, SSO Files on Arthur Greiser, Frame 61.
21. In March 1934, Greiser was promoted once again to senior storm unit leader (*Obersturmbannführer*). BAB, Former BDC Collection, SSO Files on Arthur Greiser, Frame 36.
22. Frank Fischer, *Danzig: Die zerbrochene Stadt* (Berlin: Propyläen, 2006), 326.
23. Levine, *Hitler's Free City*, 35–7.
24. Levine, *Hitler's Free City*, 40.
25. A copy of the picture is found in 'Opfer und Haltung bestimmen den Sieg,' *Ostdeutscher Beobachter* (30 January 1943).
26. Hans Hohnfeldt to Oberste Parteigericht, 1. Kammer, 21 October 1936, BAB, Former BDC Collection, OPG files for Hans Hohnfeldt, Frame 3072.
27. Vera Stroud to author, 3 May 2005.
28. Erlaubnisschein, 17 June 1930, NA, RG 319, Box 69; and Czesław Łuczak, *Arthur Greiser* (Poznań: PSO, 1997), 107.
29. Friedrich Fuchs, *Die Beziehungen zwischen der Freien Stadt Danzig und dem Deutschen Reich in der Zeit von 1920 bis 1939: Unter besonderer Berücksichtigung der Judenfrage in beiden Staaten* (Freiburg: HochschulVerlag, 1999), 52.
30. Edmund Baron von Thermann, Vermerk, 27 October 1930, PA-AA, R83194, 122.
31. Ian Kershaw, *Hitler 1936–1945: Nemesis* (New York: Norton, 2000), 912, fn. 109.
32. 'Die Rede des Staatsanwalts M. Siewierski,' BA-Ludwigsburg, ZStL, Polen 365 h 2, 78 (of document).
33. Janusz Gumkowski and Tadeusz Kułakowski, *Zbrodniarze hitlerowscy przed Najwyższym Trybunałem Narodowym* (Warsaw: Wydawnictwo Prawnicze, 1961), 5.
34. Dr. Larsen to Albert Forster, 17 June 1931, APP, Hans Hohnfeldt/17, 29–30.
35. Hans Hohnfeldt to Arthur Greiser, 7 August 1931, APP, Hans Hohnfeldt/17, 52.
36. Arthur Greiser to Hans Hohnfeldt, 8 August 1931, APP, Hans Hohnfeldt/17, 53.
37. Hans Hohnfeldt to Albert Forster, 14 August 1931, APP, Hans Hohnfeldt/17, 68–70.

38. Levine, *Hitler's Free City*, 45.
39. See 'Verzeichnis der geschichtlich wertvollen Akten in Danzig,' BAB, R3001/9803/18, 7–13.
40. Der Oberstaatsanwalt in Elbing to Preußischer Justizminister, 22 June 1931, GSA, Reichsjustizministerium, I. HA, Rep. 841 Justizministerium, 53822, 1–2. Hindenburg was President of the Reich, not the Reichstag.
41. Der Oberstaatsanwalt in Elbing to Preußischer Justizminister, 25 July 1931, GSA, Reichsjustizministerium, I. HA, Rep. 841 Justizministerium, 53822, 17 b-c.
42. Dr. Schäfer to Preußischer Justizminister, 30 September 1931, GSA, Reichsjustizministerium, I. HA, Rep. 841 Justizministerium, 53822, 17 h.
43. See documents in GSA, Reichsjustizministerium, I. HA, Rep. 841 Justizministerium, 53822, 19–46.
44. Levine, *Hitler's Free City*, 43.
45. Arthur Greiser, 'Unsere bisherige Politik in Danzig,' *Der Vorposten*, 6 February 1931, IPN, 196/206, 1.
46. *Danziger Neuesten Nachrichten*, 19 March 1931, PA-AA, R 83194, 177.
47. Schenk, *Hitlers Mann*, 39.
48. 'Dreistündige außenpolitische Aussprache im Volkstag,' *Danziger Neuesten Nachrichten*, 16 February 1933, PA-AA, R83195, 108.
49. Levine, *Hitler's Free City*, 42–54; Schenk, *Hitlers Mann*, 39–42.
50. Hermann Rauschning, *The Conservative Revolution* (New York: G. P. Putnam's Sons, 1941), 7.
51. Levine, *Hitler's Free City*, 47–53.
52. Kimmich, *The Free City*, 143.
53. Levine, *Hitler's Free City*, 61–4.
54. Levine, *Hitler's Free City*, 75.
55. Arthur Greiser to Justizabteilung, 16 August 1933, APG, 260/473, 325–6.
56. Hans L. Leonhardt, *Nazi Conquest of Danzig* (Chicago: University of Chicago Press, 1942), 71. Emphasis in original.
57. Arthur Greiser to Albert Forster, 7 November 1933, APG, 260/453, 177–81.
58. Helmer Rosting to the secretary-general of the League of Nations, 4 November 1933, PA-AA, R83197.
59. Greiser to Forster, 7 November 1933.
60. Bericht des Berichtserstatters, Völkerbundsrat, 18 January 1934, PA-AA, R83197.
61. Leonhardt, *Nazi Conquest*, 84–5. Emphasis in original.
62. Arthur Greiser to the drei Landräte, Pol. Präs., Staatskommissar Temp, Zoppot, Staatskommissar Hannemann, Tiegenhof, und stellv. Bürgermeister von Neuteich, 17 January 1934, APG, 260/473, 529.
63. Arthur Greiser to Hermann Rauschning, 23 April 1934, APG, 260/473, 649.
64. Łuczak, *Arthur Greiser*, 4.

65. Arthur Greiser to Gustav and Ida Greiser, 31 March 1917, IPN 63/3, 17.
66. Schenk, *Hitlers Mann*, 68.
67. Erwin Lichtenstein, *Die Juden der Freien Stadt Danzig unter der Herrschaft des Nationalsozialismus* (Tübingen: Mohr, 1973), 33.
68. Samuel Echt, *Die Geschichte der Juden in Danzig* (Leer: Verlag Gerhard Rautenberg, 1972), 138.
69. Vera Stroud to author.
70. See Harry Siegmund, *Rückblick: Erinnerungen eines Staatsdieners in bewegter Zeit* (Raisdorf: Ostsee Verlag, 1999), 60; Arthur Greiser to Paul Batzer, 1 August 1933, APG, 260/473, 133–4; and Arthur Greiser to Maria, 18 May 1934, IZ, I-941.
71. See Klage des Vicepräsident Arthur Greiser, 23 August 1934, and other documents in NA, XE000933, *Greiser*, Arthur.
72. Fragebogen zur Erlangung der Heiratsgenehmigung, BAB, Former BDC Collection, RS Files on Arthur Greiser, Frames 1718–20.
73. On Hans Pfitzner, see Jens Malte Fischer, 'The Very German Fate of a Composer: Hans Pfitzner,' in Michael H. Kater and Albrecht Riethmüller, eds., *Music and Nazism: Art under Tyranny, 1933–1945* (Laaber: Laaber-Verlag, 2003), 75–89; Michael H. Kater, *Composers of the Nazi Era: Eight Portraits* (New York: Oxford University Press, 2000), 144–82; Michael H. Kater, 'Culture, Society, and Politics in the Cosmos of "Hans Pfitzner the German,"' in Celia Applegate and Pamela Potter, eds., *Music and German National Identity* (Chicago: University of Chicago Press, 2002), 178–89; and John Williamson, *The Music of Hans Pfitzner* (Oxford: Clarendon Press, 1992).
74. Kater, *Composers*, 146–8; and Kater, 'Culture,' 180.
75. Mrs. Harry Siegmund, interview with author, 25 May 2005.
76. Rotraut Fülleborn, interview with author, 26 May 2005; Harry Siegmund, interview with author, 25 May 2005.
77. Arthur Greiser to Paul Batzer, 6 March 1935, APG, 260/471, 283.
78. The letters were found at Greiser's former country estate, and presented to the Instytut Zachodni in Poznań in 1975. See IZ, I-941.
79. Arthur Greiser to Maria, 2 May 1934, IZ, I-941.
80. Arthur Greiser to Maria, 18 May 1934, IZ, I-941.
81. Arthur Greiser to Maria, 15 August 1934, IZ, I-941.
82. Arthur Greiser to Maria, 24 August 1934, IZ, I-941.
83. Greiser to Maria, 2 May 1934.
84. Arthur Greiser to Maria, 21 June 1934, IZ, I-941.
85. Arthur Greiser to Maria, 9 August 1934, IZ, I-941.
86. Greiser to Maria, 15 August 1934.
87. On the Linsmayer–Greiser feud, see Levine, *Hitler's Free City*, 33, 75–6, 96–7.
88. Otto von Radowitz, Aufzeichnung, 28 November 1934, PA-AA, R35964, 33.

89. See Arthur Greiser, Vermerk, 15 November 1933, NA, XE000933, *Greiser, Arthur*; and Ernst Röhm, Befehl, 9 January 1934, BAB, Former BDC Collection, SSO Files on Arthur Greiser, Frame 67.
90. Hermann Rauschning, *Makers of Destruction: Meetings and Talks in Revolutionary Germany* (London: Eyre and Spottiswoode, 1942), 265.
91. Arthur Greiser to Maria, 31 August 1934, IZ, I-941.
92. Arthur Greiser to Maria, 1 September 1934, IZ, I-941.
93. Arthur Greiser to Maria, 3 September 1934, IZ, I-941.
94. Rotraut Fülleborn, interview with author, 30 May 2007.
95. Ruth Greiser to Heinrich Himmler, 12 October 1934, BAB, SSO Files on Arthur Greiser, Frames 80–3. Emphasis in original.
96. For the converted value of the gulden in 2008 dollars, see *http://www.answers.com/topic/danzig-gulden;* and *http://www.measuringworth.com*.
97. Urteil, Landgericht Danzig, 15 October 1934, BAB, SSO Files on Arthur Greiser, Frames 69–73.
98. Arthur Greiser to Heinrich Himmler, 10 November 1934, BAB, SSO Files on Arthur Greiser, Frame 84.
99. Arthur Greiser to Maria, 1 November 1934, IZ, I-941.
100. Arthur Greiser to Maria, 8 November 1934, IZ, I-941.
101. Arthur Greiser to Maria, 13 November 1934, IZ, I-941.
102. Arthur Greiser to Maria, 12 November 1934, IZ, I-941.
103. Greiser to Maria, 13 November 1934.
104. Arthur Greiser to Maria, 16 November 1934, IZ, I-941.
105. Walter Buch, Erklärung, 20 July 1934, NA, RG319, Box 69.
106. See 'Zusammenstellung der Vorwürfe des Pg. Reuter gegen Gauleiter Greiser,' [1943], NA, RG319, Box 69.
107. Aktennotiz, C/Hh., 26 November 1934, BAB, Former BDC Collection, SSO Files on Arthur Greiser, Frame 132.
108. Wilhelm Freiherr von Holzschuher to Arthur Greiser, 29 November 1934, NA, RG319, Box 69.
109. Arthur Greiser to Maria, November 20, 1934, IZ, I-941.
110. Levine, *Hitler's Free City*, 77–9.
111. Rauschning, *The Conservative Revolution*, 9.
112. Hermann Rauschning, Vermerk, 29 September 1934, PA-AA, R31077K.
113. On Sean Lester see Paul McNamara, *Sean Lester, Poland and the Nazi Takeover of Danzig* (Dublin: Irish Academic Press, 2009).
114. Arthur Greiser to Sean Lester, 2 October 1934, PA-AA, R31077K.
115. Koester to Auswärtiges Amt, 6 October 1934, PA-AA, R31077K.
116. Koester to Auswärtiges Amt, 10 October 1934, PA-AA, R31077K.
117. Hermann Rauschning to Arthur Greiser, 11 October 1934, PA-AA, R35964, 69.
118. Schenk, *Hitlers Mann*, 54.
119. Leonhardt, *Nazi Conquest*, 95–6, 111; Levine, *Hitler's Free City*, 81.

120. Wilhelm Huth, Arthur Greiser, *et al.* to Hermann Rauschning, 19 November 1934, BAB, R43II/14026, 41. Translation in Rauschning, *The Conservative Revolution*, 25–6.
121. Rauschning, *The Conservative Revolution*, 25, 27–8.
122. Leonhardt, *Nazi Conquest*, 97–8; and Levine, *Hitler's Free City*, 81.
123. Levine, *Hitler's Free City*, 97.
124. *Akten zur Deutschen Auswärtigen Politik 1918–1945, Serie C, 1933–1937: Das Dritte Reich: Die ersten Jahre* (Göttingen: Vandenhoeck und Ruprecht, 1973), Vol. 3, no. 1, 491–2.
125. Koester to Auswärtiges Amt, 28 November 1934, PA-AA, R83198.
126. 'Regierungserklärung des Präsidenten des Senats der Freien Stadt Danzig, Arthur Greiser, vom 28. November 1934,' PA-AA, R83198.
127. Arthur Greiser to Werner Lorenz, 6 December 1934, APG, 260/456, 21–2; and Valdis O. Lumans, *Himmler's Auxiliaries: The Volksdeutsche Mittelstelle and the German National Minorities of Europe, 1933–1945* (Chapel Hill: University of North Carolina Press, 1993), 48.
128. Levine, *Hitler's Free City*, 97.
129. Koester to Auswärtiges Amt, 29 November 1934, PA-AA, R83198.
130. Arthur Greiser to Maria, 23 January 1935, IZ, I-941.
131. Arthur Greiser to Maria, 22 March 1935, IZ, I-941.
132. Leonhardt, *Nazi Conquest*, 110–24.
133. Arthur Greiser to Maria, 26 March 1935, IZ, I-941.
134. Arthur Greiser to Marianne Wolffgram, 30 March 1935, APG, 260/455, 591–2.
135. Andrzejewski, *Opposition*, 93.
136. Levine, *Hitler's Free City*, 85.
137. Leonhardt, *Nazi Conquest*, 123.
138. Levine, *Hitler's Free City*, 81–8.
139. Ruth Greiser to Arthur Greiser, 4 February 1935, NA, XE000933, *Greiser*, Arthur.
140. Beschluss, 24. April 1939, NA, XE000933, *Greiser*, Arthur.
141. See Aufzeichnung, 5 May 1936, and many other similar documents in NA, XE000933, *Greiser*, Arthur.
142. Gerhard Gülzow, *Kirchenkampf in Danzig 1934–1945: Persönliche Erinnerungen* (Leer: Verlag Gerhard Rautenberg, 1968), 43.
143. 'NS-Ausleseschule,' *http://de.wikipedia.org/wiki/NS-Ausleseschule*, accessed 1 August 2009.
144. PA-AA, Angestellte Weibl.- 15–15, Personalakten für Ingrid Birr, Nr.125A.
145. Arthur Greiser to Maria, 26 March 1935, IZ, I-941.
146. Fülleborn, 26 May 2005.
147. Aertzlicher Untersuchungsbogen, signed Erich Grossmann, 28 February 1935, BAB, Former BDC Collection, RS Files on Arthur Greiser, Frame 1704.

148. Aerztlicher Untersuchungsbogen, signature illegible, 8 February 1935, BAB, Former BDC Collection, RS Files for Arthur Greiser, Frame 1702.
149. Steinbeck to Arthur Greiser, [1935], BAB, Former BDC Collection, SSO Files on Arthur Greiser, Frame 86.
150. Arthur Greiser to Maria, 15 March 1935, IZ, I-941.
151. Greiser to Maria, 22 March 1935.
152. Greiser to Maria, 15 March 1935.
153. Levine, *Hitler's Free City*, 87.
154. Rauschning, *Makers*, 257.
155. Schenk, *Hitlers Mann*, 62. For the calculation of Greiser's salary in 2008 dollars, see *http://www.answers.com/topic/danzig-gulden*; and *http://uwacadweb.uwyo.edu/numimage/currency.htm*, accessed 5 August 2009.
156. 'Senatspräsident Greiser gestern in Berlin getraut,' *Deutsche Allgemeine Zeitung*, 10 April 1935, BAB, NS5/VI/17583, 59.
157. Arthur Greiser to Weinrestaurant Horcher, 3 April 1935, APG, 260/457, 513.
158. 'Die Warschauer Philharmoniker in Danzig,' *Danziger Neueste Nachrichten*, 9 December 1935, APG, 260/475, 347.
159. *Il. Kur. Codzienny*, 11 December 1935, APG, 260/475, 339.
160. See Kater, *Composers*, 169–70; and 'Frau Maria Greiser-Koerfer spielte im Staatstheater,' *Danziger Vorposten*, 27 April 1936, APG, 260/475, 485.
161. BAB, Former BDC Collection, NSDAP Ortskartei 3200/G0016, Frame 2208.
162. See Joachim C. Fest, *The Face of the Third Reich: Portraits of the Nazi Leadership* (New York: Pantheon Books, 1970), 121; Ralf Melzer, *Konflikt und Anpassung: Freimauerei in der Weimarer Republik und im 'Dritten Reich'* (Vienna: Braumüller, 1999), 50; Albert Speer, *Inside the Third Reich* (New York: Macmillan, 1970), 97; and Jochen von Lang, *The Secretary: Martin Bormann: The Man Who Manipulated Hitler* (New York: Random House, 1979), 298.
163. Arthur Greiser to Maria, 23 January 1935, IZ, I-941.
164. Sean Lester, memorandum, 19 June 1935, UNOG, *http://biblio-archive.unog.ch/Dateien/0/D2248.pdf.* My thanks to Robert Nylander for pointing me to this document.
165. *Granica zbrodni Arthura Greisera* (1969).
166. See Leon Goldensohn, *The Nuremberg Interviews: Conducted by Leon Goldensohn*, ed. Robert Gellately (New York: Knopf, 2004), 32, 53.
167. Goldensohn, *The Nuremberg Interviews*, 17, 19, 82, 129, 424.
168. Fülleborn, 26 May 2005.
169. Fülleborn, 26 May 2005.
170. Eric A. Zillmer, Molly Harrower, Barry A. Ritzler, and Robert P. Archer, *The Quest for the Nazi Personality: A Psychological Investigation of Nazi War Criminals* (Hillsdale: Lawrence Erlbaum Associates, 1995), 32.

3. 'THE NICEST TIME OF MY LIFE:' SENATE PRESIDENT

1. Günter Grass, *The Tin Drum* (New York: Vintage, 1990), 117.
2. Otto von Radowitz to Auswärtiges Amt, 19 January 1935, PA-AA, R83199.
3. See Paul McNamara, *Sean Lester, Poland and the Nazi Takeover of Danzig* (Dublin: Irish Academic Press, 2009).
4. Aufzeichnung des Generalkonsuls in Danzig von Radowitz, 12 December 1934, in *Akten zur Deutschen Auswärtigen Politik 1918–1945, Serie C, 1933–1937* (Göttingen: Vandenhoeck und Ruprecht, 1973–81), Vol. 3, no. 2, 718–20 (hereafter *ADAP*).
5. Czesław Łuczak, *Arthur Greiser* (Poznań: PSO, 1997), 27.
6. 'Danzig Commissioner Jeered,' *New York Times* (30 March 1935), 8.
7. Arthur Greiser to Maria, 26 March 1935, IZ, I-941.
8. Otto von Radowitz to Auswärtiges Amt, 29 March 1935, PA-AA, R83199.
9. 'Danzig Commissioner Jeered,' 8.
10. Aufzeichnung des Reichsministers des Auswärtigen Freiherrn von Neurath, 1 April 1935, *ADAP*, Serie C, Vol. 4, no. 1, 3.
11. Friedrich Fuchs, *Die Beziehungen zwischen der Freien Stadt Danzig und dem Deutschen Reich in der Zeit von 1920 bis 1939: Unter besonderer Berücksichtigung der Judenfrage in beiden Staaten* (Freiburg: HochschulVerlag, 1999), 57.
12. Ernst Sodeikat, 'Der Nationalsozialismus und die Danziger Opposition,' *Vierteljahrshefte für Zeitgeschichte* 14 (1966): 148.
13. Herbert S. Levine, *Hitler's Free City: A History of the Nazi Party in Danzig, 1925–39* (Chicago: University of Chicago Press, 1970), 104.
14. Der Generalkonsul in Danzig von Radowitz an Ministerialdirektor Meyer, 16 May 1935, in *ADAP*, Serie C, Vol. 4, no. 1, 164–5.
15. Richard Breyer, *Das Deutsche Reich und Polen 1932–1937: Außenpolitik und Volksgruppenfragen* (Würzburg: Holzner-Verlag, 1955), 197–8.
16. Der Preußische Ministerpräsident Göring an den Reichsminister des Auswärtigen Freiherrn von Neurath, 21 May 1935, in *ADAP*, Serie C, Vol. 4, no. 1, 177–82.
17. Der Generalkonsul in Danzig von Radowitz an Ministerialdirektor Meyer, 13 June 1935, includes Arthur Greiser, Vermerk, 11 June 1935, in *ADAP*, Serie C, Vol. 4, no. 1, 297.
18. Der Generalkonsul in Danzig . . . an Ministerialdirektor Meyer, 13 June 1935, 294–300.
19. 'Migration to Reich Planned by Danzig,' *New York Times* (14 June 1935), 7.
20. Arthur Greiser, Regierungserklärung, 12 June 1935, PA-AA, R83201.
21. Jerzy Szapiro, 'Danzig Nazis Bring Crisis to Free City,' *New York Times* (30 June 1935), E5.
22. Aufzeichnung des Ministerialdirektors Meyer, 26 July 1935, in *ADAP*, Serie C, Vol. 4, no. 1, 475–7.

23. Aufzeichnung des Legationssekretärs Graf Adelmann, 1 August 1935, in *ADAP*, Serie C, Vol. 4, no. 1, 509–12.
24. Levine, *Hitler's Free City*, 92–5.
25. Viktor Böttcher, Vermerk über eine Besprechung zwischen Präsident Greiser und dem Hohen Kommissar Lester in Anwesenheit von Marchese Giustiniani und Dr. Böttcher, 17 August 1935. NA, XE000933, *Greiser*, Arthur.
26. 'Die Erfolge des Staatsmanns Greiser,' *Der Mitteldeutsche*, 5 February 1937, BAB, NS5VI/17583, 55.
27. Hans Koester to Auswärtiges Amt, 1 June 1935, PA-AA, R83201.
28. Otto von Radowitz to Auswärtiges Amt, 25 May 1935, PA-AA, R83201.
29. Sean Lester to Arthur Greiser, 12 July 1935, PA-AA, R83201.
30. Paul McNamara to author, 3 December 2008.
31. Douglas Gageby, *The Last Secretary General: Sean Lester and the League of Nations* (Dublin: Town House, 1999), 90–1.
32. Arthur Greiser, Regierungserklärung, 27 November 1935, PA-AA, R83203.
33. Levine, *Hitler's Free City*, 110–11.
34. McNamara, *Sean Lester*, 124.
35. McNamara, *Sean Lester*, 129.
36. See Arthur Greiser, Vermerk über eine Rücksprache beim Führer, [16 January 1936]; and Vermerk über eine Rücksprache mit Herrn Ministerpräsidenten Göring [15 January 1936], NA, XE000933, *Greiser*, Arthur.
37. Sodeikat, 'Der Nationalsozialismus,' 155–64.
38. Arthur Greiser to Maria, 24 January 1936, IZ, I-941.
39. McNamara, *Sean Lester*, 229–30.
40. Levine, *Hitler's Free City*, 112–13.
41. Arthur Greiser, Schlußwort des Angeklagten Artur [*sic*] Greiser im Prozess vor dem Höchsten Volksgericht, July 1946, BA-Bayreuth, Ost.Dok. 13/452, 28.
42. Levine, *Hitler's Free City*, 98.
43. McNamara, *Sean Lester*, 113.
44. Levine, *Hitler's Free City*, 99.
45. Dieter Schenk, *Hitlers Mann in Danzig: Gauleiter Forster und die NS-Verbrechen in Danzig-Westpreußen* (Bonn: Dietz, 2000), 224–8.
46. 'Jahresbericht des Senats der Freien Stadt Danzig, 1935,' December 1935, PA-AA, R83203.
47. Levine, *Hitler's Free City*, 144.
48. Arthur Greiser, Regierungserklärung, 12 June 1935.
49. Frank Fischer, *Danzig: Die zerbrochene Stadt* (Berlin: Propyläen, 2006), 333.
50. 'Konflikt in Danzig: SA Gauleiter Forstner [*sic*] fordert Rücktritt des Senatspräsidenten Greiser,' *Basler Nachrichten*, 29 October 1935, PA-AA, R83202.
51. Arthur Greiser, Auszug aus einem Vermerk über eine Besprechung mit Minister Papée, 18 November 1935, APG, 260/475, 293.
52. Otto von Radowitz to Roediger, 8 February 1936, PA-AA, R31077K.
53. McNamara, *Sean Lester*, 142–3.

54. Levine, *Hitler's Free City*, 115.
55. Gageby, *The Last Secretary General*, 119.
56. Otto von Radowitz to Auswärtiges Amt, 16 June 1936, PA-AA, R103932.
57. Schenk, *Hitlers Mann*, 64.
58. McNamara, *Sean Lester*, 148–9; and McNamara to author.
59. McNamara, *Sean Lester*, 156.
60. Levine, *Hitler's Free City*, 116.
61. McNamara, *Sean Lester*, 160–1.
62. Levine, *Hitler's Free City*, 116–17.
63. Clarence K. Streit, 'Danzig Rift Turns Poles from Reich; League Test Seen,' *New York Times* (6 July 1936), 6.
64. Gageby, *The Last Secretary General*, 125.
65. Clarence K. Streit, 'Nazi Mocks League in Danzig Hearing,' *New York Times* (5 July 1936), 1, 7.
66. Joseph Goebbels, *Die Tagebücher von Joseph Goebbels: Sämtliche Fragmente*, ed. Elke Fröhlich (Munich: K. G. Saur, 1987), Part 1, Vol. 2, 639.
67. Aufzeichnung ohne Unterschrift, July 1937, in *ADAP*, Serie C, Vol. 4, no. 2, 946.
68. Goebbels, *Die Tagebücher*, Part I, Vol. 2, 639.
69. See Arthur Greiser to Hermann Göring, 9 July 1936; Arthur Greiser to Wolff, 9 July 1936; Arthur Greiser to Heinrich Himmler, 9 July 1936; and Hermann Göring to Arthur Greiser, 11 July 1936, NA, XE000933, *Greiser*, Arthur.
70. Levine, *Hitler's Free City*, 117.
71. Breyer, *Das Deutsche Reich*, 205.
72. 'Re-enter the Nazis,' *News Chronicle*, 6 July 1936, PA-AA, R103932.
73. 'The League and Germany,' *The Times*, 6 July 1936, PA-AA, R103932.
74. 'Kultur,' *Morningpost*, 6 July 1936, PA-AA, R103932.
75. 'Cocking a Snook,' *New York Times* (26 July 1936), E8.
76. 'Editorial Cartoon 1—No Title,' *New York Times* (19 July 1936), E2.
77. For general accounts of the suppression of the Danzig opposition, see Marek Andrzejewski, *Opposition und Widerstand in Danzig 1933 bis 1939* (Bonn: Dietz, 1994); Fuchs, *Die Beziehungen*; Hans L. Leonhardt, *Nazi Conquest of Danzig* (Chicago: University of Chicago Press, 1942); Levine, *Hitler's Free City*; and Sodeikat, 'Der Nationalsozialismus,' 139–74.
78. 'Danzig Nazis Plot an Unarmed Coup,' *New York Times* (8 July 1936), 11.
79. 'Nazis Defy League; Crush Danzig Foes,' *New York Times* (19 July 1936), 1.
80. Carl J. Burckhardt, *Meine Danziger Mission 1937–1939* (Munich: Callwey, 1980), 94.
81. Andrzejewski, *Opposition*, 176–80.
82. Levine, *Hitler's Free City*, 120.
83. Arthur Greiser, Vermerk, 10 January 1935, PA-AA, R35964, 23–6.
84. McNamara, *Sean Lester*, 82.
85. Greiser, Schlußwort, 25; and McNamara to author.

86. Greiser, Vermerk, 10 January 1935, 23–6.
87. Jerzy Szapiro, 'Warsaw is Firm on Danzig Rights,' *New York Times* (13 January 1935), E2.
88. Otto von Radowitz to Auswärtiges Amt, 23 January 1935, PA-AA, R83199.
89. Rüdiger Ruhnau, *Die Freie Stadt Danzig 1919–1939* (Berg am See: Kurt Vowinckel Verlag, 1979), 150.
90. Abschrift appended to Otto von Radowitz to Auswärtiges Amt, 4 September 1935, PA-AA, R83202.
91. 'Die Jagden in Bialowiece,' *Danziger Neueste Nachrichten*, 11 February 1936, APG, 260/475, 371.
92. 'Präsident Greiser zur polnischen Staatsjagd abgereist,' *Danziger Neueste Nachrichten*, 14 February 1936, APG, 260/475, 375.
93. Breyer, *Das Deutsche Reich*, 203.
94. Arthur Greiser to Albert Forster, 15 October 1936, NA, XE000933, *Greiser*, Arthur.
95. Ruhnau, *Die Freie Stadt Danzig*, 149.
96. Diego von Bergen to Auswärtiges Amt, 30 March 1938, PA-AA, R103951.
97. Levine, *Hitler's Free City*, 121.
98. Arthur Greiser to Generalintendanten Merz, 16 August 1939, APG, 260/458, 305–6.
99. Merz to Arthur Greiser, 18 August 1939, APG, 260/458, 307.
100. Fuchs, *Die Beziehungen*, 115–16; Ernst Sodeikat, 'Die Verfolgung und der Widerstand der Juden in der Freien Stadt Danzig von 1933 bis 1945,' *Bulletin des Leo Baeck Instituts* 8 (1965): 112–13.
101. Erwin Lichtenstein, *Die Juden der Freien Stadt Danzig unter der Herrschaft des Nationalsozialismus* (Tubingen: Mohr, 1973), 13–15.
102. Samuel Echt, *Die Geschichte der Juden in Danzig* (Leer: Verlag Gerhard Rautenberg, 1972), 144.
103. Lichtenstein, *Die Juden*, 161–2; Petition an den Völkerbund wegen der Lage der Juden im Gebiet der Freien Stadt Danzig, [1935], PA-AA, R83245, 37 (of petition).
104. Petition, 7.
105. Lichtenstein, *Die Juden*, 33–5.
106. Echt, *Die Geschichte*, 154.
107. Lichtenstein, *Die Juden*, 44.
108. Otto von Radowitz to Auswärtiges Amt, 15 July 1935, PA-AA, R83245.
109. Paul Batzer to Fachgruppe Gaststätten- und Beherbergungsgewerbe im Gebiet der Freien Stadt Danzig, 26 October 1935, APG, 260/471, 349.
110. 'German Nazis Ban Greiser Radio Talk,' *New York Times* (26 July 1936), 24.
111. Levine, *Hitler's Free City*, 99.
112. Helmut Kluck, 'Die heutige innenpolitische Lage in Danzig,' 30 July 1936, BA-Bayreuth, Ost.Dok.8/105, 16.
113. Levine, *Hitler's Free City*, 99.

114. Arthur Greiser to Heinrich Himmler, 2 April 1936, NA, XE000933, *Greiser*, Arthur.
115. See Arthur Greiser to Heinrich Himmler, 7 May 1937; Beschluß, 27 April 1937; and Kreisgericht der NSDAP, Kreis Zoppot, E 1/37, 7 April 1937, BAB, Former BDC Collection, SSO Files on Arthur Greiser, Frames 119–25.
116. Der Reichsführer-SS, Der Chef des Sicherheitshauptamtes, Aktenvermerk, 5 October 1936, BAB, Former BDC Collection, SSO Files on Arthur Greiser, Frame 118.
117. Hans Hohnfeldt to Oberste Parteigericht, 1. Kammer, 21 October 1936, BAB, Former BDC Collection, OPG Files on Hans Hohnfeldt, Frames 3056–76.
118. Beschluss, Gaugericht Braunes Haus, 28 June 1937, BAB, Former BDC Collection, OPG Files on Hans Hohnfeldt, Frame 3402.
119. Hans Hohnfeldt, Vergleich, 28 June 1937; and Beschluss, Gaugericht Braunes Haus, 28 June 1937, BAB, Former BDC Collection, OPG Files on Hans Hohnfeldt, Frames 3396, 3402.
120. 'Socialists Arrested by the Danzig Nazis,' *New York Times* (5 October 1936), 12.
121. 'Danzig Arrests Continue,' *New York Times* (6 October 1936), 19.
122. 'Danzig Nazis Defy League on Inquiry,' *New York Times* (8 October 1936), 2.
123. Arthur Greiser, Vermerk, 16 October 1936, NA, XE000933, *Greiser*, Arthur.
124. Arthur Greiser to Werner Lorenz, 15 January 1937, APG, 260/456, 47.
125. 'Danzig Receives a Polish Warning,' *New York Times* (29 October 1936), 4.
126. Levine, *Hitler's Free City*, 118–19; McNamara, *Sean Lester*, 204.
127. Arthur Greiser to Heinrich Himmler, 15 January 1937, RGVA, 500-1-560. My thanks to Peter Klein for sharing this document with me.
128. See Paul Stauffer, *Zwischen Hofmannsthal und Hitler: Carl J. Burckhardt Facetten einer aussergewöhnlichen Existenz* (Zurich: Verlag Neue Zürcher Zeitung, 1991), 93–124; and Eliyu Stern, 'The Jews of Danzig under Nazi Rule—Struggle, Rescue and Destruction,' in Asher Cohen, Yehoyakim Cochavi, Yoav Gelber, eds., *Dapim: Studies on the Shoah* (New York: Peter Lang, 1991), 98–9.
129. Burckhardt, *Meine Danziger Mission*, 77.
130. See handwritten notes and other documents in NA, XE000933, *Greiser*, Arthur.
131. Arthur Greiser to Albert Forster, 28 May 1937, NA, RG319, Box 69.
132. Burckhardt, *Meine Danziger Mission*, 110.
133. Ernst von Weizsäcker, Vermerk, 23 June 1937, PA-AA, R103934.
134. Burckhardt, *Meine Danziger Mission*, 115.
135. Fuchs, *Die Beziehungen*, 78.
136. Arthur Greiser, Direktive, 25 October 1937, APG, 260/476.
137. Burckhardt, *Meine Danziger Mission*, 123.

138. Burckhardt, *Meine Danziger Mission*, 132–4.
139. Levine, *Hitler's Free City*, 140.
140. Burckhardt, *Meine Danziger Mission*, 132.
141. Arthur Greiser to Maria, 28 February 1938, IZ, I-941.
142. Arthur Greiser to Ingrid Greiser, 7 March 1938, IPN, 63/7, 6.
143. Burckhardt, *Meine Danziger Mission*, 132–3.
144. NSDAP Gauleitung Ost-Hannover to Arthur Greiser, 31 March 1938, APG, 260/466, 705.
145. Burckhardt, *Meine Danziger Mission*, 133.
146. Arthur Greiser, 14 July 1938, NA, RG319, Box 69.
147. Arthur Greiser, 19 July 1938, NA, RG319, Box 69.
148. Arthur Greiser, 20 September 1938, NA, RG319, Box 69.
149. Arthur Greiser, Vermerk, 21 June 1937, NA, XE000933, *Greiser*, Arthur.
150. Viktor Böttcher, Vermerk, 19 December 1938, NA, XE000933, *Greiser*, Arthur.
151. Lichtenstein, *Die Juden*, 117.
152. Burckhardt, *Meine Danziger Mission*, 117.
153. Burckhardt, *Meine Danziger Mission*, 104.
154. Schenk, *Hitlers Mann*, 86–7; and Stern, 'The Jews,' 98–9.
155. Lichtenstein, *Die Juden*, 64.
156. Levine, *Hitler's Free City*, 145; Stauffer, *Zwischen Hofmannsthal*, 103.
157. Schenk, *Hitlers Mann*, 99.
158. Ernst von Weizsäcker, Aufzeichnung, 17 October 1938, *ADAP*, Serie D, 1937–1941 (Baden-Baden: Imprimerie Nationale, 1953), Vol. 5, 80.
159. Schenk, *Hitlers Mann*, 99.
160. Echt, *Die Geschichte*, 189–90.
161. Arthur Greiser to Marian Chodacki, [December 1938], PA-AA, R103961.
162. Lichtenstein, *Die Juden*, 81.
163. Lichtenstein, *Die Juden*, 90.
164. Echt, *Die Geschichte*, 207.
165. Echt, *Die Geschichte*, 118–21; and Lichtenstein, *Die Juden*, 94–6.
166. See documents in Lichtenstein, *Die Juden*, 220–6; and Echt, *Die Geschichte*, 221–3.
167. Echt, *Die Geschichte*, 229.
168. Hans Viktor Böttcher, *Die Freie Stadt Danzig: Wege und Umwege in die europäische Zukunft* (Bonn: Kulturstiftung der deutschen Vertriebenen, 1995), 62.
169. Ludwig Denne, *Das Danzig Problem in der deutschen Außenpolitik 1934–1939* (Bonn: Ludwig Röhrscheid Verlag, 1959), 182.
170. Schenk, *Hitlers Mann*, 107.
171. Böttcher, *Die Freie Stadt Danzig*, 63.
172. Schenk, *Hitlers Mann*, 109.
173. Harry Siegmund, *Rückblick: Erinnerungen eines Staatsdieners in bewegter Zeit* (Raisdorf: Ostsee Verlag, 1999), 175.

174. Arthur Greiser to SS-Gruppenführer Scharfe, 10 July 1939, APG, 260/460, 383–4.
175. Böttcher, *Die Freie Stadt Danzig*, 63.
176. Schenk, *Hitlers Mann*, 109.
177. Arthur Greiser, Vermerk, 3 August 1939, and Vermerk, 25 August 1939, NA, XE000933, *Greiser*, Arthur.
178. Arthur Greiser to Ingrid Greiser, 20 March 1938, IPN, 63/7, 17.
179. Arthur Greiser to Ingrid Greiser, 22 March 1939, IPN, 63/8, 2.
180. Arthur Greiser to Erhardt Greiser, 9 June 1939, IPN, 63/8, 3–4.
181. Arthur Greiser to Ingrid Greiser, 12 July 1939, IPN, 63/8, 5–6.
182. Burckhardt, *Meine Danziger Mission*, 94.
183. Julius Hoppenrath, 'Dr. Rauschning, Forster, und Greiser als Menschen und Politiker,' 3 March 1956, BA-Bayreuth, Ost.Dok.8/155, 8.
184. Arthur Greiser to Ida and Ingrid Greiser, 3 June 1938, IPN, 63/7, 31.
185. Arthur Greiser to Ingrid Greiser, 14 June 1938, IPN, 63/7, 28.
186. Viktor Böttcher, Vermerk, 23 May 1938, *ADAP*, Serie D, Vol. 5, 42–4.
187. Arthur Greiser, Vermerk des Präsidenten des Danziger Senats, 22 December 1938, *ADAP*, Serie D, Vol. 5, 123–5.
188. Arthur Greiser, Vermerk, 17 March 1939, PA-AA, R103935.
189. Levine, *Hitler's Free City*, 147.
190. Levine, *Hitler's Free City*, 151; Denne, *Das Danzig-Problem*, 212.
191. Robert L. Koehl, *The Black Corps: The Structure and Power Struggles of the Nazi SS* (Madison: University of Wisconsin Press, 1983), 154.
192. Levine, *Hitler's Free City*, 151.
193. Denne, *Das Danzig-Problem*, 232–5.
194. Arthur Greiser to Präsident Klaus, Post- und Telegrafenverwaltung, 16 August 1939, APG, 260/464, 155–6.
195. Arthur Greiser to Kommando der Landespolizei, 22 August 1939, APG, 260/464, 157–8.
196. Arthur Greiser, Vermerk, 25 August 1939, NA, XE000933, *Greiser*, Arthur; and Böttcher, *Die Freie Stadt Danzig*, 129.
197. Schenk, *Hitlers Mann*, 122.
198. Burckhardt, *Meine Danziger Mission*, 352.
199. Julius Hoppenrath, 'Gauleiter Forster als Mensch und als Politiker,' 18 August 1955, BA-Bayreuth, Ost.Dok.8/55, 13.
200. Arthur Greiser, *Der Aufbau im Osten* (Jena: Fischer, 1942), 7.
201. Some historians caution against too much emphasis on this rivalry. See Andrzejewski, *Opposition*, 78; Anna M. Cienciala, *Poland and the Western Powers 1938–1939: A Study in the Interdependence of Eastern and Western Europe* (London: Routledge & Kegan Paul, 1968), 94; and McNamara, *Sean Lester*, 225.
202. Greiser, Schlußwort, 33.
203. 'Nach 10 Jahren Kampf,' *Ostdeutscher Beobachter* (29 November 1939), 3.

4. THE 'MODEL GAU:' THE WARTHEGAU

1. Czesław Madajczyk, *Die Okkupationspolitik Nazideutschlands in Polen 1939–1945* (Berlin: Akademie, 1987), 26.
2. Arthur Greiser, 'Die Grossdeutsche Aufgabe im Wartheland,' *Nationalsozialistische Monatshefte*, no. 130 (January 1941): 47.
3. Harry Siegmund, *Rückblick: Erinnerungen eines Staatsdieners in bewegter Zeit* (Raisdorf: Ostsee Verlag, 1999), 179–83.
4. Arthur Greiser, *Der Aufbau im Osten* (Jena: Fischer, 1942), 7.
5. Siegmund, *Rückblick*, 183.
6. Ernst von Weizsäcker, Vermerk, 7 September 1939, PA-AA, R29569.
7. Siegmund, *Rückblick*, 183–4.
8. Hans Lammers to Hans Pfundtner, 7 September 1939, RGVA, 720-5-2739. My thanks to Peter Klein for sharing this document with me.
9. Franz Halder, *Kriegstagebuch, Band I: Vom Polenfeldzug bis zum Ende der Westoffensive*, ed. Hans-Adolf Jacobsen (Stuttgart: Kohlhammer, 1962), 65; and Hans Umbreit, *Deutsche Militärverwaltungen 1938/39: Die militärische Besetzung der Tschechoslowakei und Polens* (Stuttgart: Deutsche Verlags-Anstalt, 1977), 88.
10. Martin Broszat, *Nationalsozialistische Polenpolitik 1939–1945* (Stuttgart: Deutsche Verlags-Anstalt, 1961), 26.
11. Siegmund, *Rückblick*, 184.
12. Herbert Mehlhorn, 'Tagesbefehl des C.d.Z.,' 7 September 1939, APP, 298/49, 37.
13. Siegmund, *Rückblick*, 185.
14. Herbert Mehlhorn, 'Niederschrift über die am 11. September ds. Js. stattgefundene Dienstbesprechung,' 11 September 1939, APP, 298/57, 6.
15. Siegmund, *Rückblick*, 185.
16. Herbert Mehlhorn, 'Niederschrift über den am 12. d. mts. stattgefundenen Generalappell,' 12 September 1939, APP, 298/57, 9.
17. Greiser later stated that he came to Posen on 12 September. See Greiser, *Der Aufbau*, 9. Most publications state that he came on September 13. See Czesław Łuczak, *Arthur Greiser* (Poznań: PSO, 1997), 36; Madajczyk, *Die Okkupationspolitik*, 8; and Eugen Petrull, 'Geburt und erste Lebenstage des Warthelandes,' *Ostdeutscher Beobachter* (26 October 1944). Siegmund states that he and Greiser first arrived on 14 September. See Siegmund, *Rückblick*, 186.
18. Petrull, 'Geburt.'
19. Robert M. Kennedy, *The German Campaign in Poland (1939)* (Washington, DC: Department of the Army, 1956), 102–3.
20. Greiser, 'Die Großdeutsche Aufgabe,' 46.
21. The number 10,000 for Posen and eastern Pomerania is given by Hans Freiherr von Rosen, *Die Verschleppung der Deutschen aus Posen und Pommerellen im September 1939: Eine Dokumentation* (Berlin: Westkreuz, 1990), 18. Both Rosen and Jansen and Weckbecker concur that between 10,000 and 15,000

ethnic Germans were arrested in all of Poland in September 1939. See Christian Jansen and Arno Weckbecker, *Der 'Volksdeutsche Selbstschutz' in Polen 1939/40* (Munich: Oldenbourg, 1992), 26.

22. The lower figure is found in Günter Schubert, *Das Unternehmen 'Bromberger Blutsonntag': Tod einer Legende* (Cologne: Bund, 1989), 199. The higher figure stems from Rosen, *Die Verschleppung*, 23.
23. See Schubert, *Das Unternehmen*, 7–20.
24. For the numbers killed, see Alexander B. Rossino, *Hitler Strikes Poland: Blitzkrieg, Ideology, and Atrocity* (Lawrence: University Press of Kansas, 2003), 62; and Schubert, *Das Unternehmen 'Bromberger Blutsonntag,'* 198.
25. Rossino, *Hitler*, 73.
26. Siegmund, *Rückblick*, 186.
27. Chef der Zivilverwaltung, 'Lagebericht,' 25 September 1939, APP, 298/50, 27.
28. General der Artillerie Vollard-Bockelberg, 14 September 1939, APP, 298/35, 9; and Arthur Greiser, 18 September 1939, BAB, ZR 536 A.2.
29. Michael Alberti, *Die Verfolgung und Vernichtung der Juden im Reichsgau Wartheland 1939–1945* (Wiesbaden: Harrassowitz, 2006), 39.
30. Joseph Goebbels, *Die Tagebücher von Joseph Goebbels: Sämtliche Fragmente; Teil I: Aufzeichnungen 1924–1941*, ed. Elke Fröhlich (Munich: Saur, 1987), Vol. 3, 620.
31. Arthur Greiser, 'Tagesbericht Nr.1. für die Zeit vom 13. bis 17. September 1939,' 18 September 1939, APP, 298/51, 2–4.
32. Arthur Greiser, 'Tagesbericht Nr.2. für den 18. September 1939,' 19 September 1939, APP, 298/51, 7.
33. Greiser, 'Tagesbericht Nr.1.,' 4.
34. Arthur Greiser, 'Tätigkeitsbericht Nr.4 für die Zeit vom 21. bis 28. September 1939,' 29 September 1939, APP, 298/50, 41.
35. Greiser, 'Tagesbericht Nr.2.,' 8–10.
36. Greiser, 'Tagesbericht Nr.1.,' 1–5.
37. Greiser, 'Tagesbericht Nr.2.,' 8.
38. Dr. Meyer, 'Unternehmen Tannenberg,' 23 September 1939, BAB, ZR 543 A.1, 150.
39. Gerhard Engel, *Heeresadjutant bei Hitler 1938–1943: Aufzeichnungen des Majors Engel*, ed. Hildegard von Kotze (Stuttgart: Deutsche Verlags-Anstalt, 1974), 63.
40. 'Rückgabe der Vermögenswerte: Arthur Greiser über die Ziele der Zivilverwaltung in Polen,' *Preussische Zeitung*, 11 October 1939, BAB, R8034III/163, 117.
41. Bogdan Musial, 'Das Schlachtfeld zweier totalitärer Systeme: Polen unter deutscher und sowjetischer Herrschaft 1939–1941,' in *Genesis des Genozids: Polen 1939–1941*, ed. Klaus-Michael Mallmann and Bogdan Musial (Darmstadt: Wissenschaftliche Buchgesellschaft, 2004), 15.

42. Goebbels, *Die Tagebücher*, Vol. 3, 620.
43. Rossino, *Hitler*, 59.
44. Engel, *Heeresadjutant*, 63.
45. Chef der Zivilverwaltung beim Militärbefehlshaber Posen, 'Lagebericht,' 25 September 1939, APP, 298/50, 27–9. Umbreit attributes this document to Greiser. See Umbreit, *Deutsche Militärverwaltungen*, 154.
46. Alberti, *Die Verfolgung*, 46.
47. Schulze-Annè, 17 October 1939, APP, 298/27, 5.
48. See Landrat, Der Kreiskommissar Schubin, 'Lagebericht,' 26 October 1939, APP, 298/27, 23.
49. See Broszat, *Nationalsozialistische Polenpolitik*, 45; and Jansen and Weckbecker, *Der 'Volksdeutsche Selbstschutz,'* 156.
50. Jansen and Weckbecker, *Der 'Volksdeutsche Selbstschutz'*, 8, 69, 195.
51. Der Oberbürgermeister der Regierungshauptstadt Hohensalza to Dr. Weber, 6 November 1939, BAB, R138II/6.
52. Broszat, *Nationalsozialistische Polenpolitik*, 44.
53. Dr. Ficker, Vermerk, 8 January 1940, BAB, R43II/1411a, 231–2.
54. Dr. Heinrich Hassmann to Zentralstelle zur Verfolgung von NS-Verbrechen, 8 February 1965, ZStL, 203 AR-Z 112/60, 517–19; Czesław Łuczak, *Pod niemieckim jarzmem (Kraj Warty 1939–1945)* (Poznań: PSO, 1996), 35; and Siegmund, *Rückblick*, 198.
55. 'Wyrok niem. Sądu specjalnego w Poznaniu przeciw Hirschfeldowi z dn. 23.7.1940 w sprawie mordu w inowrocławskim więzieniu,' IZ, I-110. Von Hirschfeld died in April 1945; the circumstances of his death remain unclear. See Vermerk, Staatsanwaltschaft bei dem Landgericht Göttingen, 31 December 1962, ZStL, 203 AR-Z 112/60, 527–8.
56. Siegmund, *Rückblick*, 197, 187.
57. Madajczyk, *Die Okkupationspolitik*, 22–6.
58. 'Aus dem Erlaß Adolf Hitlers vom 8. October 1939 zur völkerrechtswidrigen Angliederung polnischer Gebiete,' in Werner Röhr, ed., *Europa unterm Hakenkreuz: Die faschistische Okkupationspolitik in Polen (1939–1945)* (Berlin: Deutscher Verlag der Wissenschaften, 1989), 127–8.
59. Jochen v. Lang, *Der Sekretär: Martin Bormann: Der Mann, der Hitler beherrschte* (Munich: Herbig, 1987), 153.
60. Dieter Rebentisch, *Führerstaat und Verwaltung im Zweiten Weltkrieg: Verfassungsentwicklung und Verwaltungspolitik 1939–1945* (Stuttgart: Franz Steiner, 1989), 249.
61. [Friedrichs], Notiz für den Stabsleiter, 4 October 1939, BAB, NS6/799, 26–8.
62. Łuczak, *Arthur Greiser*, 17.
63. Wilhelm Frick to Hans Lammers, 20 October 1939, BAB, R43II/1390f, 11.
64. 'Das Reich schaut auf Posen,' *Ostdeutscher Beobachter* (4 November 1939), 1.
65. Siegmund, *Rückblick*, 204.

66. 'Der große Tag des Warthegaues,' *Ostdeutscher Beobachter* (3 November 1939), 1. See also 'Die Amtseinführung des Statthalters,' *Ostdeutscher Beobachter* (1 November 1939), 7; and 'Verwaltungsaufbau im Warthegau,' *Berliner Börsen-Zeitung*, 3 November 1939, BAB, NS5IV/17583, 46.
67. Łuczak, *Pod niemieckim jarzmem*, 3.
68. Vermerk, 16 March 1940, BAB, R43II/1390f, 27.
69. The German and Polish population figures stem from Łuczak, *Pod niemieckim jarzmem*, 83. For more on the number of Jews in the Gau, see Chapter 5.
70. 'Die Gaugebiete des Reiches,' *Ostdeutscher Beobachter* (23 March 1941), 4.
71. Alberti, *Die Verfolgung*, 95.
72. Madajczyk, *Die Okkupationspolitik*, 242.
73. Łuczak, *Pod niemieckim jarzmem*, 7–8.
74. Wilhelm Frick, 'Verlegung des Regierungssitzes des Regierungsbezirks Kalisch,' 29 March 1940, BAB, R1501/5401, 211.
75. Goebbels, *Die Tagebücher*, Part I, Vol. 4, 71.
76. Ingrid Birr, 'Bericht über die Lodzer-Reise vom 10.4.–13.4.1940,' BAB, N2313/9, 2–4. My thanks to Michael Alberti for sharing this document with me.
77. See Chapter 7.
78. For general information on the makeup of the Warthegau's territory, see Broszat, *Nationalsozialistische Polenpolitik*, 34–5; Jeanne Dingell, *Zur Tätigkeit der Haupttreuhandstelle Ost: Treuhandstelle Posen 1939 bis 1945* (Frankfurt/M: Peter Lang, 2003), 37; Łuczak, *Pod niemieckim jarzmem*, 7–9; and Werner Röhr, '"Reichsgau Wartheland" 1939–1945: Vom "Exerzierplatz des praktischen Nationalsozialismus" zum "Mustergau"?' *Bulletin für Faschismus und Weltkriegsforschung* no. 18 (2002): 34–5.
79. Alberti, *Die Verfolgung*, 51; and Dieter Pohl, 'Die Reichsgaue Danzig–Westpreußen und Wartheland: Koloniale Verwaltung oder Modell für die zukünftige Gauverwaltung?' in Jürgen John, Horst Möller, and Thomas Schaarschmidt, eds., *Die NS-Gaue: Regionale Mittelinstanzen im zentralistischen 'Führerstaat'* (Munich: Oldenbourg, 2007), 397.
80. Madajczyk, *Die Okkupationspolitik*, 31.
81. Aly argues that Lodsch was annexed to the Warthegau so as to provide an urban setting for the planned influx of Baltic ethnic Germans. See Götz Aly, *'Endlösung': Völkerverschiebung und der Mord an den europäischen Juden* (Frankfurt/M: Fischer, 1995), 68.
82. 'Gauleiter Greiser in Lodsch,' *Ostdeutscher Beobachter* (8 November 1939), 1.
83. Łuczak, *Pod niemieckim jarzmem*, 5.
84. Arthur Greiser to Adolf Hitler, 9 November 1939, BAB, NS10/73, 23.
85. Aly, *'Endlösung,'* 68.
86. Gerda Zorn, *'Nach Ostland geht unser Ritt': Deutsche Eroberungspolitik und die Folgen: Das Beispiel Lodz* (Cologne: Röderberg, 1988), 59.

87. See Ian Kershaw, 'Arthur Greiser—Ein Motor der "Endlösung,"' in Ronald Smelzer, Enrico Syring, and Rainer Zitelmann, eds., *Die Braune Elite II: 21 weitere biographische Skizzen* (Darmstadt: Wissenschaftliche Buchgesellschaft, 1993), 116.
88. Arthur Greiser to Wilhelm Frick, 15 March 1940, BAB, R43II/494a, 133.
89. Vermerk, 7 May 1940, BAB, R43II/494a, 134–5.
90. See Institut für Zeitgeschichte, ed., *Akten der Partei-Kanzlei der NSDAP: Rekonstruktion eines verlorengegangenen Bestands* (Munich: Oldenbourg, 1983), Part 1, 101 23615–33 (hereafter *Akten*); and Rebentisch, *Führerstaat*, 194–5.
91. Hans Lammers to Gauleiter, 19 December 1941, BAB, R43II/494a, 170.
92. Rebentisch, *Führerstaat*, 172.
93. See Siegmund, *Rückblick;* LKA/NW, Dez. 15, 'Zeugenvernehmung,' Harry Siegmund, 10 October 1966, ZStL, 203 AR 690/65, 76–8; and Arthur Greiser to alle Dienststellen des Staates und der Gauselbstverwaltung, alle Sonderbehörden und Aufbauorganisationen, die Selbstverwaltungen und Körperschaften der Wirtschaft und des Nährstandes, 1 October 1941, APP, 299/380, 7–9.
94. LKA/NW, Dez. 15, 'Zeugenvernehmung,' Fritz Harder, 8 November 1966, ZStL, 203 AR 690/65, 50–2; and Arthur Greiser to alle Dienststellen.
95. On Willi Bethke, see 'Defense of the Polish Office in Danzig,' *http://en.wikipedia.org/wiki/Polish_post_office_in_Danzig*, accessed 14 October 2008.
96. Siegmund, *Rückblick*, 238.
97. LKA/NW, Dez. 15, 'Zeugenvernehmung,' Elsa Claaßen, 23 August 1966, ZStL, 203 AR 690/65, 85–6.
98. Siegmund, *Rückblick*, 260.
99. Siegmund, *Rückblick*, 298.
100. Siegmund, *Rückblick*, 186.
101. 'Auszeichnung Danziger Parteigenossen,' *Ostdeutscher Beobachter* (10 August 1940), 5.
102. BAB, Former BDC Collection, PK files on August Jäger.
103. Rebentisch, *Führerstaat*, 250.
104. Broszat, *Nationalsozialistische Polenpolitik*, 55; and Dietrich Orlow, *The History of the Nazi Party: 1933–1945* (Pittsburgh: University of Pittsburgh Press, 1973), 290.
105. Martyn Housden, *Resistance and Conformity in the Third Reich* (London: Routledge, 1997), 50.
106. Arthur Greiser to Maria, 20–21 July 1946, BA-Ludwigsburg, ZStL, I-110 AR 655/73, 314–18.
107. August Jäger, 20 January 1943, APP, 299/11, 80. Jäger first issued such a directive on 29 July 1941.
108. See Peter Klein, *Die 'Gettoverwaltung Litzmannstadt' 1940–1944: Eine Dienststelle im Spannungsfeld von Kommunalbürokratie und staatlicher Verfolgungspolitik* (Hamburg: Hamburger Edition, 2009), 148–51.

109. See Ulrich Herbert, *Best: Biographische Studien über Radikalismus, Weltanschauaung und Vernunft 1903–1989* (Bonn: Dietz, 1996).
110. Alberti, *Die Verfolgung*, 59.
111. BAB, Former BDC Collection, RS and SSO files on Herbert Mehlhorn.
112. Siegmund, *Rückblick*, 213.
113. BAB, Former BDC Collection, SSO files on Wilhelm Koppe.
114. Ruth Bettina Birn, *Die Höheren SS- und Polizeiführer: Himmlers Vertreter im Reich und in den besetzten Gebieten* (Düsseldorf: Droste, 1986), 105, 205, 375, 378.
115. Klein, *Die 'Gettoverwaltung Litzmannstadt,'* 141–7.
116. 'SS-Obergruppenführer Koppe scheidet von Posen,' *Ostdeutscher Beobachter* (14 November 1943).
117. Der Oberstaatsanwalt, Bonn, Wilhelm Koppe [statement], 2 February 1960, ZStL, 203 AR-Z 69/59, 138.
118. Szymon Datner, *Wilhelm Koppe: nieukarany zbrodniarz hitlerowski* (Warsaw: Zachodnia Agencja Prasowa, 1963), 14.
119. Alberti, *Die Verfolgung*, 71.
120. This underscores Mann's argument that men from lost or borderlands areas were overrepresented among Nazi perpetrators. Michael Mann, *The Dark Side of Democracy: Explaining Ethnic Cleansing* (New York: Cambridge University Press, 2005), 239.
121. Siegmund, *Rückblick*, 3–48.
122. Ben Kiernan, *Blood and Soil: A World History of Genocide and Extermination from Sparta to Darfur* (New Haven: Yale University Press, 2007), 442.
123. See BAB, Former BDC Collection, SSO Files on Ernst Damzog, Helmut Bischoff, Hermann Krumey, and Heinz Reinefarth.
124. Rossino, *Hitler*, 44–5, 69–71.
125. Rebentisch, *Führerstaat*, 159.
126. Jeremy Noakes, ' "Viceroys of the Reich?" Gauleiters 1925–45,' in Anthony McElligott and Tim Kirk, eds., *Working Towards the Führer: Essays in Honour of Sir Ian Kershaw* (Manchester: Manchester University Press, 2003), 130.
127. Ian Kershaw, *Hitler 1936–1945: Nemesis* (New York, Norton, 2000), 315.
128. Rebentisch, *Führerstaat*, 170.
129. 'Aus dem Erlaß Adolf Hitlers vom 8. October 1939,' in *Europa*, 127–8.
130. Rebentisch, *Führerstaat*, 246, 176–80.
131. Wilhelm Frick to Reichsstatthalter in Danzig und Posen, 6 December 1939, BAB, R43II/1390f, 5.
132. 'Der große Tag.'
133. Herbert Mehlhorn, 'Übersichtsbericht über die Tätigkeit der Verwaltungsabteilung beim C.d.Z.,' 3 October 1939, APP, 298/53, 38.
134. See, for example, Martin Bormann to Alfred Rosenberg, 11 January 1940, BAB, NS8/183, 158.

135. For accounts of this conflict, see Broszat, *Nationalsozialistische Polenpolitik*, 56–7; Madajczyk, *Die Okkupationspolitik*, 43; Hans Mommsen, *Beamtentum im Dritten Reich* (Stuttgart: Deutsche Verlags-Anstalt, 1966), 110–13; Günter Neliba, *Wilhelm Frick: Der Legalist des Unrechtsstaates* (Paderborn: Schöningh, 1992), 311–12; and Rebentisch, *Führerstaat*, 160–1.
136. Rebentisch, *Führerstaat*, 186. Historians have portrayed Greiser in this affair very differently. Broszat saw Greiser as a mere tool of the Party Chancellery, while Mommsen insisted that Greiser 'determined' the Party Chancellery's stance. See Broszat, *Nationalsozialistische Polenpolitik*, 56; and Mommsen, *Beamtentum*, 113.
137. Arthur Greiser to Werner Willikens, 11 November 1939, BAB, R43II/1390f, 19.
138. R. Walther Darré to Wilhelm Frick, 29 November 1939, BAB, R43II/1390f, 22.
139. Vermerk, 14 December 1939, BAB, R43II/1390f, 23.
140. Siegmund, *Rückblick*, 299–300.
141. Diemut Majer, *'Non-Germans' under the Third Reich: The Nazi Judicial and Administrative System in Germany and Occupied Eastern Europe, with Special Regard to Occupied Poland, 1939–1945* (Baltimore: Johns Hopkins University Press, 2003), 216.
142. Majer, *'Non-Germans,'* 61.
143. *Akten*, Part I, Volume 1, 484.
144. See Majer, *'Non-Germans,'* 416, 476.
145. 'Stellungnahme Schmalz,' 23 August 1948, IfZ, ED901/52.
146. Pohl, 'Die Reichsgaue,' 399.
147. Pohl, 'Die Reichsgaue,' 398.
148. 'Stellungnahme Schmalz.'
149. Paul Batzer, 'Eidesstattliche Erklärung,' 5 August 1948, IfZ, ED901/52.
150. Batzer, 'Eidesstattliche Erklärung;' and 'Stellungnahme Schmalz.'
151. Karl Hans Fuchs, 'Gauleiter Greiser,' *Ostdeutscher Beobachter* (1 November 1939), 1.
152. '"Wer leben will, der kämpfe also,..."' *Ostdeutscher Beobachter* (17 March 1940), 3.
153. For conversion and inflation-adjusted rates, see www.history.ucsb.edu/faculty/marcuse/projects/currency.htm#tables; and *www.measuringworth.com/calculators/uscompare/result.php*, accessed 6 August 2009.
154. Siegmund, *Rückblick*, 191, 214.
155. Noakes, '"Viceroys,"' 135.
156. 'Das Wartheland in der Kriegswirtschaft,' *Ostdeutscher Beobachter* (13 December 1939), 3.
157. '"Arthur-Greiser-Schule" in Hohensalza,' *Ostdeutscher Beobachter* (3 December 1941), 9.
158. Łuczak, *Arthur Greiser*, 4.

159. 'Gauleiter Greiser Reichsverteidigungskommissar,' *Ostdeutscher Beobachter* (5 March 1940).
160. Rebentisch, *Führerstaat*, 132.
161. Harry Siegmund, interview with author, 25 May 2005.
162. For the meeting with Hitler on December 14, see Hans Lammers to Wilhelm Frick, 4 January 1940, BAB, R43II/1390f, 15–16. For the meeting on 16 September 1940, see Martin Bormann to Hans Lammers, 16 September 1940, *Akten*, 101 23615. For the meeting on 31 October 1940, see Martin Bormann to Hans Lammers, 2 November 1940, *Akten*, 101 04576. Greiser's other personal meetings with Hitler are described in future chapters.
163. Noakes, '"Viceroys,"' 134.
164. Arthur Greiser to Heinrich Himmler, 8 October 1943, BAB, Former BDC Collection, SSO Files for Arthur Greiser, 155.
165. Siegmund, interview.
166. See Chapter 3.
167. See Chapters 5 and 6; and Arthur Rosenberg, 'Aktennotiz über Unterredung mit dem Reichsmarschall am 9. August 1941,' BAB, R6/23, 22–4.
168. Arthur Greiser to Heinrich Himmler, 6 July 1942, BAB, Former BDC Collection, SSO Files for Arthur Greiser, Frame 103.
169. Arthur Greiser to Heinrich Himmler, 7 March 1944, BAB, Former BDC Collection, SSO Files for Arthur Greiser, Frame 139; and Arthur Greiser to Heinrich Himmler, 15 April 1943, BAB, NS19/3662, 65–6.
170. See Heinrich Himmler to Arthur Greiser, 12 October 1943, BAB, Former BDC Collection, SSO Files for Arthur Greiser, Frame 152.
171. Heinrich Himmler, *Der Dienstkalender Heinrich Himmlers 1941/42*, ed. Peter Witte, Michael Wildt, *et al.* (Hamburg: Christians, 1999), 192.
172. Siegmund, *Rückblick*, 210.
173. Heinrich Himmler to Arthur Greiser, 1 May 1943, BAB, Former BDC Collection, SSO Files for Arthur Greiser, Frame 156.
174. Arthur Greiser to Heinrich Himmler, 22 July 1940, BAB, NS19/2619, 4.
175. Arthur Greiser to Wilhelm Frick and Heinrich Himmler, 28 July 1941, APP, 299/1172, 31.
176. Stanisław Nawrocki, *Policja hitlerowska w tzw. Kraju Warty w latach 1939–1945* (Poznań: Instytut Zachodni, 1970), 75.
177. Siegmund, for example, has claimed that the SS was essentially a 'state within a state' in the Warthegau and that Greiser had little influence over the vicious policies that took place there. The Polish historian Nawrocki has argued just the opposite—that Greiser totally controlled the police apparatus and thus initiated and directed all the developments that characterized his Gau. See Siegmund, *Rückblick*, 210; and Stanisław Nawrocki, *Terror policyjny w 'Kraju Warty' 1939–1945* (Poznań: Wydawnictwo Poznańskie, 1973), 21.
178. Klein, *Die 'Ghettoverwaltung Litzmannstadt,'* 145.
179. Majer, *'Non-Germans,'* 215.

180. Nawrocki, *Policja*, 72.
181. Dienstlaufbahn for Arthur Greiser and Werner Best, 2 November 1939, BAB, Former BDC Collection, SSO Files on Arthur Greiser, Frames 36, 111.
182. Nawrocki, *Policja*, 71.
183. Nawrocki, *Policja*, 72–6.
184. On Gauleiter–SS tensions, see Mark Mazower, *Hitler's Empire: Nazi Rule in Occupied Europe* (London: Allen Lane, 2008), 233–4.
185. Peter Klein suggests that there were tensions between Greiser and Reinhard Heydrich, the powerful RSHA chief. See Chapter 5.
186. Siegmund, *Rückblick*, 232.
187. Goebbels, *Die Tagebücher*, Part I, Vol. 3, 655.
188. 'Danzig dankt Arthur Greiser,' *Ostdeutscher Beobachter* (29 November 1939), 1.
189. Over the years, various incorrect versions of Erhardt's death have circulated. Contemporary Polish rumor mills claimed that Erhardt was on his way to a Hitler-Youth winter meeting; that a drunken Gestapo official caused the accident; and that Erhardt was killed while riding a motorcycle from Danzig to Posen. Denne, writing in West Germany, suggested that the death was the work of the Polish resistance movement. Łuczak suggested a different timing of the accident and, in turn, a rather different picture of Greiser: that the accident happened after Erhardt had already arrived in Posen and while he was taking a sight-seeing drive around the Gau. As a way to entertain his son, so this version goes, Greiser had Schulz-Wiedemann and Hey show Erhardt the extent of his father's new territory. Greiser thus appears as a swaggering father bent on displaying his newfound power to his son. Greiser family members, however, independently corroborate that Erhardt died in a freak accident on the way home from school. See 'Arthur Greiser und "Der Engel der Musik,"' IfZ, ED901/62, 6; Ludwig Denne, *Das Danzig Problem in der deutschen Außenpolitik 1934–1939* (Bonn: Ludwig Röhrscheid Verlag, 1959), 59, fn. 36; Łuczak, *Arthur Greiser*, 104; Rotraut Fülleborn, interview with author, Hamburg, 26 May 2005; and Siegmund, interview.
190. Fülleborn, interview.
191. 'Der Sohn des Gauleiters tödlich verunglückt,' *Ostdeutscher Beobachter* (22 December 1939), 5; Protokół, Jan Goroński, 14–15 March 1946, IPN, 196/27, 85–6.
192. *Ostdeutscher Beobachter* (22 December 1939), 12.
193. 'Programm für die Beisetzung am Sonnabend, dem 23.12.1939,' BAB, N2313/7, 217.
194. Fülleborn, interview.
195. 'Der letzte Weg,' *Ostdeutscher Beobachter* (Christmas 1939), 2.
196. Arthur Greiser to Friedrich Uebelhoer, 5 January 1940, BAB, N2313/8, 20.
197. Siegmund, *Rückblick*, 226–7.
198. Paul Rüge, Tagebuchaufzeichnungen, BA-Bayreuth, Ost-Dok.13/185, 5.
199. Arthur Greiser, Schlußwort des Angeklagten Artur [*sic*] Greiser im Prozess vor dem Höchsten Volksgericht, July 1946, BA-Bayreuth, Ost-Dok.13/452, 67.

200. 'Der Sohn des Gauleiters,' 5.
201. 'Der ewige Kraftquell unseres Brauchtums,' *Ostdeutscher Beobachter* (22 December 1939), 2.

5. 'A BLONDE PROVINCE:' RESETTLEMENT, DEPORTATION, MURDER

1. Arthur Greiser, *Der Aufbau im Osten* (Jena: Fischer, 1942), 9.
2. See Chapter 4; on the date of Greiser's war enlistment, see Chapter 1.
3. Zamość, a much smaller geographical entity, also saw a very radical attempt to alter the population makeup. See Karl Heinz Roth, '"Generalplan Ost"—"Gesamtplan Ost": Forschungsstand, Quellenprobleme, neue Ergebnisse,' in Mechthild Rössler and Sabine Schleiermacher, eds., *Der 'Generalplan Ost': Hauptlinien der nationalsozialistischen Planungs- und Vernichtungspolitik* (Berlin: Akademie, 1993), 78.
4. Aly has argued that Nazi population policies involving all three groups ultimately brought on the 'Final Solution.' Götz Aly, *'Endlösung:' Völkerverschiebung und der Mord an den europäischen Juden* (Frankfurt/M: Fischer, 1995).
5. Brigitte Hamann, *Hitler's Vienna: A Dictator's Apprenticeship* (New York: Oxford University Press, 1999), 323.
6. 'Aus Adolf Hitlers "Erlaß zur Festigung deutschen Volkstums" vom 7. Oktober 1939,' in Werner Röhr, ed., *Europa unterm Hakenkreuz: Die faschistische Okkupationspolitik in Polen (1939–1945)* (Berlin: Deutscher Verlag der Wissenschaften, 1989), 126–7.
7. See Rössler and Schleiermacher, eds., *Der 'Generalplan Ost;'* and Czesław Madajczyk, ed., *Vom Generalplan Ost zum Generalsiedlungsplan: Dokumente* (Munich: Saur, 1994).
8. Roth, '"Generalplan Ost,"' 41.
9. Künzel, 'Ausführungen des Reichsführers SS anläßlich seines Besuches in der Einwanderungszentrale Posen am 12.XII.1939,' 12 December 1939, BAB, NS2/60, 16.
10. Many historians have made this point. See, for example, Chad Bryant, *Prague in Black: Nazi Rule and Czech Nationalism* (Cambridge, Mass.: Harvard University Press, 2007), 115; John Connelly, 'Nazis and Slavs: From Racial Theory to Racist Practice,' *Central European History* 32, no. 1 (1999): 29; and Isabel Heinemann, *'Rasse, Siedlung, deutsches Blut': Das Rasse- & Siedlungshauptamt der SS und die rassenpolitische Neuordnung Europas* (Göttingen: Wallstein, 2003), 30–1.
11. Jürgen von Hehn, *Die Umsiedlung der baltischen Deutschen—das letzte Kapitel baltischdeutscher Geschichte* (Marburg: Herder-Institut, 1982), 75–87.
12. Dietrich A. Loeber, *Diktierte Option: Die Umsiedlung der Deutsch-Balten aus Estland und Lettland 1939–1941* (Neumünster: Karl Wachholtz, 1974), 79–81.

13. On the resettlement of various groups of ethnic Germans, see Stephan Döring, *Die Umsiedlung der Wolhyniendeutschen in den Jahren 1939 bis 1940* (Frankfurt/M: Peter Lang, 2001); Dirk Jachomowski, *Die Umsiedlung der Bessarabien-, Bukovina- und Dobrudschadeutschen: Von der Volksgruppe in Rumänien zur 'Siedlungsbrücke' an der Reichsgrenze* (Munich: Oldenbourg, 1984); Robert L. Koehl, *RKFDV: German Resettlement and Population Policy 1939–1945: A History of the Reich Commission for the Strengthening of Germandom* (Cambridge, Mass.: Harvard University Press, 1957); Loeber, *Diktierte Option*; Harry Stossun, *Die Umsiedlungen der Deutschen aus Litauen während des Zweiten Weltkrieges: Untersuchungen zum Schicksal einer Deutschen Volksgruppe im Osten* (Marburg: Herder-Institut, 1993); and von Hehn, *Die Umsiedlung.*
14. See Valdis O. Lumans, *Himmler's Auxiliaries: The Volksdeutsche Mittelstelle and the German National Minorities of Europe, 1933–1945* (Chapel Hill: University of North Carolina Press, 1993).
15. See Heinemann, *'Rasse.'*
16. Döring, *Die Umsiedlung*, 327.
17. Koehl, *RKFDV*, 62–3.
18. Martin Sandberger to Otto Ohlendorf, 25 October 1939, BAB, R69/100, 5.
19. Martin Sandberger to the RSHA-Adjuntur, 26 October 1939, BAB, R69/100, 6–7.
20. Martin Sandberger to the Stl. Stettin, 28 October 1939, BAB, R69/981, 2.
21. Greiser, *Der Aufbau*, 13–14.
22. Martin Sandberger, Niederschrift, 11 December 1939, BAB, R69/981, 33–5.
23. Chad Carl Bryant, 'Making the Czechs German: Nationality and Nazi Rule in the Protectorate of Bohemia and Moravia, 1939–1945' (Ph.D. diss., University of California, Berkeley, 2002), 132.
24. Wilhelm Koppe, 'Abschiebung von Juden und Polen aus dem Reichsgau "Warthe-Land,"' 12 November 1939, BAB, R70 Polen/198.
25. On these deportations, see Szymon Datner, Janusz Gumkowski, and Kazimierz Leszczyński, eds., *Wysiedlanie ludności ziem polskich wcielonych do Rzeszy; Biuletyn Głównej Komisji Badania Zbrodni Hitlerowskich w Polsce 12* (Warsaw: Wydawnictwo Prawnicze, 1960); Czesław Madajczyk, *Die Okkupationspolitik Nazideutschlands in Polen 1939–1945* (Berlin: Akademie, 1987), 405–33; Phillip T. Rutherford, *Prelude to the Final Solution: The Nazi Program for Deporting Ethnic Poles, 1939–1941* (Lawrence: University Press of Kansas, 2007); and Maria Rutowska, *Wysiedlenia ludności polskiej z Kraju Warty do Generalnego Gubernatorstwa 1939–1941* (Poznań: Instytut Zachodni, 2003).
26. Rutherford, *Prelude*, 97.
27. See Rutowska, *Wysiedlenia*, 97–104.
28. Rutherford, *Prelude*, 95.
29. Arthur Greiser, Rundschreiben an alle Parteidienststellen, Staatsdienststellen, Landräte usw., 4 December 1939, APP, 298/65, 32.

30. Joseph Goebbels, *Die Tagebücher von Joseph Goebbels: Sämtliche Fragmente*, ed. Elke Fröhlich (Munich: K. G. Saur, 1987), Part I, Vol. 4, 19.
31. Peter Klein, *Die 'Gettoverwaltung Litzmannstadt' 1940–1944: Eine Dienststelle im Spannungsfeld von Kommunalbürokratie und staatlicher Verfolgungspolitik* (Hamburg: Hamburger Edition, 2009), 141–7.
32. Hans Frank, *Das Diensttagebuch des deutschen Generalgouverneurs in Polen 1939–1945*, ed. Werner Präg and Wolfgang Jacobmeyer (Stuttgart: Deutsche Verlags-Anstalt, 1975), 164.
33. Frank, *Das Diensttagebuch*, 263.
34. Datner, Gumkowski, and Leszczyński, eds., *Wysiedlanie*, 113 F.
35. Rolf-Heinz Höppner, Aktenvermerk, 6 November 1940, IPN, 196/36, 557–8.
36. Frank, *Das Diensttagebuch*, 302.
37. Rutherford, *Prelude*, 190.
38. Rutherford, *Prelude*, 9.
39. Aly, *'Endlösung,'* 20; Rutherford, *Prelude*, 222.
40. Rutherford, *Prelude*.
41. Speer described Greiser as 'an extreme anti-Semite,' while Alberti writes that 'Greiser's radical anti-Semitism is undisputed...' See Albert Speer, *Der Sklavenstaat: Meine Auseinandersetzungen mit der SS* (Stuttgart: Deutsche Verlags-Anstalt, 1981), 395; and Michael Alberti, *Die Verfolgung und Vernichtung der Juden im Reichsgau Wartheland 1939–1945* (Wiesbaden: Harrassowitz, 2006), 57.
42. Czesław Łuczak, *Arthur Greiser* (Poznań: PSO, 1997), 82.
43. 'Die deutsche Stadt Lodsch,' *Ostdeutscher Beobachter* (12 November 1939), 5.
44. For a discussion of the number of Jews in the Warthegau, see Alberti, *Die Verfolgung*, 33–4.
45. Czesław Łuczak, *Dzień po dniu w okupowanej Wielkopolsce i na ziemi łódzkiej (Kraj Warty): kalendarium wydarzeń 1939–1945* (Poznań: Lektor, 1993), 13, 16.
46. Czesław Łuczak, ed., *Położenie ludności polskiej w tzw. Kraju Warty w okresie hitlerowskiej okupacji (Documenta occupationis XIII)* (Poznań: Instytut Zachodni, 1990), 9.
47. Arthur Greiser, 'Tätigkeitsbericht Nr.4 für die Zeit vom 21. bis 28. September 1939,' 29 September 1939, APP, 298/50, 38–9.
48. Alberti, *Die Verfolgung*, 104.
49. Gerhard Pietrusky, 'Ein Jahr Aufbauarbeit der Abteilung IV/B (Siedlung und Umlegung) des Reichsstatthalters im Reichsgau Wartheland,' Posen 1940, Special Collections, Stabi, 3.
50. Alberti, *Die Verfolgung*, 106.
51. Albert Rapp, 'Abschiebung von Juden aus dem Reichsgau "Warthe-Land,"' 24 November 1939, BAB, R70 Polen/198, 17–18.
52. 'Anordnung von Heinrich Himmler, Reichsführer SS und Chef der Deutschen Polizei vom 30. Oktober 1939 zur Massendeportationen der polnischen und jüdischen Bevölkerung,' in Röhr, ed., *Europa*, 135–6.

53. Gerhard Scheffler to Wilhelm Koppe, 18 November 1939, IPN, 62/297, 42–3.
54. Alberti, *Die Verfolgung*, 133–6, 141.
55. Aly, *'Endlösung,'* 90, 111.
56. Aly, *'Endlösung,'* 203.
57. Alberti, *Die Verfolgung*, 147–50.
58. Reichsamtsleiter Schieder, Besuchs-Vermerk Akten-Vermerk, 11 January 1940, BAB, Former BDC Collection, PK files for Greiser, Frames 2862–74.
59. Christopher Browning, with contributions by Jürgen Matthäus, *The Origins of the Final Solution: The Evolution of Nazi Jewish Policy, September 1939–March 1942* (Lincoln: University of Nebraska Press, 2004), 115.
60. Ingrid Greiser to Kurt Birr, 'Bericht über die Lodzer-Reise vom 10.4–13.4.1940,' BAB, N2313/9, 2–4.
61. Wilhelm Stuckart, Vermerk über die Besprechungen betr. das Ghetto in Lodsch, 3 April 1940, BAB, R58/3518, 2–3.
62. Israel Gutman, 'Introduction: The Distinctiveness of the Lodz ghetto,' in Isaiah Trunk, *Lodz ghetto: A History* (Bloomington: Indiana University Press, 2006), xxx.
63. Browning, *The Origins*, 115.
64. Fehre, 'Bericht über die Lagerbesuche am 18.I.1940 nachm.,' undated, APP, 800/23, 39–40.
65. Günther Pancke to Dr. Grawitz, 27 February 1940, BAB, NS2/61, 74–5.
66. Doppler, Tagesbefehl Nr.538 vom 19.6.1941, BAB, R59/223, 56.
67. 'Der Gauleiter im Wolhynienlager,' *Ostdeutscher Beobachter* (13 April 1940), 6.
68. Ingrid Greiser, 'Bericht,' 4.
69. Doppler, Tagesbefehl Nr. 333 vom 19.9.1940, BAB, R59/220, 125.
70. Arthur Greiser to Werner Lorenz, 3 July 1943, BAB, NS19/20, 2.
71. Werner Lorenz to Arthur Greiser, 12 July 1943, BAB, NS19/20, 5–10.
72. Arthur Greiser to Werner Lorenz, 3 August 1943, BAB, NS19/20, 16.
73. See, for example, Rudolf Schlimmig, 'Wartheland Gau der Bauern und Soldaten,' *Deutsche Allgemeine Zeitung*, 24 October 1942, BAB, R8043III/163, 92.
74. Jachomowski, *Die Umsiedlung*, 159.
75. Lorenz to Greiser, 12 July 1943, 9.
76. Protokoll über die Besprechung der Abteilungsleiter am 2. Februar 1940, APP, 800/23, 71.
77. See, for example, Befehlshaber der Ordnungspolizei, 'Betreuung der volksdeutschen Ansiedler,' 6 May 1941, BAB, R49/3050, 72–3; and M. Baier, Bericht, 3 February 1943, BAB, R49/121, 25–6.
78. Flora Schulz, Bericht, 14 July 1942, BAB, R49/3062, 7.
79. See, for example, R., Bericht, 27 March 1942, BAB, R49/120, 5; and 'Haltung der Polen,' December 1942, BAB, R49/122, 191.
80. Wilhelm Koppe, 1 November 1941, APP, 304/2, 100.

81. See Elizabeth Harvey, *Women and the Nazi East: Agents and Witnesses of Germanization* (New Haven: Yale University Press, 2003), 147–90.
82. 'Die Partei übernimmt Umsiedlerbetreuung,' *Ostdeutscher Beobachter* (4 February 1941), 1.
83. 'Wir wollen gute Kameradschaft halten,' *Ostdeutscher Beobachter* (4 February 1941), 5.
84. Arthur Greiser to Heinrich Himmler, 15 December 1941, BAB, NS19/2617, 1.
85. Bericht eines Vertrauensmannes, 1 November 1940, BAB, R58/243, 300.
86. See, for example, Alfred Intelmann, 'Aufzeichnungen aus dem letzten Arbeitsjahr der deutschbaltischen Volksgruppe in Lettland und ihrer Umsiedlung,' BA-Bayreuth, Ost.Dok.14/11, 196; and Walter Baron Maydell to Walter Darré, 4 December 1939, BAB, NS8/173, 60–1.
87. Der Leiter der Wirtschaftsabteilung, 22 May 1941, APP, 299/1219, 30–3.
88. 'Forderung der Zeit: Ostbewährung! Gauleiter und Reichsstatthalter Greiser vor der Führerschaft des Gaues aus Partei und Staat,' *Ostdeutscher Beobachter* (3 August 1941), 5.
89. Czesław Łuczak, *Pod niemieckim jarzmem (Kraj Warty 1939–1945)* (Poznań: PSO, 1996), 71.
90. See Götz Aly, *Hitlers Volksstaat: Raub, Rassenkrieg und nationaler Sozialismus* (Frankfurt/M: Fischer, 2005), 265–6.
91. Doris L. Bergen, 'Tenuousness and Tenacity: The Volksdeutschen of Eastern Europe, World War II, and the Holocaust,' in Krista O'Donnell, Renate Bridenthal, and Nancy Reagin, eds., *The Heimat Abroad: The Boundaries of Germanness* (Ann Arbor: University of Michigan Press, 2005), 268, 272.
92. Harvey, *Women*, 79.
93. Dieter Pohl, 'Die Reichsgaue Danzig–Westpreußen und Wartheland: Koloniale Verwaltung oder Modell für die zukünftige Gauverwaltung?' in Jürgen John, Horst Möller, and Thomas Schaarschmidt, eds., *Die NS-Gaue: Regionale Mittelinstanzen im zentralistischen 'Führerstaat'* (Munich: Oldenbourg, 2007), 400.
94. On officials in the Warthegau, see David Bruce Furber II, 'Going East: Colonialism and German Life in Nazi-Occupied Poland' (Ph.D. Diss., University of New York at Buffalo, 2003); and Wiesław Porzycki, *Posłuszni aż do śmierci (niemieccy urzędnicy w Kraju Warty 1939–1945)* (Poznań: PSO, 1997).
95. Dieter Rebentisch, *Führerstaat und Verwaltung im Zweiten Weltkrieg: Verfassungsentwicklung und Verwaltungspolitik 1939–1945* (Stuttgart: Franz Steiner, 1989), 159.
96. Pohl, 'Die Reichsgaue,' 400.
97. Wilhelm Koppe to sämtliche Zivil- und Polizeibehörden im Reichsgau 'Wartheland,' 24 November 1939, BAB, R49/3033, 15.
98. 'Korruption im Warthegau nicht geduldet!' *Ostdeutscher Beobachter* (17 December 1939), 5.

99. Oskar Knofe, Tagesordnung Nr.55, 29 March 1941, APP, 1008/4, 19.
100. On negative stereotypes of the Volhynian Germans, see Der Landrat, Wreschen, to Chef der Zivilverwaltung, 16 October 1939, APP, 298/27, 3; SS-Arbeitsstab Turek, 4 October 1940, APP, 304/110, 5; and Johannes Pikarski, Erlebnisse bei der Durchschleusung der Umsiedler aus Wolhynien in der Zeit von 23. Dezember 1939 bis März 1940 in der EWZ-Nebenstelle-Pabianice, August 1942, BAB, R69/39, 175. On positive stereotypes of the Bessarabian Germans, see Doppler, Tagesbefehl Nr. 403, 6 February 1941, BAB, R59/221, 116.
101. Der Reichsstatthalter, Generalstaatsanwalt, to Reichsminister der Justiz, Dr. Thierack, 31 January 1943, BAB, R3001/altR22/3383, 106.
102. Wilhelm Fielitz, *Das Stereotyp des Wolhyniendeutschen Umsiedlers: Popularisierungen zwischen Sprachinselforschung und Nationalsozialistischer Propaganda* (Marburg: Elwert, 2000), 20.
103. Rutherford, *Prelude*, 178–81.
104. Harry Siegmund to Wilhelm Koppe, 10 May 1941, APP, 1009/2, 37. Emphasis in original.
105. 'Notiz über Ausführungen des Reichsstatthalters Arthur Greiser im Reichsgau "Wartheland" während einer Führertagung in Kutno am 1. August 1941,' in Kurt Pätzold, ed., *Verfolgung, Vertreibung, Vernichtung: Dokumente des faschistischen Antisemitismus 1933 bis 1942* (Leipzig: Verlag Philipp Reclam jun., 1984), 298.
106. Aly, *'Endlösung,'* 327, fn.1.
107. On these Polish reservations, see Hermann Krumey, 'Abschlußbericht über die Arbeit der Umwandererzentralstelle im Rahmen des erweiterten 3. Nahplanes,' 31 December 1942, BAB, R75/9, 1–15; and Łuczak, ed., *Położenie*, 153–5.
108. Heinemann, *'Rasse,'* 225, fn. 120.
109. Łuczak, *Pod niemieckim jarzmem*, 77; and Czesław Łuczak, *Polscy robotnicy przymusowi w Trzeciej Rzeszy podczas II Wojny Światowej* (Poznań: Wydawnictwo Poznańskie, 1974), 65.
110. Łuczak, ed., *Położenie*, 156.
111. Heinemann, '*Rasse*,' 282–4.
112. Madajczyk, *Die Okkupationspolitik*, 467; and Karol Marian Pospieszalski, ed., *Niemiecka lista narodowa w 'Kraju Warty': wybór dokumentów (Documenta occupationis teutonicae IV)* (Poznań: Instytut Zachodni, 1949), 202–3.
113. Pospieszalski, ed., *Niemiecka lista narodowa*, 206–35.
114. Łuczak, *Polscy robotnicy przymusowi*, 78.
115. Alberti, *Die Verfolgung*, 163, 172.
116. Klein, *Die 'Gettoverwaltung Litzmannstadt,'* 508.
117. Abteilungsleiter III, 'Verhältnis zwischen Posen und Litzmannstadt,' 22 November 1941, BAB, N2313/12, 300–1.
118. Christopher Browning, *The Path to Genocide: Essays on Launching the Final Solution* (New York: Cambridge University Press, 1992), 32.

119. Wilhelm Stuckart, Vermerk über die Besprechungen betr. das Ghetto in Lodsch, 3 April 1940, BAB, R58/3518, 2–3.
120. Alberti, *Die Verfolgung*, 174.
121. Gutman, 'Introduction,' xxxviii–xxxix.
122. Classic accounts of the Lodz ghetto include Lucjan Dobroszycki, ed., *The Chronicle of the Lodz ghetto 1941–1944* (New Haven; Yale University Press, 1984); and Trunk, *Lodz ghetto*. More recent accounts include Gordon J. Horwitz, *Łódź and the Making of a Nazi City* (Cambridge, Mass.: Harvard University Press, 2008); Klein, *Die 'Gettoverwaltung Litzmannstadt'*; and Andrea Löw, *Juden im Getto Litzmannstadt: Lebensbedingungen, Selbstwahrnehmung, Verhalten* (Göttingen: Wallstein, 2006).
123. Alberti, *Die Verfolgung*, 313.
124. Frank, *Das Diensttagebuch*, 261–4.
125. Henry Friedlander, *The Origins of Nazi Genocide: From Euthanasia to the Final Solution* (Chapel Hill: University of North Carolina Press, 1995), xii–xiii.
126. See Alberti, *Die Verfolgung*, 324–37; and Volker Rieß, *Die Anfänge der Vernichtung 'lebensunwerten Lebens' in den Reichsgauen Danzig–Westpreußen und Wartheland 1939/40* (Frankfurt/M: Peter Lang, 1995), 243–353.
127. Browning suggests 'a coordinating role of Himmler and the central "euthanasia" authorities in Berlin;' Alberti believes that the operations in the Warthegau were separate. See Browning, *The Origins*, 188; and Alberti, *Die Verfolgung*, 333.
128. Browning, *The Origins*, 188.
129. Alberti, *Die Verfolgung*, 324.
130. Rieß, *Die Anfänge*, 270.
131. Alberti argues that Greiser personally told Robert Schulz, the head of the Gau Self-Administration, to authorize the murders. Alberti, *Die Verfolgung*, 333.
132. Stanisław Nawrocki, *Terror policyjny w 'Kraju Warty' 1939–1945* (Poznań: Wydawnictwo Poznańskie, 1973), 56.
133. Rieß, *Die Anfänge*, 359.
134. Aly, *'Endlösung,'* 114–15; and Browning, *The Origins*, 189.
135. Rieß, *Die Anfänge*, 298–300.
136. Alberti, *Die Verfolgung*, 327–30.
137. Wilhelm Koppe to Jakob Sporrenberg, 18 October 1940, BAB, NS19/2576, 3–4.
138. Alberti, *Die Verfolgung*, 336.
139. Aly, *'Endlösung,'* 395–6; Browning, *The Origins*, 366; and Ian Kershaw, 'Improvised Genocide? The Emergence of the "Final Solution" in the "Warthegau,"' *Transactions of the Royal Historical Society* (1992): 75–6.
140. Alberti, *Die Verfolgung*, 351.
141. See Aly, *'Endlösung,'* 397.
142. Alberti, *Die Verfolgung*, 274–5.

143. Rolf-Heinz Höppner, memorandum, 16 July 1941, BAB, R58/954, 190–1.
144. Ian Kershaw, *Hitler 1936–1945: Nemesis* (New York: Norton, 2000), 471.
145. Rolf-Heinz Höppner, memorandum.
146. Eisenbach interpreted Höppner's sentence to mean that Greiser was biding his time, waiting for a signal from Berlin—and particularly from economics functionaries—before deciding on a particular course of action. Kershaw deduced from the memorandum that Höppner's proposals came from security officials rather than from Greiser; this fits his reasoning that it was Koppe, and not Greiser, who first suggested mass murder in the Gau. Alberti teases out another interpretation. In Höppner's memorandum, the line about Greiser is followed by a statement about Uebelhoer: 'There is an impression that District President Uebelhoer doesn't want the ghetto to disappear because he seems to profit nicely from it.' Alberti argues that by mentioning Greiser and Uebelhoer in the same point, Höppner was drawing a connection between the two: not just Uebelhoer was an obstacle to the liquidation of the ghetto, but so too was Greiser. See Artur Eisenbach, 'O należyte zrozumienie genezy zagłady Żydów,' *Biuletyn Żydowskiego Instytutu Historyczynego w Polsce* 104 (1977): 61; Kershaw, 'Improvised Genocide?' 75; and Alberti, *Die Verfolgung*, 361.
147. Alberti, *Die Verfolgung*, 366.
148. Arthur Greiser to Kurt Schmalz, August Jäger, Wilhelm Koppe, Viktor Böttcher, Hans Burckhardt, Friedrich Uebelhoer, Drendel, and Helmut Froböß, 22 July 1941, BAB, R3001(alt R22)/850, 134–7.
149. Klein further posits that the Führer's approval of Greiser taking the initiative on the 'Jewish Question' in his Gau posed a threat to Reinhard Heydrich; by definition, it undermined the RSHA-chief's overall responsibility for the Final Solution. So as to counteract a territorial decentralization of the Final Solution, Heydrich thus prepared the famous 31 July memorandum for Göring's signature that confirmed the RSHA-chief's responsibility for the 'total solution of the Jewish Question.' Klein, *Die 'Gettoverwaltung Litzmannstadt'*, 349–51.
150. Browning, *The Origins*, 283–4.
151. Klein, *Die 'Gettoverwaltung Litzmannstadt,'* 549.
152. Klein, *Die 'Gettoverwaltung Litzmannstadt,'* 349.
153. Browning, *The Origins*, 326–7.
154. Heinrich Himmler to Arthur Greiser, 18 September 1941, BAB, NS19/2655, 3.
155. Browning, *The Origins*, 330.
156. Alberti, *Die Verfolgung*, 355.
157. Klein, *Die 'Gettoverwaltung Litzmannstadt,'* 357.
158. Alberti, *Die Verfolgung*, 402–3; and Peter Longerich, *Politik der Vernichtung: Eine Gesamtdarstellung der nationalsozialistischen Judenverfolgung* (Munich: Piper, 1998), 452.

159. Arthur Greiser to Heinrich Himmler, 28 October 1941, BAB, NS19/2655, 49.
160. Łuczak, ed., *Położenie*, 40–1.
161. Alberti, *Die Verfolgung*, 402; Klein, *Die 'Gettoverwaltung Litzmannstadt,'* 386, 428; and Pohl, 'Die Reichsgaue,' 402.
162. Peter Klein, 'Die Rolle der Vernichtungslager Kulmhof (Chełmno), Belzec (Bełżec) und Auschwitz-Birkenau in den frühen Deportationsvorbereitungen,' in Dittmar Dahlmann and Gerhard Hirsch, eds., *Lager, Zwangsarbeit, Vertreibung und Deportation: Dimensionen der Massenverbrechen in der Sowjetunion und in Deutschland 1933 bis 1945* (Essen: Klartext, 1999), 475–6.
163. Alberti, *Die Verfolgung*, 440.
164. Klein, *Die 'Gettoverwaltung Litzmannstadt,'* 478.
165. Heinrich Himmler to Arthur Greiser, 11 October 1941, BAB, NS19/2655, 41.
166. Greiser to Himmler, 28 October 1941, 49.
167. H. G. Adler, *Der Verwaltete Mensch: Studien zur Deportation der Juden aus Deutschland* (Tübingen: J. C. B. Mohr, 1974), 172.
168. Greiser to Himmler, 28 October 1941, 49.
169. Alberti, *Die Verfolgung*, 395.
170. Klein, *Die 'Gettoverwaltung Litzmannstadt,'* 357.
171. Piotr Rybczyński, 'Likwidacja skupisk ludności żydowskiej w powiecie konińskim,' in *Ośrodek zagłady w Chełmnie nad Nerem i jego rola w hitlerowskiej polityce eksterminacyjnej* (Konin: Muzeum Okręgowe, 1995), 113. See also Theo Richmond, *Konin: A Quest* (New York: Pantheon, 1995), 478–82.
172. Alberti, *Die Verfolgung*, 414.
173. Rybczyński, 'Likwidacja,' 111–12.
174. Alberti, *Die Verfolgung*, 412–15.
175. Achterberg to Geheime Staatspolizei, Stapopolizeileitstelle Posen, Aussendienststelle in Lissa, 9 October 1941, BAB, R70Polen/88, 9.
176. On Chełmno, see *Ośrodek*; Łucja Pawlicka-Nowak, *The Extermination Center for Jews in Chełmno-on-Ner in the Light of the Latest Research: Symposium Proceedings September 6–7, 2004* (District Museum of Konin, 2004); Adalbert Rückerl, ed., *Nationalsozialistische Vernichtungslager im Spiegel deutscher Strafprozesse: Belzec, Sobibor, Treblinka, Chelmno* (Munich: Deutscher Taschenbuch Verlag, 1977); and Manfred Struck, ed., *Chełmno/Kulmhof: Ein vergessener Ort des Holocaust* (Bonn: Gegen Vergessen—Für Demokratie, 2001).
177. Klein, *Die 'Gettoverwaltung Litzmannstadt,'* 341.
178. Richard Breitman, *The Architect of Genocide: Himmler and the Final Solution* (Hanover: Brandeis University Press, 1991), 202.
179. This raises doubts about Aly's general argument that demographic pressures led Nazi officials to carry out the Holocaust (his argument remains more convincing for the Warthegau). See Aly, *'Endlösung.'*
180. Browning, *The Origins*, 366.
181. Alberti, *Die Verfolgung*, 329.
182. Albin Wietrzykowski, *Powrót Arthura Greisera* (Poznań: Nakładem Księgarni Wydawniczej Spółdzielni 'Pomoc,' 1946), 22.

183. Dr. Drüge, 'Beschwerde gegen die teilweise Aufhebung des Haftbefehls gegen Koppe,' BA-Ludwigsburg, 203 AR-Z 69/59, 1104–11; Kershaw, 'Improvised Genocide?' 69; and Rückerl, ed., *Nationalsozialistische Vernichtungslager*, 253.
184. Rückerl, ed., *Nationalsozialistische Vernichtungslager*, 264.
185. Aly, *'Endlösung,'* 362, fn.82.
186. Klein, *Die 'Gettoverwaltung Litzmannstadt,'* 416.
187. While a decision to liquidate Soviet Jews had already been made by August 1941, Holocaust scholars debate when the decision to murder all of Europe's Jews—including German Jews—was made. Christopher Browning and Peter Klein have argued that the October 1941 deportation of German Jews to ghettos in the east was inextricably linked with the decision to murder all of Europe's Jews. By contrast, Christian Gerlach argues that the decision to send German Jews eastwards was separate from that of their murder. He suggests that Hitler made the decision to murder all western Jews only after Germany declared war against the United States. According to Gerlach, Hitler announced his decision at a meeting of Reichsleiters and Gauleiters on 12 December 1941 (at which Greiser was present). Heydrich, in turn, used the Wannsee Conference on 20 January 1942 to inform high-ranking security officials about this and other decisions. Events in the Warthegau do not fully support one or the other position. It's not clear why the western Jews deported to Litzmannstadt were expressly excluded from murder operations that targeted ghetto inmates beginning on 16 January 1942. If Browning and Klein are correct, why weren't these Jews also deported on or after 16 January? If Gerlach is correct, why weren't they murdered shortly after the Wannsee Conference, during the first wave of deportations that ended on 2 April? See Browning, *The Origins*, 427; Gerlach, 'The Wannsee Conference,' 761, 767, 771–2, 784; and Klein, *Die 'Gettoverwaltung Litzmannstadt,'* 452–3.
188. Heinrich Himmler, *Der Dienstkalender Heinrich Himmlers 1941/42*, ed. Peter Witte, Michael Wildt, *et al.* (Hamburg: Christians, 1999), 398–9.
189. This, in turn, casts some doubt on Klein's argument that Hitler gave Greiser carte blanche to 'solve' the 'Jewish Question' in his territory in July 1941.
190. Alberti, *Die Verfolgung*, 450–1.
191. Guido Knopp, *Hitlers Helfer: Täter und Vollstrecker* (Munich: C. Bertelsmann, 1998), 142; and Jochen von Lang, *Der Hitler-Junge: Baldur von Schirach: Der Mann der Deutschlands Jugend erzog* (Hamburg: Rasch und Röhring, 1988), 311.
192. Łuczak, ed., *Położenie*, 40–2.
193. Łuczak, ed., *Położenie*, 42–5.
194. Arthur Greiser to Heinrich Himmler, 21 November 1942, BAB, NS19/1585, 17.
195. Łuczak, ed., *Położenie*, 46.
196. Greiser, *Der Aufbau*, 13–15.

197. Arthur Greiser to Heinrich Himmler, 7 March 1944, BAB, Former BDC Collection, SSO Files on Arthur Greiser.
198. 'Glaube und Beharrlichkeit Gebot der Viertelstunde vor Zwölf,' *Litzmannstädter Zeitung*, 15 March 1944, BAB, R8034III/163.
199. Łuczak, *Pod niemieckim jarzmem*, 83.

6. 'THE GERMAN IS THE MASTER:' SEGREGATION IN THE WARTHEGAU

1. Czesław Madajczyk, *Die Okkupationspolitik Nazideutschlands in Polen 1939–1945* (Berlin: Akademie, 1987), 513; and Alfred Konieczny and Herbert Szurgacz, eds., *Praca przymusowa Polaków pod panowaniem hitlerowskim 1939–1945 (Documenta occupationis X)* (Poznań: Instytut Zachodni, 1976), xlvii.
2. 'Warthegau—ein lebendiger Ostwall,' *Ostdeutscher Beobachter* (6 November 1939).
3. Karol Marian Pospiezalski, ed., *Hitlerowskie 'prawo' okupacyjne w Polsce: wybór dokumentów: część I: ziemie 'wcielone' (Documenta occupationis V)* (Poznań: Instytut Zachodni, 1959), 274–80.
4. Arthur Greiser, 'Zur Volkstumsfrage,' *Völkischer Beobachter*, 29 April 1942, BAB, NS5VI/17583, 34.
5. Arthur Greiser, *Der Aufbau im Osten* (Jena: Fischer, 1942), 8.
6. Karol Marian Pospieszalski, ed., *Niemiecka lista narodowa w 'Kraju Warty' (Documenta occupationis teutonicae IV)* (Poznań: Instytut Zachodni, 1949), 245–6.
7. Konieczny and Szurgacz, eds., *Praca*, 281–2.
8. Michael Alberti, *Die Verfolgung und Vernichtung der Juden im Reichsgau Wartheland 1939–1945* (Wiesbaden: Harrassowitz, 2006), 92.
9. On the origins of the Ethnic German Register, see Isabel Heinemann, *'Rasse, Siedlung, deutsches Blut': Das Rasse- & Siedlungshauptamt der SS und die rassenpolitische Neuordnung Europas* (Göttingen: Wallstein, 2003), 260–82; Robert L. Koehl, 'The *Deutsche Volksliste* in Poland 1939–1945,' *Journal of Central European Affairs* 15, no. 4 (1956): 354–66; and Herbert Strickner, 'Die "Deutsche Volksliste" in Posen,' in Pospieszalski, ed., *Niemiecka lista narodowa*, 36–54.
10. Strickner, 'Die "Deutsche Volksliste,"' 44–6.
11. 'Aus den Richtlinien für die Erfassung der deutschen Volkszugehörigen im Reichsgau Wartheland in der "Deutschen Volksliste," November 1939,' in Herbert Michaelis and Ernst Schraepler, eds., *Ursachen und Folgen: Vom deutschen Zusammenbruch 1918 und 1945 bis zur staatlichen Neuordnung Deutschlands in der Gegenwart* (Berlin: Dokumenten-Verlag Dr. Herbert Wendler [no date]), Vol. 14, 121–5.
12. Raul Hilberg, *The Destruction of the European Jews*, revised and definitive edition (New York: Holmes & Meier, 1985), Vol. 1, 72.

13. Strickner, 'Die "Deutsche Volksliste,"' 87.
14. Strickner, 'Die "Deutsche Volksliste,"' 45.
15. Der k. Gauamtsleiter, Gaugrenzlandamt, Eilrundschreiben, 16 August 1940, BAB, R49/62, 31–5; and Strickner, 'Die "Deutsche Volksliste,"' 65–70.
16. Czesław Łuczak, ed., *Położenie ludności polskiej w tzw. Kraju Warty w okresie hitlerowskiej okupacji (Documenta occupationis XIII)* (Poznań: Instytut Zachodni, 1990), 363.
17. Łuczak, ed., *Położenie*, 179–80.
18. E. Wetzel and G. Hecht, 'Die Frage der Behandlung der Bevölkerung der ehemaligen polnischen Gebiete nach rassenpolitischen Gesichtspunkte,' 25 November 1939, BAB, NS2/56.
19. Heinrich Himmler, 'Einige Gedanken über die Behandlung der Fremdvölkischen im Osten,' in Helmut Krausnick, ed., 'Denkschrift Himmlers über die Behandlung der Fremdvölkischen im Osten (Mai 1940),' *Vierteljahrshefte für Zeitgeschichte* 5 (1957): 196–8.
20. Krausnick, ed., 'Denkschrift,' 195–6.
21. Arthur Greiser, 'Richtlinien für den Verwaltungsaufbau in den Kreisen und Städten der Provinz Posen,' 29 September 1939, BAB, ZR 536 A.2.
22. Czesław Łuczak, ed., *Dyskryminacja Polaków w Wielkopolsce w okresie okupacji hitlerowskiej: wybór źródeł* (Poznań: Wydawnictwo Pozańskie, 1966), 359–60.
23. Łuczak, ed., *Położenie*, 180–2.
24. Łuczak, ed., *Położenie*, 182, 348–9.
25. Łuczak, ed., *Dyskryminacja*, 343–5.
26. August Jäger to alle Herren Landräte und Oberbürgermeister, 28 July 1941, IPN, 196/12, 84.
27. Chef des Führungsstabes und persönlicher Referent, 14 August 1941, IPN, 196/12, 86.
28. Partei-Kanzlei, 3 February 1943, IPN, 196/12, 112.
29. Rolf-Heinz Höppner to Steinhilber, 14 August 1943, IPN, 196/12, 116.
30. See Hans-Christian Harten, *De-Kulturation und Germanisierung: Die nationalsozialistische Rassen- und Erziehungspolitik in Polen 1939–1945* (Frankfurt/M: Campus, 1996), 92–3; and Diemut Majer, *'Non-Germans' under the Third Reich: The Nazi Judicial and Administrative System in Germany and Occupied Eastern Europe, with Special Regard to Occupied Poland, 1939–1945* (Baltimore: Johns Hopkins University Press, 2003), 208.
31. *Ostdeutscher Beobachter* (2 December 1939), 11.
32. *Ostdeutscher Beobachter* (27 June 1940), 5.
33. Łuczak, ed., *Położenie*, 350.
34. Czesław Łuczak, *Pod niemieckim jarzmem (Kraj Warty 1939–1945)* (Poznań: PSO, 1996), 195; and Łuczak, ed., *Położenie*, 374.
35. Łuczak, ed., *Położenie*, 351.
36. Harten, *De-Kulturation*, 97.
37. Majer, '*Non-Germans*,' 210.

38. Łuczak, ed., *Położenie*, 358–61.
39. Madajczyk, *Die Okkupationspolitik*, 169, n. 11.
40. Łuczak, ed., *Położenie*, 352–3.
41. Łuczak, ed., *Położenie*, 364–5.
42. Łuczak, *Pod niemieckim jarzmem*, 170.
43. Łuczak, ed., *Położenie*, 285; and Majer, *'Non-Germans,'* 259.
44. Łuczak, ed., *Położenie*, 287.
45. Łuczak, ed., *Dyskryminacja*, 275; and Łuczak, ed., *Położenie*, 283, 289.
46. Majer, *'Non-Germans,'* 258.
47. Łuczak, ed., *Dyskryminacja*, 260–1.
48. Łuczak, ed., *Położenie*, 323–5.
49. Łuczak, ed., *Dyskryminacja*, 316–20.
50. Łuczak, ed., *Dyskryminacja*, 311–13.
51. Łuczak, ed., *Dyskryminacja*, 315–16.
52. Łuczak, ed., *Dyskryminacja*, 321–3.
53. On educational policy toward Poles in the Warthegau, see Georg Hansen, *Ethnische Schulpolitik im besetzten Polen: Der Mustergau Wartheland* (Münster: Waxmann, 1995); Georg Hansen, ed., *Schulpolitik als Volkstumspolitik: Quellen zur Schulpolitik der Besatzer in Polen 1939–1945* (Münster: Waxmann, 1994); and Harten, *De-Kulturation.*
54. Pospiezalski, ed., *Hitlerowskie 'prawo' okupacyjne*, 63–4.
55. Łuczak, ed., *Położenie*, 322–3.
56. Łuczak, ed., *Położenie*, 329–31.
57. Łuczak, ed., *Położenie*, 252.
58. Łuczak, ed., *Położenie*, 325–6.
59. Majer, *'Non-Germans,'* 232.
60. Majer, *'Non-Germans,'* 234.
61. Madajczyk, *Die Okkupationspolitik*, 264; and Majer, *'Non-Germans,'* 222.
62. Łuczak, ed., *Położenie*, 264–5.
63. Pospiezalski, ed., *Hitlerowskie 'prawo' okupacyjne*, 274–80.
64. Madajczyk, *Die Okkupationspolitik*, 266.
65. Armin Ziegler, *Wer kennt schon Zabikowo . . . Ein Bericht über das 'Polizeigefängnis der Sicherheitspolizei und SS-Arbeitserziehungslager Posen-Lenzingen'* (Schönaich: Im Selbstverlag, 1994), 24–5.
66. Łuczak, ed., *Położenie*, 303.
67. Majer, *'Non-Germans,'* 256.
68. Łuczak, ed., *Położenie*, 369.
69. Łuczak, ed., *Dyskryminacja*, 258–9.
70. Łuczak, ed., *Położenie*, 297.
71. Łuczak, ed., *Położenie*, 298–9.
72. Dr. Karl Coulon, Vermerk, 27 August 1940, IPN, 62/20, 7.
73. Łuczak, ed., *Położenie*, 301–2.
74. Majer, *'Non-Germans,'* 251.

75. Majer, *'Non-Germans,'* 236–7.
76. Majer, *'Non-Germans,'* 246.
77. Institut für Zeitgeschichte, ed., *Akten der Partei-Kanzlei der NSDAP: Rekonstruktion eines verlorengegangenen Bestands* (Munich: Oldenbourg, 1983), Part I, 101 28401–7.
78. Madajczyk, *Die Okkupationspolitik*, 196; and Pospiezalski, ed., *Hitlerowskie 'prawo' okupacyjne*, 330–4.
79. Oberlandesgerichtspräsident, Der Reichsstatthalter, 9 January 1941, BAB, R3001(alt R22)/850, 55.
80. 'Schreiben von Hans Heinrich Lammers an den Reichsminister der Justiz vom 27. Mai 1941 über die "Strafrechtspflege" in den eingegliederten Ostgebieten,' in Helma Kaden and Ludwig Nestler, eds., *Dokumente des Verbrechens: Aus Akten des Dritten Reiches 1933–1945* (Berlin: Dietz, 1993), Vol. 2, 207–8.
81. Roland Freisler to Arthur Greiser, 24 June 1941, BAB, R3001(alt R22)/850, 64–5. See also Martin Broszat, *Nationalsozialistische Polenpolitik 1939–1945* (Stuttgart: Deutsche Verlags-Anstalt, 1961), 150–1; and Madajczyk, *Die Okkupationspolitik*, 197.
82. See Drendel to Arthur Greiser, 17 August 1943, BAB, R3001(alt R22)/850, 528.
83. Peter Klein, *Die 'Gettoverwaltung Litzmannstadt' 1940–1944: Eine Dienststelle im Spannungsfeld von Kommunalbürokratie und staatlicher Verfolgungspolitik* (Hamburg: Hamburger Edition, 2009), 347.
84. Arthur Greiser to Roland Freisler, 22 July 1941, BAB, R3001(alt R22)/850, 133.
85. See Chapter 5.
86. Arthur Greiser to Kurt Schmalz, August Jäger, Wilhelm Koppe, Viktor Böttcher, Hans Burckhardt, Friedrich Uebelhoer, Drendel, and Helmut Froböß, 22 July 1941, BAB, R3001(alt R22)/850, 134–7.
87. Arthur Greiser to Hans Lammers, 13 November 1941, BAB, R3001(alt R22)/850, 198–9.
88. See BAB, R3001(alt R22)/850, 200–1, 215–16.
89. Reichsminister der Justiz to the Herrn Reichsstatthalter der Reichsgaue Wartheland und Danzig–Westpreußen, and die Herren Oberpräsidenten der Provinzen Oberschlesien und Ostpreußen, 9 April 1942, BAB, R3001(alt R22)/850, 318.
90. Arthur Greiser to the Herren Regierungspräsidenten, Herren Landräte, Oberbürgermeister und Amtskommissare im Reichsgau Wartheland, 23 August 1941, BAB, R138/II/15; see also Majer, *'Non-Germans,'* 219–21.
91. Majer, *'Non-Germans,'* 220.
92. 'Verordnung über die Strafrechtspflege gegen Polen und Juden in den eingegliederten Ostgebieten,' *Reichsgesetzblatt* Teil I (16 December 1941): 759–61.

93. Czesław Łuczak, *Arthur Greiser* (Poznań: PSO, 1997), 67.
94. Marian Woźniak, 'Więźniowie więzienia policyjnego Poznańskiego gestapo w latach 1943–1945,' *Kronika Wielkopolski* 36 (1985): 147.
95. Łuczak, ed., *Położenie*, 34–6; and Pospiezalski, ed., *Hitlerowskie 'prawo' okupacyjne*, 351–2, and for numerous other examples, 351–413.
96. Łuczak, ed., *Położenie*, 76.
97. Polish scholars estimate that some 70,000 to 102,000 Poles were murdered in the Warthegau. See Łuczak, *Pod niemieckim jarzmem*, 38; and Madajczyk, *Die Okkupationspolitik*, 241. The Germans, however, did not outright execute anywhere near this number of Poles. Perhaps Łuczak and Madajczyk are also including Poles who died indirectly as a result of the Nazi occupation.
98. See Łuczak, *Pod niemieckim jarzmem*, 202–50; Edward Serwanski, 'Polityczne i wojskowe organizacje podziemne w Wielkopolsce,' *Nojnowsze Dzieje Polski: Materiały i Studia z Okresu II Wojny Światowej* no. 3 (1959): 43–72; and Woźniak, 'Więźniowie,' 145–91.
99. Łuczak, *Pod niemieckim jarzmem*, 222.
100. Łuczak, ed., *Dyskryminacja*, 111–13.
101. Hans Burckhardt to Arthur Greiser, 24 March 1942, APP, 299/1219, 177.
102. Łuczak, ed., *Położenie*, 295–6.
103. Łuczak, *Pod niemieckim Jarzmem*, 224.
104. Auszugsweise Abschrift, 1941, IPN, 62/22, 2.
105. Hans Neumann to Friedrich Uebelhoer, 28 May 1941, BAB, R75/9a, 102–4.
106. Kommandeur der Gendarmerie bei dem Regierungspräsidenten, Anordnungen des Kommandeurs der Gendarmerie Nr.7, 18 November 1941, BAB, R70 Polen/188, 7.
107. Lagebericht des Höheren SS- und Polizeiführers vom 28.2.–6.3.43, IPN, 62/21, 85–6.
108. August Jäger to sämtliche Abteilungsleiter meiner Behörde und an alle gleichgeordneten, nachgeordneten und unterstellten Behörden, 11 December 1941, IPN, 62/346, 129.
109. Kurt Schmalz, Schnellrundbrief, 19 April 1941, APP, 1009/2, 24.
110. Arthur Greiser to Roland Freisler, 26 June 1942, BAB, R3001(alt R22)/850, 345–6.
111. Arthur Greiser to Leiter der Partei-Kanzlei, Reichsminister des Innern, Reichsminister der Justiz, 27 May 1943, BAB, R3001(alt R22)/850, 388–9.
112. Reichsminister der Justiz to Arthur Greiser, 11 June 1943, BAB, R3001(alt R22)/850, 390.
113. Gauamt für Volkstumspolitik, Berichte der Kreisamtsleiter, Kreis Kolmar, March 1942, IPN, 196/36, 439.
114. Joseph Goebbels, *Die Tagebücher von Joseph Goebbels: Sämtliche Fragmente*, ed. Elke Fröhlich (Munich: K.G. Saur, 1996), Part II, Vol. 6, 457.
115. Heinrich Himmler to Arthur Greiser, 15 November 1940, BAB, R49/62, 72–8.

116. Arthur Greiser to Heinrich Himmler, 24 November 1940, BAB, R49/62, 80–2.
117. 'Aus dem Erlaß Heinrich Himmlers vom 12. September 1940 zur Überprüfung und Aussonderung der Bevölkerung im annektierten Polen,' in Werner Röhr, ed., *Europa unterm Hakenkreuz: Die faschistische Okkupationspolitik in Polen (1939–1945)* (Berlin: Deutscher Verlag der Wissenschaften, 1989), 186–8.
118. 'Verordnung über die Deutsche Volksliste und die deutsche Staatsangehörigkeit in den eingegliederten Ostgebieten,' *Reichsgesetzblatt* (4 March 1941), Part 1, 118–20.
119. Wilhelm Frick, 'Erwerb der deutschen Staatsangehörigkeit durch ehemalige polnische und Danziger Staatsangehörige,' 13 March 1941, BAB, R49/71, 14–15.
120. Arthur Greiser to the Bezirksstellen der Deutschen Volksliste, 6 April 1941, BAB, R49/62, 21–30.
121. Reichsstatthalter I/50, 26 August 1941, APP, 299/1112, 355.
122. Rolf-Heinz Höppner to Herbert Mehlhorn, 25 August 1941, APP, 299/1112, 356.
123. Heinrich Himmler, 'Rassische Musterung der Angehörigen der Abteilung 3 der Deutschen Volksliste,' Anordnung 50/I, 23 September 1941, APP, 305/67, 4–5.
124. Dr. Karl Albert Coulon to Dr. Neeße, 26 August 1941, IZ, I-236.
125. SS-Hauptsturmführer Massury to Reichsführer-SS, 23 August 1941, IZ, I-236.
126. See SD des Reichsführers-SS, SD-Abschnitt Litzmannstadt, 25 October 1941, APP, 305/67, 2–3.
127. One historian, Isabel Heinemann, writes that 'Gauleiter Greiser, after massive pressure from Himmler and the racial experts from the RuSHA, gave up his initial resistance to racial screenings and yielded.' Since Greiser prevailed, her interpretation misses the point. See Heinemann, *'Rasse,'* 274.
128. August Jäger to Herren Regierungspräsidenten in Posen, Hohensalza, und Litzmannstadt, 3 January 1942, APP 299/1115, 2–6.
129. Wilhelm Stuckart, 'Vereinfachung und Beschleunigung des Volkslistenverfahrens,' 4 May 1942, BAB, R49/189, 71–2.
130. Arthur Greiser, 'Behandlung der in die Abteilungen 3 und 4 der Deutschen Volksliste aufgenommenen Personen,' 1 January 1942, IZ, I-166, 2–5.
131. 'Aus der Allgemeinen Anordnung Nr. 12/C Heinrich Himmlers vom 9. Februar 1942 über die Behandlung der in die Abteilung 3 der "Deutschen Volksliste" eingetragenen Personen,' in Röhr, ed., *Europa unterm Hakenkreuz*, 213–15.
132. Heinrich Himmler, 'Behandlung der in Abteilung 4 der Deutschen Volksliste eingetretenen Personen,' 16 February 1942, BAB, R58/1032, 68–70.
133. 'Aus der Allgemeinen Anordnung Nr. 12/C,' in Röhr, ed., *Europa unterm Hakenkreuz*, 213–15.

134. Arthur Greiser to Heinrich Himmler, 2 April 1943, IZ, I-157, 4–5.
135. 'Pg. Höppner verläßt das Wartheland,' *Ostdeutscher Beobachter* (15 July 1944).
136. Rolf-Heinz Höppner, Vermerk, 9 March 1943, APP, 299/1166, 90.
137. Rolf-Heinz Höppner, 18 March 1943, APP, 299/1166, 92.
138. Rolf-Heinz Höppner, Vermerk, 31 January 1944, IZ, I-306, 29.
139. Peter R. Black, *Ernst Kaltenbrunner: Ideological Soldier of the Third Reich* (Princeton: Princeton University Press, 1984), 200–6.
140. Hermann Benz, 'Die deutsche Massnahmen von 1939 bis 1944,' 28 December 1955, BA-Bayreuth, Ost-Dok.8/456, 6.
141. Arthur Greiser, Schlußwort des Angeklagten Artur [*sic*] Greiser im Prozess vor dem Höchsten Volksgericht, July 1946, BA-Bayreuth, Ost-Dok.13/452, 40.
142. 'Pg. Höppner.'
143. Zofia Boda-Krężel, *Sprawa volkslisty na Górnym Śląsku koncepcje likwidacji problemu i ich realizacja* (Opole: Instytut Śląski, 1978), 22–4, 33–4.
144. Arthur Greiser to Heinrich Himmler, 16 March 1943, BAB, NS19/3662, 78–9.
145. Heinrich Himmler to Arthur Greiser, 3 April 1943, BAB, NS19/3662, 72.
146. Arthur Greiser to Heinrich Himmler, 15 April 1943, BAB, NS19/3662, 65–6.
147. Boda-Krężel, *Sprawa volkslisty*, 25.
148. 'Arbeitstagung des Gauamtes für Volkstumspolitik am 20. und 21.3.1943 in Posen,' in Pospieszalski, ed., *Niemiecka lista narodowa*, 250–3.
149. In Zichenau, Erich Koch dithered about setting up the DVL. When he finally did so in December 1942, he employed laxer guidelines than Greiser. See Karel C. Berkhoff, *Harvest of Despair: Life and Death in Ukraine under Nazi Rule* (Cambridge, Mass.: Harvard University Press, 2004), 211–12.
150. See Stansław Jankowiak, 'Einleitung,' in Włodzimierz Borodziej and Hans Lemberg, eds., *'Unsere Heimat ist uns ein fremdes Land geworden…' Die Deutschen östlich von Oder und Neiße 1945–1950: Dokumente aus polnischen Archiven*, Bd. 3: *Wojewodschaft Posen Wojewodschaft Stettin (Hinterpommern)* (Marburg: Verlag Herder-Institut, 2004), 43.
151. Arthur Greiser to Heinrich Himmler, 16 March 1943, BAB, NS19/3662, 78–9.
152. See Łuczak, ed., *Dyskryminacja*, 97–100; Łuczak, ed., *Położenie*, 23; and Hermann Krumey, 'Abschlußbericht über die Arbeit der Umwandererzentralstelle im Rahmen des erweiterten 3. Nahplanes,' BAB, R75/9, 9.
153. Majer, *'Non-Germans,'* 246–8.
154. Wilhelm Frick to Albert Forster, Arthur Greiser, Fritz Bracht, und Erich Koch, 13 April 1943, IZ, I-441, 71–2.
155. Arthur Greiser to Wilhelm Frick, 14 April 1943, IZ, I-441, 73.
156. Arthur Greiser to his Behörde, 14 April 1943, IZ, I-441, 73.
157. Herbert Mehlhorn, Vermerk, 20 April 1943, IZ, I-441, 75.
158. Arthur Greiser, Schnellbrief, 27 May 1943, IZ, I-441, 77.

159. Łuczak, ed., *Położenie*, 265–6.
160. Łuczak, ed., *Położenie*, 274–5.
161. Madajczyk, *Die Okkupationspolitik*, 253–4.
162. Pospiezalski, ed., *Hitlerowskie 'prawo' okupacyjne*, 280.
163. Łuczak, ed., *Położenie*, 173–4.
164. 'Aus der Anordnung Nr. 67/I von SS-Gruppenführer Ulrich Greifelt, Chef des Stabshauptamtes des RKF, vom 19. Februar 1942 zur Eindeutschung von Kindern aus polnischen Familien und Waisenhäusern,' in Röhr, ed., *Europa*, 215–16.
165. Harten, *De-Kulturation*, 302. Łuczak states that 12,000 Polish children were subject to Germanization. See Łuczak, *Arthur Greiser*, 71–2.
166. Dr. Gramsch, 'Sitzung über Ostfragen unter dem Vorsitz des Ministerpräsidenten Generalfeldmarschall Göring,' 12 February 1940, IZ, I-774.
167. von Hof, Vermerk, 30 January 1941, BAB, R113/7, 32–3.
168. Alexander Dolezalek, Vermerk, 12 February 1941, BAB, R49/3066, 43–7.
169. Phillip T. Rutherford, *Prelude to the Final Solution: The Nazi Program for Deporting Ethnic Poles, 1939–1941* (Lawrence: University Press of Kansas, 2007), 203.
170. Pospiezalski, ed., *Hitlerowskie 'prawo' okupacyjne*, 274–80.
171. Madajczyk, *Die Okkupationspolitik*, 271.
172. Reichsbahndirektion Posen to Reichsstatthalter, 17 October 1941, IPN, 62/75, 3–4.
173. Łuczak, ed., *Położenie*, 264.
174. Łuczak, ed., *Położenie*, 290–2.
175. Hermann Krumey, 'Abschlußbericht über die Aussiedlungen im Rahmen der Einsetzung der Beßarabiendeutschen (3. Nahplan) vom 21.1.1941–26.1.1942 im Reichsgau Wartheland,' [1942], BAB, R75/8, 1–8.
176. 'Rede des Gauleiters Parteigenossen Arthur Greiser vom 20. Dezember 1942 zur Frage der Leistungspolen,' BAB, Former BDC Collection, PK Files for Arthur Greiser, 5.
177. Wilhelm Stuckart to Heinrich Himmler, 20 November 1942, BAB, Former BDC Collection, SSHO/6980.
178. Otto Georg Thierack to Heinrich Himmler, 16 November 1942, BAB, Former BDC Collection, SSHO/6980.
179. 'Rede des Gauleiters Parteigenossen Arthur Greiser,' 6–7.
180. Pospieszalski, ed., *Niemiecka lista narodowa*, 248.
181. Arthur Greiser to the Reich minister of finance, 5 October 1944, in Institut für Zeitgeschichte, ed., *Akten*, Part I, 103 14294–5.
182. Madajczyk, *Die Okkupationspolitik*, 516.
183. Arthur Greiser, Fragebogen, 31 July 1937, BAB, Former BDC Collection, SSO Files on Arthur Greiser, Frames 40–1.
184. Arthur Greiser to Martin Bormann, 4 December 1939, BAB, R58/7581, 19.

185. Early postwar accounts of church policy in the Gau portrayed Greiser as a mere tool of Bormann, Himmler, or Heydrich; this was in keeping with the then reigning totalitarian interpretation of the Nazi regime. See Broszat, *Nationalsozialistische Polenpolitik*, 167; and J. S. Conway, *The Nazi Persecution of the Churches 1933–45* (New York: Basic Books, 1968), 313.
186. 'Bericht über die Dienstreise nach Posen am 12.12.1939,' BAB, R58/7578, 30–1.
187. Arthur Greiser to Hans Kerrl, 5 February 1940, in Institut für Zeitgeschichte, ed., *Akten*, 102 01398–401.
188. Heinrich Himmler to Arthur Greiser, 14 February 1940, in Institut für Zeitgeschichte, ed., *Akten*, 102 01405.
189. Broszat, *Nationalsozialistische Polenpolitik*, 166.
190. Vermerk, 21 June 1940, BAB, R43II/170, 25.
191. Hans Kerrl to Wilhelm Frick, 3 April 1940, BAB, R43II/170, 19–20.
192. Martin Bormann to Hans Lammers, 1 November 1940, BAB, R43II/150a, 97.
193. Paul Gürtler, *Nationalsozialismus und evangelische Kirchen im Warthegau: Trennung von Staat und Kirche im nationalsozialistischen Weltanschauungsstaat* (Göttingen: Vandenhoeck und Ruprecht, 1958), 200–1.
194. See Der Generalbevollmächtigte für die Reichsverwaltung, 26 July 1940, BAB, R43II/170, 50; and Vermerk, 5 July 1940, BAB, R43II/170, 41–2.
195. Der Reichsstatthalter to Rudolf Hess, 26 August 1940, BAB, R58/7581, 77.
196. Rolf-Heinz Höppner to RSHA, 10 December 1940, BAB, R58/7216, 22–8.
197. Gürtler, *Nationalsozialismus*, 254–5.
198. Institut für Zeitgeschichte, ed., *Akten*, 251. For a copy of the decree, see Gürtler, *Nationalsozialismus*, 260–4.
199. For a contrary view, see Richard Steigmann-Gall, *The Holy Reich: Nazi Conceptions of Christianity, 1919–1945* (Cambridge: Cambridge University Press, 2003), 229.
200. Max Winkler, 'Behandlung des Kirchenvermögens in den eingegliederten Ostgebieten,' BAB, R3001(alt R22)/4009, 11–14.
201. Broszat, *Nationalsozialistische Polenpolitik*, 171–2.
202. Höppner to RSHA, 10 December 1940, 22–8.
203. Cardinal Maglione to Joachim von Ribbentrop, 2 March 1943, PA-AA, R29818, 278141–68.
204. Bernhard Stasiewski, 'Die Kirchenpolitik der Nationalsozialisten im Warthegau 1939–1945,' *Vierteljahrshefte für Zeitgeschichte* 7, no. 1 (1959): 65.
205. Arthur Greiser to Hans Lammers, 24 January 1941, BAB, R43II/170, 71–3.
206. Vermerk, 31 January 1941, BAB, R43II/170, 74.
207. See Arthur Greiser to Ernst von Weizsäcker, 28 April 1941, PA-AA, R29815, 239835–6; and Richard Haidlen, 'Aufzeichung zu der Note des Nuntius über die religiöse Lage im Wartheland,' 23 August 1941, PA-AA, R29816, 240372.
208. Ernst von Weizsäcker to Arthur Greiser, 7 January 1942, PA-AA, R29816, 240397–8.

209. Richard Haidlen, Aufzeichnung betreffend die kirchlichen Verhältnisse im Warthegau, 20 February 1942, PA-AA, R29816, 240400.
210. Walther Hewel, Notiz für Herrn Ges. v. Steengracht, 11 June 1942, PA-AA, R29818, 278181–2.
211. Ernst Woermann, 'Zusammenstellung über die Massnahmen gegen die katholische Kirche,' 24 October 1942, PA-AA, R29817.
212. See SD reports about Kalisch, IPN, 70/33.
213. Vermerk, Erste Ortsbeauftragtentagung vom 1.–4.Oktober 1943, IZ, I-67, 3.
214. W. Thomson to Adolf Hitler, 10 September 1941, Institut für Zeitgeschichte, ed., *Akten*, 101 01483–7.
215. Harry Siegmund to Galiziendeutschen Umsiedler der Amtsgemeinden: Stavenshagen, Vorwalde, Wurzelroden, Weizenfelde, Vogelsang, 13 February 1942, IPN, 62/179, 15.
216. Conway, *The Nazi Persecution*, 321–2.
217. Auszug aus dem Lagebericht des Regierungspräsidenten Litzmannstadt vom 20. Mai für die Zeit vom 21. April bis 20. Mai 1941, IPN, 62/237, 15.
218. See Birk, Vermerk, 3 April 1942, IPN 62/239, 345–6; and Ernst Damzog to Birk, 8 May 1942, 355–6.
219. Meyer to Kurt Krüger, 18 March 1943, IPN, 62/239, 398.
220. Martin Bormann to the Generalbevollmächtigten für die Reichsverwaltung, 8 March 1943, BAB, R43II/165a, 226–8.
221. Meyer, Vermerk, 6 April 1943, IPN, 62/239, 409.
222. Hans Burckhardt, 'Gauleiter Greiser,' 6 July 1945, IPN, 196/36, 472–3.
223. Fruhwirth and Hartl, 'Vermerk über die Besprechung mit Gauleiter Greiser über die konfessionellen Maßnahmen im Reichsgau Wartheland,' 13–14 August 1940, BAB, R58/7581, 63.
224. Alexander Hohenstein, *Wartheländisches Tagebuch aus den Jahren 1941/42* (Stuttgart: Deutsche Verlags-Anstalt, 1961), 206.
225. Hohenstein, *Wartheländisches Tagebuch*, 208.
226. Martin Bormann to Arthur Greiser, 5 April 1943; and Arthur Greiser to Martin Bormann, 14 May 1943, APP, 299/1185, 27–9.
227. Arthur Greiser, Vermerk, 14 July 1944, APP, 299/1185, 59–60.

7. 'THE MOST MODERN STREETS:' EXPLOITING POLES AND JEWS TO MAKE THE GAU GERMAN

1. Karol Marian Pospiezalski, ed., *Hitlerowskie 'prawo' okupacyjne w Polsce: wybór dokumentów: część I: ziemie 'wcielone' (Documenta occupationis V)* (Poznań: Instytut Zachodni, 1959), 274–80.
2. Arthur Greiser, *Der Aufbau im Osten* (Jena: Fischer, 1942), 6.
3. Greiser, *Der Aufbau*, 11.

4. 'Rückgabe der Vermögenswerte: Arthur Greiser über die Ziele der Zivilverwaltung in Polen,' *Preussische Zeitung*, 11 October 1939, BAB, R8034III/163, 117.
5. 'So wohnt der deutsche Siedler,' *Gausonderdienst 'Die Innere Front,'* 2, no. 232/3 (26 July 1941).
6. Arthur Greiser to Gerhard Scheffler, 5 October 1939, APP, 298/75, 5.
7. On the HTO, see Jeanne Dingell, *Zur Tätigkeit der Haupttreuhandstelle Ost: Treuhandstelle Posen 1939 bis 1945* (Frankfurt/M: Peter Lang, 2003); and Bernhard Rosenkötter, *Treuhandpolitik: Die 'Haupttreuhandstelle Ost' und der Raub polnischer Vermögen 1939–1945* (Essen: Klartext, 2003).
8. Rosenkötter, *Treuhandpolitik*, 290.
9. Pospiezalski, ed., *Hitlerowskie 'prawo' okupacyjne*, 183–8.
10. 'Verordnung über die Behandlung von Vermögen der Angehörigen des ehemaligen polnischen Staates,' *Reichsgesetzblatt* Teil I (17 September 1940): 1270–3.
11. Arthur Greiser to Fritz Ohl, 15 November 1939, IPN, 196/36, 543.
12. 'Anlegung von Reichsgeldern auf Sonderkonten bei der Landesbank sowie bei Privatbanken in Posen und Abwickelung dieser Sonderkonten durch den Reichsstatthalter außerhalb der Reichshaushaltsrechnung und außerhalb der Rechnungskontrolle des Rechnungshofes,' 12 October 1944, R2301/5993, 18–19.
13. Frank Bajohr, *Parvenüs und Profiteure: Korruption in der NS-Zeit* (Frankfurt/M: Fischer, 2004), 128.
14. Reichsamtsleiter Schieder, Besuchs-Vermerk Akten-Vermerk, 11 January 1940, BAB, Former BDC Collection, PK files for Arthur Greiser, Frames 2862–2874. For conversion and inflation-adjusted rates, see *www.history.ucsb.edu/faculty/marcuse/projects/currency.htm#tables*; and *www.measuring worth.com/calculators/uscompare/result.php*, accessed 5 August 2009.
15. Office of Der Höhere SS- und Polizeiführer als Beauftragter des RKfdFdV, 3 February 1940, APP, 299/1786, 103.
16. See Rosenkötter, *Treuhandpolitik*, 225; and documents in APP, 299/1786.
17. Wilhelm Stuckart, 'Vermerk über die Besprechungen betr. das Ghetto in Lodsch,' 3 April 1940, BAB, R58/3518, 2–3.
18. Rosenkötter, *Treuhandpolitik*, 129–30.
19. Hermann Göring, Zweite Anordnung über die HTO, 17 February 1941, BAB, R186/37, 308.
20. Czesław Łuczak, ed., *Położenie ludności polskiej w tzw. Kraju Warty w okresie hitlerowskiej okupacji (Documenta occupationis XIII)* (Poznań: Instytut Zachodni, 1990), 189–90.
21. Diemut Majer, *'Non-Germans' under the Third Reich: The Nazi Judicial and Administrative System in Germany and Occupied Eastern Europe, with Special Regard to Occupied Poland, 1939–1945* (Baltimore: Johns Hopkins University Press, 2003), 255–6.

22. *Ostdeutscher Beobachter* (15 March 1940), 10.
23. See Czesław Łuczak, ed., *Dyskryminacja Polaków w Wielkopolsce w okresie okupacji hitlerowskiej: wybór źródeł* (Poznań: Wydawnictwo Pozańskie, 1966), 207–12; and Łuczak, ed., *Położenie*, 190, 192–3, 202, 209.
24. Arthur Greiser, 'Abschrift für die Landräte, die Oberbürgermeister von Posen und Gnesen und den Polizeipräsidenten von Posen,' 18 September 1939, APP, 298/65, 2.
25. Arthur Greiser, 'Anordnung betreffend Entfernung der polnischen Inschriften vom 23. September 1939,' *Verordnungsblatt des Chefs der Zivilverwaltung beim Miltärbefehlshaber von Posen*, no. 1 (3 October 1939), 9.
26. 'Der ewige Kraftquell unseres Brauchtums,' *Ostdeutscher Beobachter* (22 December 1939), 2.
27. Arthur Greiser, 'Tätigkeitsbericht Nr.4 für die Zeit vom 21. bis 28. September 1939,' 29 September 1939, APP, 298/50, 37–45.
28. Richard C. Lukas, *The Forgotten Holocaust: The Poles under German Occupation, 1939–1944* (Lexington: University Press of Kentucky, 1986), 13.
29. Heinrich Himmler, Eil-Runderlass, 16 December 1939, BAB, NS 6/331, 47–8.
30. Hanns Streit, 'Reichsuniversität Posen,' *Die Bewegung*, 11 March 1941, BAB, R4901/13132.
31. Dr. Ruhle to the RKfdFdV, Bodenamt, 23 August 1944, APP, 299/3383, 80.
32. G. J. Gooden to author, 10 November 2005.
33. Arthur Rhode, 'Beitrag zur Archiv-Sammlung der Vertriebenen beim Bundesarchiv für den Reichsgau Wartheland,' 29 June 1955, BA-Bayreuth, Ost-Dok.8/421, 13.
34. 'Posener Hallenschwimmbad bereits im Bau,' *Ostdeutscher Beobachter* (9 April 1940), 6.
35. 'Erste Wettkämpfe im Posener Hallenschwimmbad,' *Ostdeutscher Beobachter* (12 September 1942), 6.
36. Intensive efforts, however, are underway to transform the former synagogue into a site more in keeping with its original function. See the website of the Poznań Synagogue Project: *http://www.pozsynpro.org*.
37. Reichsstatthalter (Oberfinanzpräsident) to Reichsstatthalter, Abteilung I, Kommunal Referat, 1 August 1944, APP, 299/1748, 3.
38. Wilhelm Keuck, Bericht über den Weiteraufbau und die Tätigkeit der Schutzpolizei Litzmannstadt vom 20.6.1940 bis 31.12.1941, 30 January 1942, APP, 1008/7, 73.
39. Michael Alberti, *Die Verfolgung und Vernichtung der Juden im Reichsgau Wartheland 1939–1945* (Wiesbaden: Harrassowitz, 2006), 122; and Schneider, Der Landrat, Wollstein to Haupttreuhandstelle Ost, 20 July 1940, APP 299/1786, 225.
40. Eierkuchen to HTO, Treuhandnebenstelle Litzmannstadt, 17 June 1943, APP, 301/628, 1.

41. Arthur Greiser, 'Die Grossdeutsche Aufgabe im Wartheland,' *Nationalsozialistische Monatshefte* no. 130 (January 1941): 47–8.
42. 'Sitzung über Ostfragen unter dem Vorsitz des Ministerpräsidenten Generalfeldmarschall Göring,' 12 February 1940, IZ, I-774.
43. Czesław Łuczak, *Pod niemieckim jarzmem (Kraj Warty 1939–1945)* (Poznań: PSO, 1996), 102.
44. Greiser, *Der Aufbau*, 11–12.
45. Arthur Greiser to Heinrich Himmler, 18 February 1943, BAB, Former BDC Collection, SSO files on Arthur Greiser.
46. Hans Pfundtner to Augustin, 21 January 1941, BAB, R1501/2442.
47. Daniel Inkelas, 'Visions of Harmony and Violence: RFK Landscape Planning and Population Policy in Annexed Poland, 1939–1944' (Ph.D. diss., Northwestern University, 1998), 159.
48. 'Zukunftspläne im Warthegau,' *Der neue Tag* (Prag), 26 October 1940, BAB, NS5VI/17279.
49. Wolf Gruner, 'Juden bauen die "Straßen des Führers": Zwangsarbeit und Zwangsarbeitslager für nichtdeutsche Juden im Altreich 1940 bis 1943/44,' *Zeitschrift für Geschichtswissenschaft* 44, no. 9 (1996): 789.
50. Greiser, 'Die Grossdeutsche Aufgabe,' 48.
51. Greiser, *Der Aufbau*, 11.
52. See Peter Klein, *Die 'Gettoverwaltung Litzmannstadt' 1940–1944: Eine Dienststelle im Spannungsfeld von Kommunalbürokratie und staatlicher Verfolgungspolitik* (Hamburg: Hamburger Edition, 2009), 176–91.
53. Gordon J. Horwitz, *Łódź and the Making of a Nazi City* (Cambridge, Mass.: Harvard University Press, 2008), 301.
54. Łuczak, *Pod niemieckim jarzmem*, 109.
55. Klein, *Die 'Gettoverwaltung Litzmannstadt,'* 263.
56. Alberti, *Die Verfolgung*, 232.
57. Andrea Löw, *Juden im Getto Litzmannstadt: Lebensbedingungen, Selbstwahrnehmung, Verhalten* (Göttingen: Wallstein, 2006), 120.
58. Klein, *Die 'Gettoverwaltung Litzmannstadt,'* 229–30; and Dieter Rebentisch, *Führerstaat und Verwaltung im Zweiten Weltkrieg: Verfassungsentwicklung und Verwaltungspolitik 1939–1945* (Stuttgart: Franz Steiner, 1989), 112. The words are Rebentisch's, not Greiser's.
59. Götz Aly, *'Endlösung': Völkerverschiebung und der Mord an den europäischen Juden* (Frankfurt/M: Fischer, 1995), 264–5.
60. Aly, *'Endlösung,'* 283.
61. Horwitz, *Łódź*, 130.
62. Klein, *Die 'Gettoverwaltung Litzmannstadt,'* 290.
63. Israel Gutman, 'Introduction: The Distinctiveness of the Lodz ghetto,' in Isaiah Trunk, *Lodz ghetto: A History* (Bloomington: Indiana University Press, 2006), xlv.
64. Klein, *Die 'Gettoverwaltung Litzmannstadt,'* 268.

65. Klein, *Die 'Gettoverwaltung Litzmannstadt,'* 299.
66. Gruner, 'Juden,' 789–93.
67. Hermann Göring, 18 February 1941, BAB, R3901/20281, 44.
68. Gruner, 'Juden,' 792–3; and Klein, *Die 'Gettoverwaltung Litzmannstadt,'* 298.
69. Alberti, *Die Verfolgung*, 5.
70. Armin Ziegler, *Wer kennt schon Zabikowo... Ein Bericht über das 'Polizeigefängnis der Sicherheitspolizei und SS-Arbeitserziehungslager Posen-Lenzingen'* (Schönaich: Im Selbstverlag, 1994), 10.
71. Alberti, *Die Verfolgung*, 288.
72. Ezra Schilit, Vernehmungsniederschrift, 20 February 1974, BA-Ludwigsburg, ZStL, 203 AR-Z 26/72, 1714–17.
73. Anna Ziółkowska, *Obozy pracy przymusowej dla Żydów w Wielkopolsce w latach okupacji hitlerowskiej (1941–1943)* (Poznań: Wydawnictwo Poznańskie, 2005), 46–7.
74. Heinrich Schwendemann and Wolfgang Dietsche, *Hitlers Schloß: Die 'Führerresidenz' in Posen* (Berlin: Ch. Links, 2003), 152. Greiser was not alone in using Jewish labor for Germanization projects. Jewish laborers at Auschwitz, for example, helped lay the foundations for a Silesian industrial complex that was intended to rival that of the Ruhr. See Adam Tooze, *The Wages of Destruction: The Making and Breaking of the Nazi Economy* (New York: Viking, 2007), 526–7.
75. Alberti, *Die Verfolgung*, 290.
76. See Samuel D. Kassow, *Who Will Write Our History? Rediscovering A Hidden Archive from the Warsaw Ghetto* (New York: Vintage Books, 2009), 131–2.
77. See Edith Kramer, 'Meine Erfahrungen in Posen, Antoniek und Theresienstadt bis zur Rettung in der Schweiz,' *Emuna/Israel Forum* 11, no. 3 (1976): 30–6; no. 4, 28–36; no. 5, 69–74.
78. Wolf Gruner, *Jewish Forced Labor Under the Nazis: Economic Needs and Racial Aims* (New York: Cambridge University Press, 2006), 187.
79. Schilit, Vernehmungsniederschrift, 1717.
80. See, for example, Lagebericht des Inspekteurs der Sicherheitspolizei und des SD, 15 November 1942, APP, 299/1174, 176–8.
81. Ernst Kendzia, Anordnung über die Beschäftigung jüdischer Arbeitskräfte im Reichsgau Wartheland, 25 June 1942, BA-Ludwigsburg, ZStL, Polen 365b, 150–1.
82. Ingo Loose, *Kredite für NS-Verbrechen: Die deutschen Kreditinstitute in Polen und die Ausraubung der polnischen und jüdischen Bevölkerung 1939–1945* (Oldenbourg: Institut für Zeitgeschichte, 2007), 167.
83. Alberti, *Die Verfolgung*, 300.
84. Alberti, *Die Verfolgung*, 440.
85. Greiser, *Der Aufbau*, 9–10.
86. Heinrich Schwendemann, 'Der Umbau des Schlosses zur "Führer-Residenz,"' in Janusz Pazder and Evelyn Zimmermann, eds., *Kaiserschloss*

Posen: Von der 'Zwingburg im Osten' zum Kulturzentrum 'Zamek' (Potsdam and Poznań: Stiftung Preussische Schlösser und Gärten Berlin-Brandenburg and Centrum Kultury Zamek w Poznaniu, 2003), 177.

87. Joseph Goebbels, *Die Tagebücher von Joseph Goebbels: Sämtliche Fragmente; Teil I: Aufzeichnungen 1924–1941*, ed. Elke Fröhlich (Munich: Saur, 1987), Part I, Vol. 4, 19.
88. See Niels Gutschow, 'Stadtplanung im Warthegau 1939–1944,' in Mechthild Rössler and Sabine Schleiermacher, eds., *Der 'Generalplan Ost': Hauptlinien der nationalsozialistischen Planungs- und Vernichtungspolitik* (Berlin: Akademie, 1993), 234; and A.W. Schürmann, 'Posens Stadtbild wird wieder deutsch,' *Der Baukurier*, 31 July 1940, BAB, NS5VI/17279; and 'Zukunftspläne.'
89. See Pazder and Zimmermann, eds., *Kaiserschloss Posen*; Schwendemann and Dietsche, *Hitlers Schloß*; and Schwendemann, 'Der Umbau,' 175–84.
90. Arthur Greiser to Martin Bormann, 28 June 1940, BAB, R43II/1022, 11–12.
91. Arthur Greiser, 'Meine Parteigenossen,' 3 January 1944, IPN, 196/37, 647–50.
92. See Horwitz, *Łódź*.
93. Gerda Zorn, *'Nach Ostland geht unser Ritt': Deutsche Eroberungspolitik und die Folgen: Das Beispiel Lodz* (Cologne: Röderberg, 1988), 59.
94. 'Wandlungen einer Großstadt im Osten,' *Ostdeutscher Beobachter* (8 November 1940).
95. Zorn, *'Nach Ostland,'* 62.
96. 'Grosszügiges Aufbauprogramm in Litzmannstadt,' *Gausonderdienst 'Die Innere Front,'* 1, no. 156 (15 November 1940).
97. Aly, *'Endlösung,'* 288.
98. Czesław Łuczak, 'Uniwersytet Poznański w latach drugiej wojny Światowej,' in Przemysław Hauser, Tomasz Jasińsky, and Jerzy Topolsky, eds., *Alma Mater Posnaniensis w 80. rocznicę utworzenia uniwersytetu w Poznaniu* (Poznań: Wydawnictwo Naukowe, 1999), 175.
99. Arthur Greiser to Reichsministerium für Wissenschaft, Erziehung und Volksbildung, 11 December 1939, BAB, R43II/940, 78.
100. Hans Lammers to Bernhard Rust, 31 January 1940, BAB, R43II/940, 84.
101. Bernhard Rust to Hans Lammers, 13 December 1940, BAB, R43II/940, 98–100.
102. Jan M. Piskorski, 'Die Reichsuniversität Posen (1941–1945),' in Hartmut Lehmann and Otto Gerhard Oexle, eds., *Nationalsozialismus in den Kulturwissenschaften* (Göttingen: Vandenhoeck und Ruprecht, 2004), Vol. 1, 248.
103. Greiser, 'Die Großdeutsche Aufgabe,' 49.
104. 'Die Reichsuniversität Posen,' *Nürnberger Zeitung*, [1941], BAB, R4901/13132.
105. Piskorski, 'Die Reichsuniversität Posen,' 258.
106. Michael Burleigh, *Germany Turns Eastwards: A Study of Ostforschung in the Third Reich* (Cambridge: Cambridge University Press, 1988), 293; 'Drei Jahre

Reichsuniversität Posen,' *Ostdeutscher Beobachter* (21 April 1944); and '200 neue Stundenten,' *Gausonderdienst 'Die Innere Front,'* 3, no. 11/12 (24 January 1942).

107. Piskorski, 'Die Reichsuniversität Posen,' 266.
108. Der Rektor der Universität, 6 November 1941, APP, 299/1126, 9.
109. 'Ein Markstein auf dem Weg des Warthelandes,' *Ostdeutscher Beobachter* (28 April 1941).
110. Piskorski, 'Die Reichsuniversität Posen,' 268; and 'Zwei Jahre Hochschularbeit im deutschen Osten,' *Ostdeutscher Beobachter* (21 April 1943).
111. Burleigh, *Germany*, 295.
112. 'Wortlaut der Verordnung Görings,' *Ostdeutscher Beobachter* (10 March 1941).
113. Michael Imort, 'Forestopia: The Use of the Forest Landscape in Naturalizing National Socialist Ideologies of *Volk*, Race, and *Lebensraum*, 1918–1945' (Ph.D. diss., Queen's University, 2000), 388.
114. 'Institut für Ostrechtsforschung bereits bei der Arbeit,' *Ostdeutscher Beobachter* (29 January 1942).
115. Burleigh, *Germany*, 295.
116. 'Theater und Schulen sind politische Bollwerke,' *Ostdeutscher Beobachter* (19 March 1941).
117. Höhere Schulen, 17 May 1944, APP, 299/2317, 223–6.
118. Greiser, 'Die Großdeutsche Aufgabe,' 48.
119. Elizabeth Harvey, *Women and the Nazi East: Agents and Witnesses of Germanization* (New Haven: Yale University Press, 2003), 195.
120. See Der Reichsstatthalter III/2 to Herrn Abteilungsleiter III, 7 April 1942, APP, 299/2317, 10; and Georg Hansen, ed., *Schulpolitik als Volkstumspolitik: Quellen zur Schulpolitik der Besatzer in Polen 1939–1945* (Münster: Waxmann, 1994), 429–70.
121. See Harvey, *Women*, 191–213.
122. 'Gauleiter Greisers Appell an die Erzieher,' *Ostdeutscher Beobachter* (20 October 1940).
123. Dr. Sprenger, Abteilung III/4 to Sachgebiet I/22, 10 November 1941, APP, 299/2414, 91.
124. Harvey, *Women*, 195.
125. 'Gauleiter Greisers Appell.'
126. 'Theater.'
127. Goebbels, *Die Tagebücher*, Part I, Vol. 4, 544.
128. Alan E. Steinweis, 'German Cultural Imperialism in Czechoslovakia and Poland, 1938–1945,' *International History Review* 13 (1991): 477–8.
129. '"Feinde,"' *Ostdeutscher Beobachter* (17 November 1940).
130. '350000 Mark zum Sinfoniekonzert fürs WHW: Glanzvoller Auftakt des Orchesters der Gauhauptstadt mit Frau Maria Greiser als Solistin,' *Ostdeutscher Beobachter* (8 November 1940), 5.
131. Michael H. Kater, *Composers of the Nazi Era: Eight Portraits* (New York: Oxford University Press, 2000), 164.

132. 'Glanzvoller Höhepunkt der Posener Musikwoche,' *Ostdeutscher Beobachter* (7 September 1942).
133. Siegfried Rühle, 'Hervorragende deutsche Kulturstätte im Wartheland: Ein Jahr Aufbauarbeit in Kaiser Friedrich-Museum zu Posen,' *Gausonderdienst 'Die Innere Front,'* 2, no. 179/80 (22 January 1941).
134. Siegfried Rühle, 'Das Kaiser Friedrich-Museum zu Posen,' BAB, R138II/14.
135. Rühle, 'Das Kaiser Friedrich-Museum.'
136. 'Planung und Aufbau im Osten,' *Ostdeutscher Beobachter* (23 October 1941).
137. 'Ausstellung "Maler im Wartheland,"' *Ostdeutscher Beobachter* (22 October 1942).
138. Rolf-Heinz Höppner, 'Meldungen aus dem Reichsgau Wartheland für die Zeit vom 22.11 bis 28.11.1942,' IPN, 62/122, 62–3.
139. See Gauhauptmann im Reichsgau Wartheland, ed., *Der Warthegau: Landschaft und Siedlung in Werken Deutscher Maler: Ein Bildband* (Posen: Hirt-Reger und v. Schroedel-Siemau Verlag, 1943).
140. 'Das Landesamt für Vorgeschichte,' BAB, R138II/14.
141. Dr. Walter Kersten, Anlage zur Tagesordnung Nr. 49, 11 November 1940, APP, 1008/3, 143–4.
142. 'Bericht über die im letzten Jahr im Rahmen der Abt. III des Reichsstatthalters geleistete Aufbauarbeit,' 20 September 1942, APP, 299/2317, 64.
143. 'Bericht über die im letzten Jahr,' 64.
144. 'Hindenburg und seine Geburtsstadt Posen,' *Ostdeutscher Beobachter* (2 October 1940).
145. On plans for renovating Hindenburg's birth house, see documents in APP, 299/3179.
146. 'Hindenburg-Gymnasium in Posen,' *Ostdeutscher Beobachter* (25 June 1940), 5; 'Hindenburg und seine Geburtsstadt;' 'Posen ehrt seinen großen Sohn,' *Ostdeutscher Beobachter* (3 October 1941), 7; and 'Historische Stätten der Gauhauptstadt,' *Ostdeutscher Beobachter* (7 October 1943).
147. Jay W. Baird, *To Die for Germany: Heroes in the Nazi Pantheon* (Bloomington: Indiana University Press, 1990), 44.
148. Herbert Mehlhorn, 13 October 1941, APP, 299/10, 4.
149. See Chapter 6.
150. See, for example, 'Kutno—Mahnmal der Treue und des Ruhmes,' *Ostdeutscher Beobachter* (2 September 1940), 1; '"Der Geist von Kutno soll lebendig bleiben!"' *Ostdeutscher Beobachter* (2 September 1941), 1; and 'Wartheland soll Gau der Frontsoldaten werden,' *Ostdeutscher Beobachter* (2 September 1942), 1–2.
151. 'Weitere ermordete Kameraden geborgen,' *Ostdeutsche Beobachter* (16 December 1939), 7.
152. 'Wartheland soll Gau der Frontsoldaten werden,' 1–2.
153. See 'Das Wartheland in der Kriegswirtschaft,' *Ostdeutscher Beobachter* (13 December 1939), 3; and 'Gauleiter und Reichsstatthalter Greiser drei Jahre im Wartheland,' *Ostdeutscher Beobachter* (13 September 1942), 7.

154. '"Ehrenbuch der Kaufmannschaft,"' *Ostdeutscher Beobachter* (16 November 1941).
155. 'Verein für Zeitgeschichte,' *Ostdeutscher Beobachter* (22 December 1942).
156. '300 000 Wohnungen im Wartheland benötigt,' *Ostdeutscher Beobachter* (8 October 1941). Reich bureaucrats delegated to the East were given a subsidy to make the transfer more palatable.
157. See Tilman Harlander and Gerhard Fehl, eds., *Hitlers Sozialer Wohnungsbau: Wohnungspolitik, Baugestaltung und Siedlungsplanung* (Hamburg: Christians, 1986); Wolfgang König, 'Das Scheitern einer nationalsozialistischen Konsumgesellschaft: "Volksprodukte" in Politik, Propaganda, und Gesellschaft des "Dritten Reiches,"' *Zeitschrift für Unternehmensgeschichte* no. 2 (2003): 140, 150; and Ronald Smelser, *Robert Ley: Hitler's Labor Front Leader* (Oxford: Berg, 1988), 168.
158. 'Leistungsschau "Schönheit des Wohnens" eröffnet,' *Ostdeutscher Beobachter* (19 May 1942).
159. 'Haustechnik und Lebenskultur im neuen Osten,' *Ostdeutscher Beobachter* (6 June 1941), 9.
160. To date, studies on Nazi-era consumption have not focused on the annexed eastern areas. See Shelley Baranowski, *Strength Through Joy: Consumerism and Mass Tourism in the Third Reich* (Cambridge: Cambridge University Press, 2004); Irene Guenther, *Nazi Chic? Fashioning Women in the Third Reich* (Oxford: Berg, 2004); and König, 'Das Scheitern.'
161. See *Hitlers Sozialer Wohnungsbau*, 32–4; and Gutschow, 'Stadtplanung,' 238–9.
162. Hornung, 'Schönheit des Wohnens im Warthegau auch im Kriege,' [1943–44], APP, 299/3208, 62–4.
163. Arthur Greiser, memorandum, 26 May 1941, APP, 299/3208, 1–2.
164. 'Sozialer Wohnungsbau und deutsche Wohnkultur im Wartheland: Gauleiter Greiser besuchte das Gauheimstättenamt,' *Gausonderdienst 'Die Innere Front,'* 2, no. 217 (31 May 31 1941). Emphasis in original.
165. Hornung, 'Schönheit,' 62–4.
166. 'Leistungsschau.'
167. 'Schöner wohnen, besser leben, Leistungsschau der DAF im Wartheland,' *Gausonderdienst 'Die Innere Front,'* 3, no. 61/2 (22 May 1942).
168. 'Wohnstättenbau—eine politische Aufgabe!' *Ostdeutscher Beobachter* (14 June 1940), 5.
169. See Baranowski, *Strength*, 99–107.
170. O. Mann, '"Mit freiem Volk auf freiem Grund!"' Zur Frage der Gestaltung des wartheländischen Bauernhauses—Entwicklung eines gaueigenen Stils,' *Gausonderdienst 'Die Innere Front,'* 2, no. 178 (18 January 1941). Emphasis in original.
171. 'Möbel für bäuerliche Wohnhäuser,' *Ostdeutscher Beobachter* (20 February 1943).

172. 'Möbelentwürfe für bäuerliche Wohnhäuser im Wartheland,' [1943], APP, 299/3208, 21–2.
173. 'Schöner wohnen.'
174. Ernst Bährecke, *Die Maschinenfabrik Hohensalza: Ein Versuch zur Schilderung polnischer 'Kulturzustände' und Beiträge zur Wiederaufbauarbeit im Warthegau* (August, 1940).
175. See Arthur Greiser to Gustav and Ida Greiser, 2 June 1916, IPN, 63/2, 41; and Arthur Greiser to Maria, 13 September 1934, IZ, I-941.
176. See Thomas M. Lekan, *Imagining the Nation in Nature: Landscape Preservation and German Identity, 1885–1945* (Cambridge, Mass.: Harvard University Press, 2004), 1–2; and Joachim Wolschke-Bulmahn and Gert Grönig, 'The National Socialist Garden and Landscape Ideal: *Bodenständigkeit* (Rootedness in the Soil),' in Richard A. Etlin, ed., *Art, Culture, and Media Under the Third Reich* (Chicago: University of Chicago Press, 2002), 73.
177. Gunnar Brands, 'From World War I Cemeteries to the Nazi "Fortresses of the Dead:" Architecture, Heroic Landscape, and the Quest for National Identity in Germany,' in Joachim Wolschke-Bulmahn, ed., *Places of Commemoration: Search for Identity and Landscape Design* (Washington, D.C.: Dumbarton Oaks Research Library and Collection, 2001), 245; and George L. Mosse, *Fallen Soldiers: Reshaping the Memory of the World Wars* (New York: Oxford University Press, 1990), 109.
178. Mosse, *Fallen Soldiers*, 111; and Brands, 'From World War I Cemeteries,' 228.
179. For a general discussion of the link between Nazi environmental policies and Germanization schemes, see David Blackbourn, *The Conquest of Nature: Water, Landscape, and the Making of Modern Germany* (New York: Norton, 2006), 251–309.
180. Imort, 'Forestopia,' 391.
181. Inkelas, 'Visions,' 165–6.
182. Imort, 'Forestopia,' 405–6.
183. Abteilung Raumordnung und Landesplanung, 'NSBDT,' 5 August 1940, APP, 299/376, 12.
184. Imort, 'Forestopia,' 389.
185. Greiser, *Der Aufbau*, 17–18.
186. 'Der "Leslauer Reichswald,"' *Ostdeutscher Beobachter* (June 21, 1943).
187. Christian Haupt, 25 January 1953, BA-Bayreuth, Ost.Dok. 2/74, 1.
188. Heinrich May, 'Der grosse Judenmord,' in Karol Marian Pospieszlski, ed., 'Niemiecki nadleśniczy o zagładzie Żydów w Chełmnie nad Nerem,' *Przegląd Zachodni* 18, no. 3–4 (1962): 101–3.
189. 'Vorläufige Bestimmungen für die Aufstellung von Grabmalen auf deutschen Friedhöfen im Regierungsbezirk Posen,' 18 June 1941, APP, 299/3039, 64.
190. See Brands, 'From World War I Cemeteries,' 226–8, 231–2.
191. Herbert Mehlhorn, 'Erholungsgebiete im Warthegau,' 5 September 1940, BAB, R49/166, 57–61.

192. 'Erschließung der Schönheit des Warthelandes: Förderung durch das Verkehrsamt Posen,' *Gausonderdienst 'Die Innere Front,'* 1, no. 76–7 (11 June 1940).
193. Raumordnung und Landesplanung, 'Radwegeplanung,' 13 December 1941, BA-Bayreuth, Ost.Dok.13/166, 19–20.
194. Klein, *Die 'Gettoverwaltung Litzmannstadt,'* 501.
195. Arthur Greiser to Heinrich Himmler, 21 November 1942, BAB, NS19/1585, 17.
196. Alberti, *Die Verfolgung*, 460.
197. Klein, *Die 'Gettoverwaltung Litzmannstadt,'* 576.
198. Trunk, *Lodz ghetto*, 167.
199. Klein, *Die 'Gettoverwaltung Litzmannstadt,'* 528.
200. Alberti, *Die Verfolgung*, 461.
201. Klein, *Die 'Gettoverwaltung Litzmannstadt,'* 529.
202. See Alberti, *Die Verfolgung*, 277; and Christopher Browning, *The Path to Genocide: Essays on Launching the Final Solution* (New York: Cambridge University Press, 1992), 44.
203. Klein, *Die 'Gettoverwaltung Litzmannstadt,'* 480–1.
204. Friedrich Wilhelm Ribbe to Amtskommissar Deutscheneck, 8 July 1942, ZIH, 205/66.
205. Klein, *Die 'Gettoverwaltung Litzmannstadt,'* 500.
206. Alberti, *Die Verfolgung*, 452–3; Klein, *Die 'Gettoverwaltung Litzmannstadt,'* 504.
207. Klein, *Die 'Gettoverwaltung Litzmannstadt,'* 503, 512.
208. Loose, *Kredite*, 166–7.
209. Andrzej Strzelecki, *The Deportation of Jews from the Lodz Ghetto to KL Auschwitz and Their Extermination* (Oświęcim: Auschwitz-Birkenau State Muzeum, 2006), 31.
210. Alberti, *Die Verfolgung*, 453–4.
211. Protokoll über Zeugenvernehmung, Rudolf Kramp, 1 July 1945, BA-Ludwigsburg, AR-Z 141/88, Vol. III, 456.
212. 'Gauleiter Greiser auf den Baustellen Posens,' *Ostdeutscher Beobachter* (14 September 1940), 3.
213. 'Empörung in Posen,' January 1943, BAB, R43II/1022, 49.
214. Wilhelm Frick, 'Ortsnamenänderungen in den eingegliederten Ostgebieten,' 29 December 1939, BAB, R1501/1289, 1–4.
215. Alexander Dolezalek, 'Umbennung von Ortsnamen,' 10 December 1940, BAB, R49/3065, 19–20.
216. Reichsstatthalter I/21 to the Herrn Regierungspräsidenten in Posen, Hohensalza, and Litzmannstadt, 24 June 1942, APP, 299/1269, 194.
217. See Friedrich Uebelhoer to the Herrn Reichsstatthalter in Posen, 10 July 1942, APP, 299/1270, 39.
218. 'Aufzeichnungen über den Verlauf der Besprechung im RMdI. am 27. August 1943 mit Vertretern des OKW., den OKH., des Reichspostministeriums,

des Reichsstatthalters in Posen, des Reichsamts für Landesaufnahme und der Publikationsstelle Berlin-Dahlem,' BAB, R1501/1289, 15.

219. Arthur Greiser to August Jäger, 15 November 1943, APP, 299/1270, 272.
220. Dr. Wöhrl to Reichsminister des Innern, 22 December 1943, BAB, R1501/1289, 13.
221. Reichsstatthalter I/21 to the Sicherheitsdienst des Reichsführers-SS, SD-Leitabschnitt Posen, 15 November 1944, APP, 299/1270, 23. Emphasis in original.
222. Tooze, *The Wages*, 526–7.
223. Olsen to Kreisbaumt des Landkreises Lissa, 17 August 1943, BAB, R138II/5, 17.
224. Klein, *Die 'Gettoverwaltung Litzmannstadt,'* 610–11.
225. Strzelecki, *The Deportation*, 23.
226. See Klein, *Die 'Gettoverwaltung Litzmannstadt,'* 602.
227. Klein, *Die 'Gettoverwaltung Litzmannstadt,'* 604–6.
228. Peter Klein gives a very different interpretation of Greiser from the one presented in these pages. Klein argues that from late 1942 onwards, Greiser and Himmler together were eager to shut down the Litzmannstadt ghetto and have its inhabitants murdered. He points to a December 1942 discussion that Greiser had with Werner Ventzki, the lord mayor of Litzmannstadt, in which Greiser stated that all questions concerning the ghetto should be viewed from the perspective of its 'immediate (*alsbaldige*) dissolution.' In Klein's view, the ghetto continued to exist for another nineteen months due to the intransigence of Litzmannstadt city officials and the ghetto administration; the transport and other difficulties associated with moving the ghetto to Globocnik's Lublin district; and Biebow's taking on of new job contracts that had to be fulfilled. Between December 1942 and August 1943, Greiser and Himmler replaced all of the leading local officials (except for Biebow) in the city and ghetto administration. Only then, Klein argues, were Greiser and Himmler in a position to shut down the ghetto. While not without merits, Klein's interpretation begs some questions. Why and when did Greiser give up his strategy of murdering 'unproductive' while keeping alive 'productive' Jews? Why were city officials so bent on maintaining the ghetto, particularly since they knew best that the ghetto was not lucrative? Why, given that local officials had all been replaced by August 1943, was the decision to close the ghetto made only in February 1944? And why, if Greiser was so eager to have the ghetto disbanded, did he object to changing the status of the ghetto into a concentration camp? Klein, I believe, neglects that many Nazi authorities, including Greiser, thought that the ghetto was profitable; only in January 1944, did they definitely learn otherwise. See Klein, *Die 'Gettoverwaltung Litzmannstadt,'* 370, 576, 581–2, 626.
229. Arthur Greiser to Oswald Pohl, 14 February 1944, BAB, Former BDC Collection, SSHO/5163.

230. Klein, *Die 'Gettoverwaltung Litzmannstadt,'* 613–15.
231. Albert Speer, *Der Sklavenstaat: Meine Auseinandersetzungen mit der SS* (Stuttgart: Deutsche Verlags-Anstalt, 1981), 396–7.
232. Alberti, *Die Verfolgung*, 488–94.
233. Strzelecki, *The Deportation*, 127.
234. Löw, *Juden*, 498.
235. Alberti, *Die Verfolgung*, 495; Löw, *Juden*, 491; and Frank Stier, *Kriegsauftrag 160: Behelfsheimbau im Ghetto Litzmannstadt (Lodz) und im KZ-Außenlager Königs Wusterhausen durch das Deutsche Wohnungshilfswerk* (Berlin: Verlag Willmuth Arenhövel, 1999).
236. Strzelecki, *The Deportation*, 37, 53, 72–3.
237. For different estimates, see Löw, *Juden*, 498; and Strzelecki, *The Deportation*, 119.
238. Alberti, *Die Verfolgung*, 496–8.
239. Adalbert Rückerl, ed., *Nationalsozialistische Vernichtungslager im Spiegel deutscher Strafprozesse: Belzec, Sobibor, Treblinka, Chelmno* (Munich: Deutscher Taschenbuch Verlag, 1977), 243.
240. Eichmann's testimony is cited in Scheske, Aktenvermerk zur Einstellungsverfügung, 14 April 1966, BA-Ludwigsburg, 203 AR 185/65, 137.

8. 'FEUDAL DUKE:' RULE AND LOSS

1. 'Zusammenkunft der Gauleiter Greiser und Bracht anläßlich der Führertagung vom 30.4. bis 1.5.43 in Kattowitz,' 4 May 1943, BA-Berlin, NS19/995, 3–6. Heinrich Himmler, it turned out, didn't much care for this report; he ordered that the SS-leader responsible for it be replaced. See memorandum for Ernst Kaltenbrunner, 11 May 1943, BA-Berlin, NS19/955, 7.
2. Frank Bajohr, *Parvenüs und Profiteure: Korruption in der NS-Zeit* (Frankfurt/M: Fischer, 2004), 13.
3. Harry Siegmund, *Rückblick: Erinnerungen eines Staatsdieners in bewegter Zeit* (Raisdorf: Ostsee Verlag, 1999), 201, 186.
4. Institut für Zeitgeschichte, ed., *Akten der Partei-Kanzlei der NSDAP: Rekonstruktion eines verlorengegangenen Bestands* (Munich: Oldenbourg, 1983), Part I, 305 00046.
5. Siegmund, *Rückblick*, 202; and Armin Ziegler, interview with author, 1 June 2007.
6. Schnellbrief Reichsstatthalter VII A to Forstamt Ludwigsberg, 10 January 1941, APP, 299/3055, 166.
7. Otto von Estorff and Gerhard Winkler to Oberregierungsrat Bernhardt, 24 July 1940, APP, 299/3057, 18–20.
8. Reichsstatthalter VII/2 to Reichsminister des Innern, 20 May 1940, APP, 299/3056, 227–8.

9. Nelles, 'Neubau Dienstwohngebäude für den Reichsstatthalter am Mariensee,' 7 July 1942, APP, 299/3057, 56; and Heinrich Schwendemann and Wolfgang Dietsche, *Hitlers Schloß: Die 'Führerresidenz' in Posen* (Berlin: Ch. Links, 2003), 152. For conversion and inflation-adjusted rates, see *www.history.ucsb.edu/faculty/marcuse/projects/currency.htm#tables*; and *www.measuringworth.com/calculators/uscompare/result.php*, accessed 13 July 2009.
10. Hans Pfundtner to Lutz Graf Schwerin von Krosigk, 25 May 1940, APP, 299/3056, 229.
11. Nelles, 'Neubau,' 56; Hermann Mattern, 'Geländeplanung an Dienstwohngebäude des Reichsstatthalters im Warthegau,' 1941, APP, 299/3058, 2; and Hermann Mattern, 'Erläuterungsbericht,' 6 December 1941, APP 299/3059, 2–3.
12. Nelles to Lutz Graf Schwerin von Krosigk, 31 July 1942, APP, 299/3055, 116.
13. Arthur Rhode, 'Beitrag zur Archiv-Sammlung der Vertriebenen beim Bundesarchiv für den Reichsgau Wartheland,' 29 June 1955, BA-Bayreuth, Ost-Dok.8/421, 13.
14. See APP 299/3055, 444–50.
15. Hans Burckhardt, 'Gauleiter Greiser,' 6 July 1945, IPN, 196/36, 466.
16. 'Empörung in Posen,' January 1943, BA-Berlin, R43II/1022, 49.
17. Siegmund, *Rückblick*, 298.
18. 'Arthur Greiser und "Der Engel der Musik,"' IfZ, ED901/62, 2.
19. Antje Cordier, interview with author, 2 June 2007.
20. See Personnel File for Ingrid Birr, PA-AA, Angestellte Weibl.-15–15, Nr.125A; Peter R. Black, *Ernst Kaltenbrunner: Ideological Soldier of the Third Reich* (Princeton: Princeton University Press, 1984), 211; and Albert Speer, *Inside the Third Reich* (New York: Macmillan, 1970), 97.
21. Cordier; and Paul Ruge, interview with author, 31 May 2007.
22. Rotraut Fülleborn, interview with author, 26 May 2005.
23. Arthur Greiser to Friedrich Uebelhoer, 5 January 1940, BA-Berlin, N2313/8, 20.
24. Ingrid Greiser to Kurt Birr, 'Bericht über die Lodzer-Reise vom 10.4–13.4.1940,' BA-Berlin, N2313/9, 2–4.
25. Fülleborn, 26 May 2005; and Rotraut Fülleborn, interview with author, 30 May 2007.
26. Siegmund, *Rückblick*, 284.
27. See BA-Berlin, Former BDC Collection, SSO Files for Harry Siegmund.
28. Hans Lammers to Martin Bormann, 3 June 1943, Institut für Zeitgeschichte, ed., *Akten*, Part I, 101 05254–9.
29. Siegmund, *Rückblick*, 326.
30. Siegmund, *Rückblick*, 105.
31. Burckhardt, 'Gauleiter Greiser,' 463.
32. See BA-Berlin, Former BDC Collection, PK files for Otto Greiser.
33. Cordier.

34. Burckhardt, 'Gauleiter Greiser,' 464.
35. These included Schwarzenau, Oberau, Hermannsbad, and Zillerdorf. Arthur Greiser, Anordnung betreffend die Gästehäuser, 28 April 1944, APP, 299/3386, 59–62.
36. Siegmund, *Rückblick*, 228–9.
37. Joseph Goebbels, *Die Tagebücher von Joseph Goebbels: Sämtliche Fragmente*, ed. Elke Fröhlich (Munich: K. G. Saur, 1987–1996), Part I, Vol. 4, 19.
38. Heinrich Himmler, *Der Dientstkalender Heinrich Himmlers 1941/42*, ed. Peter Witte, Michael Wildt, *et al.* (Hamburg: Christians, 1999), 167.
39. See Arthur Greiser to Hans Pfundtner, 13 June 1941; and Hans Pfundtner to Arthur Greiser, 3 July 1941, BA-Berlin, R1501/5313, 297–301.
40. Arthur Greiser to Amtsgericht-Grundbuchamt in Obornik, 25 October 1939, IPN, 196/15, 28.
41. Fülleborn, 30 May 2007.
42. Siegmund, *Rückblick*, 296.
43. Cordier.
44. Arthur Greiser to August Jäger, 24 April 1940, APP, 299/3386, 1; and Cromme, Aktenvermerk, 22 May 1942, APP, 299/3015, 1.
45. *Gausonderdienst 'Die Innere Front,'* 1, no. 43/4 (12 April 1940).
46. Greiser, Anordnung betreffend die Gästehäuser, 59–62.
47. 'Arthur Greiser: Gauleiter und Reichsstatthalter im Reichsgau Wartheland,' 14 November 1941, BA-Berlin, R8034III/163, 108.
48. Oskar Knofe, Tagesordnung, no. 79, 2 July 1942, APP, 1008/5, 44.
49. Jan Goroński to Sędzia Apelacyjny Sledczy, 14–15 March 1946, IPN, 196/27, 85–6.
50. See Institut für Zeitgeschichte, ed., *Akten*, Part I, 101 08417–38.
51. Albin Wietrzykowski, *Powrót Arthura Greisera* (Poznań: Nakładem Księgarni Wydawniczej Spółdzielni 'Pomoc,' 1946), 13.
52. Ruge.
53. Walter Petzel, 'Gauleiter Greiser,' 15 June 1949, BA-Bayreuth, Ost-Dok.8/401, 2–4; Ruge; and Harry Siegmund, interview with author, 25 May 2005.
54. Siegmund, *Rückblick*, 298.
55. Hugo Heiser, 'Erlebnisbericht,' September 1955, BA-Bayreuth, Ost-Dok.8/438, 12.
56. Goebbels, *Die Tagebücher*, Part I, Vol. 4, 256.
57. Czesław Łuczak, *Arthur Greiser* (Poznań: PSO, 1997), 107.
58. Hans Wallenberg and Ernst Langendorf, German Intelligence Section Special Interrogation Series no. 12, 1 June 1945, NA, RG319, Box 69.
59. Siegmund, *Rückblick*, 215–16; and Edward Kujaciński to the Prokuratura Specjalnego Sądu Karnego w Poznaniu, 17 May 1946, IPN, 196/27, 59. For the exchange rate, see Janusz K. Tanas, 'Perspective of Polish Business: An Historical Snapshot," *www.anu.edu.au/NEC/Archive/PolishBusiness-Canberra,pdf*, accessed 23 October 2007.

60. Czesław Staniszewski to Sędzia Apelacyjny Sledczy, 1 June 1946, IPN, 196/27, 63–4.
61. Sąd Grodzki to Głównej Komisji Badania Zbordni Niemieckich w Polsce w Poznaniu, 29 March 1946; and Arthur Greiser, Vollmacht, 6 September 1943, IPN, 196/27, 26–7.
62. Burckhardt, 'Gauleiter Greiser,' 465.
63. See Bajohr, *Parvenüs*.
64. Petzel, 'Gauleiter Greiser,' 2–4.
65. Siegmund, *Rückblick*, 298.
66. Burckhardt, 'Gauleiter Greiser,' 462. Emphasis in original.
67. Burckhardt, 'Gauleiter Greiser,' 467.
68. Dieter Rebentisch, *Führerstaat und Verwaltung im Zweiten Weltkrieg: Verfassungsentwicklung und Verwaltungspolitik 1939–1945* (Stuttgart: Franz Steiner, 1989), 254–5.
69. Hans Lammers to Martin Bormann, 3 June 1943, Institut für Zeitgeschichte, ed., *Akten*, Part I, 101 05254–9; and Part I, Vol. 1, 849. See also Rebentisch, *Führerstaat*, 257.
70. Arthur Greiser, Rundschreiben an alle Dientstellen der Partei und des Staates, 8 July 1942, Institut für Zeitgeschichte, ed., *Akten*, Part I, 101 23634.
71. Emil Pax, 'Bericht über Konflikte des Reichsministerium für Wissenschaft, Erziehung und Volksbildung mit der NSDAP betr. Mittelschule-Hauptschule sowie mit dem Reichsstatthalter im Wartheland und Danzig–Westpreussen betr. Errichtung von Schulen für polnische Kinder,' 17 September 1961, BA-Bayreuth, Ost-Dok.13/159, 8.
72. Rebentisch, *Führerstaat*, 248.
73. Arthur Greiser to Hans Burckhardt, 21 October 1941, BAB, R138II/1.
74. 'Gliederung der Verwaltung im Reichsgau Wartheland, insbesondere im Verhältnis zwischen Reichsstatthalter und den Regierungspräsidenten,' [May 1942], BAB, N2313/16, 31–47. See also Wilhelm Frick, Schnellbrief to Albert Forster and Arthur Greiser, 6 December 1939, R1501/5401, 158–9.
75. Institut für Zeitgeschichte, ed., *Akten*, Part I, Vol. 1, 817.
76. Michael Alberti, *Die Verfolgung und Vernichtung der Juden im Reichsgau Wartheland 1939–1945* (Wiesbaden: Harrassowitz, 2006), 62.
77. Friedrich Uebelhoer, 'Rücksprache mit Gauleiter,' BAB, N2313/12, 339–40.
78. Arthur Greiser to Wilhelm Frick, 13 October 1942, BAB, R1501/1847.
79. Friedrich Uebelhoer to Adolf Hitler, 6 January 1943, BAB, N2313/17, 1–2.
80. See documents in BAB, NS19/2651, 70–98.
81. Alberti, *Die Verfolgung*, 63–4.
82. Wilhelm Schlau, 'Gnesen von 1940 bis 1945,' BA-Bayreuth, Ost-Dok.8/480, 5.
83. Gordon J. Horwitz, *Łódź and the Making of a Nazi City* (Cambridge, Mass.: Harvard University Press, 2008), 306.

84. Diemut Majer, *'Non-Germans' under the Third Reich: The Nazi Judicial and Administrative System in Germany and Occupied Eastern Europe, with Special Regard to Occupied Poland, 1939–1945* (Baltimore: Johns Hopkins University Press, 2003), 215, 720, fn. 14.
85. Rebentisch, *Führerstaat*, 353.
86. Michael Burleigh, *The Third Reich: A New History* (New York: Hill and Wang, 2000), 455.
87. Goebbels, *Die Tagebücher*, Part II, Vol. 8, 226.
88. Martyn Housden, *Hans Frank: Lebensraum and the Holocaust* (Houndmills: Palgrave Macmillan, 2003), 196.
89. Goebbels, *Die Tagebücher*, Part II, Vol. 8, 251.
90. Goebbels, *Die Tagebücher*, Part II, Vol. 8, 535–6.
91. Siegmund, *Rückblick*, 300.
92. 'Frankfurters Kugeln sollten Greiser treffen,' *Königsberger Allgemeine Zeitung*, 21 March 1940, BAB, R8034III/163, 113.
93. Łuczak claimed that the assassination attempt took place. Łuczak, *Arthur Greiser*, 85.
94. Bruno Streckenbach to Heinrich Himmler, 27 June 1942, IfZ, Fa 223/23.
95. Rolf-Heinz Höppner to Arthur Greiser, 22 November 1943, NA, RG319, Box 69.
96. Heinrich Himmler to Martin Bormann, 26 May 1943, NA, RG319, Box 69.
97. 'Zusammentstellung der Vorwürfe des Pg. Reuter gegen Gauleiter Greiser,' 31 August 1943, NA, RG319, Box 69.
98. Höppner to Greiser.
99. Maier, 'Begründung,' 19 November 1943, NA, RG319, Box 69.
100. Arthur Greiser to Schultz, 30 May 1944, NA, RG319, Box 69.
101. Anlage zu dem Brief an das Oberste Parteigericht, z. Hd. des Vorsitzenden der I. Kammer Parteigenossen Schultz, vom 30. Mai 1944, NA, RG319, Box 69.
102. Arthur Greiser to Schultz, 1 June 1944, NA, RG319, Box 69.
103. Robert Wistrich, *Who's Who in Nazi Germany* (New York: Macmillan, 1982), 141.
104. Tages-Programm für die Reichs- und Gauleitertagung am 6. Oktober 1943 in Posen, BAB, NS19/3124, 35. See also 'Famous Speeches by Heinrich Himmler,' *http://www.scrapbookpages.com/dachauscrapbook/HimmlerSpeeches.html*, accessed 27 January 2009.
105. *Deutsche Wochenschau*, BA-Filmarchiv, DW 688/1943.
106. Theodor Berkelmann to Heinrich Himmler, 27 November 1943, BAB, Former BDC Collection, SSO Files for Arthur Greiser, Frame 150.
107. Heinrich Himmler to Ernst-Heinrich Schmauser, 12 December 1943, BAB, Former BDC Collection, SSO Files for Arthur Greiser, Frame 149.
108. Greiser spoke a few words at the 30 December funeral of HSSPF Theodor Berkelmann. See 'Trauerfeier für SS-Obergruppenführer Berkelmann,'

Völkischer Beobachter, 31 December 1943, BAB, Former BDC Collection, SSO Files for Theodor Berkelmann.

109. Arthur Greiser to Oberste Parteigericht, 30 May 1944, NA, RG319, Box 69.
110. Arthur Greiser, 'Meine Parteigenossen,' 3 January 1944, IPN, 196/37, 647–50.
111. Ruge.
112. Goebbels, *Die Tagebücher*, Part II, Vol. 11, 175.
113. Kornel Michałowski, *Listy z okupowanego Poznania* (Poznań: Osięgłowski, 1998), 11, 66–7; and Marian Olszewski, 'Naloty bombowe zachodnich aliantów na Poznań w 1941 i 1944 roku,' *Kronika Miasta Poznania* 35, no. 2 (1967): 19–21, 28–30.
114. NSDAP-Gauleitung Wartheland, Amt für Volkswohlfahrt, Tätigkeits- und Lagebericht für die Monate Juli/August 1943, APP, NSDAP Gauleitung/13, 102–10.
115. Eugen Petrull, 'Die Berliner Umquartierten im Wartheland,' *Ostdeutscher Beobachter* (20 October 1943).
116. Greiser, 'Meine Parteigenossen,' 647–50.
117. In November 1943, Gau authorities calculated that 59,286 're-quartered' individuals were in the Gau. NSDAP-Gauleitung Wartheland, Amt für Volkswohlfahrt, 'Tätigkeits- und Lagebericht für den Monat November 1943,' APP, NSDAP Gauleitung Wartheland/13, 216.
118. NSDAP-Gauleitung Wartheland, Amt für Volkswohlfahrt, 'Tätigkeits- und Lagebericht für den Monat Dezember 1943, Hauptstelle: Organisation,' APP, NSDAP Gauleitung Wartheland/13, 226.
119. Ulrich Greifelt to Heinrich Himmler, 10 January 1944, BAB, NS19/2656, 124.
120. Arthur Greiser, Anordnung, 11 January 1944, BAB, R49/3041, 1–5.
121. Arthur Greiser to Heinrich Himmler, 28 February 1944, BAB, NS19/2656, 158.
122. Arthur Greiser, Grundsätzliche Anordnung 6/44, 13 April 1944, APP, 299/1978, 182–3.
123. Czesław Łuczak, *Pod niemieckim jarzmem (Kraj Warty 1939–1945)* (Poznań: PSO, 1996), 71.
124. Arthur Greiser, Grundsätzliche Anordnung 14/44, 14 July 1944, BAB, R49/3041, 123–4.
125. Bericht des Höheren SS- und Polizeiführers Warthe, Posen vom 19.6.1944, BAB, NS19/3114, 5–6.
126. Dr. Cropp to Arthur Greiser, 26 May 1944, APP, 299/1978, 227–8.
127. See Medizinalrat, Gesundheitsamt Konin to Reichsstatthalter II B, 24 January 1944, APP, 299/1978, 42; and Dr. Karch, Staatliche Gesundheitsamt Kalisch to Reichsstatthalter, 4 February 1944, APP, 299/1978, 92.
128. See NSDAP-Gauleitung Wartheland, Amt für Volkswohlfahrt, 'Tätigkeits- und Lagebericht für den Monat September 1944,' APP, NSDAP Gaulei-

tung/13, 324–6; and Wilhelm Maul to Reichsministerium für Volksaufklärung und Propaganda, 4 April 1944, IPN, 62/48, 99.

129. Arthur Greiser, Anordnung, 22 May 1944, APP 299/1978, 219–20.
130. NSDAP-Gauleitung Wartheland . . . Monat September 1944, 324–6.
131. See Verhandlungsbericht von Pg. Dr. Wolfram über den Arbeitseinsatz rußlanddeutscher Jugendlicher bei Anwesenheit des Gauleiters, [November 1944], IZ, I-256.
132. NSDAP-Gauleitung Wartheland, Amt für Volkswohlfahrt, 'Tätigkeits- und Lagebericht für den Monat Januar 1944,' APP, NSDAP Gauleitung Wartheland/13, 255–6.
133. Der Reichsverteidigungskomissar für den Reichsverteidigungsbezirk Wartheland to NSDAP-Gauleitung Wartheland, Amt für Volkswohlfahrt, 22 July 1944, APP, 299/1207, 23.
134. Hans-Erich Volkmann, 'Zwischen Ideologie und Pragmatismus: Zur nationalsozialistischen Wirtschaftspolitik im Reichsgau Wartheland,' in Ulrich Haustein, Georg W. Strobel, and Gerhard Wagner, eds., *Ostmitteleuropa: Berichte und Forschungen* (Stuttgart: Klett-Cotta, 1981), 439.
135. Czesław Łuczak, ed., *Położenie ludności polskiej w tzw. Kraju Warty w okresie hitlerowskiej okupacji (Documenta occupationis XIII)* (Poznań: Instytut Zachodni, 1990), 305–6.
136. Łuczak, ed., *Położenie*, 307–9.
137. Łuczak, ed., *Położenie*, 185.
138. 'Posener Polen in Katyn,' *Ostdeutscher Beobachter* (20 April 1943), 1.
139. Gissibl to all Kreisleiter, 23 April 1943, IPN, 62/368, 1.
140. Dr. Held to the Kommandeur der Gendarmerie bei dem Regierungspräsidenten, 24 April 1943, BAB, R70 Polen/188, 10.
141. Goebbels, *Die Tagebücher*, Part II, Vol. 11, 175.
142. Łuczak, ed., *Położenie*, 185.
143. Łuczak, ed., *Położenie*, 274.
144. Łuczak, ed., *Dyskryminacja*, 301–2.
145. Greiser, Anordnung, 11 January 1944, 1–5.
146. Arthur Greiser to sämtliche Kreisleiter und Landräte, 21 March 1944, BAB, R49/3041, 81.
147. 'Volk der Arbeit, Volk in Waffen,' *Ostdeutscher Beobachter* (15 August 1944), 1.
148. Letter to Arthur Greiser, [August 1944], IZ, I-820, 1–9.
149. Czesław Łuczak, ed., *Dyskryminacja Polaków w Wielkopolsce w okresie okupacji hitlerowskiej: wybór zródeł* (Poznań: Wydawnictwo Pozańskie, 1966), 307–10.
150. Greiser, 'Meine Parteigenossen,' 647–50.
151. Siegmund, *Rückblick*, 332; Herbert Mehlhorn to SS-Personalhauptamt, 16 March 1944, BAB, Former BDC Collection, SSO files for Herbert Mehlhorn; and Chapter 6.
152. August Jäger to alle Dienststellen des Staates und der Wirtschaft, 6 June 1944, APP, 299/1889, 336.

153. 'Notdienstpflichtung im Wartheland,' *Ostdeutscher Beobachter* (1 August 1944).
154. Arthur Greiser to sämtliche Behörden der Gaustufe einschl. Abteilungsleiter meiner Behörde, 28 August 1944, APP, 299/1889, 384–7.
155. Robert Schulz to Heinrich Himmler, 16 August 1944, BAB, R1501/1348.
156. 'Der Vorhang ist gefallen,' *Ostdeutscher Beobachter* (3 September 1944).
157. Arthur Greiser to Heinrich Himmler, 4 September 1944, APP, 299/1207, 167–8.
158. Eberhard Maatz, 'Erlebnisse und Beobachtungen im Reichsgau Wartheland 1940–1945,' BA-Bayreuth, Ost.Dok.8/464, 8.
159. Arthur Greiser, Rundspruch an alle Kreisleiter und Landräte, 31 July 1944, APP, 299/1889, 361–2.
160. Rudolf Bayer, Bericht, 20 September 1955, BA-Bayreuth, Ost.Dok.8/437, 8.
161. Maatz, 'Erlebnisse,' 8.
162. 'Unser Leben—Adolf Hitler,' *Ostdeutscher Beobachter* (22 July 1944).
163. Jochen von Lang, *Der Hitler-Junge: Baldur von Schirach: Der Mann der Deutschlands Jugend erzog* (Hamburg: Rasch und Röhring, 1988), 311.
164. Hennigsen to Zentralstelle der Landesjustizverwaltung, 25 February 1964, BA-Ludwigsburg, 211 AR 1507/61, 286.
165. Włodzimierz Borodziej, *The Warsaw Uprising of 1944* (Madison: University of Wisconsin Press, 2006), 99; Norman Davies, *Rising '44: The Battle for Warsaw* (New York: Viking, 2003), 252; and Arthur Greiser to Martin Bormann, 30 September 1944, in Institut für Zeitgeschichte, ed., *Akten*, Part I, 306 00798.
166. See Chapter 7.
167. Borodziej, *The Warsaw Uprising*, 78–81.
168. Paul Ruge, statement to Der Untersuchungsrichter beim Landgericht in Flensburg, 28 July 1965, BA-Ludwigsburg, 211 AR 1507/61, 538–43.
169. Aussage des SS-Obergruppenführers von dem Bach-Zalewski, Februar 1947 in Warschau, BA-Ludwigsburg, 211 AR 1507/61, Sonderband I.
170. An den Kaufmann, 21 August 1944, APP, 299/2807, 12–13.
171. Leiter des Landeswirtschaftsamtes, Vermerk, 22 August 1944, APP, 299/2807, 7.
172. Dr. Gülde, Aktenvermerk, 14 September 1944, APP, 299/2807, 130.
173. Dr. Gülde, Vermerk, 19 October 1944, APP, 299/2808, 111.
174. Wirtschaftsstab Ost to Landeswirtschaftsamt, 3 October 1944, APP, 299/2815, 25; and Giersch to Landeswirtschaftsamt, 8 November 1944, 35.
175. Łuczak, *Pod niemieckim jarzmem*, 145.
176. Landeswirtschaftsamtes, Vorläufige Übersicht, 26 September 1944, APP, 299/2807, 182–3.
177. Armin Ziegler to author, 10 June 2008.
178. Hans Frank, *Das Diensttagebuch des deutschen Generalgouverneurs in Polen 1939–1945*, ed. Werner Präg and Wolfgang Jacobmeyer (Stuttgart: Deutsche Verlags-Anstalt, 1975), 909.
179. See Goebbels, *Die Tagebücher*, Part II, Vol. 13, 367, and Vol. 14, 31.

180. David K. Yelton, *Hitler's Volkssturm: The Nazi Militia and the Fall of Germany, 1944–1945* (Lawrence: University Press of Kansas, 2002), 13.
181. 'Der Gauleiter führt den Volkssturm,' *Ostdeutscher Beobachter* (19 October 1944), 1.
182. Arthur Greiser, 'Aufbau und Kampfeinsatz des Deutschen Volkssturms im Reichsgau Wartheland,' 20 February 1945, BA-Bayreuth, Ost.Dok.8/402, 5–20; Walter Petzel to Späth-Meyken, 15 March 1953, 2–3; and Walter Petzel, 'Bericht des Gauleiters Greiser über "Aufbau und Kampfeinsatz des Deutschen Volkssturms im Reichsgau Wartheland vom 20.2.45,"' 6 March 1953, 21–2.
183. 'Ruhige Zuversicht in den Ostkreisen,' *Ostdeutscher Beobachter* (22 October 1944).
184. 'Heimat und Front sind eins,' *Ostdeutscher Beobachter* (18 October 1944).
185. Arthur Greiser, 'Kampf—Lebensinhalt des Warthelandes: Aufruf des Gauleiters und Reichsstatthalters zum "Tag der Freiheit" 1944,' *Ostdeutscher Beobachter* (26 October 1944), 1.
186. 'Schutzburg des Reiches im Osten,' *Ostdeutscher Beobachter* (7 November 1944).
187. Greiser, 'Kampf,' 1.
188. Alastair Noble, 'The Phantom Barrier: *Ostwallbau* 1944–1945,' *War in History* 8, no. 4 (2001): 467.
189. Greiser, 'Aufbau und Kampfeinsatz,' 5–20.
190. Arthur Greiser to Rotraut Greiser, 26 December 1944, Private collection of Rotraut Fülleborn.
191. Armin Ziegler, *Posen Januar 1945: Evakuierung und Flucht der deutschen Zivilbevölkerung der Stadt Posen im Januar 1945* (Schönaich: Im Selbstverlag, 1989), 24.
192. Paul Ruge, 'Tagebuch über die Zeit v. 12.1.–10.5.1945,' BA-Bayreuth, Ost.Dok.13/185, 2.
193. Ziegler, *Posen*, 24.
194. Goebbels, *Die Tagebücher*, Part II, Vol. 15, 122.
195. Ruge, interview.
196. Fritz Harder to Dr. Julius Hoppenrath, 1 June 1956, BA-Bayreuth, Ost. Dok.8/499, 2–3.
197. Hugo Heiser, 'Erlebnisbericht,' September 1944, BA-Bayreuth, Ost.Dok.8/438, 13.
198. Ziegler, *Posen*, 25.
199. Goebbels, *Die Tagebücher*, Part II, Vol. 15, 135.
200. Ziegler, *Posen*, 42.
201. See Ziegler, *Posen*, 15–20.
202. Bayer, Bericht, 8; Joachim Rogall, ed., *Die Räumung des 'Reichsgaus Wartheland' vom 16. bis 26. Januar 1945 im Spiegel amtlicher Berichte* (Sigmaringen: Jan Thorbecke, 1993), 107–10; and Siegmund, interview.

203. Blanka Meissner, *Ewakuacja niemieckich władz administracyjncy i niemieckiej ludności okupowanych ziem polskich w latach 1944–1945*, Informacja Wewnętrzna, no. 93 (Warsaw: Główna Komisja Badania Zbrodni Hitlerowskich w Polsce Instytut Pamięci Narodowej, 1987), 100; and Ziegler, *Posen*, 25.
204. Greiser, 'Aufbau und Kampfeinsatz,' 15.
205. Rogall, ed., *Die Räumung*, 74.
206. Ziegler, *Posen*, 21.
207. Harder to Hoppenrath, 3; Ruge, 'Tagebuch,' 3–4.
208. Karl-Heinz Klinter, '18.7.1944–31.1.1945: Posen—eine Zeit der Vorbereitung zum letzten Widerstand und der Zusammenbruch der Front im Osten,' 221, Private collection of Armin Ziegler.
209. Ziegler, *Posen*, 21.
210. Walter Petzel, 'Gauleiter Greiser,' 15 June 1949, BA-Bayreuth, Ost.Dok.8/401, 4.
211. Harder to Hoppenrath, 3; and Ziegler, *Posen*, 21.
212. Klinter, '18.7.1944–31.1.1945,' 223.
213. Ziegler, *Posen*, 26–8.
214. Ziegler, *Posen*, 26–8.
215. Harder to Hoppenrath, 3; and Ruge, 'Tagebuch,' 3–4.
216. Ziegler, *Posen*, 28–9.
217. Ruge, 'Tagebuch,' 5.
218. Klinter, '18.7.1944–31.1.1945,' 223. Emphasis in original.
219. Rogall, ed., *Die Räumung*, 32; and Ziegler, *Posen*, 31.
220. Ziegler, *Posen*, 43.
221. Ruge, 'Tagebuch,' 5.
222. Ziegler, *Posen*, 65.
223. Günther Baumann, *Posen '45—Bastion an der Warthe: eine Dokumentation* (Düsseldorf: Hilfsgemeinschaft Ehemaliger Posenkämpfer, 1992), 95–6.
224. Czesław Łuczak, *Dzień po dniu w okupowanej Wielkopolsce i na ziemi łódzkiej (Kraj Warty): kalendarium wydarzeń 1939–1945* (Poznań: Lektor, 1993), 336.
225. Meissner, *Ewakuacja*, 128.
226. Rogall, ed., *Die Räumung*, 125.
227. See Kulturstiftung der deutschen Vertriebenen, ed., *Vertreibung und Vertreibungsverbrechen, 1945–1948: Bericht des Bundesarchivs vom 28. Mai 1974: Archivalien und ausgewählte Erlebnisberichte* (Bonn: Kulturstiftung der deutschen Vertriebenen, 1989), 223–31; Rogall, ed., *Die Räumung*; and Theodor Schieder, ed., *Die Vertreibung der deutschen Bevölkerung aus den Gebieten östlich der Oder-Neisse*, Vol. 1 ([Berlin]: Bundesministerium für Vertriebene, [1953]), 357–84.
228. 'Reichsgau Wartheland,' *http://en.wikipedia.org/wiki/Reichsgau_Wartheland*, accessed 5 August 2009.
229. See, for example, Siegmund, *Rückblick*, 347.

230. Jürgen Thorwald, *Es begann an der Weichsel* (Stuttgart: Steingrüben, 1959), 78–9.
231. Walter Petzel, 'Gauleiter Greiser,' 15 June 1949, BA-Bayreuth, Ost.Dok.8/401, 4; and Chapter 1.

9. 'TWO SOULS IN MY BREAST:' TRIAL AND EXECUTION

1. Armin Ziegler, *Posen Januar 1945: Evakuierung und Flucht der deutschen Zivilbevölkerung der Stadt Posen im Januar 1945* (Schönaich: Im Selbstverlag, 1989), 89.
2. Paul Ruge, interview with author, 31 May 2007.
3. See, for example, Karl Warwecke, 'Bericht über meine Beobachtungen und Eindrücke aus der Zeit meiner Tätigkeit als Verwaltungsbeamter bei den Landratsämtern Gostingen und Obornik von Sept. 1939 bis zur Vertreibung am 21. Jan. 1945,' 18 June 1956, BA-Bayreuth, Ost.Dok.8/488, 6.
4. Ruge, interview.
5. Paul Ruge, 'Tagebuch über die Zeit v. 12.1.–10.5.1945,' BA-Bayreuth, Ost.Dok.13/185, 5–6.
6. Joseph Goebbels, *Die Tagebücher von Joseph Goebbels: Sämtliche Fragmente*, ed. Elke Fröhlich (Munich: K. G. Saur, 1987–1996), Part II, Vol. 15, 190.
7. Ruge, 'Tagebuch,' 5–6.
8. Goebbels, *Die Tagebücher*, 283.
9. Ruge, 'Tagebuch,' 6–7.
10. Goebbels, *Die Tagebücher*, 182.
11. Goebbels, *Die Tagebücher*, 210.
12. Goebbels, *Die Tagebücher*, 223.
13. Goebbels, *Die Tagebücher*, 357.
14. Ruge, 'Tagebuch,' 7.
15. Heinz Guderian, *Erinnerungen eines Soldaten* (Neckargemünd: Kurt Vowinkel, 1960), 408.
16. Julius Hoppenrath, 'Stellungnahme von Dr. Hoppenrath,' 23 November 1955, BA-Bayreuth, Ost.Dok.8/447, 4.
17. See Karl Höffkes, *Hitlers politische Generale: Die Gauleiter des Dritten Reichs: Ein biographisches Nachschlagewerk* (Tübingen: Grabert, 1986), 106; and Jürgen Thorwald, *Es begann an der Weichsel* (Stuttgart: Steingrüben, 1959), 85.
18. Goebbels, *Die Tagebücher*, 262.
19. Martin Bormann, 'Rundschreiben 65/45 der Parteikanzlei von 12.2.45,' 12 February 1945, BAB, NS6/353, 30.
20. Ziegler, *Posen*, 90.
21. Arthur Greiser, 'Aufbau und Kampfeinsatz des Deutschen Volkssturms im Reichsgau Wartheland,' 20 February 1945, BA-Bayreuth, Ost.Dok.8/402, 5–20.
22. According to one source, Greiser and von Gottberg planned to assassinate Bormann. When, however, they approached Himmler about the matter, the

SS-leader refused. Himmler supposedly thought that Bormann's death would be too great a blow for Hitler. This whole story seems far-fetched. Greiser was on thin ice with Hitler, and was surely reluctant to further anger his Führer. See Höffkes, *Hitlers politische Generale*, 106.

23. Ruge, 'Tagebuch,' 8–9.
24. Robert N. Proctor, *The Nazi War on Cancer* (Princeton: Princeton University Press, 1999), 42.
25. Ingrid Birr to Personalabteilung Auswärtiges Amt, 18 October 1944, PA-AA, Angestellte Weibl.-15–15, Personalakte Ingrid Birr, Nr.125A; Ruge, 'Tagebuch,' 9; and Harry Siegmund, interview with author, 25 May 2005.
26. Ruge, 'Tagebuch,' 9.
27. Sam Winters and Daniel J. Sullivan, 'Greiser, Arthur,' 20 May 1945, NA, RG 319, Box 69.
28. Armin Ziegler to author, 22 January 2009; and *http://www.usafa.af.mil/df/dfllib/SL3/germans/berger.cfm*, accessed 2 February 2009.
29. Maria Greiser to Paul Ruge, 25 October 1959; and Dr. Wilhelm Zietz to Paul Ruge, 23 April 1959, Private collection of Paul Ruge.
30. Ruge, 'Tagebuch,' 9–13.
31. 'Americans Claim Greiser,' *New York Times* (18 May 1945), 7; Arrest Report, 17 April [*sic*] 1945; Samuel Winters and Daniel J. Sullivan, 'Greiser, Arthur,' 17 May 1945; and Samuel Winters and Daniel J. Sullivan, 'Greiser, Arthur,' 20 May 1945, NA, RG319, Box 69.
32. Winters and Sullivan, 'Greiser,' 20 May 1945.
33. Paul Kubala, Disposition List of SAIC Inmates, 5 October 1945, NA, RG498, Box 74.
34. Hans Wallenberg and Ernst Langendorf, PWB-CPT–HQ Seventh Army, German Intelligence Section, Special Interrogation Series No. 12, 1 June 1945, NA, RG319, Box 69.
35. Arthur Greiser to Carl Burckhardt, 25 July 1945, NA, RG319, Box 69.
36. Richard Overy, *Interrogations: The Nazi Elite in Allied Hands, 1945* (New York: Viking, 2001), xviii.
37. Kubala, Disposition List.
38. 'Report,' 12 November 1945, NA, RG319, Box 69.
39. Krankenblatt, Station 21b; and Krankenblatt, Seventh Army Internee Hospital 2 Karlsruhe, NA, RG319, Box 69.
40. Arthur Greiser to Maria Greiser, 15 June 1946, IZ, I-439.
41. Maria Greiser to Arthur Greiser, 25 March 1946, IfZ, ED901/48.
42. Bogdan Musial, 'NS-Kriegsverbrecher vor polnischen Gerichten,' *Vierteljahreshefte für Zeitgeschichte* 47 (1999): 25–6.
43. Charles Fahy to Deputy Theater Judge Advocate, War Crimes Branch, APO 633, US Army, 21 February 1946, NA, RG446, Box 130, Case No. 98–1.
44. Arthur Greiser to Maria Greiser, 15 June 1946.

45. Janusz Gumkowski and Tadeusz Kułakowski, *Zbrodniarze hitlerowscy przed Najwyższym Trybunałem Narodowym* (Warsaw: Wydawnictwo Prawnicze, 1961), 3.
46. *Granica zbrodni Arthura Greisera* (Poland, 1969); and *The Nazis: A Warning from History*, dir. Laurence Rees (Britain: British Broadcasting Corporation, 1997).
47. Thorwald, *Es begann*, 85; and Ziegler, *Posen*, 92.
48. Arthur Greiser to Maria Greiser, 20–21 July 1946, BA-Ludwigsburg, ZStL, I-110 AR 655/73, 314–18.
49. Arthur Greiser to Maria Greiser, 15 June 1946.
50. 'Poles Stage Own "Circus" With Two Caged Nazis,' *New York Times* (4 April 1946), 16.
51. Höffkes, *Hitlers Politische Generale*, 106; and Ziegler, *Posen*, 93, 102. Both Höffkes and Ziegler rightly question the legend.
52. Bericht, 26 April 1951, BA-Bayreuth, Ost.Dok.2/96, 97.
53. 'Greiser w więzieniu na Młyńskiej,' *Głos Wielkopolski* (14 June 1946), 1.
54. Arthur Greiser to Maria Greiser, 15 June 1946.
55. 'Greiser w więzieniu na Młyńskiej,' 1.
56. Today Mariensee is the administrative seat of a national park. See Heinrich Schwendemann and Wolfgang Dietsche, *Hitlers Schloß: Die 'Führerresidenz' in Posen* (Berlin: Ch. Links, 2003), 153.
57. Arthur Greiser to Maria Greiser, 15 June 1946.
58. Musial, 'NS-Kriegsverbrecher,' 36–8.
59. Tadeuz Cyprian and Jerzy Sawicki, eds., *Siedem wyroków Najwyższego Trybunału Narodowego* (Poznań: Instytut Zachodni, 1962), xi, 3.
60. Musial, 'NS-Kriegsverbrecher,' 53–4.
61. Gumkowski and Kułakowski, *Zbrodniarze hitlerowscy*, 4–5.
62. Jerzy Sawicki, *Vor dem polnischen Staatsanwalt* (Berlin: Deutscher Militärverlag, 1962), 9–10.
63. 'Proces Greisera w połowie czerwca,' *Głos Wielkopolski* (3 June 1946), 5; Sawicki, *Vor dem polnischen Staatsanwalt*, 10.
64. 'Główny oskarżyciel angielski w Norymberdze przybywa do Polski,' *Głos Wielkopolski* (13 June 1946), 1; and 'Dziś rozpoczyna się proces Greisera,' *Głos Wielkopolski* (22 June 1946), 2.
65. Jackson was expected to come with a ten-man entourage. Besides attending the trial, the guests were to be shown around Posen and to be taken to the 'Greiser villa' (Mariensee). See Ministerstwo Sprawiedliwości Rzeczpospolita Polska to Obywatel Prezydent Prezesa Sądu Apelacyjnego, 27 June 1946, IfZ, ED901/48.
66. United Nations War Crimes Commission, ed., *Law Reports of Trials of War Criminals*, Vol. XIII (London: The United Nations War Crimes Commission, 1949), 70–4.
67. 'Prozess gegen Arthur Greiser vor dem Obersten Volkstribunal,' BA-Ludwigsburg, ZStL, Polen 365 h 2, 7–8. See also Głowna Komisja Badania

Zbrodni Niemieckich w Polsce, ed., *Proces Artura Greisera przed Najwyższym Trybunałem Narodowym* (Warsaw: Skład Głowny Polski Instytut Wydawniczy, 1946).

68. United Nations War Crimes Commission, ed., *Law Reports*, 70–4.
69. 'Prozess,' 64.
70. See Chapter 5.
71. 'Prozess,' 56.
72. Gary Jonathan Bass, *Stay the Hand of Vengeance: The Politics of War Crimes Tribunals* (Princeton: Princeton University Press, 2000), 201.
73. Arthur Greiser to Maria Greiser, 15 June 1946.
74. 'Dziś,' 1.
75. 'Greiser w więzieniu na Młyńskiej,' 1.
76. Howard A. Bowman to James F. Byrnes, 23 July 1946, NA, RG59, Decimal File, 1945–49, Box 3607.
77. *Greiser przed sądem Rzeczypospolitiej* (Poland, 1946), BA-Filmarchiv, SP 14399; and 'Pierwszy dzień procesu Greisera,' *Głos Wielkopolski* (23 June 1946), 1.
78. Gumkowski and Kułakowski, *Zbrodniarze hitlerowscy*, 4.
79. 'Proces Greisera przestrogą dla narodu polskiego,' *Głos Wielkopolski* (21 June 1946), 1.
80. Bowman to Byrnes.
81. See IPN, 196/38, 707–864; and Głowna Komisja, ed., *Proces Artura Greisera.*
82. Gumkowski and Kułakowski, *Zbrodniarze hitlerowscy*, 22.
83. Gumkowski and Kułakowski, *Zbrodniarze hitlerowscy*, 16.
84. Gumkowski and Kułakowski, *Zbrodniarze hitlerowscy*, 10.
85. Jan Kręglewski to Najwyższego Trybunała Narodowego, 17 June 1946, IPN, 196/34, 137–69.
86. 'Urteil,' BA-Ludwigsburg, ZStL, Polen 365 h 2, 29 (of document).
87. United Nations War Crimes Commission, ed., *Law Reports*, 102–3.
88. Gumkowski and Kułakowski, *Zbrodniarze hitlerowscy*, 24.
89. Gumkowski and Kułakowski, *Zbrodniarze hitlerowscy*, 52.
90. Gumkowski and Kułakowski, *Zbrodniarze hitlerowscy*, 22.
91. Gumkowski and Kułakowski, *Zbrodniarze hitlerowscy*, 18.
92. Gumkowski and Kułakowski, *Zbrodniarze hitlerowscy*, 14.
93. Hannah Arendt commented that the notion of 'inner emigration,' put forth by not a few Nazis on trial, had become a 'sort of joke.' In this context, she parenthetically mentioned Greiser and the two-souls argument that he presented to the Polish court. See Hannah Arendt, *Eichmann in Jerusalem: A Report on the Banality of Evil* (New York: Viking Penguin, 1963), 126–7.
94. Gumkowski and Kułakowski, *Zbrodniarze hitlerowscy*, 54–7.
95. Many Nazis besides Greiser tried to defend themselves with patent untruths. See Karin Orth, *Die Konzentrationslager-SS: Sozialstrukturelle Analysen und biographische Studien* (Munich: Deutscher Taschenbuch Verlag, 2004), 301–2.
96. Ian Kershaw, 'Arthur Greiser—Ein Motor der "Endlösung,"' in Ronald Smelzer, Enrico Syring, and Rainer Zitelmann, eds., *Die Braune Elite II: 21*

weitere biographische Skizzen (Darmstadt: Wissenschaftliche Buchgesellschaft, 1993), 117.

97. Gumkowski and Kułakowski, *Zbrodniarze hitlerowscy*, 60.
98. 'Die Rede des Staatsanwalts M. Siewierski,' BA-Ludwigsburg, ZStL, Polen 365 h 2, 73–82.
99. 'Die Rede des Staatsanwalts M. Siewierski,' 93–104.
100. 'Rede des Staatsanwalts J. Sawicki,' BA-Ludwigsburg, ZStL, Polen 365 h 2, 104–34.
101. Lawrence Douglas, *The Memory of Judgment: Making Law and History in the Trials of the Holocaust* (New Haven: Yale University Press, 2001), 42.
102. 'Die Rede des Verteidigers Dr. St. Hejmowski,' BA-Ludwigsburg, ZStL, Polen 365 h 2, 136–59.
103. 'Die Rede des Verteidigers Dr. J. Kręglewski, BA-Ludwigsburg, ZStL, Polen 365 h2, 159–95.
104. Arthur Greiser, Schlußwort des Angeklagten Artur [*sic*] Greiser im Prozess vor dem Höchsten Volksgericht, July 1946, BA-Bayreuth, Ost-Dok.13/452, 21–67.
105. 'Urteil,' BA-Ludwigsburg, ZStL, Polen 365 h 2, 14–15.
106. 'Urteil,' 19.
107. 'Urteil,' 16.
108. Telford Taylor, *Nuremberg and Vietnam: An American Tragedy* (Chicago: Quadrangle Books, 1970), 87.
109. Douglas, *The Memory*, 48.
110. 'Urteil,' 27.
111. 'Urteil,' 28.
112. 'Urteil,' 37.
113. Jan T. Gross, *Fear: Anti-Semitism in Poland After Auschwitz: An Essay in Historical Interpretation* (New York: Random House, 2006), 122.
114. United Nations War Crimes Commission, ed., *Law Reports*, 107–8.
115. 'Na karę śmierci,' *Głos Wielkopolski* (11 July 1946), 1–2.
116. Bowman to Byrnes.
117. Arthur Greiser to Bolesław Bierut, 9 July 1946, IPN, 196/38, 906–7.
118. Z. Kapitaniak to Najwyższy Trybunały Narodowy, 12 July 1946, IPN, 196/38, 908.
119. 'Greiser Appeals to Pope,' *New York Times* (13 July 1946), 7.
120. See Chapter 3.
121. Michael Phayer, *Pius XII, The Holocaust, and the Cold War* (Bloomington: Indiana University Press, 2008), 162; and 'Pope Made Appeal to Aid Rosenbergs; Plea One of Mercy,' *New York Times* (14 February 1953), 4.
122. 'Greiser Execution Set Today in Posen,' *New York Times* (20 July 1946), 2.
123. '15,000 Poles Watch Greiser Execution,' *New York Times* (22 July 1946), 4.
124. 'Vatican Denies Knowledge,' *New York Times* (20 July 1946), 2.
125. 'Pope Asked Poles to Spare Greiser,' *New York Times* (23 July 1946), 12.

126. 'Greiser Execution,' 2.
127. Protokoll der Zeugenaussage, Roman Śmielecki, 26 August 1985, BA-Ludwigsburg, ZStL, AR 318/97, 11–15.
128. 'Sprawiedliwości stało się zadość,' *Wola Ludu*, 22 July 1946, IfZ, ED901/49.
129. Protokoll, Śmielecki, 11–15.
130. 'Sprawiedliwości.'
131. Arthur Greiser to Maria Greiser, 20–21 July 1946.
132. Protokoll, Śmielecki, 15–16.
133. 'Sprawiedliwości.'
134. Protokoll, Śmielecki, 16.
135. *Granica zbrodni Arthura Greisera.*
136. Protokoll, Śmielecki, 17.
137. Henryk Zimniak to Zentrale Stelle Ludwigsburg, [1996], BA-Ludwigsburg, ZStL, AR 933/96, 213.
138. Protokoll, Śmielecki, 17.
139. Raimund Perkowski, telephone conversation with Armin Ziegler in author's presence, 1 June 2007.
140. Maria Greiser to Paul Ruge, 25 November 1956, Private collection of Paul Ruge.
141. Maria Greiser to Paul Ruge, 25 October 1959, Private collection of Paul Ruge.
142. Maria Greiser to Paul Ruge, 26 June 1958, Private collection of Paul Ruge. See also Norbert Frei, *Adenauer's Germany and the Nazi Past: The Politics of Amnesty and Integration* (New York: Columbia University Press, 2002), 41–66.
143. Maria Greiser to Paul Ruge, 15 August 1956, Private collection of Paul Ruge. Emphasis in original.
144. Maria Greiser to Paul Ruge, 1 July 1960, Private collection of Paul Ruge.
145. Maria Greiser to Paul Ruge, [December 1960], Private collection of Paul Ruge.
146. Maria Greiser to Paul Ruge, 11 December 1958, Private collection of Paul Ruge.
147. Greiser to Ruge, 1 July 1960.
148. Harry Siegmund to author, 31 January 2005.
149. Rotraut Fülleborn, interview with author, 26 May 2005; Siegmund, interview.
150. Rotraut Fülleborn, interviews with author, 26 May 2005 and 30 May 2007.
151. Antje Cordier, interview with author, 2 June 2007.
152. Fülleborn, 30 May 2007.
153. Vera Stroud to author, 3 May 2005.
154. Vera Stroud to author, 3 May 2005 and 20 May 2005.
155. Ian Kershaw, 'Improvised Genocide? The Emergence of the "Final Solution" in the "Warthegau,"' *Transactions of the Royal Historical Society* (1992), 77.

156. Dieter Schenk, *Hitlers Mann in Danzig: Gauleiter Forster und die NS-Verbrechen in Danzig-Westpreußen* (Bonn: Dietz, 2000), 287.
157. Kershaw, 'Improvised Genocide?' 77.
158. Kershaw, 'Improvised Genocide?' 77–8.
159. See Karl Raddatz, 'Neues über Herrn Reinefarth,' *Die Weltbühne*, August 1958, BAB, Former BDC Collection, SSO Files for Heinz Reinefarth, Frame 398; and *http://en.wikipedia.org/wiki/Heinz_Reinefarth*, accessed 13 May 2008.
160. See *http://en.wikipedia.org/wiki/Werner_Lorenz*, accessed 13 May 2008.
161. Harry Siegmund, *Rückblick: Erinnerungen eines Staatsdieners in bewegter Zeit* (Raisdorf: Ostsee Verlag, 1999), 382, 392, 422, 454.
162. Michael Mann, *The Dark Side of Democracy: Explaining Ethnic Cleansing* (Cambridge: Cambridge University Press, 2005), 227.

AFTERWORD

1. See Eric A. Zillmer, Molly Harrower, Barry A. Ritzler, and Robert P. Archer, *The Quest for the Nazi Personality: A Psychological Investigation of Nazi War Criminals* (Hillsdale: Lawrence Erlbaum Associates, 1995).
2. Marian Bartoszkiewicz, 'Arthur Greiser,' *Przegląd Zachodni* 2 (1946) : 301–20; Albin Wietrzykowski, *Powrót Arthura Greisera* (Poznań: Nakładem Księgarni Wydawniczej Spółdzielni 'Pomoc,' 1946); and 'Die Rede des Staatsanwalts M. Siewierski,' BA-Ludwigsburg, ZStL, Polen 365 h 2, 71–104.
3. See, for example, Martin Broszat, *Nationalsozialistische Polenpolitik 1939–1945* (Stuttgart: Deutsche Verlags-Anstalt, 1961), 55, 167; and J. S. Conway, *The Nazi Persecution of the Churches 1933–45* (New York: Basic Books, 1968), 313.
4. Ian Kershaw, '"Working Towards the Führer": Reflections on the Nature of the Hitler Dictatorship,' *Contemporary European History* 2, no. 2 (1993): 103–18.
5. Ian Kershaw, 'Arthur Greiser—Ein Motor der "Endlösung,"' in Ronald Smelzer, Enrico Syring, and Rainer Zitelmann, eds., *Die Braune Elite II: 21 weitere biographische Skizzen* (Darmstadt: Wissenschaftliche Buchgesellschaft, 1993), 116–27; and Ian Kershaw, 'Improvised Genocide? The Emergence of the "Final Solution" in the "Warthegau,"' *Transactions of the Royal Historical Society* (1992): 51–78.
6. See the ongoing series *Documenta occupationis teutonicae*, Vols. I-XV (Poznań: Instytut Zachodni, 1945–2005); and Czesław Madajczyk, *Die Okkupationspolitik Nazideutschlands in Polen 1939–1945* (Berlin: Akademie, 1987).
7. See Peter R. Black, *Ernst Kaltenbrunner: Ideological Soldier of the Third Reich* (Princeton: Princeton University Press, 1984), 283; and Peter H. Merkl, *Political Violence under the Swastika: 581 Early Nazis* (Princeton: Princeton University Press, 1975), 17–18.
8. See Karel C. Berkhoff, *Harvest of Despair: Life and Death in Ukraine Under Nazi Rule* (Cambridge, Mass.: Harvard University Press, 2004); Chad Bryant,

Prague in Black: Nazi Rule and Czech Nationalism (Cambridge, Mass.: Harvard University Press, 2007); Bernhard Chiari, *Alltag hinter der Front: Besatzung, Kollaboration und Widerstand in Weißrußland 1941–1944* (Düsseldorf: Droste, 1998); Christian Gerlach, *Kalkulierte Morde: Die deutsche wirtschafts- und Vernichtungspolitik in Weißrußland 1941 bis 1944* (Hamburg: Hamburger Edition, 1999); Norbert Kunz, *Die Krim unter deutscher Herrschaft 1941–1944: Germanisierungsutopie und Besatzungsrealität* (Darmstadt: Wissenschaftliche Buchgesellschaft, 2005); Wendy Lower, *Nazi Empire-Building and the Holocaust in Ukraine* (Chapel Hill: University of North Carolina Press, 2005); Richard Lukas, *The Forgotten Holocaust: The Poles under German Occupation, 1939–44* (New York: Hippocrene Books, 1997); and Valdis O. Lumans, *Latvia in World War II* (New York: Fordham University Press, 2006).

9. See Phillip T. Rutherford, *Prelude to the Final Solution: The Nazi Program for Deporting Ethnic Poles, 1939–1941* (Lawrence: University Press of Kansas, 2007); and Elizabeth Harvey, *Women and the Nazi East: Agents and Witnesses of Germanization* (New Haven: Yale University Press, 2003). On the Final Solution in the Warthegau, see Michael Alberti, *Die Verfolgung und Vernichtung der Juden im Reichsgau Wartheland 1939–1945* (Wiesbaden: Harrassowitz, 2006); Götz Aly, *'Endlösung': Völkerverschiebung und der Mord an den europäischen Juden* (Frankfurt/M: Fischer, 1995); Gordon J. Horwitz, *Ghettostadt: Łódź and the Making of a Nazi City* (Cambridge, Mass.: Harvard University Press, 2008); Peter Klein, *Die 'Gettoverwaltung Litzmannstadt' 1940–1944: Eine Dienststelle im Spannungsfeld von Kommunalbürokratie und staatlicher Verfolgungspolitik* (Hamburg: Hamburger Edition, 2009); and Andrea Löw, *Juden im Getto Litzmannstadt: Lebensbedingungen, Selbstwahrnehmung, Verhalten* (Göttingen: Wallstein, 2006).

10. See, for example, Isabel Heinemann, *'Rasse, Siedlung, deutsches Blut': Das Rasse- & Siedlungshauptamt der SS und die rassenpolitische Neuordnung Europas* (Göttingen: Wallstein, 2003).

11. Burckhardt claims that Greiser was born in the city of Posen; his father was a secondary-school teacher; his brothers died in World War I; and he had served in the famed Richthofen air squadron. Carl J. Burckhardt, *Meine Danziger Mission 1937–1939* (Munich: Callwey, 1980), 76. Denne includes some of these and several other errors: that in the 1920s, Greiser participated in beer-hall brawls in Munich; and that the Polish resistance organized the car accident in which Greiser's son died. See Ludwig Denne, *Das Danzig Problem in der deutschen Außenpolitik 1934–1939* (Bonn: Ludwig Röhrscheid Verlag, 1959), 59. Kershaw repeats the incorrect statement that Greiser began military service on 4 August 1914. He also gives an incorrect name for Greiser's son, and an incorrect date for Greiser's hanging. See Kershaw, 'Arthur Greiser,' 118, 120, 126. Majer writes that 'Greiser was taken prisoner by the British in 1945, extradited to Poland, condemned, and executed on July 9, 1946 . . .' In fact, Greiser was captured by the Americans, and executed on 21 July 1946. Diemut Majer, *'Non-Germans' under the Third Reich: The Nazi Judicial and Administrative*

System in Germany and Occupied Eastern Europe, with Special Regard to Occupied Poland, 1939–1945 (Baltimore: Johns Hopkins University Press, 2003), 699, fn. 87. Wistrich claims that Greiser was 'hanged on 20 June 1946 in front of his former palace in Poznan after being paraded around the town in a cage.' Both the date and place of the hanging are wrong, and Greiser was not paraded around town. Robert Wistrich, *Who's Who in Nazi Germany* (New York: Macmillan, 1982), 107.

12. The most comprehensive of these, *Pod niemieckim jarzmem (Kraj Warty 1939–1945)* (Under the German Yoke: Warthegau 1939–1945), is a fine overview of developments in the Warthegau. See Czesław Łuczak, *Pod niemieckim jarzmem (Kraj Warty 1939–1945)* (Poznań: PSO, 1996).

Selected Bibliography

Alberti, Michael. *Die Verfolgung und Vernichtung der Juden im Reichsgau Wartheland 1939–1945*. Wiesbaden: Harrassowitz, 2006.

Aly, Götz. *'Endlösung': Völkerverschiebung und der Mord an den europäischen Juden*. Frankfurt/M: Fischer, 1995.

Andrzejewski, Marek. *Opposition und Widerstand in Danzig 1933 bis 1939*. Bonn: Dietz, 1994.

Arendt, Hannah. *Eichmann in Jerusalem: A Report on the Banality of Evil*. New York: Viking Penguin, 1963.

Auswärtiges Amt, ed. *Akten zur Deutschen Auswärtigen Politik 1918–1945*. Baden-Baden: Imprimerie Nationale, 1950–1995.

Bajohr, Frank. *Parvenüs und Profiteure: Korruption in der NS-Zeit*. Frankfurt/M: Fischer, 2004.

Balzer, Brigitte. *Die preußische Polenpolitik 1894–1908 und die Haltung der deutschen konservativen und liberalen Parteien (unter besonderer Berücksichtigung der Provinz Posen)*. Frankfurt/M: Peter Lang, 1990.

Baranowski, Shelley. *Strength Through Joy: Consumerism and Mass Tourism in the Third Reich*. Cambridge: Cambridge University Press, 2004.

Bartoszkiewicz, Marian. 'Arthur Greiser.' *Przegląd Zachodni* 2 (1946): 301–20.

Bass, Gary Jonathan. *Stay the Hand of Vengeance: The Politics of War Crimes Tribunals*. Princeton: Princeton University Press, 2000.

Berghahn, Volker R. and Simone Lässig, eds. *Biography Between Structure and Agency: Central European Lives in International Historiography*. New York: Berghahn, 2008.

Birn, Ruth Bettina. *Die Höheren SS- und Polizeiführer: Himmlers Vertreter im Reich und in den besetzten Gebieten*. Düsseldorf: Droste, 1986.

Black, Peter R. *Ernst Kaltenbrunner: Ideological Soldier of the Third Reich*. Princeton: Princeton University Press, 1984.

Blackbourn, David. *The Conquest of Nature: Water, Landscape, and the Making of Modern Germany*. New York: Norton, 2006.

Blanke, Richard. *Orphans of Versailles: The Germans in Western Poland 1918–1939*. Lexington: University Press of Kentucky, 1993.

—— *Prussian Poland in the German Empire (1871–1900)*. Boulder: East European Monographs, 1981.

Boberach, Heinz, ed. *Meldungen aus dem Reich 1938–1945: Die geheimen Lageberichte des Sicherheitsdienstes der SS*. Herrsching: Pawlak, 1984.

Böhler, Jochen. *Auftakt zum Vernichtungskrieg: Die Wehrmacht in Polen 1939*. Frankfurt/M: Fischer, 2006.

Borodziej, Włodzimierz. *The Warsaw Uprising of 1944*. Madison: University of Wisconsin Press, 2006.

Breitinger, Hilarius. *Als Deutschenseelsorger in Posen und im Warthegau 1934–1945*. Mainz: Matthias-Grünewald-Verlag, 1984.

Breitman, Richard. *The Architect of Genocide: Himmler and the Final Solution*. Hanover: Brandeis University Press, 1991.

Breyer, Richard. *Das Deutsche Reich und Polen 1932–1937: Außenpolitik und Volksgruppenfragen*. Würzburg: Holzner-Verlag, 1955.

Broszat, Martin. *Nationalsozialistische Polenpolitik 1939–1945*. Stuttgart: Deutsche Verlags-Anstalt, 1961.

Browning, Christopher. *Ordinary Men: Reserve Police Battalion 101 and the Final Solution in Poland*. New York: HarperCollins, 1992.

——with Jürgen Matthäus. *The Origins of the Final Solution: The Evolution of Nazi Jewish Policy, September 1939–March 1942*. Lincoln: University of Nebraska Press, 2004.

Burckhardt, Carl J. *Meine Danziger Mission 1937–1939*. Munich: Callwey, 1980.

Cesarani, David. *Becoming Eichmann: Rethinking the Life, Crimes, and Trial of a 'Desk Murderer.'* Cambridge, Mass.: Da Capo, 2006.

Connelly, John. 'Nazis and Slavs: From Racial Theory to Racist Practice.' *Central European History* 32, no. 1 (1999): 1–33.

Conway, J. S. *The Nazi Persecution of the Churches 1933–45*. New York: Basic Books, 1968.

Cyprian, Tadeuz, and Jerzy Sawicki, eds. *Siedem wyroków Najwyższego Trybunału Narodowego*. Poznań: Instytut Zachodni, 1962.

Datner, Szymon, Janusz Gumkowski, and Kazimierz Leszczyński, eds. *Wysiedlanie ludności ziem polskich wcielonych do Rzeszy: Biuletyn Głównej Komisji Badania Zbrodni Hitlerowskich w Polsce 12*. Warsaw: Wydawnictwo Prawnicze, 1960.

Denne, Ludwig. *Das Danzig Problem in der deutschen Außenpolitik 1934–1939*. Bonn: Ludwig Röhrscheid Verlag, 1959.

Dingell, Jeanne. *Zur Tätigkeit der Haupttreuhandstelle Ost: Treuhandstelle Posen 1939 bis 1945*. Frankfurt/M: Peter Lang, 2003.

Douglas, Lawrence. *The Memory of Judgment: Making Law and History in the Trials of the Holocaust*. New Haven: Yale University Press, 2001.

Echt, Samuel. *Die Geschichte der Juden in Danzig*. Leer: Verlag Gerhard Rautenberg, 1972.

Eisenbach, Artur. 'O należyte zrozumienie genezy zagłady Żydów.' *Biuletyn Żydowskiego Instytutu Historycznego w Polsce* 104 (1977): 55–69.

Esch, Michael G. *'Gesunde Verhältnisse': Deutsche und polnische Bevölkerungspolitik in Ostmitteleuropa 1939–1950*. Marburg: Verlag Herder-Institut, 1998.

Fest, Joachim C. *The Face of the Third Reich: Portraits of the Nazi Leadership*. New York: Pantheon Books, 1970.

Frank, Hans. *Das Diensttagebuch des deutschen Generalgouverneurs in Polen 1939–1945*. Ed. Werner Präg and Wolfgang Jacobmeyer. Stuttgart: Deutsche Verlags-Anstalt, 1975.

Friedlander, Henry. *The Origins of Nazi Genocide: From Euthanasia to the Final Solution*. Chapel Hill: University of North Carolina Press, 1995.

Furber, David Bruce II. 'Going East: Colonialism and German Life in Nazi-Occupied Poland.' Ph.D. Diss., University of New York at Buffalo, 2003.

Gerlach, Christian. 'The Wannsee Conference, the Fate of German Jews, and Hitler's Decision in Principle to Exterminate All European Jews.' *Journal of Modern History* 70 (December 1998): 759–812.

Głowna Komisja Badania Zbrodni Niemieckich w Polsce, ed. *Proces Artura Greisera przed Najwyższym Trybunałem Narodowym*. Warsaw: Skład Głowny Polski Instytut Wydawniczy, 1946.

Goebbels, Joseph. *Die Tagebücher von Joseph Goebbels: Sämtliche Fragmente*. Ed. Elke Fröhlich. Munich: K. G. Saur, 1987–1996.

Goldensohn, Leon. *The Nuremberg Interviews: Conducted by Leon Goldensohn*. Ed. Robert Gellately. New York: Knopf, 2004.

Goldhagen, Daniel Jonah. *Hitler's Willing Executioners: Ordinary Germans and the Holocaust*. New York: Knopf, 1996.

Greiser, Arthur. *Der Aufbau im Osten*. Jena: Fischer, 1942.

—— 'Die Grossdeutsche Aufgabe im Wartheland.' *Nationalsozialistische Monatshefte* no. 130 (January 1941): 46–50.

Gröning, Gert and Joachim Wolschke-Bulmahn. *Die Liebe zur Landschaft: Teil III: Der Drang nach Osten: Zur Entwicklung der Landespflege im Nationalsozialismus und während des Zweiten Weltkrieges in den 'eingegliederten Ostgebieten.'* Munich: Minerva, 1987.

Gross, Jan T. *Fear: Anti-Semitism in Poland After Auschwitz: An Essay in Historical Interpretation*. New York: Random House, 2006.

Gruner, Wolf. *Jewish Forced Labor Under the Nazis: Economic Needs and Racial Aims*. New York: Cambridge University Press, 2006.

Gumkowski, Janusz and Tadeusz Kułakowski. *Zbrodniarze hitlerowscy przed Najwyższym Trybunałem Narodowym*. Warsaw: Wydawnictwo Prawnicze, 1961.

Gürtler, Paul. *Nationalsozialismus und evangelische Kirchen im Warthegau: Trennung von Staat und Kirche im nationalsozialistischen Weltanschauungsstaat*. Göttingen: Vandenhoeck und Ruprecht, 1958.

Hagen, William W. *Germans, Poles, and Jews: The Nationality Conflict in the Prussian East, 1772–1914*. Chicago: University of Chicago Press, 1980.

Hansen, Georg. *Ethnische Schulpolitik im besetzten Polen: Der Mustergau Wartheland*. Münster: Waxmann, 1995.

Harten, Hans-Christian. *De-Kulturation und Germanisierung: Die nationalsozialistische Rassen- und Erziehungspolitik in Polen 1939–1945*. Frankfurt/M: Campus, 1996.

Harvey, Elizabeth. *Women and the Nazi East: Agents and Witnesses of Germanization*. New Haven: Yale University Press, 2003.

Heinemann, Isabel. *'Rasse, Siedlung, deutsches Blut': Das Rasse- & Siedlungshauptamt der SS und die rassenpolitische Neuordnung Europas*. Göttingen: Wallstein, 2003.

Herbert, Ulrich. *Best: Biographische Studien über Radikalismus, Weltanschauung und Vernunft 1903–1989*. Bonn: Dietz, 1996.

Hilberg, Raul. *The Destruction of the European Jews*. Revised and Definitive Edition. New York: Holmes and Meier, 1985.

Himmler, Heinrich. *Der Dienstkalender Heinrich Himmlers 1941/42*. Ed Peter Witte, Michael Wildt, *et al*. Hamburg: Christians, 1999.

Höffkes, Karl. *Hitlers politische Generale: Die Gauleiter des Dritten Reichs: Ein biographisches Nachschlagewerk*. Tübingen: Grabert, 1986.

Hohenstein, Alexander. *Wartheländisches Tagebuch aus den Jahren 1941/42*. Stuttgart: Deutsche Verlags-Anstalt, 1961.

Horwitz, Gordon J. *Łódź and the Making of a Nazi City*. Cambridge, Mass.: Harvard University Press, 2008.

Hüttenberger, Peter. *Die Gauleiter: Studie zum Wandel des Machtgefüges in der NSDAP*. Stuttgart: Deutsche Verlags-Anstalt, 1969.

Imort, Michael. 'Forestopia: The Use of the Forest Landscape in Naturalizing National Socialist Ideologies of *Volk*, Race, and *Lebensraum*, 1918–1945.' Ph.D. Diss., Queen's University, 2000.

Inkelas, Daniel. 'Visions of Harmony and Violence: RFK Landscape Planning and Population Policy in Annexed Poland, 1939–1944.' Ph.D. Diss., Northwestern University, 1998.

Institut für Zeitgeschichte, ed. *Akten der Partei-Kanzlei der NSDAP: Rekonstruktion eines verlorengegangenen Bestands*. Munich: Oldenbourg, 1983–1992.

Instytut Zachodni, ed. *Documenta occupationis*. Poznań: Instytut Zachodni, 1945–2005.

Jansen, Christian and Arno Weckbecker. *Der 'Volksdeutsche Selbstschutz' in Polen 1939/40*. Munich: Oldenbourg, 1992.

John, Jürgen, Horst Möller, and Thomas Schaarschmidt, eds. *Die NS-Gaue: Regionale Mittelinstanzen im zentralistischen 'Führerstaat.'* Munich: Oldenbourg, 2007.

Jüdisches Historisches Institut Warschau, ed. *Faschismus—Getto—Massenmord: Dokumentation über Ausrottung und Widerstand der Juden in Polen während des zweiten Weltkrieges*. Frankfurt/M: Röderberg-Verlag [1960].

Kaden, Helma and Ludwig Nestler, eds. *Dokumente des Verbrechens: Aus Akten des Dritten Reiches 1933–1945*. Berlin: Dietz, 1993.

Kater, Michael H. *Composers of the Nazi Era: Eight Portraits*. New York: Oxford University Press, 2000.

Kershaw, Ian. 'Arthur Greiser—Ein Motor der "Endlösung."' In Ronald Smelzer, Enrico Syring, and Rainer Zitelmann, eds. *Die Braune Elite II: 21 weitere biographische Skizzen.* Darmstadt: Wissenschaftliche Buchgesellschaft, 1993, pp. 116–27.

——*Hitler 1936–1945: Nemesis.* New York: Norton, 2000.

——'Improvised Genocide? The Emergence of the "Final Solution" in the "Warthegau."' *Transactions of the Royal Historical Society* (1992): 51–78.

Kiernan, Ben. *Blood and Soil: A World History of Genocide and Extermination from Sparta to Darfur.* New Haven: Yale University Press, 2007.

Klein, Peter. *Die 'Gettoverwaltung Litzmannstadt' 1940–1944: Eine Dienststelle im Spannungsfeld von Kommunalbürokratie und staatlicher Verfolgungspolitik.* Hamburg: Hamburger Edition, 2009.

Koehl, Robert L. *RKFDV: German Resettlement and Population Policy 1939–1945: A History of the Reich Commission for the Strengthening of Germandom.* Cambridge, Mass.: Harvard University Press, 1957.

Kotowski, Albert S. *Polens Politik gegenüber seiner deutschen Minderheit 1919–1939.* Wiesbaden: Harrassowitz, 1998.

Leonhardt, Hans L. *Nazi Conquest of Danzig.* Chicago: University of Chicago Press, 1942.

Levine, Herbert S. *Hitler's Free City: A History of the Nazi Party in Danzig, 1925–39.* Chicago: University of Chicago Press, 1970.

Lichtenstein, Erwin. *Die Juden der Freien Stadt Danzig unter der Herrschaft des Nationalsozialismus.* Tubingen: Mohr, 1973.

Lifton, Robert Jay. *The Nazi Doctors: Medical Killing and the Psychology of Genocide.* New York: Basic Books, 1986.

Longerich, Peter. *Politik der Vernichtung: Eine Gesamtdarstellung der nationalsozialistischen Judenverfolgung.* Munich: Piper, 1998.

Loose, Ingo. *Kredite für NS-Verbrechen: Die deutschen Kreditinstitute in Polen und die Ausraubung der polnischen und jüdischen Bevölkerung 1939–1945.* Oldenbourg: Institut für Zeitgeschichte, 2007.

Löw, Andrea. *Juden im Getto Litzmannstadt: Lebensbedingungen, Selbstwahrnehmung, Verhalten.* Göttingen: Wallstein, 2006.

Łuczak, Czesław. *Arthur Greiser.* Poznań: PSO, 1997.

——*Dzień po dniu w okupowanej Wielkopolsce i na ziemi łódzkiej (Kraj Warty): kalendarium wydarzeń 1939–1945.* Poznań: Lektor, 1993.

——*Pod niemieckim jarzmem (Kraj Warty 1939–1945).* Poznań: PSO, 1996.

——*Polscy robotnicy przymusowi w Trzeciej Rzeszy podczas II Wojny Światowej.* Poznań: Wydawnictwo Poznańskie, 1974.

——ed. *Dyskryminacja Polaków w Wielkopolsce w okresie okupacji hitlerowskiej: wybór źródeł.* Poznań: Wydawnictwo Pozańskie, 1966.

Lumans, Valdis O. *Himmler's Auxiliaries: The Volksdeutsche Mittelstelle and the German National Minorities of Europe, 1933–1945.* Chapel Hill: University of North Carolina Press, 1993.

Madajczyk, Czesław. *Die Okkupationspolitik Nazideutschlands in Polen 1939–1945*. Berlin: Akademie, 1987.

——ed. *Vom Generalplan Ost zum Generalsiedlungsplan: Dokumente*. Munich: Saur, 1994.

Majer, Diemut. *'Non-Germans' under the Third Reich: The Nazi Judicial and Administrative System in Germany and Occupied Eastern Europe, with Special Regard to Occupied Poland, 1939–1945*. Baltimore: Johns Hopkins University Press, 2003.

Mallmann, Klaus-Michael and Gerhard Paul, eds. *Karrieren der Gewalt: Nationalsozialistische Täterbiographien*. Darmstadt: Wissenschaftliche Buchgesellschaft, 2004.

Mann, Michael. *The Dark Side of Democracy: Explaining Ethnic Cleansing*. Cambridge: Cambridge University Press, 2005.

Mazower, Mark. *Hitler's Empire: Nazi Rule in Occupied Europe*. London: Allen Lane, 2008.

McNamara, Paul. *Sean Lester, Poland and the Nazi Takeover of Danzig*. Dublin: Irish Academic Press, 2009.

Melzer, Ralf. *Konflikt und Anpassung: Freimauerei in der Weimarer Republik und im 'Dritten Reich.'* Vienna: Braumüller, 1999.

Merkl, Peter H. *Political Violence under the Swastika: 581 Early Nazis*. Princeton: Princeton University Press, 1975.

Mommsen, Hans. *Beamtentum im Dritten Reich*. Stuttgart: Deutsche Verlags-Anstalt, 1966.

Müller, Rolf-Dieter. *Hitlers Ostkrieg und die deutsche Siedlungspolitik: Die Zusammenarbeit von Wehrmacht, Wirtschaft und SS*. Frankfurt/M: Fischer, 1991.

Musial, Bogdan. 'NS-Kriegsverbrecher vor polnischen Gerichten.' *Vierteljahreshefte für Zeitgeschichte* 47 (1999): 25–56.

Naimark, Norman M. *Fires of Hatred: Ethnic Cleansing in Twentieth-Century Europe*. Cambridge, Mass.: Harvard University Press, 2001.

Nawrocki, Stanisław. *Policja hitlerowska w tzw. Kraju Warty w latach 1939–1945*. Poznań: Instytut Zachodni, 1970.

——*Terror policyjny w 'Kraju Warty' 1939–1945*. Poznań: Wydawnictwo Poznańskie, 1973.

Neubach, Helmut. *Die Ausweisungen von Polen und Juden aus Preussen 1885/86: Ein Beitrag zu Bismarcks Polenpolitik und zur Geschichte des deutsch-polnischen Verhältnisses*. Wiesbaden: Otto Harrassowitz, 1967.

Neuberger, Helmut. *Winkelmaß und Hakenkreuz: Die Freimaurer und das Dritte Reich*. Munich: Herbig, 2001.

Noakes, Jeremy. '"Viceroys of the Reich?" Gauleiters 1925–45.' In Anthony McElligott and Tim Kirk, eds. *Working Towards the Führer: Essays in Honour of Sir Ian Kershaw*. Manchester: Manchester University Press, 2003, pp. 118–52.

Orlow, Dietrich. *The History of the Nazi Party: 1933–1945*. Pittsburgh: University of Pittsburgh Press, 1973.

Orth, Karin. *Die Konzentrationslager-SS: Sozialstrukturelle Analysen und biographische Studien*. Munich: Deutscher Taschenbuch Verlag, 2004.

Pätzold, Kurt, ed. *Verfolgung, Vertreibung, Vernichtung: Dokumente des faschistischen Antisemitismus 1933 bis 1942*. Leipzig: Verlag Philipp Reclam jun., 1984.

Paul, Gerhard, ed. *Die Täter der Shoah: Fanatische Nationalsozialisten oder ganz normale Deutsche?* Göttingen: Wallstein, 2002.

Porzycki, Wiesław. *Posłuszni aż do śmierci (niemieccy urzędnicy w Kraju Warty 1939–1945)*. Poznań: PSO, 1997.

Rebentisch, Dieter. *Führerstaat und Verwaltung im Zweiten Weltkrieg: Verfassungsentwicklung und Verwaltungspolitik 1939–1945*. Stuttgart: Franz Steiner, 1989.

Rieß, Volker. *Die Anfänge der Vernichtung 'lebensunwerten Lebens' in den Reichsgauen Danzig-Westpreußen und Wartheland 1939/40*. Frankfurt/M: Peter Lang, 1995.

Rogall, Joachim, ed. *Die Räumung des 'Reichsgaus Wartheland' vom 16. bis 26. Januar 1945 im Spiegel amtlicher Berichte*. Sigmaringen: Jan Thorbecke, 1993.

Röhr, Werner. '"Reichsgau Wartheland" 1939–1945: Vom "Exerzierplatz des praktischen Nationalsozialismus" zum "Mustergau"?' *Bulletin für Faschismus und Weltkriegsforschung* no. 18 (2002): 29–54.

——ed. *Europa unterm Hakenkreuz: Die faschistische Okkupationspolitik in Polen (1939–1945)*. Berlin: Deutscher Verlag der Wissenschaften, 1989.

Roseman, Mark. 'Beyond Conviction? Perpetrators, Ideas, and Action in the Holocaust in Historiographical Perspective.' In Frank Biess, Mark Roseman, and Hanna Schissler, eds. *Conflict, Catastrophe and Continuity: Essays on Modern German History*. New York: Berghahn, 2007, pp. 83–103.

Rosenkötter, Bernhard. *Treuhandpolitik: Die 'Haupttreuhandstelle Ost' und der Raub polnischer Vermögen 1939–1945*. Essen: Klartext, 2003.

Rossino, Alexander B. *Hitler Strikes Poland: Blitzkrieg, Ideology, and Atrocity*. Lawrence: University Press of Kansas, 2003.

Rössler, Mechthild and Sabine Schleiermacher, eds. *Der 'Generalplan Ost': Hauptlinien der nationalsozialistischen Planungs- und Vernichtungspolitik*. Berlin: Akademie, 1993.

Rückerl, Adalbert, ed. *Nationalsozialistische Vernichtungslager im Spiegel deutscher Strafprozesse: Belzec, Sobibor, Treblinka, Chelmno*. Munich: Deutscher Taschenbuch Verlag, 1977.

Rutherford, Phillip T. *Prelude to the Final Solution: The Nazi Program for Deporting Ethnic Poles, 1939–1941*. Lawrence: University Press of Kansas, 2007.

Rutowska, Maria. *Wysiedlenia ludności polskiej z Kraju Warty do Generalnego Gubernatorstwa 1939–1941*. Poznań: Instytut Zachodni, 2003.

Schenk, Dieter. *Hitlers Mann in Danzig: Gauleiter Forster und die NS-Verbrechen in Danzig-Westpreußen*. Bonn: Dietz, 2000.

Schwendemann, Heinrich and Wolfgang Dietsche. *Hitlers Schloß: Die 'Führerresidenz' in Posen*. Berlin: Ch. Links, 2003.

Siegmund, Harry. *Rückblick: Erinnerungen eines Staatsdieners in bewegter Zeit*. Raisdorf: Ostsee Verlag, 1999.

Sodeikat, Ernst. 'Die Verfolgung und der Widerstand der Juden in der Freien Stadt Danzig von 1933 bis 1945.' *Bulletin des Leo Baeck Instituts* 8 (1965): 107–49.

Speer, Albert. *Infiltration.* New York: Macmillan, 1981.

Stasiewski, Bernhard. 'Die Kirchenpolitik der Nationalsozialisten im Warthegau 1939–1945.' *Vierteljahrshefte für Zeitgeschichte* 7, no. 1 (1959): 46–74.

Stauffer, Paul. *Zwischen Hofmannsthal und Hitler: Carl J. Burckhardt: Facetten einer aussergewöhnlichen Existenz.* Zurich: Verlag Neue Zürcher Zeitung, 1991.

Struck, Manfred, ed. *Chelmno/Kulmhof: Ein vergessener Ort des Holocaust.* Bonn: Gegen Vergessen—Für Demokratie, 2001.

Thorwald, Jürgen. *Es begann an der Weichsel.* Stuttgart: Steingrüben, 1959.

Tooze, Adam. *The Wages of Destruction: The Making and Breaking of the Nazi Economy.* New York: Viking, 2007.

Trunk, Isaiah. *Łódź ghetto: A History.* Bloomington: Indiana University Press, 2006.

Umbreit, Hans. *Deutsche Militärverwaltungen 1938/39: Die militärische Besetzung der Tschechoslowakei und Polens.* Stuttgart: Deutsche Verlags-Anstalt, 1977.

United Nations War Crimes Commission, ed. *Law Reports of Trials of War Criminals.* Vol. XIII. London: The United Nations War Crimes Commission, 1949.

von Lang, Jochen. *The Secretary: Martin Bormann: The Man Who Manipulated Hitler.* New York: Random House, 1979.

Waller, James. *Becoming Evil: How Ordinary People Commit Genocide and Mass Killing.* Oxford: Oxford University Press, 2002.

Welzer, Harald. *Täter: Wie aus ganz normalen Menschen Massenmörder werden.* Frankfurt/M: Fischer, 2005.

Wietrzykowski, Albin. *Powrót Arthura Greisera.* Poznań: Nakładem Księgarni Wydawniczej Spółdzielni 'Pomoc,' 1946.

Wildt, Michael. *Generation des Unbedingten: Das Führungskorps des Reichssicherheitshauptamtes.* Hamburg: Hamburger Edition, 2003.

Witte, Peter. 'Zwei Entscheidungen in der "Endlösung der Judenfrage": Deportationen nach Lodz und Vernichtung in Chelmno.' Ed. Miroslav Kárný, Raimund Kemper, and Margita Kárná. *Theresienstädter Studien und Dokumente* (1995), pp. 38–68.

Wolschke-Bulmahn, Joachim, ed. *Places of Commemoration: Search for Identity and Landscape Design.* Washington, D.C.: Dumbarton Oaks Research Library and Collection, 2001.

Ziegler, Armin. *Posen Januar 1945: Evakuierung und Flucht der deutschen Zivilbevölkerung der Stadt Posen im Januar 1945.* Schönaich: Im Selbstverlag, 1989.

—— *Wer kennt schon Zabikowo ... Ein Bericht über das 'Polizeigefängnis der Sicherheitspolizei und SS-Arbeitserziehungslager Posen-Lenzingen.'* Schönaich: Im Selbstverlag, 1994.

Zillmer, Eric A., Molly Harrower, Barry A. Ritzler, and Robert P. Archer, eds. *The Quest for the Nazi Personality: A Psychological Investigation of Nazi War Criminals.* Hillsdale: Lawrence Erlbaum Associates, 1995.

Ziółkowska, Anna. *Obozy pracy przymusowej dla Żydów w Wielkopolsce w latach okupacji hitlerowskiej (1941–1943)*. Poznań: Wydawnictwo Poznańskie, 2005.

Zorn, Gerda. *'Nach Ostland geht unser Ritt': Deutsche Eroberungspolitik und die Folgen: Das Beispiel Lodz*. Cologne: Röderberg, 1988.

Acknowledgments

Every book has a story behind it—felicitous coincidences, curious discoveries, memorable meetings, and, most important, remarkable help from unexpected sources. Imagine my surprise when one morning an unsolicited e-mail from a Greiser family member arrived in my mailbox. The family found me! I am enormously grateful to Katrin Greiser, herself a historian of the Third Reich and Arthur's grand niece, for putting me in touch with various relatives. In particular, she made it possible for me to contact Rotraut Fülleborn, Arthur's daughter, a lovely woman. This is surely not the book that Mrs. Fülleborn wants to read about her father, but I am immensely grateful to her for talking with me at such length. The two days that I spent with her are among the most special memories that I have. In addition, she made family documents and photographs available to me. Two of Greiser's nieces, Antje Cordier and Vera Stroud, also shared their recollections of their uncle with me. Together, these three individuals made it possible for me to more fully reconstruct Greiser's early life.

I was lucky enough to speak with two others who knew Greiser personally. Harry Siegmund welcomed me to his home and recounted his experiences with his cousin. Paul Ruge, in his lively, inimitable way, told me fascinating anecdotes about his times with Greiser. He also allowed me to copy his collection of postwar letters from Maria Greiser.

Armin Ziegler went well beyond typical scholarly cooperation: he shared with me his extensive knowledge of the Warthegau, provided documents from his private collection, made phone calls on my behalf, and commented on my entire manuscript in a most useful way. I benefited greatly from Paul McNamara's deep knowledge of Danzig politics in the 1930s, as well as from his advice on navigating Danzig archives. Paul also accompanied me on a wild adventure through Gdańsk and its environs in search of Greiser's old haunts—an unforgettable day!

Many others aided my research. Robert Rothstein, who taught me first-year Polish, cheerfully responded to my inquiries about Polish-language usage. Gaby Müller-Oelrichs, head of the Library at the Haus der Wannsee-Konferenz, was enormously helpful in making research materials available to me. Pierre Th. Braunschweig, David T. Curp, Eike Eckert, Gerard Gooden, and Alexander Prusin answered inquiries, provided documents, and/or otherwise helped me. Michael Alberti and Peter Klein discussed their findings on the Final Solution in the Warthegau with me; both also provided me with useful documents. I owe Richard Breitman a huge thanks: just before the manuscript was completed, he made extraordinary efforts so that I could see over 1,000 pages of material on Greiser recently declassified by the National Archives.

Research projects are expensive endeavors. To carry out the research for this book, the German Marshall Fund awarded me a Research Fellowship for the 2003–4 academic year. Amherst College provided additional funding in the form of a Karl Loewenstein Sabbatical Fellowship. I have also benefited from the College's generous Faculty Research Award Program. The College has provided a congenial work environment; it's a pleasure to work at such a supportive institution. In particular, I have benefited from my colleagues in the History Department, and from the professional staff in Information Technology and the Robert Frost Library.

Over the past few years, I have had various opportunities to speak on Greiser. I thank Omer Bartov for organizing the Borderlands Workshop at Brown University; Konrad Jarausch for having me at the Zentrum für Zeitgeschichtliche Forschung; Francis Nicosia for bringing me to the University of Vermont; Mary Sarotte for including me in a conference at St. John's College, Cambridge University; and Jonathan Zatlin for arranging talks at both Boston University and the Center for European Studies at Harvard University.

Mark Mazower brought me to Oxford University Press, and I am very glad that he did. It has been a pleasure working with Christopher Wheeler, Matthew Cotton, Kate Hind, Susan Beer, and Andrew Hawkey. Mark Roseman provided an extraordinary set of readers' comments; they made me rethink the project in a most productive way. Two other anonymous readers also supplied me with useful comments.

Many individuals read parts or all of the manuscript, and I am grateful to all of them. Peter Baldwin, Christopher Browning, Chad Bryant, Peter Carstens, Christian Gerlach, Nasser Hussain, Charles Maier, and Tara

Zahra read and/or commented on earlier versions of different parts of the manuscript. In spring 2009, students in my seminar on ethnic cleansing suggested reader-friendly changes to the manuscript. Participants in the 2008–9 Amherst College Copeland Colloquium on 'States of Violence' discussed my Introduction. In the final months of writing, Lawrence Douglas, Paul McNamara, and Jonathan Zatlin looked at particular chapters and made valuable stylistic and factual corrections. Michal Shapira read the whole manuscript and, with her sharp intellect, offered excellent suggestions for improvement. Leo Zaibert also read the entire manuscript, and his insightful comments led to important revisions. Robert Nylander carefully checked every chapter and used his arcane knowledge of weaponry, animals, and trains to save me from some egregious errors. He even managed to dig up some fascinating documents—previously unknown to me—about Greiser. Finally, in the last stages of production, Samuel Huneke put his discerning eye to the entire manuscript. Thanks to him and everyone else mentioned, this book became a significantly better read.

And then there is Susan Whitlock, a dear childhood friend. Out of touch for many years, we reconnected shortly before I finished this book. Susan graciously offered to put her professional editorial expertise to work on it. Her efforts have led to a smoother, more coherent book. While I am enormously grateful to her for her editorial assistance, I am even more so for her friendship.

Throughout work on this grim project, I enjoyed the support and company of my husband and children. In countless ways, my husband, Daniel Gordon, made this book and much more possible. Dan spent a year in Berlin that he otherwise could have spent elsewhere; enabled research trips and conference attendance; and endured innumerable days and evenings when I insisted on working on 'the book.' He has never read a word of the manuscript, but should he do so, I hope that he will be pleased. Our children, Nathan, Dora, and Stella (who was born in the midst of the project), managed not only to respect my closed study door, but also to distract me from my writing; for both, I am profoundly grateful. With lots of love, this book is dedicated to all four of them. Dan, Nathan, Dora, and Stella: you're the best!

Amherst, September 2009

Index